See what students love about LearningCurve.

Macmillan Education
LearningCurve learningcurveworks.com

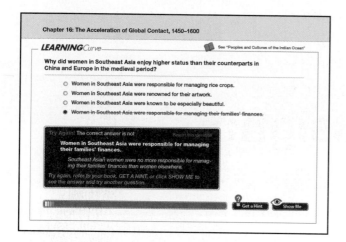

"With LearningCurve, students engage with the content and retain it better."

— Melissa Walker, *Converse College*

Students using LaunchPad receive access to LearningCurve for *Understanding World Societies*.

Each chapter-based LearningCurve activity gives students multiple chances to understand key concepts, return to the narrative textbook if they need to reread, and answer questions correctly.

Over 90% of students report satisfaction with LearningCurve's fun and accessible game-like interface.

Assigning LearningCurve in place of reading quizzes is easy for instructors, and the reporting features help instructors track overall class trends and spot topics that are giving students trouble so that they can adjust lectures and class activities.

To learn more about LearningCurve, visit learningcurveworks.com.

LearningCurve: Everyone's got a learning curve — what's yours?

Understanding
World Societies

A HISTORY

SECOND EDITION

VOLUME 1 To 1600

John P. McKay
University of Illinois at Urbana-Champaign

Bennett D. Hill
Late of Georgetown University

John Buckler
Late of University of Illinois at Urbana-Champaign

Patricia Buckley Ebrey
University of Washington

Roger B. Beck
Eastern Illinois University

Clare Haru Crowston
University of Illinois at Urbana-Champaign

Merry E. Wiesner-Hanks
University of Wisconsin–Milwaukee

Jerry Dávila
University of Illinois at Urbana-Champaign

Bedford/St. Martin's
Boston • New York

For Bedford/St. Martin's

Vice President, Editorial, Macmillan Higher Education Humanities: Edwin Hill
Publisher for History: Michael Rosenberg
Director of Development for History: Jane Knetzger
Associate Editor for History: Robin Soule
Production Editor: Annette Pagliaro Sweeney
Senior Production Supervisor: Dennis Conroy
Executive Marketing Manager: Sandra McGuire
Project Manager: Katrina Ostler, Jouve
Editorial Assistant: Arrin Kaplan
Cartography: Mapping Specialists, Ltd.
Photo Researcher: Bruce Carson
Director of Rights and Permissions: Hilary Newman
Senior Art Director: Anna Palchik
Cover Design: William Boardman
Cover Art: The Fourteenth Lohan Vanavasi (detail)
Lu Xinzhong, Chinese, late 12th–early 13th century
Chinese, Southern Song dynasty, late 12th century
Ink, color, and gold on silk
Image: 79.2 × 41.5 cm (31 3/16 × 16 5/16 in.)
Other (overall when folding screen is closed): 158.8 × 59 cm (62 1/2 × 23 1/4 in.)
Other (side panel, proper left): 158 × 31 cm (62 3/16 × 12 3/16 in.)
Other (side panel, proper right): 158 × 29.3 cm (62 3/16 × 11 9/16 in.)
Other (overall, center panel): 158.8 × 59 cm (62 1/2 × 23 1/4 in.)
Museum of Fine Arts, Boston
William Sturgis Bigelow Collection
11.6129
Photograph © 2014 Museum of Fine Arts, Boston. All rights reserved/Bridgeman Images.
Composition: Jouve
Printing and Binding: RR Donnelley and Sons

9 8 7 6 5 4
f e d c b a

For information, write: Bedford/St. Martin's, 75 Arlington Street, Boston, MA 02116
(617-399-4000)

ISBN 978-1-4576-9992-4 (Combined Edition)
ISBN 978-1-319-00837-6 (Volume 1)
ISBN 978-1-319-00838-3 (Volume 2)

Understanding
World Societies

A HISTORY

VOLUME 1

How to use this book to figure out what's really important

The **chapter title** tells you the subject of the chapter and identifies the time span that will be covered.

The **opening question** and **chapter introduction** identify the most important themes, events, and people that will be explored in the chapter.

16
THE ACCELERATION OF GLOBAL CONTACT

1450–1600

> **What new global connections were forged in the fifteenth and sixteenth centuries?** Chapter 16 examines the causes, course, and effects of European expansion in the fifteenth and sixteenth centuries. Before 1500 Europeans were relatively marginal players in a centuries-old trading system that linked Africa, Asia, and Europe. By 1550 the European search for better access to Asian trade goods had led to a new overseas empire in the Indian Ocean and the accidental discovery of the Western Hemisphere. With this discovery South and North America were drawn into an international network of trade centers and political empires, which Europeans came to dominate. The era of globalization had begun, creating new political systems and forms of economic exchange as well as cultural assimilation, conversion, and resistance.

✓ **LearningCurve**
After reading the chapter, use LearningCurve to retain what you've read.

454

Memorizing facts and dates for a history class won't get you very far. That's because history isn't just about "facts." This textbook is designed to help you focus on what's truly significant in the history of world societies and to give you practice thinking like a historian.

Nezahualpilli At the time of the arrival of Europeans, Nezahualpilli was ruler of the city-state of Texcoco, the second most important city in the Aztec Empire after Tenochtitlan. (Nezahualpilli, portrait from *Codex Ixtlilxochitl*, 1582, pigment on European paper/Bibliothèque Nationale, Paris, France/De Agostini Picture Library/akg-images)

> What was the Afroeurasian trade world like prior to the era of European exploration?

> Why and how did Europeans undertake ambitious voyages of expansion?

> What was the impact of Iberian conquest and settlement on the peoples and ecologies of the Americas?

> How was the era of global contact shaped by new commodities, commercial empires, and forced migrations?

> How did new encounters shape cultural attitudes and beliefs in Europe and the New World?

The **chapter-opening questions** are also the questions that open the new sections of the chapter and will be addressed in turn on the following pages. You should think about answers to them as you read.

Each section has tools that help you focus on what's important.

The **question in red** asks about the specific topic being discussed in this section. Pause to answer each one after you read the section.

> ## How was the era of global contact shaped by new commodities, commercial empires, and forced migrations?

A New World Sugar Refinery in Brazil

Sugar was the most important and most profitable plantation crop in the New World. This image shows the processing and refinement of sugar on a Brazilian plantation. Sugarcane was grown, harvested, and processed by African slaves who labored under brutal and ruthless conditions to generate enormous profits for plantation owners. (The Bridgeman Art Library/Getty Images)

THE CENTURIES-OLD AFROEURASIAN trade world was forever changed by the European voyages of discovery and their aftermath. For the first time, a truly global economy emerged in the sixteenth and seventeenth centuries, and it forged new links among far-flung peoples, cultures, and societies.

The Columbian Exchange

The travel of people and goods between the Old and New Worlds led to an exchange of animals, plants, and diseases, a complex process known as the **Columbian exchange.** As we have seen, the introduction of new diseases to the Americas had devastating consequences. But other results of the exchange brought benefits not only to the Europeans but also to native peoples.

Everywhere they settled, the Spanish and Portuguese brought and raised wheat. Grapes and olives brought over from Spain did well in parts of Peru and Chile. Perhaps the most significant introduction to the diet of Native Americans

Key terms in the margins give you background on important people, ideas, and events. Use these for reference while you read, but also think about which terms are emphasized and why they matter.

Columbian exchange
▶ The exchange of animals, plants, and diseases between the Old and the New Worlds.

CHAPTER LOCATOR | What was the Afroeurasian trade world like prior to the era of European exploration? | Why and how did Europeans undertake ambitious voyages of expansion?

to pay tributes in cash, rather than in labor. To respond to a shortage of indigenous workers, royal officials established a new government-run system of forced labor, called *repartimiento* in New Spain and *mita* in Peru. Administrators assigned a certain percentage of the inhabitants of native communities to labor for a set period each year in public works, mining, agriculture, and other tasks.

Spanish systems for exploiting the labor of indigenous peoples were both a cause of and a response to the disastrous decline in the numbers of such peoples that began soon after the arrival of Europeans. Some indigenous people died as a direct result of the violence of conquest and the disruption of agriculture and trade caused by warfare. The most important cause of death, however, was infectious disease. Having little or no resistance to diseases brought from the Old World, the inhabitants of the New World fell victim to smallpox, typhus, influenza, and other illnesses.

The pattern of devastating disease and population loss established in the Spanish colonies was repeated everywhere Europeans settled. Overall, population declined by as much as 90 percent or more but with important regional variations. In general, densely populated urban centers were worse hit than rural areas and tropical, low-lying regions suffered more than cooler, higher-altitude ones.

Colonial administrators responded to native population decline by forcibly combining dwindling indigenous communities into new settlements and imposing the rigors of the encomienda and the repartimiento. By the end of the sixteenth century the search for fresh sources of labor had given birth to the new tragedy of the Atlantic slave trade (see page 598).

Patterns of Settlement

The century after the discovery of silver in 1545 marked the high point of Iberian immigration to the Americas. Although the first migrants were men, soon whole families began to cross the Atlantic, and the European population began to increase through natural reproduction. By 1600 American-born Europeans, called *Creoles*, outnumbered immigrants.

Iberian settlement was predominantly urban in nature. Spaniards settled into the cities and towns of the former Aztec and Inca Empires as the native population dwindled through death and flight. They also established new cities in which settlers were quick to establish urban institutions familiar to them from home: city squares, churches, schools, and universities.

Despite the growing number of Europeans and the rapid decline of the native population, Europeans remained a small minority of the total inhabitants of the Americas. Iberians formed sexual relationships with native women leading to a substantial population of mixed Iberian and Indian descent known as *mestizos* (meh-STEE-zohz). The large-scale arrival of enslaved Africans, starting in Brazil in the mid-sixteenth century, added new ethnic and racial dimensions to the population (see pages 598–603).

QUICK REVIEW <

What factors help explain the conquest of the mighty Inca and Aztec Empires by the Spanish?

What was the impact of Iberian conquest and settlement on the peoples of the Americas?	How was the era of global contact shaped by new commodities and forced migrations?	How did new encounters shape cultural attitudes and beliefs in Europe and the New World?	LearningCurve Check what you know.

473

The **quick review** helps you check your recall of the section before you resume reading.

The **chapter locator** at the bottom of the page puts this section in the context of the chapter as a whole so you can see how this section relates to what's coming next.

The Chapter Study Guide provides a process that will build your understanding and your historical skills.

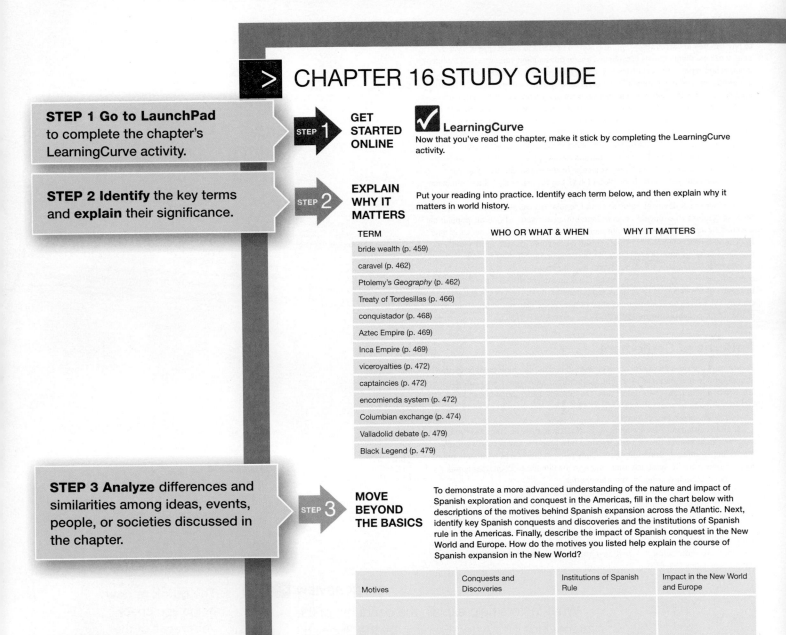

CHAPTER 16 STUDY GUIDE

STEP 1 Go to LaunchPad to complete the chapter's LearningCurve activity.

STEP 1 — GET STARTED ONLINE

✓ **LearningCurve**
Now that you've read the chapter, make it stick by completing the LearningCurve activity.

STEP 2 Identify the key terms and **explain** their significance.

STEP 2 — EXPLAIN WHY IT MATTERS

Put your reading into practice. Identify each term below, and then explain why it matters in world history.

TERM	WHO OR WHAT & WHEN	WHY IT MATTERS
bride wealth (p. 459)		
caravel (p. 462)		
Ptolemy's *Geography* (p. 462)		
Treaty of Tordesillas (p. 466)		
conquistador (p. 468)		
Aztec Empire (p. 469)		
Inca Empire (p. 469)		
viceroyalties (p. 472)		
captaincies (p. 472)		
encomienda system (p. 472)		
Columbian exchange (p. 474)		
Valladolid debate (p. 479)		
Black Legend (p. 479)		

STEP 3 Analyze differences and similarities among ideas, events, people, or societies discussed in the chapter.

STEP 3 — MOVE BEYOND THE BASICS

To demonstrate a more advanced understanding of the nature and impact of Spanish exploration and conquest in the Americas, fill in the chart below with descriptions of the motives behind Spanish expansion across the Atlantic. Next, identify key Spanish conquests and discoveries and the institutions of Spanish rule in the Americas. Finally, describe the impact of Spanish conquest in the New World and Europe. How do the motives you listed help explain the course of Spanish expansion in the New World?

Motives	Conquests and Discoveries	Institutions of Spanish Rule	Impact in the New World and Europe

STEP 4

PUT IT ALL TOGETHER

Now, take a step back and try to explain the big picture. Remember to use specific examples from the chapter in your answers.

STEP 4 Answer the big-picture questions using specific examples or evidence from the chapter.

THE AFROEURASIAN TRADE WORLD BEFORE COLUMBUS

▶ Which states were at the center of global trade prior to 1492? Why?

▶ Why were Europeans at a trading disadvantage prior to 1492? How did geography limit European participation in world trade? What role did Europe's economy and material culture play in this context?

DISCOVERY AND CONQUEST

▶ In your opinion, what was the most important motive behind European expansion? What evidence can you provide to support your position?

▶ What was the Columbian exchange? How did it transform both Europe and the Americas?

CHANGING VALUES AND BELIEFS

▶ How did European expansion give rise to new ideas about race?

▶ How did expansion complicate European's understanding of themselves and their place in the world?

LOOKING BACK, LOOKING AHEAD

▶ If Europe was at the periphery of the global trading system prior to 1492, where was it situated by the middle of the sixteenth century? What had changed? What had not?

▶ What connections can you make between our own experience of globalization in the twenty-first century and the experience of globalization in the sixteenth century? In what ways are the experiences similar? In what ways do they differ?

> **IN YOUR OWN WORDS**

Imagine that you must give an oral report to the class answering the following question: **What new global connections were forged in the fifteenth and sixteenth centuries?** What would be the most important points and why?

ACTIVE RECITATION Explain how you would answer the chapter-opening question in your own words to make sure you have a firm grasp of the most important themes and events of the chapter.

PREFACE: Why This Book This Way

Understanding World Societies grew out of many conversations we have had among ourselves and with other instructors about the teaching and learning of history. We knew that instructors wanted a world history text that introduced students to the broad sweep of history but that also re-created the lives of ordinary men and women in appealing human terms. We knew that instructors wanted a text that presented cutting-edge scholarship in new fields of historical inquiry. We also knew that many instructors wanted a text that would help students focus as they read, keep their interest in the material, and encourage them to learn historical thinking skills. It is our hope that Understanding World Societies addresses all of these concerns.

The second edition of Understanding World Societies continues to provide the social and cultural focus, comprehensive regional organization, and global perspective that have long been hallmarks of the book. All three of these qualities have been greatly enhanced by the addition of a new member to the author team, Jerry Dávila from the University of Illinois, who brings expertise in Latin America and the twentieth century. A renowned scholar of Brazil whose work focuses on race and social policy, Jerry offers a fresh perspective to our coverage of Latin America and to the final chapters in the book, which he has completely reconceptualized. Not only do we thus continue to benefit from a collaborative team of regional experts with deep experience in the world history classroom, but we are also pleased to introduce a suite of digital tools designed to save you time and help students gain confidence and learn historical thinking skills.

New Tools for the Digital Age

Because we know that your classroom needs are changing rapidly, we are excited to announce that Understanding World Societies is available with **LaunchPad**. Free when packaged with the book, or heavily discounted as a stand-alone product, LaunchPad's course space and interactive e-book is ready to use as is or can be edited and customized with your own material and assigned right away. Developed with extensive feedback from history instructors and students, LaunchPad includes the complete narrative e-book, as well as abundant primary documents, maps, images, assignments, and activities. The aims of key learning outcomes are addressed via formative and summative assessment, short-answer and essay questions, multiple-choice quizzing, and **LearningCurve**, an adaptive learning tool designed to get students to read before they come to class. Available with training and support, LaunchPad can help you take your teaching into a new era. To learn more about the benefits of LearningCurve and LaunchPad, see the "Versions and Supplements" section on page xxiii and see below on how specific skills-based features of Understanding World Societies benefit from the ability to assign and track student work in LaunchPad.

Understanding World Societies:
Bringing the Past to Life for Students

In this age of global connections, with its influence on the global economy, global migration patterns, popular culture, and global warming, among other things, the study of world history is more vital and urgent than ever before. An understanding of the broad sweep of the human past helps us comprehend today's dramatic changes and enduring continuities. People now migrate enormous distances and establish new lives far from their places of birth, yet migration has been a constant in history since the first humans walked out of Africa. Satellite and cell phones now link nearly every inch of the planet, yet the expansion of communication networks is a process that is thousands of years old. Children who speak different languages at home now sit side by side in schools and learn from one another, yet intercultural encounters have long been a source of innovation, transformation, and at times, unfortunately, conflict.

This book is designed for twenty-first-century students who will spend their lives on this small interconnected planet and for whom an understanding of only local or national history will no longer be sufficient. We believe that the study of world history in a broad and comparative context is an exciting, important, and highly practical pursuit. It is our conviction, based on considerable experience in introducing large numbers of students to world history, that a book reflecting current trends in scholarship can excite readers and inspire an enduring interest in the long human experience.

Our strategy has been twofold. First, we have made social and cultural history the core elements of our narrative. We seek to re-create the lives of ordinary people in appealing human terms and also to highlight the interplay between men's and women's lived experiences and the ways they reflect on these to create meaning. Thus, in addition to foundational works of philosophy and literature, we include popular songs and stories. We present objects along with texts as important sources for studying history, and this has allowed us to incorporate the growing emphasis on material culture in the work of many historians. At the same time, we have been mindful of the need to give great economic, political, and intellectual developments the attention they deserve. We want to give individual students and instructors an integrated perspective so that they can pursue—on their own or in the classroom—the themes and questions that they find particularly exciting and significant.

Second, we have made every effort to strike an effective global and regional balance. The whole world interacts today, and to understand the interactions and what they mean for today's citizens, we must study the whole world's history. Thus we have adopted a comprehensive regional organization with a global perspective that is clear and manageable for students. For example, Chapter 7 introduces students in depth to East Asia, and at the same time the chapter highlights the cultural connections that occurred via the Silk Road and the spread of Buddhism. We study all geographical areas, conscious of the separate histories of many parts of the world, particularly in the earliest millennia of human development. We also stress the links among cultures, political units, and economic systems, for these connections have made the world what it is today. We make comparisons and connections across time as well as space, for understanding the unfolding of the human story in time is the central task of history.

An Inquiry-Based Model Designed for Understanding

By employing innovative pedagogy, we believe that *Understanding World Societies* helps students not only understand the book's major developments but also begin to grasp the question-driven methodology that is at the heart of the historian's craft. Each chapter opens with a **new chapter-opening question** that drives students toward the overarching themes of the chapter, followed by a **brief chapter introduction** that identifies the most important events and people to be discussed. **Section-opening headings** expressed as questions and **section-ending quick review questions** further model the kinds of questions historians ask and help students engage in inquiry-based reading and understanding.

Chapter Study Guides Designed for Active Learning

At the core of the unique pedagogical features of *Understanding World Societies* are the revised **Chapter Study Guides** that provide a carefully structured four-step process to help students build deep understanding of the chapter material. In **Step 1**, students go to LaunchPad to complete the LearningCurve activity to ensure that they have a grasp of the basic content and concepts of the chapter. In **Step 2**, students not only identify the chapter's key terms but also explain why each matters. In **Step 3**, they begin to apply their understanding of the chapter material through activities that ask them to consider comparison, change over time, or cause and effect. In **Step 4**, analytical and synthetic questions require students to engage in higher-order historical thinking. And, finally, in an active recitation exercise, students **answer the chapter-opening question** to fully realize their understanding of the chapter. In LaunchPad, instructors can assign the **NEW Guided Reading Exercise** for each chapter, which prompts students to read actively to collect information that answers a broad analytic question central to the chapter as a whole.

Primary Sources for Teaching Critical Thinking and Analysis

Understanding World Societies offers an extensive program of primary source assignments to help students master a number of key learning outcomes, among them **critical thinking**, **historical thinking**, **analytical thinking**, **argumentation**, and learning about the **diversity of world cultures**. When assigned in LaunchPad, all primary source features are accompanied by multiple-choice quizzes that help you ensure that students come to class prepared.

New assignable **Online Document Projects** in LaunchPad offer students more practice in interpreting primary sources. Each project, based on the Individuals in Society feature described below, prompts students to explore a key question through analysis of multiple sources. Chapter 22, for example, asks students to analyze documents on the complexities of the Haitian Revolution and the conditions that made Toussaint L'Ouverture's story possible. Auto-graded multiple-choice questions based on the documents help students analyze the sources.

Finally, we have revised our **primary source documents collection**, *Sources for World Societies*, to add more visual sources and to closely align the readings with the chapter topics and themes of the second edition. The documents are now available in a fully assignable and assessable electronic format within each LaunchPad unit, and the accompanying multiple-choice questions measure comprehension and hold students accountable for their reading.

Student Engagement with Biography

In our years of teaching world history, we have often noted that students come alive when they encounter stories about real people in the past. To give students a chance to see the past through ordinary people's lives, each chapter includes one of the popular **Individuals in Society** biographical essays, each of which offers a brief study of an individual or a group, informing students about the societies in which the individuals lived. This feature grew out of our long-standing focus on people's lives and the varieties of historical experience, and we believe that readers will empathize with these human beings who themselves were seeking to define their own identities. The spotlighting of individuals, both famous and obscure, perpetuates the book's continued attention to cultural and intellectual developments, highlights human agency, and reflects changing interests within the historical profession as well as the development of "micro-history." As mentioned previously, the majority of these features are tied to **NEW Online Document Projects**, available in LaunchPad, that allow students to explore further the historical conditions in which these individuals lived. **NEW** features include essays on Sudatta, a lay follower of the Buddha; Cosimo and Lorenzo de' Medici; Malintzin; and Sieng, a Mnong refugee living in the United States.

Geographical and Visual Literacy

We recognize students' difficulties with geography and visual analysis, and the new edition retains our **Mapping the Past map activities** and **Picturing the Past visual activities**. Included in each chapter, these activities ask students to analyze the map or visual and make connections to the larger processes discussed in the narrative, giving them valuable practice in reading and interpreting maps and images. In LaunchPad, they are assignable, and students can submit their work. Throughout the textbook and online in LaunchPad, more than **92 full-size maps** illustrate major developments in the chapter. In addition, **74 spot maps** are embedded in the narrative to show specific areas under discussion.

Chronological Reasoning

To help students make comparisons, understand change over time, and see relationships among contemporaneous events, each chapter begins with a **chapter chronology** that reviews major developments discussed in the chapter. This chronology, available from every page in LaunchPad, allows students to compare developments over the centuries.

Better-Prepared Students

To help students fully understand their reading and come to class prepared, instructors who adopt LaunchPad for *Understanding World Societies* can assign the **LearningCurve** formative assessment activities. This online learning tool is popular with students because it helps them rehearse content at their own pace in a nonthreatening, game-like environment. LearningCurve is also popular with instructors because the reporting features allow them to track overall class trends and spot topics that are giving students trouble so they can adjust their lectures and class activities. When LearningCurve is assigned, students come to class better prepared, and instructors can better evaluate and adjust their classes.

To further encourage students to read and fully assimilate the text as well as measure how well they do this, instructors can assign the **new multiple-choice summative quizzes** in LaunchPad, where they are automatically graded. These secure tests not only encourage students to study the book, they can be assigned at specific intervals as high-stakes testing and thus provide another means for analyzing class performance.

Organizational and Textual Changes

To meet the demands of the evolving course, we have made several major changes in the organization of chapters to reflect the way the course is taught today. The most dramatic changes are the reordering of Chapter 17: "The Islamic World Powers, 1300–1800" (formerly Chapter 20) and a complete overhaul of the final section of the book, covering the postwar era. This new placement for our coverage of Islam reflects a growing interest among instructors and students in the Islamic world and highlights early Islamic cultural contributions.

To address the concerns of instructors who teach from the second volume of the text, we have added a new section on the Reformation to Chapter 18 so that students whose courses begin with Chapters 15 or 16 will now receive that coverage in Volume 2. The new section includes the Protestant and Catholic Reformations, as well as religious violence and witch-hunts.

In its examination of the age of revolution in the Atlantic world, Chapter 22 now incorporates revolutions in Latin America. In order to provide a more global perspective on European politics, culture, and economics in the early modern period, Chapter 23 on the Industrial Revolution considers industrialization more broadly as a global phenomenon with a new section titled "The Global Picture." Together, the enhanced global perspectives of these chapters help connect the different regions of the globe and, in particular, help explain the crucial period when Europe began to dominate the rest of the globe.

The final section of the text covering the post-1945 period has also been completely reworked. In addition to updating all of the postwar chapters through 2014, Jerry Dávila substantially rewrote and streamlined the last four chapters into three to create a more tightly focused and accessible section that now divides the period chronologically as follows: *Chapter 31: Decolonization, Revolution, and the Cold War, 1945–1968*; *Chapter 32: Liberalization, 1968–2000s*; *Chapter 33: The Contemporary World in Historical Perspective*. The last three chapters are now organized around two dominant themes of the postwar world: liberation movements that challenged power structures such as colonialism and racial supremacism and the spread of liberalization that characterized the end of the Cold War in particular, marking the rise of free markets and liberal political systems. The final chapter examines the significance of social movements in shaping a contemporary world that continues to struggle with historic conflicts and inequalities.

In terms of specific textual changes, we have worked hard to keep the book up to date and to strengthen our comprehensive, comparative, and connective approach. Moreover, we revised every chapter with the goal of readability and accessibility. Highlights of the new edition include:

- Chapter 1 includes new information on the recent archaeological find at Göbekli Tepe in present-day Turkey that suggests that cultural factors may have played a role in the development of agriculture.
- Chapter 2 has new coverage on Egyptian society and a discussion of gender distinctions in Sumerian society.
- In Chapter 6, the section on the founding of Rome has been completely rewritten.
- Chapter 8 contains a new section on Christian missionaries and conversion, and it explains the process of the Christianization of barbarian Europe.
- Chapter 11 now centers on the ways in which systems of religious belief shaped ancient societies of the Americas and provided tools that people used to understand and adapt their world. It also looks at the role of sources produced after the European encounter in shaping our understanding of the histories of indigenous American empires.
- An expanded discussion of witchcraft in Chapter 15 now discusses practices of indigenous peoples in the New World.
- Chapter 18 has expanded coverage of Russian imperial expansion as well as a new section called "Peoples Beyond Borders" that includes piracy and gives students a feeling for the ways in which imperial borders were often more real on the map than in real life.
- In Chapter 19, a new section called "The Early Enlightenment" clarifies the mixture of religious, political, and scientific thought that characterized the early period of the Enlightenment.
- Chapter 22 emphasizes the indigenous origins of the Haitian revolution by highlighting the African backgrounds of slaves and the considerable military experience many of them had, which helps explain how they could defeat the French and British.
- Chapter 23 has been heavily revised to reflect new scholarship on industrialization and to provide a broader, more comparative perspective.
- A new section in Chapter 24 on social and economic conflict connects the industrialization of continental Europe with the political coverage of the revolutions of 1848.
- Chapter 27 now focuses on the Americas within the framework of liberalism and examines connections between the experiences with settlement, state formation, and economic integration in the United States and Latin America.
- Chapter 29 contains more detail on the reforms of emir Amanullah Khan in the section on the modernization of Afghanistan.
- As noted previously, the final three chapters of the book have been entirely rewritten by new author Jerry Dávila.

In sum, we have tried to bring new research and interpretation into our global history, believing it essential to keep our book stimulating, accurate, and current for students and instructors.

Acknowledgments

It is a pleasure to thank the many instructors who critiqued the parent textbook, *A History of World Societies*, Tenth Edition. Their feedback helped inform the shape this book has taken.

Stewart Anderson, *Brigham Young University*

Brian Arendt, *Lindenwood University*

Stephen Auerbach, *Georgia College*

Michael Bardot, *Lincoln University*

Natalie Bayer, *Drake University*

Michael Bazemore, *William Peace University*

Brian Becker, *Delta State University*

Rosemary Bell, *Skyline College*

Chris Benedetto, *Granite State College*

Wesley L. Bishop, *Pitt Community College*

Robert Blackey, *California State University–San Bernardino*

Edward Bond, *Alabama A&M University*

Nathan Brooks, *New Mexico State University*

Jurgen Buchenau, *The University of North Carolina at Charlotte*

Paul Buckingham, *Morrisville State College*

Steven B. Bunker, *University of Alabama*

Kate Burlingham, *California State University, Fullerton*

David Bush, *The College of the Siskiyous*

Laura M. Calkins, *Texas Tech University*

Robert Caputi, *Erie Community College–North Campus*

Lucia Carter, *Mars Hill College*

Lesley Chapel, *Saginaw Valley State University*

Nevin Crouse, *Chesapeake College*

Everett Dague, *Benedictine College*

Peter de Rosa, *Bridgewater State University*

Jeffrey Demsky, *San Bernardino Valley College*

Nicholas Di Liberto, *Newberry College*

Randall Dills, *University of Louisville*

Shawn Dry, *Oakland Community College*

Roxanne Easley, *Central Washington University*

John Fielding, *Mount Wachusett Community College*

Barbara Fuller, *Indian River State College*

Dolores Grapsas, *New River Community College*

Emily Fisher Gray, *Norwich University*

Gayle Greene-Aguirre, *Mississippi Gulf Coast Community College*

Neil Greenwood, *Cleveland State Community College*

Christian Griggs, *Dalton State College*

W. Scott Haine, *Cañada College*

Irwin Halfond, *McKendree University*

Alicia Harding, *Southern Maine Community College*

Jillian Hartley, *Arkansas Northeastern College*

Robert Haug, *University of Cincinnati*

John Hunt, *Utah Valley University*

Fatima Imam, *Lake Forest College*

Rashi Jackman, *De Anza College*

Jackie Jay, *Eastern Kentucky University*

Timothy Jenks, *East Carolina University*

Andrew Kellett, *Harford Community College*

Christine Kern, *Edinboro University*

Christopher Killmer, *St. Johns River State College*

Mark Klobas, *Scottsdale Community College*

Chris Laney, *Berkshire Community College*

Erick D. Langer, *Georgetown University*

Mary Jean Lavery, *Delaware County Community College*

Mark Lentz, *University of Louisiana, Lafayette*

Darin Lenz, *Fresno Pacific University*

Yi Li, *Tacoma Community College*

Jonas Liliequist, *Umeå University*

Ron Lowe, *University of Tennessee at Chattanooga*

Mary Lyons-Carmona, *University of Nebraska at Omaha*

Elizabeth S. Manley, *Xavier University of Louisiana*

Brandon D. Marsh, *Bridgewater College*

Sean F. McEnroe, *Southern Oregon University*

John McLeod, *University of Louisville*

Brendan McManus, *Bemidji State University*

Christina Mehrtens, *University of Massachusetts-Dartmouth*

Charlotte Miller, *Middle Georgia State College*

Robert Montgomery, *Baldwin Wallace University*

Curtis Morgan, *Lord Fairfax Community College*

Richard Moss, *Harrisburg Area Community College*

Larry Myers, *Butler Community College*

Erik Lars Myrup, *University of Kentucky*

April Najjaj, *Mount Olive College*

Katie Nelson, *Weber State University*

Lily Rhodes Novicki, *Virginia Western Community College*

Monica Orozco, *Westmont College*

Neal Palmer, *Christian Brothers University*

Jenifer Parks, *Rocky Mountain College*

Melinda Pash, *Fayetteville Technical Community College*

Tao Peng, *Minnesota State University–Mankato*

Patricia Perry, *St. Edward's University*

William Plants, *University of Rio Grande/Rio Grande Community College*

Joshua Pollock, *Modesto Junior College*

Fabrizio Prado, *College of William & Mary*

Daniel Prosterman, *Salem College*

Tracie Provost, *Middle Georgia College*

Melissa Redd, *Pulaski Technical College*

Charles Reed, *Elizabeth City State University*

Leah Renold, *Texas State University*

Kim Richardson, *Front Range Community College*

David Ruffley, *Colorado Mountain College*

Martina Saltalamacchia, *University of Nebraska at Omaha*

Karl Schmidt, *South Dakota State University*

Kimberly Schutte, *SUNY–The College at Brockport*

Eva Seraphin, *Irvine Valley College*

Courtney Shah, *Lower Columbia College*

Jeffrey Shumway, *Brigham Young University*

David Simonelli, *Youngstown State University*

James Smith, *Southwest Baptist University*

Kara D. Smith, *Georgia Perimeter College*

Ilicia Sprey, *Saint Joseph's College*

Rachel Standish, *San Joaquin Delta College*

Kate Staples, *West Virginia University*

Brian Strayer, *Andrews University*

Sonia Chandarana Tandon, *Forsyth Technical Community College*

James Todesca, *Armstrong Atlantic State University*

Elisaveta Todorova, *University of Cincinnati*

Dianne Walker, *Baton Rouge Community College*

Kenneth Wilburn, *East Carolina University*

Carol Woodfin, *Hardin-Simmons University*

Laura Zeeman, *Red Rocks Community College*

It is also a pleasure to thank the many editors who have assisted us over the years, first at Houghton Mifflin and now at Bedford/St. Martin's. At Bedford/St. Martin's, these include associate editor Robin Soule; senior development editors Sara Wise and Laura Arcari; editorial assistant Arrin Kaplan; former executive editor Traci Mueller Crowell; director of development Jane Knetzger; former publisher for history Mary Dougherty; map editor Charlotte Miller; photo researcher Bruce Carson; text permissions editor Eve Lehmann; and production editor Annette Pagliaro Sweeney, with the assistance of Erica Zhang and the guidance of Sue Brown, director of editing, design, and media production, and managing editor Michael Granger. We would also like to thank former vice president for editorial humanities Denise Wydra and former president Joan E. Feinberg.

VERSIONS AND SUPPLEMENTS

Adopters of *Understanding World Societies* and their students have access to abundant print and digital resources and tools, including documents, assessment and presentation materials, the acclaimed Bedford Series in History and Culture volumes, and much more. And for the first time, the full-featured LaunchPad course space provides access to the narrative with all assignment and assessment opportunities at the ready. See below for more information, visit the book's catalog site at **bedfordstmartins.com/mckayworldunderstanding/catalog**, or contact your local Bedford/St. Martin's sales representative.

Get the Right Version for Your Class

To accommodate different course lengths and course budgets, *Understanding World Societies* is available in several different formats, including 3-hole-punched loose-leaf Budget Books versions and low-priced PDF e-books, such as the *Bedford e-Book to Go* from our Web site and other PDF e-books from other commercial sources. And for the best value of all, package a new print book with LaunchPad at no additional charge to get the best each format offers—a print version for easy portability and reading with a LaunchPad interactive e-book and course space with loads of additional assignment and assessment options.

- **Combined Volume** (Chapters 1–33): available in paperback, loose-leaf, and e-book formats and in LaunchPad
- **Volume 1, To 1600** (Chapters 1–16): available in paperback, loose-leaf, and e-book formats and in LaunchPad
- **Volume 2, Since 1450** (Chapters 16–33): available in paperback, loose-leaf, and e-book formats and in LaunchPad

As noted below, any of these volumes can be packaged with additional titles for a discount. To get ISBNs for discount packages, see the online catalog at **bedfordstmartins.com/mckayworldunderstanding/catalog** or contact your Bedford/St. Martin's representative.

NEW Assign LaunchPad — A Content-Rich and Assessment-Ready Interactive e-book and Course Space

Available for discount purchase on its own or for packaging with new books at no additional charge, LaunchPad is a breakthrough solution for today's courses. Intuitive and easy-to-use for students and instructors alike, LaunchPad is ready to use as is, but it can be edited, customized with your own material, and assigned in seconds. *LaunchPad for Understanding World Societies* includes Bedford/St.

Martin's high-quality content all in one place, including the full interactive e-book and the *Sources of World Societies* documents collection plus LearningCurve formative quizzing, guided reading activities designed to help students read actively for key concepts, additional primary sources, images, videos, chapter summative quizzes, and more.

Through a wealth of formative and summative assessments, including short-answer questions, essay questions, multiple-choice quizzing, and the adaptive learning program of LearningCurve (see the full description below), students gain confidence and get into their reading *before* class. Map and visual activities engage students with visual analysis and critical thinking as they work through each unit, while special boxed features become more meaningful through automatically graded multiple-choice exercises and short-answer questions that prompt students to analyze their reading.

LaunchPad easily integrates with course management systems, and with fast ways to build assignments, rearrange chapters, and add new pages, sections, or links, it lets teachers build the courses they want to teach and hold students accountable. For more information, visit **launchpadworks.com** or contact us at **history@bedfordstmartins.com** to arrange a demo.

✅ NEW Assign LearningCurve So Your Students Come to Class Prepared

Students using LaunchPad receive access to LearningCurve for *Understanding World Societies*. Assigning LearningCurve in place of reading quizzes is easy for instructors, and the reporting features help instructors track overall class trends and spot topics that are giving students trouble so they can adjust their lectures and class activities. This online learning tool is popular with students because it was designed to help them rehearse content at their own pace, in a nonthreatening, game-like environment. The feedback for wrong answers provides instructional coaching and sends students back to the book for review. Students answer as many questions as necessary to reach a target score, with repeated chances to revisit material they haven't mastered. When LearningCurve is assigned, students come to class better prepared.

Take Advantage of Instructor Resources

Bedford/St. Martin's has developed a rich array of teaching resources for this book and for this course. They range from lecture and presentation materials and assessment tools to course management options. Most can be found in LaunchPad or can be downloaded or ordered at **bedfordstmartins.com/mckayworldunderstanding /catalog**.

▶ **Instructor's Resource Manual.** The instructor's manual offers both experienced and first-time instructors tools for preparing lectures and running discussions. It includes chapter content learning objectives, teaching strategies, and a guide to chapter-specific supplements available for the text, plus suggestions on how to get the most out of LearningCurve and a survival guide for first-time teaching assistants.

▶ **Guide to Changing Editions.** Designed to facilitate an instructor's transition from the previous edition of *Understanding World Societies* to the second edition, this guide presents an overview of major changes as well as of changes in each chapter.

▶ **Computerized Test Bank.** The test bank includes a mix of fresh, carefully crafted multiple-choice, short-answer, and essay questions for each chapter. All questions appear in Microsoft Word format and in easy-to-use test bank software that allows instructors to add, edit, re-sequence, and print questions and answers. Instructors can also export questions into a variety of formats, including Blackboard, Desire2Learn, and Moodle.

▶ *The Bedford Lecture Kit:* **PowerPoint Maps and Images.** Look good and save time with *The Bedford Lecture Kit*. These presentation materials are downloadable individually from the Instructor Resources tab at **bedfordstmartins .com/mckayworldunderstanding/catalog**. They include all maps, figures, and images from the textbook in JPEG and PowerPoint formats.

Package and Save Your Students Money

For information on free packages and discounts up to 50%, visit **bedfordstmartins .com/mckayworldunderstanding/catalog** or contact your local Bedford/St. Martin's sales representative. The products that follow all qualify for discount packaging.

▶ **The Bedford Series in History and Culture.** More than 100 titles in this highly praised series combine first-rate scholarship, historical narrative, and important primary documents for undergraduate courses. Each book is brief, inexpensive, and focused on a specific topic or period. For a complete list of titles, visit **bedfordstmartins.com/history/series**.

▶ *Rand McNally Atlas of World History.* This collection of almost 70 full-color maps illustrates the eras and civilizations in world history from the emergence of human societies to the present.

▶ *The Bedford Glossary for World History.* This handy supplement for the survey course gives students historically contextualized definitions for hundreds of terms—from *abolitionism* to *Zoroastrianism*—that they will encounter in lectures, reading, and exams.

▶ *World History Matters: A Student Guide to World History Online.* Based on the popular "World History Matters" Web site produced by the Center for History and New Media, this unique resource, edited by Kristin Lehner (The Johns Hopkins University), Kelly Schrum (George Mason University), and T. Mills Kelly (George Mason University), combines reviews of 150 of the most useful and reliable world history Web sites, with an introduction that guides students in locating, evaluating, and correctly citing online sources.

▶ **Trade Books.** Titles published by sister companies Hill and Wang; Farrar, Straus and Giroux; Henry Holt and Company; St. Martin's Press; Picador; and Palgrave Macmillan are available at a 50% discount when packaged with Bedford/St. Martin's textbooks. For more information, visit **bedfordstmartins.com /tradeup**.

▶ *A Pocket Guide to Writing in History.* This portable and affordable reference tool by Mary Lynn Rampolla provides reading, writing, and research advice useful to students in all history courses. Concise yet comprehensive advice on approaching typical history assignments, developing critical reading skills, writing effective history papers, conducting research, using and documenting sources, and avoiding plagiarism—enhanced with practical tips and examples throughout—has made this slim reference a best-seller.

▶ *A Student's Guide to History.* This complete guide to success in any history course provides the practical help students need to be successful. In addition to introducing students to the nature of the discipline, author Jules Benjamin teaches a wide range of skills, from preparing for exams to approaching common writing assignments, and explains the research and documentation process with plentiful examples.

BRIEF CONTENTS

LearningCurve
bedfordstmartins.com
/mckayunderstanding

CONTENTS

1

THE EARLIEST HUMAN SOCIETIES

TO 2500 B.C.E. *2*

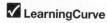

2

THE RISE OF THE STATE IN SOUTHWEST ASIA AND THE NILE VALLEY

3200–500 B.C.E. *32*

3

THE FOUNDATION OF INDIAN SOCIETY

TO 300 C.E *62*

4

CHINA'S CLASSICAL AGE

TO 221 B.C.E. *88*

5

THE GREEK EXPERIENCE

3500–30 B.C.E. *114*

6

THE WORLD OF ROME

CA. 1000 B.C.E.–400 C.E. *144*

7

EAST ASIA AND THE SPREAD OF BUDDHISM

221 B.C.E.–800 C.E. *174*

8

CONTINUITY AND CHANGE IN EUROPE AND WESTERN ASIA

250–850 *202*

9

THE ISLAMIC WORLD

600–1400 *232*

10

AFRICAN SOCIETIES AND KINGDOMS

1000 B.C.E.–1500 C.E.   *266*

11

THE AMERICAS

2500 B.C.E.–1500 C.E.   *296*

12

CULTURAL EXCHANGE IN CENTRAL AND SOUTHERN ASIA

300–1400 *328*

13

STATES AND CULTURES IN EAST ASIA

800–1400 *360*

14

EUROPE IN THE MIDDLE AGES

15

EUROPE IN THE RENAISSANCE AND REFORMATION

16

THE ACCELERATION OF GLOBAL CONTACT

1450–1600   *454*

MAPS, FIGURES, AND TABLES

SPECIAL FEATURES

Understanding
World Societies

A HISTORY

VOLUME 1

1
THE EARLIEST HUMAN SOCIETIES

TO 2500 B.C.E.

> How did human societies change and develop in the Paleolithic and Neolithic Eras? Chapter 1 examines early human history, tracing developments from the first humans through the emergence of settled agriculture. Human history began in Africa, where millions of years ago humans evolved from a primate ancestor. They migrated out of Africa in several waves, walking along coasts and over land, eventually spreading across much of the earth. Their tools were initially multipurpose sharpened stones and sticks, but gradually they invented more specialized tools. Environmental changes, such as the advance and retreat of the glaciers, shaped life dramatically and may have led to the most significant change in all of human history, the domestication of plants and animals.

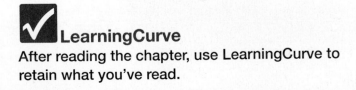

LearningCurve
After reading the chapter, use LearningCurve to retain what you've read.

> How did humans evolve, and where did they migrate?

> What were the key features of Paleolithic society?

> How did plant and animal domestication develop, and what effects did it have on human society?

> How did growing social and gender hierarchies and expanding networks of trade increase the complexity of human society in the Neolithic period?

West African Man Humans began to portray themselves on the surfaces of places where they lived and traveled as early as 50,000 B.C.E. This rock painting from the region of Niger in Africa shows a person, perhaps a shaman, wearing a large headdress. (© David Coulson/Robert Estall photo agency/Alamy)

How did humans evolve, and where did they migrate?

STUDYING THE EARLIEST ERA OF HUMAN HISTORY involves methods that seem simple—looking carefully at an object—as well as new high-tech procedures, such as DNA analysis. Through such research, scholars have examined early human evolution, traced the expansion of the human brain, and studied migration out of Africa and across the planet. Combined with spoken language, that larger brain enabled humans to adapt to many different environments and to be flexible in their responses to new challenges.

Understanding the Early Human Past

People throughout the world have developed systems of classification that help them understand things: earth and sky; seen and unseen; animal, vegetable, and mineral; past, present, and future. Among these systems of classification was

CHAPTER LOCATOR | How did humans evolve, and where did they migrate? | What were the key features of Paleolithic society?

4 CHAPTER 1
THE EARLIEST HUMAN SOCIETIES

ca. 4.4 million years ago
Ardipithecus evolve in Africa

ca. 2.5–4 million years ago
Australopithecus evolve in Africa

ca. 500,000–2 million years ago
Homo erectus evolve and spread out of Africa

ca. 250,000–9000 B.C.E.
Paleolithic era

ca. 250,000 years ago
Homo sapiens evolve in Africa

ca. 30,000–150,000 years ago
Neanderthals flourish in Europe and western Asia

ca. 120,000 years ago
Homo sapiens migrate out of Africa to Eurasia

ca. 50,000 years ago
Human migration to Australia

ca. 20,000–30,000 years ago
Possible human migration from Asia to the Americas

ca. 25,000 B.C.E.
Earliest evidence of woven cloth and baskets

ca. 15,000 B.C.E.
Earliest evidence of bows and atlatls; humans cross the Bering Strait land bridge to the Americas

ca. 15,000–10,000 B.C.E.
Final retreat of glaciers; megafaunal extinctions

ca. 9000 B.C.E.
Beginning of the Neolithic; horticulture; domestication of sheep and goats

ca. 7000 B.C.E.
Domestication of cattle; plow agriculture

ca. 5500 B.C.E.
Smelting of copper

ca. 5000 B.C.E.
Invention of pottery wheel

ca. 3200 B.C.E.
Earliest known invention of writing

ca. 3000 B.C.E.
Development of wheeled transport; beginning of bronze technology

ca. 2500 B.C.E.
Bronze technology becomes common in many areas; beginning of the Bronze Age

A note on dates: This book generally uses B.C.E. (Before the Common Era) and C.E. (Common Era) when giving dates, a system of chronology based on the Christian calendar and now used widely around the world. Scholars who study the very earliest periods of hominid and human history usually use the phrase "years ago" to date their subjects, as do astrophysicists and geologists; this is often abbreviated as B.P. (Before the Present). Because the scale of time covered in Chapter 1 is so vast, a mere 2,000 years does not make much difference, and so B.C.E. and "years ago" have similar meaning.

one invented in eighteenth-century Europe that divided all living things on earth into groups. Each of these divisions—such as that between plants and animals—is further subdivided into smaller and smaller groups, such as class, order, family, and genus. The final important division is the species, which is generally defined as a group of organisms that can interbreed with one another and produce fertile offspring of both sexes.

In their natural state, members of a species resemble one another, but over time they can become increasingly dissimilar. (Think of Chihuahuas and Great Danes, both members of the same species.) Ever since humans began shaping the world around them, this process has often been the result of human action. But in the long era before humans, the increasing dissimilarity resulted, in the opinion of most scientists, from the process of natural selection. Small variations within individuals in one species enabled them to acquire more food and better living conditions and made them more successful in breeding, thus allowing them to pass their genetic material on to the next generation. When a number of individuals within a species became distinct enough that they could no longer interbreed

How did plant and animal domestication develop, and what effects did it have on human society?

How did social hierarchies and trade increase complexity?

☑ LearningCurve
Check what you know.

successfully with others, they became a new species. Species also become extinct, particularly during periods of mass extinctions such as the one that killed the dinosaurs about 65 million years ago. Natural processes of species formation and extinction continue, although today changes in the biosphere—the living matter in the world—result far more from human action than from natural selection.

The scientists who developed this system of organizing the world placed humans within it, using the same means of classification that they used for all other living things. Humans were in the animal kingdom, the order of Primates, the family Hominidae, and the genus *Homo*. Like all classifications, this was originally based on externally visible phenomena: humans were placed in the Primates order because, like other primates, they have hands that can grasp, eyes facing forward to allow better depth perception, and relatively large brains; they were placed in the **hominid** family along with chimpanzees, gorillas, and orangutans because they shared even more features with these great apes. Over 98 percent of human DNA is the same as that of chimpanzees, which indicates to most scientists that humans and chimpanzees share a common ancestor. That common ancestor probably lived between 5 million and 7 million years ago.

Physical remains were the earliest type of evidence studied to learn about the distant human past, and scholars used them to develop another system of classification, one that distinguished between periods of time rather than types of living creatures. (Constructing models of time is called "periodization.") They gave labels to eras according to the primary materials out of which tools that survived were made. Thus the earliest human era became the Stone Age, the next era the Bronze Age, and the next the Iron Age. They further divided the Stone Age into the Old Stone Age, or **Paleolithic era**, during which people used stone, bone, and other natural products to make tools and gained food largely by **foraging**—that is, by gathering plant products, trapping or catching small animals and birds, and hunting larger prey. This was followed by the New Stone Age, or **Neolithic era**, which saw the beginning of agricultural and animal domestication. People around the world adopted agriculture at various times, and some never did, but the transition between the Paleolithic and the Neolithic is usually set at about 9000 B.C.E., the point at which agriculture was first developed.

Geologists refer to the last twelve thousand years as the Holocene (meaning very recent) epoch. The entire history of the human species fits well within the Holocene and the previous geologic epoch, the Pleistocene (PLIGH-stuh-seen), which began about 2.5 million years ago.

The Pleistocene was marked by repeated advances in glaciers and continental ice sheets. Glaciers tied up huge quantities of the earth's water, leading to lower sea levels, making it possible for animals and eventually humans to walk between places that were separated by oceans during interglacial times. Animals and humans were also prevented from migrating to other places by the ice sheets themselves, however, and the colder climate made large areas unfit to live in. Climate thus dramatically shaped human cultures.

Hominid Evolution

Using many different pieces of evidence from all over the world, archaeologists, paleontologists, and other scholars have developed a view of human evolution whose basic outline is widely shared, though there are disagreements about

hominids
▶ Members of the family Hominidae that contains humans, chimpanzees, gorillas, and orangutans.

Paleolithic era
▶ Period during which humans used tools of stone, bone, and wood and obtained food by gathering and hunting. Roughly 250,000–9,000 B.C.E.

foraging
▶ A style of life in which people gain food by gathering plant products, trapping or catching small animals and birds, and hunting larger prey.

Neolithic era
▶ Period beginning in 9000 B.C.E. during which humans obtained food by raising crops and animals and continued to use tools primarily of stone, bone, and wood.

CHAPTER LOCATOR | How did humans evolve, and where did they migrate? | What were the key features of Paleolithic society?

6 CHAPTER 1
THE EARLIEST HUMAN SOCIETIES

details. Most primates, including other hominids such as chimpanzees and gorillas, have lived primarily in trees, but at some point a group of hominids in East Africa began to spend more time on the ground, and between 6 and 7 million years ago they began to walk upright at least some of the time.

Over many generations, the skeletal and muscular structure of some hominids evolved to make upright walking easier, and they gradually became fully bipedal. The earliest fully bipedal hominids, whom paleontologists place in the genus *Australopithecus*, lived in southern and eastern Africa between 2.5 and 4 million years ago. Walking upright allowed australopithecines to carry and use things, which allowed them to survive better and may have also spurred brain development.

About 3.4 million years ago, some hominids began to use naturally occurring objects as tools, and sometime around 2.5 million years ago, one group of australopithecines in East Africa began to make and use simple tools, evolving into a different type of hominid that later paleontologists judged to be the first in the genus *Homo*. Called *Homo habilis* ("handy human"), they made sharpened stone pieces, which archaeologists call hand axes, and used them for various tasks. This suggests greater intelligence, and the skeletal remains support this, for *Homo habilis* had a larger brain than did the australopithecines.

About 2 million years ago, another species, called *Homo erectus* ("upright human"), evolved in East Africa. *Homo erectus* had still larger brains and made tools that were slightly specialized for various tasks, such as handheld axes, cleavers, and scrapers. Archaeological remains indicate that *Homo erectus* lived in larger groups than had earlier hominids and engaged in cooperative gathering, hunting, and food preparation. The location and shape of the larynx suggests that members of this species were able to make a wider range of sounds than were earlier hominids, so they may have relied more on vocal sounds than on gestures to communicate ideas to one another.

One of the activities that *Homo erectus* carried out most successfully was moving (Map 1.1). Gradually small groups migrated out of East Africa onto the open plains of central Africa, and from there into northern Africa. From 1 million to 2 million years ago, the earth's climate was in a warming phase, and these hominids ranged still farther, moving into western Asia by as early as 1.8 million years ago. Bones and other materials from China and the island of Java in Indonesia indicate that *Homo erectus* had reached there by about 1.5 million years ago, migrating over large landmasses as well as along the coasts. (Sea levels were lower than they are today, and Java could be reached by walking.) *Homo erectus* also walked north, reaching what is now Spain by at least 800,000 years ago and what is now Germany by 500,000 years ago. In each of these places, *Homo erectus* adapted gathering and hunting techniques to the local environment, learning how to find new sources of plant food and how to best catch local animals.

The Great Rift Valley

Homo Sapiens, "Thinking Humans"

Homo erectus was remarkably adaptable, but another hominid proved still more so: *Homo sapiens* ("thinking humans"). A few scientists think that *Homo sapiens* evolved from *Homo erectus* in a number of places in Afroeurasia, but the majority think that, like hominid evolution from earlier primates, this occurred only in East Africa. The evidence is partly archaeological, but also genetic. One type of DNA,

How did plant and animal domestication develop, and what effects did it have on human society?

How did social hierarchies and trade increase complexity?

☑ LearningCurve
Check what you know.

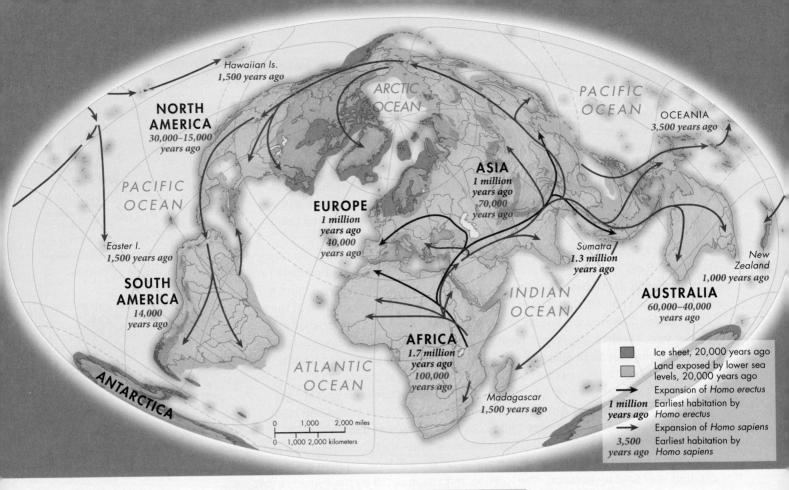

Hawaiian Is.
1,500 years ago

ARCTIC
OCEAN

PACIFIC
OCEAN

NORTH
AMERICA
30,000–15,000
years ago

OCEANIA
3,500 years ago

PACIFIC
OCEAN

ASIA
1 million
years ago
70,000
years ago

EUROPE
1 million
years ago
40,000
years ago

Easter I.
1,500 years ago

Sumatra
1.3 million
years ago

New
Zealand
1,000 years ago

SOUTH
AMERICA
14,000
years ago

INDIAN
OCEAN

AUSTRALIA
60,000–40,000
years ago

AFRICA
1.7 million
years ago
100,000
years ago

ATLANTIC
OCEAN

ANTARCTICA

Madagascar
1,500 years ago

0   1,000   2,000 miles

0 1,000 2,000 kilometers

Ice sheet, 20,000 years ago
Land exposed by lower sea
levels, 20,000 years ago
→ Expansion of *Homo erectus*
1 million Earliest habitation by
years ago *Homo erectus*
→ Expansion of *Homo sapiens*
3,500 Earliest habitation by
years ago *Homo sapiens*

MAP 1.1 ■ Human Migration
in the Paleolithic and Neolithic
Eras

> MAPPING THE PAST

ANALYZING THE MAP: What were the major similarities and differences between the migrations of *Homo erectus* and those of
Homo sapiens? How did environmental factors shape human
migration?
CONNECTIONS: What types of technology were required for the
migration patterns seen here? What do these migration patterns
suggest about the social organization of early people?

called mitochondrial DNA, indicates that modern humans are so similar genetically that they cannot have been evolving for the last 1 million or 2 million years.
This evidence suggests that the evolution of *Homo sapiens* has instead taken
place for only about 250,000 years. Because there is greater human genetic variety
today in Africa than in other parts of the world, the evidence also suggests that
Homo sapiens have lived there the longest, so that Africa is where they first
emerged.

Although there is some debate about where and when *Homo sapiens* emerged,
there is little debate about what distinguished these humans from earlier hominids: a bigger brain, in particular a bigger forebrain, the site of conscious thought.
The ability to think reflectively allowed for the creation of symbolic language, that
is, for language that follows certain rules and that can refer to things or states of

CHAPTER LOCATOR | How did humans evolve,
and where did they
migrate?

What were the key
features of Paleolithic
society?

8 CHAPTER 1
THE EARLIEST HUMAN SOCIETIES

being that are not necessarily present. Greater intelligence allowed *Homo sapiens* to better understand and manipulate the world around them, and symbolic language allowed this understanding to be communicated within a group and passed from one generation to the next. Through spoken language *Homo sapiens* began to develop collective explanations for the world around them that we would now call religion, science, and philosophy. Spoken language also enabled *Homo sapiens* to organize socially into larger groups, thus further enhancing their ability to affect the natural world.

The advantages of a larger brain seem evident to us, so we may not think to ask why hominids evolved this way. Large brains also bring disadvantages, however. They take more energy to run than other parts of the body, so that large-brained animals have to eat more than small-brained ones. Large brains create particular problems for bipedal mammals, for the narrow pelvic structure that works best for upright walking makes giving birth to a large-headed infant difficult and painful.

The question of why hominids developed ever-larger brains might best be answered by looking at how paleontologists think it happened. As *Homo habilis*, *Homo erectus*, and *Homo sapiens* made and used tools, the individuals whose mental and physical abilities allowed them to do so best were able to obtain more food and were more likely to mate and have children who survived. Thus bigger brains led to better tools, but the challenges of using and inventing better tools also created selective pressure that led to bigger brains.

The same thing may have happened with symbolic language and thought. A slightly bigger brain allowed for more complex thought and better language skills. These thinking and speaking skills enabled individuals to better attract mates and fend off rivals, which meant a greater likelihood of passing on the enhanced brain to the next generation.

The growth in brain size and complexity may also have been linked to social organization. Individuals who had better social skills were more likely to mate than those who did not—this has been observed in chimpanzees and, of course, in modern humans—and thus to pass on their genetic material. Social skills were particularly important for females, because the combination of bipedalism and growing brain size led to selective pressure for hominid infants to be born at an even earlier stage in their development than other primate infants. Thus the period when human infants are dependent on others is very long, and mothers with good social networks to assist them were more likely to have infants who survived.

All these factors operated together in processes that promoted bigger and better brains. In the Paleolithic period, *Homo sapiens'* brains invented highly specialized tools made out of a variety of materials that replaced the more general-purpose stone tools made by *Homo erectus*: barbed fishhooks and harpoons, snares and traps for catching small animals, bone needles for sewing clothing, awls for punching holes in leather, nets for catching fish, sharpened flint pieces bound to wooden or bone handles for hunting or cutting, and slings for carrying infants. By 25,000 years ago, and perhaps earlier, humans in some parts of the world were weaving cloth and baskets, and by 17,000 years ago they were using bows and atlatls (AHT-lah-tuhlz)—notched throwing sticks made of bone, wood, or antler—to launch arrows and barbs with flint points bound to wooden shafts.

| How did plant and animal domestication develop, and what effects did it have on human society? | How did social hierarchies and trade increase complexity? | ☑️ **LearningCurve** Check what you know. |

The archaeological evidence for increasingly sophisticated language and social organization is less direct than that for tool use, but it is hard to imagine how humans could have made the tools they did—or would have chosen to decorate so many of them—without both of these.

Migration and Differentiation

Like *Homo erectus* had earlier, groups of *Homo sapiens* moved. By 200,000 years ago they had begun to spread across Africa, and by 120,000 years ago they had begun to migrate out of Africa to Eurasia (see Map 1.1). They most likely walked along the coasts of India and Southeast Asia, and then migrated inland. At the same time, further small evolutionary changes led to our own subspecies of anatomically modern humans, *Homo sapiens sapiens* (which literally translates as "thinking thinking humans"). *Homo sapiens sapiens* moved into areas where there were already *Homo erectus* populations, eventually replacing them, leaving *Homo sapiens* as the only survivors and the ancestors of all modern humans.

The best-known example of interaction between *Homo erectus* and *Homo sapiens sapiens* is that between Neanderthals (named after the Neander Valley in Germany, where their remains were first discovered) and a group of anatomically modern humans called Cro-Magnons. **Neanderthals** lived throughout Europe and western Asia beginning about 150,000 years ago, had brains as large as those of modern humans, and used tools, including spears and scrapers for animal skins, that enabled them to survive in the cold climate of Ice Age central Europe and Russia. They built freestanding houses and decorated objects and themselves with red ochre, a form of colored clay. They sometimes buried their dead carefully with tools, animal bones, and perhaps flowers, which suggests that they understood death to have a symbolic meaning.

Cro-Magnon peoples moved into parts of western Asia where Neanderthals lived by about 70,000 years ago, and into Europe by about 45,000 years ago. The two peoples appear to have lived side by side for millennia, hunting the same types of animals and gathering the same types of plants. The last evidence of Neanderthals as a separate species comes from about 30,000 years ago, and it is not clear exactly how they died out. They may have been killed by Cro-Magnon peoples, or they simply may have lost the competition for food as the climate worsened around 30,000 years ago and the glaciers expanded.

Homo erectus migrated great distances, but *Homo sapiens sapiens* made use of greater intelligence and better toolmaking capabilities to migrate still farther. They used simple rafts to reach Australia by at least 50,000 years ago, and by 35,000 years ago had reached New Guinea. By at least 15,000 years ago, humans had walked across the land bridges then linking Siberia and North America at the Bering Strait and had crossed into the Americas. Because by 14,000 years ago humans were already in southern South America, ten thousand miles from the land bridges, many scholars now think that people came to the Americas much earlier. They think humans came from Asia to the Americas perhaps as early as 20,000 or even 30,000 years ago, walking or using rafts along the coasts. (See Chapter 11 for a longer discussion of this issue.)

With the melting of glaciers sea levels rose, and parts of the world that had been linked by land bridges, including North America and Asia as well as many parts of Southeast Asia, became separated by water. This cut off migratory paths

Neanderthals

▶ Group of *Homo erectus* with brains as large as those of modern humans that flourished in Europe and western Asia between 150,000 and 30,000 years ago.

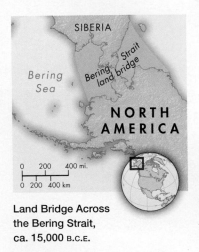

Land Bridge Across the Bering Strait, ca. 15,000 B.C.E.

but also spurred innovation. Humans designed and built ever more sophisticated boats and learned how to navigate by studying wind and current patterns, bird flights, and the position of the stars. They sailed to increasingly remote islands, including those in the Pacific, the last parts of the globe to be settled. The western Pacific islands were inhabited by about 2000 B.C.E., Hawaii by about 500 C.E., and New Zealand by about 1000 C.E. (For more on the settlement of the Pacific islands, see page 355.)

Once humans had spread out over much of the globe, groups often became isolated from one another, and people mated only with other members of their own group or those who lived nearby, a practice anthropologists call endogamy. Thus, over thousands of generations, although humans remained one species, *Homo sapiens sapiens* came to develop differences in physical features, including skin and hair color, eye and body shape, and amount of body hair. Language also changed over generations, so that thousands of different languages were eventually spoken. Groups created widely varying cultures and passed them on to their children, further increasing diversity among humans.

QUICK REVIEW

In what ways was *Homo sapiens* different from other hominids?

How did plant and animal domestication develop, and what effects did it have on human society?	How did social hierarchies and trade increase complexity?	✓ LearningCurve Check what you know.

11

> What were the key features of Paleolithic society?

Paleolithic Hand Axes

Like most Paleolithic stone tools, these two hand axes from Libya in northern Africa were made by chipping flakes off stone to form a sharpened edge. Although they are traditionally called axes, they were used for a variety of purposes, including skinning, cutting, and chopping. (Robert Harding Images/Masterfile)

EVENTUALLY HUMAN CULTURES BECAME WIDELY DIVERSE, but in the Paleolithic period people throughout the world lived in ways that were similar to one another. Archaeological evidence and studies of modern foragers suggest that people lived in small groups of related individuals and moved throughout the landscape in search of food. Most had few material possessions, only what they could carry, although in areas where food resources were especially rich, such as along seacoasts, they built structures and lived more permanently in one place. In the later Paleolithic, people in many parts of the world created art and music and developed religious ideas that linked the natural world to a world beyond.

Foraging for Food

Paleolithic peoples have often been called hunter-gatherers, but recent archaeological and anthropological research indicates that both historical and contemporary hunter-gatherers have depended much more on gathered foods than on hunted meat. Thus most scholars now call them foragers, a term that highlights

CHAPTER LOCATOR | How did humans evolve, and where did they migrate? | **What were the key features of Paleolithic society?**

CHAPTER 1
12 THE EARLIEST HUMAN SOCIETIES

the flexibility and adaptability in their search for food. Most of what foragers ate were plants, and much of the animal protein in their diet came from foods gathered or scavenged rather than hunted directly: insects, shellfish, small animals caught in traps, fish and other sea creatures caught in weirs and nets, and animals killed by other predators.

Paleolithic peoples did hunt large game. Groups working together forced animals over cliffs, threw spears, and, beginning about 15,000 B.C.E., used bows and atlatls to shoot projectiles so that they could stand farther away from their prey while hunting. The final retreat of the glaciers also occurred between 10,000 and 15,000 years ago, and the warming climate was less favorable to the very large mammals that had roamed the open spaces of many parts of the world. Wooly mammoths, mastodons, and wooly rhinos all died out in Eurasia in this **megafaunal extinction**, as did camels, horses, and sloths in the Americas and giant kangaroos and wombats in Australia. In many places, these extinctions occurred just about the time that modern humans appeared, and increasing numbers of scientists think that they were at least in part caused by human hunting.

Most foraging societies that exist today or did so until recently have some type of **division of labor** by sex, and also by age, with children and older people responsible for different tasks than adult men and women. Men are more often responsible for hunting and women for gathering plant and animal products. This has led scholars to assume that in Paleolithic society men were also responsible for hunting, and women for gathering.

Obtaining food was a constant preoccupation, but it was not a constant job. Studies of recent foragers indicate that, other than in times of environmental disasters such as prolonged droughts, people need only about ten to twenty hours a week to gather food and carry out the other tasks needed to survive, such as locating water and building shelters. Moreover, the diet of foragers is varied and nutritious. The slow pace of life and healthy diet did not mean that Paleolithic life spans approached those of the modern world, however. People avoided such contemporary killers as heart disease and diabetes, but they often died at young ages from injuries, infections, animal attacks, and interpersonal violence. Mothers and infants died in childbirth, and many children died before they reached adulthood.

Total human population thus grew very slowly during the Paleolithic. Moreover, the population was widely scattered, with small bands of people occupying very large territories. The low population density meant that human impact on the environment was relatively small, although still significant. In addition to contributing to the extinction of some large animals, Paleolithic people may have also shaped their environments by setting fires, which encouraged the growth of new

megafaunal extinction
▶ Die-off of large animals in many parts of the world about 15,000–10,000 B.C.E., caused by climate change and perhaps human hunting.

division of labor
▶ Differentiation of tasks by gender, age, training, status, or other social distinction.

> Human Population Growth in the Paleolithic and Present Eras:

30,000 years ago: 500,000
10,000 years ago: 5 million
300 years ago: 1 billion
Today: 7 billion

How did plant and animal domestication develop, and what effects did it have on human society?	How did social hierarchies and trade increase complexity?	✓ LearningCurve Check what you know.

plants and attracted animals that fed on them, making hunting or snaring game easier. This practice was a factor in the spread of plants that thrived best with occasional burning, such as the eucalyptus in Australia.

Family and Kinship Relationships

Small bands of humans—twenty or thirty people was a standard size for foragers in harsh environments—were scattered across broad areas, but this did not mean that each group lived in isolation. Their travels in search of food brought them into contact with one another, not simply for talking and celebrating, but also for providing opportunities for the exchange of sexual partners, which was essential to group survival. Mating arrangements varied in their permanence, but many groups seem to have developed a somewhat permanent arrangement whereby a man or woman left his or her original group and joined the group of his or her mate, what would later be termed marriage.

Within each band, and within the larger kin groups, individuals had a variety of identities; they were simultaneously fathers, sons, husbands, and brothers, or mothers, daughters, wives, and sisters. Each of these identities was relational (parent to child, sibling to sibling, spouse to spouse), and some of them, especially parent to child, gave one power over others. Paleolithic people were not differentiated by wealth, for in a foraging society accumulating material goods was not advantageous. But they were differentiated by such factors as age, gender, and position in a family, and no doubt by personal qualities such as intelligence, courage, and charisma.

Stereotypical representations of Paleolithic people often portray men going off to hunt while women and children crouched around a fire, waiting for the men to bring back meat. Studies of the relative importance of gathering to hunting, women's participation in hunting, and gender relations among contemporary foraging peoples have led some analysts to turn these stereotypes on their heads. They see Paleolithic bands as egalitarian groups in which the contributions of men and women to survival were recognized and valued, and in which both men and women had equal access to the limited amount of resources held by the group. Other scholars argue that this is also a stereotype, overly romanticizing Paleolithic society. They note that, although social relations among foragers were not as hierarchical as they were in other types of societies, many foraging groups had one person who held more power than others, and that person was almost always a man. This debate about gender relations is often part of larger discussions about whether Paleolithic society—and by implication, "human nature"— was primarily peaceful and nurturing or violent and brutal, and whether these qualities are gender related. Like much else about the Paleolithic, sources about gender and about violence are fragmentary and difficult to interpret; there may simply have been a diversity of patterns, as there is among more modern foragers.

Whether peaceful and egalitarian or violent and hierarchical, heterosexual relations produced children, who were cared for as infants by their mothers or other women who had recently given birth. Breast milk was the only food available that infants could easily digest, so mothers nursed their children for several years. Other than for feeding, children were most likely cared for by other male and female members of the group as well as by their mothers during the long period of human childhood.

CHAPTER LOCATOR | How did humans evolve, and where did they migrate? | **What were the key features of Paleolithic society?**

14 CHAPTER 1 THE EARLIEST HUMAN SOCIETIES

Cultural Creations and Spirituality

Beginning in the Paleolithic, human beings expressed themselves through what we would now term the arts or culture: painting and decorating walls and objects, making music with their voices and a variety of instruments, imagining and telling stories, dancing alone or in groups. Evidence from the Paleolithic, particularly from after about 50,000 years ago, includes flutes, carvings, jewelry, and paintings done on cave walls and rock outcroppings that depict animals, people, and symbols.

At the same time that people marked and depicted the world around them, they also appear to have developed ideas about supernatural forces that controlled some aspects of the natural world and the place of humans in it, what we now term spirituality or religion. Paleolithic burials, paintings, and objects suggest that people may have thought of their world as extending beyond the visible. People, animals, plants, natural occurrences, and other things around them had spirits, an idea called **animism**. The only evidence of Paleolithic animism that survives is physical, of course, but more recent animist traditions carry on this understanding of the spiritual nature and interdependence of all things.

animism
▶ Idea that people, animals, plants, natural occurrences, and other parts of the physical world have spirits.

Cave Paintings of Horses and a Horned Aurochs from Lascaux Cave, Southern France, ca. 15,000 B.C.E.

The artist who made these amazing animals in charcoal and red ochre first smoothed the surface, just as a contemporary artist might. This cave includes paintings of hundreds of animals, including predators such as lions, as well as abstract symbols. (JM Labat/Photo Researchers, Inc.)

> PICTURING THE PAST

ANALYZING THE IMAGE: The artist painted the animals so close together that they overlap. What might this arrangement have been trying to depict or convey?

CONNECTIONS: Why might Paleolithic people have made cave paintings? What do these paintings suggest about Stone Age culture and society?

How did plant and animal domestication develop, and what effects did it have on human society?

How did social hierarchies and trade increase complexity?

☑ LearningCurve
Check what you know.

Paleolithic Flute

This flute, carved from the wing bone of a griffon vulture, was unearthed in a cave in Germany along with pieces of other flutes made from mammoth ivory and stone tools. Dating from at least 33,000 B.C.E., it is the oldest musical instrument ever found and suggests that music has long been an important part of human culture.
(H. Jensen/University of Tübingen)

shamans

▶ Spiritually adept men and women who communicated with the unseen world.

Death took people from the realm of the living, but for Paleolithic groups people continued to inhabit an unseen world, along with spirits and deities, after death; thus kin groups included deceased as well as living members of a family. The unseen world regularly intervened in the visible world, for good and ill, and the actions of dead ancestors, spirits, and gods could be shaped by living people. Concepts of the supernatural pervaded all aspects of life; hunting, birth, death, and natural occurrences such as eclipses, comets, and rainbows all had religious meaning. Supernatural forces were understood to determine the basic rules for human existence, and upsetting these rules could lead to chaos.

Ordinary people learned about the unseen world through dreams and portents, and messages and revelations were also sent more regularly to shamans, spiritually adept men and women who communicated with the unseen world. Shamans created complex rituals through which they sought to ensure the health and prosperity of an individual, family, or group. Objects understood to have special power, such as carvings or masks in the form of an animal or person, could give additional protection, as could certain plants or mixtures eaten, sniffed, or rubbed on the skin. Shamans thus also operated as healers, with cures that included what we would term natural medicines and religious healing.

> QUICK REVIEW

What social relationships shaped and defined Paleolithic bands?

CHAPTER LOCATOR | How did humans evolve, and where did they migrate? | What were the key features of Paleolithic society?

16 CHAPTER 1 THE EARLIEST HUMAN SOCIETIES

How did plant and animal domestication develop, and what effects did it have on human society?

This two-handled pot, made in the Yellow River Valley of baked ceramics, is painted in a swirling red and black geometric design. Neolithic agricultural communities produced a wide array of storage containers for keeping food and other commodities from one season to the next. (Museum purchase, Fowler McCormack, Class of 1921. Fund. y1979-94. Photo: Bruce M. White/Princeton University Art Museum/Art Resource, NY)

FORAGING REMAINED THE BASIC WAY OF LIFE for most of human history. In a few especially fertile areas, however, the natural environment provided enough food that people could become more settled. As they remained in one place, they began to plant seeds as well as gather wild crops, to raise certain animals instead of hunting them, and to selectively breed both plants and animals to make them more useful to humans. This seemingly small alteration was the most important change in human history; because of its impact it is often termed the **Agricultural Revolution**. Plant and animal domestication marked the transition from the Paleolithic to the Neolithic. It allowed the human population to grow far more quickly than did foraging, but it also required more labor, which became increasingly specialized.

Agricultural Revolution
▶ Dramatic transformation in human history resulting from the change from foraging to raising crops and animals.

The Development of Horticulture

Areas of the world differed in the food resources available to foragers. In some, acquiring enough food to sustain a group was difficult, and groups had to move constantly. In others, moderate temperatures and abundant rainfall allowed for verdant plant growth; or seas, rivers, and lakes provided substantial amounts of fish and shellfish. Groups in such areas were able to become more settled. About

How did plant and animal domestication develop, and what effects did it have on human society?	How did social hierarchies and trade increase complexity?	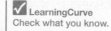 LearningCurve Check what you know.

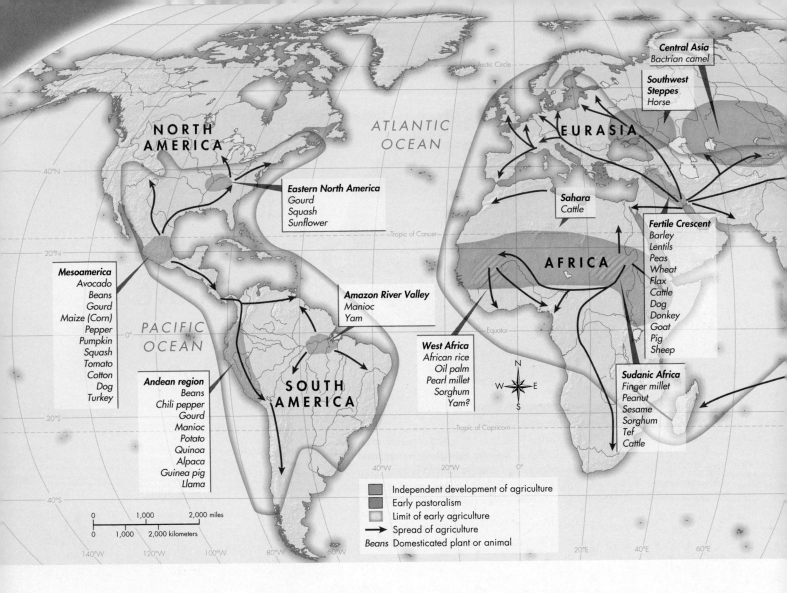

Mesoamerica
Avocado
Beans
Gourd
Maize (Corn)
Pepper
Pumpkin
Squash
Tomato
Cotton
Dog
Turkey

Andean region
Beans
Chili pepper
Gourd
Manioc
Potato
Quinoa
Alpaca
Guinea pig
Llama

Eastern North America
Gourd
Squash
Sunflower

Amazon River Valley
Manioc
Yam

West Africa
African rice
Oil palm
Pearl millet
Sorghum
Yam?

Sudanic Africa
Finger millet
Peanut
Sesame
Sorghum
Tef
Cattle

Sahara
Cattle

Fertile Crescent
Barley
Lentils
Peas
Wheat
Flax
Cattle
Dog
Donkey
Goat
Pig
Sheep

Central Asia
Bactrian camel

Southwest Steppes
Horse

Independent development of agriculture
Early pastoralism
Limit of early agriculture
Spread of agriculture
Beans Domesticated plant or animal

0   1,000   2,000 miles
0   1,000   2,000 kilometers

15,000 years ago, the earth's climate entered a warming phase, and the glaciers began to retreat. As the earth became warmer, the climate became wetter, and more parts of the world were able to support sedentary or semi-sedentary groups of foragers.

In several of these places, foragers began planting seeds in the ground along with gathering wild grains, roots, and other foodstuffs. By observation, they learned the optimum times and places for planting. They removed unwanted plants through weeding and selected the seeds they planted in order to get crops that had favorable characteristics, such as larger edible parts. Through this human intervention, certain crops became **domesticated**, that is, modified by selective breeding so as to serve human needs, in this case to provide a more reliable source of food.

This early crop planting was done by individuals using hoes and digging sticks, and it is often termed **horticulture** to distinguish it from the later agriculture using plows. Intentional crop planting developed first in the area archaeologists call the Fertile Crescent, which runs from present-day Lebanon, Israel, and Jordan north to Turkey and then south to the Iran-Iraq border (Map 1.2). About 9000 B.C.E. people there began to plant seeds of the wild wheat and barley they had already been harvesting, along with seeds of legume crops, such as peas and lentils, and

domesticated
▶ Plants and animals modified by selective breeding so as to serve human needs; domesticated animals will behave in specific ways and breed in captivity.

horticulture
▶ Crop raising done with hand tools and human power.

CHAPTER LOCATOR | How did humans evolve, and where did they migrate? | What were the key features of Paleolithic society?

East Asia
Millet
Rice
Soybean
Silkworm
Pig

Southeast Asia
Banana
Yam
Chicken
Water buffalo
Zebu cattle

New Guinea
Sugar cane
Taro
Yam

PACIFIC OCEAN

AUSTRALIA

MAP 1.2 ■ The Spread of Agriculture and Pastoralism

Local plants and animals were domesticated in many different places. Agriculturalists and pastoralists spread the knowledge of how to raise them, and spread the plants and animals themselves through migration, trade, and conquest.

Black Sea

ANATOLIA
Çatal Hüyük

MESOPOTAMIA
Tigris R.
Euphrates R.

ARABIAN DESERT

Probable ancient coastline

☐ Fertile Crescent

The Fertile Crescent

of the flax with which they made linen cloth. By about 8000 B.C.E. people were growing sorghum and millet in parts of the Nile River Valley, and perhaps yams in western Africa. By about 7000 B.C.E. they were growing domesticated rice, millet, and legumes in China; yams and taro in Papua New Guinea; and perhaps squash in Mesoamerica. In each of these places, the development of horticulture occurred independently, and it may have happened in other parts of the world as well.

Why, after living successfully as foragers for tens of thousands of years, did humans in so many parts of the world all begin raising crops at about the same time? The answer to this question is not clear, but crop raising may have resulted from population pressures in those parts of the world where the warming climate provided more food. More food meant lower child mortality and longer life spans, which allowed communities to grow. When population growth outstripped the local food supply, people had a choice: they could move to a new area—the solution that foragers had relied on when faced with the problem of food scarcity—or they could develop ways to increase the food supply to keep up with population growth, a solution that the warming climate was making possible. They chose the latter and began to plant more intensively, beginning cycles of expanding population and intensification of land use that have continued to today.

How did plant and animal domestication develop, and what effects did it have on human society?

How did social hierarchies and trade increase complexity?

 LearningCurve
Check what you know.

A recent archaeological find at Göbekli Tepe in present-day Turkey, at the northern edge of the Fertile Crescent, suggests that cultural factors may have played a role in the development of agriculture. Here, around 9000 B.C.E. hundreds of people came together to build rings of massive, multiton, elaborately carved limestone pillars and then covered them with dirt and built more. The people who created this site lived some distance away, where archaeological evidence indicates they first carved the pillars. The evidence also reveals that they ate wild game and plants, not crops. The project may have unintentionally spurred the development of new methods of food production that would allow the many workers to be fed efficiently. Indeed, it is very near here that evidence of the world's oldest domesticated wheat has been discovered.

Whatever the reasons for the move from foraging to crop raising, within several centuries of initial crop planting, people in the Fertile Crescent, parts of China, and the Nile Valley were relying on domesticated food products alone. They built permanent houses near one another in villages surrounded by fields, and they invented new ways of storing foods, such as in pottery made from clay. Villages were closer together than were the camps of foragers, so population density as well as total population grew.

A field of planted and weeded crops yields ten to one hundred times as much food — measured in calories — as the same area of naturally occurring plants. It also requires much more labor, however, which was provided both by the greater number of people in the community and by those people working longer hours. Farming peoples were often in the fields from dawn to dusk. Early farmers were also less healthy than foragers were. Their narrower range of foodstuffs made them more susceptible to disease and nutritional deficiencies such as anemia.

Foragers who lived at the edge of horticultural communities appear to have recognized the negative aspects of crop raising, for they did not immediately

Pillar at Göbekli Tepe

The huge limestone pillars arranged in rings at the Paleolithic site Göbekli Tepe are somewhat humanoid in shape, and the carvings are of dangerous animals, including lions, boars, foxes, snakes, vultures, and scorpions. The structure required enormous skill and effort of the people who built it, and clearly had great importance to them. (Vincent J. Musi/National Geographic Creative)

CHAPTER LOCATOR | How did humans evolve, and where did they migrate? | What were the key features of Paleolithic society?

adopt this new way of life. Instead farming spread when a village became too large and some residents moved to a new area. Because the population of farming communities grew so much faster than that of foragers, however, horticulture quickly spread into fertile areas. By about 6500 B.C.E. farming had spread northward from the Fertile Crescent into Greece, and by 4000 B.C.E. farther northward all the way to Britain; by 4500 B.C.E. it had spread southward into Ethiopia. At the same time, crop raising spread out from others areas in which it was first developed, and slowly larger and larger parts of China, South and Southeast Asia, and East Africa became home to horticultural villages.

People adapted crops to their local environments, choosing seeds that had qualities that were beneficial, such as drought resistance. They also domesticated new kinds of crops. In the Americas, for example, by about 3000 B.C.E. corn was domesticated in southern Mexico and potatoes and quinoa in the Andes region of South America, and by about 2500 B.C.E. squash and beans in eastern North America. These crops then spread, so that by about 1000 B.C.E. people in much of what is now the western United States were raising corn, beans, and squash. In the Indus Valley of South Asia, people were growing dates, mangoes, sesame seeds, and cotton along with grains and legumes by 4000 B.C.E. Accordingly, crop raising led to dramatic human alteration of the environment.

Certain planted crops eventually came to be grown over huge areas of land, so that some scientists describe the Agricultural Revolution as a revolution of codependent domestication: humans domesticated crops, but crops also "domesticated" humans so that they worked long hours spreading particular crops around the world. Of these, corn has probably been the most successful; more than half a million square miles around the world are now planted in corn.

In some parts of the world horticulture led to a dramatic change in the way of life, but in others it did not. Horticulture can be easily combined with gathering and hunting, as plots of land are usually small; many cultures, including some in Papua New Guinea and North America, remained mixed foragers and horticulturists for thousands of years. Especially in deeply wooded areas, people cleared small plots by chopping and burning the natural vegetation, and planted crops in successive years until the soil eroded or lost its fertility, a method termed "slash and burn." They then moved to another area and began the process again, perhaps returning to the first plot many years later, after the soil had rejuvenated itself. Groups using shifting slash-and-burn cultivation remained small and continued to rely on the surrounding forest for much of their food.

Animal Domestication and the Rise of Pastoralism

At roughly the same time that they domesticated certain plants, people also domesticated animals. The earliest animal to be domesticated was the dog, which separated genetically as a subspecies from wolves at least 15,000 years ago and perhaps much earlier. The relationship provided both humans and dogs with benefits: humans gained dogs' better senses of smell and hearing and their body warmth, and dogs gained new food sources and safer surroundings.

Dogs fit easily into a foraging lifestyle, but humans also domesticated animals that led them to completely alter their way of life. In about 9000 B.C.E., at the same

How did plant and animal domestication develop, and what effects did it have on human society? | How did social hierarchies and trade increase complexity? | 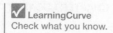 LearningCurve Check what you know.

21

Pastoral economies thrive in many parts of the world today, particularly in areas that are too dry for agriculture, including central Australia, Central Asia, northern and western Africa, and much of the U.S. West. As in early pastoralism, contemporary herders choose and breed their animals for qualities that will allow them to prosper in the local environment.

(Yvan Travert/akg-images)

time they began to raise crops, people in the Fertile Crescent domesticated wild goats and sheep, probably using them first for meat, and then for milk, skins, and eventually fleece (see Map 1.2). They learned from observation and experimentation that traits are passed down from generation to generation, and they began to breed the goats and sheep selectively for qualities that they wanted. Sometimes they trained dogs to assist them in herding, and then selectively bred the dogs for qualities that were advantageous for this task.

Sometime after goats and sheep, pigs were domesticated in both the Fertile Crescent and China, as were chickens in southern Asia. Like domesticated crops, domesticated animals eventually far outnumbered their wild counterparts. Animal domestication also shaped human evolution; groups that relied on animal milk and milk products for a significant part of their diet tended to develop the ability to digest milk as adults, while those that did not remained lactose intolerant as adults, the normal condition for mammals.

pastoralism

▶ An economic system based on herding flocks of goats, sheep, cattle, or other animals.

Sheep and goats allow themselves to be herded, and people developed a new form of living, **pastoralism**, based on herding and raising livestock. In areas with sufficient rainfall and fertile soil, pastoralism can be relatively sedentary and thus is easily combined with horticulture; people built pens for animals, or in colder climates constructed special buildings or took them into their houses. They learned that animal manure increases crop yields, so they gathered the manure from enclosures and used it as fertilizer.

Increased contact with animals and their feces also increased human contact with various sorts of disease-causing pathogens. This was particularly the case where humans and animals lived in tight quarters. Thus pastoralists and agriculturalists developed illnesses that had not plagued foragers, and the diseases became endemic, that is, widely found within a region without being deadly. Ultimately people who lived with animals developed resistance to some of these

CHAPTER LOCATOR | How did humans evolve, and where did they migrate? | What were the key features of Paleolithic society?

22 CHAPTER 1
THE EARLIEST HUMAN SOCIETIES

illnesses, but foragers' lack of resistance to many illnesses meant that they died more readily after coming into contact with new endemic diseases, as was the case when Europeans brought smallpox to the Americas in the sixteenth century.

In drier areas, flocks need to travel long distances from season to season to obtain enough food, so some pastoralists became nomadic. Nomadic pastoralists often gather wild plant foods as well, but they tend to rely primarily on their flocks of animals for food. Pastoralism was well suited to areas where the terrain or climate made crop planting difficult, such as mountains, deserts, dry grasslands, and tundras. Eventually other grazing animals, including cattle, camels, horses, yak, and reindeer, also became the basis of pastoral economies in Central and West Asia, many parts of Africa, and far northern Europe.

Plow Agriculture

Horticulture and pastoralism brought significant changes to human ways of life, but the domestication of certain large animals had an even bigger impact. Cattle and water buffalo were domesticated in some parts of Asia and North Africa in which they occurred naturally by at least 7000 B.C.E., and horses, donkeys, and camels by about 4000 B.C.E. All these animals can be trained to carry people or burdens on their backs and to pull loads dragged behind them. The domestication of large animals dramatically increased the power available to humans to carry out their tasks, which had both an immediate effect in the societies in which this happened and a long-term effect when these societies later encountered societies in which human labor remained the only source of power.

The pulling power of animals came to matter most, because it could be applied to food production. Sometime in the seventh millennium B.C.E., people attached wooden sticks to frames that animals dragged through the soil, thus breaking it up and allowing seeds to sprout more easily. Using plows, Neolithic people produced a significant amount of surplus food, which meant that some people in the community could spend their days performing other tasks, increasing the division of labor. Surplus food had to be stored, and some began to specialize in making products for storage, such as pots, baskets, and other kinds of containers. Others specialized in making tools, houses, and other items needed in village life, or for producing specific types of food. Families and households became increasingly interdependent, trading food for other commodities or services.

Stored food was also valuable and could become a source of conflict, as could other issues in villages where people lived close together. Villagers needed more complex rules than did foragers about how food was to be distributed and how different types of work were to be valued. Certain individuals began to specialize in the determination and enforcement of these rules, and informal structures of power gradually became more formalized as elites developed. These elites then distributed resources to their own advantage, often using force to attain and maintain their power.

QUICK REVIEW <

Why was the invention of the plow such a profound turning point in human history?

| How did plant and animal domestication develop, and what effects did it have on human society? | How did social hierarchies and trade increase complexity? |  LearningCurve Check what you know. |

23

How did growing social and gender hierarchies and expanding networks of trade increase the complexity of human society in the Neolithic period?

Stone Circle at Nabta Playa, Egypt, ca. 4800 B.C.E.

This circle of stones, erected when the Egyptian desert received much more rainfall than it does today, may have been a type of calendar marking the summer solstice. Circular arrangements of stones or ditches were constructed in many places during the Neolithic era, and most no doubt had calendrical, astronomical, and/or religious purposes. (Courtesy of Raymond Betz)

social hierarchies

▶ Divisions between rich and poor, elites and common people that have been a central feature of human society since the Neolithic era.

THE DIVISION OF LABOR THAT PLOW AGRICULTURE ALLOWED LED TO THE creation of **social hierarchies**, the divisions between rich and poor, elites and common people that have been a central feature of human society since the Neolithic era. Plow agriculture also strengthened differentiation based on gender, with men becoming more associated with the world beyond the household and women with the domestic realm. Social hierarchies were reinforced over generations as children inherited goods and status from their parents. People increasingly communicated ideas within local and regional networks of exchange, just as they traded foodstuffs, tools, and other products.

Social Hierarchies and Slavery

Within foraging groups, some individuals already had more authority because of their links with the world of gods and spirits, positions as heads of kin groups, or personal characteristics. These three factors gave individuals advantages in agricultural societies, and the advantages became more significant over time as there

CHAPTER LOCATOR | How did humans evolve, and where did they migrate? | What were the key features of Paleolithic society?

24 CHAPTER 1 THE EARLIEST HUMAN SOCIETIES

were more resources to control. Priests and shamans became full-time religious specialists, exchanging their services in interceding with the gods for food. In many communities, religious specialists were the first to work out formal rules of conduct that later became oral and written codes of law. The codes often required people to accord deference to priests as the representatives of the gods, so that they became an elite group with special privileges.

Individuals who were the heads of large families or kin groups had control over the labor of others, and this power became more significant when that labor brought material goods that could be stored. Material goods—plows, sheep, cattle, sheds, pots, carts—gave one the ability to amass still more material goods, and the gap between those who had them and those who did not widened. Storage also allowed wealth to be retained over long periods of time and handed down from one family member to another, so that over generations small differences in wealth grew larger. The ability to control the labor of others could also come from physical strength, a charismatic personality, or leadership talents, and such traits may have also led to greater wealth.

Wealth itself could command labor, as individuals or families could buy the services of others to work for them or impose their wishes through force, hiring soldiers to threaten or carry out violence. Eventually some individuals bought others outright. Like animals, slaves were a source of physical power for their owners, providing them an opportunity to amass still more wealth and influence.

Gender Hierarchies and Inheritance

Along with hierarchies based on wealth and power, the development of agriculture was intertwined with a hierarchy based on gender. The system in which men have more power and access to resources than women and some men are dominant over other men is called **patriarchy**.

Plow agriculture heightened patriarchy. Although farming with a hoe was often done by women, plow agriculture came to be a male task, perhaps because of men's upper-body strength or because plow agriculture was more difficult to combine with care for infants and small children than was horticulture. At the same time that cattle began to be raised for pulling plows and carts rather than for meat, sheep began to be raised primarily for wool. Spinning thread and weaving cloth became primarily women's work. Spinning and weaving were generally done indoors and involved simpler and cheaper tools than plowing; they could also be taken up and put down easily, and so could be done at the same time as other tasks.

Though in some ways this arrangement seems complementary, with each sex doing some of the necessary labor, plow agriculture increased gender hierarchy. Men's responsibility for plowing and other agricultural tasks took them outside the household more often than women's duties did, enlarging their opportunities for leadership. This role may have led to their being favored as inheritors of family land and the right to farm communally held land. Accordingly, over generations, women's independent access to resources decreased, and it became increasingly difficult for women to survive without male support.

As inherited wealth became more important, men wanted to make sure that their sons were theirs, so they restricted their wives' movements and activities. This was especially the case among elite families. Among foragers and

patriarchy
▶ Social system in which men have more power and access to resources than women and some men are dominant over other men.

How did plant and animal domestication develop, and what effects did it have on human society?

How did social hierarchies and trade increase complexity?

✅ LearningCurve
Check what you know.

25

horticulturalists, women needed to be mobile for the group to survive; their labor outdoors was essential. Among agriculturalists, the labor of animals, slaves, and hired workers could substitute for that of women in families that could afford them. Thus in some Neolithic societies, there is evidence that women spent more and more of their time within the household.

Social and gender hierarchies were enhanced over generations as wealth was passed down unequally, and they were also enhanced by rules and norms that shaped sexual relationships, particularly heterosexual ones. However their power originated, elites began to think of themselves as a group set apart from the rest by some element that made them distinctive—such as military prowess, natural superiority, or connections with a deity. They increasingly understood this distinctive quality to be hereditary and developed traditions—later codified as written laws—that stipulated which heterosexual relationships would pass this quality on, along with passing on wealth. Relationships between men and women from elite families were formalized as marriage, through which both status and wealth were generally passed down. Relationships between elite men and non-elite women generally did not function in this way, or did so to a lesser degree; the women were defined as concubines or mistresses, or simply as sexual outlets for powerful men. Relations between an elite woman and a non-elite man generally brought shame and dishonor to the woman's family and sometimes death to the man.

No elite can be completely closed to newcomers, however, because the accidents of life and death, along with the genetic problems caused by repeated close intermarriage, make it difficult for any small group to survive over generations. Thus mechanisms were developed in many cultures to adopt boys into elite families, to legitimate the children of concubines and slave women, or to allow elite girls to marry men lower on the social hierarchy. All systems of inheritance also need some flexibility. The inheritance patterns in some cultures favored male heirs exclusively, but in others close relatives were favored over those more distant, even if this meant allowing daughters to inherit. The drive to keep wealth and property within a family or kin group often resulted in women inheriting, owning, and in some cases managing significant amounts of wealth, a pattern that continues today.

Trade and Cross-Cultural Connections

The increase in food production brought by the development of plow agriculture allowed Neolithic villages to grow ever larger. By 7000 B.C.E. or so, some villages in the Fertile Crescent may have had as many as ten thousand residents. One of the best known of these, Çatal Hüyük in what is now modern Turkey, shows evidence of trade as well as of the specialization of labor. Çatal Hüyük's residents lived in mud-brick houses whose walls were covered in white plaster. The men and women of the town grew wheat, barley, peas, and almonds and raised sheep and perhaps cattle, though they also seem to have hunted. They made textiles, pots, figurines, baskets, carpets, copper and lead beads, and other goods. They gathered, sharpened, and polished obsidian, a volcanic rock that could be used for knives, blades, and mirrors, and then traded it with neighboring towns. From here the obsidian was exchanged still farther away, for Neolithic societies slowly developed local and then regional networks of exchange and communication.

INDIVIDUALS IN SOCIETY
The Iceman

On September 19, 1991, two German vacationers climbing in the Italian Alps came upon a corpse lying facedown and covered in ice. Scientists determined that the Iceman, as the corpse is generally known, died 5,300 years ago. He was between twenty-five and thirty-five years old at the time of his death, and he stood about five feet two inches tall. An autopsy revealed much about the man and his culture. The bluish tinge of his teeth showed a diet of milled grain, which proves that he came from an environment where crops were grown. The Iceman hunted as well as farmed: he was found with a bow and arrows and shoes of straw, and he wore a furry cap and a robe of animal skins that had been stitched together with thread made from grass.

The equipment discovered with the Iceman demonstrates that his people mastered several technologies. He carried a hefty copper ax, made by someone with a knowledge of metallurgy. In his quiver were numerous wooden arrow shafts and two finished arrows. The arrows had sharpened flint heads and feathers attached to the ends of the shafts with resin-like glue. Apparently the people of his culture knew the value of feathers to direct the arrow and thus had mastered the basics of ballistics. His bow was made of yew, a relatively rare wood in central Europe that is among the best for archers.

The artifacts found with the body tell scientists much about how the Iceman lived. The Iceman's shoes, made with a twine framework stuffed with straw and covered with skin, indicate that he used all parts of the animals he hunted. (discovery: Courtesy, Roger Teissl; shoes: South Tyrol Museum of Archaeology, http://www.iceman.it)

Yet a mystery still surrounds the Iceman. When his body was first discovered, scholars assumed that he was a hapless traveler overtaken in a fierce snowstorm. But the autopsy found an arrowhead lodged under his left shoulder. The Iceman was not alone on his last day. Someone was with him, and that someone had shot him from below and behind. The Iceman is the victim in the first murder mystery in Europe, and the case will never be solved.

QUESTIONS FOR ANALYSIS

1. What does the autopsy of the corpse indicate about the society in which the Iceman lived?
2. How do the objects found with the Iceman support the generalizations about Neolithic society in this chapter?

LaunchPad

ONLINE DOCUMENT PROJECT
What can artifacts tell us about Neolithic society?
Examine the objects found with the Iceman, and then complete a quiz and writing assignment based on the evidence and details from this chapter. *See inside front cover to learn more.*

Among the goods traded in some parts of the world was copper. Pure copper occurs close to the surface in some areas, and people, including those at Çatal Hüyük, hammered it into shapes for jewelry and tools. More often, copper, like most metals, occurs mixed with other materials in a type of rock called ore, and by about 5500 B.C.E. people in the Balkans had learned that copper could be extracted from ore by heating it in a smelting process. (See "Individuals in Society: The Iceman," page 27.) Smelting techniques were discovered independently in many places around the world, including China, Southeast Asia, West Africa, and the Andes region. Pure copper is soft, but through experimentation artisans learned that it would become harder if they mixed it with other metals such as arsenic, zinc, or tin during heating, creating an alloy called bronze.

Because it was stronger than copper, bronze had a far wider range of uses, so much so that later historians decided that its adoption marked a new period in human history, the Bronze Age. It began about 3000 B.C.E. in some places, and by about 2500 B.C.E. bronze technology was having an impact in many parts of the world, especially in weaponry. The end of the Bronze Age came with the adoption of iron technology, which also varied in its beginnings from 1200 B.C.E. to 300 B.C.E.

Objects were not the only things traded over increasingly long distances during the Neolithic period, for people also carried ideas as they traveled. Knowledge about the seasons and the weather was vitally important for those who depended on crop raising, and agricultural peoples in many parts of the world began to calculate recurring patterns in the world around them, slowly developing calendars. Scholars have demonstrated that people built circular structures of mounded earth or huge upright stones to help them predict the movements of the sun and stars.

The rhythms of the agricultural cycle and patterns of exchange also shaped religious beliefs and practices. Shamans and priests developed ever more elaborate rituals designed to assure fertility, in which the gods were often given something from a community's goods in exchange for their favor. In many places gods came to be associated with patterns of birth, growth, death, and regeneration. Like humans, the gods came to have a division of labor and a social hierarchy. Thus, as human society was becoming more complex, so was the unseen world.

> QUICK REVIEW

What connections can you make between the advent of agriculture and the intensification of gender hierarchies?

CHAPTER SUMMARY

Through studying the physical remains of the past, sometimes with very new high-tech procedures such as DNA analysis, scholars have determined that human evolution involved a combination of factors, including bipedalism, larger brain size, spoken symbolic language, and longer periods of infancy. Humans invented ever more complex tools, many of which were made of stone, from which later scholars derived the name for this earliest period of human history,

CHAPTER LOCATOR | How did humans evolve, and where did they migrate? | What were the key features of Paleolithic society?

CHAPTER 1
28 THE EARLIEST HUMAN SOCIETIES

the Paleolithic era. These tools allowed Paleolithic peoples to shape the world around them. During this era, humans migrated out of Africa, adapting to many different environments and developing diverse cultures. Early humans lived in small groups of related individuals, moving through the landscape as foragers in the search for food.

Beginning about 9000 B.C.E. people living in southwest Asia, and then elsewhere, began to plant seeds as well as gather wild crops, raise certain animals, and selectively breed both plants and animals to make them more useful to humans. This domestication of plants and animals was the most important change in human history and marked the beginning of the Neolithic Era. The domestication of large animals led to plow agriculture, through which humans could raise much more food, and the world's population grew. Plow agriculture allowed for a greater division of labor, which strengthened social hierarchies based on wealth and gender. Neolithic agricultural communities developed technologies to meet their needs and often traded with one another for products that they could not obtain locally. Religious ideas came to reflect the new agricultural society.

CONNECTIONS The human story is often told as a narrative of unstoppable progress toward greater complexity. The small kin groups of the Paleolithic gave way to Neolithic villages that grew ever larger until they became cities. Egalitarian foragers became stratified by divisions of wealth and power that were formalized as aristocracies, castes, and social classes. Oral rituals of worship, healing, and celebration in which everyone participated grew into a dizzying array of religions, philosophies, and branches of knowledge presided over by specialists. The rest of this book traces this story and explores the changes over time that are the central thread of history.

As you examine what can seem to be a staggering number of developments, it is also important to remember that many things were slow to change and that some aspects of human life in the Neolithic, or even the Paleolithic, continued. Foraging, horticulture, pastoralism, and agriculture have been the primary economic activities of most people throughout the entire history of the world. The social patterns set in early agricultural societies—with most of the population farming the land and a small number of elite who lived off their labor—lasted for millennia. You have no doubt recognized other similarities between the early peoples discussed in this chapter and the people you see around you, and it is important to keep these continuities in mind as you embark on your examination of human history.

🅟 LaunchPad

ONLINE DOCUMENT PROJECT
The Iceman's World

What can artifacts tell us about Neolithic society?

Examine the objects found with the Iceman, and then complete a quiz and writing assignment based on the evidence and details from this chapter. *See inside front cover to learn more.*

How did plant and animal domestication develop, and what effects did it have on human society?	How did social hierarchies and trade increase complexity?	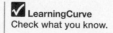 **LearningCurve** Check what you know.

CHAPTER 1 STUDY GUIDE

STEP 1 | GET STARTED ONLINE

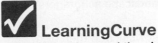 **LearningCurve**

Now that you've read the chapter, make it stick by completing the LearningCurve activity.

STEP 2 | EXPLAIN WHY IT MATTERS

Put your reading into practice. Identify each term below, and then explain why it matters in world history.

TERM	WHO OR WHAT & WHEN	WHY IT MATTERS
hominids (p. 6)		
Paleolithic era (p. 6)		
foraging (p. 6)		
Neolithic era (p. 6)		
Neanderthals (p. 10)		
megafaunal extinction (p. 13)		
division of labor (p. 13)		
animism (p. 15)		
shamans (p. 16)		
Agricultural Revolution (p. 17)		
domesticated (p. 18)		
horticulture (p. 18)		
pastoralism (p. 22)		
social hierarchies (p. 24)		
patriarchy (p. 25)		

STEP 3 | MOVE BEYOND THE BASICS

To demonstrate a more advanced understanding of the similarities and differences between Paleolithic and Neolithic society, fill in the chart below with descriptions of each society in four key areas: social organization and hierarchy, gender relations, technology and trade, and religion and spirituality. In what ways were Paleolithic and Neolithic societies the most similar? How would you explain these instances of continuity?

	Social Organization and Hierarchy	Gender Relations	Technology and Trade	Religion and Spirituality
Paleolithic Society				
Neolithic Society				

STEP 4

PUT IT ALL TOGETHER

Now, take a step back and try to explain the big picture. Remember to use specific examples from the chapter in your answers.

HUMAN EVOLUTION AND MIGRATION

▶ What explains the evolution of ever larger brains in successive hominid species?

▶ How did geography and climate shape the migration and distribution of early human communities?

PALEOLITHIC SOCIETY

▶ What role did family, kinship, and gender relations play in Paleolithic society?

▶ What do we know about the culture and spirituality of Paleolithic peoples? How do we know it?

THE AGRICULTURAL REVOLUTION AND THE DEVELOPMENT OF NEOLITHIC SOCIETY

▶ Why did some human communities make the transition from foraging to settled agriculture while others did not?

▶ How did agriculture contribute to the development of new social, political, and economic institutions in Neolithic communities?

LOOKING BACK, LOOKING AHEAD

▶ In your opinion, at what point did human history begin? With the first bipedal hominids? Later? Why did you choose the point in the past you did?

▶ Argue for or against the following statement. "The Agricultural Revolution should be considered the fundamental turning point in human history, the moment when the foundations of all future social, economic, and political institutions were laid down."

> IN YOUR OWN WORDS

Imagine that you must give an oral report to the class answering the following question: **How did human societies change and develop in the Paleolithic and Neolithic Eras?** What would be the most important points and why?

How does writing shape what we can know about the past, and how did writing develop to meet the needs of cities and states?

Clay Letter Written in Cuneiform and Its Envelope, ca. 1850 B.C.E.
In this letter from a city in Anatolia, located on the northern edge of the Fertile Crescent in what is now southern Turkey, a Mesopotamian merchant complains to his brother at home, hundreds of miles away, that life is hard and comments on the trade in silver, gold, tin, and textiles. Correspondents often enclosed letters in clay envelopes and sealed them by rolling a cylinder seal across the clay, leaving the impression of a scene, just as you might use a stamped wax seal today. Here the very faint impression of the sender's seal at the bottom shows a person, probably the owner of the seal, being led in a procession toward a king or god. (© The Trustees of the British Museum/Art Resource, NY)

Beginning about 5,000 years ago, people in some parts of the world developed a new technology, writing. Writing developed to meet the needs of more complex urban societies that are often referred to as "civilizations." In particular, writing met the needs of the state, a new political form that developed during the time covered in this chapter.

Written Sources and the Human Past

Historians who study human societies that developed systems of writing continue to use many of the same types of physical evidence as do those who study societies without writing. For some cultures, the writing or record-keeping systems have not yet been deciphered, so our knowledge of these people also depends largely on physical evidence. Scholars can read the writing of a great many societies, however, adding greatly to what we can learn about them.

Much ancient writing survives only because it was copied and recopied, sometimes years after it was first produced. The survival of a work means that someone from a later period—and often a long chain of someones—judged it

CHAPTER LOCATOR | How does writing shape what we can know about the past, and how did writing develop? | How did the peoples of Mesopotamia form states and develop new technologies?

34 CHAPTER 2
THE RISE OF THE STATE IN SOUTHWEST ASIA AND THE NILE VALLEY

ca. 3800 B.C.E. Establishment of first cities in Sumer	**ca. 1200 B.C.E.** Bronze Age Collapse; destruction and drought
ca. 3200 B.C.E. Earliest surviving cuneiform writing	**ca. 1100 B.C.E.** Iron technology improves; beginning of the Iron Age; Phoenicians begin to trade in the Mediterranean
2660–2180 B.C.E. Period of the Old Kingdom in Egypt	**ca. 965–925 B.C.E.** Hebrew kingdom ruled by Solomon
2500 B.C.E. Bronze weaponry becomes common in Mesopotamia	**ca. 900–612 B.C.E.** Assyrian Empire
ca. 2300 B.C.E. Establishment of Akkadian empire	**722 B.C.E.** Kingdom of Israel destroyed by the Assyrians
1792–1750 B.C.E. Hammurabi rules Babylon	**587 B.C.E.** Kingdom of Judah destroyed by the Babylonians
ca. 1600 B.C.E. Hittites begin to expand their empire	**550 B.C.E.** Cyrus the Great consolidates the Persian Empire
ca. 1570–1070 B.C.E. Period of the New Kingdom in Egypt	

worthy of the time, effort, and resources needed to produce copies. The copies may not be completely accurate. Historians studying ancient works thus often try to find as many early copies as they can and compare them to arrive at the version they think is closest to the original.

The works considered worthy of copying tend to be those that are about the political and military events involving major powers, those that record religious traditions, or those that come from authors who were later regarded as important. By contrast, written sources dealing with the daily life of ordinary men and women were few to begin with and were rarely saved or copied because they were not considered significant.

Some early written texts survive in their original form because people inscribed them in stone, shells, bone, or other hard materials, intending them to be permanent. Stones with inscriptions were often erected in the open in public places for all to see, so they include text that leaders felt had enduring importance, such as laws, religious proclamations, decrees, and treaties. Sometimes this permanence was accidental: in ancient Mesopotamia (in the area of modern Iraq), all writing was initially made up of indentations on soft clay tablets, which then hardened. Hundreds of thousands of these tablets have survived, the oldest dating to about 3200 B.C.E., and from them historians have learned about many aspects of everyday life. By contrast, writing in Egypt at the same time was often done in ink on papyrus sheets, made from a plant that grows abundantly in Egypt. Some of these papyrus sheets have survived, but papyrus is much more fragile than hardened clay, so most have disintegrated. In China, the oldest surviving writing is on bones and turtle shells from about 1200 B.C.E., but it is clear that writing was done much earlier on less permanent materials such as silk and bamboo. (For more on the origins of Chinese writing, see page 95.)

How did the Egyptians create a prosperous and long-lasting society?	How did the Hebrews create an enduring written religious tradition?	How did the Assyrians and the Persians consolidate their power and control the subjects?	✓ LearningCurve Check what you know.

Cities and the Idea of Civilization

Along with writing, the growth of cities has often been a way that scholars mark the increasing complexity of human societies. In the ancient world, residents of cities generally viewed themselves as more advanced and sophisticated than rural folk. They saw themselves as more "civilized," a word that comes from the Latin adjective *civilis*, which refers to either a citizen of a town or of a larger political unit such as an empire.

This depiction of people as either civilized or uncivilized was gradually extended to whole societies. Beginning in the eighteenth century European scholars described those societies in which political, economic, and social organizations operated on a large scale as "civilizations." Civilizations had cities; laws that governed human relationships; codes of manners and social conduct that regulated how people were to behave; and scientific, philosophical, and theological ideas that explained the larger world. Generally only societies that used writing were judged to be civilizations.

Until the middle of the twentieth century, historians often referred to the earliest places where writing and cities developed as the "cradles of civilization," proposing a model of development for all humanity patterned on that of an individual person. However, the idea that all human societies developed (or should develop) in a uniform process from a "cradle" to a "mature" civilization has now been largely discredited, and some world historians choose not to use the word *civilization* at all because it could imply that some societies are superior to others.

The Rise of States, Laws, and Social Hierarchies

Cities concentrated people and power, and they required more elaborate mechanisms to make them work than had small agricultural villages and foraging groups. These mechanisms were part of what political scientists call "the state," an organization in which a small share of the population is able to coerce resources out of everyone else in order to gain and then maintain power. In a state, the interest that gains power might be one particular family, a set of religious leaders, or even a charismatic or talented individual able to handle the problems of dense urban communities.

However they are established, states coerce people through violence, or the threat of violence, and develop permanent armies for this purpose. Using armed force every time they need food or other resources is not very efficient, however, so states also establish bureaucracies and systems of taxation. States also need to keep track of people and goods, so they sometimes develop systems of recording information and accounting. These systems allow for the creation of more elaborate rules of behavior, often written down in the form of law codes, which facilitate further growth in state power, or in the form of religious traditions, which specify what sort of behavior is pleasing to the gods or other supernatural forces.

Written laws and traditions generally create more elaborate social hierarchies, in which divisions between elite groups and common people are established more firmly. They also generally heighten gender hierarchies. Those who

CHAPTER LOCATOR | How does writing shape what we can know about the past, and how did writing develop? | How did the peoples of Mesopotamia form states and develop new technologies?

CHAPTER 2
36   THE RISE OF THE STATE IN SOUTHWEST ASIA AND THE NILE VALLEY

gain power in states are most often men, so they tend to establish laws and norms that favor males in marriage, property rights, and other areas.

Whether we choose to call the process "the birth of civilization" or "the growth of the state," in the fourth millennium B.C.E., Neolithic agricultural villages expanded into cities that depended largely on food produced by the surrounding countryside while people living in cities carried out other tasks. The organization of a more complex division of labor was undertaken by an elite group, which enforced its will through laws, taxes, and bureaucracies backed up by armed force or the threat of it. Social and gender hierarchies became more complex and rigid. All this happened first in Mesopotamia, then in Egypt, and then in India and China.

QUICK REVIEW

What connections can you make between the invention of writing and the emergence and growth of cities?

| How did the Egyptians create a prosperous and long-lasting society? | How did the Hebrews create an enduring written religious tradition? | How did the Assyrians and the Persians consolidate their power and control the subjects? | ✓ LearningCurve Check what you know. |

37

How did the peoples of Mesopotamia form states and develop new technologies and institutions?

States first developed in Mesopotamia, where sustained agriculture reliant on irrigation from the Euphrates and Tigris Rivers resulted in larger populations, a division of labor, and the growth of cities. Priests and rulers developed ways to control and organize these complex societies. Conquerors from the north unified Mesopotamian city-states into larger empires and spread Mesopotamian culture over a large area.

Environmental Challenges, Irrigation, and Religion

Mesopotamia was part of the Fertile Crescent, where settled agriculture first developed (see pages 17–21). The earliest agricultural villages in Mesopotamia were in the northern, hilly parts of the river valleys, where there is abundant rainfall for crops. Farmers had brought techniques of crop raising southward by about

CHAPTER LOCATOR | How does writing shape what we can know about the past, and how did writing develop? | **How did the peoples of Mesopotamia form states and develop new technologies?**

CHAPTER 2
38 THE RISE OF THE STATE IN SOUTHWEST ASIA AND THE NILE VALLEY

5000 B.C.E., to the southern part of Mesopotamia known as Sumer (soo-MAIR). In this arid climate farmers developed large-scale irrigation, which required organized group effort but allowed the population to grow. By about 3800 B.C.E. one of these agricultural villages, Uruk (OO-rook), had expanded significantly, becoming what many historians view as the world's first city. Over the next thousand years, other cities emerged in Sumer. These cities built defensive walls, marketplaces, and large public buildings; each came to dominate the surrounding countryside, becoming city-states independent from one another, though not very far apart.

The city-states of Sumer relied on irrigation systems that required cooperation and at least some level of social and political cohesion. The authority to run this system was, it seems, initially assumed by Sumerian priests. Encouraged and directed by their religious leaders, people built temples on tall platforms in the center of their cities. Temples grew into elaborate complexes of buildings with storage space for grain and other products and housing for animals. Surrounding the temple and other large buildings were the houses of ordinary citizens, each constructed around a central courtyard.

To Sumerians, and to later peoples in Mesopotamia as well, many different gods and goddesses controlled the world, a religious idea later scholars called **polytheism**. Each deity represented cosmic forces such as the sun, moon, water, and storms. The gods judged good and evil and would punish humans who lied or cheated. People believed that humans had been created to serve the gods and generally anticipated being well treated by the gods if they served them well.

polytheism
▶ The worship of many gods and goddesses.

Sumerian Politics and Society

Exactly how kings emerged in Sumerian society is not clear. Scholars have suggested that during times of crisis, a chief priest or sometimes a military leader assumed what was supposed to be temporary authority over a city. He established an army, trained it, and led it into battle. Temporary power gradually became permanent kingship, and kings in some Sumerian city-states began to hand down the kingship to their sons, establishing patriarchal hereditary dynasties in which power was handed down through the male line. The symbol of royal status was the palace, which came to rival the temple in its grandeur.

Kings made alliances with other powerful individuals, often through marriage. Royal family members were responsible for many aspects of government. Kings worked closely with religious authorities and relied on ideas about their connections with the gods, as well as the kings' military might, for their power. Acting together, priests, nobles, and kings in Sumerian cities used force, persuasion, and threats of higher taxes to maintain order, keep the irrigation systems working, and keep food and other goods flowing.

The king and the nobles held extensive tracts of land, as did the temple; these lands were worked by the palace's or the temple's clients—free men and women who were dependent on the palace or the temple. They received crops and other goods in return for their labor. Although this arrangement assured the clients of a livelihood, the land they worked remained the possession of the palace or the temple. Some individuals and families owned land outright and paid their taxes in the form of agricultural products or items they made. At the bottom rung of society were slaves. Like animals, slaves were a source of physical power for their owners, providing them an opportunity to amass more wealth and influence.

How did the Egyptians create a prosperous and long-lasting society?

How did the Hebrews create an enduring written religious tradition?

How did the Assyrians and the Persians consolidate their power and control the subjects?

✓ LearningCurve
Check what you know.

39

Each of these social categories included both men and women, but their experiences were not the same, for Sumerian society made distinctions based on gender. Most elite landowners were male, but women who held positions as priestesses or as queens ran their own estates independently of their husbands and fathers. Some women owned businesses and took care of their own accounts. They could own property and distribute it to their offspring. Sons and daughters inherited from their parents, although a daughter received her inheritance in the form of a dowry, which technically remained hers but was managed by her husband or husband's family after marriage. The Sumerians established the basic social, economic, and intellectual patterns of Mesopotamia and influenced their neighbors to the north and east.

Writing, Mathematics, and Poetry

The origins of writing probably date back to the ninth millennium B.C.E., when people in southwest Asia used clay tokens as counters for record keeping. By the fourth millennium people had realized that impressing the tokens on soft clay, or drawing pictures of the tokens on clay, was simpler than making tokens. This breakthrough in turn suggested that more information could be conveyed by adding pictures of other objects, and slowly the new technology of writing developed. The result was a complex system of pictographs in which each sign pictured an object, such as "star" (line A of Figure 2.1). These pictographs were the forerunners of the Sumerian form of writing known as **cuneiform** (kyou-NEE-uh-form).

cuneiform
▸ Sumerian form of writing; the term describes the wedge-shaped marks made by a stylus.

Pictographs were initially limited in that they could not represent abstract ideas, but the development of ideograms—signs that represented ideas—made writing more versatile. Thus the sign for "star" could also be used to indicate "heaven," "sky," or even "god." The real breakthrough came when scribes started using signs to represent sounds.

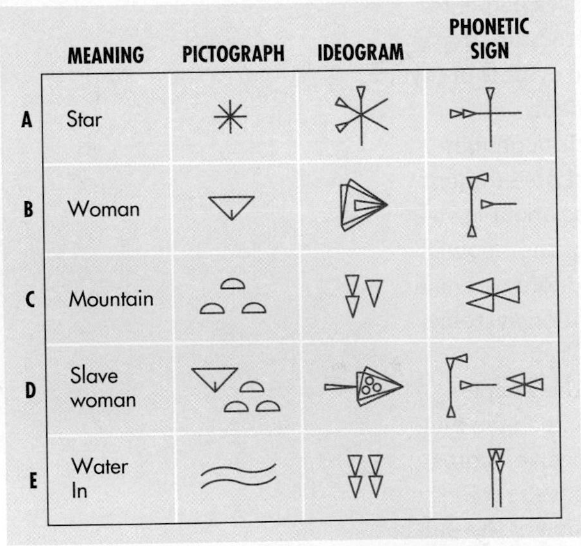
MEANING
PICTOGRAPH
IDEOGRAM
PHONETIC SIGN
A
Star
B
Woman
C
Mountain
D
Slave woman
E
Water In

FIGURE 2.1 ■ Sumerian Writing

(Source: Excerpted from S. N. Kramer, *The Sumerians: Their History, Culture, and Character.* Copyright © 1963 by the University of Chicago Press. Used by permission of The University of Chicago Press.)

The development of the Sumerian system of writing was piecemeal, with scribes making changes and additions as they were needed. The system became so complicated that the Sumerians established scribal schools, which by 2500 B.C.E. flourished throughout the region. Students at the schools were all male, and most came from families in the middle range of urban society. Scribal schools were primarily intended to produce individuals who could keep records of the property of temple officials, kings, and nobles. Thus writing first developed as a way to enhance the growing power of elites, not to record speech.

Sumerians wrote numbers as well as words on clay tablets, and some surviving tablets show multiplication and division problems. The Sumerians and later Mesopotamians made significant advances in mathematics using a numerical system based on units of sixty, ten, and six, from which we derive our division of hours into sixty minutes and minutes into sixty seconds. They also developed the concept of place value—that the value of a number depends on where it stands in relation to other numbers.

CHAPTER LOCATOR | How does writing shape what we can know about the past, and how did writing develop? | **How did the peoples of Mesopotamia form states and develop new technologies?**

Written texts were not an important part of Sumerian religious life, nor were they central to the religious practices of most of the other peoples in this region. Stories about the gods circulated orally and traveled with people when they moved up and down the rivers. Sumerians also told stories about heroes and kings, many of which were eventually reworked into the world's first **epic poem**, the *Epic of Gilgamesh* (GIL-guh-mesh), which was later written down.

Empires in Mesopotamia

The wealth of Sumerian cities also attracted conquerors from the north. Around 2300 B.C.E. Sargon, the king of a region to the north of Sumer, conquered a number of Sumerian cities with what was probably the world's first permanent army and created a large state. The symbol of his triumph was a new capital, the city of Akkad (AH-kahd). Sargon also expanded the Akkadian empire westward to northern Syria, which became the breadbasket of the empire. He encouraged trading networks that brought in goods from as far away as the Indus River in South Asia and what is now Turkey (Map 2.1). Sargon spoke a different language than did the Sumerians, one of the many languages that scholars identify as belonging to the Semitic language family, which includes modern-day Hebrew and Arabic.

MAP 2.1 ■ Spread of Cultures in Southwest Asia and the Nile Valley, ca. 3000–1640 B.C.E.

This map illustrates the spread of the Mesopotamian and Egyptian cultures through the semicircular stretch of land often called the Fertile Crescent. From this area, the knowledge and use of agriculture spread throughout western Asia, northern Africa, and Europe.

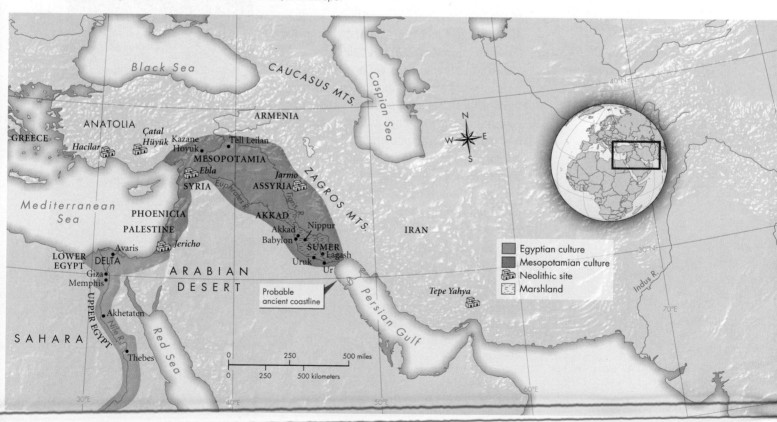

How did the Egyptians create a prosperous and long-lasting society?

How did the Hebrews create an enduring written religious tradition?

How did the Assyrians and the Persians consolidate their power and control the subjects?

✓ LearningCurve
Check what you know.

Akkadians adapted cuneiform writing to their own language, and Akkadian became the diplomatic language used over a wide area.

Sargon tore down the defensive walls of Sumerian cities and appointed his own sons as their rulers to help him cement his power. He also appointed his daughter, Enheduana (2285–2250 B.C.E.), as high priestess in the city of Ur. Here she wrote a number of hymns, becoming the world's first author to put her name to a literary composition.

Sargon's dynasty appears to have ruled Mesopotamia for about 150 years, and then collapsed, in part because of a period of extended drought. Various city-states then rose to power, one of which was centered on the city of Babylon. Babylon was in an excellent position to dominate trade on both the Tigris and Euphrates Rivers, and it was fortunate in having a very able ruler in Hammurabi (hahm-moo-RAH-bee) (r. 1792–1750 B.C.E.). Initially a typical king of his era, he unified Mesopotamia later in his reign by using military force, strategic alliances with the rulers of smaller territories, and religious ideas. As had earlier rulers, Hammurabi linked his success with the will of the gods. He connected himself with the sun-god Shamash, the god of law and justice, and encouraged the spread of myths that explained how Marduk, the primary god of Babylon, had been elected king of the gods by the other deities in Mesopotamia. Babylonian ideas and beliefs thus became part of the cultural mixture of Mesopotamia.

Life Under Hammurabi

Hammurabi's law code

▶ A proclamation issued by Babylonian king Hammurabi to establish laws regulating many aspects of life.

Hammurabi's most memorable accomplishment was the proclamation of an extensive law code, introduced about 1755 B.C.E. **Hammurabi's law code** set a variety of punishments for breaking the law, including fines and physical punishment such as mutilation, whipping, and burning. It demanded that the punishment fit the crime, calling for "an eye for an eye and a tooth for a tooth," at least among social equals, although higher-ranking people could pay a fine to lower-ranking victims instead of having an arm broken or losing an eye.

Law Code of Hammurabi

Hammurabi ordered his code to be inscribed on stone pillars and set up in public throughout the Babylonian empire. At the top of the pillar Hammurabi (left) is depicted receiving the rod and ring of authority from Shamash, the god of law and justice. (© RMN-Grand Palais/Art Resource, NY)

CHAPTER LOCATOR | How does writing shape what we can know about the past, and how did writing develop? | **How did the peoples of Mesopotamia form states and develop new technologies?**

42 CHAPTER 2
THE RISE OF THE STATE IN SOUTHWEST ASIA AND THE NILE VALLEY

Hammurabi's code provides a wealth of information about daily life in Mesopotamia. Because of farming's fundamental importance, the code dealt extensively with agriculture. Tenants faced severe penalties for neglecting the land or not working it at all. The code also regulated other trades, and artisans had to guarantee the quality of their goods and services to consumers. Hammurabi gave careful attention to marriage and the family. As elsewhere in the area, marriage had aspects of a business agreement. The groom or his father offered the prospective bride's father a gift, and if this was acceptable, the bride's father provided his daughter with a dowry, which technically remained hers. A father could not disinherit a son without just cause, and the code ordered the courts to forgive a son for his first offense. On family matters and other issues, Hammurabi's code influenced other law codes, including those later written down in Hebrew Scripture (see page 53).

QUICK REVIEW

What role did kings play in Mesopotamian society?
What about priests?

How did the Egyptians create a prosperous and long-lasting society?	How did the Hebrews create an enduring written religious tradition?	How did the Assyrians and the Persians consolidate their power and control the subjects?	✔ LearningCurve Check what you know.

> How did the Egyptians create a prosperous and long-lasting society?

Egyptian Home Life

This grave painting depicts an intimate moment in the life of an aristocratic family, with the father and mother in the center and their children around them. (Gianni Dagli Orti/ The Art Archive at Art Resource, NY)

> PICTURING THE PAST

ANALYZING THE IMAGE: What evidence do you find in the painting that Egyptian artists based the size of figures on people's status in the household?

CONNECTIONS: Based on your reading, how might an image of a poor family differ from this depiction?

At about the same time that Sumerian city-states expanded and fought with one another in the Tigris and Euphrates Valleys, a more cohesive state under a single ruler grew in the valley of the Nile River in North Africa. This was Egypt, which for long stretches of history was prosperous and secure. At various times groups invaded and conquered Egypt or migrated into Egypt seeking better lives. Often these newcomers adopted aspects of Egyptian culture, and Egyptians also carried their traditions with them when they established an empire and engaged in trade.

The Nile and the God-King

No other single geographical factor had such a fundamental and profound impact on Egyptian life, society, and history as the Nile River (see Map 2.2, page 47). The Nile flooded once a year for a period of several months, bringing fertile soil

CHAPTER LOCATOR | How does writing shape what we can know about the past, and how did writing develop? | How did the peoples of Mesopotamia form states and develop new technologies?

44 CHAPTER 2 THE RISE OF THE STATE IN SOUTHWEST ASIA AND THE NILE VALLEY

and moisture for farming. Through the fertility of the Nile and their own hard work, Egyptians produced an annual agricultural surplus, which in turn sustained a growing and prosperous population. The Nile also unified Egypt, serving as a highway that promoted easy communication.

The political power structures that developed in Egypt came to be linked with the Nile. Somehow the idea developed that a single individual, a king, was responsible for the rise and fall of the Nile. The king came to be viewed as a descendant of the gods and thus a god himself. Political unification most likely proceeded slowly, but stories told about early kings highlighted one who had united Upper Egypt—the upstream valley in the south—and Lower Egypt—the delta area of the Nile that empties into the Mediterranean Sea—into a single kingdom around 3100 B.C.E. The political unification of Egypt in the Archaic Period (3100–2660 B.C.E.) ushered in the period known as the Old Kingdom (2660–2180 B.C.E.).

The focal point of religious and political life in the Old Kingdom was the king, who commanded the wealth, resources, and people of Egypt. The king's surroundings had to be worthy of a god, and only a magnificent palace was suitable for his home; in fact, the word **pharaoh**, which during the New Kingdom (1570–1070 B.C.E.) came to be used for the king, originally meant "great house." Just as the kings occupied a great house in life, so they reposed in great pyramids after death. Built during the Old Kingdom, these massive stone tombs contained all the things needed by the king in his afterlife and also symbolized the king's power and his connection with the sun-god.

Like the Mesopotamians, the Egyptians were polytheistic, worshipping many gods of all types, some mightier than others. They developed complex ideas of their gods that reflected the world around them, and these views changed over the many centuries of Egyptian history as gods took on new attributes and often merged with one another. During the Old Kingdom, Egyptians considered the sun-god Ra the creator of life. Much later, during the New Kingdom (see page 46), the pharaohs of a new dynasty favored the worship of a different sun-god, Amon. As his cult grew, Amon came to be identified with Ra, and eventually the Egyptians combined them into one sun-god, Amon-Ra.

The Egyptians likewise developed views of an afterlife that reflected the world around them and that changed over time. During the later part of the Old Kingdom, the walls of kings' tombs were carved with religious texts that provided spells that would bring the king back to life and help him ascend to heaven. Toward the end of the Old Kingdom, the tombs of powerful nobles also contained such inscriptions, an indication that more people expected to gain everlasting life. In the Middle Kingdom (2080–1640 B.C.E.), new types of spells appeared on the coffins of even more people, a further expansion in admissions to the afterlife.

PERIODS OF EGYPTIAN HISTORY

Period	Dates	Significant Events
Archaic	3100–2660 B.C.E.	Unification of Egypt
Old Kingdom	2660–2180 B.C.E.	Construction of the pyramids
First Intermediate	2180–2080 B.C.E.	Political chaos
Middle Kingdom	2080–1640 B.C.E.	Recovery and political stability
Second Intermediate	1640–1570 B.C.E.	Hyksos migrations; struggles for power
New Kingdom	1570–1070 B.C.E.	Creation of an Egyptian empire; growth in wealth
Third Intermediate	1100–653 B.C.E.	Political fragmentation and conquest by outsiders

pharaoh
▶ The title given to the king of Egypt in the New Kingdom, from a word that meant "great house."

How did the Egyptians create a prosperous and long-lasting society?

How did the Hebrews create an enduring written religious tradition?

How did the Assyrians and the Persians consolidate their power and control the subjects?

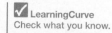
LearningCurve
Check what you know.

45

During the New Kingdom, a time when Egypt came into greater contact with the cultures of the Fertile Crescent, Egyptians developed even more complex ideas about the afterlife, recording these in written funerary manuscripts that have come to be known as the *Book of the Dead*. These texts explained that the soul left the body to become part of the divine after death and told of the god Osiris (oh-SIGH-ruhs), who died each year and was then brought back to life by his wife Isis (IGH-suhs) when the Nile flooded. Osiris eventually became king of the dead, weighing dead humans' hearts to determine whether they had lived justly enough to deserve everlasting life.

Egyptian Society and Work

Egyptian society reflected the pyramids that it built. At the top stood the pharaoh, who relied on a circle of nobles, officials, and priests to administer his kingdom. All of them were assisted by scribes, who used a writing system perhaps adapted from Mesopotamia or perhaps developed independently. Egyptian scribes actually created two writing systems: one called hieroglyphics for engraving important religious or political texts on stone or writing them on papyrus made from reeds growing in the Nile Delta, and a much simpler system called hieratic that allowed scribes to write more quickly and was used for the documents of daily life. The cities of the Nile Valley were also home to artisans of all types, along with merchants and other tradespeople. A large group of farmers made up the broad base of the social pyramid.

For Egyptians, the Nile formed an essential part of daily life. During the flooding season—from June to October—farmers worked on the pharaoh's building programs and other tasks away from their fields. When the water began to recede, they diverted some of it into ponds for future irrigation and began planting wheat and barley, using plows pulled by oxen or people. From October to February, farmers planted and tended crops, and from February until the next flood, they harvested them. As in Mesopotamia, common people paid their obligations to their superiors in products and in labor. Some young men were drafted into the pharaoh's army, which served as both a fighting force and a labor corps.

The lives of all Egyptians centered around the family. Just as in Mesopotamia, marriage was a business arrangement. A couple's parents arranged the marriage, which seems to have taken place at a young age. Once couples were married, having children, especially sons, was a high priority. Most Egyptian men had only one wife, but among the wealthy some had several wives or concubines. Ordinary women were expected to obey their fathers, husbands, and other men, but they possessed considerable economic and legal rights. They could own land in their own names, operate businesses, and testify in court. Literature and art depict a world in which ordinary husbands and wives enjoyed each other's company.

Migrations, Revivals, and Collapse

While Egyptian civilization flourished in the Nile Valley, various groups migrated throughout the Fertile Crescent and then accommodated themselves to local cultures (Map 2.2). Some settled in the Nile Delta, including a group the Egyptians called Hyksos. Although they were later portrayed as a conquering horde, the

CHAPTER LOCATOR | How does writing shape what we can know about the past, and how did writing develop? | How did the peoples of Mesopotamia form states and develop new technologies?

CHAPTER 2
46   THE RISE OF THE STATE IN SOUTHWEST ASIA AND THE NILE VALLEY

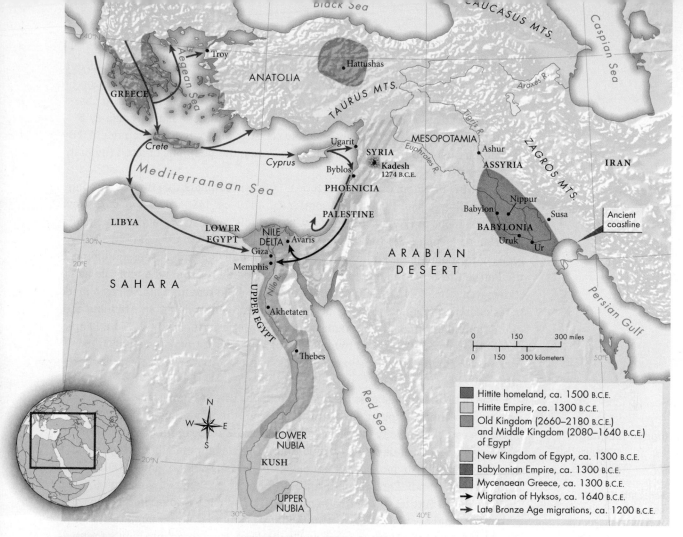

MAP 2.2 ■ Empires and Migrations in the Eastern Mediterranean

The rise and fall of empires in the eastern Mediterranean were shaped by internal developments, military conflicts, and the migration of peoples to new areas.

> MAPPING THE PAST

ANALYZING THE MAP: At what point was the Egyptian Empire at its largest? The Hittite Empire? What were the other major powers in the eastern Mediterranean at this time?

CONNECTIONS: What were the major effects of the migrations of the Hyksos? Of the late Bronze Age migrations? What clues does the map provide as to why the late Bronze Age migrations had a more powerful impact than those of the Hyksos?

Hyksos were actually migrants looking for good land, and their entry into the delta, which began around 1800 B.C.E., was probably gradual and generally peaceful. The newcomers began to worship Egyptian deities and modeled their political structures on those of the Egyptians.

The Hyksos brought with them methods of making bronze (see Chapter 1) and casting it into weapons that became standard in Egypt. They thereby brought Egypt fully into the Bronze Age culture of the Mediterranean world. The Hyksos also introduced horse-drawn chariots and the composite bow, made of multiple materials for greater strength, which along with bronze weaponry revolutionized Egyptian warfare. The migration of the Hyksos, combined with a series of famines and internal struggles for power, led Egypt to fragment politically.

| How did the Egyptians create a prosperous and long-lasting society? | How did the Hebrews create an enduring written religious tradition? | How did the Assyrians and the Persians consolidate their power and control the subjects? | ✓ LearningCurve Check what you know. |

In about 1570 B.C.E. a new dynasty of pharaohs arose, pushing the Hyksos out of the delta and conquering territory to the south and northeast. These warrior-pharaohs inaugurated what scholars refer to as the New Kingdom, a period characterized not only by enormous wealth and conscious imperialism but also by a greater sense of insecurity because of new contacts and military engagements. By expanding Egyptian power beyond the Nile Valley, the pharaohs created the first Egyptian empire.

The New Kingdom pharaohs include a number of remarkable figures. Among these was Hatshepsut (haht-SHEP-soot) (r. ca. 1479–ca. 1458 B.C.E.), one of the few female pharaohs in Egypt's long history. (See "Individuals in Society: Hatshepsut and Nefertiti," page 49.) Amenhotep III (ah-men-HOE-tep) (r. ca. 1388–ca. 1350 B.C.E.) corresponded with other powerful kings in Babylonia and other kingdoms in the Fertile Crescent. Amenhotep III was succeeded by his son, who took the name Akhenaten (ah-keh-NAH-tuhn) (r. 1351–1334 B.C.E.). He renamed himself as a mark of his changing religious ideas, choosing to worship a new sun-god, Aten, instead of the traditional Amon or Ra. Akhenaten's wife Nefertiti (nehf-uhr-TEE-tee) supported his religious ideas, but this new religion, imposed from above, failed to find a place among the people, and after his death traditional religious practices returned.

One of the key challenges facing the pharaohs after Akhenaten was the expansion of the kingdom of the Hittites. At about the same time that the Sumerians were establishing city-states, speakers of **Indo-European languages** migrated into Anatolia, modern-day Turkey. Indo-European is a large family of languages that includes English, most of the languages of modern Europe, ancient Greek, Latin, Persian, Hindi, Bengali, and Sanskrit (for more on Sanskrit, see page 67). It also includes Hittite, the language of one of the peoples who migrated into this area. Beginning about 1600 B.C.E., Hittite kings began to conquer more territory (see Map 2.2). As the Hittites expanded southward, they came into conflict with the Egyptians, who were establishing their own larger empire. There were a number of battles, but both sides seem to have recognized the impossibility of defeating the other, and in 1258 the Egyptian king Ramesses II (r. ca. 1290–1224 B.C.E.) and the Hittite king Hattusili III (r. ca. 1267–1237 B.C.E.) concluded a peace treaty.

The treaty brought peace between the Egyptians and the Hittites for a time, but this stability did not last. Within several decades of the treaty, groups of seafaring peoples whom the Egyptians called "Sea Peoples" raided, migrated, and marauded in the eastern Mediterranean, disrupting trade and in some cases looting and destroying cities. These raids, combined with the expansion of the Assyrians (see page 55), led to the collapse of the Hittite Empire and the fragmentation of the Egyptian empire. There is evidence of drought, and some scholars have suggested that a major volcanic explosion in Iceland cooled the climate for several years, leading to a series of poor harvests. All of these developments are part of a general "Bronze Age Collapse" in the period around 1200 B.C.E. that historians see as a major turning point.

Indo-European languages
▶ A large family of languages that includes English, most of the languages of modern Europe, ancient Greek, Latin, Persian, Hindi, Bengali, and Sanskrit, the sacred tongue of ancient India.

The Emergence of New States

The Bronze Age Collapse was a time of massive political and economic disruption, but it was also a period of the spread of new technologies, especially iron. The

CHAPTER LOCATOR | How does writing shape what we can know about the past, and how did writing develop? | How did the peoples of Mesopotamia form states and develop new technologies?

48 CHAPTER 2 THE RISE OF THE STATE IN SOUTHWEST ASIA AND THE NILE VALLEY

INDIVIDUALS IN SOCIETY
Hatshepsut and Nefertiti

Egyptians understood the pharaoh to be the living embodiment of the god Horus, the source of law and morality, and the mediator between gods and humans. His connection with the divine stretched to members of his family, so his siblings and children were also viewed as in some ways divine. Because of this, a pharaoh often took his sister or half-sister as one of his wives. This concentrated divine blood set the pharaonic family apart from other Egyptians (who did not marry close relatives) and allowed the pharaohs to imitate the gods, who in Egyptian mythology often married their siblings. A pharaoh chose one of his wives to be the "Great Royal Wife," or principal queen. Often this was a relative, though sometimes it was one of the foreign princesses who married pharaohs to establish political alliances.

The familial connection with the divine allowed a handful of women to rule in their own right in Egypt's long history. We know the names of four female pharaohs, of whom the most famous was Hatshepsut. She was the sister and wife of Thutmose II and, after he died, served as regent — as adviser and co-ruler — for her young stepson Thutmose III, who was the son of another woman. Hatshepsut sent trading expeditions and sponsored artists and architects, ushering in a period of artistic creativity and economic prosperity. She built one of the world's great buildings, an elaborate terraced temple at Deir el Bahri, which eventually served as her tomb. Hatshepsut's status as a powerful female ruler was difficult for Egyptians to conceptualize, and she is often depicted in male dress or with a false beard, thus looking more like the male rulers who were the norm. After her death, Thutmose III tried to destroy all evidence that she had ever ruled, smashing statues and scratching her name off inscriptions, perhaps because of personal animosity and perhaps because he wanted to erase the fact that a woman had once been pharaoh. Only within recent decades have historians and archaeologists begun to (literally) piece together her story.

Though female pharaohs were very rare, many royal women had power through their position as Great Royal Wives. The most famous was Nefertiti (ca. 1370–1330 B.C.E.), the wife of Akhenaten. Her name means "the perfect (or beautiful) woman has come," and inscriptions give her many other titles.

Nefertiti used her position to spread the new religion of the sun-god Aten. Together she and Akhenaten built a new palace at Akhetaten, the present-day Amarna, away from the old centers of power. There they developed the cult of Aten to the exclusion of the traditional deities. Nearly the only literary survivor of their religious belief is the "Hymn to Aten," which declares Aten to be the only god. It describes Nefertiti as "the great royal consort whom

Painted limestone bust of Nefertiti. (bpk, Berlin/ Aegyptisches Museum, Staaliche Museen, Berlin, Germany/Photo: Margarete Buesing/Art Resource, NY)

Granite head of Hatshepsut. (bpk, Berlin/Aegyptisches Museum, Staaliche Museen, Berlin, Germany/Photo: Margarete Buesing/Art Resource, NY)

he, Akhenaten, loves. The mistress of the Two Lands, Upper and Lower Egypt."

Nefertiti is often shown as being the same size as her husband, and in some inscriptions she is performing religious rituals that would normally have been carried out only by the pharaoh. The exact details of her power are hard to determine, however. An older theory held that her husband removed her from power, though there is also speculation that she may have ruled secretly in her own right after his death. Her tomb has long since disappeared, though some scholars believe that an unidentified mummy discovered in 2003 in Egypt's Valley of the Kings may be Nefertiti's.

QUESTIONS FOR ANALYSIS

1. Why might it have been difficult for Egyptians to accept a female ruler?
2. What opportunities do hereditary monarchies such as that of ancient Egypt provide for women? How does this fit with gender hierarchies in which men are understood as superior?

LaunchPad

ONLINE DOCUMENT PROJECT
Considering Egyptian views of gender roles, what complexities did Egyptian writers and artists face in depicting Hatshepsut? Analyze written and visual representations of Hatshepsut, and then complete a quiz and writing assignment based on the evidence and details from this chapter. *See inside front cover to learn more.*

Iron Age
▶ Period beginning about 1100 B.C.E. when iron became the most important material for weapons and tools in some parts of the world.

Iron Age began in about 1100 B.C.E. Iron weapons became important items of trade around the Mediterranean and throughout the Tigris and Euphrates Valleys, and the technology for making them traveled as well.

The decline of Egypt allowed new powers to emerge. South of Egypt along the Nile was a region called Nubia, which as early as 2000 B.C.E. served as a conduit of trade through which a variety of products flowed north from sub-Saharan Africa. As Egypt expanded during the New Kingdom, it took over northern Nubia, incorporating it into the growing Egyptian empire. The Nubians adopted many features of Egyptian culture, including Egyptian gods, the use of hieroglyphs, and the building of pyramids. Many Nubians became officials in the Egyptian bureaucracy and officers in the army, and there was significant intermarriage between the two groups.

With the contraction of the Egyptian empire, an independent kingdom, Kush, rose to power in Nubia, with its capital at Napata in what is now Sudan. The Kushites conquered southern Egypt, and in 727 B.C.E. the Kushite king Piye (r. ca. 747–716 B.C.E.) swept through the entire Nile Valley to the delta in the north. United once again, Egypt enjoyed a brief period of peace during which the Egyptian culture continued to influence that of its conquerors. In the seventh century B.C.E. invading Assyrians pushed the Kushites out of Egypt, and the Kushite rulers moved their capital farther up the Nile to Meroë, where they built hundreds of pyramids. Meroë became a center of iron production, exporting iron goods to much of Africa and across the Red Sea and the Indian Ocean to India. Gold and cotton textiles also provided wealth to the Kushite kingdom, which in the third century B.C.E. developed its own alphabet.

While Kush expanded in the southern Nile Valley, another group rose to prominence along the Mediterranean coast of modern Lebanon. These people established the prosperous commercial centers of Tyre, Sidon, and Byblos. These peoples were master shipbuilders, and from about 1100 B.C.E. to 700 B.C.E. many of the residents of these cities became the seaborne merchants of the Mediterranean. Their most valued products were purple and blue textiles, from which originated their Greek name, **Phoenicians**, meaning "Purple People."

Phoenicians
▶ People of the prosperous city-states in what is now Lebanon who traded and founded colonies throughout the Mediterranean and spread the phonetic alphabet.

The variety and quality of the Phoenicians' trade goods generally made them welcome visitors. They established colonies and trading posts throughout the Mediterranean and as far west as the Atlantic coast of modern-day Portugal. The Phoenicians' voyages brought them into contact with the Greeks, to whom they introduced many aspects of the older and more urbanized cultures of Mesopotamia and Egypt.

> **> Phoenician Trade Goods:**

- Dyed textiles
- Bronze
- Iron
- Wine
- Hunting dogs
- Gold
- Ivory

CHAPTER LOCATOR | How does writing shape what we can know about the past, and how did writing develop? | How did the peoples of Mesopotamia form states and develop new technologies?

CHAPTER 2
50   THE RISE OF THE STATE IN SOUTHWEST ASIA AND THE NILE VALLEY

FIGURE 2.2 ■ Origins of the Alphabet

List of hieroglyphic, Ugaritic, Phoenician, Greek, and Roman sign forms. (Source: A. B. Knapp, *The History and Culture of Ancient Western Asia and Egypt.* © 1988 Wadsworth, a division of Cengage Learning, Inc. Reproduced by permission, www.cengage.com/permissions.)

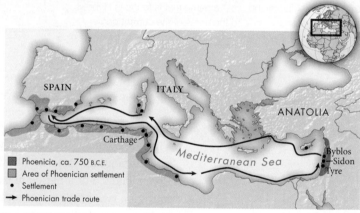

HIEROGLYPHIC	REPRESENTS	UGARITIC	PHOENICIAN	GREEK	ROMAN
	Throw stick			Γ	G
	Man with raised arms			E	E
	Basket with handle			K	K
	Water			M	M
	Snake			N	N
	Eye			O	O
	Mouth			Π	P
	Head			P	R
	Pool with lotus flowers			Σ	S
	House			B	B
	Ox-head			A	A

The Phoenicians' overwhelming cultural achievement was the spread of a completely phonetic system of writing—that is, an alphabet (see Figure 2.2). Writers of cuneiform and hieroglyphics had developed signs that were used to represent sounds, but these were always used with a much larger number of ideograms. Sometime around 1800 B.C.E., workers in the Sinai Peninsula, which was under Egyptian control, began to use only phonetic signs to write, with each sign designating one sound. The Greeks modified this alphabet for their own language, and the Romans later based their alphabet—the script we use to write English today—on Greek. Alphabets based on the Phoenician alphabet were also created in the Persian Empire and formed the basis of Hebrew, Arabic, and various alphabets of South and Central Asia.

Phoenician Settlements in the Mediterranean

QUICK REVIEW ◄

How did the Nile shape the society and culture of ancient Egypt?

How did the Egyptians create a prosperous and long-lasting society?

How did the Hebrews create an enduring written religious tradition?

How did the Assyrians and the Persians consolidate their power and control the subjects?

✓ LearningCurve
Check what you know.

> How did the Hebrews create an enduring written religious tradition?

Yahweh
▶ All-powerful god of the Hebrew people and the basis for the enduring religious traditions of Judaism.

The legacy of another people who took advantage of Egypt's collapse to found an independent state may have been even more far-reaching than that of the Phoenicians. For a period of several centuries, the Hebrews controlled first one and then two small states on the western end of the Fertile Crescent. The Hebrews created a new form of religious belief, a monotheism based on the worship of an all-powerful god they called **Yahweh** (YAH-way). Beginning in the late seventh century B.C.E. the Hebrews began to write down their religious ideas, traditions, laws, advice literature, prayers, hymns, history, and prophecies in a series of books. These were gathered together centuries later to form the Hebrew Bible. These writings later became the core of the Hebrews' religion, Judaism. Jews today revere these texts, as do many Christians, and Muslims respect them, all of which gives them particular importance.

The Hebrew State

The Hebrews were nomadic pastoralists who may have migrated into the Nile Delta from the east seeking good land for their herds of sheep and goats. According to the Hebrew Bible, they were enslaved by the Egyptians but were led out

CHAPTER LOCATOR | How does writing shape what we can know about the past, and how did writing develop? | How did the peoples of Mesopotamia form states and develop new technologies?

52 CHAPTER 2 THE RISE OF THE STATE IN SOUTHWEST ASIA AND THE NILE VALLEY

of Egypt by a charismatic leader named Moses. The Hebrews settled in the area between the Mediterranean and the Jordan River known as Canaan and were organized into tribes, each tribe consisting of numerous families who thought of themselves as related to one another. They slowly adopted agriculture and, not surprisingly, at times worshipped the agricultural gods of their neighbors. In this they followed the common historical pattern of newcomers by adapting the culture of an older, well-established people.

The Bible reports that the greatest danger to the Hebrews came from a group known as the Philistines (FIH-luh-steenz), who migrated to and established a kingdom in Canaan. The Hebrews found a leader in Saul, who with his men fought the Philistines. Saul subsequently established a monarchy over the Hebrew tribes, an event conventionally dated to about 1025 B.C.E. Saul's work was carried on by David of Bethlehem, who captured the city of Jerusalem, which he made the religious and political center of the realm. David's son Solomon (r. ca. 965–925 B.C.E.) launched a building program that the biblical narrative describes as including cities, palaces, fortresses, and roads. The most symbolic of these projects was the Temple of Jerusalem. The Temple of Jerusalem was intended to be the religious heart of the kingdom, a symbol of Hebrew unity and of Yahweh's approval of the Hebrew state.

This state did not last long. At Solomon's death his kingdom broke into political halves. The northern part became Israel, with its capital at Samaria, and the southern half was Judah, with Jerusalem remaining its center. War broke out between the northern and southern halves, and the Assyrians wiped out the northern kingdom in 722 B.C.E. Judah survived numerous invasions until the Babylonians crushed it in 587 B.C.E. The survivors were sent into exile in Babylonia, a period commonly known as the Babylonian Captivity. In 538 B.C.E. the Persian king Cyrus the Great conquered the Babylonians and permitted some forty thousand exiles to return to Jerusalem (see page 56).

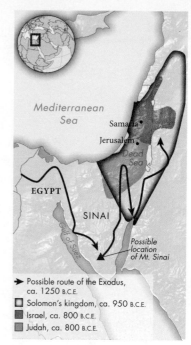

➤ Possible route of the Exodus, ca. 1250 B.C.E.
☐ Solomon's kingdom, ca. 950 B.C.E.
■ Israel, ca. 800 B.C.E.
■ Judah, ca. 800 B.C.E.

The Hebrew Exodus and State, ca. 1250–800 B.C.E.

The Jewish Religion

During and especially after the Babylonian Captivity, the most important Hebrew texts of history, law, and ethics were edited and brought together in the Torah, the first five books of the Hebrew Bible. Fundamental to an understanding of the Jewish religion is the concept of the Covenant, an agreement that people believed to exist between themselves and Yahweh. According to the Bible, Yahweh appeared to the tribal leader Abraham, promising him that he would be blessed, as would his descendants, if they followed Yahweh. Yahweh next appeared to Moses when he was leading the Hebrews out of Egypt, and Yahweh made a covenant with the Hebrews: if they worshipped Yahweh as their only god, he would consider them his chosen people and protect them from their enemies. Individuals such as Abraham and Moses who acted as intermediaries between Yahweh and the Hebrew people were known as "prophets." Much of the Hebrew Bible consists of writings in the prophets' voices, understood as messages from Yahweh to the Hebrews.

Worship was embodied in a series of rules of behavior, the Ten Commandments, which Yahweh gave to Moses; these required certain kinds of religious observances and forbade the Hebrews to steal, kill, lie, or commit adultery, thus

How did the Egyptians create a prosperous and long-lasting society? | **How did the Hebrews create an enduring written religious tradition?** | How did the Assyrians and the Persians consolidate their power and control the subjects? | ✓ LearningCurve Check what you know.

53

creating a system of ethical absolutes. From the Ten Commandments a complex system of rules of conduct was created and later written down as Hebrew law. The later prophets such as Isaiah created a system of ethical monotheism, in which goodness was understood to come from a single transcendent god, and in which religious obligations included fair and just behavior toward other people as well as rituals.

Like Mesopotamian deities, Yahweh punished people, but the Hebrews also believed he would protect them all, not simply kings and powerful priests, and make them prosper if they obeyed his commandments. The religion of the Hebrews was thus addressed to not only the elites but also the individual. Because kings or other political leaders were not essential to its practice, the rise or fall of a kingdom was not crucial to the religion's continued existence. Religious leaders were important in Judaism, but personally following the instructions of Yahweh was the central task for observant Jews in the ancient world.

Hebrew Society

The Hebrews were originally nomadic, but they adopted settled agriculture in Canaan, and some lived in cities. Over time, communal use of land gave way to family or private ownership, and devotions to the traditions of Judaism replaced tribal identity.

Family relationships reflected evolving circumstances. Marriage and the family were fundamentally important in Jewish life. Celibacy was frowned upon, and almost all major Jewish thinkers and priests were married. As in Mesopotamia and Egypt, marriage was a family matter, too important to be left solely to the whims of young people. The bearing of children was seen in some ways as a religious function. Sons were especially desired because they maintained the family bloodline while keeping ancestral property in the family. A firstborn son became the head of the household upon his father's death. Mothers oversaw the early education of the children, but as boys grew older, their fathers provided more of their education.

The development of urban life among Jews created new economic opportunities, especially in crafts and trade. People specialized in certain occupations, and, as in most ancient societies, these crafts were family trades.

> **QUICK REVIEW**

How did the religion of the Hebrews differ from that of
their Near Eastern neighbors?

CHAPTER LOCATOR | How does writing shape what we can know about the past, and how did writing develop? | How did the peoples of Mesopotamia form states and develop new technologies?

CHAPTER 2

54   THE RISE OF THE STATE IN SOUTHWEST ASIA AND THE NILE VALLEY

Assyrian Warriors Attack a City

In this Assyrian carving from a royal throne room made about 865 B.C.E., warriors cross a river on inflated skins, which both support them and provide air for breathing underwater. Such innovative techniques, combined with a large army and effective military organization, allowed the Assyrians to establish a large empire. (Werner Forman Archive/British Museum, London. Location: 10. © 2004 Werner Forman/TopFoto/The Image Works)

Small kingdoms like those of the Phoenicians and the Jews could exist only in the absence of a major power. In the ninth century B.C.E. one major power arose in the form of the Assyrians, who starting in northern Mesopotamia created an empire through often-brutal military conquests. And from a base in what is now southern Iran, the Persians established an even larger empire, developing effective institutions of government.

Assyria, the Military Monarchy

Starting from a base in northern Mesopotamia around 900 B.C.E., the Assyrians began a campaign of expansion and domination, conquering, exacting tribute, and building new fortified towns, palaces, and temples. By means of almost constant warfare, the Assyrians created an empire that stretched from their capital of Nineveh on the Tigris River to central Egypt. Revolt against the Assyrians inevitably promised the rebels bloody battles and cruel sieges followed by surrender, accompanied by systematic torture and slaughter, and sometimes deportations.

Assyrian methods were certainly harsh, but in practical terms Assyria's success was due primarily to the size of its army and to the army's sophisticated and effective military organization. In addition, the Assyrians developed a wide variety of siege machinery and techniques. Never before in this area had anyone

How did the Egyptians create a prosperous and long-lasting society?	How did the Hebrews create an enduring written religious tradition?	**How did the Assyrians and the Persians consolidate their power and control the subjects?**	 LearningCurve Check what you know.

applied such technical knowledge to warfare. The Assyrians also knew how to coordinate their efforts, both in open battle and in siege warfare. Not only did the Assyrians know how to win battles, but they also knew how to take advantage of their victories. As early as the eighth century B.C.E., the Assyrian kings began to organize their conquered territories into an empire. The lands closest to Assyria became provinces governed directly by Assyrian officials. Kingdoms beyond the provinces were not annexed but became dependent states.

By the seventh century B.C.E. Assyrian power seemed firmly established. Yet the downfall of Assyria was swift and complete. Babylon won its independence in 626 B.C.E. and joined forces with a new group, the Medes, an Indo-European-speaking people from Persia. Together the Babylonians and the Medes destroyed the Assyrian Empire in 612 B.C.E., paving the way for the rise of the Persians.

The Rise and Expansion of the Persian Empire

As we have seen, Assyria rose to power from a base in the Tigris and Euphrates River Valleys of Mesopotamia, which had seen many earlier empires. The Assyrians were defeated by a coalition that included not only a Mesopotamian power—

MAP 2.3 ■ The Assyrian and Persian Empires, ca. 1000–500 B.C.E.

The Assyrian Empire at its height around 650 B.C.E. included almost all of the old centers of power in the ancient Near East. By 500 B.C.E., however, the Persian Empire was far larger, extending from the Mediterranean Sea to the Indus River.

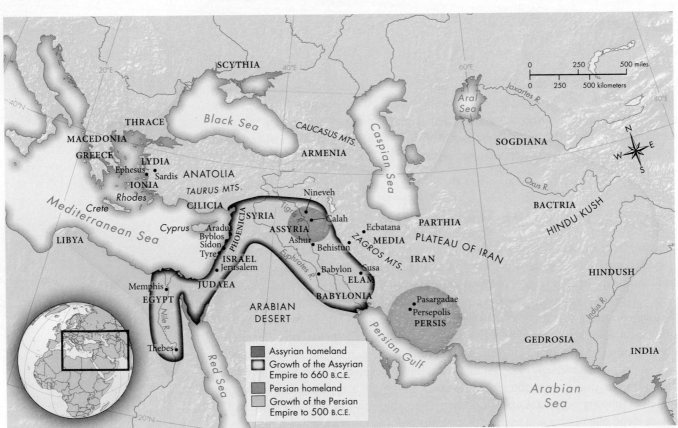

CHAPTER LOCATOR | How does writing shape what we can know about the past, and how did writing develop? | How did the peoples of Mesopotamia form states and develop new technologies?

CHAPTER 2
56 THE RISE OF THE STATE IN SOUTHWEST ASIA AND THE NILE VALLEY

Babylon—but also a people with a base of power in a part of the world that had not been the site of earlier urbanized states: Persia (modern-day Iran) (Map 2.3).

Iran's geographical position and topography explain its traditional role as the highway between western and eastern Asia. Nomadic peoples migrating south from the broad steppes of Russia and Central Asia have streamed into Iran throughout much of history. (For an in-depth discussion of these groups, see Chapter 12.) Confronting the uncrossable salt deserts, most have turned either westward or eastward, moving on until they reached the advanced and wealthy urban centers of Mesopotamia and India. Cities did emerge along these routes, however, and Iran became the area where nomads met urban dwellers.

Among these nomads were Indo-European-speaking peoples who migrated into this area about 1000 B.C.E. with their flocks and herds. They were also horse breeders, and the horse gave them a decisive military advantage over those who already lived in the area. One of these groups was the Medes, who settled in northern Iran. With the rise of the Medes, the balance of power in western Asia shifted east of Mesopotamia for the first time.

In 550 B.C.E. Cyrus the Great (r. 559–530 B.C.E.), king of the Persians (another Indo-European-speaking group) and one of the most remarkable statesmen of antiquity, conquered the Medes. Cyrus then set out to win control of the shore of the Mediterranean and thus of the terminal ports of the great trade routes that crossed Iran and Anatolia and to secure eastern Iran from the threats of nomadic invasions. In a series of major campaigns Cyrus achieved both goals.

After his victories, Cyrus made sure the Persians were portrayed as liberators, and in some cases he was more benevolent than most conquerors. According to his own account, he freed all the captive peoples, including the Hebrews, who were living in forced exile in Babylon.

Cyrus's successors continued the Persian conquests, creating the largest empire the world had yet seen. Darius (r. 521–486 B.C.E.) conquered Scythia in Central Asia, along with much of Thrace and Macedonia, areas north of the Aegean Sea (see Map 2.3, page 56). Darius began to call himself "King of Kings." Invasions of Greece by Darius and his son Xerxes were unsuccessful, but the Persian Empire lasted another two hundred years, until it became part of the empire of Alexander the Great (see page 131).

The Persians also knew how to preserve the peace they had won on the battlefield. To govern the empire, they created an efficient administrative system based in their newly built capital city of Persepolis. Under Darius, they divided the empire into districts and appointed either Persian or local nobles as administrators called satraps to head each one. The satrap controlled local government, collected taxes, heard legal cases, and maintained order. He was assisted by a council and also by officials and army leaders sent from Persepolis who made sure that he knew the will of the king and that the king knew what was going on in the provinces.

Scythian Saddlecloth

This red felt saddlecloth, dating from the fifth century B.C.E., is decorated with appliqués showing a winged griffon vulture with its claws in the back of a horned ibex. It was made by one of the nomadic peoples of western Asia, an area the Greeks called Scythia, some of which was conquered by the Persians. Items of daily use decorated with animals may have been thought to offer protection or assist in a hunt; this cloth was placed in a tomb, where it was preserved through the millennia by being frozen. (Hermitage, St. Petersburg, Russia/Photo © Boltin Picture Library/The Bridgeman Art Library)

How did the Egyptians create a prosperous and long-lasting society?

How did the Hebrews create an enduring written religious tradition?

How did the Assyrians and the Persians consolidate their power and control the subjects?

☑ LearningCurve
Check what you know.

The Persians allowed the peoples they conquered to maintain their own customs and beliefs as long as they paid the proper amount of taxes and did not rebel.

Communication and trade were eased by a sophisticated system of roads linking the empire from the coast of Asia Minor to the valley of the Indus River. These roads meant that the king was usually in close touch with officials and subjects, and they simplified the defense of the empire by making it easier to move Persian armies. The roads also aided the flow of trade, which Persian rulers further encouraged by building canals, including one that linked the Red Sea and the Nile.

The Religion of Zoroaster

Persian religion was originally polytheistic and tied to nature, with Ahuramazda (ah-HOOR-uh-MAZ-duh) as the chief god. Around 600 B.C.E. the ideas of Zoroaster (zoh-roh-ASS-tuhr), a thinker and preacher whose dates are uncertain, began to gain prominence. Zoroaster is regarded as the author of key religious texts, which were later gathered together in a collection of sacred texts called the Avesta. He introduced new spiritual concepts, stressing devotion to Ahuramazda alone and emphasizing the individual's responsibility to choose between the forces of creation, truth, and order and those of nothingness, chaos, falsehood, and disorder. At the end of time, the forces of order would win, and the victorious Ahuramazda, like the Egyptian god Osiris, would preside over a last judgment to determine each person's eternal fate.

Zoroaster's writings were communicated by teachers, and King Darius began to use Zoroastrian language and images. Under the protection of the Persian kings, Zoroastrian ideas spread throughout Iran and the rest of the Persian Empire, and then into central China. **Zoroastrianism** survived the fall of the Persian Empire to influence Christianity, Islam, and Buddhism, largely because of its belief in a just life on earth and a happy afterlife. Good behavior in the world, even though unrecognized at the time, would receive ample reward in the hereafter. Evil, no matter how powerful a person had been in life, would be punished after death. In some form or another, Zoroastrian concepts still pervade many modern religions and Zoroastrianism still exists as a religion.

Zoroastrianism
► Religion based on the teachings of Zoroaster that emphasized the individual's responsibility to choose between good and evil.

> **QUICK REVIEW**

How did the Assyrians treat subject peoples?
What about the Persians?

CHAPTER SUMMARY

Beginning about 5,000 years ago, people in some parts of the world invented writing, in large part to meet the needs of the state. States first developed in the southern part of Mesopotamia known as Sumer, where priests and rulers invented ways to control and organize people who lived in cities reliant on irrigation. Conquerors from the north unified Mesopotamian city-states into larger empires and spread Mesopotamian culture over a large area.

CHAPTER LOCATOR | How does writing shape what we can know about the past, and how did writing develop? | How did the peoples of Mesopotamia form states and develop new technologies?

During the third millennium B.C.E. Egypt grew into a cohesive state under a single ruler. For long stretches of history, Egypt was prosperous and secure in the Nile Valley, although at times various groups migrated in or invaded and conquered this kingdom. During the period known as the New Kingdom, warrior-kings created a large Egyptian empire. After the collapse of the New Kingdom, the Nubian rulers of Kush conquered Egypt, and another group, the Phoenicians, came to dominate trade in the Mediterranean, spreading a letter alphabet. Another group, the Hebrews, created a new form of religious belief based on the worship of a single all-powerful god.

In the ninth century B.C.E. the Assyrians used a huge army and sophisticated military tactics to create an empire from a base in northern Mesopotamia. The Persians established an even larger empire, developing effective institutions of government and building roads. The Persians generally allowed their subjects to continue their own customs, traditions, and religions. Around 600 B.C.E. a new religion grew in Persia based on the teachings of the prophet Zoroaster.

 **CONNECTIONS** Writing was invented to serve the needs of people who lived close to one another in cities and states, and almost everyone who could write lived in states. Because most history, including this book, concentrates on areas with states, the next two chapters examine the states that were developing in India and China during the period discussed in this chapter. In Chapter 5 we pick up on developments in the Mediterranean that link to those in Mesopotamia, Egypt, and Persia discussed in this chapter.

It is important to remember that, as was the spread of agriculture, the growth of the state was a slow process. States became the most powerful and most densely populated forms of human society, and today almost everyone on the planet is at least hypothetically a citizen of a state. In 500 B.C.E. perhaps only a little over 5 percent of the world's population lived in states. In his *Histories*, Herodotus pays primary attention to the Persians and the Greeks, both of whom had writing and states, but he also discusses many peoples who had neither. In their attempts to provide a balanced account of all the world's peoples, historians today are also looking beyond written sources.

How did the Egyptians create a prosperous and long-lasting society?	How did the Hebrews create an enduring written religious tradition?	How did the Assyrians and the Persians consolidate their power and control the subjects?	✓ LearningCurve Check what you know.

CHAPTER 2 STUDY GUIDE

 STEP 1

GET STARTED ONLINE

 LearningCurve

Now that you've read the chapter, make it stick by completing the LearningCurve activity.

STEP 2

EXPLAIN WHY IT MATTERS

Put your reading into practice. Identify each term below, and then explain why it matters in World history.

TERM	WHO OR WHAT & WHEN	WHY IT MATTERS
polytheism (p. 39)		
cuneiform (p. 40)		
epic poems (p. 41)		
Hammurabi's law code (p. 42)		
pharaoh (p. 45)		
Indo-European languages (p. 48)		
Iron Age (p. 50)		
Phoenicians (p. 50)		
Yahweh (p. 52)		
Zoroastrianism (p. 58)		

 **STEP 3**

MOVE BEYOND THE BASICS

To demonstrate a more advanced understanding of the development of regional powers in Mesopotamia, Egypt, Assyria, and Persia, fill in the chart below with descriptions of the factors contributing to the emergence of a powerful state in each region, focusing on four key areas: government, method of expansion, role of religion, and role of trade. How would you characterize the relationship between each state and the other cultures and societies that came under its control?

	Government	Methods of Expansion	Role of Religion	Role of Trade
Mesopotamia				
Egypt				
Assyria				
Persia				

Now, take a step back and try to explain the big picture. Remember to use specific examples from the chapter in your answers.

GOVERNMENT AND SOCIETY IN ANCIENT MESOPOTAMIA AND EGYPT

▶ What role did religion play in legitimizing the power of Mesopotamian and Egyptian rulers?

▶ What similarities and differences do you note in the structure of Mesopotamian and Egyptian society? How would you explain these similarities and differences?

HEBREW RELIGION AND SOCIETY

▶ How did the experience of subjugation and exile shape Hebrew religion and culture?

▶ How did the Hebrew's relationship with Yahweh differ from that of their neighbors' relationships with their deities?

IMPERIAL POWERS: ASSYRIA AND PERSIA

▶ How did the brutality of Assyrian rule contribute both to the rise and fall of their empire?

▶ How did the Persians build and maintain their empire? What explains its long-term stability?

LOOKING BACK, LOOKING AHEAD

▶ How did the states of Mesopotamia, Egypt, Assyria, and the Persian Empire differ from earlier forms of social and political organization?

▶ How would you explain the fact that, over time, the state became the dominant form of political organization in societies around the world?

> **IN YOUR OWN WORDS**

Imagine that you must give an oral report to the class answering the following question: **Where, how, and why did the first states emerge?** What would be the most important points and why?

3

THE FOUNDATION OF INDIAN SOCIETY

TO 300 C.E.

> **What were the defining social and cultural characteristics of ancient India?** Chapter 3 examines the development of ancient India from its first civilization to the collapse of its first empire. From about 2800 B.C.E. to 1800 B.C.E., the Indus Valley, or Harappan culture, thrived and expanded over a huge area. A very different Indian society emerged after the decline of this civilization. It was dominated by the Aryans, warriors who spoke an early version of Sanskrit. It was in this period that Buddhism and Jainism were founded and the early Brahmanic religion of the Aryans developed into Hinduism. The Mauryan Dynasty emerged in the wake of the Greek invasion of north India in 326 B.C.E. The empire proved short-lived, however, and for several centuries India was politically divided. Nonetheless, cultural elements dating back to the ancient period spread through trade and other contact.

Female Spirit from an Indian Stupa Royal patronage aided the spread of Buddhism in India, especially the patronage of King Ashoka, who sponsored the construction of numerous Buddhist monuments. This head of a female spirit (called a *yakshini*) is from the stupa that Ashoka had built at Bharhut in central India. (Sudarsana Yakshini, relief from Stupa of Bharhut, Madhya Pradesh, India/De Agostini Picture Library/G. Nimatallah/The Bridgeman Art Library)

> What does archaeology tell us about the Harappan civilization in India?

> What kind of society and culture did the Indo-European Aryans create?

> What ideas and practices were taught by the founders of Jainism, Buddhism, and Hinduism?

> What was the result of Indian contact with the Persians and Greeks, and what were the consequences of unification under the Mauryan Empire?

> How was India shaped by political disunity and contacts with other cultures during the five centuries from 185 B.C.E. to 300 C.E.?

✓ LearningCurve
After reading the chapter, use LearningCurve to retain what you've read.

What does archaeology tell us about the Harappan civilization in India?

Mohenjo-daro

Mohenjo-daro was a planned city built of fired mud brick. Its streets were straight, and covered drainpipes were installed to carry away waste. From sites like this, we know that the early Indian political elite had the power and technical expertise to organize large, coordinated building projects. Found in Mohenjo-daro, this small ceramic figurine (right) shows a woman adorned with necklaces and an elaborate headdress. (site: © M. Kenoyer/Harrapa.com. Courtesy, Department of Archeology and Museums, Government of Pakistan; figurine: © Angelo Hornak/Alamy)

I In India, as elsewhere, the possibilities for both agriculture and communication have always been shaped by geography. Monsoon rains sweep northward from the Indian Ocean each summer. The lower reaches of the Himalaya Mountains in the northeast are covered by dense forests. Immediately to the south are the fertile valleys of the Indus and Ganges Rivers. These lowland plains, which stretch all the way across the subcontinent, were tamed for agriculture over time, and India's great empires were centered there. To their west are the deserts of Rajasthan and southeastern Pakistan, historically important in part because their flat terrain enabled invaders to sweep into India from the northwest. South of the great river valleys rise the Vindhya Mountains and the dry, hilly Deccan Plateau. Only along the western coast of this part of India do the hills give way to narrow plains where crop agriculture flourished (Map 3.1). India's long coastlines and predictable winds fostered maritime trade with other countries bordering the Indian Ocean.

Agriculture was well established in India by about 7000 B.C.E. Wheat and barley were the early crops, probably having spread in their domesticated form from what is today the Middle East. Farmers also domesticated cattle, sheep, and goats and learned to make pottery.

CHAPTER LOCATOR | **What does archaeology tell us about the Harappan civilization in India?** | What kind of society and culture did the Indo-European Aryans create?

64 CHAPTER 3 THE FOUNDATION OF INDIAN SOCIETY

2800–2000 B.C.E. Height of Harappan civilization	**326 B.C.E.** Alexander the Great enters Indus Valley
ca. 1500–500 B.C.E. Vedic Age; flourishing of Aryan civilization; *Rig Veda*	**ca. 322–185 B.C.E.** Mauryan Empire
ca. 1000 B.C.E. Introduction of iron	**ca. 300 B.C.E.** Jain religion splits into two sects
750–500 B.C.E. *Upanishads*	**ca. 269–232 B.C.E.** Reign of Ashoka
ca. 513 B.C.E. Persians conquer the Indus Valley and Kashmir	**ca. 150 B.C.E.–250 C.E.** Classical period of Tamil culture
ca. 500 B.C.E. Founding of Buddhism and Jainism	**ca. 100 C.E.** More inclusive Mahayana form of Buddhism emerges
ca. 400 B.C.E.–200 C.E. Gradual evolution of the Brahmanic religion into Hinduism	**ca. 200 C.E.** *Code of Manu*

India's first civilization is known today as the Indus Valley or the **Harappan** (huh-RAH-puhn) civilization, from the modern names of the river and city near where the first ruins were discovered. Archaeologists have discovered some three hundred Harappan cities and many more towns and villages in both Pakistan and India (see Map 3.1). It was a literate civilization, but no one has been able to decipher the more than four hundred symbols inscribed on stone seals and copper tablets. The civilization flourished most from 2500 B.C.E. to 2000 B.C.E.

Harappan
▶ The first Indian civilization; also known as the Indus Valley civilization.

The Harappan civilization extended over nearly five hundred thousand square miles in the Indus Valley, making it more than twice as large as ancient Egypt or Sumer. Yet Harappan civilization was marked by striking uniformity. Throughout the region, for instance, even in small villages, bricks were made to the same standard proportion (4:2:1). Figurines of pregnant women have been found throughout the area, suggesting common religious ideas and practices.

Like Mesopotamian cities, Harappan cities were centers for crafts and trade and were surrounded by extensive farmland. The Harappans were the earliest known manufacturers of cotton cloth. Trade was extensive. As early as the reign of Sargon of Akkad in the third millennium B.C.E. (see page 41), trade between India and Mesopotamia carried goods and ideas between the two cultures, probably by way of the Persian Gulf.

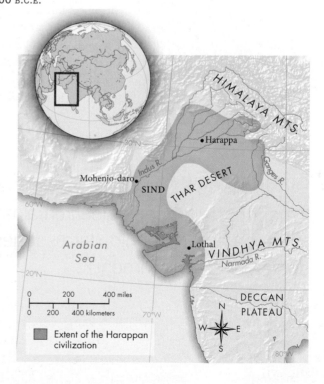

MAP 3.1 ■ Harappan Civilization, ca. 2500 B.C.E.
The earliest civilization in India developed in the Indus River Valley in the west of the subcontinent.

What ideas were taught by the founders of Jainism, Buddhism, and Hinduism?	What was the result of Indian contact with the Persians and Greeks?	How was India shaped by political disunity and contacts with other cultures?	✔️ LearningCurve Check what you know.

The cities of Mohenjo-daro in southern Pakistan, and Harappa, some 400 miles to the north, were huge for this period, more than 3 miles in circumference, with populations estimated at 35,000 to 40,000. Both were defended by great citadels that were 40 to 50 feet high. The cities had obviously been planned and built before being settled. Streets were straight and varied from 9 to 34 feet in width. The houses were substantial, many two stories tall, some perhaps three. The focal point of a house was a central courtyard onto which the rooms opened.

Perhaps the most surprising aspect of the elaborate planning of these cities was their complex system of drainage. Each house had a bathroom with a drain connected to brick-lined sewers located under the major streets. Openings allowed the refuse to be collected, probably to be used as fertilizer on nearby fields. No other ancient city had such an advanced sanitation system.

Both Mohenjo-daro and Harappa also contained numerous large structures, which archaeologists think were public buildings. One of the most important was the large ventilated storehouse for the community's grain. Mohenjo-daro also had a marketplace or place of assembly, a palace, and a huge pool some 39 feet long by 23 feet wide by 8 feet deep. Like the later Roman baths, it had spacious dressing rooms for the bathers.

The prosperity of the Indus civilization depended on constant and intensive cultivation of the rich river valley. Although rainfall seems to have been greater then than in recent times, the Indus, like the Nile, flowed through a relatively dry region made fertile by annual floods and irrigation. And as in Egypt, agriculture was aided by a long, hot growing season and near-constant sunshine.

Because no one has yet deciphered the written language of the Harappan people, their political, intellectual, and religious life is largely unknown. There clearly was a political structure with the authority to organize city planning and facilitate trade, but we do not even know whether there were hereditary kings.

Soon after 2000 B.C.E., the Harappan civilization mysteriously declined. The decline cannot be attributed to the arrival of powerful invaders, as was once thought. Rather it was internally generated. Environmental theories include an earthquake that led to a shift in the course of the river, or a severe drought. Some scholars speculate that long-distance commerce collapsed, leading to an economic depression. Others theorize that the population fell prey to diseases, such as malaria, that caused people to flee the cities.

> **QUICK REVIEW**

What do the archeological remains of the great cities of Harappa and Mohenjo-daro suggest about Harappan society and government?

CHAPTER LOCATOR | What does archaeology tell us about the Harappan civilization in India? | What kind of society and culture did the Indo-European Aryans create?

66 CHAPTER 3 THE FOUNDATION OF INDIAN SOCIETY

What kind of society and culture did the Indo-European Aryans create?

Bronze Sword

This bronze sword, with a rib in the middle of the blade for strength, is a striking example of the quality of Aryan arms. Superior weapons gave the Aryans military advantage. (© The Trustees of the British Museum/Art Resource, NY)

After the decline of the Harappan civilization, a people who called themselves Aryans became dominant in north India. They were speakers of an early form of Sanskrit, an Indo-European language closely related to ancient Persian and more distantly related to Latin, Greek, Celtic, and their modern descendants, such as English. The Aryans flourished during the Vedic Age (ca. 1500–500 B.C.E.). Named for the Vedas, a large and significant body of ancient sacred works written in Sanskrit, this period witnessed the Indo-Aryan development of the caste system and the Brahmanic religion and the writing of the great epics that represent the earliest form of Indian literature.

Aryans

▶ The dominant people in north India after the decline of the Indus Valley civilization; they spoke an early form of Sanskrit.

Aryan Dominance in North India

Until relatively recently, the dominant theory was that the Aryans came into India from outside, perhaps as part of the same movements of people that led to the Hittites

> **Links Between English and Sanskrit:**

Sanskrit Word:	Meaning:	Related English Word:
nava	ship	*naval*
deva	god	*divine*
raja	ruler	*regal*

What ideas were taught by the founders of Jainism, Buddhism, and Hinduism?	What was the result of Indian contact with the Persians and Greeks?	How was India shaped by political disunity and contacts with other cultures?	✓ LearningCurve Check what you know.

occupying parts of Anatolia, the Achaeans entering Greece, and the Kassites conquering Sumer—all in the period from about 1900 B.C.E. to 1750 B.C.E. Some scholars, however, have proposed that the Indo-European languages spread to this area much earlier; to them it seems possible that the Harappan people were speakers of an early Indo-European language. If that was the case, the Aryans would be one of the groups descended from this early population.

The central source of information on the early Aryans is the *Rig Veda*, the earliest of the Vedas, originally an oral collection of hymns, ritual texts, and philosophical treatises composed in Sanskrit between 1500 B.C.E. and 500 B.C.E. The *Rig Veda* portrays the Aryans as warrior tribes who glorified military skill and heroism; loved to drink, hunt, race, and dance; and counted their wealth in cattle. The Aryans did not sweep across India in a quick campaign, nor were they a disciplined army led by one conqueror. Rather they were a collection of tribes that frequently fought with each other and only over the course of several centuries came to dominate north India.

The key to the Aryans' success probably lay in their superior military technology, including two-wheeled chariots, horses, and bronze swords and spears. Their epics present the struggle for north India in religious terms, describing their chiefs as godlike heroes and their opponents as irreligious savages who did not perform the proper sacrifices. In time, however, the Aryans clearly absorbed much from those they conquered, such as agricultural techniques and foods.

At the head of each Aryan tribe was a chief, or raja (RAH-juh), who led his followers in battle and ruled them in peacetime. The warriors in the tribe elected the chief for his military skills. Next in importance to the chief was the priest. In time, priests evolved into a distinct class possessing precise knowledge of the complex rituals and of the invocations and formulas that accompanied them. Below them in the pecking order was a warrior nobility who rode into battle in chariots and perhaps on horseback. The warrior class met at assemblies to reach decisions and advise the raja. The common tribesmen tended herds and worked the land. To the conquered non-Aryans fell the drudgery of menial tasks. It is difficult to define precisely their social status. Though probably not slaves, they were certainly subordinate to the Aryans and worked for them in return for protection.

Over the course of several centuries, the Aryans pushed farther east into the valley of the Ganges River, at that time a land of thick jungle populated by aboriginal forest peoples. The tremendous challenge of clearing the jungle was made somewhat easier by the introduction of iron around 1000 B.C.E., probably by diffusion from Mesopotamia.

As Aryan rulers came to dominate large settled populations, the style of political organization changed from tribal chieftainship to territorial kingship. In other words, the ruler now controlled an area with people living in permanent settlements, not a nomadic tribe that moved as a group. Moreover, kings no longer needed to be elected by the tribe; it was enough to be invested by priests and to perform the royal ceremonies they designed. The priests, or **Brahmins**, supported the growth of royal power in return for confirmation of their own power and status. The Brahmins also served as advisers to the kings. In the face of this royal-priestly alliance, the old tribal assemblies of warriors withered away. By the time Persian armies reached the Indus around 513 B.C.E., there were sixteen major Aryan kingdoms in north India.

Rig Veda

▶ The earliest collection of Indian hymns, ritual texts, and philosophical treatises, it is the central source of information on early Aryans.

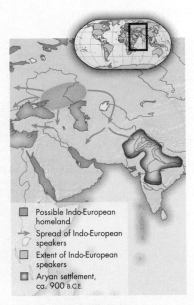

Indo-European Migrations and the Vedic Age

Possible Indo-European homeland

Spread of Indo-European speakers

Extent of Indo-European speakers

Aryan settlement, ca. 900 B.C.E.

Brahmins

▶ Priests of the Aryans; they supported the growth of royal power in return for royal confirmation of their own religious rights, power, and status.

CHAPTER LOCATOR | What does archaeology tell us about the Harappan civilization in India? | **What kind of society and culture did the Indo-European Aryans create?**

CHAPTER 3
68 THE FOUNDATION OF INDIAN SOCIETY

Life in Early India

Caste was central to the social life of these north Indian kingdoms. Early Aryan society had distinguished among the warrior elite, the priests, ordinary tribesmen, and conquered subjects. These distinctions gradually evolved into the **caste system**, which divided society into strictly defined hereditary groups. Society was conceived of as four hierarchical strata whose members did not eat with or marry each other. These strata, or varnas, were Brahmin (priests), Kshatriya (warriors and officials), Vaishya (merchants), and Shudra (peasants and laborers). The caste system thus allowed the numerically outnumbered Aryans to maintain dominance over their subjects and not be culturally absorbed by them.

Social and religious attitudes supported the caste system. Aryans considered the work of artisans impure. They left all such work to the local people, who were probably superior to them in these arts anyway. Trade, by contrast, was not viewed as demeaning. Brahmanic texts of the period refer to trade as equal in value to farming, serving the king, or being a priest.

As priests, the Brahmins were expected to memorize every syllable and tone of the Vedas so that their rituals would please the gods. They not only conducted the traditional ceremonies but also developed new ones for new circumstances. As agriculture became more important to the Aryans, for example, Brahmins acted as agents of Agni, the god of fire, to purify the land for crops. The Brahmins also knew the formulas and spells that were effective against diseases and calamities.

Those without places in the four varnas—that is, newly conquered peoples and those who had lost their caste status through violations of ritual—were outcastes. That simply meant that they belonged to no caste. In time, some of them became "untouchables" because they were "impure." They were scorned because they earned their living by performing such "polluting" jobs as slaughtering animals and dressing skins.

Slavery was a feature of early social life in India. People captured in battle often became slaves, but captives could also be ransomed by their families. Later, slavery was less connected with warfare and became more of an economic and social institution. At birth, slave children automatically became the slaves of their parents' masters. Indian slaves could be bought, used as collateral, or given away.

Like most nomadic tribes, the Aryans were patrilineal and patriarchal (tracing descent through males and placing power in the senior men of the family). Thus the roles of women in Aryan society probably were more subordinate than were the roles of women in local Dravidian groups, many of which were matrilineal (tracing descent through females). But even in Aryan society women were treated somewhat more favorably than in later Indian society. In epics such as the *Ramayana*, women are often portrayed as forceful personalities, able to achieve their goals both by using feminine ploys to cajole men and by direct action.

Brahmanism

The Aryans recognized a multitude of gods who shared some features with the gods of other early Indo-European societies such as the Persians and Greeks. Ordinary people dealt with these gods through priests who made animal sacrifices to them. By giving valued things to the gods, people strengthened both the power of the gods and their own relationships with them. Gradually, under the

caste system
▸ The Indian system of dividing society into hereditary groups whose members interacted primarily within the group, and especially married within the group.

What ideas were taught by the founders of Jainism, Buddhism, and Hinduism?	What was the result of Indian contact with the Persians and Greeks?	How was India shaped by political disunity and contacts with other cultures?	✓ LearningCurve Check what you know.

priestly monopoly of the Brahmins, correct sacrifice and proper ritual became so important that most Brahmins believed that a properly performed ritual would force a god to grant a worshipper's wish. Ordinary people could watch a ceremony, but could not perform the key steps in the ritual.

The *Upanishads* (oo-PAH-nih-shadz), composed between 750 B.C.E. and 500 B.C.E., record speculations about the mystical meaning of sacrificial rites and about cosmological questions of man's relationship to the universe. They document a gradual shift from the mythical worldview of the early Vedic Age to a deeply philosophical one. Associated with this shift was a movement toward asceticism (uh-SEH-tuh-sihz-uhm)—severe self-discipline and self-denial.

Ancient Indian cosmology (theories of the universe) focused not on a creator who made the universe out of nothing, but rather on endlessly repeating cycles. Key ideas were **samsara**, the reincarnation of souls by a continual process of rebirth, and **karma**, the tally of good and bad deeds that determined the status of an individual's next life. Good deeds led to better future lives, evil deeds to worse future lives. Reward and punishment worked automatically; there was no all-knowing god who judged people and could be petitioned to forgive a sin, and each individual was responsible for his or her own destiny in a just and impartial world.

To most people, especially those on the low end of the economic and social scale, these ideas were attractive. By living righteously and doing good deeds, people could improve their lot in the next life. Yet there was another side to these ideas: the wheel of life could be seen as a treadmill, giving rise to a yearning for release from the relentless cycle of birth and death. One solution offered in the *Upanishads* was moksha, or release from the wheel of life. Brahmanic mystics claimed that life in the world was actually an illusion and that the only way to escape the wheel of life was to realize that ultimate reality was unchanging.

The unchanging ultimate reality was called **brahman**. Brahman was contrasted to the multitude of fleeting phenomena that people consider important in their daily lives. The individual soul or self was ultimately the same substance as the universal brahman, in the same way that each spark is in substance the same as a large fire.

The *Upanishads* gave the Brahmins a high status to which the poor and lowly could aspire in a future life. Consequently, the Brahmins greeted the concepts presented in these works and those who taught them with tolerance and understanding and made a place for them in traditional religious practice. The rulers of Indian society also encouraged the new trends, since the doctrines of samsara and karma encouraged the poor and oppressed to labor peacefully and dutifully. Thus, although the new doctrines were intellectually revolutionary, in social and political terms they supported the existing power structure.

samsara
▶ The transmigration of souls by a continual process of rebirth.

karma
▶ The tally of good and bad deeds that determines the status of an individual's next life.

brahman
▶ The unchanging ultimate reality, according to the *Upanishads*.

> QUICK REVIEW

How did religion reinforce social hierarchy in Aryan society?

CHAPTER LOCATOR | What does archaeology tell us about the Harappan civilization in India? | What kind of society and culture did the Indo-European Aryans create?

CHAPTER 3
70 THE FOUNDATION OF INDIAN SOCIETY

What ideas and practices were taught by the founders of Jainism, Buddhism, and Hinduism?

The God Vishnu

Vishnu is depicted here coming to the rescue of an elephant in the clutches of a crocodile. It comes from the fifth-century-c.e. Dasavatara Temple in Uttar Pradesh. (© akg-images/Jean-Louis Nou/The Image Works)

By the sixth and fifth centuries B.C.E., cities had reappeared in India, and merchants and trade were thriving. Bricks were again baked in kilns and used to build ramparts around cities. One particular kingdom, Magadha, had become much more powerful than any of the other states in the Ganges plain. Written language had also reappeared.

This was a period of intellectual ferment throughout Eurasia—the period of the early Greek philosophers, the Hebrew prophets, Zoroaster in Persia, and Confucius and the early Daoists in China. In India it led to numerous sects that rejected various elements of Brahmanic teachings. The two most influential were Jainism and Buddhism. Hinduism emerged in response to these new religions but at the same time was the most direct descendant of the old Brahmanic religion.

What ideas were taught by the founders of Jainism, Buddhism, and Hinduism?	What was the result of Indian contact with the Persians and Greeks?	How was India shaped by political disunity and contacts with other cultures?	✓ LearningCurve Check what you know.

The most extreme Jain ascetics not only endured the elements without the help of clothes, but also were generally indifferent to bodily comfort. The Jain saint depicted in this eighth-century-C.E. cave temple has maintained his posture for so long that vines have grown up around him. (Courtesy, Robert Fisher)

Jainism

The key figure of Jainism, Vardhamana Mahavira (fl. ca. 520 B.C.E.), was the son of the chief of a small state and a member of the warrior class. Like many ascetics of the period, he left home to become a wandering holy man. For twelve years he traveled through the Ganges Valley until he found enlightenment and became a "completed soul." Mahavira taught his doctrines for about thirty years, founding a disciplined order of monks and gaining the support of many lay followers, male and female.

Jainism

▶ Indian religion whose followers consider all life sacred and avoid destroying other life.

Mahavira accepted the Brahmanic doctrines of karma and rebirth but developed these ideas in new directions, founding the religion referred to as **Jainism**. He asserted that human beings, animals, plants, and even inanimate objects all have living souls enmeshed in matter, accumulated through the workings of karma. The ascetic, who willingly undertakes suffering, can dissipate some of the accumulated karma and make progress toward liberation. If a soul at last escapes from all the matter weighing it down, it becomes lighter than ordinary objects and floats to the top of the universe, where it remains forever in bliss.

Mahavira's followers pursued such liberation by living ascetic lives and avoiding evil thoughts and actions. The Jains considered all life sacred and tried to live without destroying other life. A Jain who wished to avoid violence to life became a vegetarian and took pains not to kill any creature, even tiny insects in the air and soil. Among the most conservative Jains, priests practiced nudity, for clinging to clothes, even a loincloth, was a form of attachment. Lay Jains could pursue Jain teachings by practicing nonviolence and not eating meat.

Although Jainism never took hold as widely as Hinduism and Buddhism (discussed below), it has been an influential strand in Indian thought and has several million adherents in India today. Fasting and nonviolence as spiritual practices in

CHAPTER LOCATOR | What does archaeology tell us about the Harappan civilization in India? | What kind of society and culture did the Indo-European Aryans create?

CHAPTER 3
72 THE FOUNDATION OF INDIAN SOCIETY

India owe much to Jain teachings. In the twentieth century Mohandas Gandhi, leader of the Indian independence movement, was influenced by these ideas through his mother, and the American civil rights leader Dr. Martin Luther King, Jr., was influenced by Gandhi.

Siddhartha Gautama and Buddhism

Siddhartha Gautama (fl. ca. 500 B.C.E.), also called Shakyamuni ("sage of the Shakya tribe"), is best known as the Buddha ("enlightened one"). He was a contemporary of Mahavira and came from the same warrior social class. At age twenty-nine, unsatisfied with his life of comfort and troubled by the suffering he saw around him, he left home to become a wandering ascetic. He traveled south to the kingdom of Magadha, where he studied with yoga masters, but later took up extreme asceticism. According to tradition, while meditating under a bo tree at Bodh Gaya, he reached enlightenment. After several weeks of meditation, he preached his first sermon, urging a "middle way" between asceticism and worldly life. For the next forty-five years, the Buddha traveled through the Ganges Valley,

Gandharan Frieze Depicting the Buddha

This carved stone from ca. 200 C.E. is one in a series portraying scenes from the life of the Buddha. From the Gandharan kingdom (located in modern Pakistan), this frieze depicts the Buddha seated below the bo tree, where he was first enlightened. (Scenes from the life of the Buddha, Kushan Dynasty (stone)/Freer Gallery, Smithsonian Institution, Washington, D.C., U.S.A./The Bridgeman Art Library)

> PICTURING THE PAST

ANALYZING THE IMAGE: What are the people around the Buddha doing? What animals are portrayed?

CONNECTIONS: Does this frieze effectively convey any Buddhist principles? If so, which ones?

What ideas were taught by the founders of Jainism, Buddhism, and Hinduism?	What was the result of Indian contact with the Persians and Greeks?	How was India shaped by political disunity and contacts with other cultures?	✓ LearningCurve Check what you know.

propounding his ideas, refuting his adversaries, and attracting followers. Probably because he refused to recognize the divine authority of the Vedas and dismissed sacrifices, he attracted followers mostly from among merchants, artisans, and farmers, rather than Brahmins.

In his first sermon the Buddha outlined his main message, summed up in the **Four Noble Truths** and the **Eightfold Path**. The Four Noble Truths are as follows: (1) pain and suffering, frustration, and anxiety are ugly but inescapable parts of human life; (2) suffering and anxiety are caused by human desires and attachments; (3) people can understand these weaknesses and triumph over them; and (4) this triumph is made possible by following a simple code of conduct, the Eightfold Path. The basic insight of Buddhism is thus psychological. The deepest human longings can never be satisfied, and even those things that seem to give pleasure cause anxiety because we are afraid of losing them. Attachment to people and things causes sorrow at their loss.

Buddhism differed from Brahmanism and later Hinduism in that it ignored the caste system. Everyone, noble and peasant, educated and ignorant, male and female, could follow the Eightfold Path. Moreover, the Buddha was extraordinarily nondogmatic. In his view, there was no harm in honoring local gods or observing traditional ceremonies, as long as one remembered the goal of enlightenment and did not let sacrifices become snares or attachments. The willingness of Buddhists to tolerate a wide variety of practices aided the spread of the religion.

The Buddha's followers transmitted his teachings orally until they were written down in the second or first century B.C.E. These scriptures are called sutras. The form of monasticism that developed among the Buddhists was less strict than that of the Jains. Buddhist monks moved about for eight months of the year (except the rainy season), begging for their one meal a day, but they could bathe and wear clothes. Within a few centuries Buddhist monks began to overlook the rule that they should travel. They set up permanent monasteries, generally on land donated by kings or other patrons. Orders of nuns also appeared, giving women the opportunity to seek truth in ways men had traditionally used. The main ritual that monks and nuns performed in their monastic establishments was the communal recitation of the sutras. Lay Buddhists could aid the spread of the Buddhist teachings by providing food for monks and support for their monasteries, and they could pursue their own spiritual progress by adopting practices such as abstaining from meat and alcohol. (See "Individuals in Society: Sudatta, Lay Follower of the Buddha," page 76.)

Because Buddhism had no central ecclesiastical authority, early Buddhist communities developed several divergent traditions and came to stress different sutras. One of the most important of these, associated with the monk-philosopher Nagarjuna (fl. ca. 100 C.E.), is called **Mahayana**, or "Great Vehicle," because it was a more inclusive form of the religion. One branch of Mahayana taught that reality is empty (that is, nothing exists independently of itself). Another branch held that ultimate reality is consciousness, that everything is produced by the mind.

Just as important as the metaphysical literature of Mahayana Buddhism was its devotional side, influenced by the religions then prevalent in Central Asia, such as Zoroastrianism (see page 58). The Buddha became deified and was placed at the head of an expanding pantheon of other Buddhas and **bodhisattvas** (boh-dih-SUHT-vuhz). Bodhisattvas were Buddhas-to-be who had stayed in the world after enlightenment to help others on the path to salvation. The Buddhas and

Four Noble Truths

▶ The Buddha's message that pain and suffering are inescapable parts of life; suffering and anxiety are caused by human desires and attachments; people can understand and triumph over these weaknesses; and the triumph is made possible by following a simple code of conduct.

Eightfold Path

▶ The code of conduct set forth by the Buddha in his first sermon, beginning with "right conduct" and ending with "right contemplation."

Mahayana

▶ The "Great Vehicle," a tradition of Buddhism that aspires to be more inclusive.

bodhisattvas

▶ Buddhas-to-be who stayed in the world after enlightenment to help others on the path to salvation.

| What does archaeology tell us about the Harappan civilization in India? | What kind of society and culture did the Indo-European Aryans create? |

bodhisattvas became objects of veneration. With the growth of Mahayana, Buddhism attracted more and more laypeople.

Buddhism remained an important religion in India until about 1200 c.e. By that time it had spread widely through East, Central, and Southeast Asia. After 1200 c.e. Buddhism declined in India, losing out to both Hinduism and Islam, and the number of Buddhists in India today is small. Buddhism never lost its hold in Nepal and Sri Lanka, however, and today it is also a major religion in Southeast Asia, Tibet, China, Korea, and Japan.

Hinduism

Both Buddhism and Jainism were direct challenges to the old Brahmanic religion. Both rejected animal sacrifice, which by then was a central element in the rituals performed by Brahmin priests. Even more important, both religions tacitly rejected the caste system, accepting people of any caste into their ranks. Over the next several centuries (ca. 400 b.c.e.–200 c.e.), in response to this challenge, the Brahmanic religion evolved in a more devotional direction, developing into the religion commonly called Hinduism. In Hinduism Brahmins retained their high social status, but it became possible for individual worshippers to have more direct contact with the gods, showing their devotion without using priests as intermediaries.

The bedrock of Hinduism is the belief that the Vedas are sacred revelations and that a specific caste system is implicitly prescribed in them. Hinduism is a guide to life, the goal of which is to reach union with brahman, the unchanging ultimate reality. There are four steps in this search, progressing from study of the Vedas in youth to complete asceticism in old age. In their quest for brahman, people are to observe **dharma** (DAHR-muh), the moral law.

Hinduism assumes that there are innumerable legitimate ways of worshipping brahman, including devotion to personal gods. After the third century b.c.e. Hinduism began to emphasize the roles and personalities of thousands of powerful gods. These gods were usually represented by images, either small ones in homes or larger ones in temples. People could show devotion to their personal gods by reciting hymns or scriptures and by making offerings of food or flowers before these images. Hinduism's embrace of a large pantheon of gods enabled it to incorporate new sects, doctrines, beliefs, rites, and deities.

A central ethical text of Hinduism is the *Bhagavad Gita* (BAH-guh-vahd GEE-tuh), a part of the world's longest ancient epic, the *Mahabharata*. The *Bhagavad Gita* offers guidance on the most serious problem facing a Hindu—how to live in the world and yet honor dharma and thus achieve release from the wheel of life. The heart of the *Bhagavad Gita* is the spiritual conflict confronting Arjuna, a human hero about to ride into battle against his kinsmen. As he surveys the battlefield, struggling with the grim notion of killing his relatives, Arjuna voices his doubts to his charioteer, none other than the god Krishna. When at last Arjuna refuses to spill his family's blood, Krishna explains compassionately to Arjuna the duty to act—to live in the world and carry out his duties as a warrior. Indeed, the *Bhagavad Gita* emphasizes the necessity of action, which is essential for the welfare of the world. For Arjuna the warrior's duty is to wage war in compliance with his dharma. Only those who live within the divine law without complaint will be

dharma
▶ The Sanskrit word for moral law, central to both Buddhist and Hindu teachings.

| What ideas were taught by the founders of Jainism, Buddhism, and Hinduism? | What was the result of Indian contact with the Persians and Greeks? | How was India shaped by political disunity and contacts with other cultures? | ✓ LearningCurve Check what you know. |

75

Sudatta, Lay Follower of the Buddha

During the decades when the Buddha traveled around north India spreading his teachings, he attracted both disciples and lay followers. Stories of the Buddha's interactions with them were passed down orally for centuries, and undoubtedly were elaborated over time. Still, these accounts give us a sense of what life was like in early India. The wealthy banker or merchant Sudatta is a good example of an ardent lay follower. He was so generous to others that he is normally referred to by his epithet, Anathapindada, which means "benefactor of the needy."

The people depicted here are performing the Buddhist ritual of circumambulating a stupa (a mound containing the ashes or other relics of a monk). (British Museum, London/Erich Lessing/Art Resource, NY)

Sudatta met the Buddha in the first year after his enlightenment. In one early conversation with him, Sudatta asks if he must leave the world to attain nirvana:

> Now, I have heard thy disciples praise the bliss of the hermit and denounce the unrest of the world. "The Holy One," they say, "has given up his kingdom and his inheritance, and has found the path of righteousness, thus setting an example to all the world how to attain Nirvana." My heart yearns to do what is right and to be a blessing unto my fellows. Let me then ask you, Must I give up my wealth, my home, and my business enterprises, and, like you, go into homelessness in order to attain the bliss of a religious life?

The Buddha replied that the crucial issue was the way an individual looked on wealth. Anyone who cleaves to wealth needs to cast it aside, but anyone who "possessing riches, uses them rightly, will be a blessing unto his fellows." It is cleaving to wealth and power that enslaves people, not the mere possession of wealth. Artisans, merchants, or officers of the king who stay in the world should concentrate on performing their duties well. "If they live in the world not a life of self but a life of truth, then surely joy, peace, and bliss will dwell in their minds."*

Sudatta purchased a large park to provide a place where the Buddha and his disciples could live during the rainy season and had many buildings built there. The Buddha returned to this Jetavana Monastery many times and frequently gave sermons there. Sudatta also provided food for monks and gave generously to the poor and needy. As a result of his generosity, Sudatta was gradually reduced to poverty himself. Then, through divine intervention, those who owed him money returned it, making him wealthy once again.

Stories recounted that Sudatta's family, including his three daughters, became pious followers. Although Sudatta's son initially resisted the Buddha, he eventually became a generous patron himself. The Buddha himself helped convert Sudatta's unpleasant daughter-in-law. Once when the Buddha was preaching at Sudatta's home, he was disrupted by the sounds of Sudatta's son's wife scolding the servants. The Buddha asked to have her brought to him, and he instructed her on the proper conduct of wives. There were three types of bad wives, he told her: the destructive wife, who is pitiless, fond of other men, and contemptuous of her husband; the thievish wife, who squanders the family wealth; and the mistress wife, who is rude, lazy, and domineering. These he contrasted with the four kinds of good wives: the motherly wife, who cares for her husband as a mother for her son; the sisterly wife, who defers to her husband in the same affectionate way that a younger sister defers to her older brother; the friend wife, who loves her husband as if he were her best friend; and the handmaiden wife, who is calm, patient,

*Paul Carus, *The Gospel of Buddha* (Chicago: Open Court, 1894/1915), pp. 61–63, slightly modified.

and obedient. Deeply moved by these teachings, the daughter-in-law determined to be a handmaiden wife.

Sudatta died before the Buddha. A sutra that survives purports to be the sermon two of the Buddha's chief disciples preached to him on his deathbed. They counseled Sudatta on how to face his situation by training himself to decide not to cling to what is seen, heard, sensed, thought, attained, sought after, or pondered by the intellect.

QUESTIONS FOR ANALYSIS

1. What can you infer about the circumstances of the early followers of the Buddha from the life of Sudatta?
2. What insights does the life of Sudatta provide into the ways faith in Buddhism was spread?

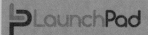

ONLINE DOCUMENT PROJECT

What made Buddhism accessible to everyone? Read a selection of Buddhist parables, and then complete a quiz and writing assignment based on the evidence and details from this chapter. *See inside front cover to learn more.*

released from rebirth. One person's dharma may be different from another's, but both individuals must follow their own dharmas.

Hinduism provided a complex and sophisticated philosophy of life and a religion of enormous emotional appeal that was attractive to ordinary Indians. Over time it grew to be the most common religion in India. Hinduism validated the caste system, adding to the stability of everyday village life, since people all knew where they stood in society. Hinduism also inspired the preservation of literary masterpieces in Sanskrit and the major regional languages of India. Among these are the *Puranas*, which are stories of the gods and great warrior clans, and the *Mahabharata* and *Ramayana*, which are verse epics of India's early kings.

QUICK REVIEW

What elements of Buddhism and Jainism were incorporated into Hinduism?

What was the result of Indian contact with the Persians and Greeks, and what were the consequences of unification under the Mauryan Empire?

Hellenistic Influences in Gandharan Art

Because Alexander the Great's army had reached Gandhara and Hellenistic states and subsequently controlled it for more than a century, the art of this region was strongly influenced by Greek artistic styles. This stucco figure was excavated from a site in eastern Afghanistan where some twenty-three thousand Greco-Buddhist sculptures were found. Hellenistic influence, as evidenced by the drape of the clothing and the modeling of the head, is particularly easy to recognize in this piece. (Erich Lessing/Art Resource, NY)

In the late sixth century B.C.E., with the creation of the Persian Empire that stretched from the west coast of Anatolia to the Indus River (see pages 56–58), west India was swept up in events that were changing the face of the ancient Near East. A couple of centuries later, by 322 B.C.E., the Greeks had supplanted the Persians in northwest India. Chandragupta saw this as an opportunity to expand his territories, and he successfully unified all of north India. The Mauryan (MAWR-ee-uhn) Empire that he founded flourished under the reign of his grandson, Ashoka, but after Ashoka's death the empire declined.

CHAPTER LOCATOR | What does archaeology tell us about the Harappan civilization in India? | What kind of society and culture did the Indo-European Aryans create?

Encounters with the West

India became involved in the turmoil of the sixth century B.C.E. when the Persian emperor Darius conquered the Indus Valley and Kashmir about 513 B.C.E. Persian control did not reach eastward beyond the Punjab, but even so it fostered increased contact between India and the Near East and led to the introduction of new ideas, techniques, and materials into India.

The Persian Empire in turn succumbed to Alexander the Great, and in 326 B.C.E. Alexander led his Macedonian and Greek troops through the Khyber Pass into the Indus Valley (discussed in Chapter 5 on page 131). The India that Alexander encountered was composed of many rival states. He defeated some of these states in the northwest and heard reports of others.

The Greeks were intrigued by the Indian culture they encountered. Alexander had heard of the sophistication of Indian philosophers and summoned some to instruct him or debate with him. The Greeks were also impressed with Indian cities, most notably Taxila, a major center of trade in the Punjab. From Taxila, Alexander followed the Indus River south, hoping to find the end of the world. His men, however, mutinied and refused to continue. When Alexander turned back, he left his general Seleucus (suh-LOO-kuhs) in charge of his easternmost region.

Chandragupta and the Founding of the Mauryan Empire

The one to benefit most from Alexander's invasion was Chandragupta, the ruler of a growing state in the Ganges Valley. He took advantage of the crisis caused by Alexander's invasion to expand his territories, and by 322 B.C.E. he had made himself sole master of north India (Map 3.2). In 304 B.C.E. he defeated the forces of Seleucus.

With stunning effectiveness, Chandragupta applied the lessons learned from Persian rule. He adopted the Persian practice of dividing the area into provinces. Each province was assigned a governor, usually drawn from Chandragupta's own family. He established a complex bureaucracy to see to the operation of the state and a bureaucratic taxation system that financed public services through taxes on agriculture. He also built a regular army, complete with departments for everything from naval matters to the collection of supplies.

For the first time in Indian history, one man governed most of the subcontinent, exercising control through delegated power. From his capital at Pataliputra in the Ganges Valley, Chandragupta sent agents to the provinces to oversee the workings of government and to keep him informed of conditions in his realm. In designing his bureaucratic system, Chandragupta enjoyed the able assistance of his great minister Kautilya, who wrote a treatise called the *Arthashastra* on how a king should seize, hold, and manipulate power.

Megasthenes, a Greek ambassador sent by Seleucus, spent fourteen years in Chandragupta's court. He left a lively description of life there. He described the city as square and surrounded by wooden walls, twenty-two miles on each side, with 570 towers and 64 gates. It had a university, a library, and magnificent palaces, temples, gardens, and parks. The king personally presided over court

| What ideas were taught by the founders of Jainism, Buddhism, and Hinduism? | **What was the result of Indian contact with the Persians and Greeks?** | How was India shaped by political disunity and contacts with other cultures? | ✔ LearningCurve Check what you know. |

79

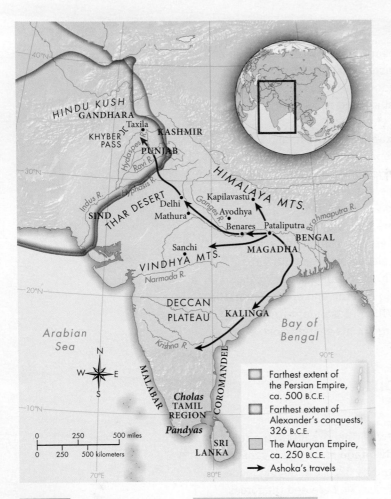

MAP 3.2 ■ The Mauryan Empire, ca. 250 B.C.E.

The Ganges River Valley was the heart of the Mauryan Empire. Although India is protected from the cold by mountains in the north, mountain passes in the northwest allowed both migration and invasion.

> **MAPPING THE PAST**

ANALYZING THE MAP: Where are the major rivers of India? How close are they to mountains?

CONNECTIONS: Can you think of any reasons that the Persian Empire and Alexander's conquests both reached into the same region of northwest India?

sessions where legal cases were heard and petitions received. The king claimed for the state all mines and forests, and there were large state farms, granaries, shipyards, and spinning and weaving factories. Even prostitution was controlled by the state. Only a portion of the empire was ruled so directly, according to Megasthenes. In outlying areas, local kings were left in place if they pledged loyalty.

According to Jain tradition, Chandragupta became a Jain ascetic and died a peaceful death in 298 B.C.E. Although he personally adopted a nonviolent philosophy, he left behind a kingdom with the military might to maintain order and defend India from invasion.

The Reign of Ashoka, ca. 269–232 B.C.E.

Chandragupta's grandson Ashoka proved to be one of India's most remarkable figures. The era of Ashoka was enormously important in the religious history of the world, because Ashoka embraced Buddhism and promoted its spread beyond India.

As a young prince, Ashoka served as governor of two prosperous provinces where Buddhism flourished. At the death of his father about 274 B.C.E., Ashoka rebelled against his older brother, who had succeeded as king, and after four years of fighting won his bid for the throne. Crowned king, Ashoka ruled intelligently and energetically.

In the ninth year of his reign, 261 B.C.E., Ashoka conquered Kalinga, on the east coast of India. In a grim and savage campaign, Ashoka reduced Kalinga by wholesale slaughter. Instead of exulting like a conqueror, however, Ashoka was consumed with remorse and revulsion at the horror of war. He embraced Buddhism and used the machinery of his empire to spread Buddhist teachings throughout India. He supported the doctrine of not hurting humans or animals that was then spreading among religious people of all sects in India. Two years after his conversion, he undertook a 256-day pilgrimage to all the holy sites of Buddhism, and on his return he sent missionaries to all known countries. Ashoka's remarkable crisis of conscience changed the way he ruled. He emphasized compassion, nonviolence, and adherence to dharma. He appointed officials to oversee the moral welfare of the realm and required local officials to govern humanely. He may have perceived dharma as a kind of civic virtue, a universal ethical model capable of uniting the diverse peoples of his extensive empire.

CHAPTER LOCATOR | What does archaeology tell us about the Harappan civilization in India? | What kind of society and culture did the Indo-European Aryans create?

CHAPTER 3
80 THE FOUNDATION OF INDIAN SOCIETY

Ashoka felt the need to protect his new religion and to keep it pure. He warned Buddhist monks that he would not tolerate schism—divisions based on differences of opinion about doctrine or ritual. According to Buddhist tradition, a great council of Buddhist monks was held at Pataliputra, where the earliest canon of Buddhist texts was codified. At the same time, Ashoka honored India's other religions, even building shrines for Hindu and Jain worshippers.

Despite his devotion to Buddhism, Ashoka never neglected his duties as emperor. He tightened the central government of the empire and kept a close check on local officials. He built roads and rest spots to improve communication within the realm. These measures also facilitated the march of armies and the armed enforcement of Ashoka's authority.

Ashoka directly administered the central part of the **Mauryan Empire**, focusing on Magadha. Beyond it were four large provinces under princes who served as viceroys, each with its own sets of smaller districts and officials. The interior of south India was described as inhabited by undefeated forest tribes. Farther south,

Mauryan Empire
▶ The first Indian empire founded by Chandragupta.

What ideas were taught by the founders of Jainism, Buddhism, and Hinduism?

What was the result of Indian contact with the Persians and Greeks?

How was India shaped by political disunity and contacts with other cultures?

✓ LearningCurve
Check what you know.

81

along the coasts, were peoples that Ashoka maintained friendly relations with but did not rule, such as the Cholas and Pandyas. Relations with Sri Lanka were especially close under Ashoka.

Ashoka ruled for thirty-seven years. After he died in about 232 B.C.E., the Mauryan Dynasty went into decline, and India broke up into smaller units, much like those in existence before Alexander's invasion. Even though Chandragupta had instituted bureaucratic methods of centralized political control and Ashoka had vigorously pursued the political and cultural integration of the empire, the institutions they created were not entrenched enough to survive periods with weaker kings.

> **QUICK REVIEW**

What steps did Ashoka take to strengthen and consolidate Mauryan rule?

CHAPTER LOCATOR | What does archaeology tell us about the Harappan civilization in India? | What kind of society and culture did the Indo-European Aryans create?

82   CHAPTER 3
THE FOUNDATION OF INDIAN SOCIETY

How was India shaped by political disunity and contacts with other cultures during the five centuries from 185 B.C.E. to 300 C.E.?

After the Mauryan Dynasty collapsed in 185 B.C.E., and for much of subsequent Indian history, political unity would be the exception rather than the rule. By this time, however, key elements of Indian culture—the caste system; the religious traditions of Hinduism, Buddhism, and Jainism; and the great epics and legends—had given India a cultural unity strong enough to endure even without political unity.

In the years after the fall of the Mauryan Dynasty, a series of foreign powers dominated the Indus Valley and adjoining regions. The first were hybrid Indo-Greek states ruled by the inheritors of Alexander's defunct empire stationed in what is now Afghanistan. The city of Taxila became a major center of trade, culture, and education, fusing elements of Greek and Indian culture.

The great, slow movement of nomadic peoples out of East Asia that brought the Scythians to the Near East brought the Shakas to northwest India. They controlled the region from about 94 B.C.E. to 20 B.C.E., when they were displaced by a new nomadic invader, the Kushans, who ruled the region of today's Afghanistan, Pakistan, and west India as far south as Gujarat.

During the Kushan period, Greek culture had a considerable impact on Indian art. Indo-Greek artists and sculptors working in India adorned Buddhist shrines, modeling the earliest representation of the Buddha on Hellenistic statues of Apollo. Another contribution from the Indo-Greek states was coin cast with images of the king, which came to be widely adopted by Indian rulers, aiding commerce and adding evidence of rulers' names and sequence to the historical record. Places where coins are found also show patterns of trade.

Cultural exchange also went in the other direction. Old Indian animal folktales were translated into Syriac and Greek and these translated versions eventually made their way to Europe. South India in this period was also the center of active seaborne trade, with networks reaching all the way to Rome. Indian sailing technology was highly advanced, and much of this trade was in the hands of Indian merchants. In the first century C.E. a Greek merchant involved in this trade reported that the traders sold coins, topaz, coral, crude glass, copper, tin, and lead

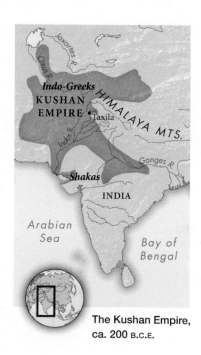

The Kushan Empire, ca. 200 B.C.E.

What ideas were taught by the founders of Jainism, Buddhism, and Hinduism?	What was the result of Indian contact with the Persians and Greeks?	**How was India shaped by political disunity and contacts with other cultures?**	✔ LearningCurve Check what you know.

and bought pearls, ivory, silk (probably originally from China), jewels of many sorts (probably many from Southeast Asia), and above all cinnamon and pepper.

During these centuries there were significant advances in science, mathematics, and philosophy. Indian astronomers charted the movements of stars and planets and recognized that the earth was spherical. In the realm of physics, Indian scientists, like their Greek counterparts, conceived of matter in terms of five elements: earth, air, fire, water, and ether. This was also the period when Indian law was codified. The *Code of Manu*, which lays down family, caste, and commercial law, was compiled in the second or third century C.E., drawing on older texts.

Regional cultures tend to flourish when there is no dominant unifying state, and the Tamils of south India were one of the major beneficiaries of the collapse of the Mauryan Dynasty. The period from 200 B.C.E. to 200 C.E. is considered the classical period of Tamil culture, when many great works of literature were written under the patronage of the regional kings. Some of the poems written then provide evidence of lively commerce, mentioning bulging warehouses, ships from many lands, and complex import-export procedures. From contact of this sort, the south came to absorb many cultural elements from the north, but also retained differences. Castes were present in the south before contact with the Sanskrit north, but they took distinct forms, as the Kshatriya (warrior) and Vaishya (merchant) varnas were hardly known in the far south.

Code of Manu
▶ The codification of early Indian law that lays down family, caste, and commercial law.

> **QUICK REVIEW**

What impact did the Kushans have on Indian society and culture?

CHAPTER SUMMARY

Civilization first emerged in the Indus River Valley of India in the third millennium B.C.E. The large cities of this Harappan civilization were carefully planned, with straight streets and sewers; buildings were of kiln-dried brick. Harappan cities were largely abandoned by 1800 B.C.E. for unknown reasons.

A few centuries later, the Aryans, speakers of an early form of the Indo-European language Sanskrit, rose to prominence in north India, marking the beginning of the Vedic Age. Aryan warrior tribes fought using chariots and bronze swords and spears, gradually expanding into the Ganges River Valley. The first stages of the Indian caste system date to this period, when warriors and priests were ranked above merchants, artisans, and farmers. The Vedas document the religious ideas of this age, such as the importance of sacrifice and the notions of karma and rebirth.

Beginning around 500 B.C.E. three of India's major religions emerged. Mahavira, the founder of the Jain religion, taught his followers to live ascetic lives, avoid harming any living thing, and renounce evil thoughts and actions. The founder of Buddhism, Siddhartha Gautama, or the Buddha, similarly taught his followers a path to liberation that involved freeing themselves from desires, avoiding violence, and gaining insight. Hinduism developed in response to the popularity of

CHAPTER LOCATOR | What does archaeology tell us about the Harappan civilization in India? | What kind of society and culture did the Indo-European Aryans create?

84 CHAPTER 3 THE FOUNDATION OF INDIAN SOCIETY

Jainism and Buddhism. Hindu traditions validated sacrifice and caste and developed devotional practice, giving individuals a more personal relationship with the gods they worshipped.

From contact with the Persians and Greeks in the sixth century B.C.E. and fourth century B.C.E., respectively, new political techniques, ideas, and art styles and the use of money entered the Indian repertoire. Shortly after the arrival of the Greeks, much of north India was politically unified by the Mauryan Empire under Chandragupta. His grandson Ashoka converted to Buddhism, promoted its spread inside and outside of India.

After the decline of the Mauryan Empire, India was politically fragmented for several centuries. Indian cultural identity remained strong, however, because of shared literature and religious ideas. In the northwest, new monadic groups, the Shakas and the Kushans, emerged. Cultural interchange was facilitated through trade both overland and by sea.

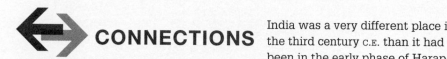 **CONNECTIONS** India was a very different place in the third century C.E. than it had been in the early phase of Harappan civilization more than two thousand years earlier. The region was still divided into many different polities, but people living there in 300 shared much more in the way of ideas and traditions. The great epics such as the *Mahabharata* and the *Ramayana* provided a cultural vocabulary for groups that spoke different languages and had rival rulers. New religions had emerged, notably Buddhism and Jainism, and Hinduism was much more a devotional religion. Contact with ancient Mesopotamia, Persia, Greece, and Rome had brought new ideas, practices, and products.

During this same time period, civilization in China underwent similar expansion and diversification. China was farther away than India from other Eurasian centers of civilization, and its developments were consequently not as closely linked. Logographic writing appeared with the Bronze Age Shang civilization and was preserved into modern times, in striking contrast to India and lands to its west, which developed alphabetical writing systems. Still, some developments affected both India and China, such as the appearance of chariots and horseback riding. The next chapter takes up the story of these developments in early China. In Chapter 12, after considering early developments in Europe, Asia, Africa, and the Americas, we return to the story of India.

| What ideas were taught by the founders of Jainism, Buddhism, and Hinduism? | What was the result of Indian contact with the Persians and Greeks? | How was India shaped by political disunity and contacts with other cultures? | ✓ **LearningCurve** Check what you know. |

CHAPTER 3 STUDY GUIDE

STEP 1

GET STARTED ONLINE

 LearningCurve

Now that you've read the chapter, make it stick by completing the LearningCurve activity.

STEP 2

EXPLAIN WHY IT MATTERS

Put your reading into practice. Identify each term below, and then explain why it matters in world history.

TERM	WHO OR WHAT & WHEN	WHY IT MATTERS
Harappan (p. 65)		
Aryans (p. 67)		
Rig Veda (p. 68)		
Brahmins (p. 69)		
caste system (p. 70)		
samsara (p. 70)		
karma (p. 70)		
brahman (p. 70)		
Jainism (p. 72)		
Four Noble Truths (p. 74)		
Eightfold Path (p. 74)		
Mahayana (p. 74)		
bodhisattva (p. 74)		
dharma (p. 75)		
Mauryan Empire (p. 81)		
Code of Manu (p. 84)		

STEP 3

MOVE BEYOND THE BASICS

To demonstrate a more advanced understanding of India's great indigenous religious traditions, fill in the chart below with descriptions of three key aspects of these religions: core beliefs, social and ethical implications, appeal and spread. What aspects of Brahmanic belief and practice did Jainism and Buddhism reject? What core Brahmanic beliefs remained a part of Hinduism?

	Core Beliefs	Social and Ethical Implications	Appeal and Spread
Jainism			
Buddhism			
Hinduism			

STEP 4 PUT IT ALL TOGETHER

Now, take a step back and try to explain the big picture. Remember to use specific examples from the chapter in your answers.

EARLY INDIAN CIVILIZATIONS

▶ What similarities were there between Harappan civilization and the civilizations of Mesopotamia and Egypt?

▶ How did Brahmanism shape early Indian society and politics?

INDIA'S GREAT RELIGIONS

▶ What beliefs do Jainism, Buddhism, and Hinduism have in common?

▶ How would you explain the fact that Hinduism eventually grew to be the most common religion in India?

THE RISE AND FALL OF THE MAURYAN EMPIRE

▶ What were the keys to Mauryan political success?

▶ How did encounters with outsiders contribute to both the rise of the Mauryan Empire and to Indian development in the centuries after the empire's fall?

LOOKING BACK, LOOKING AHEAD

▶ How did geography and climate shape the development of commercial connections both within India and between India and the larger world?

▶ How would you explain the fact that, up until the establishment of the Mughal Empire in the sixteenth century, periods of political unification of the Indian subcontinent have been the exception and not the rule? What light does the early history of India shed on this question?

> IN YOUR OWN WORDS

Imagine that you must give an oral report to the class answering the following question: **What were the defining social and cultural characteristics of ancient India? What would be the most important points and why?**

What was the impact of China's geography on the development of Chinese societies?

Neolithic Jade Plaque

This small plaque (2½ inches by 3¼ inches), dating from about 2000 B.C.E., is similar to others of the Liangzhu area near modern Shanghai. It is incised to depict a human figure that merges into a monster mask. The lower part could be interpreted as his arms and legs but at the same time resembles a monster mask with bulging eyes, prominent nostrils, and a large mouth. (Zhejiang Provincial Institute of Cultural Relics and Archeology/Uniphoto Press, Japan/Ancient Art & Architecture Collection, Ltd.)

The term *China*, like the term *India*, does not refer to the same geographical entity at all points in history. The historical China, also called China proper, was smaller than present-day China. The contemporary People's Republic of China includes Tibet, Inner Mongolia, Turkestan, Manchuria, and other territories that in premodern times were neither inhabited by Chinese nor ruled directly by Chinese states.

The Impact of Geography

China proper, about a thousand miles north to south and east to west, occupies much of the temperate zone of East Asia (Map 4.1). The northern part, drained by the Yellow River, is colder, flatter, and more arid than the south. Wheat and millet were the region's most important crops. The dominant soil is **loess**—fine wind-driven earth that is fertile and easy to work even with simple tools. Because so much of the loess ends up as silt in the Yellow River, the riverbed rises and easily

loess
▶ Soil deposited by wind; it is fertile and easy to work.

CHAPTER LOCATOR | **What was the impact of China's geography on the development of Chinese societies?** | What was life like during the Shang Dynasty, and how did writing affect Chinese culture?

> CHRONOLOGY

ca. 5000 B.C.E. Emergence of regional Neolithic settlements	**500–200 B.C.E.** Golden age of Chinese philosophy
ca. 1500–1050 B.C.E. Shang Dynasty	**453–403 B.C.E.** *The Art of War*
ca. 1200 B.C.E. Evidence of writing found in royal tombs; chariots come into use	**403–221 B.C.E.** Warring States Period; decline of the Zhou Dynasty
ca. 1050–256 B.C.E. Zhou Dynasty	**ca. 370–300 B.C.E.** Mencius
ca. 900 B.C.E. *Book of Songs*, *Book of Changes*, *Book of Documents*	**ca. 350 B.C.E.** Infantry armed with crossbows
551–479 B.C.E. Confucius	**ca. 310–215 B.C.E.** Xunzi
ca. 500 B.C.E. Iron technology in wide use; cities spread across the central Zhou states	**ca. 300–200 B.C.E.** Early Daoist teachings outlined in *Laozi* and the *Zhuangzi*

floods unless diked. Drought is another perennial problem for farmers in the north. The Yangzi (YANG-zuh) River is the dominant feature of the warmer, wetter, and more lush south, a region well suited to rice cultivation. The Yangzi and its many tributaries are navigable, so boats were traditionally the preferred means of transportation in the south.

Mountains, deserts, and grasslands separated China proper from other early civilizations. Between China and India lay Tibet, with its vast mountain ranges and high plateaus. North of Tibet are great expanses of desert, and north of the desert, grasslands stretch from Ukraine to eastern Siberia. Chinese civilization did not spread into any of these Inner Asian regions, above all because they were not suited to growing crops. Inner Asia, where raising animals is a more productive use of land than planting crops, became the heartland of China's traditional enemies, such as the nomadic tribes of the Xiongnu (SHUHNG-noo) and Mongols.

Early Agricultural Societies of the Neolithic Age

From about 10,000 B.C.E. agriculture was practiced in China. It apparently originated independently of somewhat earlier developments in Egypt and Mesopotamia but was perhaps influenced by developments in Southeast Asia, where rice was also cultivated very early. By 5000 B.C.E. there were Neolithic village settlements in several regions of China. The primary Neolithic crops were drought-resistant millet, grown in the loess soils of the north, and rice, grown in the wetlands of the lower reaches of the Yangzi River. In both areas pigs, dogs, and cattle were domesticated, and by 3000 B.C.E. sheep had become important in the north and water buffalo in the south. Silk production can also be traced back to this period.

| How was China governed, and what was life like during the Zhou Dynasty? | How did advances in military technology contribute to the rise of independent states? | What ideas did Confucius teach, and how were they spread after his death? | How did the teachings of Daoism, Legalism, and other schools differ from Confucianism? | ✓ LearningCurve
Check what you know. |

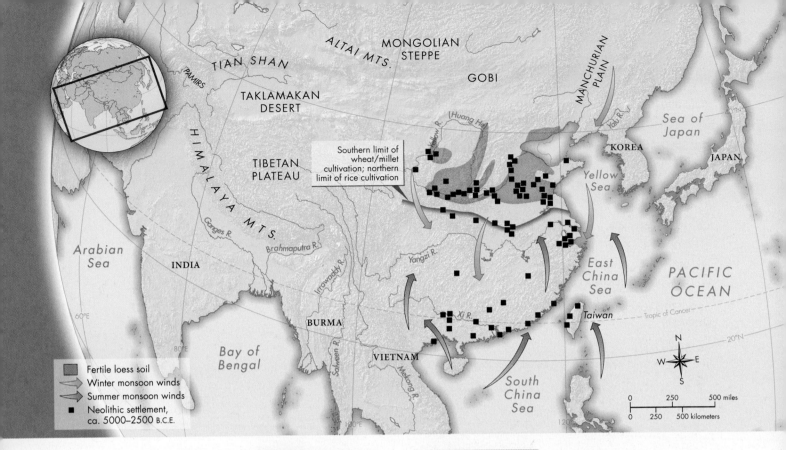

MAP 4.1 ■ **The Geography of Historical China**

Chinese civilization developed in the temperate regions drained by the Yellow and Yangzi Rivers.

Map legend:
- Fertile loess soil
- Winter monsoon winds
- Summer monsoon winds
- Neolithic settlement, ca. 5000–2500 B.C.E.

> MAPPING THE PAST

ANALYZING THE MAP: Trace the routes of the Yellow and Yangzi Rivers. Where are the areas of loess soil? Where are the Neolithic sites concentrated?

CONNECTIONS: Does China's geography explain much about its history? (See also Map 4.2.) What geographical features had the greatest impact in the Neolithic Age? How might the fact that the Yellow and Yangzi Rivers flow west to east, rather than north to south, have influenced the development of Chinese society?

Over the course of the fifth to third millennia B.C.E., many distinct regional Neolithic cultures emerged. These Neolithic societies left no written records, but we know from the material record that over time they came to share more social and cultural practices. Many practices related to the treatment of the dead spread to other groups from their original area. Fortified walls made of rammed earth were built around settlements in many places, suggesting not only increased contact between Neolithic societies but also increased conflict. (For more on life in Neolithic societies, see Chapter 1.)

> QUICK REVIEW

What were the most important differences between the region around the Yellow River and the region around the Yangzi River?

CHAPTER LOCATOR | What was the impact of China's geography on the development of Chinese societies? | **What was life like during the Shang Dynasty, and how did writing affect Chinese culture?**

What was life like during the Shang Dynasty, and what effect did writing have on Chinese culture and government?

Royal Burials at Anyang

Eleven large tombs and more than a thousand small graves have been excavated at the royal burial ground at Anyang. In 2005 seven pits were discovered in which horses and chariots had been buried to accompany a king in the afterlife. (© CHINA NEWSPHOTO/Reuters/Corbis)

Archaeological evidence indicates that after 2000 B.C.E. a Bronze Age civilization appeared in north China that shared traits with Bronze Age civilizations elsewhere in Eurasia, such as Mesopotamia, Egypt, and Greece. These traits included writing, metalworking, domestication of the horse, class stratification, and cult centers. The archaeological findings are linked to the Shang Dynasty, long known from early texts.

Shang Society

Shang civilization was not as densely urban as that of Mesopotamia, but Shang kings ruled from large settlements (Map 4.2). The best excavated is **Anyang**, from which the Shang kings ruled for more than two centuries. At the center of Anyang were large palaces, temples, and altars. Outside the central core were industrial

Anyang
▶ One of the Shang Dynasty capitals from which the Shang kings ruled for more than two centuries.

| How was China governed, and what was life like during the Zhou Dynasty? | How did advances in military technology contribute to the rise of independent states? | What ideas did Confucius teach, and how were they spread after his death? | How did the teachings of Daoism, Legalism, and other schools differ from Confucianism? | ☑ **LearningCurve** Check what you know. |

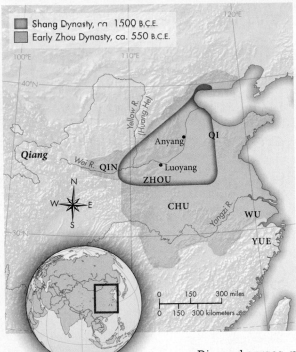

■ Shang Dynasty, ca 1500 B.C.E.
■ Early Zhou Dynasty, ca. 550 B.C.E.

MAP 4.2 ■ **The Shang and Early Zhou Dynasties, ca. 1500–400 B.C.E.**

The early Zhou government controlled larger areas than the Shang did, but the independent states of the Warring States Period were more aggressive about pushing out their frontiers, greatly extending the geographical boundaries of Chinese civilization.

areas where bronzeworkers, potters, stone carvers, and other artisans lived and worked. Beyond these urban settlements were farming areas and large forests.

Texts found in the Shang royal tombs at Anyang show that Shang kings were military chieftains. They fought rebellious vassals and foreign tribes, but the situation constantly changed as vassals became enemies and enemies accepted offers of alliance. War booty was an important source of the king's revenue, especially the war captives who could be made into slaves.

Bronze-tipped spears and battle axes were widely used by Shang warriors, giving them an advantage over less technologically advanced groups. Bronze was also used for the fittings of the chariots that came into use around 1200 B.C.E. Chariot technology apparently spread by diffusion across Asia, passing from one society to the next.

Shang power did not rest solely on military supremacy. The Shang king was also the high priest, the one best qualified to offer sacrifices to the royal ancestors and the high god Di. Royal ancestors were viewed as able to intervene with Di, send curses, produce dreams, assist the king in battle, and so on. The king divined his ancestors' wishes by interpreting the cracks made in heated cattle bones or tortoise shells prepared for him by professional diviners.

Shang palaces were undoubtedly splendid but were constructed of perishable material like wood, and nothing of them remains today, giving China none of the ancient stone buildings and monuments so characteristic of the West. What has survived are the lavish underground tombs built for Shang kings and their consorts.

The one royal tomb not robbed before it was excavated was for Lady Hao, one of the many wives of the king Wu Ding (ca. 1200 B.C.E.). The tomb was filled with almost 500 bronze vessels and weapons, over 700 jade and ivory ornaments, and 16 people who would tend to Lady Hao in the afterlife. Human sacrifice did not occur only at funerals. Inscribed bones report sacrifices of war captives in the dozens and hundreds.

Shang society was marked by sharp status distinctions. The king and other noble families had family and clan names transmitted along patrilineal lines, from father to son. Kingship similarly passed along patrilineal lines. The kings and the aristocrats owned slaves, many of whom had been captured in war. In the urban centers there were substantial numbers of craftsmen who worked in stone, bone, and bronze.

Shang farmers were obligated to work for their lords (making them essentially serfs). Their lives were not that different from the lives of their Neolithic ancestors, and they worked the fields with similar stone tools. They usually lived in small, compact villages surrounded by fields.

Bronze Metalworking

As in Egypt, Mesopotamia, and India, the development of more complex forms of social organization in Shang China coincided with the mastery of metalworking, specifically bronze. The bronze industry required the coordination of a large labor

CHAPTER LOCATOR | What was the impact of China's geography on the development of Chinese societies? | **What was life like during the Shang Dynasty, and how did writing affect Chinese culture?**

94 CHAPTER 4 CHINA'S CLASSICAL AGE

force and skilled artisans. Bronze was used more for ritual than for war in Shang times. Most surviving Shang bronze objects are vessels that would have originally been used during sacrificial ceremonies.

The decoration on Shang bronzes seems to say something interesting about Shang culture, but scholars do not agree about what that is. In the art of ancient Egypt, Assyria, and Babylonia, representations of agriculture and of social hierarchy are very common, matching our understandings of the social, political, and economic development of those societies. In Shang China, by contrast, images of wild animals predominate. Some animal images readily suggest possible meanings. Birds, for example, suggest to many the idea of messengers that can communicate with other realms, especially realms in the sky. More problematic is the most common image, the stylized animal face called the **taotie** (taow-tyeh). To some it is a monster—a fearsome image that would scare away evil forces. Others imagine a dragon—an animal whose vast powers had more positive associations. Some hypothesize that it reflects masks used in rituals. Others associate it with animal sacrifices, totemism, or shamanism. Still others see these images as hardly more than designs. Without new evidence, scholars can only speculate.

taotie
▶ A stylized animal face commonly seen in Chinese bronzes.

The Development of Writing

The survival of divination texts inscribed on bones from Shang tombs demonstrates that writing was already a major element in Chinese culture by 1200 B.C.E. Writing must have been developed earlier, but the early stages cannot be traced, probably because writing was done on wood, bamboo, silk, or other perishable materials.

The invention of writing had profound effects on China's culture and government. A written language made possible a bureaucracy capable of keeping records and corresponding with commanders and governors far from the palace. Hence literacy became the ally of royal rule, facilitating control over a wide realm. Literacy also preserved the learning, lore, and experience of early Chinese society and facilitated the development of abstract thought.

Like ancient Egyptian and Sumerian scripts, the Chinese script was **logographic**: each word was represented by a single symbol (Figure 4.1). In western Eurasia

logographic
▶ A system of writing in which each word is represented by a single symbol, such as the Chinese script.

FIGURE 4.1 ■ The Origins of Chinese Writing

The modern Chinese writing system (bottom row) evolved from the script employed by diviners in the Shang period (top row). (Source: Adapted from Patricia Buckley Ebrey, *The Cambridge Illustrated History of China* [Cambridge: Cambridge University Press, 1996], p. 26. Reprinted by permission of Cambridge University Press.)

WORD	ox	goat, sheep	tree	moon	earth	water	to show, declare	then (men and bowl)	heaven	to pray
SHANG SYMBOL	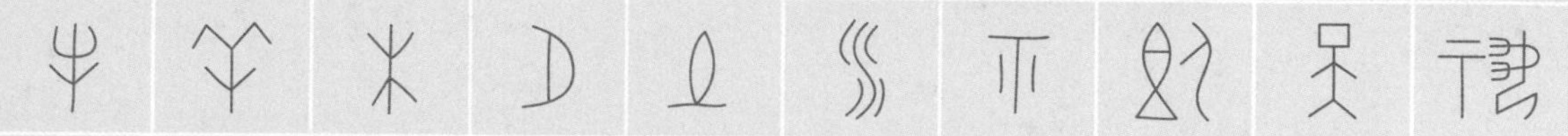 ψ	⋎	木	D	⏃	⦀	示	訃	吴	祝
MODERN CHARACTER	牛	羊	木	月	土	水	示	就	天	祝

How was China governed, and what was life like during the Zhou Dynasty?

How did advances in military technology contribute to the rise of independent states?

What ideas did Confucius teach, and how were they spread after his death?

How did the teachings of Daoism, Legalism, and other schools differ from Confucianism?

✔ LearningCurve
Check what you know.

logographic scripts were eventually modified or replaced by phonetic scripts, but that never happened in China. Because China retained its logographic writing system, many years were required to gain full mastery of reading and writing, which added to the prestige of education.

Why did China retain a logographic writing system even after encounters with phonetic ones? Although phonetic systems have many real advantages, especially with respect to ease of learning to read, there are some costs to dropping a logographic system. Since characters did not change when the pronunciation changed, educated Chinese could read texts written centuries earlier without the need for translation. Moreover, as the Chinese language developed regional variants, readers of Chinese could read books and letters by contemporaries whose oral language they could not comprehend. Thus the Chinese script played a large role in holding China together and fostering a sense of connection with the past. In addition, many of China's neighbors (Japan, Korea, and Vietnam, in particular) adopted the Chinese script, allowing communication through writing between people whose languages were totally unrelated. In this regard, Chinese characters were like Arabic numerals, which have the same meaning however they are pronounced (Table 4.1).

TABLE 4.1 ■ Pronouncing Chinese Words

Letter	Phonetic Equivalent in Chinese
Phonetic equivalents for the vowels and especially perplexing consonants are given here.	
a	ah
e	uh
i	ee; except after z, c, and ch, when the sound is closer to i in it
u	oo; as in English food
c	ts (ch, however, is like English ch)
q	ch
z	dz
zh	j
x	sh

> **QUICK REVIEW**

What were the sources of Shang power and wealth?

CHAPTER LOCATOR | What was the impact of China's geography on the development of Chinese societies? | What was life like during the Shang Dynasty, and how did writing affect Chinese culture?

96 CHAPTER 4 CHINA'S CLASSICAL AGE

How was China governed, and what was life like during the Zhou Dynasty?

Winged Immortal

Less than 8 inches tall, this bronze candelabra is in the shape of an immortal. Those who mastered the secrets of not dying were thought to be able to fly through the heavens. (Werner Forman/akg-images)

The Shang campaigned constantly against enemies in all directions. To the west of the Shang were the fierce Qiang (chyang). Between the Shang capital and the Qiang were the Zhou (joe). In about 1050 B.C.E. the Zhou rose against the Shang and defeated them in battle. Their successors maintained the cultural and political advances that the Shang rulers had introduced.

Zhou Politics

The early Zhou period is the first one for which transmitted texts exist in some abundance. The ***Book of Documents*** (ca. 900 B.C.E.) describes the Zhou conquest of the Shang as the victory of just and noble warriors over decadent courtiers led by an irresponsible and sadistic king.

Book of Documents
▶ One of the earliest Chinese books, containing documents, speeches, and historical accounts about early Zhou rule.

How was China governed, and what was life like during the Zhou Dynasty?	How did advances in military technology contribute to the rise of independent states?	What ideas did Confucius teach, and how were they spread after his death?	How did the teachings of Daoism, Legalism, and other schools differ from Confucianism?	✓ LearningCurve Check what you know.

Like the Shang kings, the Zhou kings sacrificed to their ancestors, but they also sacrificed to Heaven. The *Book of Documents* assumes a close relationship between Heaven and the king, who was called the Son of Heaven. According to the documents, Heaven gives the king a mandate to rule only as long as he rules in the interests of the people. Because the last king of the Shang had been decadent and cruel, Heaven took the mandate away from him and entrusted it to the virtuous Zhou kings. This theory of the **Mandate of Heaven** remained a central feature of Chinese political ideology from the early Zhou period on.

Rather than attempt to rule all their territories directly, the early Zhou rulers set up a decentralized feudal system. They sent relatives and trusted subordinates with troops to establish walled garrisons in the conquered territories. Such a vassal was generally able to pass his position on to a son, so that in time the domains became hereditary. By 800 B.C.E. there were about two hundred lords with domains large and small.

As generations passed and ties of loyalty and kinship grew more distant, the regional lords became so powerful that they no longer obeyed the commands of the king. In 771 B.C.E. the Zhou king was killed by an alliance of non-Chinese tribesmen and Zhou vassals. One of his sons was put on the throne, and then for safety's sake the capital was moved east to modern Luoyang, just south of the Yellow River in the heart of the central plains (see Map 4.2, page 94). However, the revived Zhou Dynasty never fully regained control over its vassals, and China entered a prolonged period without a strong central authority.

Life During the Zhou Dynasty

During the early Zhou period, aristocratic attitudes and privileges were strong. Inherited ranks placed people in a hierarchy ranging downward from the king to the rulers of states with titles like duke and marquis, to the hereditary great officials of the states, to the lower ranks of the aristocracy — known as **shi** — and finally to the ordinary people (farmers, craftsmen, and traders). Patrilineal family ties were very important in this society, and at the upper reaches, at least, sacrifices to ancestors were one of the key rituals used to forge social ties.

Glimpses of what life was like at various social levels in the early Zhou Dynasty can be found in the *Book of Songs* (ca. 900 B.C.E.), which contains the earliest Chinese poetry. Some of the songs are hymns used in court religious ceremonies, such as offerings to ancestors. Others clearly had their origins in folk songs. The seasons set the pace for rural life, and the songs contain many references to seasonal changes. Some of these songs depict farmers clearing fields, plowing and planting, gathering mulberry leaves for silkworms, and spinning and weaving.

Social and economic change quickened after 500 B.C.E. Cities began appearing all over north China. Thick earthen walls were built around the palaces and ancestral temples of the ruler and other aristocrats, and often an outer wall was added to protect the artisans, merchants, and farmers who lived outside the inner wall. Accounts of sieges launched against these walled citadels are central to descriptions of military confrontations in this period.

The development of iron technology in the early Zhou Dynasty promoted economic expansion and allowed some people to become very rich. By the fifth

Mandate of Heaven
▶ The theory that Heaven gives the king a mandate to rule only as long as he rules in the interests of the people.

shi
▶ The lower ranks of Chinese aristocracy; these men could serve in either military or civil capacities.

Book of Songs
▶ The earliest collection of Chinese poetry; it provides glimpses of what life was like in the early Zhou Dynasty.

CHAPTER LOCATOR | What was the impact of China's geography on the development of Chinese societies? | What was life like during the Shang Dynasty, and how did writing affect Chinese culture?

98   CHAPTER 4   CHINA'S CLASSICAL AGE

Music played a central role in court life in ancient China, and bells are among the most impressive bronze objects of the period. The tomb of a minor ruler who died about 400 B.C.E. contained 124 musical instruments, including drums, flutes, mouth organs, pan pipes, zithers, a set of 32 chime stones, and this 64-piece bell set. The bells bear inscriptions that name the two tones each bell could make, depending on where it was struck. Five men, using poles and mallets and standing on either side of the set of bells, would have played the bells by hitting them from outside. (Hubei Provincial Museum/Uniphoto Press, Japan/Ancient Art & Architecture Collection, Ltd.)

century B.C.E. iron was being widely used for both farm tools and weapons. In the early Zhou, inherited status and political favor had been the main reasons some people had more power than others. Beginning in the fifth century wealth alone was also an important basis for social inequality. Late Zhou texts frequently mention trade across state borders. People who grew wealthy from trade or industry began to rival rulers for influence. Rulers who wanted trade to bring prosperity to their states welcomed traders and began making coins to facilitate trade.

Social mobility increased over the course of the Zhou period. Rulers often sent out their own officials rather than delegate authority to hereditary lesser lords. This trend toward centralized bureaucratic control created opportunities for social advancement for the shi on the lower end of the old aristocracy. Competition among such men guaranteed rulers a ready supply of able and willing subordinates, and competition among rulers for talent meant that ambitious men could be selective in deciding where to offer their services. (See "Individuals in Society: Lord Mengchang," page 100.)

Religion in Zhou times was not simply a continuation of Shang practices. The practice of burying the living with the dead—so prominent in the royal tombs of the Shang—steadily declined in the middle Zhou period. New deities and cults also appeared, especially in the southern state of Chu, where areas that had

| How was China governed, and what was life like during the Zhou Dynasty? | How did advances in military technology contribute to the rise of independent states? | What ideas did Confucius teach, and how were they spread after his death? | How did the teachings of Daoism, Legalism, and other schools differ from Confucianism? | ✓ LearningCurve Check what you know. |

99

During the Warring States Period, men could rise to high rank on the basis of talent. Lord Mengchang rose on the basis of his people skills: he treated his retainers so well that he attracted thousands of talented men to his service, enabling him to rise to prime minister of his native state of Qi (chee) in the early third century B.C.E.

Lord Mengchang's beginnings were not promising. His father, a member of the Qi royal family, already had more than forty sons when Mengchang was born, and he ordered the mother, one of his many concubines, to leave the baby to die. She, however, secretly reared him, and while still a child he was able to win his father's approval through his cleverness.

At his father's death Mengchang succeeded him. Because Mengchang would provide room and board to men who sought to serve him, he soon attracted a few thousand retainers, many of humble background, some fleeing justice. Every night, we are told, he ate with them all in his hall, treating them equally no matter what their social origins.

Most of the stories about Mengchang revolve around retainers who solved his problems in clever ways. Once, when Mengchang had been sent as an envoy to Qin, the king of Qin was persuaded not to let so talented a minister return to help Qi. Under house arrest, Mengchang was able to ask one of the king's consorts to help him, but in exchange she wanted a fur coat kept in the king's treasury. A former thief among Mengchang's retainers stole it for him, and Mengchang was soon on his way. By the time he reached the barrier gate, Qin soldiers were pursuing him, and he knew that he had to get through quickly. One of his retainers imitated the crowing of a cock, which got the other cocks to crow, making the guards think it was dawn, so they opened the gates and let his party through.

When Mengchang served as prime minister of Qi, his retainers came up with many clever stratagems that convinced the nearby states of Wei and Han to join Qi in resisting Qin. Several times, one of his retainers of modest origins, Feng Xuan (schwan), helped Mengchang withstand the political vicissitudes of the day. When sent to collect debts owed to Mengchang in his fief of Xue, Feng Xuan instead forgave all the debts of those too poor to repay their loans. Later, when Lord Mengchang lost his post at court and returned to his fief, most of his retainers deserted him, but he found himself well loved by the local residents, all because of Feng Xuan's generosity in his name. After Mengchang reattained his court post and was traveling back to Qi, he complained to Feng Xuan about those who had deserted him. Feng Xuan, we are told, got down from the carriage and bowed to Lord Mengchang, and when pressed said that the lord should accept the retainers' departures as part of the natural order of things:

Mengchang promoted trade by issuing bronze coins. Some Zhou coins, like the one shown here with the mold used to cast it, were shaped like miniature knives. (© The Trustees of the British Museum/Art Resource, NY)

Wealth and honor attract while poverty and lowliness repel; such is the nature of things. Think of it like the market. In the morning it is crowded and in the evening it is deserted. This is not because people prefer the morning to the evening, but rather because what they want can not be found there [in the evening]. Do not let the fact that your retainers left when you lost your position lead you to bar them from returning. I hope that you will treat them just the way you did before.*

QUESTIONS FOR ANALYSIS

1. How did Mengchang attract his many retainers, and how did their service benefit him?
2. Who in this story benefited from hereditary privilege, and who advanced because of ability? What does this suggest about social mobility during the Warring States Period?
3. Many of the stories about Mengchang are included in *Intrigues of the Warring States*, a book that Confucians disapproved of. What do you think they found objectionable?

*Shi ji 75.2362. Translated by Patricia Ebrey.

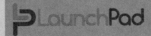

ONLINE DOCUMENT PROJECT

How did rulers and their subordinates interact during the Warring States Period? Read a selection of stories from the Warring States Period, and then complete a quiz and writing assignment based on the evidence and details from this chapter. *See inside front cover to learn more.*

earlier been considered barbarian were being incorporated into the cultural sphere of the Central States, as the core region of China was called. The state of Chu expanded rapidly in the Yangzi Valley, defeating and absorbing fifty or more small states as it extended its reach north to the heartland of Zhou and east to absorb the old states of Wu and Yue. By the late Zhou period, Chu was on the forefront of cultural innovation and produced the greatest literary masterpiece of the era, the *Songs of Chu*, a collection of fantastical poems full of images of elusive deities and shamans who can fly through the spirit world.

QUICK REVIEW

What were the most important differences between Shang and Zhou society and culture?

| How was China governed, and what was life like during the Zhou Dynasty? | How did advances in military technology contribute to the rise of independent states? | What ideas did Confucius teach, and how were they spread after his death? | How did the teachings of Daoism, Legalism, and other schools differ from Confucianism? | ✓ LearningCurve Check what you know. |

> How did advances in military technology contribute to the rise of independent states?

Mounted Swordsman

This depiction of a warrior fighting a leopard decorates a bronze mirror inlaid with gold and silver dating from the Warring States Period. (From *Gugong wenwu yuekan*, 91 [1990])

Warring States Period

▶ The period of Chinese history between 403 B.C.E. and 221 B.C.E. when states fought each other and one state after another was destroyed.

By 400 B.C.E. advances in military technology were undermining the old aristocratic social structure of the Zhou. Large, well-drilled infantry armies able to withstand and defeat chariot-led forces became potent military forces in the **Warring States Period**, which lasted from 403 B.C.E. to 221 B.C.E. Fueled by the development of new weaponry and war tactics, the Chinese states destroyed each other one by one until only one state was left standing—the state of Qin (chin).

New Technologies for War

By 300 B.C.E. states were sending out armies of a few hundred thousand drafted foot soldiers, usually accompanied by horsemen. Adding to their effectiveness was the development of the **crossbow** around 350 B.C.E. The intricate bronze trigger of the crossbow allowed a foot soldier to shoot farther than could a horseman carrying a light bow. To defend against crossbows, soldiers began wearing armor and helmets. Most of the armor was made of leather strips tied with cords. Helmets were sometimes made of iron.

crossbow

▶ A powerful mechanical bow developed during the Warring States Period.

CHAPTER LOCATOR | What was the impact of China's geography on the development of Chinese societies? | What was life like during the Shang Dynasty, and how did writing affect Chinese culture?

The introduction of cavalry in this period further reduced the need for a chariot-riding aristocracy. Shooting bows and arrows from horseback was first perfected by non-Chinese peoples to the north of China proper, who at that time were making the transition to a nomadic pastoral economy. The northern state of Jin developed its own cavalry to defend itself from the attacks of these horsemen. Once it started using cavalry against other Chinese states, they too had to master the new technology. From this time on, acquiring and pasturing horses was a key component of military preparedness.

Because of these developments, rulers wanted to increase their populations, to have more commoners to serve as foot soldiers and more craftsmen to supply more weapons. To increase agricultural output, they brought new land into cultivation, drained marshes, and dug irrigation channels. Rulers began surveying their land and taxing farmers. They wanted to undermine the power of lords over their subjects in order to get direct access to the peasants' labor power. Serfdom thus gradually declined.

The development of infantry armies also created the need for a new type of general, and rulers became less willing to let men lead troops merely because of aristocratic birth. In *The Art of War* (453–403 B.C.E.), Sun Wu described the ideal general as a master of maneuver, illusion, and deception. He argued that heroism is a useless virtue that leads to needless deaths. Discipline, however, is essential, and he insisted that the entire army had to be trained to follow the orders of its commanders without questioning them.

The Warring States, 403–221 B.C.E.

The Victorious States

During the Warring States Period, states on the periphery of the Zhou realm had more room to expand than states in the center. With access to more resources, they were able to pick off their neighbors, one after the other. Still, for two centuries the final outcome was far from clear, as alliances among states were regularly made and nearly as regularly broken.

By the third century B.C.E. there were only seven important states remaining. These states were much more centralized than their early Zhou predecessors. Their kings had eliminated indirect control through vassals and in their place dispatched royal officials to remote cities. Before the end of the third century B.C.E. one state, Qin, conquered all of the others, a development discussed in Chapter 7.

QUICK REVIEW <

What connections can you make between military and social developments in the Warring States Period?

How was China governed, and what was life like during the Zhou Dynasty?

How did advances in military technology contribute to the rise of independent states?

What ideas did Confucius teach, and how were they spread after his death?

How did the teachings of Daoism, Legalism, and other schools differ from Confucianism?

☑ LearningCurve
Check what you know.

> What ideas did Confucius teach, and how were they spread after his death?

Serving Parents with Filial Piety

This twelfth-century-c.e. illustration of a passage in the *Classic of Filial Piety* shows how commoners should serve their parents: by working hard at productive jobs such as farming and tending to their parents' daily needs. The married son and daughter-in-law offer food or drink to the older couple as their own children look on, thus learning how they should treat their own parents after they become aged. (National Palace Museum, Taiwan/The Art Archive at Art Resource, NY)

The Warring States Period was the golden age of Chinese philosophy, the era when the "Hundred Schools of Thought" contended. During the same period in which Indian sages and mystics were developing religious speculation about karma, souls, and ultimate reality (see Chapter 3), Chinese thinkers were arguing about the ideal forms of social and political organization and man's connections to nature.

Confucius

As a young man, Confucius (traditional dates: 551–479 B.C.E.) served in the court of his home state of Lu without gaining much influence. After leaving Lu, he set out with a small band of students and wandered through neighboring states in search of a ruler who would take his advice. We know what he taught from the *Analects*, a collection of his sayings put together by his followers after his death.

The thrust of Confucius's thought was ethical rather than theoretical or metaphysical. He talked repeatedly of an ideal age in the early Zhou Dynasty when

CHAPTER LOCATOR | What was the impact of China's geography on the development of Chinese societies? | What was life like during the Shang Dynasty, and how did writing affect Chinese culture?

everyone was devoted to fulfilling his or her role: superiors looked after those dependent on them; inferiors devoted themselves to the service of their superiors; parents and children, husbands and wives all wholeheartedly embraced what was expected of them. Confucius saw five relationships as the basis of society: between ruler and subject; between father and son; between husband and wife; between elder brother and younger brother; and between friend and friend. Mutual obligations of a hierarchical sort underlay the first four of these relationships—the senior leads and protects; the junior supports and obeys. The exception was the relationship between friends, which was conceived in terms of mutual obligations between equals.

A man of moderation, Confucius was an earnest advocate of gentlemanly conduct. He redefined the term *gentleman* (*junzi*) to mean a man of moral cultivation rather than a man of noble birth. He repeatedly urged his followers to aspire to be gentlemen rather than petty men intent on personal gain. Confucius did not advocate social equality, but his teachings minimized the importance of class distinctions and opened the way for intelligent and talented people to rise in the social scale. The Confucian gentleman found his calling in service to the ruler. Loyal advisers should encourage their rulers to govern through ritual, virtue, and concern for the welfare of their subjects, and much of the *Analects* concerns the way to govern well. To Confucius the ultimate virtue was **ren** (humanity). A person of humanity cares about others and acts accordingly.

In the Confucian tradition, studying texts came to be valued over speculation, meditation, and mystical identification with deities. Confucius encouraged the men who came to study with him to master the poetry, rituals, and historical traditions that we know today as Confucian classics.

ren
▶ The ultimate Confucian virtue; it is translated as perfect goodness, benevolence, humanity, human-heartedness, and nobility.

The Spread of Confucian Ideas

The eventual success of Confucian ideas owes much to Confucius's followers in the three centuries following his death. The most important of them were Mencius (ca. 370–300 B.C.E.) and Xunzi (ca. 310–215 B.C.E.).

Mencius, like Confucius, traveled around offering advice to rulers of various states. Over and over he tried to convert them to the view that the ruler able to win over the people through benevolent government would succeed in unifying "all under Heaven." Mencius proposed concrete political and financial measures to ease tax burdens and otherwise improve the people's lot. Men willing to serve an unworthy ruler earned his contempt, especially when they worked hard to fill the ruler's coffers or expand his territory.

With his disciples and fellow philosophers, Mencius also discussed other issues in moral philosophy, arguing strongly, for instance, that human nature is fundamentally good, as everyone is born with the capacity to recognize what is right and act on it. Xunzi, a half century later, took the opposite view of human nature, arguing that people are born selfish and that only through education and ritual do they learn to put moral principle above their own interest. In his view, much of what is desirable is not inborn but must be taught.

Neither Confucius nor Mencius had had much actual political or administrative experience, but Xunzi had worked for many years in the court of his home state. Not surprisingly, he showed more consideration than either Confucius or

| How was China governed, and what was life like during the Zhou Dynasty? | How did advances in military technology contribute to the rise of independent states? | **What ideas did Confucius teach, and how were they spread after his death?** | How did the teachings of Daoism, Legalism, and other schools differ from Confucianism? | ✓ LearningCurve Check what you know. |

105

Mencius for the difficulties a ruler might face in trying to rule through ritual and virtue. Xunzi was also a more rigorous thinker than his predecessors and developed the philosophical foundations of many ideas merely outlined by Confucius and Mencius. Confucius, for instance, had declined to discuss gods, portents, and anomalies and had spoken of sacrificing as if the spirits were present. Xunzi went further and explicitly argued that Heaven does not intervene in human affairs.

Still, Xunzi did not propose abandoning traditional rituals. In his view, rulers and educated men should continue traditional ritual practices such as complex funeral protocols because the rites themselves have positive effects on performers and observers. Not only do they let people express feelings and satisfy desires in an orderly way, but because they specify graduated ways to perform the rites according to social rank, ritual traditions sustain the social hierarchy.

The Confucian vision of personal ethics and public service found a small but ardent following during the Warring States Period. In later centuries rulers came to see men educated in Confucian virtues as ideal advisers and officials. Neither revolutionaries nor flatterers, Confucian scholar-officials opposed bad government and upheld the best ideals of statecraft. Confucian political ideals shaped Chinese society into the twentieth century.

The Confucian vision also provided a moral basis for the Chinese family that continues into modern times. Repaying parents and ancestors came to be seen as a sacred duty. Because people owe their very existence to their parents, they should reciprocate by respecting their parents, making efforts to please them, honoring their memories, and placing the interests of the family line above personal preferences, all of which were aspects of **filial piety**. Since the family line is a patrilineal line from father to son to grandson, placing great importance on it has had the effect of devaluing women.

filial piety
▶ Reverent attitude of children to their parents extolled by Confucius.

> **QUICK REVIEW**
How did ideas about the family shape Confucian philosophy?

CHAPTER LOCATOR | What was the impact of China's geography on the development of Chinese societies? | What was life like during the Shang Dynasty, and how did writing affect Chinese culture?

106 CHAPTER 4 CHINA'S CLASSICAL AGE

How did the teachings of Daoism, Legalism, and other schools of thought differ from Confucianism?

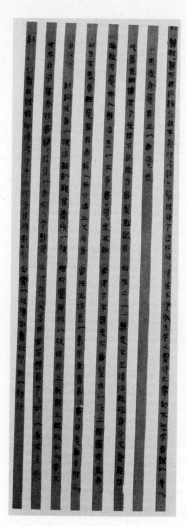

Inscribed Bamboo Slips

In 1993 Chinese archaeologists discovered a late-fourth-century-B.C.E. tomb in Hubei province that contained 804 bamboo slips bearing some 12,000 Chinese characters. Scholars have been able to reconstruct more than a dozen books from them, many of them previously unknown. (Private Collection/Archives Charmet/The Bridgeman Art Library)

> PICTURING THE PAST
ANALYZING THE IMAGE: Can you spot any repeated characters? Can you see any very simple characters?
CONNECTIONS: What were the consequences of recording texts on bamboo or wooden strips? How might doing so have shaped reading and writing in Zhou times? For modern archaeologists who discover these texts in tombs, would the medium used pose any challenges?

During the Warring States Period, rulers took advantage of the destruction of states to recruit newly unemployed men to serve as their advisers and court assistants. Lively debate often resulted as these strategists proposed policies and refuted opponents, and new schools of thought emerged. Many of these schools directly opposed the ideas of Confucius and his followers. Most notable were the Daoists, who believed that the act of striving to improve society only made it worse, and the Legalists, who argued that a strong government depended not so much on moral leadership as on effective laws and procedures.

Daoism

Confucius and his followers believed in moral action. They thought men of virtue should devote themselves to making the government work to the benefit of the people. Those who came to be labeled Daoists disagreed. They thought striving to make things better generally made them worse. They sought to go beyond

How was China governed, and what was life like during the Zhou Dynasty?

How did advances in military technology contribute to the rise of independent states?

What ideas did Confucius teach, and how were they spread after his death?

How did the teachings of Daoism, Legalism, and other schools differ from Confucianism?

✓ LearningCurve
Check what you know.

107

Dao

▶ The Way, a term used by Daoists to refer to the natural order and by Confucians to refer to the moral order.

everyday concerns and to let their minds wander freely. Rather than making human beings and human actions the center of concern, they focused on the larger scheme of things, the whole natural order identified as the Way, or **Dao**.

Early Daoist teachings are known from two surviving books, the *Laozi* and the *Zhuangzi*, both dating to the third century B.C.E. Laozi, the putative author of the *Laozi*, may not be a historical figure, but the text ascribed to him has been of enduring importance. A recurrent theme in this brief, aphoristic text is the mystical superiority of yielding over assertion and silence over words. Because purposeful action is counterproductive, the ruler should let people return to a natural state of ignorance and contentment. In the philosophy of the *Laozi*, the people would be better off if they knew less, gave up tools, renounced writing, stopped envying their neighbors, and lost their desire to travel or engage in war.

Zhuangzi (369–286 B.C.E.), the author of the book of the same name, shared many of the central ideas of the *Laozi*. The *Zhuangzi* is filled with parables, flights of fancy, and fictional encounters between historical figures, including Confucius and his disciples. A more serious strain of Zhuangzi's thought concerned death. He questioned whether we can be sure life is better than death. People fear what they do not know, the same way a captive girl will be terrified when she learns she is to become the king's concubine. Perhaps people will discover that death has as many delights as life in the palace.

Zhuangzi was similarly iconoclastic in his political philosophy. In one parable a wheelwright insolently tells a duke that books are useless because all they contain are the dregs of men long dead. The duke, offended, threatens execution unless the wheelwright can explain his remark. The wheelwright responds by arguing that truly skilled craftsmen respond to situations spontaneously; they do not analyze or reason or even keep in mind the rules they have mastered. The most important truths they know cannot be written down or even explained to others. They are simply the result of experience. This strain of Daoist thought denies the validity of verbal reasoning and the sorts of knowledge conveyed through words.

Daoism can be seen as a response to Confucianism, a rejection of many of its basic premises. Nevertheless, over the course of Chinese history, many people felt the pull of both Confucian and Daoist ideas and studied the writings of both schools. Even Confucian scholars who had devoted much of their lives to public service might find that the teachings of the *Laozi* or *Zhuangzi* helped to put their frustrations in perspective.

Legalism

Legalists

▶ Political theorists who emphasized the need for rigorous laws and laid the basis for China's later bureaucratic government.

Over the course of the fourth and third centuries B.C.E., one small state after another was conquered, and the number of surviving states dwindled. Rulers fearful that their states might be next were ready to listen to political theorists who claimed expertise in the accumulation of power. These theorists, labeled **Legalists** because of their emphasis on the need for rigorous laws, argued that strong government depended not on the moral qualities of the ruler and his officials, as Confucians claimed, but on establishing effective laws and procedures. Legalism, though eventually discredited, laid the basis for China's later bureaucratic government.

CHAPTER LOCATOR | What was the impact of China's geography on the development of Chinese societies? | What was life like during the Shang Dynasty, and how did writing affect Chinese culture?

CHAPTER 4

108 CHINA'S CLASSICAL AGE

In the fourth century B.C.E. the state of Qin radically reformed itself along Legalist lines. The king of Qin abolished the aristocracy. Social distinctions were to be based on military ranks determined by the objective criterion of the number of enemy heads cut off in battle. In place of the old fiefs, the Qin king created counties and appointed officials to govern them according to the laws he decreed at court. To increase the population, Qin recruited migrants from other states. To encourage farmers to work hard and improve their land, they were allowed to buy and sell it. Ordinary farmers were thus freed from serf-like obligations to the local nobility, but direct control by the state could be even more onerous. Taxes and labor service obligations were heavy. Travel required a permit, and vagrants could be forced into penal labor service. All families were grouped into mutual responsibility groups of five and ten families; whenever anyone in the group committed a crime, all the others were equally liable unless they reported it.

Legalism found its greatest exponent in Han Feizi (ca. 280–233 B.C.E.). In his writings he warned rulers of the political pitfalls awaiting them. They had to be careful where they placed their trust, for "when the ruler trusts someone, he falls under that person's control." Given subordinates' propensities to pursue their own selfish interests, the ruler should keep them ignorant of his intentions and control them by manipulating competition among them. Warmth, affection, or candor should have no place in his relationships with others.

In Han Feizi's view, the Confucian notion that government could be based on virtue was naïve. If rulers would make the laws and prohibitions clear and the rewards and punishments automatic, then the officials and common people would be easy to govern. Uniform laws get people to do things they would not otherwise be inclined to do, such as work hard and fight wars; such laws are thus essential to the goal of establishing hegemony over all the other states.

The laws of the Legalists were designed as much to constrain officials as to regulate the common people. The third-century-B.C.E. tomb of a Qin official has yielded statutes detailing the rules for keeping accounts, supervising subordinates, managing penal labor, conducting investigations, and many other responsibilities of officials. Infractions were generally punishable through the imposition of fines.

Legalism saw no value in intellectual debate or private opinion. Divergent views of right and wrong lead to weakness and disorder. The ruler should not allow others to undermine his laws by questioning them. In Legalism, there were no laws above or independent of the wishes of the rulers, no laws that might set limits on rulers' actions.

Yin and Yang

Confucians, Daoists, and Legalists had the greatest long-term impact on Chinese civilization, but the Hundred Schools of Thought also included everyone from logicians, hedonists, and utopians to natural philosophers who analyzed the workings of nature.

A key idea developed by the natural philosophers was the concept of **yin and yang**, first described in the divination manual called the *Book of Changes* (ca. 900 B.C.E.), and developed into much more elaborate theories by late Zhou theorists. Yin is the feminine, dark, receptive, yielding, negative, and weak; yang is the masculine, bright, assertive, creative, positive, and strong. Yin and yang are

yin and yang
▶ A concept of complementary poles, one of which represents the feminine, dark, and receptive, and the other the masculine, bright, and assertive.

How was China governed, and what was life like during the Zhou Dynasty?

How did advances in military technology contribute to the rise of independent states?

What ideas did Confucius teach, and how were they spread after his death?

How did the teachings of Daoism, Legalism, and other schools differ from Confucianism?

☑ LearningCurve
Check what you know.

109

complementary poles rather than distinct entities or opposing forces. The movement of yin and yang accounts for the transition from day to night and from summer to winter. These models based on observation of nature were extended to explain not only phenomena we might classify as natural, but also social phenomena, such as the rise and fall of states and conflict in families. In all these realms, unwanted things happen when the balance between yin and yang gets disturbed.

In recent decades archaeologists have further complicated our understanding of early Chinese thought by unearthing records of the popular religion of the time— astrological manuals, handbooks of lucky and unlucky days, medical prescriptions, exercises, and ghost stories. The tomb of an official who died in 316 B.C.E., for example, has records of divinations showing that illness was seen as the result of unsatisfied spirits or malevolent demons, best dealt with through performing exorcisms or offering sacrifices to the astral god Taiyi (Grand One).

Phoenix and Tigers

Divine animals, such as dragons and phoenixes, are often portrayed in the art of the Warring States Period, especially in the south, where the art of lacquered wood was perfected. (Werner Forman/ akg-images)

> **Competing Views of Politics and Government in Chinese Philosophy:**

Confucianism:	Men of virtue should devote themselves to making government work to the benefit of all people.
Daoism:	Political reforms generally made things worse and individuals should avoid participation in government.
Legalism:	Strong government did not depend on the moral qualities of rulers and officials, but on clear, effective laws and procedures.

> **QUICK REVIEW**

How did ideas about human nature shape Daoism and Legalism?

CHAPTER SUMMARY

After several thousand years of Neolithic cultures, beginning after 2000 B.C.E., Bronze Age civilization developed in China, with cities, writing, and sharp social distinctions. Shang kings led armies and presided at sacrifices to the high god Di and the imperial ancestors. The Shang armies' bronze-tipped weapons and chariots gave them technological superiority over their neighbors.

The Zhou Dynasty, which overthrew the Shang in about 1050 B.C.E., parceled out its territory to hereditary lords. The earliest Chinese books date to this period. The *Book of Documents* provides evidence of the belief in the Mandate of Heaven,

CHAPTER LOCATOR | What was the impact of China's geography on the development of Chinese societies? | What was life like during the Shang Dynasty, and how did writing affect Chinese culture?

CHAPTER 4
110 CHINA'S CLASSICAL AGE

which justified Zhou rule. The *Book of Songs* offers glimpses into what life was like for elites and ordinary people alike in the early Zhou.

By the Warring States Period, which began in 403 B.C.E., the old domains had become independent states. As states destroyed each other, military technology made many advances, including the introduction of cavalry, infantry armies, and the crossbow. Despite its name, the Warring States Period was the golden age of Chinese philosophy. Confucius and his followers promoted the virtues of sincerity, loyalty, benevolence, filial piety, and duty. Mencius urged rulers to rule through goodness and argued that human nature is good. Xunzi stressed the power of ritual and argued that human nature is selfish and must be curbed through education. Daoists and Legalists rejected all these ideas. The Daoists Laozi and Zhuangzi looked beyond the human realm to the entire cosmos and spoke of the relativity of concepts such as good and bad and life and death. Legalists heaped ridicule on the Confucian idea that a ruler could get his people to be good by being good himself and proposed instead rigorous laws with strict rewards and punishments. Natural philosophers explained the changes of seasons and health and illness in terms of the complementary forces of yin and yang.

 **CONNECTIONS** China's transition from Neolithic farming villages to a much more advanced civilization occurred centuries later than in Mesopotamia or India, but by the Warring States Period China was at much the same stage of development as other advanced societies in Eurasia. Although many elements of China's civilization were clearly invented in China—such as its writing system, its method of casting bronze, and its Confucian philosophy—it also adopted elements that diffused across Asia, such as the cultivation of wheat, the horse-driven chariot, and riding horseback.

Greece, the subject of the next chapter, is located very close to the ancient Near Eastern civilizations, so its trajectory was quite different from China's. It was also much smaller than China, yet in time had enormous impact on the wider world. With India and China in mind, the originality of the political forms and ideas of early Greece will stand out more clearly. We return to China's history in Chapter 7, after looking at Greece and Rome.

LaunchPad

ONLINE DOCUMENT PROJECT
The Limits of Loyalty

How did rulers and their subordinates interact during the Warring States Period?

Read a selection of stories from the Warring States Period, and then complete a quiz and writing assignment based on the evidence and details from this chapter. *See inside front cover to learn more.*

| How was China governed, and what was life like during the Zhou Dynasty? | How did advances in military technology contribute to the rise of independent states? | What ideas did Confucius teach, and how were they spread after his death? | How did the teachings of Daoism, Legalism, and other schools differ from Confucianism? | ✓ **LearningCurve** Check what you know. |

CHAPTER 4 STUDY GUIDE

STEP 1

GET STARTED ONLINE

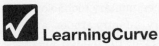 **LearningCurve**

Now that you've read the chapter, make it stick by completing the LearningCurve activity.

STEP 2

EXPLAIN WHY IT MATTERS

Put your reading into practice. Identify each term below, and then explain why it matters in world history.

TERM	WHO OR WHAT & WHEN	WHY IT MATTERS
loess (p. 90)		
Anyang (p. 93)		
taotie (p. 95)		
logographic (p. 95)		
Book of Documents (p. 97)		
Mandate of Heaven (p. 98)		
shi (p. 98)		
Book of Songs (p. 98)		
Warring States Period (p. 102)		
crossbow (p. 102)		
ren (p. 105)		
filial piety (p. 106)		
Dao (p. 108)		
Legalists (p. 108)		
yin and yang (p. 109)		

STEP 3

MOVE BEYOND THE BASICS

To demonstrate a more advanced understanding of the three philosophical traditions that originated during China's Classical Age, fill in the chart below with descriptions of three key aspects of these philosophies: core beliefs, social and ethical teachings, and vision of politics and public life. What problems and tensions in Chinese society did each of these philosophies attempt to remedy?

	Core Beliefs	Social and Ethical Teachings	Vision of Politics and Public Life
Confucianism			
Daoism			
Legalism			

STEP 4

PUT IT ALL TOGETHER

Now, take a step back and try to explain the big picture. Remember to use specific examples from the chapter in your answers.

DEVELOPMENT OF EARLY CHINESE SOCIETY

▶ How did geography shape the way Chinese culture spread and developed?

▶ What role did the Shang king play in Shang society? What was the source of his power and legitimacy?

ZHOU DYNASTY AND THE WARRING STATES PERIOD

▶ What innovations did the Zhou introduce into Chinese society and politics? What were there consequences?

▶ What were the social and cultural consequences of political decentralization during the Warring States Period?

CHINESE PHILOSOPHY IN THE CLASSICAL AGE

▶ What role do hierarchical relationships play in Confucian's philosophy? What light does this shed on Chinese beliefs and values in the Classical Age?

▶ How would you explain the fact that the Warring States period, a time of unrest and conflict, was also the golden age of Chinese philosophy?

LOOKING BACK, LOOKING AHEAD

▶ What similarities and differences do you see between Chinese society and government under the Shang and society and government in the early kingdoms of Mesopotamia? How would you explain the similarities and differences you note?

▶ How would you explain the long-term influence of Confucianism on Chinese society and culture? What elements of Confucianism might explain its enduring appeal?

> IN YOUR OWN WORDS

Imagine that you must give an oral report to the class answering the following question: **How did war and conquest shape China's development in the Classical Age?** What would be the most important points and why?

How did the geography of Greece shape its earliest history?

Hellas, as the Greeks call their land, encompasses the Greek peninsula with its southern peninsular extension, known as the Peloponnesus (peh-luh-puh-NEE-suhs), and the islands surrounding it, an area known as the Aegean (ah-JEE-uhn) basin (Map 5.1). During the Bronze Age, which for Greek history is called the "Helladic period," early settlers in Greece began establishing small communities contoured by the mountains and small plains that shaped the land. The geographical fragmentation of Greece encouraged political fragmentation. Early in Greek history several kingdoms did emerge—the Minoan on the island of Crete and the Mycenaean on the mainland—but the rugged terrain prohibited the growth of a great empire like those of Mesopotamia or Egypt.

The Minoans and Mycenaeans

On the large island of Crete, Bronze Age farmers and fishermen began to trade their surpluses with their neighbors, and cities grew, housing artisans and merchants. Beginning about 2000 B.C.E. Cretans voyaged throughout the eastern Mediterranean and the Aegean, carrying the copper and tin needed to make bronze as well as many other goods. Social hierarchies developed, and in many cities certain individuals came to hold power. The Cretans began to use writing about 1900 B.C.E., in a form later scholars called Linear A. At about the same time that writing began, rulers in several cities of Crete began to build large structures with hundreds of interconnected rooms. The archaeologists who discovered these huge structures called them palaces, and they named the flourishing and vibrant culture of this era Minoan, after the mythical king of Crete, Minos.

CHAPTER LOCATOR | **How did the geography of Greece shape its earliest history?** | What was the role of the polis in Greek society?

ca. 3000–1200 B.C.E.
Helladic period

ca. 2000–1100 B.C.E.
Minoan and Mycenaean civilizations

ca. 1200–323 B.C.E.
Hellenic period

ca. 1100–800 B.C.E.
Greece's Dark Age; population declines, trade decreases, writing disappears

ca. 800–500 B.C.E.
Archaic age; rise of the polis; Greek colonization of the Mediterranean

ca. 700–500 B.C.E.
Sparta and Athens develop distinctive political institutions

ca. 500–338 B.C.E.
Classical period; development of drama, philosophy, and major building projects in Athens

499–404 B.C.E.
Persian and Peloponnesian wars

323–30 B.C.E.
Hellenistic period

336–324 B.C.E.
Alexander the Great's military campaigns

323–ca. 300 B.C.E.
Civil wars lead to the establishment of the Ptolemaic, Antigonid, and Seleucid dynasties

168 B.C.E.
Roman overthrow of the Antigonid dynasty

30 B.C.E.
Roman conquest of Egypt; Ptolemaic dynasty ends

Few specifics are known about Minoan political life except that a king and a group of nobles stood at its head. Minoan society was long thought to have been relatively peaceful, but new excavations are revealing more and more walls around cities, which has called the peaceful nature of Minoan society into question. In terms of their religious life, Minoans appear to have worshipped goddesses far more than gods. Whether this translated into more egalitarian gender roles for real people is unclear, but surviving Minoan art suggests that it might have.

As Minoan culture was flourishing on Crete, a different type of society developed on the mainland. This society was founded by groups who had migrated in during the period after 2000 B.C.E. By about 1650 B.C.E. one group of these immigrants had raised palaces and established cities at Thebes, Athens, Mycenae (migh-SEE-nee) and elsewhere. These palace-centers ruled by local kings formed a loose hegemony under the authority of the king of Mycenae, and the archaeologists who first discovered traces of this culture called it the Mycenaean (migh-see-NEE-ahn).

As in Crete, the political unit was the kingdom, and the king and his warrior aristocracy stood at the top of society. The seat and symbol of the king's power was his palace, which was also the economic center of the kingdom. Palace scribes kept records with a script known as Linear B.

The available evidence suggests a society in which war was common. Mycenaean cities were all fortified by thick stone walls, and graves contain spears, javelins, swords, helmets, and the first examples of metal armor known in the world.

How did war influence Greece, and how did the arts, religion, and philosophy develop?

How did Alexander the Great's conquests shape society in the Hellenistic period?

How did religion, philosophy, and science develop in the Hellenistic world?

✓ **LearningCurve**
Check what you know.

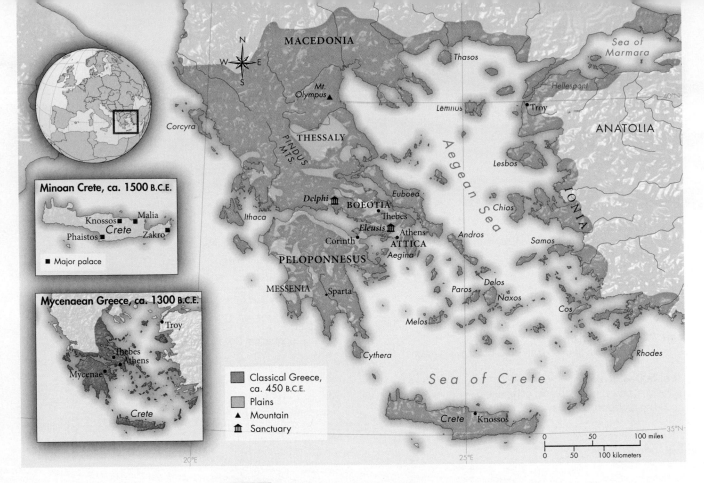

MAP 5.1 ■ Classical Greece, ca. 450 B.C.E.

In antiquity the home of the Greeks included the islands of the Aegean and the western shore of Turkey as well as the Greek peninsula itself. Crete, the home of Minoan civilization, is the large island at the bottom of the map. The Peloponnesian peninsula, where Sparta is located, is connected to the rest of mainland Greece by a very narrow isthmus at Corinth.

Contacts between the Minoans and Mycenaeans were originally peaceful, and Minoan culture and trade goods flooded the Greek mainland. But most scholars think that around 1450 B.C.E., possibly in the wake of an earthquake that left Crete vulnerable, the Mycenaeans attacked Crete, destroying many towns and occupying Knossos, Crete's leading city. For about the next fifty years, the Mycenaeans ruled much of the island. Then, between about 1300 B.C.E. and 1000 B.C.E., various kingdoms in and beyond Greece ravaged one another in a savage series of wars that destroyed both the Minoan and Mycenaean civilizations.

The fall of the Minoans and Mycenaeans was part of what some scholars see as a general collapse of Bronze Age civilizations in the eastern Mediterranean, including the end of the Egyptian New Kingdom and the fall of the Hittite Empire (see Chapter 2). This collapse appears to have had a number of causes: internal economic and social problems; invasions and migrations by outsiders; changes in warfare and weaponry, particularly the adoption of iron weapons, which made foot soldiers the most important factor in battles and reduced the power of kings and wealthy nobles fighting from chariots; and natural disasters such as volcanic eruptions, earthquakes, and droughts.

CHAPTER LOCATOR | **How did the geography of Greece shape its earliest history?** | What was the role of the polis in Greek society?

The "Dark Age"

In Greece these invasions, migrations, disasters, and social problems worked together to usher in a period of poverty and disruption that historians have traditionally called the "Dark Age" of Greece (ca. 1100–800 B.C.E.). Cities were destroyed, population declined, villages were abandoned, and trade decreased. Even writing, which was not widespread before this period, was a casualty of the chaos.

The Bronze Age Collapse led to the widespread and prolonged movement of Greek peoples, both within Greece itself and beyond. They dispersed beyond mainland Greece farther south to the islands of the Aegean Sea and in greater strength across the Aegean to the shores of Anatolia (see Map 5.1). By the conclusion of the Dark Age, the Greeks had spread their culture throughout the Aegean basin, and like many other cultures around the Mediterranean and the Near East, they had adopted iron.

Archaeological sources from the Dark Age are less rich than those from the periods that came after, so they are often used in conjunction with literary sources written in later centuries to give us a more complete picture of the era. These included tales of the heroic deeds of legendary heroes similar to the epic poems of Mesopotamia and the *Ramayana* in India. Sometime in the eighth or seventh century B.C.E. many of these were gathered together in two long epic poems: the *Iliad*, which tells the story of the Trojan War, a war similar to those fought by Mycenaean kings, and the *Odyssey*, which records the adventures of one of the heroes of that war. These poems were recited orally, and once writing was reintroduced to Greece, they were written down and attributed to a poet named Homer, though scholars debate whether Homer was an actual historical individual. The two poems present human and divine characters who are larger than life but also petty, vindictive, pouting, and deceitful, flaws that drive the action forward, usually with tragic results.

QUICK REVIEW <

What role did trade play in Minoan and Mycenaean society?

| How did war influence Greece, and how did the arts, religion, and philosophy develop? | How did Alexander the Great's conquests shape society in the Hellenistic period? | How did religion, philosophy, and science develop in the Hellenistic world? | ✓ LearningCurve Check what you know. |

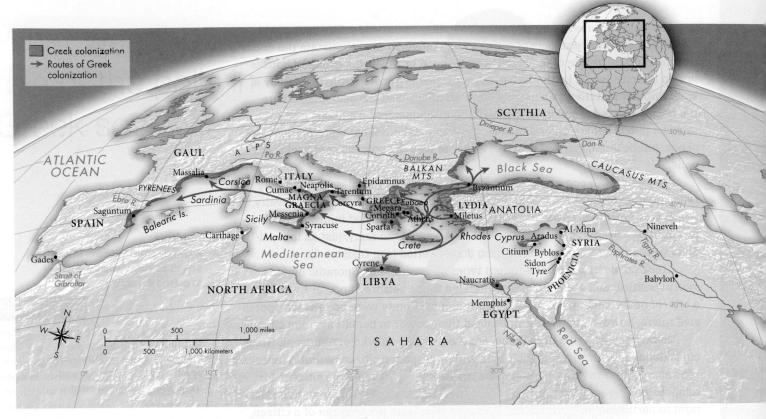

Greek colonization

→ Routes of Greek colonization

MAP 5.2 ■ Greek Colonization, ca. 750–550 B.C.E.

The Greeks established colonies along the shores of the Mediterranean and Black Seas, spreading Greek culture and creating a large trading network.

The Growth of Sparta

During the Archaic period Sparta became the leading military power in Greece. To expand their polis, the Spartans did not establish colonies but instead conquered Messenia (muh-SEE-nee-uh), a region in the southwestern Peloponnesus. They turned the Messenians into helots (HEH-luhts), unfree residents forced to work state lands. The helots soon rose in a revolt that took the Spartans thirty years to crush. Afterward, non-nobles who had shared in the fighting as foot soldiers appear to have demanded rights equal to those of the nobility and a voice in the government. Under intense pressure the aristocrats agreed to remodel the state into a new system.

The plan for the new system in Sparta was attributed to the lawgiver Lycurgus (ligh-KUHR-guhs), who may or may not have been an actual person. Political distinctions among Spartan men were eliminated, and all citizens became legally equal. Two kings, who were primarily military leaders, and a council of nobles shared executive power with five ephors (EH-fuhrs), overseers elected by the citizens. Helots worked the land, while Spartan citizens devoted their time to military training, and Sparta became extremely powerful.

In the system attributed to Lycurgus, every citizen owed primary allegiance to Sparta. Suppression of the individual along with an emphasis on military prowess led to a barracks state. Even family life was sacrificed to the polis. After long,

CHAPTER LOCATOR | How did the geography of Greece shape its earliest history? | **What was the role of the polis in Greek society?**

CHAPTER 5
122 THE GREEK EXPERIENCE

hard military training that began at age seven, citizens became lifelong soldiers. Because men often did not see their wives or other women for long periods, not only in times of war but also in times of peace, their most meaningful relations were same-sex ones.

Spartans expected women in citizen families to be good wives and strict mothers of future soldiers. With men in military service much of their lives, women in citizen families ran the estates and owned land in their own right, and they were not physically restricted or secluded.

The Evolution of Athens

Like Sparta, Athens faced pressing social and economic problems during the Archaic period, but instead of creating a state devoted to the military, the Athenians created a state that became a democracy. For Athens, the late seventh century B.C.E. was a time of turmoil. In 621 B.C.E. Draco (DRAY-koh), an Athenian aristocrat, under pressure from small landholders and with the consent of the nobles, published the first law code of the Athenian polis. His code was harsh, but it embodied the ideal that the law belonged to all citizens. Yet the aristocracy still governed Athens oppressively, and the social and economic situation remained dire. Noble landholders continued to force small farmers and artisans into economic dependence. Many families were sold into slavery as settlement for debts, while others were exiled and their land mortgaged to the rich.

One person who recognized these problems was the aristocrat Solon (SOH-luhn). Solon condemned his fellow aristocrats for their greed and dishonesty. According to later sources, Solon's sincerity and good sense convinced other aristocrats that he was no crazed revolutionary. Moreover, he gained the trust of the common people. Around 594 B.C.E. the nobles elected him *archon* (AHR-kahn), chief magistrate of the polis, and gave him extraordinary power to reform the state.

Solon immediately freed all people enslaved for debt, recalled all exiles, canceled all debts on land, and made enslavement for debt illegal. Solon allowed non-nobles into the old aristocratic assembly, where they could vote in the election of magistrates. Later sixth-century-B.C.E. leaders further broadened the opportunities for commoners to take part in government, transforming Athens into a democracy.

The democracy functioned on the ideal that all full citizens should play a role in government. In 487 B.C.E. the election of the city's nine archons was replaced by reappointment by lot, which meant that any citizen with a certain amount of property had a chance of becoming an archon. Making laws was the responsibility of two bodies, the *boule* (BOO-lee), or council, composed of five hundred members, and the *ecclesia* (ee-KLEE-zhee-uh), the assembly of all citizens.

QUICK REVIEW ◀

How did the Greek polis differ from Near Eastern city-states?

How did war influence Greece, and how did the arts, religion, and philosophy develop?

How did Alexander the Great's conquests shape society in the Hellenistic period?

How did religion, philosophy, and science develop in the Hellenistic world?

✓ LearningCurve
Check what you know.

In the classical period, how did war influence Greece, and how did the arts, religion, and philosophy develop?

Religious Procession in Hellenic Greece

This painted wooden slab from about 540 B.C.E., found in a cave near Corinth, shows adults and children about to sacrifice a sheep to the deities worshipped in this area. The participants are dressed in their finest clothes and crowned with garlands. Music adds to the festivities. Rituals such as this were a common part of religious life throughout Greece. The boys are shown with tanned skin and women with white, reflecting the ideal that men's lives took place largely outside in the sun-filled public squares, and women's in the shaded interiors of homes. The woman at the front of the procession has her hair up, indicating her married status, while the women at the rear have the long uncovered hair of unmarried women. (Pitsa/National Archeological Museum, Athens, Greece/Gianni Dagli Orti/De Agostini Picture Library/The Bridgeman Art Library)

From the time of the Mycenaeans, violent conflict was common in Greek society, and this did not change in the fifth century B.C.E., the beginning of what scholars later called the classical period of Greek history. First, the Greeks beat back the armies of the Persian Empire. Then, turning their spears against one another, they destroyed their own political system in a century of warfare that began with the Peloponnesian War. Although warfare was one of the hallmarks of the classical period, intellectual and artistic accomplishments were as well.

The Deadly Conflicts, 499–404 B.C.E.

In 499 B.C.E. the Greeks who lived in Ionia unsuccessfully rebelled against the Persian Empire, which had ruled the area for fifty years (see Chapter 2). The Athenians provided halfhearted help to the Ionians, and in retaliation the Persians struck at Athens, only to be surprisingly defeated by the Athenian hoplites at the Battle of Marathon. In 480 B.C.E. the Persian king Xerxes (ZUHRK-seez) personally led a massive invasion of Greece. Under the leadership of Sparta, many

CHAPTER LOCATOR | How did the geography of Greece shape its earliest history? | What was the role of the polis in Greek society?

Greek poleis, though not all, united to fight the Persians. The larger Persian army enjoyed early success, but the tide quickly turned and the invasion ended in failure.

The victorious Athenians and their allies then formed the Delian League, a military alliance intended to liberate Ionia from Persian rule and keep the Persians out of Greece. The Athenians, however, turned the league into an Athenian empire. They reduced their allies to the status of subjects. Athenian ideas of freedom and democracy did not extend to the citizens of other cities, and cities that objected to or revolted over Athenian actions were put down.

Under their great leader Pericles (PEHR-uh-kleez) (ca. 494–429 B.C.E.), the Athenians grew so powerful and aggressive that they alarmed Sparta and its allies. In 431 B.C.E. Athenian imperialism finally drove Sparta into the conflict known as the Peloponnesian War. The Peloponnesian War lasted a generation (431–404 B.C.E.) and brought in its wake disease, widespread civil wars, destruction, famine, and huge loss of life. In 404 B.C.E. the Athenians finally surrendered to Sparta and its allies, and Sparta stripped it of its empire. Conflicts among the states of Greece continued, however.

☐ Areas of Persian control
☐ Greek states at war with Persia
☐ Neutral Greek states

The Persian Wars, 499–479 B.C.E.

Athenian Arts in the Age of Pericles

In the midst of the warfare of the fifth century B.C.E., Pericles turned Athens into the showplace of Greece. He appropriated Delian League money to pay for a huge building program to rebuild the city that had been destroyed during the Persian occupation in 480 B.C.E. and to display to all Greeks the glory of the Athenian polis. The Acropolis in the center of the city was crowned by the Parthenon, a temple that celebrated the greatness of Athens and its patron goddess, Athena, who was represented by a huge statue.

Other aspects of Athenian culture were also rooted in the life of the polis. The polis sponsored plays as part of the city's religious festivals and required wealthy citizens to pay the expenses of their production. Many plays were highly controversial, with overt political and social commentary, but they were neither suppressed nor censored. Not surprisingly, given the incessant warfare, conflict was a constant element in Athenian drama, and playwrights used their art in attempts to portray, understand, and resolve life's basic conflicts.

Aeschylus (EHS-kuh-luhs) (525–456 B.C.E.) was the first dramatist to explore such basic questions as the rights of the individual, the conflict between the individual and society, and the nature of good and evil. In his trilogy of plays, *The Oresteia*, he treats the themes of betrayal, murder, and reconciliation, urging the use of reason and justice to reconcile fundamental conflicts.

The plays of Sophocles (SAH-fuh-kleez) (496–406 B.C.E.) also deal with matters personal, political, and divine. In *Antigone*—which tells of how a king's mistakes in judgment lead to the suicides of his son, his son's fiancée, and his wife—Sophocles emphasizes the precedence of divine law over political law and family custom. In *Oedipus the King*, Sophocles tells the story of a good man doomed by the gods to kill his father and marry his mother. When Oedipus fails to avoid his fate, he blinds himself in despair and flees into exile. In *Oedipus at Colonus*, Sophocles treats the last days of the broken man, whose patient suffering and uncomplaining piety ultimately win the blessings and honor of the gods.

The Delian League, ca. 478–431 B.C.E.

☐ Delian League
☐ Allied with Delian League, 446 B.C.E.
● Athenian military settlement

How did war influence Greece, and how did the arts, religion, and philosophy develop?

How did Alexander the Great's conquests shape society in the Hellenistic period?

How did religion, philosophy, and science develop in the Hellenistic world?

✔ LearningCurve
Check what you know.

125

The Acropolis of Athens

The natural rock formation of the Acropolis probably had a palace on top as early as the Mycenaean period, when it was also surrounded by a defensive wall. Temples were constructed beginning in the sixth century B.C.E., and after the Persian wars Pericles ordered the reconstruction and expansion of many of these, as well as the building of new and more magnificent temples and an extension of the defensive walls. The largest building is the Parthenon, a temple dedicated to the goddess Athena, which originally housed a 40-foot-tall statue of Athena made of ivory and gold sheets attached to a wooden frame. Much of the Parthenon was damaged when it was shelled during a war between Venice and the Ottoman Empire in the seventeenth century, and air pollution continues to eat away at the marble. (Marie Mauzy/Art Resource, NY)

> PICTURING THE PAST

ANALYZING THE IMAGE: Imagine yourself as an Athenian walking up the hill toward the Parthenon. What impression would the setting and the building itself convey?

CONNECTIONS: What were the various functions of the Acropolis?

Euripides (yoo-RIH-puh-deez) (ca. 480–406 B.C.E.) likewise explored the theme of personal conflict within the polis and sounded the depths of the individual. With Euripides drama entered a new and more personal phase. To him the gods mattered far less than people.

Athens also produced writers of comedies, who used humor as political commentary in an effort to suggest and support the best policies for the polis. Best known of the comedians is Aristophanes (eh-ruh-STAH-fuh-neez) (ca. 445–386 B.C.E.), a merciless critic of cranks, quacks, and fools. He used his art of sarcasm to dramatize his ideas on the right conduct of citizens and their leaders for the good of the polis.

Families and Sexual Relations

The Athenians, like other Greeks, lived with comparatively few material possessions in houses that were rather simple. A typical Athenian house consisted of a series of rooms opening onto a central courtyard that contained a well, an altar,

CHAPTER LOCATOR | How did the geography of Greece shape its earliest history? | What was the role of the polis in Greek society?

126 CHAPTER 5 THE GREEK EXPERIENCE

and a washbasin. Meals consisted primarily of various grains, especially wheat and barley, as well as lentils, olives, figs, grapes, fish, and a little meat.

In the city a man might support himself as a craftsman, or he could contract with the polis to work on public buildings. Certain crafts, including spinning and weaving, were generally done by women. Men and women without skills worked as paid laborers. Slavery was commonplace in Greece. Slaves, who were paid for their work, were usually foreigners.

The available sources suggest that women rarely played notable roles in public affairs. The status of a free woman was strictly protected by law. Only her sons could be citizens. Only she was in charge of the household and the family's possessions, yet the law gave her these rights primarily to protect her husband's interests. Women in Athens and elsewhere in Greece, like those in Mesopotamia, brought dowries to their husbands upon marriage, which went back to their fathers in cases of divorce.

In ancient Athens the main function of women from citizen families was to bear and raise children. Women in citizen families probably spent most of their time at home, leaving the house only to attend religious festivals, and perhaps occasionally plays, although this is debated. In their quarters of the house they oversaw domestic slaves and hired labor, and together with servants and friends worked wool into cloth. Women from noncitizen families lived freer lives, although they worked harder and had fewer material comforts. They performed manual labor in the fields or sold goods and services in the agora, going about their affairs much as men did.

Same-sex relations were generally accepted in all of ancient Greece. In classical Athens part of a male adolescent citizen's training might entail a hierarchical sexual and tutorial relationship with an older man, who most likely was married and may have had female sexual partners as well. A small number of sources refer to female-female sexual desire, the most famous of which are a few of the poems of Sappho (SEH-FOH), a female poet of the sixth century B.C.E.

Same-sex relations did not mean that people did not marry, for Athenians saw the continuation of the family line as essential. Sappho, for example, appears to have been married and had a daughter. Sexual desire and procreation were both important aspects of life, but ancient Greeks did not necessarily link them.

Hetaera and Young Man

In this scene painted on the inside of a drinking cup, a hetaera holds the head of a young man who has clearly had too much to drink. Sexual and comic scenes were common on Greek pottery, particularly on objects that would have been used at a private dinner party hosted by a citizen, known as a symposium. Wives did not attend symposia, but hetaerae and entertainers were often hired to perform for the male guests. (© Martin Von Wagner Museum der Universität Würzburg. Foto: P. Neckermann, respectively E. Oehrlein)

How did war influence Greece, and how did the arts, religion, and philosophy develop?

How did Alexander the Great's conquests shape society in the Hellenistic period?

How did religion, philosophy, and science develop in the Hellenistic world?

 LearningCurve
Check what you know.

127

Public and Personal Religion

Like most peoples of the ancient world, the Greeks were polytheists, worshipping a variety of gods and goddesses who were immortal but otherwise acted just like people. As elsewhere, Greek religion was primarily a matter of ritual, with rituals designed to appease the divinities believed to control the forces of the natural world. Processions, festivals, and sacrifices offered to the gods were frequently occasions for people to meet together socially. Migration, invasion, and colonization brought the Greeks into contact with other peoples and caused their religious beliefs to evolve.

By the classical era, the primary gods were understood to live metaphorically on Mount Olympus, the highest mountain in Greece. Besides these Olympian gods, each polis had its own minor deities, each with his or her own local group of worshippers. The polis administered the cults and religious festivals, and everyone was expected to participate in these civic rituals. In contrast to Mesopotamia, Egypt, and Vedic India, priests held little power in Greece; their purpose was to care for temples and sacred property and to conduct the proper rituals, but not to make religious or political rules or doctrines. Much religion was local and domestic, and individual families honored various deities privately in their homes. Many people also believed that magic rituals and spells were effective and sought the assistance of individuals reputed to have special knowledge or powers.

> The Olympian Gods:

Zeus	King of the gods
Hera	Wife and sister of Zeus
Ares	God of war
Apollo	Patron god of music and poetry
Athena	Goddess of wisdom and patron goddess of Athens

mystery religions
▶ Belief systems that were characterized by secret doctrines, rituals of initiation, and sometimes the promise of rebirth or an afterlife.

Along with public and family forms of honoring the gods, some Greeks also participated in what later historians have termed **mystery religions**, in which participants underwent an initiation ritual and gained secret knowledge that they were forbidden to reveal to the uninitiated. Many of these religions promised rebirth or an afterlife to adherents.

The Greeks also shared some Pan-Hellenic festivals, the chief of which were held at Olympia to honor the god Zeus and at Delphi to honor the god Apollo. The festivities at Olympia included athletic contests that inspired the modern Olympic games. Held every four years after they started in 776 B.C.E., the contests attracted visitors from all over the Greek world. The Pythian games at Delphi were also held every four years, and these contests included musical and literary competitions.

The Flowering of Philosophy

Just as the Greeks developed rituals to honor gods, they spun myths and epics to explain the origins of the universe. Over time, however, some Greeks began to question their old gods and myths, and they sought rational rather than super-

CHAPTER LOCATOR | How did the geography of Greece shape its earliest history? | What was the role of the polis in Greek society?

128 CHAPTER 5 THE GREEK EXPERIENCE

natural explanations for natural phenomena. These Greek thinkers, based in Ionia, are called the Pre-Socratics because their rational efforts preceded those of the better-known Socrates. Taking individual facts, they wove them into general theories that led them to conclude that, despite appearances, the universe is actually simple and subject to natural laws.

Drawing on their observations, the Pre-Socratics speculated about the basic building blocks of the universe, and most decided that all things were made of four simple substances: fire, air, earth, and water. Democritus (dih-MAW-kruh-tuhs) (ca. 460 B.C.E.) broke this down further and created the atomic theory that the universe is made up of invisible, indestructible particles. The stream of thought started by the Pre-Socratics branched into several directions. Hippocrates (hih-PAW-kruh-teez) (ca. 470–400 B.C.E.) became the most prominent physician and teacher of medicine of his time. He sought natural explanations for diseases and natural means to treat them. Illness was caused not by evil spirits, he asserted, but by physical problems in the body, particularly by imbalances in what he saw as four basic bodily fluids: blood, phlegm, black bile, and yellow bile.

The Sophists (SOFF-ihsts), a group of thinkers in fifth-century-B.C.E. Athens, applied philosophical speculation to politics and language, questioning the beliefs and laws of the polis to understand their origin. They believed that excellence in both politics and language could be taught, and they provided lessons for the young men of Athens who wished to learn how to persuade others.

Socrates (SOK-ruh-teez) (ca. 470–399 B.C.E.), whose ideas are known only through the works of others, also applied philosophy to politics and to people. His approach when exploring ethical issues and defining concepts was to start with a general topic or problem and to narrow the matter to its essentials. He did so by continuously questioning participants in a discussion or argument rather than lecturing, a process known as the Socratic method. Many Athenians viewed Socrates with suspicion because he challenged the traditional beliefs and values of Athens. His views brought him into conflict with the government. The leaders of Athens tried him for corrupting the youth of the city, and for impiety, that is, for not believing in the gods honored in the city. In 399 B.C.E. they executed him.

Most of what we know about Socrates comes from his student Plato (427–347 B.C.E.), who wrote dialogues in which Socrates asks questions and who also founded the Academy, a school dedicated to philosophy. Plato developed the theory that there are two worlds: the impermanent, changing world that we know through our senses, and the eternal, unchanging realm of "forms" that constitute the essence of true reality. According to Plato, true knowledge and the possibility of living a virtuous life come from contemplating ideal forms—what later came to be called **Platonic ideals**—not from observing the visible world.

Plato's student Aristotle (384–322 B.C.E.) believed that true knowledge came from observation of the world, analysis of natural phenomena, and logical reasoning, not contemplation. Aristotle thought that everything had a purpose, so that to know something, one also had to know its function. The range of Aristotle's thought is staggering. His interests embraced logic, ethics, natural science, physics, politics, poetry, and art. He studied the heavens as well as earth and judged the earth to be the center of the universe, with the stars and planets revolving around it.

Platonic ideals
▶ In Plato's thought, the eternal unchanging ideal forms that are the essence of true reality.

How did war influence Greece, and how did the arts, religion, and philosophy develop?

How did Alexander the Great's conquests shape society in the Hellenistic period?

How did religion, philosophy, and science develop in the Hellenistic world?

✔ LearningCurve
Check what you know.

The philosophers of ancient Athens lived at roughly the same time as major thinkers in religious and philosophical movements in other parts of the world, including Mahavira (the founder of Jainism), the Buddha, Confucius, and several prophets in Hebrew Scripture. All of these individuals thought deeply about how to live a moral life, and all had tremendous influence on later intellectual, religious, and social developments. There is no evidence that they had any contact with one another, but the parallels among them are strong enough that some historians describe the period from about 800 B.C.E. to 200 B.C.E. as the "Axial Age," by which they mean that this was a pivotal period of intellectual and spiritual transformation.

How did Athenian art, drama, and religion reflect Athenian values and beliefs?

CHAPTER LOCATOR | How did the geography of Greece shape its earliest history? | What was the role of the polis in Greek society?

CHAPTER 5
130   THE GREEK EXPERIENCE

How did Alexander the Great's conquests shape society in the Hellenistic period?

Harbor and Marketplace at Delos

During the Hellenistic period, the tiny island of Delos in the Aegean became a thriving trading center, with a paved marketplace filled with shops and stands, as well as temples paid for by merchants and ship captains. From Delos cargoes were shipped to virtually every part of the Mediterranean. Liquids such as wine and oil were generally shipped in amphoras (inset) made of baked clay. Amphoras were easy and cheap to make and surprisingly durable. (harbor: age fotostock/SuperStock; amphora: Alexis Rosenfeld/Photo Researchers, Inc.)

The Greek city-states wore themselves out fighting one another, and Philip II, the ruler of Macedonia, a kingdom in the north of Greece, gradually conquered one after another and took over their lands. He then turned against the Persian Empire but was killed by an assassin. His son Alexander continued the fight. Alexander conquered the entire Persian Empire from Libya in the west to Bactria in the east (see Map 5.3, page 133). He also founded new cities in which Greek and local populations mixed, although he died while planning his next campaign. Alexander left behind an empire that quickly broke into smaller kingdoms, but more important, his death in 323 B.C.E. ushered in an era, the **Hellenistic**, in which Greek culture, the Greek language, and Greek thought spread as far as India, blending with local traditions.

Hellenistic

▶ Literally means "like the Greek"; describes the period from the death of Alexander the Great in 323 B.C.E. to the Roman conquest of Egypt in 30 B.C.E., when Greek culture spread.

How did war influence Greece, and how did the arts, religion, and philosophy develop?	**How did Alexander the Great's conquests shape society in the Hellenistic period?**	How did religion, philosophy, and science develop in the Hellenistic world?	 **LearningCurve** Check what you know.

From Polis to Monarchy, 404–200 B.C.E.

Immediately after the Peloponnesian War, Sparta began striving for empire over all of the Greeks but could not maintain its hold. In 371 B.C.E. an army from the polis of Thebes destroyed the Spartan army, but the Thebans were unable to bring peace to Greece. Philip II, ruler of the kingdom of Macedonia on the northern border of Greece (r. 359–336 B.C.E.), turned the situation to his advantage. By clever use of his wealth and superb army, Philip won control of the northern Aegean, and in 338 B.C.E. he defeated a combined Theban-Athenian army, conquering Greece.

After his victory, Philip united the Greek states with his Macedonian kingdom and got the states to cooperate in a crusade to liberate the Ionian Greeks from Persian rule. Before he could launch his crusade, Philip fell to an assassin's dagger in 336 B.C.E. His son Alexander vowed to carry on Philip's mission and led an army of Macedonians and Greeks into western Asia. He won major battles against the Persians and seized Egypt from them without a fight.

By 330 B.C.E. the Persian Empire had fallen, but Alexander had no intention of stopping, and he set out to conquer much of the rest of Asia. After four years of fighting his soldiers crossed the Indus River (in the area that is now Pakistan), and finally, at the Hyphasis River, the troops refused to go farther. Alexander was enraged by the mutiny, but the army stood firm. Still eager to explore the limits of the world, Alexander turned south to the Arabian Sea and then back west (Map 5.3).

Alexander died in Babylon in 323 B.C.E. from fever, wounds, and excessive drinking. In just thirteen years he had created an empire that stretched from his homeland of Macedonia to India. His campaign swept away the Persian Empire, and in its place he established a Macedonian monarchy, although this fell apart with his death. Several of the chief Macedonian generals aspired to become sole ruler, which led to a civil war that lasted for decades and tore Alexander's empire apart. By the end of this conflict, the most successful generals had carved out their own smaller monarchies, although these continued to be threatened by internal splits and external attacks.

Ptolemy (TAH-luh-mee) seized Egypt, and his descendants, the Ptolemies, ruled Egypt for nearly three hundred years, until the death of the last Ptolemaic ruler, Cleopatra VII, in 30 B.C.E. Antigonus and his descendants, the Antigonids (an-TIH-guh-nuhds), gained control of the Macedonian kingdom in Europe, which they held until they were overthrown by the Romans in 168 B.C.E. (see Chapter 6). Seleucus won the bulk of Alexander's empire, his monarchy extending from western Asia to India (see page 133), gradually broke into smaller states. In terms of political stability and peace, these monarchies were no improvement on the Greek polis.

To encourage obedience, Hellenistic kings often created ruler cults that linked the king's authority with that of the gods, or they adopted ruler cults that already existed. This created a symbol of unity within kingdoms ruling different peoples who at first had little in common. Kings sometimes gave the cities in their territory all the external trappings of a polis, such as a council or an assembly of citizens, but these had no power. The city was not autonomous, as the polis had been, but had to follow royal orders. Hellenistic rulers generally relied on paid professionals to staff their bureaucracies and on trained, paid, full-time soldiers rather than citizen hoplites to fight their wars.

CHAPTER LOCATOR | How did the geography of Greece shape its earliest history? | What was the role of the polis in Greek society?

CHAPTER 5
132 THE GREEK EXPERIENCE

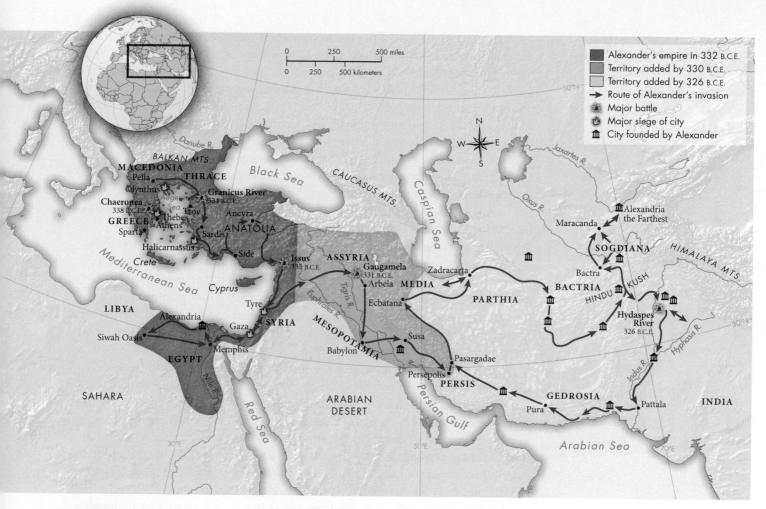

MAP 5.3 ■ Alexander's Conquests, 336–324 B.C.E.

Alexander's campaign of conquest was extensive and speedy. More important than the great success of his military campaigns was his founding of Hellenistic cities.

> **MAPPING THE PAST**

ANALYZING THE MAP: Where are most of the cities founded by Alexander located in relation to Greece? What does this suggest about his aims?

CONNECTIONS: Compare this map with Map 5.2, which shows Greek colonization in the Hellenic period (page 122). What are the major differences between the two processes of expansion?

Building a Hellenized Society

Alexander's most important legacy was the spread of Greek ideas and traditions across a wide area, a process scholars later called **Hellenization**. To maintain contact with the Greek world as he moved farther eastward, Alexander founded new cities and military colonies and settled Greek and Macedonian troops and veterans in them. This practice continued after his death. These cities and colonies became powerful instruments in the spread of Hellenism and in the blending of Greek and other cultures. Wherever it was established, the Hellenistic city resembled a modern city. It was a cultural center with theaters, temples, and libraries—a seat of learning and a place for amusement. The Hellenistic city was also an economic center—a marketplace and a scene of trade and manufacturing.

Hellenization

▶ The spread of Greek ideas, culture, and traditions to non-Greek groups across a wide area.

| How did war influence Greece, and how did the arts, religion, and philosophy develop? | **How did Alexander the Great's conquests shape society in the Hellenistic period?** | How did religion, philosophy, and science develop in the Hellenistic world? | ✓ LearningCurve Check what you know. |

The ruling dynasties of the Hellenistic world were Macedonian in origin, and Greeks and Macedonians initially filled all important political, military, and diplomatic positions. The prevailing institutions and laws were Greek, and Greek became the common spoken language of the entire eastern Mediterranean. Everyone who wanted to find an official position or compete in business had to learn it. Those who did gained an avenue of social mobility, and as early as the third century B.C.E. local people in some Greek cities began to rise in power and prominence. Cultural influences in the other direction occurred less frequently because they brought fewer advantages. Few Greeks learned a non-Greek language unless they were required to because of their official position. Greeks did begin to worship local deities, but often these were somewhat Hellenized and their qualities blended with those of an existing Greek god or goddess.

In the booming city of Alexandria, the Ptolemies generally promoted Greek culture over that of the local Egyptians. This favoritism eventually led to civil unrest, but it also led the Ptolemies to support anything that enhanced Greek learning or traditions. Ptolemaic kings established what became the largest library in the ancient world. Alexandria was also home to the largest Jewish community in the ancient world, and here Jewish scholars translated the Hebrew Bible into Greek for the first time.

The kings of Bactria and Parthia spread Greek culture far to the east, and their kingdoms became outposts of Hellenism. Some Bactrian and Parthian rulers converted to Buddhism, and the Buddhist ruler of the Mauryan Empire in northern India, Ashoka, may have ordered translations of his laws into Greek for the Greek-speaking residents of Bactria and Parthia. In the second century B.C.E., after the collapse of the Mauryan Empire, Bactrian armies conquered part of northern India, establishing several small Indo-Greek states where the mixing of religious and artistic traditions was particularly pronounced (see Chapter 3).

Yet the spread of Greek culture was wider than it was deep, as it generally did not extend far beyond the reaches of the cities. Many urban residents adopted the aspects of Hellenism that they found useful, but people in the countryside generally did not embrace it, nor were they encouraged to.

The Growth of Trade and Commerce

Not only did Alexander's conquests change the political face of the ancient world, but the spread of Greeks eastward also created new markets, causing trade to flourish. The economic connections of the Hellenistic world later proved valuable to the Romans, allowing them to trade products and ideas more easily over a broad area.

Alexander used the wealth of the Persian Empire to finance the building of roads, the development of harbors, and especially, as noted earlier, the founding of new cities. These cities opened whole new markets to merchants. Whenever possible, merchants sent their goods by water, but overland trade also became more prominent in the Hellenistic era. This period also saw the development of standardized business customs, so that merchants of different nationalities communicated in a way understandable to them all. Trade was further facilitated by the coining of money, which provided merchants with a standard way to value goods as well as a convenient method of payment.

CHAPTER LOCATOR | How did the geography of Greece shape its earliest history? | What was the role of the polis in Greek society?

The increased volume of trade helped create prosperity that made luxury goods affordable to more people. As a result, overland traders brought easily transportable luxuries such as gold, silver, and precious stones to market. They extended their networks into China, from which the most prominent good in terms of volume was silk. The trade in silk later gave the major east-west route its name: the Great Silk Road. In return the peoples of the eastern Mediterranean sent east manufactured or extracted goods, especially metal weapons, cloth, wine, and olive oil. (For more on the Silk Road in East Asia, see Chapter 7.)

More economically important than trade in exotic goods were commercial dealings in essential commodities like raw materials and grain and industrial products such as pottery. Most trade in bulk commodities like grain and wood was seaborne.

For the cities of Greece and the Aegean the trade in grain was essential, because many of them could not grow enough in their mountainous terrain. Fortunately for them, abundant wheat supplies were available nearby in Egypt and in the area north of the Black Sea. The Greek cities often paid for their grain by exporting olive oil, wine, honey, dried fruit, nuts, and vegetables. Another significant commodity supplied by the Greeks was fish, which for export was salted, pickled, or dried.

Slaves were a staple of Hellenistic trade, traveling in all directions on both land and sea routes. War provided prisoners for the slave market; to a lesser extent, so did kidnapping and capture by pirates, although the origin of most slaves is unknown. Both old Greek states and new Hellenistic kingdoms were ready slave markets, and throughout the Mediterranean world slaves were almost always in demand.

Despite the increase in trade, the Hellenistic period did not see widespread improvements in the way most people lived and worked. Cities flourished, but many people who lived in rural areas were actually worse off than they had been before, because of higher levels of rents and taxes. Technology was applied to military needs, but not to the production of food or other goods. Manual labor, not machinery, continued to turn out the agricultural produce, raw materials, and manufactured goods the Hellenistic world used.

QUICK REVIEW <

How did the Hellenistic city differ from the Hellenic polis?

How did war influence Greece, and how did the arts, religion, and philosophy develop?

How did Alexander the Great's conquests shape society in the Hellenistic period?

How did religion, philosophy, and science develop in the Hellenistic world?

✓ LearningCurve
Check what you know.

135

> How did religion, philosophy, and science develop in the Hellenistic world?

Hellenistic Married Life

This small terra-cotta figurine from Myrina in what is now Turkey, made in the second century B.C.E., shows a newly married couple sitting on a bridal bed. The groom is drawing back the bride's veil, and she is exhibiting the modesty that was a desired quality in young women. Figurines representing every stage of life became popular in the Hellenistic period and were used for religious offerings in temples and sacred places. This one was found in a tomb. (Louvre, Paris, France/Erich Lessing/Art Resource, NY)

The mixing of peoples in the Hellenistic era influenced religion, philosophy, and science. The Hellenistic kings built temples to the old Olympian gods and promoted rituals and ceremonies like those in earlier Greek cities, but new deities also gained prominence. More people turned to mystery religions that blended Greek and non-Greek elements. Others turned to practical philosophies that provided advice on how to live a good life. In the scholarly realm, Hellenistic thinkers made advances in mathematics, astronomy, and mechanical design. Additionally, physicians used observation and dissection to better understand the way the human body works.

Religion in the Hellenistic World

When Hellenistic kings founded cities, they also built temples for the old Olympian gods. In this way they spread Greek religious beliefs throughout the Hellenistic world. Greeks and non-Greeks in the Hellenistic world also honored and

CHAPTER LOCATOR | How did the geography of Greece shape its earliest history? | What was the role of the polis in Greek society?

136 CHAPTER 5
THE GREEK EXPERIENCE

worshipped deities that had not been important in the Hellenic period or that were a blend of imported Greek and indigenous gods and goddesses. Tyche (TIGH-kee), for example, was a new deity, the goddess and personification of luck, fate, chance, and fortune.

Increasingly, many people were attracted to mystery religions, which in the Hellenic period had been linked to specific gods in particular places, so that people who wished to become members had to travel. But new mystery religions, like Hellenistic culture in general, were not tied to a particular place; instead they were spread throughout the Hellenistic world, and temples of the new deities sprang up wherever Greeks lived.

Mystery religions incorporated aspects of both Greek and non-Greek religions and claimed to save their adherents from the worst that fate could do. Most taught that by the rites of initiation, in which the secrets of the religion were shared, devotees became united with a deity who had also died and risen from the dead. The sacrifice of the god and his victory over death saved the devotee from eternal death. Similarly, mystery religions demanded a period of preparation in which the converts strove to become pure and holy, that is, to live by the religion's precepts. Once aspirants had prepared themselves, they went through the initiation, usually a ritual of great emotional intensity symbolizing the entry into a new life.

Among the mystery religions the Egyptian cult of Isis took the Hellenistic world by storm. In Egyptian mythology Isis brought her husband, Osiris, back to life (see page 44), and during the Hellenistic era this power came to be understood by her followers as extending to them as well. She promised to save any mortal who came to her, and her priests asserted that she had bestowed on humanity the gift of civilization and founded law and literature. Isis was understood to be a devoted mother as well as a devoted wife, and she became the goddess of marriage, conception, and childbirth. She became the most important goddess of the Hellenistic world.

Philosophy and Its Guidance for Life

While some people turned to mystery religions to overcome Tyche and provide something permanent in a world that seemed unstable, others turned to philosophy. Several new schools of philosophical thought emerged in the Hellenistic period. One of these was **Epicureanism**, a practical philosophy of serenity in an often-tumultuous world. Epicurus (340–270 B.C.E.) decided that the principal goods of human life were contentment and pleasure, which he defined as the absence of pain, fear, and suffering. By encouraging the pursuit of pleasure, he was not advocating drunken revels or sexual excess, which he thought caused pain, but promoting moderation. Epicurus also taught that individuals could most easily attain peace and serenity by ignoring the outside world and looking instead into their personal feelings. His followers ignored politics because it led to tumult, which would disturb the soul.

Zeno (335–262 B.C.E.), a philosopher from Cyprus, advanced a different concept of human beings and the universe. Zeno first came to Athens to form his own school, the Stoa. His philosophy, **Stoicism** (STOH-uh-sih-zuhm), in turn, came to be named for his school. Zeno and his followers considered nature an expression

Epicureanism
▶ A system of philosophy based on the teachings of Epicurus, who viewed a life of contentment, free from fear and suffering, as the greatest good.

Stoicism
▶ A philosophy, based on the ideas of Zeno, that held that people could only be happy when living in accordance with nature and accepting whatever happened.

| How did war influence Greece, and how did the arts, religion, and philosophy develop? | How did Alexander the Great's conquests shape society in the Hellenistic period? | **How did religion, philosophy, and science develop in the Hellenistic world?** | ✔ LearningCurve Check what you know. |

137

Archimedes, Scientist and Inventor

Archimedes was born in the Greek city of Syracuse in Sicily, an intellectual center in which he pursued scientific interests. He was the most original thinker of his time and a practical inventor. In his book *On Plane Equilibriums*, he dealt for the first time with the basic principles of mathematics, including the principle of the lever. He once said that if he were given a lever and a suitable place to stand, he could move the world. He also demonstrated how easily his compound pulley could move huge weights with little effort:

> A three-masted merchant ship of the royal fleet had been hauled on land by hard work and many hands. Archimedes put aboard her many men and the usual freight. He sat far away from her; and without haste, but gently working a compound pulley with his hand, he drew her towards him smoothly and without faltering, just as though she were running on the surface.*

He likewise invented the Archimedian screw, a pump to bring subterranean water up to irrigate fields, which quickly came into common use. In his treatise *On Floating Bodies*, Archimedes founded the science of hydrostatics. He concluded that an object will float if it weighs less than the water it displaces, and that whenever a solid floats in a liquid, the weight of the solid equals the weight of the liquid displaced. This discovery and his reaction to it has become famous:

> When he was devoting his attention to this problem, he happened to go to a public bath. When he climbed down into the bathtub there, he noticed that water in the tub equal to the bulk of his body flowed out. Thus, when he observed this method of solving the problem, he did not wait. Instead, moved with joy, he sprang out of the tub, and rushing home naked he kept indicating in a loud voice that he had indeed discovered what he was seeking. For while running he was shouting repeatedly in Greek, "Eureka, eureka" ("I have found it, I have found it").†

*Plutarch, *Life of Marcellus*.
†Vitruvius, *On Architecture*, 9 Preface, 10.

Several of Archimedes's treatises were found on a palimpsest, a manuscript that has been scraped and washed so that another text can be written over it, thus reusing the expensive parchment. Reusing parchment was a common practice in the Middle Ages, but the original text can sometimes be reconstructed. Using digital processing with several types of light and X-rays to study this thirteenth-century-C.E. prayer book, scientists were slowly able to decipher the texts by Archimedes that were underneath, including one that had been completely lost. (Image by the Rochester Institute of Technology. Copyright resides with the owner of the Archimedes Palimpsest, but digital images of the entire manuscript can be found at www.archimedespalimpsest.org.)

War between Rome and Syracuse unfortunately interrupted Archimedes's scientific life. In 213 B.C.E., during the Second Punic War, the Romans besieged the city. Hiero, its king and Archimedes's friend, asked the scientist for help in repulsing Roman attacks. Archimedes began to build remarkable devices that served as artillery. One weapon shot missiles to break up infantry attacks. Others threw huge masses of stones that fell on the enemy with incredible speed and noise. They tore gaping holes in the Roman lines and broke up attacks. For use against Roman warships he is said to have designed a machine with beams from which large claws dropped onto the hulls of enemy warships, hoisted them into the air, and dropped them back into the sea. Later Greek authors reported that he destroyed Roman ships with a series of polished mirrors that focused sunlight and caused the ships to catch fire. Modern experiments recreating Archimedes's weapons have found that the claw may have been workable, but the mirrors probably were not, as they required a ship to remain stationary for the fire to ignite. It is not certain whether his war machines were actually effective, but later people recounted tales that the Romans became so fearful that whenever they saw a bit of rope or a stick of timber projecting over one of the walls protecting Syracuse, they shouted, "There it is. Archimedes is trying some engine on us" and fled. After many months the Roman siege was successful, however, and Archimedes was killed by a Roman soldier.

QUESTIONS FOR ANALYSIS

1. How did Archimedes combine theoretical mathematics and practical issues in his work?
2. What applications do you see in the world around you of the devices Archimedes improved or invented, such as the lever, the pulley, and artillery?

ONLINE DOCUMENT PROJECT

What advances in technological warfare occurred during the Hellenistic period? Read accounts of the siege of Syracuse, and then complete a quiz and writing assignment based on the evidence and details from this chapter. *See inside front cover to learn more.*

of divine will; in their view, people could be happy only when living in accordance with nature. They stressed the unity of humans and the universe, stating that all people were obliged to help one another.

The Stoics' most lasting practical achievement was the creation of the concept of natural law. They concluded that as all people were kindred, partook of divine reason, and were in harmony with the universe, one natural law governed them all.

Hellenistic Science and Medicine

Hellenistic thinkers made advances in mathematics, astronomy, and mechanical design. The most notable of the Hellenistic astronomers was Aristarchus of Samos (ca. 310–230 B.C.E.). Aristarchus rightly concluded that the sun is far larger than the earth and that the stars are enormously distant from the earth. He also argued against Aristotle's view that the earth is the center of the universe, instead propounding the heliocentric theory—that the earth and planets revolve around the sun.

In geometry Euclid (YOO-kluhd) (fl. ca. 300 B.C.E.), a mathematician living in Alexandria, compiled a valuable textbook of existing knowledge. His *The Elements of Geometry* became the standard introduction to the subject.

The greatest thinker of the Hellenistic period was Archimedes (ahr-kuh-MEE-deez) (ca. 287–212 B.C.E.). A clever inventor, he devised new artillery for military purposes. In peacetime he created the water screw to draw water from a lower to a higher level. (See "Individuals in Society: Archimedes, Scientist and Inventor," page 138.) He also invented the compound pulley to lift heavy weights. His chief interest, however, lay in pure mathematics. He founded the science of hydrostatics (the study of fluids at rest) and discovered the principle that the weight of a solid floating in a liquid is equal to the weight of the liquid displaced by the solid.

Eratosthenes (ehr-uh-TOSS-thuh-neez) (285–ca. 204 B.C.E.), who was the librarian of the vast Ptolemaic royal library in Alexandria, used mathematics to further the geographical studies for which he is most famous. He concluded that the earth is a spherical globe and calculated the circumference of the earth geometrically with remarkable accuracy.

As the new artillery devised by Archimedes indicates, Hellenistic science was used for purposes of war as well as peace. Theories of mechanics were applied to build military machines. The catapult became the most widely used artillery piece. As the Assyrians had earlier, engineers built siege towers, large wooden structures that served as artillery platforms, and put them on wheels so that soldiers could roll them up to a town's walls. Generals added battering rams to bring down large portions of walls. If these new engines made warfare more efficient, they also added to the misery of the people, as war often directly involved the populations of cities. War and illness fed the need for medical advances, and doctors as well as scientists combined observation with theory during the Hellenistic period. Herophilus, who lived in the first half of the third century B.C.E., worked in Alexandria and studied the writings attributed to Hippocrates. He approached the study of medicine in a systematic, scientific fashion: he dissected dead bodies and measured what he observed. His students carried on his work, searching for the causes and nature of illness and pain.

> **QUICK REVIEW**

What connections can you make between political turmoil and cultural trends during the Hellenistic period?

CHAPTER SUMMARY

Greece's mountainous terrain encouraged the development of small, independent communities and political fragmentation. Sometime after 2000 B.C.E. two kingdoms—the Minoan on Crete and the Mycenaean on the mainland—did emerge, but these remained smaller than the great empires of Mesopotamia, India, and China. The fall of these kingdoms led to a period of disruption and decline known as the Greek Dark Age (ca. 1100–800 B.C.E.). However, Greek culture survived, and Greeks developed the independent city-state, known as the polis. Greeks also established colonies and traveled and traded as far east as the Black Sea and as far west as the Atlantic Ocean. Two poleis became especially powerful: Sparta, which created a military state in which men remained in the army most of their lives, and Athens, which created a democracy in which male citizens had a direct voice. In the classical period, between 500 B.C.E. and 338 B.C.E., Greeks engaged in war with the Persians and with one another, but they also created drama, philosophy, and magnificent art and architecture.

In the middle of the fourth century B.C.E. the Greek city-states were conquered by the Macedonians under King Philip II and his son Alexander. Alexander conquered the entire Persian Empire and founded new cities in which Greek and local populations mixed. His successors continued to build cities and colonies, which were centers of trade and spread Greek culture over a broad area, extend-

CHAPTER LOCATOR | How did the geography of Greece shape its earliest history? | What was the role of the polis in Greek society?

CHAPTER 5
140 THE GREEK EXPERIENCE

ing as far east as India. The mixing of peoples in the Hellenistic era influenced religion, philosophy, and science. New deities gained prominence, and many people turned to mystery religions that blended Greek and non-Greek elements as they offered followers secret knowledge and eternal life. Others turned to practical philosophies that provided advice on how to live a good life. Advances were made in technology, mathematics, science, and medicine, but these were applied primarily to military purposes, not to improving the way ordinary people lived and worked.

 **CONNECTIONS** The Greek world was largely conquered by the Romans, as you will learn in the following chapter, and the various Hellenistic monarchies became part of the Roman Empire. In cultural terms the lines of conquest were reversed: the Romans derived their alphabet from the Greek alphabet, though they changed the letters somewhat. Roman statuary was modeled on Greek and was often, in fact, made by Greek sculptors, who found ready customers among wealthy Romans. Furthermore, the major Roman gods and goddesses were largely the same as Greek ones, though they had different names. Although the Romans did not seem to have been particularly interested in the speculative philosophy of Socrates and Plato, they were drawn to the more practical philosophies of the Epicureans and Stoics. And like the Hellenistic Greeks, many Romans turned to mystery religions that offered secret knowledge and promised eternal life.

The influence of the ancient Greeks was not limited to the Romans, of course. As discussed in Chapter 3, art and thought in northern India was shaped by the blending of Greek and Buddhist traditions. And as you will see in Chapter 15, European thinkers and writers made conscious attempts to return to classical ideals in art, literature, and philosophy during the Renaissance. In America political leaders from the Revolutionary era on decided that important government buildings should be modeled on the Parthenon or other temples. In some ways, capitol buildings in the United States are good symbols of the legacy of Greece—gleaming ideals of harmony, freedom, democracy, and beauty that (as with all ideals) do not always correspond with realities.

ONLINE DOCUMENT PROJECT
Technological Warfare

What advances in technological warfare occurred during the Hellenistic period?

Read accounts of the siege of Syracuse, and then complete a quiz and writing assignment based on the evidence and details from this chapter. *See inside front cover to learn more.*

How did war influence Greece, and how did the arts, religion, and philosophy develop?	How did Alexander the Great's conquests shape society in the Hellenistic period?	How did religion, philosophy, and science develop in the Hellenistic world?	✓ LearningCurve Check what you know.

CHAPTER 5 STUDY GUIDE

STEP 1

GET STARTED ONLINE

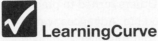

LearningCurve

Now that you've read the chapter, make it stick by completing the LearningCurve activity.

STEP 2

EXPLAIN WHY IT MATTERS

Put your reading into practice. Identify each term below, and then explain why it matters in world history.

TERM	WHO OR WHAT & WHEN	WHY IT MATTERS
polis (p. 120)		
hoplites (p. 121)		
democracy (p. 121)		
oligarchy (p. 121)		
mystery religions (p. 128)		
Platonic ideals (p. 129)		
Hellenistic (p. 131)		
Hellenization (p. 133)		
Epicureanism (p. 137)		
Stoicism (p. 137)		

STEP 3

MOVE BEYOND THE BASICS

To demonstrate a more advanced understanding of Greek identity in the Hellenic and Hellenistic worlds, fill in the chart below with descriptions of key aspects of Hellenic Greece and the Hellenistic world. How did the Greek sense of identity change after Alexander's conquests?

	Government	Economy	Religion and Philosophy	Cultural Diversity and Exchange
Hellenic Greece				
The Hellenistic World				

6

THE WORLD OF ROME

CA. 1000 B.C.E.–400 C.E.

> **How did the Romans build and control an empire that spanned the Mediterranean world?**

Chapter 6 examines the Roman Empire. With a republican government under the leadership of the Senate, the Romans conquered Italy, then the western Mediterranean basin, and then areas in the East that had been part of Alexander the Great's empire. The wars of conquest led, however, to serious problems that the Senate proved unable to handle. After a period of civil war that ended in 31 B.C.E., the emperor Augustus restored peace and expanded Roman power and law as far east as the Euphrates River. Later emperors extended Roman authority farther still, so that at its largest the Roman Empire stretched from England to Egypt and from Portugal to Persia.

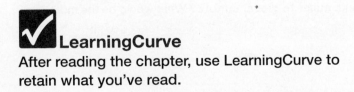 **LearningCurve**

After reading the chapter, use LearningCurve to retain what you've read.

STEP 4 **PUT IT ALL TOGETHER** Now, take a step back and try to explain the big picture. Remember to use specific examples from the chapter in your answers.

THE ORIGINS AND EARLY DEVELOPMENT OF HELLENIC GREECE

▶ How did the polis embody key aspects of Greek society and culture? Is it fair to say that, in a sense, the polis was the essence of Greek civilization? Why or why not?

▶ Compare and contrast Sparta and Athens. To what extent do these two city-states represent different solutions to the same basic challenges?

THE CLASSICAL PERIOD

▶ What were the causes and consequences of the Peloponnesian War?

▶ How was Athens's emergence as an imperial power reflected in Athenian thought and culture?

THE HELLENISTIC WORLD

▶ Why did Alexander's empire split apart shortly after his death? What impact did this political fragmentation have on the development of the Hellenistic world?

▶ What characterized the relationship between Greeks and Easterners in the Hellenistic period? To what extent were Easterners "Hellenized"?

LOOKING BACK, LOOKING AHEAD

▶ Classical Greece was a period of almost constant warfare. With this in mind, compare and contrast classical Greece with earlier periods of endemic warfare in the Near East. What factors seem to have been conducive to peace in the ancient world? What conditions tended to produce war?

▶ How would you explain the enduring influence of Greek ideas and ideals? What examples of the continuing influence of Greek culture can you identify in the contemporary world?

> **IN YOUR OWN WORDS**

Imagine that you must give an oral report to the class answering the following question: **What unique contributions did the Greeks make to global culture?** What would be the most important points and why?

753 B.C.E.
Traditional founding of the city of Rome

509 B.C.E.
Traditional date of the establishment of the Roman Republic

451–449 B.C.E.
Laws of the Twelve Tables written and issued

ca. 265 B.C.E.
Romans control most of Italy

264–241 B.C.E.; 218–201 B.C.E.; 149–146 B.C.E.
Punic Wars

53–31 B.C.E.
Civil wars among rival claimants to power

44 B.C.E.
Assassination of Julius Caesar

31 B.C.E.
Octavian (Augustus) defeats Antony and Cleopatra

27 B.C.E.
Senate grants Octavian the title "Augustus"; date marks the beginning of the Roman Empire

27 B.C.E.–68 C.E.
Julio-Claudian emperors; expansion into northern and western Europe

ca. 3 B.C.E.–29 C.E.
Life of Jesus

69–96 C.E.
Flavian emperors; restoration of order after civil wars

96–192 C.E.
Antonine emperors; prosperity and the height of the pax Romana

235–284 C.E.
Third-century crisis; civil war; invasions; economic decline

284–337 C.E.
Diocletian and Constantine attempt to reconstruct the empire

313 C.E.
Emperor Constantine issues Edict of Milan, allowing practice of all religions in the Roman Empire

380 C.E.
Emperor Theodosius makes Christianity the official religion of the empire

476 C.E.
Odoacer deposes the last Roman emperor in the West

The Etruscans

The culture that is now called Etruscan developed in north-central Italy about 800 B.C.E. The Etruscans most likely originated in Turkey or elsewhere in southwest Asia, although when they migrated to Italy is not clear. The Etruscans spoke a language that was very different from Greek and Latin, but they adopted the Greek alphabet to write their language.

The Etruscans established permanent settlements that evolved into cities resembling the Greek city-states (see page 120). They spread their influence over the surrounding countryside, which they farmed and mined for its rich mineral resources. From an early period the Etruscans began to trade natural products, especially iron, with their Greek neighbors to the south and with other peoples throughout the Mediterranean in exchange for luxury goods. Etruscan cities appear to have been organized in leagues, and beginning about 750 B.C.E. the Etruscans expanded southward into central Italy through military actions and through the establishment of colony cities. In the process they encountered a small collection of villages subsequently called Rome.

The Etruscans, ca. 500 B.C.E.

| What was life like in Rome, and what was it like in the provinces? | What was Christianity, and how did it affect life in the Roman Empire? | How did emperors respond to political and religious issues? | ✓ LearningCurve Check what you know. |

The Founding of Rome

Archaeological evidence indicates that the ancestors of the Romans began to settle on the hills east of the Tiber during the early Iron Age, around 1000 B.C.E. to 800 B.C.E. Later Romans told a number of stories about the founding of Rome. These mix legend and history, but they illustrate the traditional ethics, morals, and ideals of Rome.

According to legend, Romulus and Remus founded the city of Rome, an event later Roman authors dated precisely to 753 B.C.E. These twin brothers were the sons of the war god Mars, and their mother, Rhea Silvia, was a descendant of Aeneas, a brave and pious Trojan who left Troy after it was destroyed by the Greeks in the Trojan War. The brothers, who were left to die by a jealous uncle, were raised by a female wolf. When they were grown they decided to build a city, but quarreled over its location; Romulus killed Remus and named the city after himself. He also established a council of advisers later called the **Senate**. He and his mostly male followers expanded their power over neighboring peoples, in part by abducting and marrying their women. The women then arranged a peace by throwing themselves between their brothers and their husbands, convincing them that killing kin would make the men cursed. The Romans, favored by the gods, continued their rise to power. This founding myth ascribes positive traits to the Romans: they are descended from gods and heroes, can thrive in wild and tough settings, will defend their boundaries at all costs, and mix with other peoples rather than simply conquering them. Also, the story portrays women who were ancestors of Rome as virtuous and brave.

Later Roman historians continued the story by describing a series of kings after Romulus, each elected by the Senate. According to tradition, the last three kings were Etruscan, and another tale about female virtue was told to explain why the Etruscan kings were overthrown. In this story, the son of King Tarquin, the Etruscan king who ruled Rome, raped Lucretia, a virtuous Roman wife, in her own home. She demanded that her husband and father seek vengeance and then committed suicide in front of them. Her father and husband and the other Roman nobles swore to avenge Lucretia's death by throwing out the Etruscan kings, and they did. The Romans generally accepted this story as historical fact and dated the expulsion of the Etruscan kings to 509 B.C.E. They thus saw this year as marking the end of the monarchical period and the dawn of the republic, which had come about because of a wronged woman and her demands.

Most historians today view the idea that Etruscan kings ruled the city of Rome as legendary, but they stress the influence of the Etruscans on Rome. The Etruscans transformed Rome into a real city with walls, temples, a drainage system, and other urban structures. The Romans adopted the Etruscan alphabet, which the Etruscans themselves had adopted from the Greeks. Even the toga came from the Etruscans, as did gladiatorial combat honoring the dead. In engineering and architecture the Romans adopted some design elements and the basic plan of their temples, along with paved roads, from the Etruscans.

In this early period the city of Rome does appear to have been ruled by kings. A hereditary aristocracy also developed which advised the kings and may have played a role in choosing them. And sometime in the sixth century B.C.E. a group of aristocrats revolted against these kings and established a government in which the main institution of power would be the Senate, an assembly of aristocrats, rather than a single monarch. Executive power was in the hands of leaders called

Senate

▶ The assembly that was the main institution of power in the Roman Republic, originally composed only of aristocrats.

CHAPTER LOCATOR | How did the Romans dominate Italy, and what political institutions did they create? | How did Rome expand its power beyond Italy, and what were the effects of this expansion?

148 CHAPTER 6 THE WORLD OF ROME

consuls, but there were always two of them and they were elected for one-year terms only, not for life. Rome thereby became a republic, not a monarchy.

The Roman Conquest of Italy

In the years following the establishment of the republic, the Romans fought numerous wars with their neighbors on the Italian peninsula. The Roman army was made up primarily of citizens of Rome, who were organized for military campaigns into legions. War also involved diplomacy, at which the Romans became masters.

In 387 B.C.E. the Romans suffered a major setback when the Celts—or Gauls, as the Romans called them—invaded the Italian peninsula from the north and sacked the city of Rome. The Celts agreed to abandon Rome in return for a thousand pounds of gold. In the century that followed, the Romans rebuilt their city and recouped their losses. They brought Latium and their Latin allies fully under their control and conquered Etruria. In a series of bitter wars the Romans also subdued southern Italy and then turned north. Their superior military institutions, organization, and manpower allowed them to conquer or bring under their influence most of Italy by about 265 B.C.E. (Map 6.1).

As they expanded their territory, the Romans spread their religious traditions throughout Italy, blending them with local beliefs and practices. Religion for the Romans was largely a matter of honoring the state and the family. The main goal of religion was to secure the peace of the gods and to harness divine power for public and private enterprises. Religious rituals were an important way of expressing common values, which for Romans meant those evident in their foundation myths: bravery, morality, seriousness, family, and home. Victorious generals made sure to honor the gods of people they had conquered and by doing so transformed them into gods they could also call on for assistance in their future campaigns. As the Romans conquered the cities of Magna Graecia, the Greek deities were absorbed into the Roman pantheon.

Once they had conquered an area, the Romans did what the Persians had earlier done to help cement their new territory: they built roads. Roman roads facilitated the flow of communication, trade, and armies from the capital to outlying areas.

In politics the Romans shared full Roman citizenship with many of their oldest allies, particularly the inhabitants of the cities of Latium. In other instances they granted citizenship without the franchise, that is, without the right to vote or hold Roman office. These allies were subject to Roman taxes and calls for military service but ran their own local affairs.

The Roman State

Along with citizenship, the republican government was another important institution of Roman political life. In the early republic, social divisions determined the shape of politics. Political power was in the hands of a hereditary aristocracy—the **patricians**, whose privileged legal status was determined by their birth as members of certain families. The common people of Rome, the **plebeians** (plih-BEE-uhns), were free citizens with a voice in politics, but they had few of the patricians' political and social advantages. While some plebeian merchants rivaled the patricians in wealth, most plebeians were poor artisans, small farmers, and landless urban dwellers.

consuls
▶ Primary executives in the Roman Republic, elected for one-year terms, who commanded the army in battle, administered state business, and supervised financial affairs.

patricians
▶ The Roman hereditary aristocracy, who held most of the political power in the republic.

plebeians
▶ The common people of Rome, who were free but had few of the patricians' advantages.

What was life like in Rome, and what was it like in the provinces?

What was Christianity, and how did it affect life in the Roman Empire?

How did emperors respond to political and religious issues?

☑ LearningCurve
Check what you know.

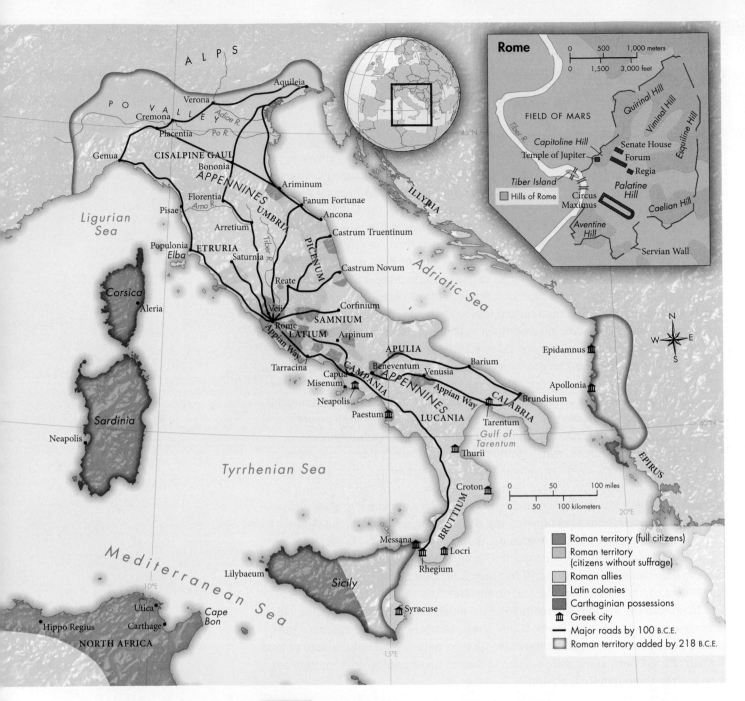

MAP 6.1 ■ **Roman Italy and the City of Rome, ca. 218 B.C.E.**

As Rome expanded, it built roads linking major cities and offered various degrees of citizenship to the territories it conquered or with which it made alliances. The territories outlined in green that are separate from the Italian peninsula were added by 218 B.C.E., largely as a result of the Punic Wars.

The Romans created several assemblies through which men elected high officials and passed ordinances. The most important of these was the Senate. During the republic, the Senate advised the consuls and other officials about military and political matters and handled government finances. Because the Senate sat year after year with the same members, while the consuls changed annually, it provided stability, and its advice came to have the force of law. Another responsibility of the Senate was to handle relations between Rome and other powers.

CHAPTER LOCATOR | **How did the Romans dominate Italy, and what political institutions did they create?** | How did Rome expand its power beyond Italy, and what were the effects of this expansion?

The highest officials of the republic were the two consuls, positions initially open only to patrician men. The consuls commanded the army in battle, administered state business, and supervised financial affairs. When the consuls were away from Rome, praetors (PREE-tuhrz) could act in their place. After the age of overseas conquests (see below), the Romans divided their lands in the Mediterranean into provinces governed by ex-consuls and ex-praetors.

A lasting achievement of the Romans was their development of law. Roman civil law, the *ius civile*, consisted of statutes, customs, and forms of procedure that regulated the lives of citizens. As the Romans came into more frequent contact with foreigners, the praetors applied a broader *ius gentium*, the "law of the peoples," to such matters as peace treaties, the treatment of prisoners of war, and the exchange of diplomats. In the ius gentium, all sides were to be treated the same regardless of their nationality. By the late republic, Roman jurists had widened this still further into the concept of *ius naturale*, "natural law" based in part on Stoic beliefs (see page 137). Natural law, according to these thinkers, is made up of rules that govern human behavior that come from applying reason rather than customs or traditions, and so apply to all societies.

Social Conflict in Rome

Inequality between plebeians and patricians led to a conflict known as the Struggle of the Orders. In this conflict the plebeians sought to increase their power by taking advantage of the fact that Rome's survival depended on its army, which needed plebeians to fill the ranks of the infantry. According to tradition, in 494 B.C.E. the plebeians literally walked out of Rome and refused to serve in the army. Their general strike worked, and the patricians made important concessions. They allowed the plebeians to elect their own officials, the tribunes, who could bring plebeian grievances to the Senate for resolution and could also veto the decisions of the consuls.

The law itself was the plebeians' primary target. Only the patricians knew what the law was, and only they could argue cases in court. All too often they used the law for their own benefit. The plebeians wanted the law codified and published. After much struggle, in 449 B.C.E. the patricians surrendered their legal monopoly and codified and published the Laws of the Twelve Tables. The patricians also made legal procedures public so that plebeians could argue cases in court. Several years later the patricians passed a law that for the first time allowed patricians and plebeians to marry one another.

After a ten-year battle, the Licinian-Sextian laws passed in 367 B.C.E. gave wealthy plebeians access to all the offices of Rome, including the right to hold one of the two consulships. Once plebeians could hold the consulship, they could also sit in the Senate and advise on policy. Though decisive, this victory did not automatically end the Struggle of the Orders. That happened only in 287 B.C.E. with the passage of the *lex Hortensia*, which gave the resolutions of the *concilium plebis*, the plebeian assembly, the force of law for patricians and plebeians alike.

QUICK REVIEW <

How did social tensions and conflict shape early Roman government?

What was life like in Rome, and what was it like in the provinces?

What was Christianity, and how did it affect life in the Roman Empire?

How did emperors respond to political and religious issues?

LearningCurve
Check what you know.

How did Rome expand its power beyond Italy, and what were the effects of this expansion?

Two Triremes Race

In this fresco painting from the temple of Isis in Pompeii, two triremes — narrow warships powered by several banks of long oars — race in what was most likely a festival celebrating the goddess. Greeks, Carthaginians, and Romans all used triremes, which had bronze front pieces designed to smash into enemy ships. The one hundred to two hundred oarsmen had to row in time to achieve the necessary speed, which took long practice, so this religious celebration also served a military purpose. (© Ministero per i Beni le Attivita Culturali — Soprintendenza archeologia de Napoli/Scala/Art Resource, NY)

As the republican government was developing, Roman territory continued to expand. The Romans conquered lands all around the Mediterranean, bringing them unheard-of power and wealth. As a result, many Romans became more cosmopolitan and comfortable, and they were especially influenced by the culture of one conquered land: Greece. Yet social unrest also came in the wake of the wars, opening unprecedented opportunities for ambitious generals who wanted to rule Rome like an empire. A series of civil wars ensued, wars which republican government did not survive.

Overseas Conquests and the Punic Wars, 264–133 B.C.E.

The Romans did not map out grandiose strategies to conquer the world. Rather they responded to situations as they arose. This meant that they sought to eliminate any state they saw as a military threat.

Their presence in southern Italy brought the Romans to the island of Sicily, where they confronted another great power in the western Mediterranean, Carthage (CAHR-thij). The city of Carthage had been founded by Phoenicians as a trading colony in the eighth century B.C.E. (see page 50). By the fourth century

CHAPTER LOCATOR | How did the Romans dominate Italy, and what political institutions did they create? | **How did Rome expand its power beyond Italy, and what were the effects of this expansion?**

CHAPTER 6
152 THE WORLD OF ROME

B.C.E. the Carthaginians began to expand their holdings. At the end of a long string of wars, the Carthaginians had created a mercantile empire that stretched from western Sicily to beyond Gibraltar.

The conflicting ambitions of the Romans and Carthaginians led to the first of the three **Punic Wars**. During the course of the first war, which lasted from 264 B.C.E. to 241 B.C.E., Rome built a navy and defeated Carthage in a series of sea battles. Sicily became Rome's first province, but despite a peace treaty, the conflict was not over.

Carthaginian armies moved into Spain, where Rome was also claiming territory. The brilliant Carthaginian general Hannibal (ca. 247–183 B.C.E.) marched an army of tens of thousands of troops from Spain across what is now France and over the Alps into Italy, beginning the Second Punic (PYOO-nik) War (218–201 B.C.E.). Hannibal won three major victories, including a devastating blow at Cannae in southeastern Italy in 216 B.C.E. He then spread devastation throughout Italy. Yet Hannibal was not able to win areas near Rome in central Italy.

Punic Wars

▶ A series of three wars between Rome and Carthage in which Rome emerged the victor.

The Roman general Scipio Africanus (ca. 236–ca. 183 B.C.E.) took Spain from the Carthaginians and then struck directly at Carthage itself, prompting the Carthaginians to recall Hannibal from Italy to defend the homeland. In 202 B.C.E., near the town of Zama, Scipio defeated Hannibal in one of the world's truly decisive battles. Scipio's victory meant that the world of the western Mediterranean would henceforth be Roman.

The Second Punic War contained the seeds of still other wars. Unabated fear of Carthage led to the Third Punic War (149–146 B.C.E.), a needless, unjust, and savage conflict that ended with obliteration of the city of Carthage itself.

The Carthaginian Empire and the Roman Republic, 264 B.C.E.

After the Second Punic War, the Romans turned east. Roman victory in Macedonia turned Antigonid Macedonia into a Roman province. Then they moved farther east and defeated the Seleucid monarchy. In 133 B.C.E. the king of Pergamum in Asia Minor willed his kingdom to Rome when he died. The Ptolemies of Egypt retained formal control of their kingdom, but they obeyed Roman wishes in terms of trade policy. Declaring the Mediterranean *mare nostrum*, "our sea," the Romans began to create a political and administrative machinery to hold the Mediterranean together under a system of provinces ruled by governors sent from Rome.

New Influences and Old Values in Roman Culture

With the conquest of the Mediterranean world, Rome became a great city. The spoils of war went to build theaters, stadiums, and other places of amusement, and Romans and Italian townspeople began to spend more of their time in leisure pursuits. This new urban culture reflected Hellenistic influences. Romans developed a liking for Greek literature and art, and it became common for an educated Roman to speak both Latin and Greek.

| What was life like in Rome, and what was it like in the provinces? | What was Christianity, and how did it affect life in the Roman Empire? | How did emperors respond to political and religious issues? | ✔️ **LearningCurve** Check what you know. |

The Greek custom of bathing also gained popularity in the Roman world. Increasingly, Romans built large public buildings containing pools supplied by intricate systems of aqueducts. These structures were more than just places to bathe. Baths included gymnasia where men exercised, snack bars and halls where people chatted and read, and even libraries and lecture halls. Women had opportunities to bathe, generally in separate facilities or at separate times, and both women and men went to the baths to see and be seen.

New customs did not change the core Roman social structures. The male head of the household was called the **paterfamilias**, and he had great power over his children. Fathers had the power to decide how family resources should be spent, and sons did not inherit until after their fathers had died. Women could inherit and own property, though they generally received a smaller portion of any family inheritance than their brothers. Very young children were under their mother's care, and most children learned the skills they needed from their own parents. For children from wealthier urban families, opportunities for formal education increased in the late republic. Boys and girls might be educated in their homes by tutors, and boys also might go to a school, paid for by their parents.

An influx of slaves from Rome's conquests provided labor for the fields, mines, and cities. To the Romans slavery was a misfortune that befell some people, but it did not entail any racial theories. For loyal slaves the Romans always held out the possibility of freedom, and manumission—the freeing of individual slaves by their masters—became common. Nonetheless, slaves rebelled from time to time in large-scale revolts put down by Roman armies.

Membership in a family did not end with death, as the spirits of the family's ancestors were understood to remain with the family. They and other gods regarded as protectors of the household were represented by small statues that stood in a special cupboard, were honored at family celebrations, and were taken with the family when they moved.

paterfamilias

▶ The oldest dominant male of the family, who held great power over the lives of family members.

The Late Republic and the Rise of Augustus, 133–27 B.C.E.

The wars of conquest eventually created serious political problems for the Romans. When the soldiers returned home, they found their farms practically in ruins. Many were forced to sell their land to ready buyers who had grown rich from the wars. These wealthy men created huge estates called latifundia. Now landless, veterans moved to the cities, especially Rome, but could not find work. These developments not only created unrest in the city but also threatened Rome's army by reducing its ranks, because landless men, even if they were Romans and lived in Rome, were forbidden to serve in the Roman army. The landless veterans found a leader in Tiberius Gracchus (163–133 B.C.E.), an aristocrat who was appalled by the situation. He proposed dividing public land among the poor. But a group of wealthy senators murdered him, launching a long era of political violence that would destroy the republic. Still, Tiberius's brother Gaius Gracchus (153–121 B.C.E.) passed a law providing the urban poor with cheap grain and urged practical reforms. Once again senators tried to stem the tide of reform by murdering him.

The next reformer, Gaius Marius (ca. 157–86 B.C.E.), recruited landless men into the army to put down a rebel king in Africa. He promised them land for their service. But after his victory, the Senate refused to honor his promise. From then

CHAPTER LOCATOR | How did the Romans dominate Italy, and what political institutions did they create?

How did Rome expand its power beyond Italy, and what were the effects of this expansion?

154 CHAPTER 6 THE WORLD OF ROME

on, Roman soldiers looked to their commanders, not to the Senate or the state, to protect their interests. Rome was also dividing into two political factions, both of which wanted political power. Both factions named individuals as supreme military commander and each led Roman troops against an external enemy but also against each other. One of these generals, Sulla, gained power in Rome, and in 81 B.C.E. the Senate made him dictator, an official office in the Roman Republic given to a man who was granted absolute power temporarily to handle emergencies such as war. Dictators were supposed to step down after six months, but Sulla held this position for nine years, and after that it was too late to restore the republican constitution.

The history of the late republic is the story of power struggles among many famous Roman figures against a background of unrest at home and military campaigns abroad. Pompey (PAHM-pee) used military victories in Spain to force the Senate to allow him to run for consul. In 59 B.C.E. he was joined in a political alliance called the First Triumvirate by Crassus, another ambitious politician and the wealthiest man in Rome, and by Julius Caesar (100–44 B.C.E.). Recognizing that military success led to power, Caesar led his troops to victory in Spain and Gaul, modern France. The First Triumvirate fell apart after Crassus was killed in battle in 53 B.C.E. while trying to conquer Parthia, leaving Caesar and Pompey in competition with each other for power. The result was civil war. The Ptolemaic rulers of Egypt became mixed up in this war, particularly Cleopatra VII, who allied herself with Caesar and had a son by him. (See "Individuals in Society: Queen Cleopatra," page 156.) Caesar emerged victorious, and he began to make a number of legal and economic reforms, acting on his own authority, though often with the approval of the Senate, which he packed with his supporters. He issued laws about debt, the collection of taxes, and the distribution of grain and land. Roman allies in Italy were to have full citizenship. He founded new colonies, which were to be populated by veterans and the poor.

Caesar was wildly popular with most people in Rome, but some senators opposed his rise to what was becoming absolute power. In 44 B.C.E. a group of conspirators assassinated him and set off another round of civil war. His grandnephew, the eighteen-year-old Octavian (63 B.C.E.–14 C.E.), joined with two of Caesar's followers, Marc Antony and Lepidus, in the Second Triumvirate. After defeating Caesar's murderers, they had a falling-out. Octavian forced Lepidus out of office and waged war against Antony, who had now also become allied with Cleopatra. In 31 B.C.E. Octavian defeated the combined forces of Antony and Cleopatra at the Battle of Actium in Greece. His victory ended the age of civil war.

The Successes of Augustus

After Augustus ended the civil wars, he faced the monumental problems of reconstruction. He had to rebuild effective government, pay his army for its services, care for the welfare of the provinces, and address the danger of various groups on Rome's frontiers. Augustus was highly successful in meeting these challenges.

Augustus claimed that he was restoring the republic, but he was actually transforming the government into one in which all power was held by a single ruler. Augustus fit his own position into the republican constitution not by creating a new office for himself but by gradually taking over many of the offices that traditionally had been held by separate people.

Augustus as Imperator

In this marble statue, found in the villa of Augustus's widow, Augustus is dressed in a military uniform and in a pose usually used to show leaders addressing their troops. This emphasizes his role as imperator, the head of the army. The figures on his breastplate show various peoples the Romans had defeated or with whom they had made treaties, along with assorted deities. Although Augustus did not declare himself a god — as later Roman emperors would — this statue shows him barefoot, just as gods and heroes were in classical Greek statuary, and accompanied by Cupid riding a dolphin, both symbols of the goddess Venus, whom he claimed as an ancestor. (Scala/Art Resource, NY)

| What was life like in Rome, and what was it like in the provinces? | What was Christianity, and how did it affect life in the Roman Empire? | How did emperors respond to political and religious issues? |  LearningCurve Check what you know. |

Cleopatra VII (69–30 B.C.E.) was a Ptolemy, a member of the dynasty of Hellenistic rulers of Egypt who had established power in the third century B.C.E. Although she was a Greek, she was passionately devoted to her Egyptian subjects and was the first in her dynasty who could speak Egyptian as well as Greek. Just as ancient pharaohs had linked themselves with the gods, she had herself portrayed as the goddess Isis and may have seen herself as a reincarnation of Isis (see page 44).

At the same time that civil war was raging in the late Roman Republic, Cleopatra and her brother Ptolemy XIII were in a dispute over who would be supreme ruler in Egypt. Julius Caesar captured the Egyptian capital of Alexandria, Cleopatra arranged to meet him, and the two became lovers, although Cleopatra was much younger and Caesar was married. The two apparently had a son, Caesarion, and Caesar's army defeated Ptolemy's army, ending the power struggle. In 46 B.C.E. Cleopatra arrived in Rome, where Caesar put up a statue of her as Isis in one of the city's temples. The Romans hated her because they saw her as a decadent Eastern queen and a threat to what were considered traditional Roman values.

After Caesar's assassination, Cleopatra returned to Alexandria. There she became involved in the continuing Roman civil war that now pitted Octavian, Caesar's heir, against Marc Antony, who commanded the Roman army in the East. When Antony visited Alexandria in 41 B.C.E. he met Cleopatra, and though he was already married to Octavian's sister, he became her lover. He abandoned (and later divorced) his Roman wife, married Cleopatra in 37 B.C.E., and changed his will to favor his children by Cleopatra. Antony's wedding present to Cleopatra was a huge grant of territory, much of it Roman, that greatly increased her power and that of all her children, including Caesarion. Antony also declared Caesarion to be Julius Caesar's rightful heir.

Octavian used the wedding gift as the reason to declare Antony a traitor. He and other Roman leaders described Antony as a romantic fool captivated by the seductive Cleopatra. Roman troops turned against Antony and joined with Octavian, and at the Battle of Actium in 31 B.C.E. Octavian defeated the army and navy of Antony and Cleopatra. Antony committed suicide, as did Cleopatra shortly afterward. Octavian ordered the teenage Caesarion killed, but the young children of Antony and Cleopatra were allowed to go back to Rome, where they were raised by Antony's widow. In another consequence of Octavian's victory, Egypt became a Roman province.

Roman sources are viciously hostile to Cleopatra, and she became the model of the alluring woman

The only portraits of Cleopatra that date from her own lifetime are on the coins that she issued. This one, made at the mint of Alexandria, shows her as quite plain, reinforcing the point made by Cicero that her attractiveness was based more on intelligence and wit than physical beauty. The reverse of the coin shows an eagle, a symbol of rule. (© The Trustees of the British Museum/Art Resource, NY)

whose sexual attraction led men to their doom. Stories about her beauty, sophistication, lavish spending, desire for power, and ruthlessness abounded and were retold for centuries. The most dramatic story was that she committed suicide through the bite of a poisonous snake, which may have been true and which has been the subject of countless paintings. Her tumultuous relationships with Caesar and Antony have been portrayed in plays, novels, movies, and television programs.

QUESTIONS FOR ANALYSIS

1. How did Cleopatra benefit from her relationships with Caesar and Antony? How did they benefit from their relationships with her?
2. How did ideas about gender and Roman suspicion of the more sophisticated Greek culture combine to shape Cleopatra's fate and the way she is remembered?
3. "Individuals in Society: Hatshepsut and Nefertiti" in Chapter 2 (see page 49) also focuses on leading female figures in Egypt, but these two women lived more than a thousand years before Cleopatra. How would you compare their situation with hers?

ᑊᒧ LaunchPad

ONLINE DOCUMENT PROJECT

What do Roman depictions of Cleopatra reveal about the attitudes and values of her time? Explore Roman accounts of Cleopatra to see what light they shed on political, social, and cultural values in the late republic and early empire, and then complete a quiz and writing assignment based on the evidence and details from this chapter. *See inside front cover to learn more.*

The Senate named him often as both consul and tribune. He was also named imperator (ihm-puh-RAH-tuhr), a title given to victorious commanders, and held control of the army, which he made a permanent standing organization. Furthermore, recognizing the importance of religion, he had himself named *pontifex maximus*, or chief priest. The Senate also gave him the honorary title *princeps civitatis*, "first citizen of the state."

Considering what had happened to Julius Caesar, Augustus wisely wielded all this power in the background, and his period of rule is officially called the "principate." The Senate continued to exist as a court of law and deliberative body. Without specifically saying so, however, Augustus created the office of emperor. In other reforms, Augustus made provincial administration more orderly and improved its functioning. He further professionalized the army and awarded grants of land in the frontier provinces to veterans. He encouraged local self-government and the development of cities. As a spiritual bond between the provinces and Rome, Augustus encouraged the cult of *Roma et Augustus* (Rome and Augustus) as the guardian of the state. In addition, he had temples, stadiums, marketplaces, and public buildings constructed in Rome and other cities.

In the social realm, Augustus promoted marriage and childbearing through legal changes that released free women and freedwomen (female slaves who had been freed) from male guardianship if they had given birth to a certain number of

Ara Pacis

In the middle years of Augustus's reign, the Roman Senate ordered a huge altar, the Ara Pacis, built to honor him and the peace he had brought to the empire. This was decorated with life-size reliefs of Augustus and members of his family, prominent Romans, and other people and deities. One side, shown here, depicts a goddess figure, most likely the goddess Peace herself, with twin babies on her lap, flanked by nymphs representing land and sea, and surrounded by plants and animals. (Scala/Art Resource, NY)

> PICTURING THE PAST

ANALYZING THE IMAGE: What do the elements depicted here most likely symbolize?

CONNECTIONS: The Ara Pacis was a work of public art designed to commemorate the deeds of Augustus. Why might the Senate have commissioned such a work? Can you think of contemporary parallels?

What was life like in Rome, and what was it like in the provinces?

What was Christianity, and how did it affect life in the Roman Empire?

How did emperors respond to political and religious issues?

✓ LearningCurve
Check what you know.

children. Men and women who were unmarried or had no children were restricted in the inheritance of property.

Aside from addressing legal issues and matters of state, Augustus actively encouraged poets and writers. For this reason the period of his rule is known as the "golden age" of Latin literature. Roman poets and prose writers celebrated human accomplishments in works that were highly polished, elegant in style, and intellectual in conception.

Rome's greatest poet was Virgil (70–19 B.C.E.), whose masterpiece is the *Aeneid* (uh-NEE-id), an epic poem that is the Latin equivalent of the Greek *Iliad* and *Odyssey* (see page 119). Virgil's account of the founding of Rome and the early years of the city gave final form to the legend of Aeneas, the Trojan hero (and ancestor of Romulus and Remus; see page 149) who escaped to Italy at the fall of Troy.

One of the most significant aspects of Augustus's reign was Roman expansion into northern and western Europe (Map 6.2). Augustus completed the conquest of Spain, founded twelve new towns in Gaul, and saw that the Roman road system linked new settlements with one another and with Italy. After hard fighting, he made the Rhine River the Roman frontier in Germania (Germany). Meanwhile, generals conquered areas as far as the Danube River, and Roman legions penetrated the areas of modern Austria, southern Bavaria, and western Hungary. The regions of modern Serbia, Bulgaria, and Romania also fell. Within this area the legionaries built fortified camps. Roads linked these camps with one another, and settlements grew up around the camps, eventually becoming towns. Traders began to frequent the frontier and to do business with the people who lived there; as a result, for the first time, central and northern Europe came into direct and continuous contact with Mediterranean culture.

Romans did not force their culture on native people in Roman territories. However, just as earlier ambitious people in the Hellenistic world knew that the surest path to political and social advancement lay in embracing Greek culture and learning to speak Greek (see page 133), those determined to get ahead now learned Latin and adopted aspects of Roman culture.

CHAPTER LOCATOR | How did the Romans dominate Italy, and what political institutions did they create? | How did Rome expand its power beyond Italy, and what were the effects of this expansion?

CHAPTER 6
158   THE WORLD OF ROME

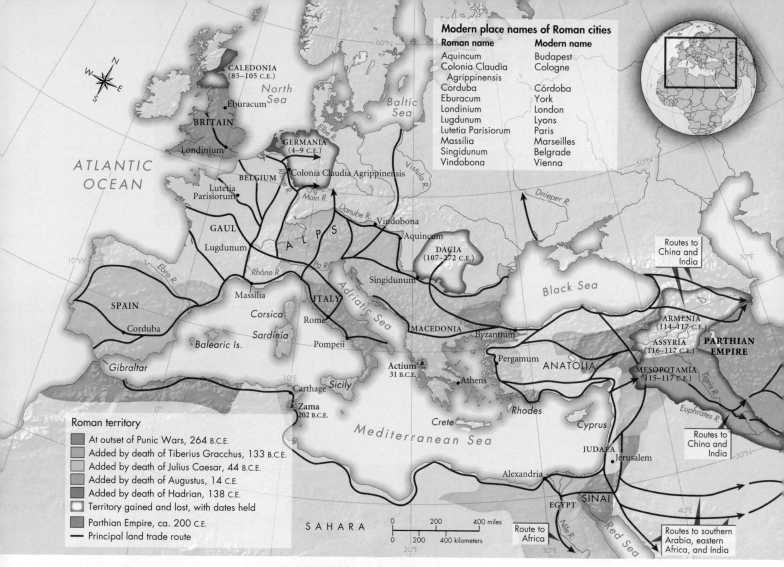

Modern place names of Roman cities

Roman name	Modern name
Aquincum	Budapest
Colonia Claudia Agrippinensis	Cologne
Corduba	Córdoba
Eburacum	York
Londinium	London
Lugdunum	Lyons
Lutetia Parisiorum	Paris
Massilia	Marseilles
Singidunum	Belgrade
Vindobona	Vienna

Roman territory

- At outset of Punic Wars, 264 B.C.E.
- Added by death of Tiberius Gracchus, 133 B.C.E.
- Added by death of Julius Caesar, 44 B.C.E.
- Added by death of Augustus, 14 C.E.
- Added by death of Hadrian, 138 C.E.
- Territory gained and lost, with dates held
- Parthian Empire, ca. 200 C.E.
- — Principal land trade route

MAP 6.2 ■ Roman Expansion, 262 B.C.E.–180 C.E.

Rome expanded in all directions, eventually controlling every shore of the Mediterranean and vast amounts of land.

> MAPPING THE PAST

ANALYZING THE MAP: How would you summarize the pattern of Roman expansion — that is, which areas were conquered first and which later? How long was Rome able to hold on to territories at the outermost boundaries of its empire?

CONNECTIONS: Many of today's major cities in these areas were founded as Roman colonies. Why do you think so many of these cities were founded along the northern border of Roman territory?

QUICK REVIEW <

Why did military commanders grow increasingly powerful in Late Republican Rome?

What was life like in Rome, and what was it like in the provinces?	What was Christianity, and how did it affect life in the Roman Empire?	How did emperors respond to political and religious issues?	 LearningCurve Check what you know.

What was life like in Rome, and what was it like in the provinces?

Roman Architecture

These three structures demonstrate the beauty and utility of Roman architecture. The Coliseum in Rome (below), a sports arena that could seat fifty thousand spectators, built between 70 C.E. and 80 C.E., was the site of gladiatorial games, animal spectacles, and executions. The Pantheon in Rome (right), a temple dedicated to all the gods, was built in its present form about 130 C.E., after earlier temples on the site had burned down. Its dome, 140 feet in diameter, remains the largest unreinforced concrete dome in the world. Romans also used concrete for more everyday purposes. The Pont du Gard at Nîmes in France (above) is a bridge over a river that carried an aqueduct supplying millions of gallons of water per day to the Roman city of Nîmes in Gaul; the water flowed in a channel at the very top. Although this bridge was built largely without mortar or concrete, many Roman aqueducts and bridges relied on concrete and sometimes iron rods for their strength.

(Pont du Gard: © Vanni Archive/Art Resource, NY; Pantheon: Gianni Dagli Orti/The Art Archive at Art Resource, NY; Coliseum: Scala/Art Resource, NY)

pax Romana
▶ The "Roman peace," a period during the first and second centuries C.E. of political stability and relative peace.

I In the late eighteenth century the English historian Edward Gibbon dubbed the stability and relative peace within the empire that Augustus created the **pax Romana**, the "Roman peace," which he saw as lasting about two hundred years. During this time the growing city of Rome saw great improvements, and trade and production flourished in the provinces. Rome also expanded eastward and came into indirect contact with China.

CHAPTER LOCATOR | How did the Romans dominate Italy, and what political institutions did they create? | How did Rome expand its power beyond Italy, and what were the effects of this expansion?

Political and Military Changes in the Empire

For fifty years after Augustus's death in 14 C.E. the dynasty that he established—known as the Julio-Claudians because all were members of the Julian and Claudian clans—provided the emperors of Rome. Some of the Julio-Claudians, such as Tiberius and Claudius, were sound rulers and created a bureaucracy of able administrators to help them govern. Others, including Caligula and Nero, were weak and frivolous.

In 68 C.E. Nero's inept rule led to military rebellion and widespread disruption. Two years later Vespasian (r. 69–79 C.E.), who established the Flavian dynasty, restored order. He also turned Augustus's principate into a hereditary monarchy and expanded the emperor's powers. During the brief reign of Vespasian's son Titus, Mount Vesuvius in southern Italy erupted, destroying Pompeii and other cities and killing thousands of people. The Flavians (69–96 C.E.) paved the way for the Antonines (96–192 C.E.), a dynasty of emperors under whose leadership the Roman Empire experienced a long period of prosperity and the height of the pax Romana. Wars generally ended victoriously and were confined to the frontiers. Second-century emperors made further changes in government that helped the empire run more efficiently while increasing the authority of the emperor.

The Roman army also saw changes, transforming from a mobile unit to a much larger defensive force, with more and more troops who were noncitizens. Because army service could lead to citizenship, non-Romans joined the army willingly to gain citizenship, receive a salary, and learn a trade. The frontiers became firmly fixed and were defended by a system of forts and walls. Behind these walls, the network of roads was expanded and improved, both to supply the forts and to reinforce them in times of trouble.

Life in Imperial Rome

The expansion and stabilization of the empire created great wealth, much of which flowed into Rome. The city, with a population of over a million, may have been the largest city in the world at that time. Fire and crime were perennial problems even in Augustus's day, and sanitation was poor. In the second century urban planning and new construction greatly improved the situation. For example, engineers built an elaborate system that collected sewage from public baths, the ground floors of buildings, and public latrines. They also built hundreds of miles of aqueducts, most of them underground, to bring fresh water into the city from the surrounding hills.

Rome grew so large that it became ever more difficult to feed its residents. Emperors solved the problem by providing citizens with free oil, wine, and grain for bread. By doing so, they also stayed in favor with the people. They and other sponsors also entertained the people with gladiatorial contests in which participants fought using swords and other weapons. Some gladiators were criminals or prisoners of war, but by the imperial period increasing numbers were volunteers, often poor immigrants who saw gladiatorial combat as a way to support themselves. All gladiators were trained in gladiatorial schools and were legally slaves, although they could keep their winnings and a few became quite wealthy. The Romans were even more addicted to chariot racing than to gladiatorial shows. Winning charioteers were idolized just as sports stars are today.

| What was life like in Rome, and what was it like in the provinces? | What was Christianity, and how did it affect life in the Roman Empire? | How did emperors respond to political and religious issues? | ✓ LearningCurve Check what you know. |

161

Prosperity in the Roman Provinces

As the empire grew and stabilized, many Roman provinces grew prosperous through the growth of agriculture, trade, and industry, among other factors. Peace and security opened Britain, Gaul, and the lands of the Danube to settlers from other parts of the Roman Empire. Veterans were given small parcels of land in the provinces, becoming tenant farmers. The garrison towns that grew up around provincial military camps became the centers of organized political life, and some grew into major cities,

The rural population throughout the empire left few records, but the inscriptions that remain point to a melding of cultures. Latin blended with the original language of an area and with languages spoken by those who came into the area later. Slowly what would become the Romance languages of Spanish, Italian, French, Portuguese, and Romanian evolved. Religion was another site of cultural exchange and mixture. Romans moving into an area learned about and began to venerate local gods, and local people learned about Roman ones. Gradually hybrid deities and rituals developed.

The Romans were the first to build cities in northern Europe, but in the eastern Mediterranean they ruled cities that had existed before Rome itself was even a village. Here there was much continuity in urban life from the Hellenistic period. There was less construction than in the Roman cities of northern and western Europe because existing buildings could simply be put to new uses.

The expansion of trade during the pax Romana made the Roman Empire an economic as well as a political force. Britain and Belgium became prime grain producers, and Britain's wool industry probably got its start under the Romans. Italy and southern Gaul produced huge quantities of wine. Roman colonists introduced the olive to southern Spain and northern Africa, which soon produced most of the oil consumed in the western part of the empire. In the East the olive oil production of Syrian farmers reached an all-time high, and Egypt produced tons of wheat that fed the Roman populace.

The growth of industry in the provinces was another striking development of this period. Cities in Gaul and Germany eclipsed the old Mediterranean manufacturing centers, and in the second century C.E. Gaul and Germany took over the pottery market. Lyons in Gaul and later Cologne in Germany became the new centers of the glassmaking industry, and the cities of Gaul were nearly unrivaled in the manufacture of bronze and brass. Aided by all this growth in trade and industry, Europe and western Asia were linked in ways they had not been before.

Eastward Expansion and Contacts Between Rome and China

As the Romans drove farther eastward, they encountered the Parthians, who had established a kingdom in what is now Afghanistan and Iran in the Hellenistic period (see page 133). In the second century the Romans tried unsuccessfully to drive out the Parthians, who came to act as a link between Roman and Chinese merchants. Chinese merchants sold their wares to the Parthians, who then carried the goods overland to Mesopotamia or Egypt, from which they were shipped throughout the Roman Empire.

CHAPTER LOCATOR | How did the Romans dominate Italy, and what political institutions did they create? | How did Rome expand its power beyond Italy, and what were the effects of this expansion?

162 CHAPTER 6
THE WORLD OF ROME

Although warfare disrupted parts of western Asia, it did not stop trade that had prospered from Hellenistic times (see pages 134–135). Silk was still a major commodity from east to west, along with other luxury goods. In return the Romans traded glassware, precious gems, and slaves. The Parthians added exotic fruits, rare birds, rugs, and other products.

The pax Romana was also an era of maritime trade, and Roman ships sailed from Egyptian ports to the mouth of the Indus River, where they purchased local merchandise and wares imported by the Parthians. Some hardy mariners pushed down the African coast and into the Indian Ocean. Roman coins have been found in Sri Lanka and Vietnam, clear evidence of trade connections.

The period of this contact coincided with the era of Han greatness in China (see page 178). During the reign of the Roman emperor Nerva (r. 96–98 C.E.), a Han emperor sent an ambassador, Gan Ying, to make contact with the Roman Empire. Gan Ying made it as far as the Persian Gulf ports, where he heard about the Romans from Parthian sailors and reported back to his emperor that the Romans were wealthy, tall, and strikingly similar to the Chinese. His report became part of a group of accounts about the Romans and other "western" peoples that circulated widely among scholars and officials in Han China.

QUICK REVIEW

What were the economic consequences of
Roman expansion?

| What was life like in Rome, and what was it like in the provinces? | What was Christianity, and how did it affect life in the Roman Empire? | How did emperors respond to political and religious issues? | ✓ LearningCurve Check what you know. |

163

> What was Christianity, and how did it affect life in the Roman Empire?

This mural, from a Roman camp at Dura-Europos on the Euphrates River, may be the earliest known depiction of Jesus. Dating to 235 c.e., it depicts Jesus healing a paralytic man, an incident described in the New Testament. Early Christians used art to spread their message. (Yale University Art Gallery, Dura-Europos Collection)

During the reign of the emperor Tiberius (r. 14–37 c.e.), in the Roman province of Judaea a Jewish man named Jesus of Nazareth preached, attracted a following, and was executed on the order of the Roman prefect Pontius Pilate. Christianity, the religion created by Jesus's followers, came to have an enormous impact first in the Roman Empire and later throughout the world.

Factors Behind the Rise of Christianity

The civil wars that destroyed the Roman Republic left their mark on Judaea, where Jewish leaders had taken sides in the conflict. The turmoil created a climate of violence throughout the area, and among the Jews movements in opposition to the Romans spread. Many Jews came to believe that a final struggle was near and that it would lead to the coming of a savior, or **Messiah**, who would destroy the Roman legions and inaugurate a period of happiness and

Messiah

▶ In Jewish belief, a savior who would bring a period of peace and happiness for Jews; many Christians came to believe that Jesus was that Messiah.

CHAPTER LOCATOR | How did the Romans dominate Italy, and what political institutions did they create? | How did Rome expand its power beyond Italy, and what were the effects of this expansion?

164 CHAPTER 6 THE WORLD OF ROME

plenty for Jews. This apocalyptic belief was an old one among Jews, but by the first century C.E. it had become more widespread than ever.

The pagan world also played its part in the story of early Christianity. The term **pagan**, which originally referred to those who lived in the countryside, came to refer to those who practiced religions other than Judaism or Christianity. This included religions devoted to the traditional Roman gods of the hearth, home, and countryside. Known as syncretistic religions, these religions blended Roman and indigenous deities. The cult of the emperor spread through the erection of statues, temples, and monuments, and mystery religions offered the promise of life after death (see Chapter 5). Many people in the Roman Empire practiced all of these religions, combining them in whatever way seemed most beneficial or satisfying to them.

pagan
▶ Originally referring to those who lived in the countryside, the term came to mean those who practiced religions other than Judaism or Christianity.

The Life and Teachings of Jesus

Into this climate of Messianic hope and Roman religious blending came Jesus of Nazareth (ca. 3 B.C.E.–29 C.E.). According to Christian Scripture, he was born to deeply religious Jewish parents and raised in Galilee. His ministry began when he was about thirty, and he taught by preaching and telling stories.

Like Socrates and the Buddha, Jesus left no writings. Accounts of his sayings and teachings first circulated orally among his followers and were later written down. The principal evidence for his life and deeds are the four Gospels of the Bible (Matthew, Mark, Luke, and John). These Gospels are records of Jesus's teachings, written sometime in the late first century to build a community of faith. Their authors had probably heard many different people talk about what Jesus said and did, and there are discrepancies among the four accounts. These differences indicate that early followers had a diversity of beliefs about Jesus's nature and purpose.

However, almost all the early sources agree on certain aspects of Jesus's teachings: he preached of a heavenly kingdom of eternal happiness in a life after death and of the importance of devotion to God and love of others. His teachings were based on Hebrew Scripture and reflected a conception of God and morality that came from Jewish tradition. The Greek translation of the Hebrew word *Messiah* is *Christus*, the origin of the English word *Christ*. Was Jesus the Messiah, the Christ? A small band of followers thought so, and Jesus claimed that he was. Yet Jesus had his own conception of the Messiah. He would establish a spiritual kingdom, not an earthly one.

The Roman official Pontius Pilate knew little about Jesus's teachings. He was concerned with maintaining peace and order. According to the New Testament, crowds followed Jesus into Jerusalem at the time of Passover, a highly emotional point in the Jewish year that marked the Jewish people's departure from Egypt under the leadership of Moses (see page 52). The prospect that these crowds would spark violence alarmed Pilate. Some Jews believed that Jesus was the long-awaited Messiah. Others hated and feared him because they thought him religiously dangerous. To avert riot and bloodshed, Pilate condemned Jesus to death, and his soldiers carried out the sentence. On the third day after Jesus's crucifixion, some of his followers claimed that he had risen from the dead. For his earliest followers and for generations to come, the resurrection of Jesus became a central element of faith.

| What was life like in Rome, and what was it like in the provinces? | **What was Christianity, and how did it affect life in the Roman Empire?** | How did emperors respond to political and religious issues? | ✓ LearningCurve Check what you know. |

165

The Spread of Christianity

Believers in Jesus's divinity met in small assemblies or congregations, often in one another's homes, to discuss the meaning of Jesus's message and to celebrate a ritual (later called the Eucharist or Lord's Supper) commemorating his last meal with his disciples before his arrest. Because they expected Jesus to return to the world very soon, they regarded earthly life and institutions as unimportant. Only later did these congregations evolve into what came to be called the religion of Christianity, with a formal organization and set of beliefs.

The catalyst in the spread of Jesus's teachings and the formation of the Christian Church was Paul of Tarsus, a well-educated Hellenized Jew. Paul traveled all over the Roman Empire and wrote letters of advice to many groups. These letters were copied and widely circulated, transforming Jesus's ideas into more specific moral teachings. As a result of his efforts, Paul became the most important figure in changing Christianity from a Jewish sect into a separate religion.

Though most of the earliest converts seem to have been Jews, Paul urged that Gentiles, or non-Jews, be accepted on an equal basis. The earliest Christian converts included people from all social classes. These people were reached by missionaries and others who spread the Christian message through family contacts, friendships, and business networks. Many women were active in spreading Christianity. Paul greeted male and female converts by name in his letters and noted that women often provided financial support for his activities. The growing Christian communities differed over the extent to which women should participate in the workings of the religion; some favored giving women a larger role in church affairs, while others were more restrictive.

People were attracted to Christian teachings for a variety of reasons. It was in many ways a mystery religion, offering its adherents special teachings that would give them immortality. But in contrast to traditional mystery religions, Christianity promised this immortality widely, not only to a select few. Christianity also offered the possibility of forgiveness, for believers accepted that human nature is weak and that even the best Christians could fall into sin. But Jesus loved sinners and forgave those who repented. Christianity was also attractive to many because it gave the Roman world a cause. By spreading the word of Christ, Christians played their part in God's plan for the triumph of Christianity on earth. Christianity likewise gave its devotees a sense of identity and community. To stress the spiritual kinship of this new type of community, Christians often called one another brother and sister. Also, many Christians took Jesus's commandment to love one another as a guide and provided support for widows, orphans, and the poor, just as they would for family members.

The Growing Acceptance and Evolution of Christianity

At first, most Roman officials largely ignored the followers of Jesus, viewing them simply as one of the many splinter groups within Judaism, but slowly some came to oppose Christian practices and beliefs. They considered Christians to be subversive dissidents because they stopped practicing traditional rituals and they objected to the cult of the emperor. Some Romans thought that Christianity was

CHAPTER LOCATOR | How did the Romans dominate Italy, and what political institutions did they create? | How did Rome expand its power beyond Italy, and what were the effects of this expansion?

166 CHAPTER 6 THE WORLD OF ROME

one of the worst of the mystery cults, with immoral and indecent rituals. Pagans also feared that the Greco-Roman gods would withdraw their favor from the Roman Empire because of the Christian insistence that the pagan gods either did not exist or were evil spirits. And many worried that Christians were trying to destroy the Roman family with their insistence on a new type of kinship.

Persecutions of Christians, including torture and executions, were organized by governors of Roman provinces and sometimes by the emperor, beginning with Nero. Most persecutions were, however, local and sporadic in nature. Responses to Christianity on the part of Roman emperors varied. Some left Christians in peace, while others ordered them to sacrifice to the emperor and the Roman gods or risk death.

By the second century Christianity was changing. The belief that Jesus was soon coming again gradually waned, and as the number of converts increased, permanent institutions were established. These included buildings and a hierarchy of officials often modeled on those of the Roman Empire. **Bishops**, officials with jurisdiction over a certain area, became especially important. They began to assert that they had the right to determine the correct interpretation of Christian teachings and to choose their successors.

Christianity also began to attract more highly educated individuals who developed complex theological interpretations of issues that were not clear in scripture. Bishops and theologians often modified teachings that seemed upsetting to Romans, such as Jesus's harsh words about wealth and family ties. Given all these changes, Christianity became more formal in the second century, with power more centralized.

bishop
▶ A Christian Church official with jurisdiction over a certain area and the power to determine the correct interpretation of Christian teachings.

QUICK REVIEW <

How did Christianity change in the centuries following the death of Jesus?

| What was life like in Rome, and what was it like in the provinces? | **What was Christianity, and how did it affect life in the Roman Empire?** | How did emperors respond to political and religious issues? | ☑ LearningCurve Check what you know. |

167

How did the emperors respond to political, economic, and religious issues in the third and fourth centuries?

Gladiator Mosaic

Made in the first half of the fourth century c.e., this mosaic from an estate outside Rome includes the name of each gladiator next to the figure. At the top a gladiator stands in a victory pose, while the fallen gladiator at the bottom is marked with the symbol Ø, indicating that he has died in combat. Many of the gladiators in this mosaic, such as those at the left, appear less fit and fearsome than the gladiators depicted in movies, more closely reflecting the reality that gladiatorial combat was a job undertaken by a variety of people. (Galleria Borghese, Rome, Italy/Scala/Art Resource, NY)

The prosperity and stability of the second century gave way to a period of domestic upheaval and foreign invasion in the Roman Empire that historians have termed the "crisis of the third century." Trying to repair the damage was the major work of the emperors Diocletian (r. 284–305) and Constantine (r. 306–337).

Political Measures

During the crisis of the third century the Roman Empire was stunned by civil war, as different individuals, generally military commanders from the border provinces, claimed rights to leadership of the empire. Beginning in 235, emperors often ruled for only a few years or even months. Non-Roman groups on the frontiers took advantage of the chaos to invade Roman-held territory along the Rhine and Danube, occasionally even crossing the Alps to maraud in Italy. In the East, Sassanid armies advanced all the way to the Mediterranean. By the time peace was

CHAPTER LOCATOR | How did the Romans dominate Italy, and what political institutions did they create? | How did Rome expand its power beyond Italy, and what were the effects of this expansion?

restored, the empire's economy was shattered, cities had shrunk in size, and many farmers had left their lands.

Diocletian, who had risen through the ranks of the military to become emperor in 284, ended the period of chaos. Under Diocletian the princeps became *dominus*, "lord," reflecting the emperor's claim that he was "the elect of god." To underscore the emperor's exalted position, Diocletian and his successor, Constantine, adopted the court ceremonies and trappings of the Persian Empire.

Diocletian recognized that the empire had become too large for one man to handle and so in 293 divided it into a western and an eastern half. He assumed direct control of the eastern part, giving a colleague the rule of the western part along with the title *augustus*. Diocletian and his fellow augustus further delegated power by appointing two men to assist them. Each man was given the title *caesar* to indicate his exalted rank.

The Division of the Roman World, 293 C.E.

After a brief civil war following Diocletian's death, Constantine eventually gained authority over the entire empire but ruled from the East. Here he established a new capital for the empire at Byzantium, an old Greek city on the Bosporus, a strait on the boundary between Europe and Asia. He named it "New Rome," though it was soon called Constantinople. In addition, he built defensive works along the borders of the empire, trying hard to keep it together, as did his successors. Despite their efforts, however, the eastern and the western halves drifted apart.

The emperors ruling from Constantinople could not provide enough military assistance to repel invaders in the western half of the Roman Empire, and Roman authority there slowly disintegrated. In 476 a Germanic chieftain, Odoacer, deposed the Roman emperor in the West. This date thus marks the official end of the Roman Empire in the West, although the Roman Empire in the East, later called the Byzantine Empire, would last for nearly another thousand years.

Economic Issues

Along with political challenges, major economic problems also confronted Diocletian and Constantine, including inflation and declining tax revenues. In an attempt to curb inflation, Diocletian issued an edict that fixed maximum prices and wages throughout the empire. He and his successors dealt with the tax system just as strictly and inflexibly. Taxes became payable in kind, that is, in goods and services instead of money. All those involved in the growing, preparation, and transportation of food and other essentials were locked into their professions, as the emperors tried to assure a steady supply of these goods. In this period of severe depression, many localities could not pay their taxes. In such cases local tax collectors, who were themselves locked into service, had to make up the difference from their own funds. This system soon wiped out a whole class of moderately wealthy people and set the stage for the lack of social mobility that was a key characteristic of European society for many centuries to follow.

The emperors' measures did not really address Rome's central economic problems. During the turmoil of the third and fourth centuries, many free farmers and their families were killed by invaders or renegade soldiers, or abandoned farms ravaged in the fighting. Consequently, large tracts of land lay untended. Landlords with ample resources began at once to claim as much of this land as they

What was life like in Rome, and what was it like in the provinces? | What was Christianity, and how did it affect life in the Roman Empire? | **How did emperors respond to political and religious issues?** | ☑ LearningCurve Check what you know.

169

could. The huge estates that resulted, called villas, were self-sufficient and became islands of stability in an unsettled world. In return for the protection and security landlords could offer, many small landholders gave over their lands and their freedom. To guarantee a supply of labor, landlords denied them the freedom to move elsewhere. Free men and women were becoming tenant farmers bound to the land, what would later be called serfs.

The Acceptance of Christianity

By the late third century most Romans tolerated Christianity, even if they did not practice it. Constantine ordered toleration of all religions in the Edict of Milan, issued in 313. He supported the church throughout his reign, expecting in return the support of church officials in maintaining order, and late in his life he was baptized as a Christian. Constantine also freed the clergy from imperial taxation and endowed the building of Christian churches.

Helped in part by its favored position in the empire, Christianity slowly became the leading religion, and emperors after Constantine continued to promote it. In 380 the emperor Theodosius (r. 379–395) made Christianity the official religion of the empire. He allowed the church to establish its own courts and to use its own body of law, called "canon law." With this he laid the foundation for later growth in church power (see Chapter 8).

> **QUICK REVIEW**

What challenges did Roman emperors face in the third and fourth centuries?

CHAPTER SUMMARY

The Italian peninsula was settled by many different groups, including Greeks in the south and Etruscans in the north. The Etruscans expanded southward into central Italy, where they influenced the culture of the small town that was growing into the city of Rome. Rome prospered and expanded its own territories, establishing a republican government led by the Senate. In a series of wars the Romans conquered the Mediterranean, creating an overseas empire that brought them unheard-of power and wealth, but also social unrest and civil war. The meteoric rise to power of Julius Caesar in the first century B.C.E. led to his assassination, but his grandnephew Augustus finally restored peace and order to Rome. Under Augustus, the republic became an empire.

Augustus and his successors further expanded Roman territories. The city of Rome became the magnificent capital of the empire. The Roman provinces and frontiers also saw extensive prosperity through the growth of agriculture, industry, and trade connections. Christianity, a religion created by the followers of Jesus of Nazareth, spread across the empire, beginning in the first century C.E.

CHAPTER LOCATOR | How did the Romans dominate Italy, and what political institutions did they create? | How did Rome expand its power beyond Italy, and what were the effects of this expansion?

170 CHAPTER 6 THE WORLD OF ROME

Initially some Roman officials and emperors persecuted Christians, but gradually hostility decreased. Emperors in the fourth century first allowed Christianity and then made it the official religion of the empire, one of many measures through which they attempted to solve the problems created by invasions and political turmoil. Their measures were successful in the East, where the Roman Empire lasted for another thousand years, but not in the West, where the Roman Empire ended in the fifth century.

 **CONNECTIONS** Despite the efforts of emperors and other leaders, the Western Roman Empire slowly broke apart and by the fifth century C.E. no longer existed. By the fourteenth century European scholars were beginning to see the fall of the Roman Empire as one of the great turning points in Western history, the end of the classical era. That began the practice of dividing Western history into different periods—eventually, the ancient, medieval, and modern eras. Those categories still shape the way that Western history is taught and learned.

This three-part conceptualization also shapes the periodization of world history. As you saw in Chapter 4 and will see in Chapter 7, China is also understood to have had a classical age, and, as you will read in Chapter 11, the Maya of Mesoamerica did as well. The dates of these ages are different from those of the classical period in the Mediterranean, but there are striking similarities among all three places: successful large-scale administrative bureaucracies were established, trade flourished, cities grew, roads were built, and new cultural forms developed. In all three places this period was followed by an era of less prosperity and more warfare and destruction.

🄻 LaunchPad

ONLINE DOCUMENT PROJECT

Queen Cleopatra

What do Roman depictions of Cleopatra reveal about the attitudes and values of her time?

Explore Roman accounts of Cleopatra to see what light they shed on political, social, and cultural values in the late republic and early empire, and then complete a quiz and writing assignment based on the evidence and details from this chapter. *See inside front cover to learn more.*

| What was life like in Rome, and what was it like in the provinces? | What was Christianity, and how did it affect life in the Roman Empire? | How did emperors respond to political and religious issues? | ✅ **LearningCurve** Check what you know. |

CHAPTER 6 STUDY GUIDE

STEP 1

GET STARTED ONLINE

✓ **LearningCurve**

Now that you've read the chapter, make it stick by completing the LearningCurve activity.

STEP 2

EXPLAIN WHY IT MATTERS

Put your reading into practice. Identify each term below, and then explain why it matters in world history.

TERM	WHO OR WHAT & WHEN	WHY IT MATTERS
Senate (p. 148)		
consuls (p. 149)		
patricians (p. 149)		
plebeians (p. 149)		
Punic Wars (p. 153)		
paterfamilias (p. 154)		
pax Romana (p. 160)		
Messiah (p. 164)		
pagan (p. 165)		
bishop (p. 167)		

STEP 3

MOVE BEYOND THE BASICS

To demonstrate a more advanced understanding of the impact of expansion on Roman identity, fill in the chart below with descriptions of the social, cultural, and political consequences of Roman expansion. What steps did the Romans take to "Romanize" subject peoples? How was Roman life, in turn, altered by contact and connections with diverse peoples?

Social Consequences of Roman Expansion	Political Consequences of Roman Expansion	Cultural Consequences of Roman Expansion

STEP 4 ▶ **PUT IT ALL TOGETHER**

Now, take a step back and try to explain the big picture. Remember to use specific examples from the chapter in your answers.

THE ORIGINS AND DEVELOPMENT OF THE ROMAN REPUBLIC

▶ How did the Romans integrate conquered Italian territories into their state? How did their policies in this regard create a foundation for further expansion?

▶ How did the evolution of Roman political institutions reflect the evolution of Roman society?

ROMAN IMPERIALISM AND ITS CONSEQUENCES

▶ What explains the instability that characterized Roman politics in the century following the Punic Wars? Why did republican institutions fail to produce the kinds of reforms and compromises that had resolved earlier political conflicts?

▶ How did Rome help connect greater Europe to the economic and cultural life of the Mediterranean world?

ROMAN DECLINE AND THE RISE OF CHRISTIANITY

▶ What factors facilitated the spread of Christianity throughout the Roman Empire? Why did many Romans initially fear Christianity? Why did such fears diminish over time?

▶ How and why did the political, cultural, and economic center of the Roman Empire shift from west to east starting in the third century C.E.?

LOOKING BACK, LOOKING AHEAD

▶ How was Roman society and culture shaped by Greek ideas and ideals? Why was Greek civilization so appealing to so many Romans?

▶ What are the implications of the claim that, together, Greek and Roman civilization represent the "classical era" in Western history? What does this claim suggest about the connections between these two civilizations and the contemporary Western world?

> **IN YOUR OWN WORDS**

Imagine that you must give an oral report to the class answering the following question: **How did the Romans build and control an empire that spanned the Mediterranean world?** What would be the most important points and why?

7

EAST ASIA AND THE SPREAD OF BUDDHISM

221 B.C.E.–800 C.E.

> **How did China come to play a dominant role in the development of East Asia?** Chapter 7 examines major developments in East Asia between 221 B.C.E. and 800 C.E. At the beginning of this era, China had just been unified into a single state. War, trade, diplomacy, missionary activity, and the pursuit of learning led the Chinese to travel to distant lands and people from distant lands to go to China. Among the results were the spread of Buddhism from India and Central Asia to China and the adaptation of many elements of Chinese culture by near neighbors, especially Korea and Japan. Increased communication also stimulated state formation among China's neighbors: Tibet, Korea, Manchuria, Vietnam, and Japan.

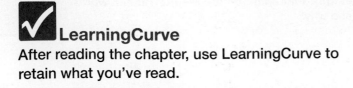

✔ LearningCurve
After reading the chapter, use LearningCurve to retain what you've read.

Palace Maid Ceramic models of attractive young women were often placed in Chinese tombs, reflecting hopes for the afterlife. (© Panorama/The Image Works)

> What were the social, cultural, and political consequences of the unification of China under the strong centralized governments of the Qin and Han empires?

> How did Buddhism find its way into East Asia, and what was its appeal and impact?

> What were the lasting accomplishments of the Sui and Tang Dynasties?

> What elements of Chinese culture were adopted by Koreans, Vietnamese, and Japanese, and how did they adapt them to their own circumstances?

> # What were the social, cultural, and political consequences of the unification of China under the strong centralized governments of the Qin and Han empires?

Army of the First Emperor

The thousands of life-size ceramic soldiers buried in pits about a half mile from the First Emperor's tomb help us imagine the Qin military machine. It was the Qin emperor's concern with the afterlife that led him to construct such a lifelike guard. The soldiers were originally painted in bright colors, and they held real bronze weapons. (Robert Harding World Imagery)

I Like the Roman Empire (see Chapter 6), the Chinese empire was put together through force of arms and held in place by sophisticated centralized administrative machinery. The governments created by the Qin and Han Dynasties affected many facets of Chinese social, cultural, and intellectual life.

The Qin Unification, 221–206 B.C.E.

In 221 B.C.E., after decades of constant warfare, Qin (chin), the state that had adopted Legalist policies during the Warring States Period (see page 108), succeeded in defeating the last of its rivals, and China was unified for the first time in many centuries. The king of Qin decided to call himself the First Emperor (*Shihuangdi*) in anticipation of a long line of successors. His state, however, did not long outlast him.

Once he ruled all of China, the First Emperor and his shrewd Legalist minister Li Si embarked on a sweeping program of centralization that touched the

CHAPTER LOCATOR | **What were the social, cultural, and political consequences of the unification of China?** | How did Buddhism find its way into East Asia, and what was its appeal and impact?

CHAPTER 7
176 EAST ASIA AND THE SPREAD OF BUDDHISM

ca. 230–208 B.C.E. Construction of Great Wall	**372** C.E. Buddhism introduced in Korea
221 B.C.E. China unified under Qin Dynasty	**538** C.E. Buddhism introduced in Japan
206 B.C.E.–**220** C.E. Han Dynasty	**581–618** C.E. Sui Dynasty
145–ca. 85 B.C.E. Sima Qian, Chinese historian	**604** C.E. Prince Shōtoku introduces Chinese-style government in Japan
114 B.C.E. Han government gains control over Silk Road trade routes across Central Asia	**605** C.E. Introduction of merit-based examination system for the selection of officials in China
111 B.C.E. Emperor Wu conquers Nam Viet	**618–907** C.E. Tang Dynasty; great age of Chinese poetry
108 B.C.E. Han government establishes colonies in Korea	**668** C.E. First political unification of Korea under Silla
105 C.E. Chinese invention of paper	**690** C.E. Empress Wu declares herself emperor, becoming the only Chinese woman emperor
ca. 200 C.E. Buddhism begins rapid growth in China	**710** C.E. Nara made the capital of Japan
220–589 C.E. Age of Division in China	**735–737** C.E. Smallpox epidemic in Japan
313–668 C.E. Three Kingdoms Period in Korea	**845** C.E. Tang emperor begins persecution of Buddhism

lives of nearly everyone in China. To cripple the nobility of the defunct states, the First Emperor ordered the nobles to leave their lands and move to the capital. The private possession of arms was outlawed to make it more difficult for subjects to rebel. The First Emperor dispatched officials to administer the territory that had been conquered and controlled the officials through a long list of regulations, reporting requirements, and penalties for inadequate performance.

To harness the enormous human resources of his people, the First Emperor ordered a census of the population. To make it easier to administer all regions uniformly, the Chinese script was standardized, outlawing regional variations in the ways words were written. The First Emperor also standardized weights, measures, coinage, and even the axle lengths of carts. To make it easier for Qin armies to move rapidly, thousands of miles of roads were built. Good roads indirectly facilitated trade.

Hundreds of thousands of subjects were drafted to build the **Great Wall** (ca. 230–208 B.C.E.), a rammed-earth fortification along the northern border between the Qin realm and the land controlled by the nomadic Xiongnu.

Great Wall
► A rammed-earth fortification built along the northern border of China during the reign of the First Emperor.

What were the lasting accomplishments of the Sui and Tang Dynasties?	What elements of Chinese culture were adopted by Koreans, Vietnamese, and Japanese?	✓ **LearningCurve** Check what you know.

After Li Si complained that scholars (especially Confucians) used records of the past to denigrate the emperor's achievements and undermine popular support, the emperor had all writings other than useful manuals on topics such as agriculture, medicine, and divination collected and burned. As a result of this massive book burning, many ancient texts were lost.

After the First Emperor died in 210 B.C.E., the Qin state unraveled. The Legalist institutions designed to concentrate power in the hands of the ruler made the stability of the government dependent on his strength and character, and his heir proved ineffective. The heir was murdered by his younger brother, and uprisings soon followed.

The Han Dynasty, 206 B.C.E.–220 C.E.

The eventual victor in the struggle for power that ensued in the wake of the collapse of the Qin Dynasty was Liu Bang, known in history as Emperor Gaozu (r. 202–195 B.C.E.). The First Emperor of Qin was from the Zhou aristocracy. Gaozu was, by contrast, from a modest family of commoners, so his elevation to emperor is evidence of how thoroughly the Qin Dynasty had destroyed the old order.

Gaozu did not disband the centralized government created by the Qin, but he did remove its most unpopular features. Harsh laws were canceled, taxes were sharply reduced, and a policy of noninterference was adopted in an effort to promote economic recovery. With policies of this sort, relative peace, and the extension of China's frontiers, the Chinese population grew rapidly (Map 7.1).

The Han government was largely supported by the taxes and forced labor demanded of farmers, but this revenue regularly fell short of the government's needs. To pay for his military campaigns, Emperor Wu, the "Martial Emperor" (r. 141–87 B.C.E.), took over the minting of coins, confiscated the land of nobles, sold offices and titles, and increased taxes on private businesses. A widespread suspicion of commerce made it easy to levy especially heavy assessments on merchants. The worst blow to businessmen, however, was the government's decision to enter into market competition with them by selling the commodities that had been collected as taxes. In 119 B.C.E. government monopolies were established in the production of iron, salt, and liquor. These enterprises had previously been sources of great profit for private entrepreneurs. Large-scale grain dealing also had been a profitable business, and the government now took that over as well.

Han Intellectual and Cultural Life

In contrast to the Qin Dynasty, which favored Legalism, the Han came to promote Confucianism. The Han government's efforts to recruit men trained in the Confucian classics marked the beginning of the Confucian scholar-official system, one of the most distinctive features of imperial China.

However, the Confucianism that made a comeback during the Han Dynasty was a changed Confucianism. Although Confucian texts had fed the First Emperor's bonfires, some dedicated scholars had hidden their books, and others had memorized whole works. The ancient books recovered in this way—called the **Confucian classics**—were revered as repositories of the wisdom of the past. Confucian scholars treated these classics with piety and attempted to make them more useful as sources of moral guidance by writing commentaries on them.

Confucian classics
▶ The ancient texts recovered during the Han Dynasty that Confucian scholars treated as sacred scriptures.

CHAPTER LOCATOR | What were the social, cultural, and political consequences of the unification of China?

How did Buddhism find its way into East Asia, and what was its appeal and impact?

CHAPTER 7
178 EAST ASIA AND THE SPREAD OF BUDDHISM

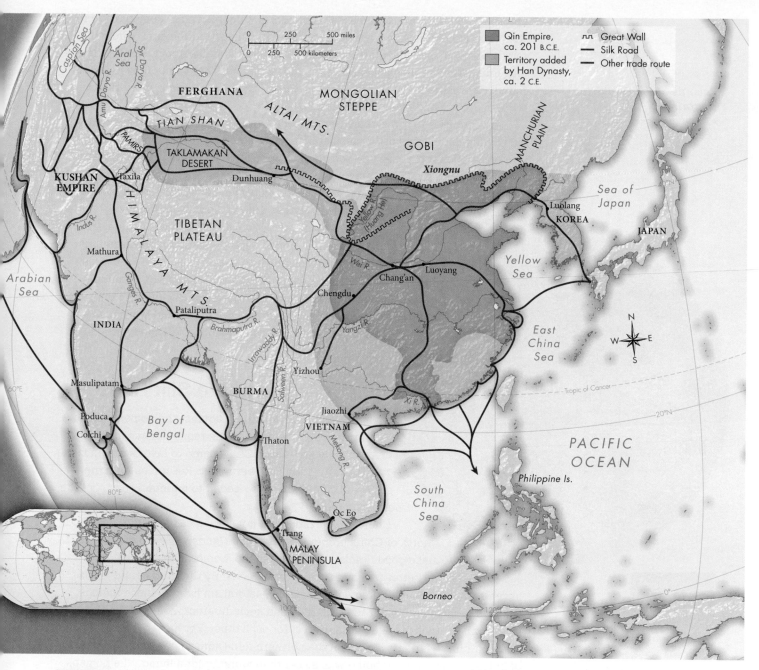

MAP 7.1 ■ **The Han Empire, 206 B.C.E.–220 C.E.**

The Han Dynasty asserted sovereignty over vast regions from Korea in the east to Central Asia in the west and Vietnam in the south. Once garrisons were established, traders were quick to follow, leading to considerable spread of Chinese material culture in East Asia. Chinese goods, especially silk, were in demand far beyond East Asia, promoting long-distance trade across Eurasia.

A major intellectual accomplishment of the Han Dynasty was history writing. Sima Qian (145–ca. 85 B.C.E.) wrote a comprehensive history of China from the time of the mythical sage-kings of high antiquity to his own day, dividing his account into a chronology recounting political events; biographies of key individuals; and treatises on subjects such as geography, taxation, and court rituals. As an

| What were the lasting accomplishments of the Sui and Tang Dynasties? | What elements of Chinese culture were adopted by Koreans, Vietnamese, and Japanese? | ✓ LearningCurve Check what you know. |

official of the emperor, he had access to important people and documents and to the imperial library. Sima Qian believed fervently in visiting the sites where history was made, examining artifacts, and questioning people about events. He was also interested in China's geography and local history. The result of his research, ten years or more in the making, was *Records of the Grand Historian*, a massive work of literary and historical genius.

For centuries to come, Sima Qian's work set the standard for Chinese historical writing, although most of the histories modeled after it covered only a single dynasty. The first of these was the work of three members of the Ban family in the first century C.E. (See "Individuals in Society: The Ban Family," page 181.)

The circulation of books like Sima Qian's was made easier by the invention of paper, which the Chinese traditionally date to 105 C.E. Scribes had previously written on strips of bamboo and wood or rolls of silk. Cai Lun, to whom the Chinese attribute the invention of paper, worked the fibers of rags, hemp, bark, and other scraps into sheets of paper. Paper, thus, was somewhat similar to the papyrus made from pounded reeds in ancient Egypt. Though much less durable than wood, paper was far cheaper than silk and became a convenient means of conveying the written word.

Records of the Grand Historian
▶ A comprehensive history of China written by Sima Qian.

Bronze Mirror

The backs of bronze mirrors were frequently decorated with images of deities and animals and with auspicious words. As viewers turned the mirrors, they saw different scenes. This Han mirror features an outer border with semicircles decorated with cloud patterns and squares with words written on them. In the center are deities. (Mirror Featuring Deities and Kings in Three Sections Surrounded by Rings of Squares and Semicircles [bronze]. Eastern Han Dynasty [25–220]/Cleveland Museum of Art, Ohio, U.S.A./Gift of Drs. Thomas and Martha Carter in Honor of Sherman E. Lee/The Bridgeman Art Library)

Inner Asia and the Silk Road

The difficulty of defending against the nomadic pastoral peoples to the north in the region known as Inner Asia is a major reason China came to favor a centralized bureaucratic form of government. Resources from the entire subcontinent were needed to maintain control of the northern border.

Chinese civilization did not spread easily to the grasslands north of China proper because those lands were too dry and cold to make good farmland. Herding sheep, horses, camels, and other animals made better economic use of those lands. By the third century B.C.E. several different peoples practicing nomadic pastoralism lived in those regions. Chinese farmers and Inner Asian herders had such different modes of life that it is not surprising that they had little respect for each other. For most of the imperial period, Chinese farmers looked on the northern non-Chinese horsemen as gangs of bullies who thought robbing was easier than working for a living. The nomads identified glory with military might and viewed farmers as contemptible weaklings.

In the late third century B.C.E. the Xiongnu (possibly the same group that was known in the West as the Huns) formed the first great confederation of nomadic tribes (see Map 7.1). The Qin's Great Wall was built to defend against the Xiongnu, and the Qin sent out huge armies in pursuit of them. The early Han emperors tried to make peace with them, offering generous gifts of silk, rice, cash, and even imperial princesses as brides. Xiongnu power did not wane, and in 166 B.C.E. 140,000 Xiongnu raided to within a hundred miles of the Chinese capital.

Emperor Wu then decided that China had to push the Xiongnu back. He sent several enormous armies deep into Xiongnu territory. These costly campaigns were of limited value because the Xiongnu were a moving target. If the Xiongnu

CHAPTER LOCATOR | What were the social, cultural, and political consequences of the unification of China?

How did Buddhism find its way into East Asia, and what was its appeal and impact?

CHAPTER 7
180 EAST ASIA AND THE SPREAD OF BUDDHISM

Ban Biao (3–54 C.E.), a successful official from a family with an envied library, had three highly accomplished children: his twin sons, the general Ban Chao (32–102) and the historian Ban Gu (32–92); and his daughter, Ban Zhao (ca. 45–120). After distinguishing himself as a junior officer in campaigns against the Xiongnu, Ban Chao was sent in 73 C.E. to the western regions to see about the possibility of restoring Chinese overlordship there, which had been lost several decades earlier. Ban Chao spent most of the next three decades in Central Asia. Through patient diplomacy and a show of force, he re-established Chinese control over the oasis cities of Central Asia, and in 92 he was appointed protector general of the area.

His twin brother, Ban Gu, was one of the most accomplished writers of his age, excelling in a distinctive literary form known as the rhapsody *(fu)*. His "Rhapsody on the Two Capitals" is in the form of a dialogue between a guest from Chang'an and his host in Luoyang. It describes the palaces, spectacles, scenic spots, local products, and customs of the two great cities. Emperor Zhang (r. 76–88) was fond of literature and often had Ban Gu accompany him on hunts or travels. He also had him edit a record of the court debates he held on issues concerning the Confucian classics.

Ban Biao was working on the *History of the Former Han Dynasty* when he died in 54. Ban Gu took over this project, modeling it on Sima Qian's *Records of the Grand Historian*. He added treatises on law, geography, and bibliography, the last a classified list of books in the imperial library.

Because of his connection to a general out of favor, Ban Gu was sent to prison in 92, where he soon died. At that time the *History of the Former Han Dynasty* was still incomplete. The emperor called on Ban Gu's widowed sister, Ban Zhao, to finish it. She came to the palace, where she not only worked on the history but also became a teacher of the women of the palace. According to the *History of the Later Han*, she taught them the classics, history, astronomy, and mathematics. In 106 an infant succeeded to the throne, and the widow of an earlier emperor became regent. This empress frequently turned to Ban Zhao for advice on government policies.

Ban Zhao credited her own education to her learned father and cultured mother and became an advocate of the education of girls. In her *Admonitions for Women,* Ban Zhao objected that many families taught their sons to read but not their daughters. She did not claim girls should have the same education as boys; after all, "just as yin and yang differ, men and women have different characteristics." Women, she

Ban Zhao, Han Dynasty historian. (© Fotoe/Uniphoto Press, Japan/Ancient Art & Architecture Collection, Ltd.)

wrote, will do well if they cultivate womanly virtues such as humility. "Humility means yielding and acting respectful, putting others first and oneself last, never mentioning one's own good deeds or denying one's own faults, enduring insults and bearing with mistreatment, all with due trepidation."* In subsequent centuries Ban Zhao's *Admonitions* became one of the most commonly used texts for the education of Chinese girls.

QUESTIONS FOR ANALYSIS

1. What inferences can you draw from the fact that a leading general had a brother who was a literary man?
2. What does Ban Zhao's life tell us about women in her society? How do you reconcile her personal accomplishments with the advice she gave for women's education?

*Patricia Buckley Ebrey, ed., *Chinese Civilization: A Sourcebook*, 2d ed., revised and expanded (New York: Free Press, 1993), p. 75.

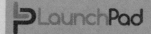

ONLINE DOCUMENT PROJECT

What do Ban Zhao's writings reveal about attitudes toward women during her time? Read sources by and about Ban Zhao, and then complete a quiz and writing assignment based on the evidence and details from this chapter. *See the inside front cover to learn more.*

Xiongnu Metalwork

The metal ornaments of the Xiongnu provide convincing evidence that they were in contact with nomadic pastoralists farther west in Asia, such as the Scythians, who also fashioned metal plaques and buckles in animal designs. This buckle or ornament is made of gold and is about 3 inches tall. (Image copyright © The Metropolitan Museum of Art/Image source: Art Resource, NY)

Silk Road
▶ The trade routes across Central Asia linking China to western Eurasia.

tributary system
▶ A system first established during the Han Dynasty to regulate contact with foreign powers. States and tribes beyond its borders sent envoys bearing gifts and received gifts in return.

did not want to fight the Chinese troops, they simply moved their camps. To try to find allies and horses, Emperor Wu turned his attention west, toward Central Asia. From an envoy he sent into Bactria, Parthia, and Ferghana in 139 B.C.E., the Chinese learned for the first time of other civilized states comparable to China.

In 114 B.C.E. Emperor Wu sent an army into Ferghana and gained recognition of Chinese overlordship in the area, thus obtaining control over the trade routes across Central Asia commonly called the **Silk Road** (see Map 7.1). The city-states along this route could carry out the trade on which they depended more conveniently with Chinese garrisons to protect them.

At the same time, Emperor Wu sent troops into northern Korea to establish military districts that would flank the Xiongnu on their eastern border. By 111 B.C.E. the Han government also had extended its rule south into Nam Viet, which extended from south China into what is now northern Vietnam.

During the Han Dynasty, China developed a **tributary system** to regulate contact with foreign powers. States and tribes beyond its borders sent envoys bearing gifts and received gifts in return. Over the course of the dynasty, the Han government's outlay on these gifts was huge, perhaps as much as 10 percent of state revenue. Although the tributary system was a financial burden to the Chinese, it reduced the cost of defense and offered China confirmation that it was the center of the civilized world.

Silk given to the Xiongnu and other northern tributaries as part of the tributary system often entered the trading networks of Persian, Parthian, and Indian merchants, who carried it by caravans across Asia. There was a market both for skeins of silk thread and for silk cloth woven in Chinese or Syrian workshops. Caravans returning to China carried gold, horses, and occasionally handicrafts of West Asian origin, such as glass beads and cups. Through the trade along the Silk Road, the Chinese learned of new foodstuffs, including walnuts, pomegranates, sesame, and coriander, all of which came to be grown in China.

Maintaining a military presence so far from the center of China was expensive. To cut costs, the government set up self-supporting military colonies, recruited Xiongnu tribes to serve as auxiliary forces, and established vast government horse farms. Still, military expenses threatened to bankrupt the Han government.

CHAPTER LOCATOR | What were the social, cultural, and political consequences of the unification of China? | How did Buddhism find its way into East Asia, and what was its appeal and impact?

CHAPTER 7
182 EAST ASIA AND THE SPREAD OF BUDDHISM

Life in Han China

How were ordinary people's lives affected by the creation of a huge Han bureaucratic empire? The lucky ones who lived in Chang'an or Luoyang, the great cities of the empire, got to enjoy the material benefits of increased long-distance trade and a boom in the production of luxury goods.

The government did not promote trade per se. The Confucian elite, like ancient Hebrew wise men, considered trade necessary but lowly. Agriculture and crafts were more honorable because they produced something, but merchants merely took advantage of others' shortages to make profits as middlemen. This attitude justified the government's takeover of the grain, iron, and salt businesses. Still, the government indirectly promoted commerce by building roads and defending cities.

Markets were the liveliest places in the cities. Besides stalls selling goods of all kinds, markets offered fortune-tellers and entertainers. The markets were also used for the execution of criminals, to serve as a warning to onlookers.

Government patronage helped maintain the quality of craftsmanship in the cities. By the beginning of the first century C.E. China also had about fifty state-run ironworking factories. Chinese metalworking was the most advanced in the world at the time. In contrast to Roman blacksmiths, who hammered heated iron to make wrought iron tools, the Chinese knew how to liquefy iron and pour it into molds, producing tools with a higher carbon content that were harder and more durable.

Iron was replacing bronze in tools, but bronzeworkers still turned out a host of goods. Bronze was prized for jewelry, mirrors, and dishes. Bronze was also used for minting coins and for precision tools such as carpenters' rules and adjustable wrenches. Han metal-smiths were mass-producing superb crossbows long before the crossbow was dreamed of in Europe.

The bulk of the population consisted of peasants living in villages of a few hundred households. Because the Han empire, much like the contemporaneous Roman Empire, drew its strength from a large population of free peasants who contributed both taxes and labor services to the state, the government had to try to keep peasants independent and productive.

To fight peasant poverty, the government kept land taxes low (one-thirtieth of the harvest), provided relief in time of famine, and promoted up-to-date agricultural methods. Still, many hard-pressed peasants were left to choose between migration to areas where new lands could be opened and quasi-servile status as the dependents of a magnate. Throughout the Han period, Chinese farmers in search of land to till pushed into frontier areas, expanding Chinese domination at the expense of other ethnic groups, especially in central and south China.

The Chinese family in Han times was much like Roman (see page 153) and Indian (see page 69) families. In all three societies senior males had great authority, parents arranged their children's marriages, and brides normally joined their husbands' families. Other practices were more distinctive to China, such as the universality of patrilineal family names, the practice of dividing land equally among the sons in a family, and the great emphasis placed on the virtue of filial piety. One of the most commonly used texts for the education of women is Ban Zhao's *Admonitions for Women*, in which she extols the feminine virtues, such as humility. (See "Individuals in Society: The Ban Family," page 181.)

What were the lasting accomplishments of the Sui and Tang Dynasties?

What elements of Chinese culture were adopted by Koreans, Vietnamese, and Japanese?

✔ LearningCurve
Check what you know.

China and Rome

The empires of China and Rome (discussed in Chapter 6) were large, complex states governed by monarchs, bureaucracies, and standing armies. Both reached the people directly through taxation and conscription policies, and both invested in infrastructure such as roads and waterworks. The empires faced the similar challenge of having to work hard to keep land from becoming too concentrated in the hands of hard-to-tax wealthy magnates. In both empires people in neighboring areas that came under political domination were attracted to the conquerors' material goods, productive techniques, and other cultural products, resulting in gradual cultural assimilation. China and Rome also had similar frontier problems and tried similar solutions, such as recruiting "barbarian" soldiers and settling soldier-colonists.

Nevertheless, the differences between Rome and Han China are worth as much notice as the similarities. The Roman Empire was linguistically and culturally more diverse than China. In China there was only one written language; people in the Roman Empire still wrote in Greek and several other languages, and people in the eastern Mediterranean could claim more ancient civilizations. Politically the dynastic principle was stronger in China than in Rome, nor were there republican ideals in China. In contrast to the graduated forms of citizenship in Rome, Han China drew no distinctions between original and added territories. The social and economic structures also differed in the two empires. Slavery was much more important in Rome than in China, and merchants were more favored.

The Fall of the Han and the Age of Division

In the second century C.E. the Han government suffered a series of blows. A succession of child emperors required regents to rule in their place until they reached maturity, allowing the families of empresses to dominate the court. Emperors, once grown, turned to **eunuchs** (castrated palace servants) for help in ousting the empresses' families, only to find that the eunuchs were just as difficult to control. In 166 and 169 scholars who had denounced the eunuchs were arrested, killed, or banished from the capital and official life. Then in 184 a millenarian religious sect rose in massive revolt. The armies raised to suppress the rebels soon took to fighting among themselves. After years of fighting, a stalemate was reached, with three warlords each controlling distinct territories in the north, the southeast, and the southwest. In 220 one of them forced the last of the Han emperors to abdicate, formally ending the Han Dynasty.

The period after the fall of the Han Dynasty is often referred to as the **Age of Division** (220–589). A brief reunification from 280 to 316 came to an end when non-Chinese who had been settling in north China since Han times seized the opportunity afforded by the political turmoil to take power. For the next two and a half centuries, north China was ruled by one or more non-Chinese dynasties (the Northern Dynasties), and the south was ruled by a sequence of four short-lived Chinese dynasties (the Southern Dynasties) centered in the area of the present-day city of Nanjing.

In the south a hereditary aristocracy entrenched itself in the higher reaches of officialdom. They saw themselves as maintaining the high culture of the Han and looked on the emperors of the successive dynasties as upstarts. In this aristocratic

eunuchs
▶ Castrated males who played an important role as palace servants.

Age of Division
▶ The period after the fall of the Han Dynasty, when China was politically divided.

CHAPTER LOCATOR | What were the social, cultural, and political consequences of the unification of China?

How did Buddhism find its way into East Asia, and what was its appeal and impact?

CHAPTER 7
184 EAST ASIA AND THE SPREAD OF BUDDHISM

culture the arts of poetry and calligraphy flourished, and people began collecting writings by famous calligraphers.

Establishing the capital at Nanjing, south of the Yangzi River, had a beneficial effect on the economic development of the south. To pay for an army and to support the imperial court and aristocracy in a style that matched their pretensions, the government had to expand the area of taxable agricultural land. The south, with its temperate climate and ample supply of water, offered nearly unlimited possibilities for such development.

The Northern Dynasties are interesting as the first case of alien rule in China. Ethnic tensions flared from time to time. In the late fifth century the Northern Wei (way) Dynasty (386–534) moved the capital from near the Great Wall to the ancient city of Luoyang, adopted Chinese-style clothing, and made Chinese the official language. But the armies remained in the hands of the non-Chinese Xianbei tribesmen. Soldiers who saw themselves as marginalized by the pro-Chinese reforms rebelled in 524. For the next fifty years north China was torn apart by struggles for power.

QUICK REVIEW <

How did the Han emperors respond to the challenges presented by nomadic peoples?

What were the lasting accomplishments of the Sui and Tang Dynasties?	What elements of Chinese culture were adopted by Koreans, Vietnamese, and Japanese?	✓ LearningCurve Check what you know.

How did Buddhism find its way into East Asia, and what was its appeal and impact?

This monk, wearing the traditional patchwork robe, sits in the crossed-legged meditation position. His small niche is to the left of the main image of the Buddha in cave 285 at Dunhuang, a cave completed in 539 C.E. under the patronage of a prince of the Northern Wei imperial house who was then the local governor. (Photo: Lois Conner. Courtesy, Dunhuang Academy)

I In much the same period that Christianity was spreading out of its original home in ancient Israel, Buddhism was spreading beyond India. Buddhism came to Central, East, and Southeast Asia with merchants and missionaries along the overland Silk Road, by sea from India and Sri Lanka, and also through Tibet. Like Christianity, Buddhism was shaped by its contact with cultures in the different areas into which it spread, leading to several distinct forms.

Buddhism's Path Through Central Asia

Under Ashoka in India (see pages 80–82), Buddhism began to spread to Central Asia. This continued under the Kushan empire (ca. 50–250 C.E.). Over the next several centuries most of the city-states of Central Asia became centers of Buddhism, from Bamiyan northwest of Kabul, to Kucha, Khotan, Loulan, Turfan, and Dunhuang (Map 7.2).

CHAPTER LOCATOR | What were the social, cultural, and political consequences of the unification of China? | **How did Buddhism find its way into East Asia, and what was its appeal and impact?**

CHAPTER 7
186 EAST ASIA AND THE SPREAD OF BUDDHISM

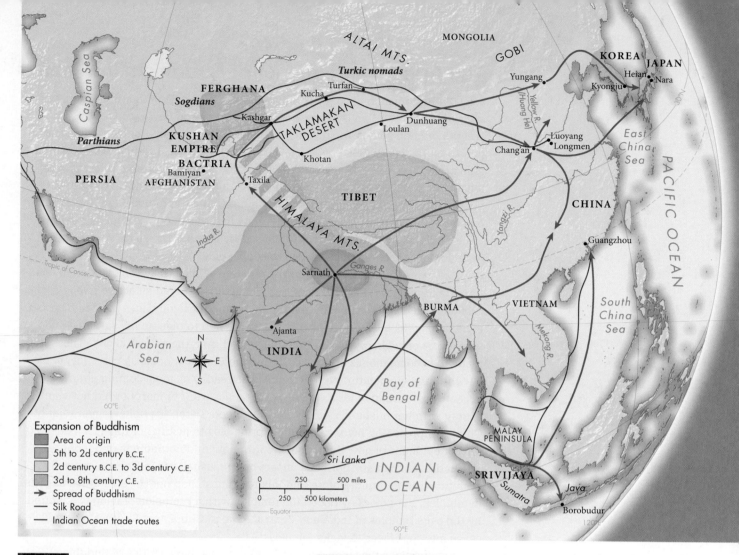

Expansion of Buddhism

- ▨ Area of origin
- ▨ 5th to 2d century B.C.E.
- ▢ 2d century B.C.E. to 3d century C.E.
- ▨ 3d to 8th century C.E.
- → Spread of Buddhism
- — Silk Road
- — Indian Ocean trade routes

MAP 7.2 ■ **The Spread of Buddhism,**
ca. 500 B.C.E.–800 C.E.

Buddhism spread throughout India in Ashoka's time and
beyond India in later centuries. The different forms of
Buddhism found in Asia today reflect this history. The
Mahayana Buddhism of Japan came via Central Asia, China,
and Korea, with a secondary later route through Tibet. The
Theravada Buddhism of Southeast Asia came directly from
India and indirectly through Sri Lanka.

> MAPPING THE PAST

ANALYZING THE MAP: Trace the routes of
the spread of Buddhism by time period.
How fast did Buddhism spread?
CONNECTIONS: Why do you think Buddhism spread more to the east of India
than to the west?

The form of Buddhism that spread from Central Asia to China, Japan, and
Korea was called Mahayana, which means "Great Vehicle" (see page 73), reflecting the claims of its adherents to a more inclusive form of the religion. Influenced
by the Iranian religions then prevalent in Central Asia, Buddhism became more
devotional. The Buddha came to be treated as a god, the head of an expanding
pantheon of other Buddhas and bodhisattvas (Buddhas-to-be). With the growth of
this pantheon, Buddhism became as much a religion for laypeople as for monks
and nuns.

What were the lasting accomplishments of the Sui and Tang Dynasties?	What elements of Chinese culture were adopted by Koreans, Vietnamese, and Japanese?	✓ LearningCurve Check what you know.

The Appeal and Impact of Buddhism in China

Why did Buddhism find so many adherents in China during the three centuries after the fall of the Han Dynasty in 220? There were no forced conversions, but still the religion spread rapidly. In the unstable political environment, many people were open to new ideas. To Chinese scholars the Buddhist concepts of the reincarnation of souls, karma, and nirvana posed a stimulating intellectual challenge. To rulers the Buddhist religion offered a source of magical power and a political tool to unite Chinese and non-Chinese. In a tumultuous age Buddhism's emphasis on kindness, charity, and eternal bliss was deeply comforting. As in India, Buddhism posed no threat to the social order, and the elite who were drawn to Buddhism encouraged its spread to people of all classes.

The monastic establishment grew rapidly in China. Like their Christian counterparts in medieval Europe, Buddhist monasteries played an active role in social, economic, and political life. Given the importance of family lines in China, becoming a monk was a major decision, since a man had to give up his surname and take a vow of celibacy, thus cutting himself off from the ancestral cult. Those not ready to become monks or nuns could pursue Buddhist goals as pious laypeople.

In China women turned to Buddhism as readily as men. Joining a nunnery became an alternative for a woman who did not want to marry or did not want to stay with her husband's family in widowhood. Later, the only woman ruler of China, Empress Wu, invoked Buddhist principles to justify her role (see page 190), further evidence of how Buddhism brought new understandings of gender.

Buddhism had an enormous impact on the visual arts in China, especially sculpture and painting. Before Buddhism, Chinese had not set up statues of gods in temples, but now they decorated temples with a profusion of images. Inspired by the cave temples of India and Central Asia, in China, too, Buddhists carved caves into rock faces to make temples.

Not everyone was won over by Buddhist teachings. Critics of Buddhism labeled it immoral, unsuited to China, and a threat to the state since monastery land was not taxed and monks did not perform labor service.

> ## QUICK REVIEW

To which groups in Chinese society did Buddhism appeal? Why?

CHAPTER LOCATOR | What were the social, cultural, and political consequences of the unification of China? | How did Buddhism find its way into East Asia, and what was its appeal and impact?

CHAPTER 7
188 EAST ASIA AND THE SPREAD OF BUDDHISM

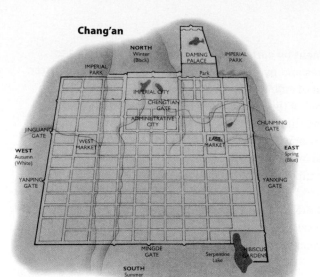

Chang'an

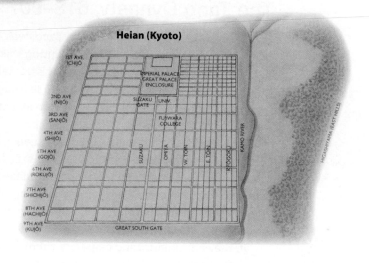

Heian (Kyoto)

What were the lasting accomplishments of the Sui and Tang Dynasties?

Urban Planning

Chang'an in Tang times attracted merchants, pilgrims, and students from all over East Asia. The city was laid out on a square grid (left) and divided into walled wards, the gates to which were closed at night. Temples were found throughout the city, but trade was limited to two government-supervised markets. In the eighth and ninth centuries the Japanese copied the general plan of Chang'an in designing their capitals — first at Nara, then at Heian, shown on the right. (Cradles of Civilization/Visual Connection Archive)

P olitical division was finally overcome when the Sui Dynasty conquered its rivals to reunify China in 581. Although the dynasty lasted only thirty-seven years, it left a lasting legacy in the form of political reform, the construction of roads and canals, and the institution of written merit-based exams for the appointment of officials. The Tang Dynasty that followed would build upon the Sui's accomplishments to create an era of impressive cultural creativity and political power.

The Sui Dynasty, 581–618

In the 570s and 580s the long period of division in China was brought to an end under the leadership of the Sui (sway) Dynasty. In addition to reunifying China, the Sui reasserted Chinese control over northern Vietnam and campaigned into Korea and against the new force on the steppe, the Turks. The Sui strengthened

What were the lasting accomplishments of the Sui and Tang Dynasties?	What elements of Chinese culture were adopted by Koreans, Vietnamese, and Japanese?	 LearningCurve Check what you know.

189

central control of the government by curtailing the power of local officials to appoint their own subordinates and by instituting in 605 C.E. competitive written examinations for the selection of officials.

The crowning achievement of the Sui Dynasty was the construction of the **Grand Canal**, which connected the Yellow and Yangzi River regions. Henceforth the rice-growing Yangzi Valley and south China played an ever more influential role in the country's economic and political life, strengthening China's internal cohesion and facilitating maritime trade with Southeast Asia, India, and areas farther west.

Despite these accomplishments, the Sui Dynasty lasted for only two reigns. The ambitious projects of the two Sui emperors led to exhaustion and unrest, and in the ensuing warfare Li Yuan seized the throne.

Grand Canal

▶ A canal, built during the Sui Dynasty, that connected the Yellow and Yangzi Rivers, notable for strengthening China's internal cohesion and economic development.

The Tang Dynasty, 618–907

The dynasty founded by Li Yuan, the Tang, was one of the high points of traditional Chinese civilization. Especially during this dynasty's first century, its capital, Chang'an, was the cultural center of East Asia. This position of strength gave the Chinese the confidence to be open to learning from the outside world, leading to a more cosmopolitan culture than in any other period before the twentieth century.

The first two Tang rulers, Gaozu (Li Yuan, r. 618–626) and Taizong (r. 626–649), were able monarchs. Adding to their armies auxiliary troops composed of Turks, Tanguts, Khitans, and other non-Chinese led by their own chieftains, they campaigned into Korea, Vietnam, and Central Asia. In 630 the Chinese turned against their former allies, the Turks, gaining territory from them and winning for Taizong the title of Great Khan.

In the civil sphere Tang emperors subdivided the administration of the empire into departments, much like the numerous agencies of modern governments. They built on the Sui precedent of using written examinations to select officials. Candidates had to master the Confucian classics and the rules of poetry, and they had to be able to analyze practical administrative and political matters. Government schools were founded to prepare the sons of officials and other young men for service as officials.

The mid-Tang Dynasty saw two women—Empress Wu and Consort Yang Guifei—rise to positions of great political power. Empress Wu was the consort of Emperor Gaozong. After Gaozong suffered a stroke in 660, she took charge. She continued to rule after Gaozong's death, summarily deposing her own two sons and dealing harshly with all opponents. In 690 she proclaimed herself emperor, the only woman who took that title in Chinese history. Although despised by later Chinese historians as an evil usurper, Empress Wu was an effective leader. It was not until she was over eighty that members of the court were able to force her out in favor of her son.

Her grandson, the emperor Xuanzong (r. 713–756), presided over a brilliant court in his early years. In his later years, however, after he became enamored of his consort Yang Guifei, he did not want to be bothered by the details of government. The emperor allowed her to place friends and relatives in important posi-

Tang China, ca. 750 C.E.

CHAPTER LOCATOR | What were the social, cultural, and political consequences of the unification of China? | How did Buddhism find its way into East Asia, and what was its appeal and impact?

CHAPTER 7
190 EAST ASIA AND THE SPREAD OF BUDDHISM

tions in the government. One of her favorites was the general An Lushan, who rebelled in 755. Xuanzong had to flee the capital, and the troops that accompanied him forced him to have Yang Guifei executed.

The rebellion of An Lushan was devastating to the Tang Dynasty. Peace was restored only by calling on the Uighurs (WEE-gurz), a Turkish people allied with the Tang, who looted the capital after taking it from the rebels. After the rebellion was finally suppressed in 763, the central government had to keep meeting the extortionate demands of the Uighurs. Many military governors came to treat their provinces as hereditary kingdoms. In addition, eunuchs gained increasing power at court.

Tang Culture

The reunification of north and south led to cultural flowering. The Tang capital cities of Chang'an and Luoyang became great metropolises. The cities were laid out in rectangular grids and contained a hundred-odd walled "blocks" inside their walls. Like the gates of the city, the gates of each block were locked at night.

In these cosmopolitan cities, knowledge of the outside world was stimulated by the presence of envoys, merchants, pilgrims, and students who came from neighboring states in Central Asia, Japan, Korea, Tibet, and Southeast Asia. Because of the presence of foreign merchants, many religions were practiced. Foreign fashions in hair and clothing were often copied, and foreign amusements such as the Persian game of polo found followings among the well-to-do. The introduction of new musical instruments and tunes from India, Iran, and Central Asia brought about a major transformation in Chinese music.

The Tang Dynasty was the great age of Chinese poetry. Skill in composing poetry was tested in the civil service examinations, and educated men had to be able to compose poems at social gatherings. The pain of parting, the joys of nature, and the pleasures of wine and friendship were all common poetic topics.

In Tang times Buddhism fully penetrated Chinese daily life. Stories of Buddhist origin became widely known, and Buddhist festivals became among the most popular holidays. Buddhist monasteries became an important part of everyday life. They ran schools for children. In remote areas they provided lodging for travelers. Merchants entrusted their money and wares to monasteries for safekeeping, in effect transforming the monasteries into banks and warehouses. The wealthy often donated money or land to support temples and monasteries, making monasteries among the largest landlords.

At the intellectual and religious level, Buddhism was developing in distinctly Chinese directions. Two schools that thrived were Pure Land and Chan. **Pure Land** appealed to laypeople because its simple act of calling on the Buddha Amitabha and his chief helper, the compassionate bodhisattva Guanyin, could lead to rebirth in Amitabha's paradise, the Pure Land. Among the educated elite the **Chan** school (known in Japan as Zen) also gained popularity. Chan teachings rejected the authority of the sutras and claimed the superiority of mind-to-mind transmission of Buddhist truths.

Opposition to Buddhism re-emerged in the late Tang period. In addition to concerns about the fiscal impact of removing so much land from the tax rolls and

Pure Land
▶ A school of Buddhism that taught that by calling on the Buddha Amitabha, one could achieve rebirth in Amitabha's Pure Land paradise.

Chan
▶ A school of Buddhism (known in Japan as Zen) that rejected the authority of the sutras and claimed the superiority of mind-to-mind transmission of Buddhist truths.

What were the lasting accomplishments of the Sui and Tang Dynasties?

What elements of Chinese culture were adopted by Koreans, Vietnamese, and Japanese?

☑ LearningCurve
Check what you know.

so many men from government labor service, there were concerns about Buddhism's foreign origins. As China's international position weakened, xenophobia surfaced. During the persecution of 845, more than 4,600 monasteries and 40,000 temples and shrines were destroyed, and more than 260,000 Buddhist monks and nuns were forced to return to secular life. Although this ban was lifted after a few years, the monastic establishment never fully recovered.

QUICK REVIEW

How did Chinese Buddhism develop under the Tang?

CHAPTER LOCATOR | What were the social, cultural, and political consequences of the unification of China? | How did Buddhism find its way into East Asia, and what was its appeal and impact?

CHAPTER 7

192 EAST ASIA AND THE SPREAD OF BUDDHISM

What elements of Chinese culture were adopted by Koreans, Vietnamese, and Japanese, and how did they adapt them to their own circumstances?

Five-Stringed Pipa/Biwa

This musical instrument, decorated with fine wood marquetry, was probably presented by the Tang court to a Japanese envoy. It was among the objects placed in a Japanese royal storage house (Shōsōin) in 756.
(Kyodo News International, Inc.)

During the millennium from 200 B.C.E. to 800 C.E., China exerted a powerful influence on its immediate neighbors, who began forming states of their own. By Tang times China was surrounded by independent states in Korea, Manchuria, Tibet, the area that is now Yunnan province, Vietnam, and Japan. All of these states were much smaller than China in area and population, making China by far the dominant force politically and culturally. Nevertheless, each of these separate states developed a strong sense of its independent identity.

The earliest information about each of these countries is found in Chinese sources. Han armies brought Chinese culture to Korea and Vietnam, but even in those cases much cultural borrowing was entirely voluntary as the elite, merchants, and craftsmen adopted the techniques, ideas, and practices they found appealing. In Japan much of the process of absorbing elements of Chinese culture was mediated via Korea. In Korea, Japan, and Vietnam the fine arts—painting, architecture, and ceramics in particular—were all strongly influenced by Chinese models. Tibet was as much in the Indian sphere of influence as in the Chinese and thus followed a somewhat different trajectory. Most significantly, it never

What were the lasting accomplishments of the Sui and Tang Dynasties?

What elements of Chinese culture were adopted by Koreans, Vietnamese, and Japanese?

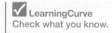 LearningCurve
Check what you know.

adopted Chinese characters as its written language, nor was it as influenced by Chinese artistic styles as were other areas. Moreover, the form of Buddhism that became dominant in Tibet came directly from India, not through Central Asia and China.

In each area Chinese-style culture was at first adopted by elites, but in time many Chinese products and ideas became incorporated into everyday life. By the eighth century the written Chinese language was used by educated people throughout East Asia. The books that educated people read included the Chinese classics, histories, and poetry, as well as Buddhist sutras translated into Chinese. The great appeal of Buddhism known primarily through Chinese translation was a powerful force promoting cultural borrowing.

Vietnam

Vietnam's climate is much like that of southernmost China—subtropical, with abundant rain and rivers. The Vietnamese first appear in Chinese sources as a people of south China called the Yue, who gradually migrated farther south as the Chinese state expanded. The people of the Red River Valley in northern Vietnam had achieved a relatively advanced level of Bronze Age civilization by the first century B.C.E. Power was held by hereditary tribal chiefs who served as civil, religious, and military leaders, with the king as the most powerful chief.

The collapse of the Qin Dynasty in 206 B.C.E. had an impact on this area because a former Qin general, Zhao Tuo (Trieu Da in Vietnamese), finding himself in the far south, set up his own kingdom of Nam Viet (Nan Yue in Chinese). This kingdom covered much of south China and was ruled by Trieu Da from his capital near the present site of Guangzhou. Its population consisted chiefly of the Viet people. After killing all officials loyal to the Chinese emperor, Trieu Da adopted the customs of the Viet and made himself the ruler of a vast state that extended as far south as modern-day Da Nang.

After almost a hundred years of diplomatic and military duels between the Han Dynasty and Trieu Da and his successors, Nam Viet was conquered in 111 B.C.E. by Chinese armies. Chinese administrators were assigned to replace the local nobility. Chinese political institutions were imposed, and Confucianism was treated as the official ideology. The Chinese language was introduced as the medium of official and literary expression, and Chinese characters were adopted as the written form for the Vietnamese spoken language. The Chinese built roads, waterways, and harbors to facilitate communication within the region and to ensure that they maintained administrative and military control over it. Chinese art, architecture, and music had a powerful impact on their Vietnamese counterparts.

Chinese innovations that were beneficial to the Vietnamese were readily integrated into the indigenous culture, but the local elite were not reconciled to Chinese political domination. The most famous early revolt took place in 39 C.E., when two widows of local aristocrats, the Trung sisters, led an uprising against foreign rule. After overwhelming Chinese strongholds, they declared themselves queens of an independent Vietnamese kingdom. Three years later a powerful army sent by the Han emperor re-established Chinese rule.

China retained at least nominal control over northern Vietnam through the Tang Dynasty. The local elite became culturally dual, serving as brokers between the Chinese governors and the native people.

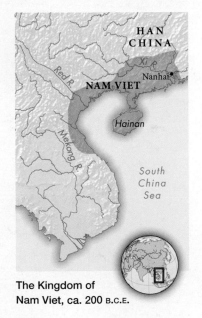

The Kingdom of Nam Viet, ca. 200 B.C.E.

CHAPTER LOCATOR | What were the social, cultural, and political consequences of the unification of China? | How did Buddhism find its way into East Asia, and what was its appeal and impact?

194 CHAPTER 7 EAST ASIA AND THE SPREAD OF BUDDHISM

Korea

Korea is a mountainous peninsula some 600 miles long extending south from Manchuria and Siberia (Map 7.3). Archaeological, linguistic, and anthropological evidence indicates that the Korean people share a common ethnic origin with other peoples of North Asia, including those of Manchuria, Siberia, and Japan. Linguistically, Korean is not related to Chinese.

Korea began adopting elements of technology from China in the first millennium B.C.E., including bronze and iron technology. Chinese-Korean contact expanded during the Warring States Period, when the state of Yan extended into part of Korea. In about 194 B.C.E. Wiman, an unsuccessful rebel against the Han Dynasty, fled to Korea and set up a state called Choson in what is now northwest Korea and southern Manchuria. In 108 B.C.E. this state was overthrown by Han armies and four prefectures were established there.

The impact of the Chinese prefectures in Korea was similar to that of the contemporaneous Roman colonies in Britain in encouraging the spread of culture and political forms. The prefectures survived not only through the Han Dynasty, but also for nearly a century after the fall of the dynasty, until 313 C.E. The Chinese never controlled the entire Korean peninsula, however. The Han commanderies coexisted with the native Korean kingdom of Koguryŏ, founded in the first century B.C.E. After the Chinese colonies were finally overthrown, the kingdoms of Paekche and Silla emerged farther south on the peninsula in the third and fourth centuries C.E., leading to what is called the Three Kingdoms Period (313–668 C.E.).

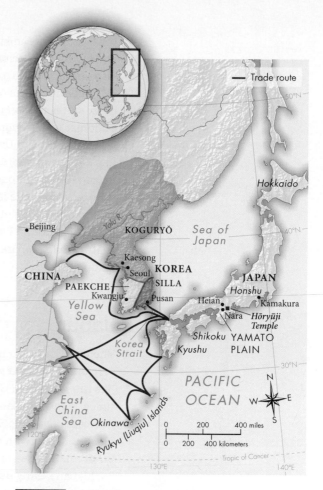

MAP 7.3 ■ Korea and Japan, ca. 600 C.E.

Korea and Japan are of similar latitude, but Korea's climate is more continental, with harsher winters. Of Japan's four islands, Kyushu is closest to Korea and mainland Asia.

Iron Artifacts from Korean Tomb

In the third and second centuries B.C.E. iron and bronze was being used in Korea to make mirrors, bells, and practical tools.
(National Museum of Gwangju, Korea/EuroCreon/ Ancient Art & Architecture Collection, Ltd.)

What were the lasting accomplishments of the Sui and Tang Dynasties?

What elements of Chinese culture were adopted by Koreans, Vietnamese, and Japanese?

✓ LearningCurve
Check what you know.

In all three Korean kingdoms Chinese was used as the language of government and learning. Each of the three kingdoms had hereditary kings, but their power was curbed by the existence of very strong hereditary elites.

Buddhism was officially introduced in Koguryŏ from China in 372 and in the other states not long after. Buddhism connected Korea to societies across Asia. Buddhist monks went back and forth between China and Korea.

When the Sui Dynasty finally reunified China in 589, it tried, unsuccessfully, to establish control of at least a part of Korea. The Tang government then tried allying itself with one state, Silla, to fight the others. Silla and Tang jointly destroyed Paekche in 660 and Koguryŏ in 668. With its new resources Silla was able to repel Tang efforts to make Korea a colony but agreed to vassal status. The unification under Silla marked the first political unification of Korea. For the next century Silla embarked on a policy of wholesale borrowing of Chinese culture and institutions.

Japan

The heart of Japan is four mountainous islands off the coast of Korea (see Map 7.3). Since the land is rugged and lacking in navigable waterways, the Inland Sea, like the Aegean in Greece, was the easiest avenue of communication in early times. Hence the land bordering the Inland Sea—Kyushu, Shikoku, and Honshu—developed as the political and cultural center of early Japan. Geography also blessed Japan with a moat to protect it against external interference—the Korea Strait and the Sea of Japan.

Japan's early development was closely tied to that of the mainland, especially to Korea. Anthropologists have discerned several major waves of immigrants into Japan. People of the Jōmon culture, established by about 10,000 B.C.E., after an influx of people from Southeast Asia, practiced hunting and fishing and fashioned clay pots. New arrivals from northeast Asia brought agriculture and a distinct culture called Yayoi (ca. 300 B.C.E.–300 C.E.). During the Han Dynasty, objects of Chinese and Korean manufacture found their way into Japan, an indication that people were traveling back and forth as well. In the third century C.E. Chinese histories begin to report on the land called Wa made up of mountainous islands. It had numerous communities with markets, granaries, tax collection, and class distinctions.

During the fourth through sixth centuries new waves of migrants from Korea brought the language that evolved into Japanese. They also brought sericulture (silkmaking), bronze swords, crossbows, iron plows, and the Chinese written language. In this period a social order similar to Korea's emerged, dominated by a warrior aristocracy organized into clans. Each clan had its own chieftain, who marshaled clansmen for battle and served as chief priest. Over time the clans fought with each other, and their numbers were gradually reduced through conquest and alliance. By the fifth century the chief of the clan that claimed descent from the sun-goddess, located in the Yamato plain around modern Osaka, had come to occupy the position of Great King—or Queen, as female rulers were not uncommon in this period.

The Yamato rulers used their religion to subordinate the gods of their rivals, much as Hammurabi had used Marduk in Babylonia (see page 41). This native religion was later termed **Shinto**, the Way of the Gods. Buddhism was formally

Shinto

▶ The Way of the Gods, Japan's native religion.

CHAPTER LOCATOR | What were the social, cultural, and political consequences of the unification of China? | How did Buddhism find its way into East Asia, and what was its appeal and impact?

CHAPTER 7

196   EAST ASIA AND THE SPREAD OF BUDDHISM

introduced in 538 c.e. and coexisted with the Shinto reverence for the spirits of ancestors and all living things.

In the sixth century Prince Shōtoku (574–622) undertook a sweeping reform of the state designed to strengthen Yamato rule by adopting Chinese-style bureaucratic practices. Near his seat of government, Prince Shōtoku built the magnificent Hōryūji Temple and staffed it with Buddhist monks from Korea. He also opened direct relations with China, sending four missions during the brief Sui Dynasty.

State-building efforts continued through the seventh century and culminated in the establishment in 710 of Japan's first long-term true city, the capital at **Nara**, north of modern Osaka. Nara, which was modeled on the Tang capital of Chang'an, gave its name to an era that lasted until 794 and was characterized by the avid importation of Chinese ideas and methods. As Buddhism developed a stronghold in Japan, it inspired many trips to China to acquire sources and to study at Chinese monasteries. Chinese and Korean craftsmen were often brought back to Japan. Musical instruments and tunes were imported as well, many originally from Central Asia. Chinese practices were instituted, such as the compilation of histories and law codes, the creation of provinces, and the appointment of governors to

> **> Prince Shōtoku's Reforms: The Seventeen Principles of 604**

- Drew from both Confucian and Buddhist teachings
- Likened the ruler to Heaven
- Instructed officials to put their duty to the ruler above the interest of their families
- Instituted a ladder of official ranks similar to China's
- Admonished the nobility to avoid strife and opposition
- Urged adherence to Buddhist precepts

Nara

▶ Japan's capital and first true city; it was established in 710 and modeled on the Tang capital of Chang'an.

Hōryūji Temple

Japanese Buddhist temples, like those in China and Korea, consisted of several buildings within a walled compound. The buildings of the Hōryūji Temple (built between 670 and 711, after Prince Shōtoku's original temple burned down) include the oldest wooden structures in the world and house some of the best early Buddhist sculpture in Japan. The three main buildings depicted here are the pagoda, housing relics; the main hall, with the temple's principal images; and the lecture hall, for sermons. The five-story pagoda could be seen from far away, much like the steeples of cathedrals in medieval Europe. (Michael Hitoshi/The Image Bank/Getty Images)

> PICTURING THE PAST

ANALYZING THE IMAGE: How are the buildings arranged? How large is the compound? What is interesting about the roofs?

CONNECTIONS: Was this temple laid out primarily for the convenience of monks who resided there or more for lay believers coming to worship? How would their needs differ?

| What were the lasting accomplishments of the Sui and Tang Dynasties? | **What elements of Chinese culture were adopted by Koreans, Vietnamese, and Japanese?** | ✓ LearningCurve Check what you know. |

collect taxes from them. By 750 some seven thousand men staffed the central government.

Increased contact with the mainland had unwanted effects as well. In contrast to China and Korea, Japan had been relatively isolated from many deadly diseases, so when diseases arrived with travelers, people did not have immunity. The great smallpox epidemic of 735–737 is thought to have reduced the population of about 5 million by 30 percent.

The Buddhist monasteries that ringed Nara were both religious centers and wealthy landlords, and the monks were active in the political life of the capital. Copying the policy of the Tang Dynasty in China, the government ordered every province to establish a Buddhist temple with twenty monks and ten nuns to chant sutras and perform other ceremonies on behalf of the emperor and the state. When an emperor abdicated in 749 in favor of his daughter, he became a Buddhist monk, a practice many of his successors would later follow.

> QUICK REVIEW

Why did elites in Korea, Vietnam, and Japan find aspects of Chinese culture and government so appealing?

CHAPTER SUMMARY

After unifying China in 221 B.C.E., the Qin Dynasty created a strongly centralized government that did away with noble privilege. The First Emperor standardized script, coinage, weights, and measures. He also built roads, the Great Wall, and a huge tomb for himself. During the four centuries of the subsequent Han Dynasty, the harsher laws of the Qin were lifted, but the strong centralized government remained. The Han government promoted internal peace by providing relief in cases of floods, droughts, and famines and by keeping land taxes low for the peasantry. The Han government sent huge armies against the nomadic Xiongnu, whose confederation threatened them in the north, but the Xiongnu remained a potent foe. Still, Han armies expanded Chinese territory in many directions. For nearly four centuries after the fall of the Han Dynasty, China was divided among contending states. After 316 the north was in the hands of non-Chinese rulers, while the south had Chinese rulers.

In the first and second centuries C.E. merchants and missionaries brought Buddhism to China. Many elements of Buddhism were new to China—a huge body of scriptures, celibate monks and nuns, traditions of depicting Buddhas and bodhisattvas in statues and paintings, and a strong proselytizing tradition. Rulers became major patrons in both north and south.

Unlike the Roman Empire, China was successfully reunified in 589 C.E. The short Sui Dynasty was followed by the longer Tang Dynasty. Tang China regained overlordship of the Silk Road cities in Central Asia. The Tang period was one of cultural flowering. Tang power declined after 755, when a powerful general

CHAPTER LOCATOR | What were the social, cultural, and political consequences of the unification of China? | How did Buddhism find its way into East Asia, and what was its appeal and impact?

CHAPTER 7
198 EAST ASIA AND THE SPREAD OF BUDDHISM

turned his army against the government. Although the rebellion was suppressed, the government was not able to regain its strong central control. Moreover, powerful states were formed along Tang's borders.

Over the ten centuries covered in Chapter 7, Korea, Japan, and Vietnam developed distinct cultures while adopting elements of China's material, political, and religious culture, including the Chinese writing system. During the Tang era, ambitious Korean and Japanese rulers sought Chinese expertise and Chinese products, including Chinese-style centralized governments and the Chinese written language.

 **CONNECTIONS** East Asia was transformed in the millennium between the Qin unification in 221 B.C.E. and the end of the eighth century C.E. The Han Dynasty and four centuries later the Tang Dynasty proved that a centralized, bureaucratic monarchy could bring peace and prosperity. By 800 C.E. neighboring societies along China's borders, from Korea and Japan on the east to the Uighurs and Tibetans to the west, had followed China's lead, forming states and building cities. Buddhism had transformed the lives of all of these societies, bringing new ways of thinking about life and death and new ways of pursuing spiritual goals.

In the same centuries that Buddhism was adapting to and simultaneously transforming the culture of much of eastern Eurasia, comparable processes were at work in western Eurasia, where Christianity continued to spread. The spread of these religions was aided by increased contact among different cultures, facilitated in Eurasia by the merchants traveling the Silk Road or sailing the Indian Ocean. Where contact among cultures wasn't as extensive, as in Africa (discussed in Chapter 10), religious beliefs were more localized. The collapse of the Roman Empire in the West during this period was not unlike the collapse of the Han Dynasty, but in Europe the empire was never put back together at the level that it was in China. The story of these centuries in western Eurasia is taken up in the next two chapters, which trace the rise of Christianity and Islam and the movement of peoples throughout Europe and Asia. Before returning to the story of East Asia after 800 in Chapter 13, we will also examine the empires in Africa (Chapter 10) and the Americas (Chapter 11).

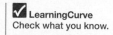

ONLINE DOCUMENT PROJECT

Ban Zhao Offers Advice to Elite Women

What do Ban Zhao's writings reveal about attitudes toward women during her time?

Read sources by and about Ban Zhao, and then complete a quiz and writing assignment based on the evidence and details from this chapter. *See the inside front cover to learn more.*

What were the lasting accomplishments of the Sui and Tang Dynasties?	What elements of Chinese culture were adopted by Koreans, Vietnamese, and Japanese?	✓ **LearningCurve** Check what you know.

CHAPTER 7 STUDY GUIDE

 STEP 1

GET STARTED ONLINE

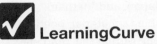 **LearningCurve**

Now that you've read the chapter, make it stick by completing the LearningCurve activity.

 STEP 2

EXPLAIN WHY IT MATTERS

Put your reading into practice. Identify each term below, and then explain why it matters in world history.

TERM	WHO OR WHAT & WHEN	WHY IT MATTERS
Great Wall (p. 177)		
Confucian classics (p. 178)		
Records of the Grand Historian (p. 180)		
Silk Road (p. 182)		
tributary system (p. 182)		
eunuchs (p. 184)		
Age of Division (p. 184)		
Grand Canal (p. 190)		
Pure Land (p. 191)		
Chan (p. 191)		
Shinto (p. 196)		
Nara (p. 197)		

 STEP 3

MOVE BEYOND THE BASICS

To demonstrate a more advanced understanding of the similarities and differences between the Han and Roman Empires, fill in the chart below with descriptions of the society, economy, and government of the Han and Roman Empires (you may want to review Chapter 6 for this exercise). Based on your comparison of these two empires, what generalizations might you make about the emergence, expansion, and decline of empires?

	Society	Economy	Government
Han Empire			
Roman Empire			

STEP 4 PUT IT ALL TOGETHER

Now, take a step back and try to explain the big picture. Remember to use specific examples from the chapter in your answers.

IMPERIAL CHINA

▶ What role did political philosophy play in Chinese imperial government? How did Legalism shape Qin government? How did Confucianism shape Han government?

▶ What common aspirations and challenges linked the Qin, Han, Sui, and Tang Dynasties?

THE SPREAD OF BUDDHISM

▶ How did Buddhism change as it spread throughout East Asia? How did the malleability of Buddhism aid its spread?

▶ What role did monasticism play in the promotion and spread of Buddhism?

CHINA AND ITS NEIGHBORS

▶ Compare and contrast the adoption of Chinese culture in Korea, Vietnam, and Japan. How would you explain the similarities and differences you note?

▶ What role did Chinese military expansion play in the spread of Chinese culture? What role did commerce and trade play?

LOOKING BACK, LOOKING AHEAD

▶ Compare and contrast China under the Han and Tang with China under the Shang and Zhou. How did unification during the later period differ from unification during the earlier period?

▶ What role did Buddhism play in facilitating the emergence of shared culture in East Asia? In your opinion, does Christianity continue to play a similar role in contemporary Western societies? Why or why not?

> IN YOUR OWN WORDS

Imagine that you must give an oral report to the class answering the following question: **How did China come to play a dominant role in the development of East Asia?** What would be the most important points and why?

8

CONTINUITY AND CHANGE IN EUROPE AND WESTERN ASIA

250–850

> What role did Christianity play in the development of Europe and Western Asia in the centuries following the collapse of the Western Roman Empire? Chapter 8 examines developments in Europe and western Asia in the centuries following the collapse of the Western Roman Empire. Scholars have long seen this era as one of the great turning points in Western history, but during the last several decades focus has shifted to continuities as well as changes. What is now usually termed "late antiquity" has been recognized as a period of creativity and adaptation in Europe and western Asia, not simply of decline and fall. The two main agents of continuity were the Eastern Roman (or Byzantine) Empire and the Christian Church. The main agent of change in late antiquity was the migration of barbarian groups throughout much of Europe and western Asia.

Orthodox Icon of Jesus In this painted icon, made for the monastery of Saint Catherine in Egypt in the eighth century, Jesus is shown on the cross, with two angels above him. Icons were important objects of veneration in the Eastern Christian, or Orthodox, Church, although they were also a source of controversy, as some church leaders thought that people were not simply using them as an aide to piety, but worshipping the image. (Kharbine-Tapabor/The Art Archive at Art Resource, NY)

> How did the Byzantine Empire preserve the legacy of Rome?

> How did the Christian Church become a major force in Europe?

> How did Christian thinkers adapt classical ideas to Christian teachings, and what new religious concepts and practices did they develop?

> How did the barbarians shape social, economic, and political structures in Europe and western Asia?

> How did the church convert barbarian peoples to Christianity?

> How did the Franks build and govern a European empire?

✓**LearningCurve**
After reading the chapter, use LearningCurve to retain what you've read.

How did the Byzantine Empire preserve the legacy of Rome?

In this illustration from a twelfth-century manuscript, sailors shoot Greek fire toward an attacking ship from a pressurized tube that looks strikingly similar to a modern flamethrower. The exact formula for Greek fire has been lost, but it was probably made from a petroleum product because it continued burning on water. Greek fire was particularly important in Byzantine defenses of Constantinople from Muslim forces in the late seventh century. (Prado, Madrid, Spain/The Bridgeman Art Library)

The Byzantine (or Eastern Roman) Empire (Map 8.1) preserved the forms, institutions, and traditions of the old Roman Empire, and its people even called themselves Romans. Most important, however, is how Byzantium protected the intellectual heritage of Greco-Roman civilization and then passed it on.

Sources of Byzantine Strength

While the western parts of the Roman Empire gradually succumbed to barbarian invaders, the Byzantine Empire survived Germanic, Persian, and Arab attacks. In 540 a force of Xiongnu and Bulgars reached the gates of Constantinople. In 583 the Avars, a mounted Mongol people who had swept across Russia and the Balkans, seized Byzantine forts along the Danube and also reached the walls of Constantinople. Between 572 and 630 the Greeks were repeatedly at war with the Sassanid Persians (see page 206). Beginning in 632 Muslim forces pressured the Byzantine Empire (see Chapter 9).

Why didn't one or a combination of these enemies capture Constantinople? The answer lies in strong military leadership and even more in the city's location and excellent fortifications. During the long reign of the emperor Justinian (r. 527–565), Byzantine generals were able to reconquer much of Italy and North Africa. The Byzantines ruled most of Italy from 535 to 572 and the southern part of the peninsula until the eleventh century. They ruled North Africa until it was con-

CHAPTER LOCATOR | **How did the Byzantine Empire preserve the legacy of Rome?** | How did the Christian Church become a major force in Europe?

204 CHAPTER 8
CONTINUITY AND CHANGE IN EUROPE AND WESTERN ASIA

224–651 Sassanid dynasty	**ca. 481–511** Reign of Clovis
325 Nicene Creed produced	**527–565** Reign of Justinian
340–419 Life of Saint Jerome	**529** Writing of *The Rule of Saint Benedict*
354–430 Life of Saint Augustine	**535–572** Byzantines reconquer and rule Italy
380 Theodosius makes Christianity official religion of Roman Empire	**730–843** Iconoclastic controversy
ca. 385–461 Life of Saint Patrick	**768–814** Reign of Charlemagne
476 Odoacer deposes the last Roman emperor in the West	**843** Treaty of Verdun divides Carolingian kingdom

quered by Muslim forces in the late seventh century. Massive triple walls, built by the emperors Constantine and Theodosius II (408–450) and kept in good repair by later emperors, protected Constantinople from sea invasion. Within the walls huge cisterns provided water, and vast gardens and grazing areas supplied food so the defending people could hold out far longer than the besieging army. Attacking Constantinople by land posed greater geographical and logistical problems

MAP 8.1 ■ The Byzantine and Sassanid Empires, ca. 600

Both the Byzantine and Sassanid Empires included territory that had earlier been part of the Roman Empire. The Sassanid Persians fought Roman armies before the founding of the Byzantine Empire. Later Byzantium and the Sassanids engaged in a series of wars that weakened both and brought neither lasting territorial acquisitions.

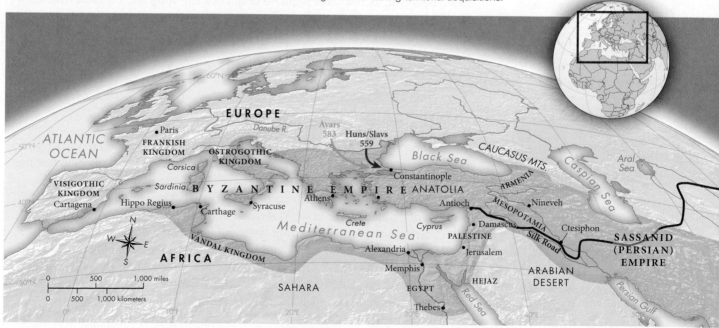

How did Christian thinkers adapt classical ideas to Christian teachings, and develop new practices?	How did the barbarians shape social, economic, and political structures in Europe and west Asia?	How did the church convert barbarian peoples to Christianity?	How did the Franks build and govern a European empire?	☑ **LearningCurve** Check what you know.

than a seventh- or eighth-century government could solve. Because the city survived, the empire, though reduced in territory, endured.

The Sassanid Empire and Conflicts with Byzantium

For several centuries the Sassanid empire of Persia was Byzantium's most regular foe. Ardashir I (r. 224–243), the ruler of a small state and the first of the Sassanid dynasty, conquered the Parthian empire in 226 (see Map 6.2, page 158). Ardashir kept expanding his holdings to the east and northwest. Like all empires, the Sassanid depended on agriculture for its economic prosperity, but its location also proved well suited for commerce (see Map 8.1). A lucrative caravan trade linked the Sassanid empire to the Silk Road and China. This trade brought about considerable cultural contact between the Sassanids and the Chinese.

Whereas the Parthians had tolerated many religions, the Sassanid Persians made Zoroastrianism the official state religion. The king's power rested on the support of nobles and Zoroastrian priests who monopolized positions in the court and in the imperial bureaucracy. A highly elaborate court ceremonial and ritual exalted the status of the king and emphasized his semidivine pre-eminence over his subjects. Adherents to religions other than Zoroastrianism, such as Jews and Christians, faced discrimination.

An expansionist foreign policy brought Persia into frequent conflict with Rome and then with Byzantium. Neither side was able to achieve a clear-cut victory until the early seventh century, when the Sassanids advanced all the way to the Mediterranean and even took Egypt in 621. Their victory would be very short-lived, however, as the taxes required to finance the wars and conflicts over the succession to the throne had weakened the Persians. The Byzantines crushed the Persians in a series of battles ending with one at Nineveh in 627. Just five years later, the first Arabic forces inspired by Islam entered Persian territories, and by 651 the Sassanid dynasty had collapsed (see page 238).

Sassanid Cameo

In this cameo — a type of jewelry made by carving into a multicolored piece of rock — the Sassanid king Shapur and the Byzantine emperor Valerian fight on horseback, each identifiable by his distinctive clothing and headgear. This does not record an actual hand-to-hand battle, but uses the well-muscled rulers as symbols of their empires.
(Erich Lessing/Art Resource, NY)

Justinian's Code of Law

Byzantine emperors organized and preserved Roman law, making a lasting contribution to the medieval and modern worlds. By the fourth century Roman law had become a huge, bewildering mass. Its sheer bulk made it almost unusable.

The emperor Justinian appointed a committee of eminent jurists to sort through and organize the laws. The result was the *Corpus Juris Civilis* (Body of Civil Law), a multipart collection of laws and legal commentary issued from 529 to 534 that is often simply termed **Justinian's *Code***. Like so much of classical culture, Justinian's *Code* was lost in western Europe with the end of the Roman Empire, but it was rediscovered in the eleventh century and came to form the foundation of law for nearly every modern European nation.

Justinian's *Code*
▶ Multipart collection of laws and legal commentary issued in the sixth century by the emperor Justinian.

CHAPTER LOCATOR | **How did the Byzantine Empire preserve the legacy of Rome?** | How did the Christian Church become a major force in Europe?

- The *Codex*: brought together all the existing imperial laws into a coherent whole, eliminated outmoded laws and contradictions, and clarified the law itself
- The *Digest*: a collection of the opinions of the foremost Roman jurists on complex legal problems
- The *Institutes*: a handbook of civil law designed for students and beginning jurists

Byzantine Intellectual Life

Just as they valued the law, the Byzantines prized education. As a result, many masterpieces of ancient Greek literature survived to influence the intellectual life of the modern world. Among members of the large reading public, history was a favorite subject. The most remarkable Byzantine historian was Procopius (ca. 500–ca. 562), who wrote the *Secret History*, a vicious and uproarious attack on Justinian and his wife, the empress Theodora. (See "Individuals in Society: Theodora of Constantinople," page 208.)

Although the Byzantines discovered little that was new in mathematics and geometry, they made advances in military applications. For example, they invented an explosive liquid that came to be known as "Greek fire." The liquid was heated and propelled by a pump through a bronze tube, and as the jet left the tube, it was ignited—somewhat like a modern flamethrower.

The Byzantines devoted a great deal of attention to medicine, and their general level of medical competence was far higher than that of western Europeans. Yet their physicians could not cope with the terrible disease, often called "the Justinian plague," that swept through the Byzantine Empire and parts of western Europe between 542 and 560. Probably originating in northwestern India and carried to the Mediterranean region by ships, the disease was similar to the bubonic plague. The epidemic had profound political as well as social consequences. It weakened Justinian's military resources, thus hampering his efforts to restore unity to the Mediterranean world.

Life in Constantinople

By the seventh century Constantinople was the greatest city in the Christian world: a large population center, the seat of the imperial court and administration, and the pivot of a large volume of international trade. Given that the city was a natural geographical connecting point between East and West, its markets offered goods from many parts of the world. At the end of the eleventh century Constantinople may have been the world's third-largest city, with only Córdoba in Spain and Kaifeng in China larger.

Although merchants could become fabulously wealthy, the landed aristocracy always held the dominant social position, as in western Europe and China. Aristocrats and monasteries usually invested their wealth in real estate, which involved little risk but brought little gain.

Constantinople did not enjoy constant political stability. Between the accession of Emperor Heraclius in 610 and the fall of the city to Western Crusaders in 1204 (see page 401), four separate dynasties ruled at Constantinople. Imperial

| How did Christian thinkers adapt classical ideas to Christian teachings, and develop new practices? | How did the barbarians shape social, economic, and political structures in Europe and west Asia? | How did the church convert barbarian peoples to Christianity? | How did the Franks build and govern a European empire? | ✓ LearningCurve Check what you know. |

207

The most powerful woman in Byzantine history was the daughter of a bear trainer for the circus. Theodora (ca. 497–548) grew up in what her contemporaries regarded as an undignified and morally suspect atmosphere, and she worked as a dancer and actress, both dishonorable occupations in the Roman world. Despite her background, she caught the eye of Justinian, who was then a military leader and whose uncle (and adoptive father) Justin had himself risen from obscurity to become the ruler of the Byzantine Empire. Under Justinian's influence, Justin changed the law to allow an actress who had left her disreputable life to marry whom she liked, and Justinian and Theodora married in 525. When Justinian was proclaimed co-emperor with his uncle Justin on April 1, 527, Theodora received the rare title of *augusta*, empress. Thereafter her name was linked with Justinian's in the exercise of imperial power.

Most of our knowledge of Theodora's early life comes from the *Secret History*, a tell-all description of the vices of Justinian and his court written by Procopius around 550. Procopius was the official court historian and thus spent his days praising those same people. In the *Secret History*, however, he portrays Theodora and Justinian as demonic, greedy, and vicious, killing courtiers to steal their property. In scene after detailed scene, Procopius portrays Theodora as particularly evil, sexually insatiable, and cruel, a temptress who used sorcery to attract men, including the hapless Justinian.

In one of his official histories, *The History of the Wars of Justinian*, Procopius presents a very different Theodora. Riots between the supporters of two teams in chariot races had turned deadly, and Justinian wavered in his handling of the perpetrators. Both sides turned against the emperor, besieging the palace while Justinian was inside it. Shouting *"Nika!"* (Victory), the rioters swept through the city, burning and looting. Justinian's counselors urged flight, but, according to Procopius, Theodora rose and declared:

> For one who has reigned, it is intolerable to be an exile. . . . If you wish, O Emperor, to save yourself, there is no difficulty: we have ample funds and there are the ships. Yet reflect whether, when you have once escaped to a place of security, you will not prefer death to safety. I agree with an old saying that the purple [that is, the color worn only by emperors] is a fair winding sheet [to be buried in].

Justinian rallied, ordered more than thirty thousand men and women executed, and crushed the revolt.

A sixth-century mosaic of the empress Theodora, made of thousands of tiny cubes of glass, shows her with a halo — a symbol of power — and surrounded by officials, priests, and court ladies. (Scala/Art Resource, NY)

Other sources describe or suggest Theodora's influence on imperial policy. Justinian passed a number of laws that improved the legal status of women, such as allowing women to own property and to be guardians over their own children. He forbade the exposure of unwanted infants, which happened more often to girls than to boys because boys were valued more highly. Theodora presided at imperial receptions for Arab sheiks, Persian ambassadors, Germanic princesses from the West, and barbarian chieftains from southern Russia. When Justinian fell ill from the bubonic plague in 542, Theodora took over his duties. Justinian is reputed to have consulted her every day about all aspects of state policy, including religious policy regarding the doctrinal disputes that continued throughout his reign.

Theodora's influence over her husband and her power in the Byzantine state continued until she died, perhaps of cancer, twenty years before Justinian. Her influence may have even continued after death, for Justinian continued to pass reforms favoring women and, at the end of his life, accepted an interpretation of Christian doctrine she had favored. Institutions that she established, including hospitals and churches, continued to be reminders of her charity and piety.

Theodora has been viewed as a symbol of the use of beauty and cleverness to attain position and power, and also as a strong and capable co-ruler who held the empire together during riots, revolts, and deadly epidemics. Just as she fascinated Procopius, she continues to intrigue writers today, who make her a character not only in historical works, but also in science fiction and fantasy.

QUESTIONS FOR ANALYSIS

1. How would you assess the complex legacy of Theodora?
2. Since Procopius's public and private views of the empress are so different, should he be trusted at all as a historical source? Why or why not?

ONLINE DOCUMENT PROJECT

What do Procopius's descriptions of Theodora and Justinian tell us about the problems and challenges his society faced? Examine sources that reveal the connections Procopius saw between Byzantium's rulers and the rapid decline he perceived in Byzantine society, and then complete a quiz and writing assignment based on the evidence and details from this chapter. *See the inside front cover to learn more.*

government involved such intricate court intrigue, assassination plots, and military revolts that the word *byzantine* is sometimes used in English to mean extremely entangled and complicated politics.

The typical household in the city included family members and servants, some of whom were slaves. Artisans lived and worked in their shops, while clerks, civil servants, minor officials, and business people commonly dwelled in multistory buildings perhaps comparable to the apartment complexes of modern American cities. Wealthy aristocrats resided in freestanding mansions.

In the homes of the upper classes, the segregation of women seems to have been the first principle of interior design. As in ancient Athens, private houses contained a *gynaeceum* (jihn-uh-SEE-uhm), or women's apartment, where women were kept strictly separated from the outside world. The fundamental reason for this segregation was the family's honor.

As it was throughout the world, marriage was part of a family's strategy for social advancement. Both the immediate family and the larger kinship group participated in the selection of a bride or a groom, choosing a spouse who might enhance the family's wealth or prestige.

QUICK REVIEW

Why did Roman government in the east survive long after it collapsed in the west?

> How did the Christian Church become a major force in Europe?

Sarcophagus of Helena

This marble sarcophagus was made for Helena, the mother of Emperor Constantine, at her death. Its detailed carvings show victorious Roman horsemen and barbarian prisoners. Like her son, Helena became a Christian, and she was sent by Constantine on a journey to bring sacred relics from Jerusalem to Constantinople as part of his efforts to promote Christianity in the empire. (© Vanni Archive/Art Resource, NY)

A s the Western Roman Empire disintegrated, the Christian Church survived and grew. The church developed permanent institutions that drew on the Greco-Roman tradition but also expressed Christian values.

The Evolution of Church Leadership and Orthodoxy

Believers in early Christian communities chose their own leaders, but over time appointment by existing church leaders or secular rulers became the common practice. During the reign of Diocletian (r. 284–305), the Roman Empire had been divided for administrative purposes into geographical units called **dioceses**, and Christianity adopted this pattern. Each diocese was headed by a bishop. The center of a bishop's authority was his cathedral, a word deriving from the Latin *cathedra*, meaning "chair."

The early Christian Church benefited from the administrative abilities of church leaders. Bishop Ambrose of Milan (339–397) was typical of the Roman

dioceses
▶ Geographic administrative districts of the church, each under the authority of a bishop and centered around a cathedral.

CHAPTER LOCATOR | How did the Byzantine Empire preserve the legacy of Rome? | **How did the Christian Church become a major force in Europe?**

210   CHAPTER 8
CONTINUITY AND CHANGE IN EUROPE AND WESTERN ASIA

aristocrats who held high public office, converted to Christianity, and subsequently became bishops. Like many bishops, Ambrose had a solid education in classical law and rhetoric, which he used to become an eloquent preacher. He had a strong sense of his authority and even successfully resisted Emperor Theodosius's (r. 379–395) efforts to take control of church property. Ambrose's assertion that the church was supreme in spiritual matters and the state in secular issues was to serve as the cornerstone of the church's position on church-state relations for centuries.

Although conflicts between religious and secular leaders were frequent, the church also received support from the emperors. In 380 Theodosius made Christianity the official religion of the empire, and later in his reign he authorized the closure or destruction of temples and holy sites dedicated to the traditional Roman and Greek gods. In return for such support, the emperors expected the Christian Church's assistance in maintaining order and unity.

Christians disagreed with one another about many issues. In the fourth and fifth centuries disputes arose over the nature of Christ. For example, Arianism, developed by Arius (ca. 250–336), a priest of Alexandria, held that Jesus was created by the will of God the Father and thus was not co-eternal with him. Emperor Constantine, who legalized Christianity in 312, rejected the Arian interpretation. In 325 he summoned a council of church leaders to Nicaea in Asia Minor and presided over it personally. The council produced the Nicene (nigh-SEEN) Creed, which defined the position that Christ is "eternally begotten of the Father" and of the same substance as the Father. Arius and those who refused to accept Nicene Christianity were banished. Their interpretation of the nature of Christ was declared a **heresy**, that is, a belief that contradicted the interpretation the church leaders declared was correct, which was termed orthodoxy. These actions did not end Arianism, however. Several later emperors were Arian Christian, and Arian missionaries converted many barbarian tribes. The Nicene interpretation eventually became the most widely held understanding of the nature of Christ.

heresy
▶ A religious practice or belief judged unacceptable by church officials.

Nonetheless, disputes about the nature of Christ also continued, with factions establishing themselves as separate Christian groups. The Nestorians, for example, regarded the divine and human natures in Jesus as distinct from one another, whereas the orthodox opinion was that they were united. The Nestorians split from the rest of the church in the fifth century after their position was outlawed and settled in Persia. Nestorian Christian missionaries later founded churches in Central Asia, India, and China (see Chapter 12).

The Western Church and the Eastern Church

The leader of the church in the West, the bishop of Rome, became more powerful than his counterpart in the Byzantine East for a variety of reasons. Most significantly, bishops of Rome asserted that Rome had a special place in Christian history. According to tradition, Saint Peter, chief of Jesus's disciples, had lived in Rome and been its first bishop. Thus, as successors of Peter, the bishops of Rome—known as **popes**, claimed a privileged position in the church hierarchy, an idea called the Petrine Doctrine. They urged other churches to appeal to Rome for the resolution of disputed issues and sent letters of guidance to other bishops. (The Christian Church headed by the pope in Rome was generally called the Roman Church in this era, and later the Roman Catholic Church.)

popes
▶ Heads of the Roman Catholic Church, who became political as well as religious authorities. The period of a pope's term in office is called a pontificate.

| How did Christian thinkers adapt classical ideas to Christian teachings, and develop new practices? | How did the barbarians shape social, economic, and political structures in Europe and west Asia? | How did the church convert barbarian peoples to Christianity? | How did the Franks build and govern a European empire? | ☑ LearningCurve Check what you know. |

This wood carving shows Saint Ambrose and Saint Jerome, two of the most important early church fathers, hard at work writing. Divine inspiration appears in the form of an angel and a dove. (Duomo, Modena, Italy/Alinari/Art Resource, NY)

The popes also expanded the church's secular authority. They made treaties with barbarian leaders, charged taxes, enforced laws, and organized armies. The Western Christian Church headed by the pope in Rome would become the most enduring nongovernmental institution in world history.

By contrast, in the East the emperor's jurisdiction over the church was fully acknowledged. As in Rome, there was a head of the church in Constantinople, called the patriarch, but he did not develop the same powers that the pope did in the West because there was never a similar power vacuum into which he needed to step. He and other high church officials were appointed by the emperor. The Eastern emperors looked on religion as a branch of the state, and they considered it their duty to protect the faith not only against heathen outsiders but also against heretics within the empire. Following the pattern set by Constantine, the emperors summoned councils of bishops and theologians to settle doctrinal disputes. They and the Eastern bishops did not accept Rome's claim to primacy, and gradually the Byzantine Christian Church, generally called the **Orthodox Church**, and the Roman Church began to diverge.

Orthodox Church
▶ Another name for the Eastern Christian Church, over which emperors continued to have power.

Christian Monasticism

Christianity began and spread as a city religion. With time, however, some especially pious Christians started to feel that a life of asceticism (extreme material sacrifice, including fasting and the renunciation of sex) was a better way to show their devotion to Christ's teachings, just as followers of Mahavira or the Buddha had centuries earlier in South Asia (see Chapter 3).

Ascetics often separate themselves from their families and normal social life, and this is what Christian ascetics did. Individuals and small groups withdrew from cities and moved to the Egyptian desert, where they sought God through prayer in caves and shelters in the desert or mountains. These individuals were called hermits or monks. Gradually, large groups of monks emerged in the deserts of Upper Egypt, creating a style of life known as monasticism. Many devout women were also attracted to this eremitical type of monasticism, becoming nuns. Although monks and nuns led isolated lives, ordinary people soon recognized them as holy people and sought them as spiritual guides.

CHAPTER LOCATOR | How did the Byzantine Empire preserve the legacy of Rome? | **How did the Christian Church become a major force in Europe?**

Church leaders did not really approve of eremitical life. Hermits sometimes claimed to have mystical experiences—direct communications with God. If hermits could communicate directly with the Lord, what need had they for priests, bishops, and the institutional church? The church hierarchy instead encouraged those who wanted to live ascetic lives of devotion to do so in communities. Consequently, in the fourth, fifth, and sixth centuries many different kinds of communal monasticism developed in Gaul, Italy, Spain, Anglo-Saxon England, and Ireland.

In 529 Benedict of Nursia (ca. 480–547) wrote a brief set of regulations for the monks who had gathered around him at Monte Cassino, between Rome and Naples. Benedict's guide for monastic life, known as *The Rule of Saint Benedict*, slowly replaced all others, and it has influenced all forms of organized religious life in the Roman Church. The guide outlined a monastic life of regularity, discipline, and moderation in an atmosphere of silence. Under Benedict's regulations, monks spent part of each day in formal prayer, chanting psalms and other prayers from the Bible. The rest of the day was passed in manual labor, study, and private prayer. The monastic life as conceived by Saint Benedict provided opportunities for men of different abilities and talents—from mechanics to gardeners to literary scholars. The Benedictine form of religious life also appealed to women, because it allowed them to show their devotion and engage in study. Benedict's twin sister, Scholastica (480–543), adapted the *Rule* for use by her community of nuns.

Benedictine monasticism also succeeded partly because it was so materially successful. In the seventh and eighth centuries Benedictine monasteries pushed back forests and wastelands, drained swamps, and experimented with crop rotation, making a significant contribution to the agricultural development of Europe. Monasteries also conducted schools for local young people. Some learned about prescriptions and herbal remedies and went on to provide medical treatment for their localities. Others copied manuscripts and wrote books. Local and royal governments drew on the services of the literate men and able administrators the monasteries produced.

Monasticism in the Orthodox world differed in fundamental ways from the monasticism that evolved in western Europe. First, while *The Rule of Saint Benedict* gradually became the universal guide for all western European monasteries, each monastic house in the Byzantine world developed its own set of rules for organization and behavior. Second, education never became a central feature of the Orthodox houses. Since bishops and patriarchs of the Orthodox Church were recruited only from the monasteries, however, these institutions did exercise cultural influence.

QUICK REVIEW

What were the most important differences between the Roman and Orthodox Churches? How would you explain these differences?

How did Christian thinkers adapt classical ideas to Christian teachings, and develop new practices?

How did the barbarians shape social, economic, and political structures in Europe and west Asia?

How did the church convert barbarian peoples to Christianity?

How did the Franks build and govern a European empire?

LearningCurve
Check what you know.

How did Christian thinkers adapt classical ideas to Christian teachings, and what new religious concepts and practices did they develop?

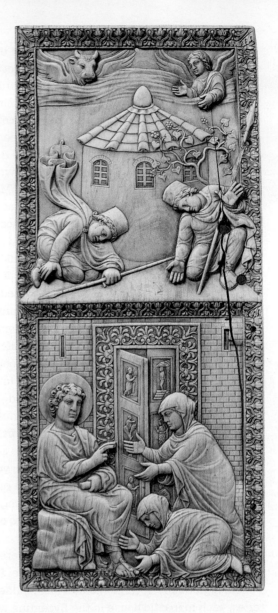

The Marys at Jesus's Tomb

This late-fourth-century ivory panel tells the biblical story of Mary Magdalene and another Mary who went to Jesus's tomb to anoint the body (Matthew 28:1–7). At the top guards collapse when an angel descends from Heaven, and at the bottom the Marys listen to the angel telling them that Jesus has risen. Here the artist uses Roman artistic styles to convey Christian subject matter, synthesizing classical form and Christian teaching.

(Castello Sforzesco Milan, Italy/Scala/Art Resource, NY)

The growth of Christianity was tied not just to institutions such as the papacy and monasteries but also to ideas. Initially, Christians rejected Greco-Roman culture. Gradually, however, Christian leaders and thinkers developed ideas that drew on classical influences, though there were also areas of controversy that differed in the Western and Eastern Churches.

Christianity and Classical Culture

In the first century Christians believed that Christ would soon fulfill his promise to return and that the end of the world was near; therefore, they saw no point in

CHAPTER LOCATOR | How did the Byzantine Empire preserve the legacy of Rome? | How did the Christian Church become a major force in Europe?

CHAPTER 8
214 CONTINUITY AND CHANGE IN EUROPE AND WESTERN ASIA

devoting time to learning. By the second century, however, these apocalyptic expectations were diminishing, and church leaders began to incorporate elements of Greek and Roman philosophy and learning into Christian teachings (see page 166). They found support for this incorporation in the written texts that circulated among Christians. In the third and fourth centuries these texts were brought together as the New Testament of the Bible, with general agreement about most of what should be included but sharp disputes about some books. Although some of Jesus's sermons as recorded in the Gospels (see page 165) urged followers to avoid worldly attachments, other parts of the Bible advocated acceptance of existing social, economic, and political structures. Christian thinkers built on these, adapting Christian teachings to fit with Roman realities and Roman ideas to fit with Christian aims, just as Buddhist thinkers adapted Buddhist teachings when they spread them to Central Asia, China, Korea, and Japan (see Chapter 7).

Saint Jerome (340–419) translated the Old Testament and New Testament from Hebrew and Greek, respectively, into vernacular Latin. Called the Vulgate, his edition of the Bible served as the official translation until the sixteenth century. Familiar with the writings of classical authors such as Cicero and Virgil, Saint Jerome believed that Christians should study the best of ancient thought because it would direct their minds to God. He maintained that the best ancient literature should be interpreted in light of the Christian faith.

Christian attitudes toward gender and sexuality provide a good example of the ways early Christians first challenged and then largely adopted the views of their contemporary world. In his plan of salvation Jesus considered women the equal of men. Women were among the earliest converts to Christianity and took an active role in its spread, preaching, acting as missionaries, being martyred alongside men, and perhaps even baptizing believers. Some women embraced the ideal of virginity and either singly or in monastic communities declared themselves "virgins in the service of Christ." All this initially made Christianity seem dangerous to many Romans who viewed marriage as the foundation of society and the proper patriarchal order.

Not all Christian teachings about gender were radical, however. In the first century male church leaders began to place restrictions on female believers. Women were forbidden to preach and were gradually excluded from holding official positions in Christianity other than in women's monasteries. In so limiting the activities of female believers, Christianity was following well-established social patterns, just as it modeled its official hierarchy after that of the Roman Empire.

Christian teachings about sexuality also built on and challenged classical models. The rejection of sexual activity involved an affirmation of the importance of a spiritual life, but it also incorporated hostility toward the body found in some Hellenistic philosophies. Just as spirit was superior to matter, the thinking went, the mind was superior to the body. Though Christian teachings affirmed that God had created the material world and sanctioned marriage, most Christian thinkers also taught that celibacy was the better life and that anything that distracted one's attention from the spiritual world performed an evil function. For most clerical writers (who were themselves male), this temptation came from women, and in some of their writings women themselves are portrayed as evil, the "devil's gateway."

How did Christian thinkers adapt classical ideas to Christian teachings, and develop new practices?

How did the barbarians shape social, economic, and political structures in Europe and west Asia?

How did the church convert barbarian peoples to Christianity?

How did the Franks build and govern a European empire?

LearningCurve
Check what you know.

215

Saint Augustine on Sin, Grace, and Redemption

One thinker had an especially strong role in shaping Christian views about sexual activity and many other issues: Saint Augustine of Hippo (354–430). Augustine was born into an urban family in what is now Algeria in North Africa. His father was a pagan; his mother, Monica, was a devout Christian. He gained an excellent education, fathered a son, and experimented with various religious ideas. In adulthood he converted to his mother's religion, eventually becoming bishop of the city of Hippo Regius.

Written in the rhetorical style and language of late Roman antiquity, Augustine's autobiography, *The Confessions*, marks a synthesis of Greco-Roman forms and Christian thought. *The Confessions* describes Augustine's moral struggle, the conflict between his spiritual aspirations and his sensual self. Many Greek and Roman philosophers had taught that knowledge would lead to virtue. Augustine came to reject this idea, claiming that people do not always act on the basis of rational knowledge. Instead the basic or dynamic force in any individual is the will. When Adam ate the fruit forbidden by God in the Garden of Eden (Genesis 3:6), he committed the "original sin" and corrupted the will, wrote Augustine. Adam's sin did not simply remain his own but was passed on to all later humans through sexual intercourse. Original sin thus became a common social stain, in Augustine's opinion, transmitted by sexual desire. According to Augustine, because Adam disobeyed God, all human beings have an innate tendency to sin: their will is weak. But Augustine held that God restores the strength of the will through grace, which is transmitted in certain rituals that the church defined as **sacraments**. Augustine's ideas on sin, grace, and redemption became the foundation of all subsequent Western Christian theology, Protestant as well as Catholic.

sacraments
▶ Certain rituals of the church believed to act as a conduit of God's grace, such as the Eucharist and baptism.

The Iconoclastic Controversy

In the centuries after Constantine, the most serious dispute within the Orthodox Church concerned icons—images or representations of God the Father, Jesus, and the saints in painting, bas-relief, or mosaic. Since the third century the church had allowed people to venerate icons. Although all prayer was to be directed to God the Father, Christian teaching held that icons representing the saints fostered reverence and that Jesus and the saints could most effectively plead a cause to God the Father. (For more about the role of saints, see page 223.) Iconoclasts, those who favored the destruction of icons, argued that people were worshipping the image itself rather than what it signified. This, they claimed, constituted idolatry, a violation of one of the Ten Commandments, the religious and moral code found in Hebrew Scripture that was also sacred to Christians.

The result of this dispute was a terrible theological conflict, the **iconoclastic controversy**, that split the Byzantine world for a century. In 730 the emperor Leo III (r. 717–741) ordered the destruction of icons. The removal of these images from Byzantine churches provoked a violent reaction: entire provinces revolted, and the Byzantine Empire and the Roman papacy severed relations. Since Eastern monasteries were the fiercest defenders of icons, Leo's son Constantine V (r. 741–775) seized their property, executed some of the monks, and forced other monks

iconoclastic controversy
▶ The conflict over the veneration of religious images in the Byzantine Empire.

CHAPTER LOCATOR | How did the Byzantine Empire preserve the legacy of Rome? | How did the Christian Church become a major force in Europe?

CHAPTER 8
216 CONTINUITY AND CHANGE IN EUROPE AND WESTERN ASIA

into the army. Theological disputes and civil disorder over the icons continued intermittently until 843, when the icons were restored.

The implications of the iconoclastic controversy extended far beyond strictly theological issues. Iconoclasm raised the question of the right of the emperor to intervene in religious disputes. Iconoclasm antagonized the pope and served to encourage him in his quest for an alliance with the Frankish monarchy (see page 226). This further divided the two parts of Christendom, and in 1054 a theological disagreement led the pope in Rome and the patriarch of Constantinople to declare each other a heretic. The outcome was a continuing schism between the Roman Catholic and the Orthodox Churches.

QUICK REVIEW <

How did the works of Saint Augustine both embrace and challenge Greco-Roman ideas?

| How did Christian thinkers adapt classical ideas to Christian teachings, and develop new practices? | How did the barbarians shape social, economic, and political structures in Europe and west Asia? | How did the church convert barbarian peoples to Christianity? | How did the Franks build and govern a European empire? | ✓ LearningCurve Check what you know. |

217

How did the barbarians shape social, economic, and political structures in Europe and western Asia?

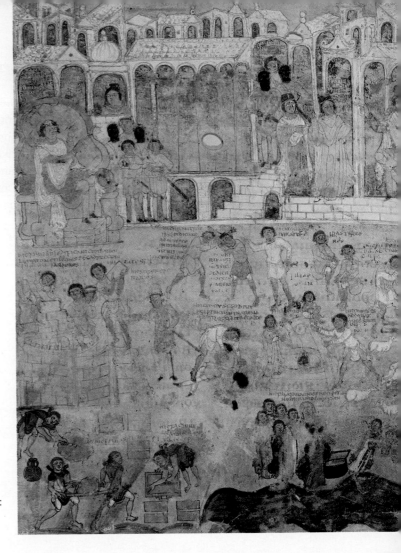

Visigothic Work and Play

This page comes from one of the very few manuscripts from the time of the barbarian invasions to have survived, a copy of the first five books of the Old Testament — the Pentateuch — made around 600, perhaps in Visigothic Spain or North Africa. The top shows biblical scenes, while the bottom shows people engaged in everyday activities: building a wall, drawing water from a well, and trading punches.
(Bibliothèque Nationale, Paris, France/The Art Archive at Art Resource, NY)

The word *barbarian* comes from the Greek *barbaros*, meaning someone who did not speak Greek. The Greeks used this word to include people such as the Egyptians, whom the Greeks respected. The Romans usually used the Latin version of *barbarian* to mean the peoples who lived beyond the northeastern boundary of Roman territory, whom they regarded as unruly, savage, and primitive. That value judgment is generally also present when we use *barbarian* in English, but there really is no other word to describe the many different peoples who lived to the north of the Roman Empire. Thus historians of late antiquity use the word *barbarian* to designate these peoples, who spoke a variety of languages but had similarities in their basic social, economic, and political structures.

Barbarians included many different ethnic groups with social and political structures, languages, laws, and beliefs developed in central and northern Europe and western Asia over many centuries. Among the largest barbarian groups were the Celts and Germans; Germans were further subdivided into various tribes, such as Ostrogoths, Visigoths, Burgundians, and Franks. *Celt* and *German* are

CHAPTER LOCATOR | How did the Byzantine Empire preserve the legacy of Rome? | How did the Christian Church become a major force in Europe?

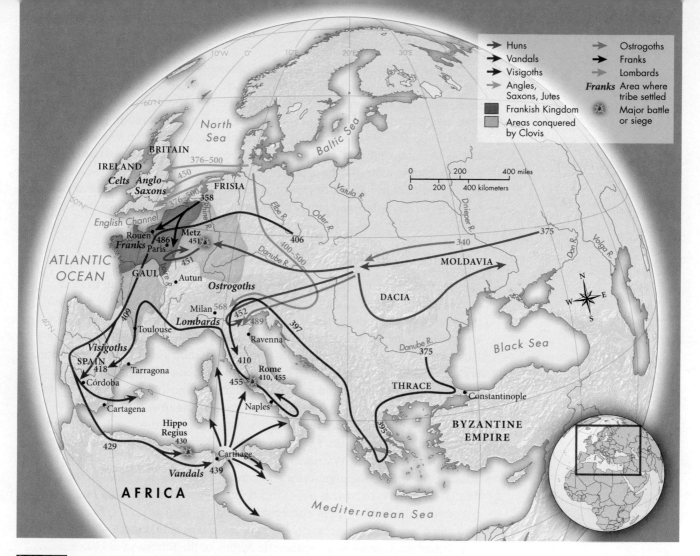

MAP 8.2 ■ The Barbarian Migrations, ca. 340–500

Various barbarian groups migrated throughout Europe and western Asia in late antiquity, pushed and pulled by a number of factors. Many of them formed loosely structured states, of which the Frankish kingdom would become the most significant.

often used as ethnic terms, but they are better understood as linguistic terms, a Celt being a person who spoke a Celtic language and a German one who spoke a Germanic language. Celts, Germans, and other barbarians brought their customs and traditions with them when they moved south and west, and these gradually combined with classical and Christian customs and beliefs to form new types of societies. From this cultural mix the Franks emerged as an especially strong and influential force, and they built a lasting empire (see page 226).

Social and Economic Structures

Barbarian groups usually resided in small villages, and climate and geography determined the basic patterns of agricultural and pastoral life. Many groups settled on the edges of clearings where they raised barley, wheat, oats, peas, and beans. Men and women tilled their fields with simple scratch plows and harvested their grain with small iron sickles. Most of people's caloric intake came from grain in some form.

| How did Christian thinkers adapt classical ideas to Christian teachings, and develop new practices? | **How did the barbarians shape social, economic, and political structures in Europe and west Asia?** | How did the church convert barbarian peoples to Christianity? | How did the Franks build and govern a European empire? | ✓ LearningCurve Check what you know. |

Within the villages, there were great differences in wealth and status. Free men and their families constituted the largest class, and the number of cattle these men possessed indicated their wealth and determined their social status. Free men also took part in tribal warfare. Slaves acquired through warfare worked as farm laborers, herdsmen, and household servants. Barbarian society was patriarchal. Some wealthy and powerful men had more than one wife, a pattern that continued even after they became Christian, but polygamy was not widespread among ordinary people. Once women were widowed, they sometimes assumed their husbands' rights over family property and took guardianship of their children.

Tribes, Warriors, and Laws

The basic social and political unit among barbarian groups was the tribe or confederation, made up of kin groups whose members believed they were all descended from a common ancestor. Tribes were led by chieftains, who were elected from among the male members of the most powerful family. The chief led the tribe in war, settled disputes among its members, conducted negotiations with outside powers, and offered sacrifices to the gods. As barbarian groups migrated into and conquered parts of the Western Roman Empire, their chiefs became even more powerful. Often chiefs adopted the title of king.

Closely associated with the chief in some tribes was the comitatus (kuhm-ee-TAH-tuhs), or war band. The warriors swore loyalty to the chief and fought alongside him in battle. Warriors may originally have been relatively equal to one another, but during the migrations and warfare of the second through the fourth centuries, the war band was transformed into a system of stratified ranks. When tribes settled down, warriors also began to acquire land as both a mark of prestige and a means to power. Social inequalities emerged and gradually grew stronger. These inequalities help explain the origins of the European noble class.

Beginning in the late fifth century some chieftains began to collect, write, and publish lists of their customs and laws. Barbarian law codes often included clauses designed to reduce interpersonal violence. Any crime that involved a personal injury, such as assault, rape, and murder, was given a particular monetary value, called the **wergeld** (WUHR-gehld) that was to be paid by a person accused of a crime to the victim or the victim's family. The wergeld varied according to the severity of the crime and also the social status and gender of the victim.

Like most people of the ancient world, barbarians worshipped hundreds of gods and goddesses with specialized functions. They regarded certain mountains, lakes, rivers, or groves of trees as sacred because these were linked to deities. Among the Celts, religious leaders called druids had legal and educational as well as religious functions, orally passing down laws and traditions from generation to generation. Bards singing poems and ballads also passed down myths and stories of heroes and gods, which were written down much later.

Migrations and Political Change

Migrating groups that the Romans labeled barbarians had moved southward and eastward off and on since about 100 C.E. (see page 168). Why did the barbarians migrate? In part, they were searching for more regular supplies of food, better

wergeld
▶ Compensatory payment for death or injury set in many barbarian law codes.

CHAPTER LOCATOR | How did the Byzantine Empire preserve the legacy of Rome? | How did the Christian Church become a major force in Europe?

220   CHAPTER 8
CONTINUITY AND CHANGE IN EUROPE AND WESTERN ASIA

farmland, and a warmer climate. Conflicts within and among barbarian groups also led to war and disruption, which motivated groups to move. Roman expansion led to further movement of barbarian groups but also to the blending of cultures.

The spread of the Celts presents a good example of both conflict and assimilation. Celtic-speaking peoples had lived in central Europe since at least the fifth century B.C.E. and had spread out from there to the Iberian Peninsula in the west, Hungary in the east, and the British Isles in the north. As Julius Caesar advanced northward into what he termed Gaul (present-day France), he defeated many Celtic tribes (see page 154). Celtic peoples conquered by the Romans often assimilated to Roman ways, intermarrying with Romans, adopting the Latin language and many aspects of Roman culture. By the fourth century C.E., however, Gaul and Britain were under pressure from Germanic groups moving westward. Roman troops withdrew from Britain, and Celtic-speaking peoples clashed with Germanic-speaking invaders, of whom the largest tribes were the Angles and the Saxons. Some Celtic-speakers moved farther west. Others remained and intermarried with Germanic peoples, their descendants forming a number of small Anglo-Saxon kingdoms.

In eastern Europe, a significant factor in barbarian migration and the merging of various Germanic groups was pressure from nomadic steppe peoples from central Asia, most prominently the Huns, who attacked the Black Sea area and the Eastern Roman Empire beginning in the fourth century. Under the leadership of their warrior-king Attila, the Huns attacked the Byzantine Empire in 447 and then turned westward, allying with some Germanic groups and moving into what is now France. After Attila turned his army southward and crossed the Alps into Italy. Though papal diplomacy was later credited with stopping the advance of the Huns, their dwindling food supplies and a plague that spread among their troops were probably much more important factors. The Huns retreated from Italy, and within a year Attila was dead. The Huns never again played a significant role in European history. Their conquests had pushed many Germanic groups together, however, which transformed smaller bands of people into larger, more unified peoples who could more easily pick the Western Roman Empire apart.

After they conquered an area, barbarians generally established states ruled by kings. However, the kingdoms did not have definite geographical borders, and their locations shifted as tribes moved. Eventually, barbarian kingdoms came to include Italy itself. From Constantinople, Eastern Roman emperors such as Justinian (see page 206) worked to reconquer at least some of the West from barbarian tribes. They were occasionally successful but could not hold the empire together for long.

Anglo-Saxon Helmet

This ceremonial bronze helmet from seventh-century England was found inside a ship buried at Sutton Hoo. The nearly 100-foot-long ship was dragged overland before being buried completely. It held one body and many grave goods, including swords, gold buckles, and silver bowls made in Byzantium. The unidentified person who was buried here was clearly wealthy and powerful, and so was very likely a chief. (© The Trustees of the British Museum/Art Resource, NY)

QUICK REVIEW <

How were barbarian societies organized?

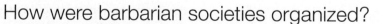

How did Christian thinkers adapt classical ideas to Christian teachings, and develop new practices?

How did the barbarians shape social, economic, and political structures in Europe and west Asia?

How did the church convert barbarian peoples to Christianity?

How did the Franks build and govern a European empire?

☑ LearningCurve
Check what you know.

> How did the church convert barbarian peoples to Christianity?

The Mediterranean served as the highway over which Christianity spread to the cities of the Roman Empire. Christian teachings were often spread into the countryside and into areas beyond the borders of the empire by those who had dedicated their lives to the church, such as monks. Such missionaries were often sent by popes specifically to convert certain groups.

Missionaries' Actions

Throughout barbarian Europe, religion was not a private or individual matter; it was a social affair, and the religion of the chieftain or king determined the religion of the people. Thus missionaries concentrated their initial efforts not on ordinary people but on kings or tribal chieftains and the members of their families. Because they had more opportunity to spend time with missionaries, queens and other female members of the royal family were often the first converts in an area, and they influenced their husbands and brothers.

Many barbarian groups were converted by Arian missionaries, who also founded dioceses. Bishop Ulfilas (ca. 310–383), for example, an Ostrogoth himself, translated the Bible from Greek into the Gothic language even before Jerome wrote the Latin Vulgate, creating a new Gothic script in order to write it down. In the sixth and seventh centuries most Goths and other Germanic tribes converted to Roman Christianity, sometimes peacefully and sometimes as a result of conquest. Ulfilas's Bible—and the Gothic script he invented—were forgotten and rediscovered only a thousand years later.

Tradition identifies the conversion of Ireland with Saint Patrick (ca. 385–461). After a vision urged him to Christianize Ireland, Patrick studied in Gaul and in 432 was consecrated a bishop. He then returned to Ireland, where he converted the Irish tribe by tribe, first baptizing the king.

The Christianization of the English began in earnest in 597, when Pope Gregory I (pontificate 590–604) sent a delegation of monks to England. The conversion of the English had far-reaching consequences because Britain later served as a base for the Christianization of Germany and other parts of northern Europe (Map 8.3). Between the fifth and tenth centuries the majority of people living on the European continent and the nearby islands accepted the Christian religion.

In eastern Europe missionaries traveled far beyond the boundaries of the Byzantine Empire. In 863 the emperor Michael III (r. 842–867) sent the brothers

CHAPTER LOCATOR | How did the Byzantine Empire preserve the legacy of Rome? | How did the Christian Church become a major force in Europe?

CHAPTER 8
222 CONTINUITY AND CHANGE IN EUROPE AND WESTERN ASIA

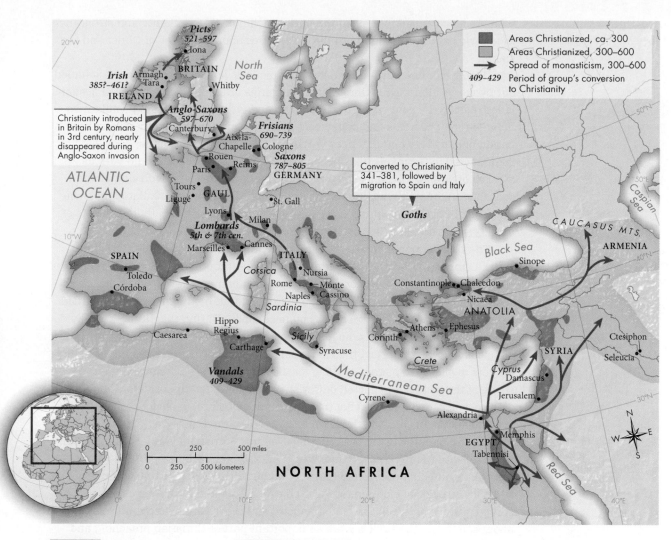

MAP 8.3 ■ **The Spread of Christianity, ca. 300–800**

Originating in the area near Jerusalem, Christianity spread throughout and then beyond the Roman world.

> MAPPING THE PAST

ANALYZING THE MAP: Based on the map, how did the roads and sea-lanes of the Roman Empire influence the spread of Christianity?

CONNECTIONS: How does the map support the conclusion that Christianity began as an urban religion and then spread into more rural areas?

Cyril (826–869) and Methodius (815–885) to preach Christianity in Moravia (an eastern region of the modern Czech Republic). Cyril invented a Slavic alphabet using Greek characters, later called the Cyrillic alphabet. In the tenth century other missionaries spread Christianity, the Cyrillic alphabet, and Byzantine art and architecture to Russia.

The Process of Conversion

How did missionaries and priests get masses of pagan and illiterate peoples to understand Christian ideals and teachings? They did it through preaching, assimilation of pagan customs, the ritual of penance, and veneration of the saints. Those

| How did Christian thinkers adapt classical ideas to Christian teachings, and develop new practices? | How did the barbarians shape social, economic, and political structures in Europe and west Asia? | **How did the church convert barbarian peoples to Christianity?** | How did the Franks build and govern a European empire? |  LearningCurve Check what you know. |

223

who preached aimed to present the basic teachings of Christianity and strengthen the newly baptized in their faith through stories about the lives of Christ and the saints.

Deeply ingrained pagan customs and practices, however, could not be stamped out by words alone. Thus Christian missionaries often pursued a policy of assimilation, easing the conversion of pagan men and women by stressing similarities between their customs and beliefs and those of Christianity and by mixing barbarian pagan ideas and practices with Christian ones. For example, bogs and lakes sacred to Germanic gods became associated with saints, as did various aspects of ordinary life, such as traveling, planting crops, and worrying about a sick child. Aspects of existing midwinter celebrations were assimilated into celebrations of Christmas. Spring rituals involving eggs and rabbits (both symbols of fertility) were added to celebrations of Easter.

penance
▶ Ritual in which Christians asked a priest for forgiveness for sins and the priest set certain actions to atone for the sins.

The ritual of **penance** was also instrumental in teaching people Christian ideas. Christianity taught that certain actions and thoughts were sins. Only by confessing sins and asking forgiveness could a sinning believer be reconciled with God. Confession was initially a public ritual, but by the fifth century individual confession to a parish priest was more common. During this ritual the individual knelt before the priest, who questioned him or her about sins he or she might have committed. The priest then set a penance such as fasting or saying specific prayers to allow the person to atone for the sin. Penance gave new converts a sense of the behavior expected of Christians, encouraged the private examination of conscience, and offered relief from the burden of sinful deeds.

saints
▶ People who were venerated for having lived or died in a way that was spiritually heroic or noteworthy.

Veneration of **saints**, people who had lived (or died) in a way that was spiritually heroic or noteworthy, was another way that Christians formed stronger connections with their religion. Saints were understood to provide protection and assistance to worshippers, and parish churches often housed saints' relics, that is, bones, articles of clothing, or other objects associated with them. The relics served as links between the material world and the spiritual, and miracle stories about saints and their relics were an important part of Christian preaching and writing.

Christians came to venerate the saints as powerful and holy. They prayed to saints or to the Virgin Mary to intercede with God, or they simply asked the saints to assist and bless them. The entire village participated in processions marking saints' days or important points in the agricultural year, often carrying images of saints or their relics around the houses and fields. The decision to adopt Christianity was often made first by an emperor or king, but actual conversion was a local matter, as people came to feel that the parish priest and the saints provided them with benefits in this world and the world to come.

> **QUICK REVIEW**

What role did kings and other elites play in the conversion of barbarian peoples to Christianity?

CHAPTER LOCATOR | How did the Byzantine Empire preserve the legacy of Rome? | How did the Christian Church become a major force in Europe?

CHAPTER 8
224 CONTINUITY AND CHANGE IN EUROPE AND WESTERN ASIA

Charlemagne and His Wife

This illumination from a ninth-century manuscript portrays Charlemagne with one of his wives. Marriage was an important tool of diplomacy for Charlemagne, and he had a number of wives and concubines. (Erich Lessing/Art Resource, NY)

> PICTURING THE PAST

ANALYZING THE IMAGE: What does Charlemagne appear to be doing? How would you characterize his wife's reaction?

CONNECTIONS: Does this depiction of a Frankish queen match what you've read about female rulers in this era, such as Theodora and Clotild?

How did the Franks build and govern a European empire?

Most barbarian kingdoms did not last very long, but one that did—and that came to have a decisive role in history—was that of the confederation of Germanic peoples known as the Franks. In the fourth and fifth centuries the Franks settled within the empire and allied with the Romans, some attaining high military and civil positions. Though at that time the Frankish kingdom was simply one barbarian kingdom among many, rulers after the influential Clovis used a variety of tactics to expand their holdings, enhance their authority, and create a stable system. Charles the Great (r. 768–814), generally known by the French version of his name, Charlemagne (SHAHR-luh-mayne), created the largest state in western Europe since the Roman Empire.

| How did Christian thinkers adapt classical ideas to Christian teachings, and develop new practices? | How did the barbarians shape social, economic, and political structures in Europe and west Asia? | How did the church convert barbarian peoples to Christianity? | **How did the Franks build and govern a European empire?** | ✔ LearningCurve Check what you know. |

The Merovingians and Carolingians

The Franks believed that Merovech, a semi-legendary figure, founded their ruling dynasty, which was thus called Merovingian (mehr-uh-VIHN-jee-uhn). The reign of Clovis (r. ca. 481–511) was decisive in the development of the Franks as a unified people. Through military campaigns, Clovis acquired the central provinces of Roman Gaul and began to conquer southern Gaul from other Germanic tribes. His wife, Clotild, a Roman Christian, pressured him to convert, but he refused. His later biographer Gregory of Tours, a bishop in the Frankish kingdom in the sixth century, attributed his conversion to a battlefield vision, just as Emperor Constantine's biographers had reported about his conversion.

Most historians today conclude that Clovis's conversion to Roman Christianity was a pragmatic choice: it brought him the crucial support of the bishops of Gaul in his campaigns against tribes that were still pagan or had accepted the Arian version of Christianity. As the defender of Roman Christianity against heretical tribes, Clovis went on to conquer the Visigoths, extending his domain to include much of what is now France and southwestern Germany.

Following Frankish traditions in which property was divided among male heirs, at Clovis's death his kingdom was divided among his four sons. For the next two centuries rulers of the various kingdoms fought one another in civil wars, and other military leaders challenged their authority.

Merovingian kings based some aspects of their government on Roman principles. For example, they adopted the Roman concept of the *civitas*—Latin for a city and its surrounding territory. A count presided over the civitas, raising troops, collecting royal revenues, and providing justice. Within the royal household, Merovingian politics provided women with opportunities, and some queens not only influenced but occasionally also dominated events. Because the finances of the kingdom were merged with those of the royal family, queens often had control of the royal treasury just as more ordinary women controlled household expenditures.

At the king's court an official called the mayor of the palace supervised legal, financial, and household officials; the mayor of the palace also governed in the king's absence. In the seventh century the position as mayor was held by members of an increasingly powerful family, the **Carolingians** (ka-ruh-LIHN-jee-uhns), who advanced themselves through advantageous marriages, a well-earned reputation for military strength, and the help of the church.

Eventually the Carolingians replaced the Merovingians as rulers of the Frankish kingdom, cementing their authority when the Carolingian Charles Martel defeated Muslim invaders in 732 at the Battle of Poitiers (pwah-tee-AY) in central France. The Battle of Poitiers helped the Carolingians acquire more support from the church, perhaps their most important asset. They further strengthened their ties to the church by supporting the work of missionaries who preached Christian principles—including the duty to obey secular authorities—to pagan peoples and by allying themselves with the papacy against other Germanic tribes.

The Warrior-Ruler Charlemagne

The most powerful of the Carolingians was Charlemagne. Through brutal military expeditions that brought wealth and by peaceful travel, personal appearances, shrewd marital alliances, and the sheer force of his personality, Charlemagne

Carolingian

▶ A dynasty of rulers that took over the Frankish kingdom from the Merovingians in the seventh century; *Carolingian* derives from the Latin word for "Charles," the name of several members of this dynasty.

CHAPTER LOCATOR | How did the Byzantine Empire preserve the legacy of Rome? | How did the Christian Church become a major force in Europe?

226 CHAPTER 8 CONTINUITY AND CHANGE IN EUROPE AND WESTERN ASIA

sought to awe newly conquered peoples and rebellious domestic enemies. By around 805 the Frankish kingdom included all of continental Europe except Spain, Scandinavia, southern Italy, and the Slavic fringes of the East.

For administrative purposes, Charlemagne divided his entire kingdom into counties. Each of the approximately six hundred counties was governed by a count. As a link between local authorities and the central government, Charlemagne appointed officials called *missi dominici*, "agents of the lord king." Each year beginning in 802 two missi, usually a count and a bishop or abbot, visited assigned districts. They checked up on the counts and their districts' judicial, financial, and clerical activities.

In the autumn of the year 800 Charlemagne visited Rome, where on Christmas Day Pope Leo III crowned him emperor. The event had momentous consequences. In taking as his motto *Renovatio romani imperi* (Revival of the Roman Empire), Charlemagne was deliberately perpetuating old Roman imperial ideas while identifying with the new Rome of the Christian Church. The Byzantines regarded his papal coronation as rebellious and Charlemagne as a usurper. His crowning as emperor thus marked a decisive break between Rome and Constantinople and gave church authorities in the West proof that the imperial title could only be granted by the pope.

As he built an empire through conquest and strategic alliances, Charlemagne also set in motion a cultural revival that later historians called the "Carolingian Renaissance." The Carolingian Renaissance was a rebirth of interest in, study of, and preservation of the language, ideas, and achievements of classical Greece and Rome. Scholars at Charlemagne's capital of Aachen copied Greco-Roman and Christian books and manuscripts and created libraries housed in churches and monasteries. Furthermore, Charlemagne urged monasteries to promote Christian learning.

Charlemagne left his vast empire to his sole surviving son, Louis the Pious (r. 814–840), who attempted to keep the empire intact. This proved to be impossible. Members of the nobility engaged in plots and open warfare against the emperor, often allying themselves with one of Louis's three sons. In 843, shortly after Louis's death, those sons agreed to the **Treaty of Verdun**, which divided the empire into three parts: Charles the Bald received the western part, Lothair the middle and the title of emperor, and Louis the eastern part, from which he acquired the title "the German."

The weakening of central power was hastened by invasions and migrations from the north, south, and east. Thus Charlemagne's empire ended in much the same way that the Roman Empire had earlier, from a combination of internal weakness and external pressure.

Charlemagne's Conquests, ca. 768–814

- Frankish Kingdom, 768
- Areas conquered by Charlemagne
- Tributary peoples
- Byzantine Empire

The Treaty of Verdun, 843

Treaty of Verdun
▶ A treaty ratified in 843 that divided Charlemagne's territories among his three surviving grandsons; their kingdoms set the pattern for the modern states of Germany, France, and Italy.

QUICK REVIEW

What role did the Roman Church play in the rise of the Carolingians to power?

How did Christian thinkers adapt classical ideas to Christian teachings, and develop new practices?	How did the barbarians shape social, economic, and political structures in Europe and west Asia?	How did the church convert barbarian peoples to Christianity?	**How did the Franks build and govern a European empire?**	✓ LearningCurve Check what you know.

227

CHAPTER SUMMARY

During the sixth and seventh centuries the Byzantine Empire survived waves of attacks, owing to effective military leadership and to fortifications around Constantinople. Byzantine emperors organized and preserved Roman institutions, and the Byzantine Empire survived until 1453. The emperor Justinian oversaw creation of a new uniform code of Roman law. The Byzantines prized education, and because of them many aspects of ancient Greek thought survived to influence the intellectual life of the Muslim world and eventually that of western Europe.

Christianity gained the support of the fourth-century emperors, and the church gradually adopted the Roman system of hierarchical organization. The church possessed able administrators and leaders. Bishops expanded their activities, and in the fifth century the bishops of Rome, taking the title "pope," began to stress their supremacy over other Christian communities. Monasteries offered opportunities for individuals to develop deeper spiritual devotion and also provided a model of Christian living and places for education and learning. Christian thinkers reinterpreted the classics in a Christian sense, incorporating elements of Greek and Roman philosophy into Christian teachings.

Barbarian groups migrated throughout Europe and Central Asia beginning in the second century. Among barbarians, the basic social unit was the tribe, made up of kin groups and led by a tribal chieftain. Missionaries and priests persuaded pagan and illiterate peoples to accept Christianity. Most barbarian kingdoms were weak and short-lived, though the kingdom of the Franks was relatively more unified and powerful. Rulers first in the Merovingian dynasty, and then in the Carolingian, used military victories, carefully calculated marriage alliances, and the help of the church to enhance their authority. Carolingian government reached the peak of its power under Charlemagne, who brought much of Europe under his authority through military conquest and strategic alliances.

CONNECTIONS For centuries the end of the Roman Empire in the West was seen as a major turning point in history, the fall of the sophisticated and educated classical world to uncouth and illiterate tribes. Over the last several decades, however, many historians have put a greater emphasis on continuities. Barbarian kings relied on officials trained in Roman law, and Latin remained the language of scholarly communication and the Christian Church. Greco-Roman art and architecture still adorned the land, and people continued to use Roman roads, aqueducts, and buildings. In eastern Europe and western Asia, the Byzantine Empire preserved the traditions of the Roman Empire and protected the intellectual heritage of Greco-Roman culture for another millennium.

In the middle of the era covered in this chapter, a new force emerged that had a dramatic impact on much of Europe and western Asia—Islam. In the seventh and eighth centuries Sassanid Persia, much of the Byzantine Empire, and the barbarian kingdoms in the Iberian Peninsula fell to Arab forces carrying this new religion. As

CHAPTER LOCATOR | How did the Byzantine Empire preserve the legacy of Rome? | How did the Christian Church become a major force in Europe?

CHAPTER 8
228 CONTINUITY AND CHANGE IN EUROPE AND WESTERN ASIA

we have seen in this chapter, a reputation as victors over Islam helped the Franks establish the most powerful state in Europe. As we will see when we pick up the story of Europe again in Chapter 14, Islam continued to shape European culture and politics in subsequent centuries. In terms of world history, the expansion of Islam may have been an even more dramatic turning point than the fall of the Roman Empire. Here, too, however, there were continuities, as the Muslims adopted and adapted Greek, Byzantine, and Persian political and cultural institutions.

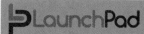

ONLINE DOCUMENT PROJECT
Theodora of Constantinople

What do Procopius's descriptions of Theodora and Justinian tell us about the problems and challenges his society faced?

Examine sources that reveal the connections Procopius saw between Byzantium's rulers and the rapid decline he perceived in Byzantine society, and then complete a quiz and writing assignment based on the evidence and details from this chapter. *See the inside front cover to learn more.*

| How did Christian thinkers adapt classical ideas to Christian teachings, and develop new practices? | How did the barbarians shape social, economic, and political structures in Europe and west Asia? | How did the church convert barbarian peoples to Christianity? | How did the Franks build and govern a European empire? | ✓ LearningCurve
Check what you know. |

STEP 1 GET STARTED ONLINE

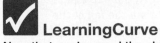 **LearningCurve**

Now that you've read the chapter, make it stick by completing the LearningCurve activity.

STEP 2 EXPLAIN WHY IT MATTERS

Put your reading into practice. Identify each term below, and then explain why it matters in world history.

TERM	WHO OR WHAT & WHEN	WHY IT MATTERS
Justinian's *Code* (p. 206)		
dioceses (p. 210)		
heresy (p. 211)		
popes (p. 211)		
Orthodox Church (p. 212)		
sacraments (p. 216)		
iconoclastic controversy (p. 216)		
wergeld (p. 220)		
penance (p. 224)		
saints (p. 224)		
Carolingian (p. 226)		
Treaty of Verdun (p. 227)		

STEP 3 MOVE BEYOND THE BASICS

To demonstrate a more advanced understanding of the role of the Byzantine Empire and the Christian Church in preserving the legacy of Greco-Roman civilization, fill in the chart below with descriptions of the contributions of the Byzantine Empire and the Christian Church in this context in two key areas: politics and government and culture and ideas. Why was the church so important to the preservation of the Greco-Roman legacy in the West? How did church and state work together to preserve the Greco-Roman legacy in the East?

	Politics and Government	Culture and Ideas
Byzantine Empire		
Christian Church		

PUT IT ALL TOGETHER

Now, take a step back and try to explain the big picture. Remember to use specific examples from the chapter in your answers.

THE BYZANTINE EMPIRE

► Compare and contrast the Western Roman Empire and the Eastern Roman Empire in the period just prior to the fall of the Western Roman Empire. Why was the Eastern Roman Empire able to withstand the pressure of barbarian migrations, while the Western Roman Empire was not?

► How did conflicts and connections with neighboring peoples shape the development of the Byzantine Empire?

THE SPREAD AND DEVELOPMENT OF CHRISTIANITY

► Is it more accurate to say that Rome was Christianized or that the Christian church was Romanized? What evidence can you present to support your position?

► Why did so many barbarian elites aid in the spread of Christianity in Europe? What does the receptivity of such elites to Christianity tell us about barbarian society and culture?

MIGRATING PEOPLES

► How did barbarian society and culture compare to Roman society and culture? Were there any areas of similarity?

► How were Germanic and Roman influences combined in the structure and institutions of the Frankish kingdom?

LOOKING BACK, LOOKING AHEAD

► Compare and contrast Europe and western Asia before and after the fall of the Roman Empire in the West. What were the most important areas of continuity?

► How did the Byzantine Empire and the Christian Church lay the foundation in late antiquity for the subsequent medieval European civilization? What contributions did barbarian peoples make in this context?

> IN YOUR OWN WORDS

Imagine that you must give an oral report to the class answering the following questions: **What role did Christianity play in the development of Europe and Western Asia in the centuries following the collapse of the Western Roman Empire?** What would be the most important points and why?

9

THE ISLAMIC WORLD

600–1400

> **How did Islamic civilization both build on and transform earlier civilizations?** Chapter 9 examines the emergence and development of Islamic civilization. Around 610 in the city of Mecca in what is now Saudi Arabia, a merchant called Muhammad had a religious vision that inspired him to preach God's revelations. By the time he died in 632, he had many followers in Arabia, and a century later his followers controlled what is now Syria, Palestine, Egypt, Iraq, Iran, northern India, northern Africa, Spain, and southern France. Within another century Muhammad's beliefs had been carried across Central Asia to the borders of China and India. The brilliant civilization that grew out of Muhammad's vision profoundly influenced the development of both Eastern and Western civilizations.

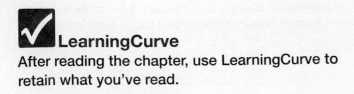

LearningCurve
After reading the chapter, use LearningCurve to retain what you've read.

Egyptian Man Life remained gracious in the great cities of North Africa and the Middle East even as Islam brought new traditions. This image of a man wearing a turban and holding a cup is from a wall painting. Found in Egypt, it dates to the eleventh century, during the Fatimid caliphate. (Museum of Islamic Art, Cairo, Egypt/Gianni Dagli Orti/The Art Archive at Art Resource, NY)

> From what kind of social and economic environment did Muhammad arise, and what did he teach?

> What made possible the spread of Islam, and what forms of government were established to rule Muslim lands?

> How were the Muslim lands governed from 900 to 1400, and what new challenges did rulers face?

> What social distinctions were important in Muslim society?

> Why did trade thrive in Muslim lands?

> What new ideas and practices emerged in the arts, sciences, education, and religion?

> How did Muslims and Christians come into contact with each other, and how did they view each other?

From what kind of social and economic environment did Muhammad arise, and what did he teach?

Much of the Arabian peninsula is desert. By the seventh century C.E. farming prevailed in the southwestern mountain valleys with their ample rainfall. In other areas scattered throughout the peninsula, oasis towns sustained sizable populations. Outside the towns were Bedouin (BEH-duh-uhn) nomadic pastoralist tribe. Though always small in number, Bedouins were the most important political and military force in the region. Mecca became the economic and cultural center of western Arabia, in part because pilgrims came to visit the Ka'ba, a temple containing a black stone thought to be a god's dwelling place. Muhammad's roots were in this region.

Arabian Social and Economic Structure

The basic social unit of the Bedouins and other Arabs was the tribe. Consisting of people connected through kinship, tribes provided protection and support and in turn expected members' total loyalty. Like the Germanic peoples in the age of

CHAPTER LOCATOR | **From what kind of environment did Muhammad arise, and what did he teach?** | What made possible the spread of Islam and what government was established? | How were Muslim lands governed and what challenges did rulers face?

234 CHAPTER 9 THE ISLAMIC WORLD

622 Muhammad and his followers emigrate from Mecca to Medina	**750–1258** Abbasid caliphate
632 Muhammad dies; Abu Bakr becomes the first caliph	**762** Baghdad founded by Abbasids
642 Muslim defeat of the Persians marks end of the Sassanid empire	**800–1300** Height of Muslim learning and creativity
651 Publication of the Qur'an	**869–883** Zanj (slave) revolts
661 Ali assassinated; split between Shi'a and Sunnis	**950–1100** Entry on a large scale of Turks into the Middle East
711 Muslims defeat Visigothic kingdom in Spain	**1055** Baghdad falls to Seljuk Turks
722–1492 Progressive loss of most of Spain to the Christian reconquest (*reconquista*)	**1099–1187** Christian Crusaders hold Jerusalem
	1258 Mongols capture Baghdad and kill the last Abbasid caliph

their migrations (see pages 218–221), Arab tribes were not static entities but rather continually evolving groups. A particular tribe might include both nomadic and sedentary members.

In northern and central Arabia in the early seventh century, tribal confederations led by their warrior elite were dominant. In the southern parts of the peninsula, however, priestly aristocracies tended to hold political power.

The power of the northern warrior class rested on its fighting skills. The southern religious aristocracy, by contrast, depended on its religious and economic power. The political genius of Muhammad was to bind together these different tribal groups into a strong, unified state.

Muhammad's Rise as a Religious Leader

Much like the earliest sources for Jesus and the Buddha, the earliest account of the life of Muhammad (ca. 570–632) comes from oral traditions passed down among followers. According to these traditions, at about age forty, Muhammad had a vision of an angelic being who commanded him to preach the revelations that God would be sending him. Muhammad began to preach to the people of Mecca, urging them to give up their idols and to submit to the one indivisible God. After his death, scribes organized the revelations jotted down by followers or memorized into chapters. In 651 they published the version of them that Muslims consider authoritative, the **Qur'an** (kuh-RAHN).

For the first two or three centuries after the death of Muhammad, there was considerable debate about theological and political issues. Likewise, religious scholars had to sort out and assess the **hadith** (huh-DEETH), collections of the

Qur'an
▶ The sacred book of Islam.

hadith
▶ Collections of the sayings of and anecdotes about Muhammad.

What social distinctions were important in Muslim society?	Why did trade thrive in Muslim lands?	What new ideas and practices emerged in the arts, sciences, education, and religion?	How did Muslims and Christians come into contact with and view each other?	☑ **LearningCurve** Check what you know.

sayings of or anecdotes about Muhammad. Muhammad's example as revealed in the hadith became the legal basis for the conduct of every Muslim. The life of Muhammad provides the "normative example," or **Sunna**, for the Muslim believer. Muhammad's example became central to the Muslim way of life.

Sunna

▶ An Arabic term meaning "trodden path." The term refers to the deeds and sayings of Muhammad, which constitute the obligatory example for Muslim life.

The Tenets of Islam

Islam, the strict monotheistic faith that is based on the teachings of Muhammad, rests on the principle of the oneness and omnipotence of God (Allah). Muslims believe that Muhammad was the last of the prophets, completing the work begun by Abraham, Moses, and Jesus. The Qur'an holds that the holy writings of both Jews and Christians represent divine revelation, but it claims that both Jews and Christians tampered with the books of God.

Muslims believe that they worship the same God as Jews and Christians. Islam appropriates much of the Old and New Testaments of the Bible but often retells the narratives with significant shifts in meaning. Muhammad insisted that he was not preaching a new message; rather, he was calling people back to the one true God, urging his contemporaries to reform their lives, to return to the faith of Abraham, the first monotheist.

The Qur'an prescribes a strict code of moral behavior. A Muslim must recite the profession of faith in God and in Muhammad as his prophet: "There is no God but God, and Muhammad is his Prophet." A believer must also pray five times a day, fast and pray during the sacred month of Ramadan, make a pilgrimage (hajj) to the holy city of Mecca once during his or her lifetime, and give alms to the Muslim poor. These fundamental obligations are known as the **Five Pillars of Islam**.

Islam forbids alcoholic beverages and gambling. It condemns usury in business — that is, lending money and charging the borrower interest — and taking advantage of market demand for products by charging high prices. Muslim jurisprudence condemned licentious behavior by both men and women and specified the same punishments for both.

Like the Christian Judgment Day, on the Islamic Judgment Day God will separate the saved and the damned. The Qur'an describes in detail the frightful tortures with which God will punish the damned and the heavenly rewards of the saved and the blessed.

Five Pillars of Islam

▶ The basic tenets of the Islamic faith; they include reciting a profession of faith in God and in Muhammad as God's prophet, praying five times daily, fasting and praying during the month of Ramadan, making a pilgrimage to Mecca once in one's lifetime, and contributing alms to the poor.

> QUICK REVIEW

What connections did Muslims see between their own religion and Christianity and Judaism?

CHAPTER LOCATOR | From what kind of environment did Muhammad arise, and what did he teach? | **What made possible the spread of Islam and what government was established?** | How were Muslim lands governed and what challenges did rulers face?

CHAPTER 9
236 THE ISLAMIC WORLD

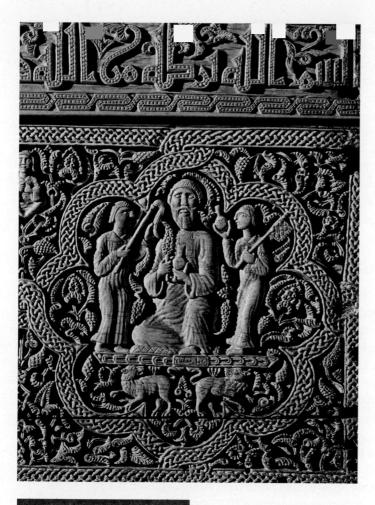

Ivory Chest of Pamplona, Spain

The court of the Spanish Umayyads prized small, intricately carved ivory chests, often made in a royal workshop and used to store precious perfumes. This exquisite side panel depicts an eleventh-century caliph flanked by two attendants. An inscription on the front translates as "In the Name of God. Blessings from God, goodwill, and happiness." (Museo Navarra, Pamplona, Spain/Institut Amatller d'Art Hispanic)

What made possible the spread of Islam, and what forms of government were established to rule Muslim lands?

According to Muslim tradition, Muhammad's preaching at first did not appeal to many people. In preaching a transformation of the social order and calling for the destruction of the idols in the Ka'ba, Muhammad challenged the power of the local elite and the pilgrimage-based economy. As a result, the townspeople of Mecca turned against him, and he and his followers were forced to flee to Medina. This *hijra* (hih-JIGH-ruh), or emigration, occurred in 622, and Muslims later dated the beginning of their era from it.

What social distinctions were important in Muslim society?	Why did trade thrive in Muslim lands?	What new ideas and practices emerged in the arts, sciences, education, and religion?	How did Muslims and Christians come into contact with and view each other?	✓ LearningCurve Check what you know.

At Medina, Muhammad attracted increasing numbers of believers, many of whom were Bedouins who supported themselves by raiding caravans en route to Mecca, setting off a violent conflict between Mecca and Medina. After eight years of strife, Mecca capitulated. In this way, by the time Muhammad died in 632, he had welded together all the Bedouin tribes.

Muhammad displayed genius as both a political strategist and a religious teacher. He gave Arabs the idea of a unique and unified **umma** (UH-muh), or community, that consisted of all those whose primary identity and bond was a common religious faith. The umma was to be a religious and political community led by Muhammad for the achievement of God's will on earth. The Islamic notion of an absolute higher authority transcended the boundaries of individual tribal units and fostered political consolidation.

Islam's Spread Beyond Arabia

After the Prophet's death, Islam quickly spread far beyond Arabia. In the sixth century two powerful empires divided the Middle East: the Greek-Byzantine empire centered at Constantinople and the Persian-Sassanid empire concentrated at Ctesiphon (near Baghdad in present-day Iraq). From the fourth through sixth centuries the Byzantines and Sassanids fought each other fiercely, each trying to expand its territories at the expense of the other and to control and tax the rich trade coming from Arabia and the Indian Ocean region. Many peripheral societies were drawn into the conflict. The resulting disorder facilitated the growth of Muslim states.

The second and third successors of Muhammad, Umar (r. 634–644) and Uthman (r. 644–656), launched a two-pronged attack against the Byzantine and Sassanid Empires. One force moved north from Arabia against the Byzantine provinces of Syria and Palestine (see page 204). From Syria, the Muslims conquered the rich province of Egypt. Simultaneously, Arab armies swept into the Sassanid empire. The Muslim defeat of the Persians at Nihawand in 642 signaled the collapse of this empire (Map 9.1).

The Muslims continued their drive eastward and in the mid-seventh century occupied the province of Khurasan, where the city of Merv became the center of Muslim control over eastern Persia and the base for campaigns farther east. By 700 the Muslims had crossed the Oxus River and swept toward Kabul, today the capital of Afghanistan. They then penetrated Kazakhstan and seized Tashkent. From southern Persia, a Muslim force marched into the Indus Valley in northwest India and in 713 founded an Islamic community there. Beginning in the eleventh century Muslim dynasties from Ghazni in Afghanistan carried Islam deeper into the Indian subcontinent (see page 345).

To the west, Arab forces moved across North Africa and crossed the Strait of Gibraltar. In 711 at the Guadalete River they easily defeated the Visigothic kingdom of Spain. Muslims controlled most of Spain until the thirteenth century. Advances into France were stopped in 732 when the Franks defeated Arab armies in a battle near the city of Tours, and Muslim occupation of parts of southern France did not last long.

CHAPTER LOCATOR | From what kind of environment did Muhammad arise, and what did he teach? | **What made possible the spread of Islam and what government was established?** | How were Muslim lands governed and what challenges did rulers face?

238 CHAPTER 9 THE ISLAMIC WORLD

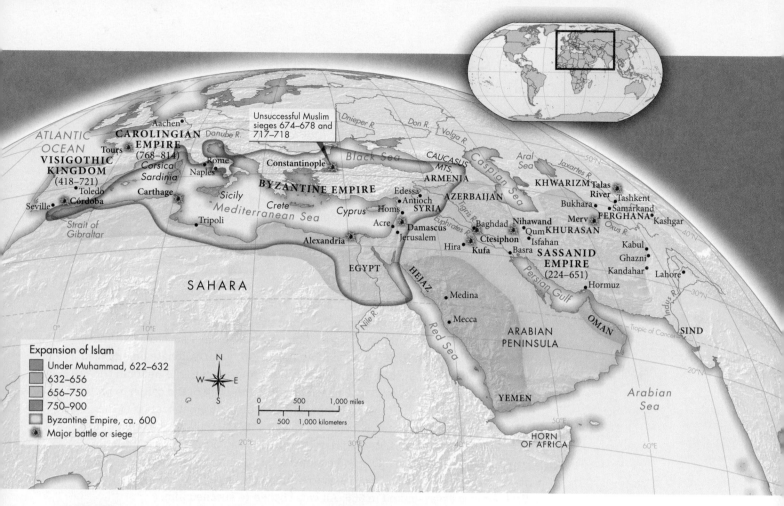

MAP 9.1 ■ The Expansion of Islam, 622–900

The rapid expansion of Islam in a relatively short span of time testifies to the Arabs' superior fighting skills, religious zeal, and economic ambition as well as to their enemies' weakness. Plague, famine, and political troubles in Sassanid Persia contributed to Muslim victory there.

> **MAPPING THE PAST**

ANALYZING THE MAP: Trace the routes of the spread of Islam by time period. How fast did it spread? How similar were the climates of the regions that became Muslim?

CONNECTIONS: Which were the most powerful and populous of the societies that were absorbed into the Muslim world? What regions or societies were more resistant?

Reasons for the Spread of Islam

By the beginning of the eleventh century the crescent of Islam had flown from the Iberian heartlands to northern India. How can this rapid and remarkable expansion be explained? Most historians point to a combination of the Arabs' military advantages and the political weaknesses of their opponents. The Byzantine and Sassanid Empires had just fought a grueling century-long war and had also been weakened by the plague. Equally important are the military strength and tactics of the Arabs. For example, rather than scattering as landlords of peasant farmers over conquered lands, Arab soldiers remained together in garrison cities, where their Arab ethnicity, tribal organization, religion, and military success set them apart. All soldiers were registered in the **diwān** (dih-WAHN), an administrative organ adopted from the Persians or Byzantines. Soldiers received a monthly ration of food for themselves and their families and an annual cash stipend. In return, they had to be available for military service.

diwān
▶ A unit of government.

| What social distinctions were important in Muslim society? | Why did trade thrive in Muslim lands? | What new ideas and practices emerged in the arts, sciences, education, and religion? | How did Muslims and Christians come into contact with and view each other? | ✓ LearningCurve Check what you know. |

The Caliphate and the Split Between Shi'a and Sunni Alliances

When Muhammad died in 632, he left a large Muslim umma, but this community stood in danger of disintegrating into separate tribal groups. How was the vast empire that came into existence within one hundred years of his death to be governed? Neither the Qur'an nor the Sunna offered guidance concerning the succession.

In this crisis, according to tradition, a group of Muhammad's ablest followers elected Abu Bakr (573–634), the Prophet's father-in-law and close supporter, and hailed him as caliph, a term combining the ideas of leader, successor, and deputy (of the Prophet). This election marked the victory of the concept of a universal community of Muslim believers.

In the two years of his rule (632–634), Abu Bakr governed on the basis of his personal prestige within the Muslim umma. He sent out military expeditions, collected taxes, dealt with tribes on behalf of the entire community, and led the community in prayer. Gradually, under Abu Bakr's first three successors, Umar (r. 634–644), Uthman (r. 644–656), and Ali (r. 656–661), the caliphate emerged as an institution. Umar succeeded in exerting his authority over the Bedouin tribes involved in ongoing conquests. Uthman asserted the right of the caliph to protect the economic interests of the entire umma. Also, Uthman's publication of the definitive text of the Qur'an showed his concern for the unity of the umma. However, Uthman was from a Mecca family that had resisted the Prophet until the capitulation of Mecca in 630, and he aroused resentment when he gave favors to members of his family. Opposition to Uthman coalesced around Ali, and when Uthman was assassinated in 656, Ali was chosen to succeed him.

Uthman's cousin Mu'awiya, a member of the Umayyad family who had built a power base as governor of Syria, refused to recognize Ali as caliph. In the ensuing civil war Ali was assassinated, and Mu'awiya (r. 661–680) assumed the caliphate. Mu'awiya founded the Umayyad Dynasty and shifted the capital of the Islamic state from Medina in Arabia to Damascus in Syria. Although electing caliphs remained the Islamic ideal, beginning with Mu'awiya, the office of caliph increasingly became hereditary. Two successive dynasties, the Umayyad (661–750) and the Abbasid (750–1258), held the caliphate.

From its inception the caliphate rested on the theoretical principle that Muslim political and religious unity transcended tribalism. Mu'awiya sought to enhance the power of the caliphate by making tribal leaders dependent on him for concessions and special benefits. At the same time, his control of a loyal and well-disciplined army enabled him to take the caliphate in an authoritarian direction. Through intimidation he forced the tribal leaders to accept his son Yazid as his heir, thereby establishing the dynastic principle of succession.

The assassination of Ali and the assumption of the caliphate by Mu'awiya had another profound consequence. It gave rise to a fundamental division in the umma and in Muslim theology. Ali had claimed the caliphate on the basis of family ties — he was Muhammad's cousin and son-in-law. When Ali was murdered, his followers argued that Ali had been the Prophet's designated successor — partly because of the blood tie, partly because Muhammad had designated Ali **imam** (ih-MAHM), or leader in community prayer. These supporters of Ali were called

imam

▶ The leader in community prayer.

CHAPTER LOCATOR | From what kind of environment did Muhammad arise, and what did he teach? | **What made possible the spread of Islam and what government was established?** | How were Muslim lands governed and what challenges did rulers face?

CHAPTER 9
240 THE ISLAMIC WORLD

Shi'a (SHEE-uh), meaning "supporters" or "partisans" of Ali (Shi'a are also known as Shi'ites). In succeeding generations, opponents of the Umayyad Dynasty emphasized their blood descent from Ali and claimed to possess divine knowledge that Muhammad had given them as his heirs.

Those who accepted Mu'awiya as caliph insisted that the central issue was adhering to the practices and beliefs of the umma based on the precedents of the Prophet. They came to be called **Sunnis** (SOO-neez), which derived from *Sunna* (examples from Muhammad's life). When a situation arose for which the Qur'an offered no solution, Sunni scholars searched for a precedent in the Sunna, which gained an authority comparable to the Qur'an itself.

Both Sunnis and Shi'a maintain that authority within Islam lies first in the Qur'an and then in the Sunna. Who interprets these sources? Shi'a claim that the imam does, for he is invested with divine grace and insight. Sunnis insist that interpretation comes from the consensus of the **ulama**, the group of religious scholars.

Throughout the Umayyad period, the Shi'a constituted a major source of discontent. They condemned the Umayyads as worldly and sensual rulers, in contrast to the pious true successors of Muhammad. A rival Sunni clan, the Abbasid (uh-BA-suhd), exploited the situation, agitating the Shi'a and encouraging dissension among tribal factions. The Abbasid contrasted their own piety with the pleasure-loving style of the Umayyads.

The Abbasid Caliphate

In 747 the Abbasid leader Abu' al-Abbas led a rebellion against the Umayyads, and in 750 he won general recognition as caliph. Damascus had served as the headquarters of Umayyad rule. Abu' al-Abbas's successor, al-Mansur (r. 754–775), founded the city of Baghdad in 762 and made it his capital. Thus the geographical center of the caliphate shifted eastward to former Sassanid territories. The first three Abbasid caliphs crushed their opponents, turned against many of their supporters, and created a new ruling elite drawn from newly converted Persian families. The Abbasid revolution established a basis for rule and citizenship more cosmopolitan and Islamic than the narrow, elitist, and Arab basis that had characterized Umayyad government.

The Abbasids worked to identify their rule with Islam. They patronized the ulama, built mosques, and supported the development of Islamic scholarship. Although at first Muslims represented only a small minority of the conquered peoples, Abbasid rule provided the religious-political milieu in which Islam gained, over time, the allegiance of the vast majority of the populations from Spain to Afghanistan.

The Abbasids also borrowed heavily from Persian culture. Following Persian tradition, the Abbasid caliphs claimed to rule by divine right. A majestic palace with hundreds of attendants and elaborate court ceremonies deliberately isolated the caliph from the people he ruled. Subjects had to bow before the caliph and kiss the ground, symbolizing his absolute power.

Under the third caliph, Harun al-Rashid (r. 786–809), Baghdad emerged as a flourishing commercial, artistic, and scientific center. Its population of about a million people created a huge demand for goods and services, and Baghdad became

Shi'a
▶ Arabic term meaning "supporters of Ali"; they make up one of the two main divisions of Islam.

Sunnis
▶ Members of the larger of the two main divisions of Islam; the division between Sunnis and Shi'a began in a dispute about succession to Muhammad, but over time many differences in theology developed.

ulama
▶ A group of religious scholars whom Sunnis trust to interpret the Qur'an and the Sunna.

What social distinctions were important in Muslim society?	Why did trade thrive in Muslim lands?	What new ideas and practices emerged in the arts, sciences, education, and religion?	How did Muslims and Christians come into contact with and view each other?	✓ LearningCurve Check what you know.

an entrepôt (trading center) for textiles, slaves, and foodstuffs coming from Oman, East Africa, and India. The city also became intellectually influential. Harun al-Rashid organized the translation of Greek medical and philosophical texts. As part of this effort the Christian scholar Hunayn Ibn Ishaq (808–873) translated Galen's medical works into Arabic and made Baghdad a center for the study and practice of medicine. Likewise, impetus was given to the study of astronomy, and through a program of astronomical observations, Muslim astronomers sought to correct and complement Ptolemaic astronomy. Above all, studies in Qur'anic textual analysis, history, poetry, law, and philosophy — all in Arabic — reflected the development of a distinctly Islamic literary and scientific culture.

An important innovation of the Abbasids was the use of slaves as soldiers. The caliph al-Mu'taşim (r. 833–842) acquired several thousand Turkish slaves who were converted to Islam and employed in military service. Scholars have offered varied explanations for this practice: that the use of slave soldiers was a response to a manpower shortage; that as highly skilled horsemen, the Turks had military skills superior to those of the Arabs and other peoples; and that al-Mu'taşim felt he could trust the Turks more than other recruits. In any case, slave soldiers — later including Slavs, Indians, and sub-Saharan blacks — became a standard feature of Muslim armies in the Middle East until the twentieth century.

Administration of the Islamic Territories

The Islamic conquests brought into being a new imperial system. The Muslims adopted the patterns of administration used by the Byzantines in Egypt and Syria and by the Sassanids in Persia. Specifically, Arab **emirs**, or governors, were appointed and given overall responsibility for public order, maintenance of the armed forces, and tax collection. Below them, experienced native officials remained in office. Thus there was continuity with previous administrations.

The Umayyad caliphate witnessed the further development of the imperial administration. At the head stood the caliph. Theoretically, he had the ultimate

emirs
▶ Arab governors who were given overall responsibility for public order, maintenance of the armed forces, and tax collection.

CHAPTER LOCATOR | From what kind of environment did Muhammad arise, and what did he teach? | **What made possible the spread of Islam and what government was established?** | How were Muslim lands governed and what challenges did rulers face?

CHAPTER 9
242 THE ISLAMIC WORLD

responsibility for the interpretation of the sacred law. In practice, however, the ulama interpreted the law as revealed in the Qur'an and the Sunna. In the course of time, the ulama's interpretations constituted a rich body of law, the **shari'a** (shuh-REE-uh). The ulama enjoyed great prestige in the Muslim community and was consulted by the caliph on difficult legal and spiritual matters. The *qadis* (KAH-dees), or judges, who were well versed in the sacred law, carried out the judicial functions of the state.

The central administrative organ was the diwān, which collected the taxes that paid soldiers' salaries (see page 239) and financed charitable and public works. Another important undertaking was a relay network established to rapidly convey letters and intelligence reports between the capital and distant outposts.

The early Abbasid period witnessed considerable economic expansion and population growth, complicating the work of government. New and specialized departments emerged, each with a hierarchy of officials. The most important new official was the vizier (vuh-ZEER), a position that the Abbasids adopted from the Persians. The vizier was the caliph's chief assistant. Depending on the caliph's personality, viziers could acquire extensive power, and some used their offices for personal gain.

shari'a
▶ Muslim law, which covers social, criminal, political, commercial, and religious matters.

QUICK REVIEW <

How did Islamic government evolve in the two centuries following the death of Muhammad?

| What social distinctions were important in Muslim society? | Why did trade thrive in Muslim lands? | What new ideas and practices emerged in the arts, sciences, education, and religion? | How did Muslims and Christians come into contact with and view each other? | ✔ LearningCurve Check what you know. |

How were the Muslim lands governed from 900 to 1400, and what new challenges did rulers face?

The Patio of the Lions at Alhambra, Fourteenth Century

The fortress that the Moorish rulers of Spain built at Granada is considered one of the masterpieces of Andalusian art, notable for the fine carving of geometrical designs and Arabic calligraphy. (George Holton/Photo Researchers, Inc.)

In theory, the caliph and his central administration governed the whole empire, but in practice, the many parts of the empire enjoyed considerable local independence. At the same time, the enormous distance between many provinces and the imperial capital made it difficult for the caliph to prevent provinces from breaking away. Consequently, regional dynasties emerged in much of the Islamic world, including Spain, Persia, Central Asia, northern India, and Egypt. None of these states repudiated Islam, but they did stop sending tax revenues to Baghdad. Moreover, states frequently fought costly wars against their neighbors in their attempts to expand. Sometimes these conflicts were worsened by Sunni-Shi'a antagonisms. All these developments, as well as invasions by Turks and Mongols, posed challenges to central Muslim authority.

Breakaway Territories and Shi'a Gains

One of the first territories to break away from the Baghdad-centered caliphate was Spain. In 755 an Umayyad prince who had escaped death at the hands of the Abbasids and fled to Spain set up an independent regime at Córdoba (see

CHAPTER LOCATOR | From what kind of environment did Muhammad arise, and what did he teach? | What made possible the spread of Islam and what government was established? | **How were Muslim lands governed and what challenges did rulers face?**

244 CHAPTER 9 THE ISLAMIC WORLD

Map 9.1). Other territories soon followed. In 800 the emir in Tunisia in North Africa set himself up as an independent ruler. And in 820 Tahir, the son of a slave, was rewarded with the governorship of Khurasan because he had supported the caliphate. Once he took office, however, Tahir ruled independently of Baghdad.

In 946 a Shi'a Iranian clan overran Iraq and occupied Baghdad. The caliph was forced to recognize the clan's leader as commander in chief and to allow the celebration of Shi'a festivals. A year later the caliph was accused of plotting against his new masters, snatched from his throne, dragged through the streets, and blinded. This incident marked the practical collapse of the Abbasid caliphate. Abbasid caliphs, however, remained as puppets of a series of military commanders and symbols of Muslim unity until the Mongols killed the last Abbasid caliph in 1258 (see page 246).

In another Shi'a advance, the Fatimids, a Shi'a dynasty that claimed descent from Muhammad's daughter Fatima, conquered North Africa and then expanded into the Abbasid province of Egypt, founding the city of Cairo as their capital in 969. For the next century or so, Shi'a were in ascendancy in much of the western Islamic world.

The Fatimid Caliphate, 909–1171

The Ascendancy of the Turks

In the mid-tenth century the Turks began to enter the Islamic world in large numbers. First appearing in Mongolia in the sixth century, groups of Turks, such as the Seljuks, gradually appeared across the grasslands of Eurasia. Skilled horsemen, they became prime targets for Muslim slave raids, as they made good slave soldiers. Once the Turks understood that Muslims could not be captured for slaves, more and more of them converted to Sunni Islam and often became *ghazi*, frontier raiders, who attacked unconverted Turks to capture slaves.

In the 1020s and 1030s Seljuk Turks overran Persia and then pushed into Iraq and Syria. Baghdad fell to them on December 18, 1055, and the caliph became a puppet of the Turkish sultan. The Turkic elite rapidly gave up pastoralism and took up the sedentary lifestyle of the people they governed.

The Turks brought badly needed military strength to the Islamic world. They played a major part in recovering Jerusalem after it was held for nearly a century, from 1099 to 1187, by the European Crusaders (who had fought to take Christian holy lands back from the Muslims; see page 401). They also were important in preventing the later Crusades from accomplishing much. Moreover, the Turks became staunch Sunnis and led a campaign against the Shi'a.

The Seljuk Empire in 1000

The influx of Turks from 950 to 1100 also helped provide a new expansive dynamic. At the Battle of Manzikert in 1071, Seljuk Turks broke through Byzantine border defenses, opening Anatolia to Turkish migration. Over the next couple of centuries, perhaps a million Turks entered the area—including bands of ghazis and dervishes (Sufi brotherhoods, see page 258).

| What social distinctions were important in Muslim society? | Why did trade thrive in Muslim lands? | What new ideas and practices emerged in the arts, sciences, education, and religion? | How did Muslims and Christians come into contact with and view each other? | ✓ LearningCurve Check what you know. |

The Mongol Invasions

In tho early thirteenth century the Mongols arrived in the Middle East. Originally from the grasslands of Mongolia, in 1206 thcy proclaimed Chinggis Khan (ca. 1162–1227) as their leader, and he welded Mongol, Tartar, and Turkish tribes into a strong confederation that rapidly subdued neighboring settled societies (see pages 335–340). After conquering much of north China, the Mongols swept westward.

In 1219–1221, when the Mongols first reached the Islamic lands, the areas from Persia through the Central Asian cities of Herat and Samarkand were part of the kingdom of Khwarizm. The ruler—the son of a Turkish slave who had risen to governor of a province—had the audacity to execute Chinggis's envoy, and Chinggis retaliated with a force of a hundred thousand soldiers that sacked city after city. Millions are said to have died.

Not many Mongol forces were left in Persia after the campaign of 1219–1221, and another army, sent in 1237, captured the Persian city of Isfahan. In 1251 the decision was taken to push farther west. Chinggis Khan's grandson Hülegü (1217–1265) led an attack on the Abbasids in Baghdad, sacking and burning the city and killing the last Abbasid caliph in 1258. The fall of Damascus followed in 1260. Mamluk soldiers from Egypt, however, were able to withstand the Mongols and win a major victory at Ayn Jalut in Syria, which has been credited with saving Egypt and the Muslim lands in North Africa and perhaps Spain. At any rate, the desert ecology of the region did not provide suitable support for the Mongol armies, which required five horses for each soldier. Moreover, in 1260 the Great Khan (ruler of Mongolia and China) died, and the top Mongol generals withdrew to Mongolia for the selection of the next Great Khan.

Hülegü and his descendants ruled the central Muslim lands (referred to as the Il-Khanate) for eighty years. In 1295 his descendant Ghazan embraced Islam and worked for the revival of Muslim culture. As the Turks had done earlier, the Mongols, once converted, injected new vigor into the faith and spirit of Islam. In the Il-Khanate the Mongols governed through Persian viziers and native financial officials.

> **QUICK REVIEW**

Why did the caliphate find it so difficult to maintain control over the Islamic empire?

CHAPTER LOCATOR | From what kind of environment did Muhammad arise, and what did he teach? | What made possible the spread of Islam and what government was established? | How were Muslim lands governed and what challenges did rulers face?

CHAPTER 9
246 THE ISLAMIC WORLD

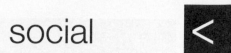

What social distinctions were important in Muslim society?

Separating Men and Women in a Mosque

In this mid-sixteenth-century illustration of the interior of a mosque, a screen separates the women, who are wearing veils and tending children, from the men. The women can hear what is being said, but the men cannot see them. (Bodleian Library, Oxford, UK/The Art Archive at Art Resource, NY)

When the Prophet appeared, Arab society consisted of independent Bedouin tribal groups loosely held together by loyalty to a strong leader and by the belief that all members of a tribe were descended from a common ancestor. Heads of families elected the sheik, or tribal chief. He was usually chosen from among elite warrior families who believed their bloodlines made them superior. According to the Qur'an, however, birth counted for nothing; piety was the only criterion for honor. The idea of social equality was a basic Muslim doctrine.

When Muhammad defined social equality, he was thinking about equality among Muslims alone. But even among Muslims, a sense of pride in ancestry could not be destroyed by a stroke of the pen. Claims based on birth remained strong among the first Muslims, and after Islam spread outside of Arabia, full-blooded Arab tribesmen regarded themselves as superior to foreign converts.

What social distinctions were important in Muslim society?	Why did trade thrive in Muslim lands?	What new ideas and practices emerged in the arts, sciences, education, and religion?	How did Muslims and Christians come into contact with and view each other?	✓ LearningCurve Check what you know.

The Social Hierarchy

In the Umayyad period, Muslim society was distinctly hierarchical. At the top of the hierarchy were the caliph's household and the ruling Arab Muslims. Descended from Bedouin tribespeople, this class constituted the ruling elite. It was a relatively small group, greatly outnumbered by Muslim villagers and country people.

Converts constituted the second class in Islamic society, one that grew slowly over time. Converts to Islam had to attach themselves to one of the Arab tribes in a subordinate capacity. From the Muslim converts eventually came the members of the commercial and learned professions—merchants, traders, teachers, doctors, artists, and interpreters of the shari'a. Second-class citizenship led some Muslim converts to adopt Shi'ism (see page 240). Even so, over the centuries, converts to Islam intermarried with their Muslim conquerors. Gradually, assimilation united peoples of various ethnic backgrounds.

dhimmis

▶ A term meaning "protected peoples"; they included Jews, Christians, and Zoroastrians.

Dhimmis (zih-MEEZ)—including Jews, Christians, and Zoroastrians—formed the third stratum. Considered "protected peoples" because they worshipped only one God, they were allowed to practice their religions, maintain their houses of worship, and conduct their business affairs as long as they gave unequivocal recognition to Muslim political supremacy and paid a small tax. Because many Jews and Christians were well educated, they were often appointed to high positions in government. However, their social position deteriorated during the Crusades and the Mongol invasions, when there was a general rise of religious loyalties. At those times, Muslims suspected the dhimmis, often rightly, of collaborating with the enemies of Islam.

How did the experience of Jews under Islam compare with that of Jews living in Christian Europe? Recent scholarship shows that, in Europe, Jews were first marginalized in the Christian social order and then completely expelled from it. In Islam, Jews, though marginalized, participated fully in commercial and professional activities, some attaining economic equality with their Muslim counterparts.

Slavery

Slavery had long existed in the ancient Middle East, and Muslim expansion ensured a steady flow of slaves captured in war. Moreover, the Qur'an accepted slavery much the way the Old and New Testaments did. But the Qur'an prescribes

CHAPTER LOCATOR | From what kind of environment did Muhammad arise, and what did he teach? | What made possible the spread of Islam and what government was established? | How were Muslim lands governed and what challenges did rulers face?

CHAPTER 9
248 THE ISLAMIC WORLD

just and humane treatment of slaves, explicitly encourages the freeing of slaves, and urges owners whose slaves ask for their freedom to give them the opportunity to buy it.

Women slaves worked as cooks, cleaners, laundresses, and nursemaids. A few performed as singers, musicians, dancers, and reciters of poetry. Many female slaves also served as concubines. Not only rulers but also high officials and rich merchants owned many concubines. Down the economic ladder, artisans and tradesmen often had a few concubines who assumed domestic as well as sexual duties.

According to tradition, the seclusion of women in a harem protected their virtue (see below), and when men had the means the harem was secured by eunuch (castrated) guards. Muslims also employed eunuchs as secretaries, tutors, and commercial agents, possibly because eunuchs were said to be more manageable and dependable than men with ordinary desires. Male slaves, eunuchs or not, were also set to work as longshoremen on the docks, as oarsmen on ships, in construction crews, in workshops, and in gold and silver mines. Male slaves also fought as soldiers.

Slavery in the Islamic world differed in at least two fundamental ways from the slavery later practiced in the Americas. First, race had no particular connection to slavery among Muslims, who were as ready to take slaves from Europe as from Africa. Second, slavery in the Islamic world was not the basis for plantation agriculture, as it was in the southern United States, the Caribbean, and Brazil in the eighteenth and nineteenth centuries.

Slavery was rarely hereditary in the Muslim world. Most slaves who were taken from non-Muslim peoples later converted, which often led to emancipation. The children of female slaves by Muslim masters were by definition Muslim and thus free. To give Muslim slavery the most positive possible interpretation, one could say that it provided a means to fill certain socioeconomic and military needs and that it assimilated rather than segregated outsiders.

Slaves Dancing

A few women slaves performed as dancers, singers, and musicians, usually before an elite audience of rulers, officials, and wealthy merchants. This reconstructed wall painting from the ninth century adorned a harem in a royal palace in Samarra. (bpk, Berlin/Art Resource, NY)

Women in Classical Islamic Society

Before Islam, Arab tribal law gave women virtually no legal powers. Girls were sold into marriage by their guardians, and their husbands could terminate the union at will. Also, women had virtually no property or succession rights. Seen from this perspective, the Qur'an sought to improve the social position of women.

The Qur'an, like the religious writings of other traditions, represents moral precept rather than social practice, and the texts are open to different interpretations. Modern scholars tend to agree that the Islamic sacred book intended women to be the spiritual equals of men and gave them considerable economic

| What social distinctions were important in Muslim society? | Why did trade thrive in Muslim lands? | What new ideas and practices emerged in the arts, sciences, education, and religion? | How did Muslims and Christians come into contact with and view each other? | ✓ LearningCurve Check what you know. |

249

rights. In the early Umayyad period, moreover, women played active roles in the religious, economic, and political life of the community. They owned property, had freedom of movement and traveled widely, and participated with men in public religious rituals and observances. But this Islamic ideal of women and men having equal value to the community did not last, and, as Islamic society changed, the precepts of the Qur'an were interpreted in more patriarchal ways.

Although the hadith—records of what Muhammad said and did, and what believers in the first two centuries after his death believed he said and did (see page 235)—usually depict women in terms of moral virtue, domesticity, and saintly ideals, they also show some prominent women in political roles. For example, Aisha, daughter of the first caliph and probably Muhammad's favorite wife, played a leading role in rallying support for the movement opposing Ali, who succeeded Uthman in 656 (see page 240). However, by the Abbasid period the status of women had declined. The practices of the Byzantine and Persian lands that had been conquered, including seclusion of women, were absorbed. The supply of slave women increased substantially. Some scholars speculate that as wealth replaced ancestry as the main criterion of social status, men more and more viewed women as possessions, as a form of wealth.

Men were also seen as dominant in their marriages. The Qur'an states that "men are in charge of women because Allah hath made the one to excel the other, and because they (men) spend of their property (for the support of women). So good women are obedient, guarding in secret that which Allah hath guarded."[1] A thirteenth-century commentator on this passage argued from it that women are incapable of and unfit for any public duties. This view came to be accepted, and later interpreters further categorized the ways in which men were superior to women.

The practices of veiling and seclusion of women have their roots in pre-Islamic times, and they took firm hold in classical Islamic society. As Arab conquerors subjugated various peoples, they adopted some of the vanquished peoples' customs. Veiling was probably of Byzantine or Persian origin. The Qur'an contains no specific rule about the veil, but its few vague references have been interpreted as sanctioning the practice. An even greater restriction on women than veiling was the practice of seclusion, the harem system. The practice of secluding women also derives from Arabic contacts with Persia and other Eastern cultures. By 800 women in more prosperous households stayed out of sight.

Marriage, the Family, and Sexuality

As in medieval Europe and traditional India and China, marriage in Muslim society was considered too important an undertaking to be left to the romantic emotions of the young. Families or guardians, not the prospective bride and groom, identified suitable partners and finalized the contract. Because it was absolutely essential that the bride be a virgin, marriages were arranged shortly after the onset of the girl's menstrual period at age twelve or thirteen. Husbands were commonly ten to fifteen years older. Youthful marriages ensured a long period of fertility.

A wife's responsibilities depended on the wealth and occupation of her husband. A farmer's wife helped in the fields, ground the corn, carried water, prepared food, and did the myriad tasks necessary in rural life. Shopkeepers' wives in the cities sometimes helped in business. In an upper-class household, the wife supervised servants, looked after all domestic arrangements, and did whatever was needed for her husband's comfort.

In every case, children were the wife's special domain. A mother exercised authority over her children and enjoyed their respect. Thus, as in Chinese culture, the prestige of the young wife depended on the production of children—especially sons—as rapidly as possible. A wife's failure to have children was one of the main reasons for a man to divorce his wife or take a second wife.

Like the Jewish tradition, Muslim law permits divorce. Although divorce is allowed, it is not encouraged. One commentator cited the Prophet as saying, "The lawful thing which God hates most is divorce."[2]

In contrast to the traditional Christian view of sexual activity as inherently shameful and only a cure for lust even within marriage, Islam maintains a healthy acceptance of sexual pleasure for both males and females. The Qur'an permits a man to have four wives, provided that all are treated justly. The vast majority of Muslim males, however, were monogamous because only the wealthy could afford to support more than one wife.

QUICK REVIEW

How did ideas about gender roles shape life in classical Islamic society?

What social distinctions were important in Muslim society?	Why did trade thrive in Muslim lands?	What new ideas and practices emerged in the arts, sciences, education, and religion?	How did Muslims and Christians come into contact with and view each other?	✔ LearningCurve Check what you know.

> Why did trade thrive in Muslim lands?

Unlike the Christian West or the Confucian East, Islam looked favorably on profit-making enterprises. The Qur'an, moreover, has no prohibition against trade with Christians or other unbelievers. In fact, non-Muslims, including the Jews of Cairo and the Armenians in the central Islamic lands, were prominent in mercantile networks.

Waterways served as the main commercial routes of the Islamic world (Map 9.2). They included the Mediterranean and Black Seas; the Caspian Sea and the Volga River, which gave access deep into Russia; the Aral Sea, from which caravans departed for China; the Gulf of Aden; and the Arabian Sea and the Indian Ocean, which linked the Persian Gulf region with eastern Africa, the Indian subcontinent, and eventually Indonesia and the Philippines.

Cairo was a major Mediterranean entrepôt for intercontinental trade. Foreign merchants sailed up the Nile to the Aswan region, traveled east from Aswan by caravan to the Red Sea, and then sailed down the Red Sea to Aden, where they entered the Indian Ocean on their way to India. They exchanged textiles, glass, gold, silver, and copper for Asian spices, dyes, and drugs and for Chinese silks and porcelains. Muslim and Jewish merchants dominated the trade with India, and all spoke and wrote Arabic. Their commercial practices included the *sakk*, an order to a banker to pay money held on account to a third party. Muslims also developed other business innovations, such as the bill of exchange, a written order from one person to another to pay a specified sum of money to a designated person or party, and the idea of the joint stock company, an arrangement that lets a group of people invest in a venture and share its profits (and losses) in proportion to the amount each has invested.

Trade also benefited from improvements in technology. The adoption from the Chinese of the magnetic compass greatly helped navigation of the Arabian Sea and the Indian Ocean. The construction of larger ships led to a shift in long-distance cargoes from luxury goods such as pepper, spices, and drugs to bulk goods such as sugar, rice, and timber.

In this period Egypt became the center of Muslim trade, benefiting from the decline of Iraq caused by the Mongol capture of Baghdad and the fall of the Abbasid caliphate (see page 246). Beginning in the late twelfth century Persian and Arab seamen sailed down the east coast of Africa and established trading towns between Somalia and Sofala (see pages 288–290). These thirty to fifty urban centers linked Zimbabwe in southern Africa with the Indian Ocean trade and the Middle Eastern trade.

CHAPTER LOCATOR | From what kind of environment did Muhammad arise, and what did he teach? | What made possible the spread of Islam and what government was established? | How were Muslim lands governed and what challenges did rulers face?

252 CHAPTER 9 THE ISLAMIC WORLD

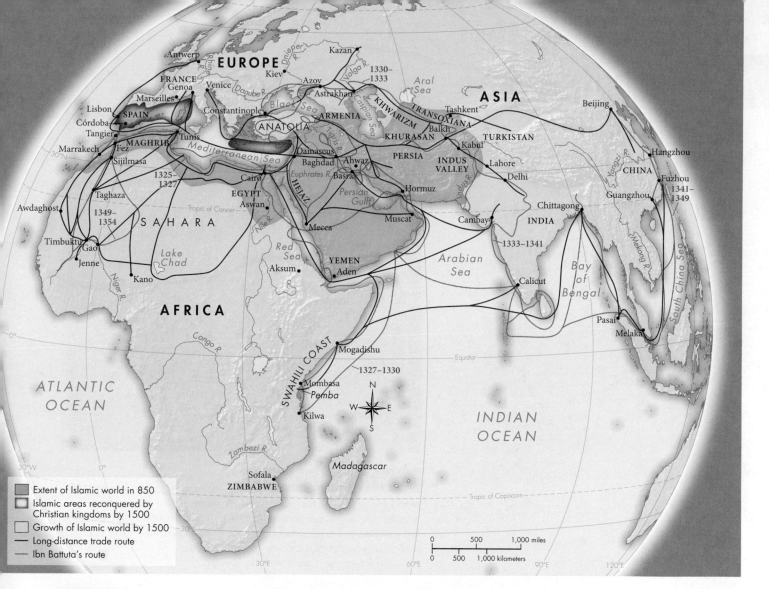

Map labels (clockwise / by region):

EUROPE · ASIA · AFRICA · CHINA

Antwerp · FRANCE · Genoa · Venice · Marseilles · Lisbon · SPAIN · Córdoba · Tangier · MAGHRIB · Marrakech · Fez · Sijilmasa · Tunis · Constantinople · Mediterranean Sea · Black Sea · ANATOLIA · ARMENIA · Damascus · Baghdad · Ahwaz · Basra · Cairo · EGYPT · Aswan · HEJAZ · Mecca · Red Sea · Aksum · YEMEN · Aden

Kazan · Kiev · Azov · Astrakhan · KHWARIZM · Aral Sea · Caspian Sea · TRANSOXIANA · Tashkent · Balkh · KHURASAN · TURKISTAN · Kabul · PERSIA · INDUS VALLEY · Lahore · Delhi · Hormuz · Muscat · Persian Gulf · Cambay · INDIA · Beijing · Hangzhou · CHINA · Fuzhou · Guangzhou · Chittagong · Calicut · Pasai · Melaka · Bay of Bengal · Arabian Sea · South China Sea

Rivers & features: Rhine R. · Dnieper R. · Volga R. · Danube R. · Tigris · Euphrates R. · Nile R. · Indus R. · Yangzi R. · Mekong R. · Congo R. · Niger R. · Zambezi R. · Lake Chad

SAHARA · Taghaza · Awdaghost · Timbuktu · Gao · Jenne · Kano · AFRICA · ATLANTIC OCEAN · SWAHILI COAST · Mogadishu · Mombasa · Pemba · Kilwa · Sofala · ZIMBABWE · Madagascar · INDIAN OCEAN · Equator · Tropic of Cancer · Tropic of Capricorn

Route dates: 1330–1333 · 1325–1327 · 1349–1354 · 1333–1341 · 1341–1349 · 1327–1330

Legend:
- Extent of Islamic world in 850
- Islamic areas reconquered by Christian kingdoms by 1500
- Growth of Islamic world by 1500
- Long-distance trade route
- Ibn Battuta's route

Scale: 0 · 500 · 1,000 miles / 0 · 500 · 1,000 kilometers

MAP 9.2 ■ The Expansion of Islam and Its Trading Networks in the Thirteenth and Fourteenth Centuries

By 1500 Islam had spread extensively in North and East Africa, and into the Balkans, the Caucasus, Central Asia, India, and the islands of Southeast Asia. Muslim merchants played a major role in bringing their religion as they extended their trade networks. They were active in the Indian Ocean long before the arrival of Europeans.

One byproduct of the extensive trade through Muslim lands was the spread of useful plants. Cotton, sugarcane, and rice spread from India to other places with suitable climates. Citrus fruits made their way to Muslim Spain from Southeast Asia and India. The value of this trade contributed to the prosperity of the Abbasid era.

QUICK REVIEW <

How did Islamic political and religious leaders view trade and commerce?

| What social distinctions were important in Muslim society? | **Why did trade thrive in Muslim lands?** | What new ideas and practices emerged in the arts, sciences, education, and religion? | How did Muslims and Christians come into contact with and view each other? | ✓ LearningCurve Check what you know. |

> What new ideas and practices emerged in the arts, sciences, education, and religion?

Teachers Disputing in a Madrasa

Although Islamic education relied heavily on memorization of the Qur'an, religious scholars frequently debated the correct interpretation of a particular text. Listening to this lively disputation, the students illustrated in this 1222 book are learning to think critically and creatively. (From *The Schefer Magamat*, Ms. Arabe 5847, fol. 118v/R. and S. Michaud/akg-images)

Long-distance trade provided the wealth that made possible a gracious and sophisticated culture in the cities of the Muslim world. (See "Individuals in Society: Ibn Battuta," page 255.) Education helped foster achievements in the arts and sciences, and Sufism brought a new spiritual and intellectual tradition.

The Cultural Centers of Baghdad and Córdoba

Although cities and mercantile centers dotted the entire Islamic world, the cities of Baghdad and Córdoba, at their peak in the tenth century, stand out as the finest examples of cosmopolitan Muslim civilization. On Baghdad's streets thronged representatives of a kaleidoscope of races, creeds, and cultures. Shops and marketplaces offered a dazzling and exotic array of goods from all over the world.

The caliph Harun al-Rashid presided over a glamorous court. He invited writers, dancers, musicians, poets, and artists to live in Baghdad. This brilliant era

CHAPTER LOCATOR | From what kind of environment did Muhammad arise, and what did he teach? | What made possible the spread of Islam and what government was established? | How were Muslim lands governed and what challenges did rulers face?

CHAPTER 9
THE ISLAMIC WORLD
254

In 1354 the sultan of Morocco appointed a scribe to write an account of the travels of Abu 'Abdallah Ibn Battuta (1304–1368), who between 1325 and 1354 had traveled through most of the Islamic world. The two men collaborated. The result was a travel book written in Arabic and later hailed as the richest eyewitness account of fourteenth-century Islamic culture. It has often been compared to the slightly earlier *Travels* of the Venetian Marco Polo (see page 341).

Ibn Battuta was born in Tangiers to a family of legal scholars. As a youth, he studied Muslim law, gained fluency in Arabic, and acquired the qualities considered essential for a civilized Muslim gentleman: courtesy, manners, and the social polish that eases relations among people.

At age twenty-one he left Tangiers to make the hajj (pilgrimage) to Mecca. He crossed North Africa and visited Alexandria, Cairo, Damascus, and Medina. Reaching Mecca in October 1326, he immediately praised God for his safe journey, kissed the Holy Stone at the Ka'ba, and recited the ritual prayers. There he decided to see more of the world.

In the next four years Ibn Battuta traveled to Iraq and to Basra and Baghdad in Persia, then returned to Mecca before sailing down the coast of Africa as far as modern Tanzania. On the return voyage he visited Oman and the Persian Gulf region, then traveled by land across central Arabia to Mecca. Strengthened by his stay in the holy city, he decided to go to India by way of Egypt, Syria, and Anatolia; across the Black Sea to the plains of western Central Asia, detouring to see Constantinople; back to the Asian steppe; east to Khurasan and Afghanistan; and down to Delhi in northern India.

For eight years Ibn Battuta served as a judge in the service of the sultan of Delhi. In 1341 the sultan chose him to lead a diplomatic mission to China. After the expedition was shipwrecked off the southeastern coast of India, Ibn Battuta traveled through southern India, Sri Lanka, and the Maldive Islands. Then he went to China, stopping in Bengal and Sumatra before reaching the southern coast of China, then under Mongol rule. Returning to Mecca in 1346, he set off for home, getting to Morocco in 1349. After a brief trip across the Strait of Gibraltar to Granada, he undertook his last journey, by camel caravan across the Sahara to Mali in the West African Sudan (see page 281), returning home in 1354. Scholars estimate that he had traveled about seventy-five thousand miles.

Ibn Battuta had a driving intellectual curiosity to see and understand the world. At every stop, he sought the learned jurists and pious men at the mosques and madrasas. He marveled at the Lighthouse of Alexandria, then in ruins; at the vast harbor at Kaffa (in southern Ukraine on the Black Sea), whose two hundred Genoese ships were loaded with

Travelers to Baghdad would have seen slave markets like this one. (© BnF, Dist, RMN–Grand Palais/Art Resource, NY)

silks and slaves for the markets at Venice, Cairo, and Damascus; and at the elephants in the sultan's procession in Delhi, which carried machines that tossed gold and silver coins to the crowds.

Ibn Battuta must have had an iron constitution. Besides walking long distances on his land trips, he endured fevers, dysentery, malaria, the scorching heat of the Sahara, and the freezing cold of the steppe. His thirst for adventure was stronger than his fear of nomadic warriors and bandits on land and the dangers of storms and pirates at sea.

Source: R. E. Dunn, *The Adventures of Ibn Battuta: A Muslim Traveler of the Fourteenth Century* (Berkeley: University of California Press, 1986).

QUESTIONS FOR ANALYSIS

1. Trace the routes of Ibn Battuta's travels on Map 9.2 (page 253).
2. How did a common Muslim culture facilitate Ibn Battuta's travels?

LaunchPad

ONLINE DOCUMENT PROJECT

How did Ibn Battuta describe his travels? Read parts of Ibn Battuta's account of his travels, and then complete a quiz and writing assignment based on the evidence and details from this chapter. *See the inside front cover to learn more.*

> Córdoba by the Numbers:

- Population: 1 million
- Mosques: 1,600
- Public Baths: 900
- Houses and Mansions: 273,177
- Shops: 80,455
- Weavers: 13,000
- Free Schools: 27
- Volumes in Library: 400,000

provided the background for the tales that appear in *The Thousand and One Nights.*

Córdoba in southern Spain competed with Baghdad for the cultural leadership of the Islamic world. Córdoba's scholars made contributions in chemistry, medicine and surgery, music, philosophy, and mathematics. In the tenth century no city in Asia or Europe could equal dazzling Córdoba. It's streets were well paved and lighted, and the city had an abundant supply of fresh water. The contemporary Saxon nun Hrosthwita of Gandersheim (d. 1000) described Córdoba as the "ornament of the world."[3]

Education and Intellectual Life

Muslim culture valued learning, especially religious learning, because knowledge provided the guidelines by which men and women should live. Parents thus established elementary schools for the training of their children. From the eighth century onward, formal education for young men involved reading, writing, and the study of the Qur'an, believed essential for its religious message and for its training in proper grammar and syntax.

madrasa
▶ A school for the study of Muslim law and religion.

Islam is a religion of the law, taught at **madrasas** (muh-DRA-suhs), schools for the study of Muslim law and religion. Schools were urban phenomena. Wealthy merchants endowed them, providing salaries for teachers, stipends for students, and living accommodations for both. All Islamic higher education rested on a close relationship between teacher and students, so in selecting a teacher, the student (or his father) considered the character and intellectual reputation of the teacher, not that of the institution. Students built their subsequent careers on the reputation of their teachers.

Learning depended heavily on memorization. In primary school, which was often attached to an institution of higher learning, a boy began his education by memorizing the entire Qur'an. In adolescence a student learned by heart an introductory work in one of the branches of knowledge, such as jurisprudence or grammar. Later he analyzed the texts in detail. Every class day, the teacher examined the student on the previous day's learning and determined whether the student fully understood what he had memorized. Students, of course, learned to write, for they had to record the teacher's commentary on a particular text. But the overwhelming emphasis was on the oral transmission of knowledge.

Because Islamic education focused on particular books, when the student had mastered a text to his teacher's satisfaction, the teacher issued the student a certificate stating that he had studied the book or collection of traditions with his teacher. The certificate allowed the student to transmit a text to the next generation on the authority of his teacher.

As the importance of books suggests, the Muslim transmission and improvement of papermaking techniques had special significance to education. After Chinese papermaking techniques spread westward, Muslim papermakers improved on them by adding starch to fill the pores in the surfaces of the sheets. Muslims carried this new method to Baghdad in Iraq, Damascus in Syria, Cairo in Egypt, and the Maghrib (North Africa), from which it entered Spain. Even before the

CHAPTER LOCATOR | From what kind of environment did Muhammad arise, and what did he teach? | What made possible the spread of Islam and what government was established? | How were Muslim lands governed and what challenges did rulers face?

256 CHAPTER 9 THE ISLAMIC WORLD

invention of printing, papermaking had a revolutionary impact on the collection and diffusion of knowledge.

Muslim higher education, apart from its fundamental goal of preparing men to live wisely and in accordance with God's law, aimed at preparing them to perform religious and legal functions as Qur'an—or hadith—readers; as preachers in the mosques; as professors, educators, or copyists; and especially as judges. Judges issued fatwas, or legal opinions, in the public courts; their training was in the Qur'an, hadith, or some text forming part of the shari'a.

On the issue of female education, Islamic culture was ambivalent. Tradition holds that Muhammad said, "The seeking of knowledge is a duty of every Muslim," but, because of the basic Islamic principle that "men are the guardians of women, because God has set the one over the other," the law excluded women from participating in the legal, religious, or civic occupations for which the madrasa prepared young men. Moreover, educational theorists insisted that men should study in a sexually isolated environment. Nevertheless, many young women received substantial educations at home. According to one biographical dictionary covering the lives of 1,075 women, 411 of them had memorized the Qur'an, studied with a particular teacher, and received a certificate.

In comparing Islamic higher education during the twelfth through fourteenth centuries with that available in Europe or China at the same time (see pages 368, 407), there are some striking similarities and some major differences. In both Europe and the Islamic countries religious authorities ran most schools, while in China the government, local villages, and lineages ran schools, and private tutoring was very common. In the Islamic world, as in China, the personal relationship of teacher and student was seen as key to education. In Europe the reward for satisfactorily completing a course of study was a degree granted by the university. In China, at the very highest levels, the state ran a civil service examination system that rewarded achievement with appointments in the state bureaucracy. In Muslim culture, by contrast, it was not the school or the state but the individual teacher whose evaluation mattered and who granted certificates.

Still, there were also some striking similarities in the practice of education. Students in all three cultures had to master a sacred language. In all three cultures education rested heavily on the study of basic religious, legal, or philosophical texts. Also, in all three cultures memorization played a large role in the acquisition and transmission of learning. Furthermore, teachers in all three societies lectured on particular passages, and leading teachers might disagree fiercely about the correct interpretations of a particular text, forcing students to question, to think critically, and to choose among divergent opinions. All these similarities in educational practice contributed to cultural cohesion and ties among the educated living in scattered localities.

In the Muslim world the spread of the Arabic language, not only among the educated classes but also among all the people, was the decisive element in the creation of a common culture. Arabic became the official language of the state and its bureaucracies in former Byzantine and Sassanid territories, and Muslim conquerors forbade Persian-speaking people to use their native language. Islamic rulers required tribute from monotheistic peoples—the Persians and Greeks—but they did not force them to change their religions. Conquered peoples were, however, compelled to submit to a linguistic conversion—to adopt the Arabic language.

| What social distinctions were important in Muslim society? | Why did trade thrive in Muslim lands? | **What new ideas and practices emerged in the arts, sciences, education, and religion?** | How did Muslims and Christians come into contact with and view each other? | ✓ LearningCurve Check what you know. |

257

In time Arabic produced a cohesive and "international" culture over a large part of the Eurasian world. Among those who wrote in Arabic was the erudite Gregory Bar-Hebraeus (1226–1286), a bishop of the Syrian Orthodox Church.

As a result of Muslim creativity and vitality, modern scholars consider the years from 800 to 1300 to be one of the most brilliant periods in the world's history. Near the beginning of this period the Persian scholar al-Khwarizmi (d. ca. 850) harmonized Greek and Indian findings to produce astronomical tables that formed the basis for later Eastern and Western research. Al-Khwarizmi's textbook on algebra (from the Arabic *al-Jabr*) was the first work in which the word *algebra* is used to mean the "transposing of negative terms in an equation to the opposite side."

Muslim medical knowledge far surpassed that of the West. Muslim medical science reached its peak in the work of Ibn Sina of Bukhara (980–1037), known in the West as Avicenna. His *al-Qanun* codified all Greco-Arabic medical thought, described the contagious nature of tuberculosis and the spreading of diseases, and listed 760 drugs.

Muslim scholars also wrote works on geography, jurisprudence, and philosophy. Al-Kindi (d. ca. 870) was the first Muslim thinker to try to harmonize Greek philosophy and the religious precepts of the Qur'an. Avicenna maintained that the truths found by human reason cannot conflict with the truths revealed in the Qur'an. Ibn Rushid, or Averroës (1126–1198), of Córdoba, paraphrased and commented on the works of Aristotle. He insisted on the right to subject all knowledge, except the dogmas of faith, to the test of reason and on the essential harmony of religion and philosophy.

The Mystical Tradition of Sufism

Like the world's other major religions—Buddhism, Hinduism, Judaism, and Christianity—Islam also developed a mystical tradition: Sufism (SOO-fih-zuhm). It arose in the ninth and tenth centuries as a popular reaction to the materialism and worldliness of the later Umayyad regime. Sufis sought a personal union with God—divine love and knowledge through intuition rather than through rational deduction and study of the shari'a. The earliest of the Sufis followed an ascetic routine (denial of physical desires to achieve a spiritual goal), dedicating themselves to fasting, prayer, meditation on the Qur'an, and the avoidance of sin.

The woman mystic Rabi'a (717–801) epitomized this combination of renunciation and devotion. An attractive woman who refused marriage so that nothing would distract her from a total commitment to God, Rabi'a attracted followers, for whom she served as a spiritual guide.

Between the tenth and the thirteenth centuries groups of Sufis gathered around prominent leaders called *shaykhs*; members of these groups were called *dervishes*. Dervishes entered hypnotic or ecstatic trances, either through the constant repetition of certain prayers or through physical exertions such as whirling or dancing.

Some Sufis acquired reputations as charismatic holy men to whom ordinary Muslims came seeking spiritual consolation, healing, charity, or political mediation between tribal and factional rivals. Other Sufis became known for their writings. Probably the most famous medieval Sufi was the Spanish mystic-philosopher Ibn al'Arabi (1165–1240). The author of a number of important works, he traveled widely in Spain, North Africa, and Arabia seeking masters of Sufism.

CHAPTER LOCATOR | From what kind of environment did Muhammad arise, and what did he teach? | What made possible the spread of Islam and what government was established? | How were Muslim lands governed and what challenges did rulers face?

258 CHAPTER 9
THE ISLAMIC WORLD

> PICTURING THE PAST

ANALYZING THE IMAGE: What sort of architectural space is depicted here? What distinctions do you see among the people in terms of how they dress and what they are doing?

CONNECTIONS: How common are music and dance in religion? What do they provide?

QUICK REVIEW <

How did Islamic education compare to education in Europe and China?

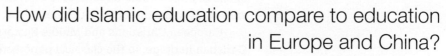

How did Muslims and Christians come into contact with each other, and how did they view each other?

Playing Chess

This page from a thirteenth-century book on chess and other games depicts a Moor and a Christian playing chess together. (Biblioteca Monasterio del Escorial, Madrid, Spain/Index/The Bridgeman Art Library)

During the early centuries of its development, Islam came into contact with the other major religions of Eurasia—Hinduism in India, Buddhism in Central Asia, Zoroastrianism in Persia, and Judaism and Christianity in western Asia and Europe. However, the relationship that did the most to define Muslim identity was the one with Christianity. The close physical proximity and the long history of military encounters undoubtedly contributed to making the Christian-Muslim encounter so important to both sides.

European Christians and Middle Eastern Muslims shared a common Judeo-Christian heritage. In the classical period of Islam, Muslims learned about Christianity from the Christians they met in conquered territories; from the Old and New Testaments; from Jews; and from Jews and Christians who converted to Islam.

In the Middle Ages, Christians and Muslims met frequently in business and trade. Commercial contacts, especially when European merchants resided for a

CHAPTER LOCATOR

From what kind of environment did Muhammad arise, and what did he teach?

What made possible the spread of Islam and what government was established?

How were Muslim lands governed and what challenges did rulers face?

CHAPTER 9
THE ISLAMIC WORLD

260

long time in the Muslim East, gave Europeans familiarity with Muslim art and architecture. Likewise, when in the fifteenth century Muslim artists in the Ottoman Empire and in Persia became acquainted with Western artists they admired and imitated them. Also, Christians very likely borrowed aspects of their higher education system from Islam.

In the Christian West, Islam had the greatest cultural impact in Andalusia in southern Spain. Between roughly the eighth and twelfth centuries Muslims, Christians, and Jews lived in close proximity in Andalusia, and some scholars believe the period represents a remarkable era of interfaith harmony. Many Christians adopted many aspects of Arabic culture. These assimilated Christians, called **Mozarabs** (moh-ZAR-uhbz), did not attach much importance to the doctrinal differences between the two religions.

However, Mozarabs soon faced the strong criticism of both Muslim scholars and Christian clerics. Muslim teachers feared that close contact between people of the two religions would lead to Muslim contamination and become a threat to the Islamic faith. Christian bishops worried that a knowledge of Islam would lead to confusion about essential Christian doctrines. Both Muslim scholars and Christian theologians argued that assimilation led to moral decline.

Thus, beginning in the late tenth century, Muslim regulations closely defined what Christians and Muslims could do. A Christian, however much assimilated, remained an unbeliever, a word that carried a pejorative connotation. Mozarabs had to live in special sections of cities; could not learn the Qur'an, employ Muslim workers or servants, or build new churches; and had to be buried in their own cemeteries. A Muslim who converted to Christianity was sentenced to death. By about 1250 the Christian reconquest of Muslim Spain had brought most of the Iberian Peninsula under Christian control. With their new authority, Christian kings set up schools that taught both Arabic and Latin to train missionaries.

Beyond Andalusian Spain, mutual animosity limited contact between people of the two religions. The Muslim assault on Christian Europe in the eighth and ninth centuries left a legacy of bitter hostility. Christians felt threatened by a faith that acknowledged God as creator of the universe but denied the Trinity and that accepted Jesus as a prophet but denied his divinity. Europeans' perception of Islam as a menace helped inspire the Crusades of the eleventh through thirteenth centuries (see page 401).

Despite the conflicts between the two religions, Muslim scholars often wrote sympathetically about Jesus. For example, the great historian al-Tabari (d. 923), relying on Arabic sources, wrote positively of Jesus's life, focusing on his birth and crucifixion. The prominent theologian and qadi (judge) of Teheran, Abd al-Jabbar (d. 1024), though not critical of Jesus, argued that Christians failed to observe the laws of Moses and Jesus and distorted Jesus's message.

In the Christian West, both positive and negative views of Islam appeared in literature. The Bavarian knight Wolfram von Eschenbach's *Parzival* and the Englishman William Langland's *Piers the Plowman* reveal broad-mindedness and tolerance toward Muslims. Some travelers in the Middle East were impressed by the kindness and generosity of Muslims and with the strictness and devotion with which Muslims observed their faith. Frequently, however, Christian literature portrayed Muslims as the most dreadful of Europe's enemies, guilty of every kind of crime.

Mozarabs
▶ Christians who adopted some Arabic customs but did not convert.

| What social distinctions were important in Muslim society? | Why did trade thrive in Muslim lands? | What new ideas and practices emerged in the arts, sciences, education, and religion? | **How did Muslims and Christians come into contact with and view each other?** | ☑ LearningCurve Check what you know. |

261

Even when they rejected each other most forcefully, the Christian and Muslim worlds had a significant impact on each other. Art styles, technology, and even institutional practices spread in both directions. During the Crusades Muslims adopted Frankish weapons and methods of fortification. Christians in contact with Muslim scholars recovered ancient Greek philosophical texts that survived only in Arabic translation.

> QUICK REVIEW

Why did Christian-Muslim relations deteriorate over the course of the Middle Ages?

CHAPTER SUMMARY

Muhammad, born in the Arabian peninsula, experienced a religious vision, after which he preached to the people to give up their idols and submit to the one indivisible God. He believed in the same God as the Christians and Jews and taught strict monotheism. After Muhammad's death, his followers gathered his revelations, eventually producing the Qur'an.

Within the span of a century, Muslims carried their faith from the Arabian peninsula through the Middle East, to North Africa and Spain, and to the borders of China and India. Successors to Muhammad established the caliphate, which through two successive dynasties coordinated rule over Muslim lands. A key challenge faced by the caliphate was a fundamental division in Muslim theology between the Sunnis and the Shi'a.

Over time, many parts of the Muslim empire gained considerable local independence. By the tenth century Turks played a more important role in the armies and came to be the effective rulers in much of the Middle East. They were succeeded by the Mongols, who invaded the Middle East in the thirteenth century.

Muslim society was distinctly hierarchical. In addition to a structure that privileged the ruling Arab Muslims over converts to Islam, then over Jews, Christians, and Zoroastrians, there were also a substantial number of slaves. Distinctions between men and women in Islamic society were strict. Over time, the seclusion and veiling of women became common practices.

Islam did not discourage trade and profitmaking. By land and sea Muslim merchants transported a rich variety of goods across Asia, the Middle East, Africa, and western Europe. As trade thrived, technical innovations aided the conduct of business.

Wealth from trade made possible a gracious and sophisticated culture in the cities of the Muslim world. During this period Muslim scholars produced important work in many disciplines, especially mathematics, medicine, and philosophy. A new spiritual and intellectual tradition arose in the mystical practices of Sufism. Muslims, Christians, and Jews interacted in many ways during this period. Many Christians converted in the early centuries of the spread of Islam. Others such as the Mozarabs assimilated into Muslim culture while retaining their religion.

CHAPTER LOCATOR | From what kind of environment did Muhammad arise, and what did he teach? | What made possible the spread of Islam and what government was established? | How were Muslim lands governed and what challenges did rulers face?

CHAPTER 9
THE ISLAMIC WORLD
262

CONNECTIONS During the five centuries that followed Muhammad's death, his teachings came to be revered in large parts of the world. Although in some ways similar to the earlier spread of Buddhism out of India and Christianity out of Palestine, the spread of Islam occurred largely through military conquests that extended Muslim lands.

Muslim civilization in these centuries drew from many sources, including Persia and Byzantium, and in turn had broad impact beyond its borders. Muslim scholars preserved much of early Greek philosophy and science through translation into Arabic. Trade connected the Muslim lands both to Europe and to India and China.

During the first and second centuries after Muhammad, Islam spread along the Mediterranean coast of North Africa. The next chapter explores other developments in Africa during this time. Many of the written sources that tell us about the African societies of these centuries were written in Arabic by visitors from elsewhere in the Muslim world. Africa's history is introduced in the next chapter.

LaunchPad

ONLINE DOCUMENT PROJECT

Long-Distance Travel in the Fourteenth Century

How did Ibn Battuta describe his travels?

Read parts of Ibn Battuta's account of his travels, and then complete a quiz and writing assignment based on the evidence and details from this chapter. *See the inside front cover to learn more.*

| What social distinctions were important In Muslim society? | Why did trade thrive in Muslim lands? | What new ideas and practices emerged in the arts, sciences, education, and religion? | How did Muslims and Christians come into contact with and view each other? | ☑ LearningCurve Check what you know. |

CHAPTER 9 STUDY GUIDE

STEP 1 **GET STARTED ONLINE**

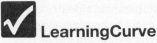 **LearningCurve**

Now that you've read the chapter, make it stick by completing the LearningCurve activity.

STEP 2 **EXPLAIN WHY IT MATTERS**

Put your reading into practice. Identify each term below, and then explain why it matters in world history.

TERM	WHO OR WHAT & WHEN	WHY IT MATTERS
Qur'an (p. 235)		
hadith (p. 235)		
Sunna (p. 236)		
Five Pillars of Islam (p. 236)		
umma (p. 238)		
diwān (p. 239)		
imam (p. 240)		
Shi'a (p. 241)		
Sunnis (p. 241)		
ulama (p. 241)		
emirs (p. 242)		
shari'a (p. 243)		
dhimmis (p. 248)		
madrasa (p. 256)		
Mozarabs (p. 261)		

STEP 3 **MOVE BEYOND THE BASICS**

To demonstrate a more advanced understanding of the relationship between Islamic beliefs and social, economic, and cultural developments in the Islamic world, fill in the first column of the chart below with a description of the core Islamic beliefs. Then, fill in the remaining three columns with descriptions of the impact of those beliefs on social, economic, and cultural developments. How did the advent of Islam impact the status of women in Islamic lands?

Core Islamic Beliefs	Impact on Social Developments	Impact on Economic Developments	Impact on Cultural Developments

STEP 4

PUT IT ALL TOGETHER

Now, take a step back and try to explain the big picture. Remember to use specific examples from the chapter in your answers.

THE ORIGINS OF ISLAM

▶ What characterized the social and economic environment in which Muhammad lived and preached?

▶ What are the core teachings of Islam? How do they compare to the core teachings of Christianity and Judaism?

ISLAMIC EXPANSION

▶ Argue for or against the following proposition: "The single most important factor explaining the rapid expansion of Islamic territories was the religious fervor of Muslim leaders and their armies." What evidence can you present to support your position?

▶ What explains the fragmentation of the Islamic world after 900? How did internal factors contribute to this trend? What about external threats?

ISLAMIC SOCIETY, COMMERCE, AND CULTURE

▶ Compare and contrast Roman (Chapter 6) and Islamic slavery. What role did slaves play in each society? How would you explain the similarities and differences you note?

▶ Compare and contrast Islamic and Confucian ideas (Chapter 7) about merchants and trade. How did such attitudes shape the social and economic trajectories of the Islamic and Chinese civilizations?

LOOKING BACK, LOOKING AHEAD

▶ What older Persian and Byzantine institutions and ideas did Islamic states incorporate into their own governments? How were those ideas and institutions modified by Islamic beliefs and practices?

▶ What connections can you make between the history of Muslim-Christian interactions and the contemporary relationship between Western and Islamic societies? How do long-held beliefs shape each society's view of the other?

> **IN YOUR OWN WORDS**

Imagine that you must give an oral report to the class answering the following question: **How did Islamic civilization both build on and transform earlier civilizations?** What would be the most important points and why?

10

AFRICAN SOCIETIES AND KINGDOMS

1000 B.C.E.–1500 C.E.

> What role did trade play in the development of African kingdoms and empires? Chapter 10 examines Africa's history to 1500. Between about 400 and 1500 highly centralized, bureaucratized, and socially stratified civilizations developed in Africa alongside communities with looser forms of social organization that were often held together through common kinship bonds. In West Africa several large empires closely linked to the trans-Saharan trade arose during this period. After 700 this trade connected West Africa with Muslim societies in North Africa and the Middle East. Meanwhile, Bantu-speaking peoples spread ironworking and domesticated crops and animals from modern Cameroon to Africa's southern tip, and the Swahili established large and prosperous city-states along the Indian Ocean coast.

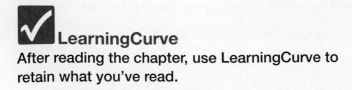

LearningCurve

After reading the chapter, use LearningCurve to
retain what you've read.

Ife Ruler West African rulers, such as the one shown in this bronze head of a Yoruban king, or *Oni*, from the thirteenth or fourteenth century, were usually male.

> How did Africa's geography shape its history and contribute to its diverse population?

> How did agriculture affect life among the early societies in the western Sudan and among the Bantu-speaking societies of central and southern Africa?

> What characterized trans-Saharan trade, and how did it affect West African society?

> How were the East African city-states, Aksum, and Great Zimbabwe different from and similar to the kingdoms of the western Sudan?

> How did Africa's geography shape its history and contribute to its diverse population?

Five main climatic zones roughly divide the African continent. Fertile land with unpredictable rainfall borders parts of the Mediterranean in the north and the southwestern coast of the Cape of Good Hope in the south. Inland from these areas are dry steppes with little plant life. These steppes gradually give way to Africa's great deserts: the Sahara in the north and the Namib (NAH-mihb) and Kalahari in the south. The Sahara's southern sub-desert fringe is called the Sahel (SA-hihl). The savannas—flat grasslands—extend in a swath across the continent's widest part—parts of south-central Africa and along the eastern coast. Dense, humid tropical rain forests stretch along coastal West Africa and on both sides of the equator in central Africa. Africa's climate is mostly tropical, with subtropical climates limited to the northern and southern coasts and the regions of high elevation. Rainfall is seasonal on most of the continent and is very sparse in desert and semidesert areas.

Geography and climate have significantly shaped African economic development. In the eastern African plains, the earliest humans hunted wild animals. The drier steppe regions favored herding. Wetter savanna regions, like the Nile Valley, encouraged grain-based agriculture. Tropical forests favored hunting and gathering and, later, root-based agriculture. Rivers and lakes supported economies based on fishing.

CHAPTER LOCATOR | **How did Africa's geography shape its history and contribute to its diverse population?** | How did agriculture affect life in the western Sudan and central and southern Africa?

ca. 1000 B.C.E.–1500 C.E. Bantu-speakers expand across central and southern Africa	**ca. 900–1100 C.E.** Kingdom of Ghana; bananas and plantains arrive in Africa from Asia
ca. 600 C.E. Christian missionaries convert Nubian rulers	**ca. 1100–1400 C.E.** Great Zimbabwe is built, flourishes
639–642 C.E. Islam introduced to Africa	**ca. 1200–1450 C.E.** Kingdom of Mali
642 C.E. Muslim conquest of Egypt	**ca. 1312–1337 C.E.** Reign of Mansa Musa in Mali
650–1500 C.E. Slave trade from sub-Saharan Africa to the Mediterranean	**1314–1344 C.E.** Reign of Amda Siyon in Ethiopia
700–900 C.E. Berbers develop caravan routes	**1324–1325 C.E.** Mansa Musa's pilgrimage to Mecca

Africa's peoples are as diverse as the continent's topography. In North Africa contacts with Asian and European civilizations date back to the ancient Phoenicians, Greeks, and Romans (see Chapters 5 and 6). Groups living on the coast or along trade routes had the greatest degree of contact with outside groups. The Berbers of North Africa, living along the Mediterranean, intermingled with many different peoples—with Muslim Arabs, who first conquered North Africa in the seventh and eighth centuries C.E. (see page 238); with Spanish Muslims and Jews, many of whom settled in North Africa after their expulsion from Spain in 1492 (see page 433); and with sub-Saharan peoples, with whom they traded across the Sahara Desert. The Swahili peoples along the East African coast developed a maritime civilization and had rich commercial contacts with southern Arabia, the Persian Gulf, India, China, and the Malay Archipelago.

South of the Sahara, short-statured peoples, sometimes inaccurately referred to as Pygmies, inhabited the equatorial rain forests. South of those forests, in the continent's southern third, lived the Khoisan (KOI-sahn), people who were primarily hunters but also had domesticated livestock.

Ancient Egypt, at the crossroads of three continents, was a melting pot of different cultures and peoples. Many diverse peoples contributed to the great achievements of Egyptian culture. Many scholars believe that Africans originating in the sub-Sahara resided in ancient Egypt, primarily in Upper Egypt (south of what is now Cairo), but that other ethnic groups constituted the majority of the population.

QUICK REVIEW

Which groups of Africans had the most contact with outside peoples? Why?

| What characterized trans-Saharan trade, and how did it affect West African society? | How did the East African city-states compare to the kingdoms of the western Sudan? | ✔ LearningCurve
Check what you know. |

How did agriculture affect life among the early societies in the western Sudan and among the Bantu-speaking societies of central and southern Africa?

Rock Painting at Tassili, Algeria

This scene of cattle grazing while a man stands guard over them was found on a rock face in Tassili n'Ajjer, a mountainous region in the Sahara where over fifteen thousand of these paintings have been catalogued. The oldest date back 9,000–12,000 years. Behind the man are perhaps his two children at play and his two wives working together in the compound. A cow stands in the enclosure to the right. (George Holton/Photo Researchers, Inc. Colorization by Robin Treadwell)

New crops introduced from Asia and the establishment of settled agriculture profoundly changed many African societies, although the range of possibilities largely depended on local variations in climate and geography. Bantu-speakers took the knowledge of domesticated livestock and agriculture, along with the ironworking skills that had developed in northern and western Africa, and spread them south across central and southern Africa. The most prominent feature of early West African society was a strong sense of community based on blood relationships and religion.

Agriculture and Its Impact

Agriculture began very early in Africa. Knowledge of plant cultivation moved west from the Levant (modern Israel and Lebanon), arriving in the Nile Delta in Egypt about the fifth millennium B.C.E. Settled agriculture then traveled down the Nile Valley and moved west across the Sahel to the central and western Sudan. West

CHAPTER LOCATOR | How did Africa's geography shape its history and contribute to its diverse population? | **How did agriculture affect life in the western Sudan and central and southern Africa?**

CHAPTER 10
270 AFRICAN SOCIETIES AND KINGDOMS

Africans were living in agricultural communities by the first century B.C.E. From there plant cultivation spread to the equatorial forests. Gradually most Africans evolved a sedentary way of life: living in villages, clearing fields, relying on root crops, and fishing. Hunting-and-gathering societies survived only in scattered parts of Africa, particularly in the central rain forest region and in southern Africa.

Between 1500 B.C.E. and 1000 B.C.E. agriculture also spread southward from Ethiopia along the Great Rift Valley of present-day Kenya and Tanzania. Archaeological evidence reveals that the peoples of East Africa grew cereals, raised cattle, and used wooden and stone tools.

Cereals such as millet and sorghum are indigenous to Africa. Scholars speculate that traders brought bananas, taros (a type of yam), sugarcane, and coconut palms to Africa from Southeast Asia. Because tropical forest conditions were ideal for banana plants, their cultivation spread rapidly. Throughout sub-Saharan Africa native peoples also domesticated donkeys, pigs, chickens, geese, and ducks, although all these came from outside Africa.

The evolution from a hunter-gatherer life to a settled life had profound effects. In contrast to nomadic societies, settled societies made shared or common needs more apparent, and those needs strengthened ties among extended families. Agricultural and pastoral populations also increased, though scholars speculate that this increase did not remain steady, but rather fluctuated over time. Nor is it clear that population growth was accompanied by a commensurate increase in agricultural output.

Early African societies were similarly influenced by the spread of ironworking, though scholars dispute the route by which this technology spread to sub-Saharan Africa. Some believe the Phoenicians brought the iron-smelting technique to northwestern Africa, from which it spread southward. Others insist it spread westward from the Meroë (MEHR-oh-ee) region of the Nile. The great trans-Saharan trade routes (see page 275) may have carried ironworking south from the Mediterranean coast. In any case, ancient iron tools found at the village of Nok on the Jos Plateau in present-day Nigeria seem to prove that ironworking industries existed in West Africa by at least 700 B.C.E.

Bantu Migrations

The spread of ironworking is linked to the migrations of Bantu-speaking peoples. Today the overwhelming majority of the 70 million people living south of the Congo River speak a **Bantu** language. Lacking written sources, modern scholars have tried to reconstruct the history of Bantu-speakers on the basis of linguistics, oral traditions, archaeology, and anthropology. Botanists and zoologists have played particularly critical roles in providing information about early diets and environments.

Bantu
▶ Speakers of a Bantu language living south and east of the Congo River.

Bantu-speaking peoples originated in the Benue region, the borderlands of modern Cameroon and Nigeria. In the second millennium B.C.E. they began to spread south and east into the equatorial forest zone. Historians still debate why they began this movement. Some hold that rapid population growth sent people in search of land. Others believe that the evolution of centralized kingdoms allowed rulers to expand their authority, while causing newly subjugated peoples to flee in the hope of regaining their independence.

What characterized trans-Saharan trade, and how did it affect West African society?

How did the East African city-states compare to the kingdoms of the western Sudan?

LearningCurve
Check what you know.

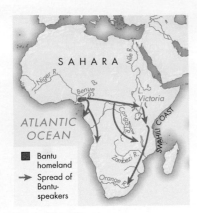

**Bantu Migrations,
ca. 1000 B.C.E.–1500 C.E.**

During the next fifteen hundred years, Bantu-speakers migrated throughout the savanna, adopted mixed agriculture, and learned ironworking. Mixed agriculture (cultivating cereals and raising livestock) and ironworking were practiced in western East Africa (the region of modern Burundi) in the first century B.C.E. In the first millennium C.E. Bantu-speakers migrated into eastern and southern Africa. Here the Bantu-speakers, with their iron weapons, either killed, drove off, or assimilated the hunting-gathering peoples they met. Some of the assimilated inhabitants gradually adopted a Bantu language, contributing to the spread of Bantu culture.

The settled cultivation of cereals, the keeping of livestock, and the introduction of new crops such as the banana—together with Bantu-speakers' intermarriage with indigenous peoples—led over a long period to considerable population increases and the need to migrate farther. The so-called Bantu migrations should not be seen as a single movement sweeping across Africa from west to east to south and displacing all peoples in its path. Rather, those migrations were an extended series of group interactions between Bantu-speakers and pre-existing peoples in which bits of culture, languages, economies, and technologies were shared and exchanged to produce a wide range of cultural variation across central and southern Africa.[1]

The Bantu-speakers' expansion and subsequent land settlement that dominated eastern and southern African history in the first fifteen hundred years of the Common Era were uneven. Significant environmental differences determined settlement patterns. Some regions had plenty of water, while others were very arid. These differences resulted in very uneven population distribution. The greatest population density seems to have been in the region bounded on the west by the Congo River and on the north, south, and east by Lakes Edward and Victoria and Mount Kilimanjaro. The rapid growth of the Bantu-speaking population led to further migration southward and eastward. By the eighth century the Bantu-speaking people had crossed the Zambezi River and had begun settling in the region of present-day Zimbabwe. By the fifteenth century they had reached Africa's southeastern coast.

Life in the Kingdoms of the Western Sudan, ca. 1000 B.C.E.–800 C.E.

Sudan

▶ The African region surrounded by the Sahara, the Gulf of Guinea, the Atlantic Ocean, and the mountains of Ethiopia.

The **Sudan** is the region bounded by the Sahara to the north, the Gulf of Guinea to the south, the Atlantic Ocean to the west, and the mountains of Ethiopia to the east (see Map 10.1). In the western Sudan savanna a series of dynamic kingdoms emerged in the millennium before European intrusion began in the 1400s and 1500s.

Between 1000 B.C.E. and 200 C.E. the peoples of the western Sudan made the momentous shift from nomadic hunting to settled agriculture. The rich savanna proved ideally suited to cereal production, especially rice, millet, and sorghum. People situated near the Senegal River and Lake Chad supplemented their diet with fish. Food supply affects population, and the region's inhabitants increased dramatically in number. By 400 C.E. the entire savanna, particularly around Lake Chad, the Niger River bend, and present-day central Nigeria, had a large population.

Families and clans affiliated by blood kinship lived together in villages or small city-states. The extended family formed the basic social unit. A chief, in

CHAPTER LOCATOR | How did Africa's geography shape its history and contribute to its diverse population? | **How did agriculture affect life in the western Sudan and central and southern Africa?**

272 CHAPTER 10 AFRICAN SOCIETIES AND KINGDOMS

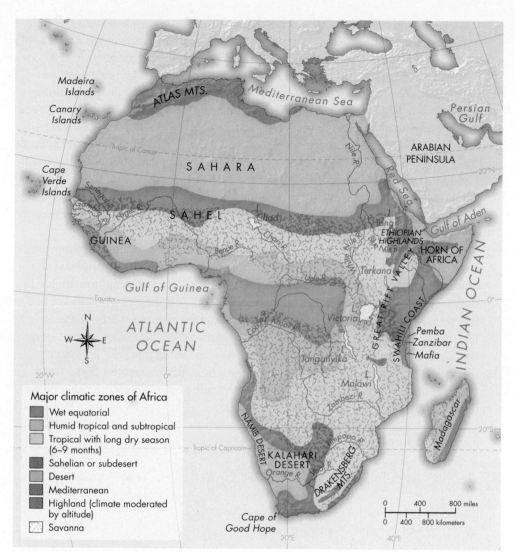

MAP 10.1 ■ The Geography of Africa

Africa's climate zones have always played a critical role in the history of the continent and its peoples. These zones mirror each other north and south of the equator: tropical forest, savanna, sub-desert, desert, and Mediterranean climate.

Major climatic zones of Africa

- Wet equatorial
- Humid tropical and subtropical
- Tropical with long dry season (6–9 months)
- Sahelian or subdesert
- Desert
- Mediterranean
- Highland (climate moderated by altitude)
- Savanna

consultation with a council of elders, governed a village. Some villages seem to have formed kingdoms. In this case, village chiefs were responsible to regional heads, who answered to provincial governors, who in turn were responsible to a king. The kings and their families formed an aristocracy.

Kingship in the Sudan may have emerged from the priesthood. African kings always had religious sanction or support for their authority and were often considered divine. In this respect, early African kingship bears a strong resemblance to Germanic kingship of the same period (discussed in Chapter 14).

Women exercised significant power and autonomy in many African societies. Among the Asante in modern-day Ghana, one of the most prominent West African peoples, the king was considered divine but shared some royal power with the Queen Mother. Among the Yoruba in modern Nigeria, the Queen Mother held the royal insignia and could refuse it if the future king did not please her. The institutions of female chiefs, known as *iyalode* among the Yoruba and *omu* among the Igbo in modern Nigeria, were established to represent women in the political process. The *omu* was even considered a female co-ruler with the male chief.

What characterized trans-Saharan trade, and how did it affect West African society?

How did the East African city-states compare to the kingdoms of the western Sudan?

✓ LearningCurve
Check what you know.

Western Sudanese religious practices, like African religions elsewhere, were animistic and polytheistic. Most people believed that a supreme being had created the universe and was the source of all life. Most African religions also recognized ancestral spirits, which might seek God's blessings for families' and communities' prosperity and security as long as these groups behaved appropriately. Some African religions believed as well that nature spirits lived in such things as the sky, forests, rocks, and rivers. These spirits controlled natural forces and had to be appeased. Because special ceremonies were necessary to satisfy the spirits, special priests with the knowledge and power to communicate with them through sacred rituals were needed. Family and village heads were often priests. Each family head was responsible for ceremonies honoring the family's dead and living members.[2] In some West African societies, oracles who spoke for the gods were particularly important.

Kinship patterns and shared religious practices helped to bind together the early western Sudan kingdoms. Islam's spread across the Sahara by at least the ninth century c.e., however, created a north-south religious and cultural divide in the western Sudan. Islam advanced across the Sahel but halted when it reached the West African savanna and forest zones. Societies in these southern zones maintained their traditional animistic religious practices. Muslim empires along the Niger River's great northern bend evolved into formidable powers ruling over sizable territory as they seized control of the southern termini of the trans-Saharan trade. What made this long-distance trade possible was the "ship of the desert," the camel.

> **QUICK REVIEW**

How did the Bantu migrations shape early Africa?

CHAPTER LOCATOR | How did Africa's geography shape its history and contribute to its diverse population? | How did agriculture affect life in the western Sudan and central and southern Africa?

What characterized trans-Saharan trade, and how did it affect West African society?

"Trans-Saharan trade" refers to the north-south trade across the Sahara (Map 10.2). The camel had an impact on this trade comparable to the very important impact of horses and oxen on European agriculture. Although scholars dispute exactly when the camel was introduced from Central Asia—first into North Africa, then into the Sahara and the Sudan—they agree that it was before 200 c.e. The trans-Saharan trade brought lasting economic and social change to Africa, facilitating the spread of Islam via Muslim Arab traders, and affected the development of world commerce.

The Berbers of North Africa

Sometime in the fifth century c.e. the North African **Berbers** fashioned a saddle for use on the camel. The saddle gave the Berbers and later the region's Arabian inhabitants maneuverability on the animal and thus a powerful political and military advantage: they came to dominate the desert and to create lucrative routes across it. The Berbers determined who could enter the desert, and they extracted large sums of protection money from merchant caravans in exchange for a safe trip.

Between 700 c.e. and 900 c.e. the Berbers developed a network of caravan routes between the Mediterranean coast and the Sudan (see Map 10.2). Ibn Battuta, an Arab traveler in the fourteenth century, when the trade was at its height, left one of the best descriptions of the trans-Saharan traffic. (See "Individuals in Society: Ibn Battuta," page 255.)

Berbers
▶ North African peoples who controlled the caravan trade between the Mediterranean and the Sudan.

What characterized trans-Saharan trade, and how did it affect West African society?	How did the East African city-states compare to the kingdoms of the western Sudan?	✔ LearningCurve Check what you know.

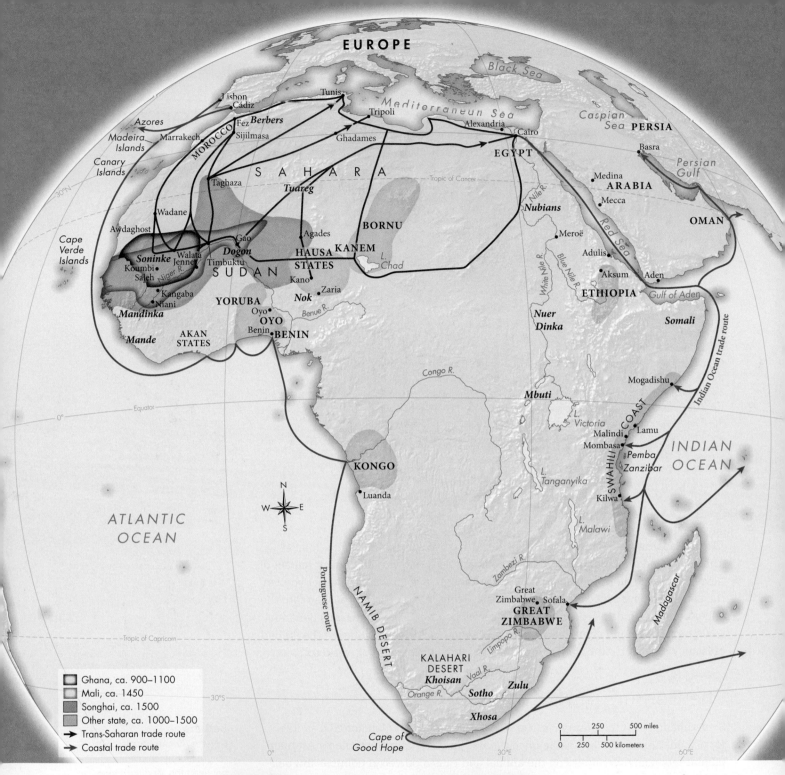

MAP 10.2 ■ African Kingdoms and Trade, ca. 800–1500
Throughout world history powerful kingdoms have generally been closely connected to far-flung trade networks.

> MAPPING THE PAST

ANALYZING THE MAP: Which kingdoms, empires, and city-states were linked to the trans-Saharan trade network? Which were connected to the Indian Ocean trade network? To the Portuguese route?

CONNECTIONS: How were the kingdoms, empires, and city-states shown on this map shaped by their proximity to trade routes?

CHAPTER LOCATOR | How did Africa's geography shape its history and contribute to its diverse population? | How did agriculture affect life in the western Sudan and central and southern Africa?

276 CHAPTER 10
AFRICAN SOCIETIES AND KINGDOMS

Nomadic raiders, the Tuareg (TWAH-rehg), posed a serious threat to trans-Saharan traders. The Tuareg were Berbers who lived in the desert uplands and preyed on the caravans as a way of life. To avoid being victimized, merchants made safe-conduct agreements with them and selected guides from among them. Large numbers of merchants crossed the desert together to discourage attack; caravans of twelve thousand camels were reported in the fourteenth century.

Berber merchants from North Africa controlled the caravan trade that carried dates, salt from the Saharan salt mines, and some manufactured goods—silk and cotton cloth, beads, mirrors—to the Sudan. These products were exchanged for the much-coveted commodities of the West African savanna—gold, ivory, gum, kola nuts (eaten as a stimulant), and enslaved West African men and women who were sold to Muslim slave markets in Morocco, Algiers, Tripoli, and Cairo.

Effects of Trade on West African Society

The steady growth of trans-Saharan trade had three important effects on West African society. First, trade stimulated gold mining. Parts of modern-day Senegal, Nigeria, and Ghana contained rich veins of gold, and scholars estimate that by the eleventh century nine tons of gold were exported to the Mediterranean coast and Europe annually. Some of this metal went to Egypt. From there it was transported down the Red Sea and eventually to India (see Map 9.2, page 253) to pay for the spices and silks demanded by Mediterranean commerce. In this way, African gold linked the entire world, exclusive of the Western Hemisphere.

Second, trade in gold and other goods created a desire for slaves. Slaves were West Africa's second-most valuable export (after gold). Slaves worked the gold and salt mines, and in Muslim North Africa, southern Europe, and southwestern Asia there was a high demand for household slaves among the elite. African slaves, like their early European and Asian counterparts, seem to have been peoples captured in war. Recent research suggests, moreover, that large numbers of black slaves were also recruited for Muslim military service through the trans-Saharan trade. Table 10.1 shows the scope of the trans-Saharan slave trade. The total number of blacks enslaved over an 850-year period may be tentatively estimated at more than 4 million.[3]

The third important effect of trans-Saharan trade on West African society was its role in stimulating the development of urban centers. Scholars date the growth of African cities from around the early ninth century. Families that had profited from trade tended to congregate in the border zones between the savanna and the Sahara. They acted as middlemen between the miners to the south and the Muslim merchants from the north. By the early thirteenth century these families had become powerful merchant dynasties. Muslim traders from the Mediterranean settled permanently in the trading depots, from which they organized the trans-Saharan caravans. The concentration of people stimulated agriculture and the craft industries. Gradually cities of sizable population emerged, including: Jenne, Gao, and Timbuktu, Sijilmasa, and Koumbi Saleh. Between 1100 and 1400 these cities played a dynamic role in West Africa's commercial life and became centers of intellectual creativity.

TABLE 10.1 ■ Estimated Magnitude of Trans-Saharan Slave Trade, 650–1500

Years	Annual Average of Slaves Traded	Total
650–800	1,000	150,000
800–900	3,000	300,000
900–1100	8,700	1,740,000
1100–1400	5,500	1,650,000
1400–1500	4,300	430,000

Source: R. A. Austen, "The Trans-Saharan Slave Trade: A Tentative Census," in *The Uncommon Market: Essays in the Economic History of the Atlantic Slave Trade*, ed. H. A. Gemery and J. S. Hogendorn (New York: Academic Press, 1979). Used with permission.

> **Major Effects of Trade on West African Society:**

- Stimulation of gold mining
- Increased demand for slaves
- Development of urban centers

What characterized trans-Saharan trade, and how did it affect West African society?

How did the East African city-states compare to the kingdoms of the western Sudan?

✓ LearningCurve
Check what you know.

The Spread of Islam in Africa

The Spread of Islam in Africa

Perhaps the most influential consequence of the trans-Saharan trade was the introduction of Islam to West Africa. In the eighth century Arab invaders overran all of coastal North Africa. They introduced the Berbers living there to Islam (see page 239), and gradually the Berbers became Muslims. As traders, these Berbers carried Islam to sub-Saharan West Africa. From the eleventh century onward militant Almoravids, a coalition of fundamentalist western Saharan Berbers, preached Islam to the rulers of Ghana, Mali, Songhai, and Kanem-Bornu. These rulers, admiring Muslim administrative techniques and wanting to protect their kingdoms from Muslim Berber attacks, converted to Islam. Some merchants also sought to preserve their elite mercantile status with the Berbers by adopting Islam. Muslims quickly became integral to West African government and society. Hence, from roughly 1000 to 1400, Islam in West Africa was a class-based religion with conversion inspired by political or economic motives. Rural people in the Sahel region and the savanna and forest peoples farther south, however, largely retained their traditional animism.

Conversion to Islam introduced West Africans to a rich and sophisticated culture. By the late eleventh century Muslims were guiding the ruler of Ghana in the operation of his administrative machinery. Because efficient government depends on keeping and preserving records, Islam's arrival in West Africa marked the advent of written documents there. Arab Muslims also taught Ghana's rulers how to manufacture bricks, and royal palaces and mosques began to be built of brick. African rulers corresponded with Arab and North African Muslim architects, theologians, and other intellectuals, who advised them on statecraft and religion. Islam accelerated the development of the West African empires of the ninth through fifteenth centuries.

After the Muslim conquest of Egypt in 642 (see page 238), Islam spread southward from Egypt up the Nile Valley and west to Darfur and Wadai. This Muslim penetration came not suddenly by military force but, as in the trans-Saharan trade routes in West Africa, gradually through commercial networks.

Muslim expansion from the Arabian peninsula across the Red Sea to the Horn of Africa, then southward along the coast of East Africa, represents a third direction of Islam's growth in Africa. From ports on the Red Sea and the Gulf of Aden, maritime trade carried Islam to East Africa and the Indian Ocean. Muslims founded the port city of **Mogadishu** between the eighth and tenth centuries, today Somalia's capital. In the twelfth century Mogadishu developed into a Muslim sultanate. Archaeological evidence, confirmed by Arabic sources, reveals a rapid Islamic expansion along Africa's east coast in the thirteenth century as far south as Kilwa, where Ibn Battuta visited a center for Islamic law in 1331.

Mogadishu

▶ A Muslim port city in East Africa founded between the eighth and tenth centuries; today it is the capital of Somalia.

> QUICK REVIEW

What connections were there between trade and the spread of Islam in Africa?

CHAPTER LOCATOR | How did Africa's geography shape its history and contribute to its diverse population? | How did agriculture affect life in the western Sudan and central and southern Africa?

How were the East African city-states, Aksum, and Great Zimbabwe different from and similar to the kingdoms of the western Sudan?

Ruins of Great Zimbabwe

Considered the most impressive monument in the African interior south of the Ethiopian highlands, these ruins of Great Zimbabwe consist of two complexes of dry-stone buildings, some surrounded by a massive serpentine wall 32 feet high and 17 feet thick at its maximum. (Robert Harding World Imagery)

All African societies shared one basic feature: a close relationship between political and social organization. Ethnic or blood ties bound clan members together. What scholars call **stateless societies** were culturally homogeneous ethnic societies, generally organized around kinship groups. These societies lacked a central authority figure, such as a king, capital city, or military. A village or group of villages might recognize a chief who held very limited powers and whose position was not hereditary, but more commonly they were governed by local councils, whose members were either elders or persons of merit. Although stateless societies functioned successfully, their weakness lay in their inability to organize and defend themselves against attack by the powerful armies of neighboring kingdoms or by the European powers of the colonial era.

While stateless societies were relatively common in Africa, the period from about 800 to 1500 is best known as the age of Africa's great empires (see Map 10.2). This period witnessed the flowering of several powerful African states. In the western Sudan the large empires of Ghana, Mali, and Songhai developed, complete with sizable royal bureaucracies. On the east coast emerged thriving city-states based on sophisticated mercantile activities and, like the western Sudan, heavily influenced by Islam. In Ethiopia, in central East Africa, kings relied

stateless societies
▶ African societies bound together by ethnic or blood ties rather than by being political states.

What characterized trans-Saharan trade, and how did it affect West African society?

How did the East African city-states compare to the kingdoms of the western Sudan?

✔ LearningCurve
Check what you know.

on their peoples' Christian faith to strengthen political authority. In southern Africa the empire of Great Zimbabwe, built on the gold trade with the east coast, flourished.

The Kingdom of Ghana, ca. 900–1100

Ghana
▶ From the word for "ruler," the name of a large and influential African kingdom inhabited by the Soninke people.

So remarkable was the kingdom of **Ghana** during the age of Africa's great empires that Arab and North African visitors praised it as a model for other rulers. The Soninke people inhabited the nucleus of the territory that became the Ghanaian kingdom. They called their ruler *ghana*, or war chief. By the late eighth century Muslim traders and other foreigners applied the king's title to the region where the Soninke lived, the kingdom south of the Sahara. The Soninke themselves called their land Wagadou (WAH-guh-doo). Only the southern part of Wagadou received enough rainfall to be agriculturally productive, and it was here that the civilization of Ghana developed (see Map 10.2). Skillful farming and efficient irrigation systems led to abundant crop production, which eventually supported a population of as many as two hundred thousand.

In 992 Ghana captured the Berber town of Awdaghost, strategically situated on the trans-Saharan trade route. Thereafter Ghana controlled the southern portion of a major caravan route. Before the year 1000 Ghana's rulers had extended their influence almost to the Atlantic coast and had captured a number of small kingdoms in the south and east. By the early eleventh century the Ghanaian king exercised sway over a territory approximately the size of Texas. No other power in the western Sudan could successfully challenge him.

Throughout this vast West African territory, all authority sprang from the king. Religious ceremonies and court rituals emphasized the king's sacredness and were intended to strengthen his authority. The king's position was hereditary in the matrilineal line—that is, the ruling king's heir was one of the king's sister's sons (presumably the eldest or fittest for battle).

A council of ministers assisted the king in the work of government, and from the ninth century on most of these ministers were Muslims. The royal administration was well served by ideas, skills, and especially literacy brought from the North African and Arab Muslim worlds. The king and his people, however, clung to their ancestral religion and basic cultural institutions.

Koumbi Saleh
▶ The city in which the king of Ghana held his court.

The Ghanaian king held court in the city of **Koumbi Saleh**, which was actually two towns, one inhabited by the king and the other by Muslims. Either to protect themselves or to preserve their special identity, the Muslims of Koumbi Saleh lived separately from the African artisans and tradespeople. Ghana's Muslim community was large and prosperous, and Muslim religious leaders exercised civil authority over their fellow Muslims. The presence of religious leaders and other learned Muslims suggests that Koumbi Saleh was a city of vigorous intellectual activity.

The king's elaborate court, the administrative machinery he built, and the extensive territories he governed were all expensive. To support the kingdom, the royal estates—some hereditary, others conquered in war—produced annual revenue, mostly in the form of foodstuffs for the royal household. The king also received tribute annually from subordinate chieftains. Customs duties on goods entering and leaving the country generated revenues as well. Salt was the largest import. Berber merchants paid a tax to the king on the cloth, metalwork, weapons,

CHAPTER LOCATOR | How did Africa's geography shape its history and contribute to its diverse population? | How did agriculture affect life in the western Sudan and central and southern Africa?

280 CHAPTER 10 AFRICAN SOCIETIES AND KINGDOMS

and other goods they brought into the country from North Africa; in return these traders received royal protection from bandits. African traders bringing gold into Ghana from the south also paid the customs duty. Finally, the royal treasury held a monopoly on the export of gold. The gold industry was undoubtedly the king's largest source of income.

The governing aristocracy—the king, his court, and Muslim administrators—occupied the highest rung on the Ghanaian social ladder. On the next rung stood the merchant class. Considerably below the merchants stood the farmers, cattle breeders, gold mine supervisors, and skilled craftsmen and weavers—what today might be called the middle class. Some merchants and miners must have enjoyed great wealth, but, as in all aristocratic societies, money alone did not grant prestige. High status was based on blood and royal service. On the social ladder's lowest rung were slaves, who worked in households, on farms, and in the mines. As in Asian and European societies of the time, slaves accounted for only a small percentage of the population.

Apart from these social classes stood the army. Ghana's king maintained at his palace a standing force of a thousand men, comparable to the bodyguards of the Roman emperors. These thoroughly disciplined, well-armed, totally loyal troops protected the king and the royal court. They lived in special compounds, enjoyed the king's favor, and sometimes acted as his personal ambassadors to subordinate rulers. In wartime this regular army was augmented by levies of soldiers from conquered peoples and by the use of slaves and free reserves.

The reasons for ancient Ghana's decline are still a matter of much debate. The most commonly accepted theory for Ghana's rapid decline is that the Berber Almoravid dynasty of North Africa invaded and conquered Ghana around 1100 and forced its rulers and people to convert to Islam. Some historians examining this issue have concluded that while Almoravid and Islamic pressures certainly disrupted the empire, weakening it enough for its incorporation into the rising Mali empire, there was no Almoravid military invasion and subsequent forced conversion to Islam.[4]

The Kingdom of Mali, ca. 1200–1450

Ghana and its capital of Koumbi Saleh were in decline between 1100 and 1200. The old empire split into several small kingdoms that feuded among themselves. One people, the Mandinka, from the kingdom of Kangaba on the upper Niger River, gradually asserted their dominance over these kingdoms. The Mandinka had long been part of the Ghanaian empire, and the Mandinka and Soninke belonged to the same language group. Kangaba formed the core of the new empire of Mali. Building on Ghanaian foundations, Mali developed into a better-organized and more powerful state than Ghana.

Mali owed its greatness to two fundamental assets. First, its strong agricultural and commercial base supported a large population and provided enormous wealth. Second, Mali had two rulers, Sundiata (soon-JAH-tuh) and Mansa Musa, who combined military success with exceptionally creative personalities.

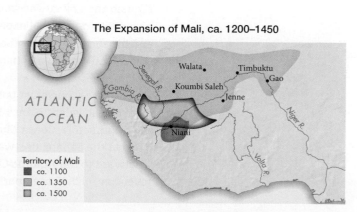

The Expansion of Mali, ca. 1200–1450

Territory of Mali
- ca. 1100
- ca. 1350
- ca. 1500

What characterized trans-Saharan trade, and how did it affect West African society?

How did the East African city-states compare to the kingdoms of the western Sudan?

✓ LearningCurve
Check what you know.

The Great Friday Mosque, Jenne

The mosque at Jenne was built in the form of a parallelogram. Inside, nine long rows of adobe columns run along a north-south axis and support a flat roof of palm logs. A pointed arch links each column to the next in its row, forming nine east-west archways facing the *mihrab*, the niche in the wall of the mosque indicating the direction of Mecca, and from which the imam speaks. This mosque (rebuilt in 1907 based on the original thirteenth-century structure) testifies to the considerable wealth, geometrical knowledge, and manpower of Mali. (Gerard Degeorge/akg-images)

The earliest surviving evidence about the Mandinka, dating from the early eleventh century, indicates that they were extremely successful at agriculture. Consistently large harvests throughout the twelfth and thirteenth centuries meant a plentiful food supply, which encouraged steady population growth. Kangaba's geographical location also ideally positioned the Mandinka in the heart of the West African trade networks. Earlier, during the period of Ghanaian hegemony, the Mandinka had acted as middlemen in the gold and salt traffic flowing north and south. In the thirteenth century Mandinka traders formed companies, traveled widely, and gradually became a major force in the entire West African trade.

Mali's founder, Sundiata (r. ca. 1230–1255) set up his capital at Niani, transforming the city into an important financial and trading center. He then embarked on a policy of imperial expansion. Through a series of military victories, Sundiata and his successors absorbed into Mali other territories of the former kingdom of Ghana and established hegemony over the trading cities of Gao, Jenne, and Walata.

These expansionist policies were continued in the fourteenth century by Sundiata's descendant Mansa Musa (r. ca. 1312–1337), early Africa's most famous ruler. Ultimately Mansa Musa's influence extended northward to several Berber cities in the Sahara, eastward to the trading cities of Timbuktu and Gao, and westward to the Atlantic Ocean. Throughout his territories, he maintained strict royal control over the flourishing trans-Saharan trade. Thus this empire, roughly

CHAPTER LOCATOR | How did Africa's geography shape its history and contribute to its diverse population? | How did agriculture affect life in the western Sudan and central and southern Africa?

twice the size of the Ghanaian kingdom and containing perhaps 8 million people, brought Mansa Musa fabulous wealth.

Mansa Musa built on the foundations of his predecessors. Malian society's stratified aristocratic structure perpetuated the pattern set in Ghana, as did the system of provincial administration and annual tribute. The emperor took responsibility for the territories that formed the heart of the empire and appointed governors to rule the outlying provinces and dependent kingdoms. But Mansa Musa made a significant innovation: in a practice strikingly similar to a system used in both China and France at the time, he appointed royal family members as provincial governors.

In another aspect of administration, Mansa Musa also differed from his predecessors. He became a devout Muslim. Although most of the Mandinka remained animists, Islamic practices and influences in Mali multiplied.

The most celebrated event of Mansa Musa's reign was his pilgrimage to Mecca in 1324–1325, during which he paid a state visit to the Egyptian sultan. Mansa Musa's entrance into Cairo was magnificent. Preceded by five hundred slaves, each carrying a six-pound staff of gold, he followed with a huge host of retainers, including one hundred elephants each bearing one hundred pounds of gold. The emperor lavished his wealth on the citizens of the Egyptian capital.

As a result of this pilgrimage, for the first time, the Mediterranean world learned firsthand of Mali's wealth and power, and the kingdom began to be known as one of the world's great empires. Mali retained this international reputation into the fifteenth century. Musa's pilgrimage also had significant consequences within Mali. He gained some understanding of the Mediterranean countries and opened diplomatic relations with the Muslim rulers of Morocco and Egypt. His zeal for the Muslim faith and Islamic culture increased. Musa brought back from Arabia the distinguished architect al-Saheli, whom he commissioned to build new mosques in Timbuktu and other cities. These mosques served as centers for African conversion to Islam.

Timbuktu began as a campsite for desert nomads, but under Mansa Musa it grew into a thriving entrepôt (trading center), attracting merchants and traders from North Africa and all parts of the Mediterranean world. In the fifteenth century Timbuktu developed into a great center for scholarship and learning. Architects, astronomers, poets, lawyers, mathematicians, and theologians flocked there. One hundred fifty schools, for men only, were devoted to Qur'anic studies. The school of Islamic law enjoyed a distinction comparable to the prestige of the Cairo school (see page 256). The vigorous traffic in books that flourished in Timbuktu made them the most common items of trade. Timbuktu's tradition and reputation for African scholarship lasted until the eighteenth century.

Moreover, in the fourteenth and fifteenth centuries many Arab and North African Muslim intellectuals and traders married native African women. The necessity of living together harmoniously, the traditional awareness of diverse cultures, and Timbuktu's cosmopolitan atmosphere contributed to a rare degree of racial tolerance and understanding.

The third great West African empire, Songhai, succeeded Mali in the fourteenth century. It encompassed the old empires of Ghana and Mali and extended its territory farther north and east to become one of the largest African empires in history (see Map 10.2).

Timbuktu

▶ Originally a campsite for desert nomads, it grew into a thriving city under Mansa Musa, king of Mali and Africa's most famous ruler.

What characterized trans-Saharan trade, and how did it affect West African society?

How did the East African city-states compare to the kingdoms of the western Sudan?

✓ LearningCurve
Check what you know.

Ethiopia: The Christian Kingdom of Aksum

Just as the ancient West African empires were significantly affected by Islam and the Arab culture that accompanied it, the African kingdoms that arose in modern Sudan and Ethiopia in northeast Africa were heavily influenced by Egyptian culture, and they influenced it in return. This was particularly the case in ancient Nubia. Nubia's capital was at Meroë (see Map 10.2); thus the country is often referred to as the Nubian kingdom of Meroë.

As part of the Roman Empire, Egypt was subject to Hellenistic and Roman cultural forces, and it became an early center of Christianity. Nubia, however, was never part of the Roman Empire; its people retained ancient Egyptian religious ideas. Christian missionaries traveled to the Upper Nile region and successfully converted the Nubian rulers around 600 C.E. By that time, there were three separate Nubian states, of which the kingdom of Nobatia, centered at Dongola, was the strongest. The Christian rulers of Nobatia had close ties with the **Aksum** kingdom in Ethiopia, and through this relationship Egyptian culture spread to Ethiopia.

Two-thirds of Ethiopia consists of the Ethiopian highlands, the rugged plateau region of East Africa. The Great Rift Valley divides this territory into two massifs (mountain masses), of which the Ethiopian Plateau is the larger. Sloping away from each side of the Great Rift Valley are a series of mountains and valleys. Together with this mountainous environment, the three Middle Eastern religions—Judaism, Christianity, and Islam—have all influenced Ethiopian society.

By the first century C.E. the Aksum kingdom in northwestern Ethiopia was a sizable trading state. Merchants at Adulis, its main port on the Red Sea, sold ivory, gold, emeralds, rhinoceros horns, shells, and slaves to the Sudan, Arabia, Yemen, and various cities across the Indian Ocean in exchange for glass, ceramics, fabrics, sugar, oil, spices, and precious gems. Adulis contained temples, stone-built houses, and irrigated agriculture. Between the first and eighth centuries Aksum served as the capital of an empire extending over much of what is now northern Ethiopia. The empire's prosperity rested on trade.

Islam's expansion into northern Ethiopia in the eighth century (see page 278) weakened Aksum's commercial prosperity. The Arabs first ousted the Greek Byzantine merchants who traded on the Dahlak Archipelago (in the southern Red Sea) and converted the islands' inhabitants. Then Muslims attacked and destroyed Adulis. Some Aksumites converted to Islam; many others found refuge in the rugged mountains north of the kingdom, where they were isolated from outside contacts. Thus began the insularity that characterized later Ethiopian society.

Tradition ascribes to Frumentius (ca. 300–380 C.E.), a Syrian Christian trader, the introduction of Coptic Christianity, an Orthodox form of Christianity that originated in Egypt, into Ethiopia. Kidnapped as a young boy en route from India to Tyre (in southern Lebanon), Frumentius was taken to Aksum, given his freedom, and appointed tutor to the future king, Ezana. Upon Ezana's accession to the throne, Frumentius went to Alexandria, Egypt, where he was consecrated the first bishop of Aksum around 328 C.E. He then returned to Ethiopia with some priests to spread Christianity. Shortly after members of the royal court accepted Christianity, it became the Ethiopian state religion.

Ethiopia's acceptance of Christianity led to the production of ecclesiastical documents and royal chronicles, making Ethiopia the first sub-Saharan African

Aksum

▶ A kingdom in northwestern Ethiopia that was a sizable trading state and the center of Christian culture.

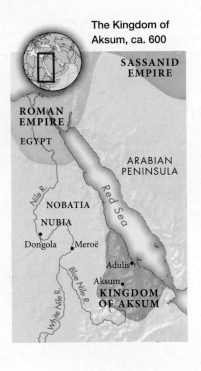

The Kingdom of Aksum, ca. 600

SASSANID EMPIRE

ROMAN EMPIRE

EGYPT

ARABIAN PENINSULA

Nile R.

Red Sea

NOBATIA

NUBIA

Dongola   Meroë

Adulis

Blue Nile R.

Aksum

KINGDOM OF AKSUM

White Nile R.

CHAPTER LOCATOR | How did Africa's geography shape its history and contribute to its diverse population? | How did agriculture affect life in the western Sudan and central and southern Africa?

society that can be studied from written records. The Scriptures were translated into Ge'ez (gee-EHZ), an ancient language and script used in Ethiopia and Aksum. Pagan temples were dedicated to Christian saints, and, as in early medieval Ireland and in the Orthodox Church of the Byzantine world, monasteries were the Christian faith's main cultural institutions in Ethiopia. As the Ethiopian state expanded, vibrant monasteries provided inspiration for the establishment of convents for nuns, as in medieval Europe (see page 396).

Monastic records provide fascinating information about early Ethiopian society. Settlements were formed on the warm and moist plateau lands. Farmers used a scratch plow (unique in sub-Saharan Africa) to cultivate wheat and barley, and they regularly rotated these cereals. Plentiful rainfall seems to have helped produce abundant crops, which in turn led to population growth. Because of ecclesiastical opposition to polygyny (the practice of having multiple wives), monogamy was the norm, other than for kings and the very rich. An abundance of land meant that young couples could establish independent households. Widely scattered farms, with the parish church as the central social unit, seem to have been the usual pattern of existence.

Above the broad class of peasant farmers stood warrior-nobles. Their wealth and status derived from their fighting skills. To acquire lands and to hold warriors' loyalty, Ethiopian kings pursued a policy of constant territorial expansion. (See "Individuals in Society: Amda Siyon," page 286.) Nobles maintained order in their regions, supplied kings with fighting men, and displayed their superior status by the size of their households and their generosity to the poor.

Sometime in the fourteenth century, six scribes in the Tigrayan highlands of Ethiopia combined oral tradition, Jewish and Islamic commentaries, apocryphal

What characterized trans-Saharan trade, and how did it affect West African society?

How did the East African city-states compare to the kingdoms of the western Sudan?

✓ LearningCurve
Check what you know.

Scholars consider Amda Siyon (r. 1314–1344) the greatest ruler of Ethiopia's Solomonic dynasty. Yet we have no image or representation of him. We know nothing of his personal life, though if he followed the practice of most Ethiopian kings, he had many wives and children. Nor do we know anything about his youth and education. The evidence of what he did, however, suggests a tough military man who personified the heroic endurance and physical pain expected of warriors. According to a chronicle of Siyon's campaign against the Muslim leader of Ifat,

> [Siyon] clove the ranks of the rebels and struck so hard that he transfixed two men as one with the blow of his spear, through the strength of God. Thereupon the rebels scattered and took to flight, being unable to hold their ground in his presence.

Amda Siyon reinforced control over his kingdom's Christian areas. He then expanded into the neighboring regions of Shewa, Gojam, and Damot. Victorious there, he gradually absorbed the Muslim states of Ifat and Hedya to the east and southeast. These successes gave him effective control of the central highlands and also the Indian Ocean trade routes to the Red Sea (see Map 10.2). He governed in a quasi-feudal fashion. Theoretically the owner of all land, he assigned *gults*, or fiefs, to his ablest warriors. In return for nearly complete authority in their regions, these warrior-nobles conscripted soldiers for the king's army, required agricultural services from the farmers working on their land, and collected taxes in kind.

Ethiopian rulers received imperial coronation at Aksum, but their kingdom had no permanent capital. Rather, the ruler and court were peripatetic. They constantly traveled around the country to crush revolts, to check the warrior-nobles' management of the gults, and to impress ordinary people with royal dignity.

Territorial expansion had important economic and religious consequences. Amda Siyon concluded trade agreements with Muslims by which they were allowed to trade with his country in return for Muslim recognition of his authority and their promise to accept his administration and pay taxes. Economic growth followed. As a result of these agreements, the flow of Ethiopian gold, ivory, and slaves to Red Sea ports for export to the Islamic heartlands and to South Asia accelerated. Profits from commercial exchange improved people's lives, or at least the lives of the upper classes.

Colorful biblical scenes adorn the interior of the Urai Kidane Miharet Church, one of the many monasteries established by Amda Siyon. (De Agostini Picture Library/akg-images)

Monk-missionaries from traditional Christian areas flooded newly conquered regions, stressing that Ethiopia was a new Zion, or a second Israel — a Judeo-Christian nation defined by religion. Ethiopian Christianity focused on the divinity of the Old Testament Yahweh, rather than on the humanity of the New Testament Jesus. Jewish dietary restrictions, such as the avoidance of pork and shellfish, shaped behavior, and the holy Ark of the Covenant had a prominent place in the liturgy. But the monks also taught New Testament values, especially the importance of charity and spiritual reform. Following the Byzantine pattern, the Ethiopian priest-king claimed the right to summon church councils and to issue doctrinal degrees. Christianity's stress on monogamous marriage, however, proved hard to enforce. As in other parts of Africa (and in Islamic lands, China, and South Asia), polygyny remained common, at least among the upper classes.

Sources: G. W. B. Huntingford, ed., *The Glorious Victories of Amda Seyon* (Oxford: Oxford University Press, 1965), pp. 89–90; H. G. Marcus, *A History of Ethiopia*, updated ed. (Berkeley: University of California Press, 2002); J. Iliffe, *Africans: The History of a Continent*, 2d ed. (New York: Cambridge University Press, 2007).

QUESTIONS FOR ANALYSIS

1. What features mark Ethiopian culture as unique and distinctive among early African societies?
2. Referring to Solomonic Ethiopia, assess the role of legend in history.

ONLINE DOCUMENT PROJECT

What role did religion play in the formation of Ethiopian identity? Explore early Ethiopian chronicles, and then complete a quiz and writing assignment based on the evidence and details from this chapter. *See inside the front cover to learn more.*

(noncanonical) Christian texts, and the writings of the early Christian Church fathers to produce the *Kebra Nagast* (The Glory of Kings). This history served the authors' goals: it became an Ethiopian national epic, glorifying a line of rulers descended from the Hebrew king Solomon (see page 52), arousing patriotic feelings, and linking Ethiopia's identity to the Judeo-Christian tradition. The book mostly deals with the origins of Emperor Menilek I of Ethiopia in the tenth century B.C.E.

The *Kebra Nagast* asserts that Queen Makeda of Ethiopia (called Sheba in the Jewish tradition) had little governmental experience when she came to the throne. So she sought the advice and wise counsel of King Solomon (r. 965–925 B.C.E.) in Jerusalem. During this visit, Solomon tricked Makeda into allowing him into her bed. Their son, Menilek, was born some months later. When Menilek reached maturity, he visited Solomon in Jerusalem. There Solomon anointed him crown prince of Ethiopia and sent a retinue of young Jewish nobles to accompany him home as courtiers. Unable to face life without the Hebrews' Ark of the Covenant, the courtiers stole the cherished wooden chest, which the Hebrews believed contained the Ten Commandments. God apparently approved the theft, for he lifted the youths, pursued by Solomon's army, across the Red Sea and into Ethiopia. Thus, according to the *Kebra Nagast*, Menilek avenged his mother's shame, and God gave his legal covenant to Ethiopia, Israel's successor.[5] Although written around twenty-three hundred years after the events, the myths and legends contained in the *Kebra Nagast* effectively served the purpose of building nationalistic fervor.

Based on this lineage, from the tenth to the sixteenth centuries, and even in the Ethiopian constitution of 1955, Ethiopia's rulers claimed they belonged to the Solomonic line of succession. In the later thirteenth century the dynasty of the Solomonic kings witnessed a literary and artistic renaissance particularly notable for works of hagiography (biographies of saints), biblical exegesis (critical explanation or interpretation of the Bible), and manuscript illumination. The most striking feature of Ethiopian society from 500 to 1500 was the close relationship between the church and the state. Christianity inspired fierce devotion and equated doctrinal heresy with political rebellion, thus reinforcing central monarchical power.

Great Mosque at Kilwa

Built between the thirteenth and fifteenth centuries to serve the Muslim commercial aristocracy of Kilwa on the Indian Ocean, the mosque attests to the wealth and power of the East African city-states. (© Ulrich Doering/Alamy)

wealth rested on the ruler's monopolistic control of all trade in the area. Some coastal cities manufactured goods for export, such as cloth and iron tools. The bulk of the cities' exports, however, consisted of animal products—leopard skins, tortoise shell, ambergris, ivory—and gold. The gold originated in the Mutapa region south of the Zambezi River, where the Bantu mined it. As in tenth-century Ghana, gold was a royal monopoly in the fourteenth-century coastal city-states. Kilwa's prosperity rested on its traffic in gold.

African goods satisfied the global aristocratic demand for luxury goods. In Arabia leopard skins were made into saddles, shells were made into combs, and ambergris was used in the manufacture of perfumes. Because African elephants' tusks were larger and more durable than those of Indian elephants, African ivory was in great demand in India. Wealthy Chinese also valued African ivory for use in sedan chair construction. In exchange for these natural products, the Swahili cities brought in, among many other items, incense, glassware, glass beads, and carpets from Arabia; textiles, spices, rice, and cotton from India; and grains, fine porcelain, silk, and jade from China.

Slaves were another export from the East African coast. Reports of East African slave trading began with the publication of the *Periplus*. The trade accelerated with the establishment of Muslim settlements in the eighth century and continued up through the arrival of the Portuguese in the late fifteenth century, which provided a market for African slaves in the New World (discussed in Chapter 15). In fact, the global slave market fueled the East African coastal slave trade until at least the beginning of the twentieth century.

As in West Africa, traders obtained slaves primarily through raids and kidnapping. The Arabs called the northern Somalia coast *Ras Assir* (Cape of Slaves). From there, Arab traders transported slaves northward up the Red Sea to the markets of Arabia and Persia. Muslim dealers also shipped blacks from the Zanzibar region across the Indian Ocean to markets in India.

As early as the tenth century sources mention persons with "lacquer-black bodies" in the possession of wealthy families in Song China.[7] In 1178 a Chinese official noted in a memorial to the emperor that Arab traders were shipping thousands of blacks from East Africa to the Chinese port of Guangzhou (Canton) by way of the Malay Archipelago.

CHAPTER LOCATOR | How did Africa's geography shape its history and contribute to its diverse population? | How did agriculture affect life in the western Sudan and central and southern Africa?

CHAPTER 10
290 AFRICAN SOCIETIES AND KINGDOMS

Southern Africa and Great Zimbabwe

Southern Africa, bordered on the northwest by the Kalahari Desert and on the northeast by the Zambezi River (see Map 10.2), enjoys a mild and temperate climate. Desert conditions prevail along the Atlantic coast. Eastward toward the Indian Ocean rainfall increases, amounting to fifty to ninety inches a year in some places. Temperate grasslands characterize the interior highlands. Considerable variations in climate occur throughout much of southern Africa from year to year.

Southern Africa has enormous mineral resources: gold, copper, diamonds, platinum, and uranium. Preindustrial peoples mined some of these deposits in open excavations down several feet, but fuller exploitation required modern technology.

Southern Africa has a history that is very different from those of West Africa, the Nile Valley, and the East African coast. Unlike the rest of coastal Africa, southern Africa remained far removed from the outside world until the Portuguese arrived in the late fifteenth century — with one important exception. Bantu-speaking people reached southern Africa in the eighth century. They brought skills in ironworking and mixed farming (settled crop production plus cattle and sheep raising) and immunity to the kinds of diseases that later decimated the Amerindians of South America (discussed in Chapter 16).

The earliest residents of southern Africa were hunters and gatherers. In the first millennium c.e. new farming techniques from the north arrived. Lack of water and timber slowed the spread of iron technology and tools and thus of crop production in southwestern Africa. These advances reached the western coastal region by 1500. By that date, Khoisan-speakers were tending livestock in the arid western regions. To the east, descendants of Bantu-speaking immigrants grew sorghum, raised cattle and sheep, and fought with iron-headed spears.

The nuclear family was the basic social unit among early southern African peoples, who practiced polygyny and traced descent in the male line. Several families formed bands numbering between twenty and eighty people. Such bands were not closed entities; people in neighboring territories identified with bands speaking the same language. As in most preindustrial societies, a division of labor existed whereby men hunted and women cared for children and raised edible plants. People lived in caves or in camps made of portable material, and they moved from one watering or hunting region to another as seasonal or environmental needs required.

In 1871 a German explorer came upon the ruined city of **Great Zimbabwe** southeast of what is now Masvingo in Zimbabwe. The ruins consist of two vast complexes of dry-stone buildings, a fortress, and an elliptically shaped enclosure commonly called the Temple. Stone carvings, gold and copper ornaments, and Asian ceramics once decorated the buildings. The ruins extend over sixty acres and are encircled by a massive wall. The entire city was built from local granite between the eleventh and fifteenth centuries without any outside influence.

These ruins tell a remarkable story. Great Zimbabwe was the political and religious capital of a vast empire. During the first millennium c.e. settled crop cultivation, cattle raising, and work in metal led to a steady buildup in population in the Zambezi-Limpopo region. The area also contained a rich gold-bearing belt. Gold ore lay near the surface; alluvial gold lay in the Zambezi River tributaries. In the tenth century the inhabitants collected the alluvial gold by panning and

Great Zimbabwe

▶ A ruined South African city discovered by a German explorer in 1871; it is considered the most powerful monument south of the Nile Valley and Ethiopian highlands.

What characterized trans-Saharan trade, and how did it affect West African society?

How did the East African city-states compare to the kingdoms of the western Sudan?

✓ LearningCurve
Check what you know.

washing; after the year 1000 the gold was worked in open mines with iron picks. Traders shipped the gold eastward to Sofala (see Map 10.2). Great Zimbabwe's wealth and power rested on this gold trade.

Great Zimbabwe declined in the fifteenth century, perhaps because the area had become agriculturally exhausted and could no longer support the large population. Some people migrated northward and settled in the Mazoe River Valley, a tributary of the Zambezi. This region also contained gold, and the settlers built a new empire in the tradition of Great Zimbabwe. This empire's rulers were called Mwene Mutapa, and their power was also based on the gold trade down the Zambezi River to Indian Ocean ports. It was this gold that the Portuguese sought when they arrived on the East African coast in the late fifteenth century.

> **QUICK REVIEW**

What connections were there among the kingdoms of West Africa, the city-states of East Africa, and the larger Islamic world?

CHAPTER SUMMARY

Africa is a huge continent with many different climatic zones and diverse geography. The African peoples are as varied as the topography. North African peoples were closely connected with the Middle Eastern and European civilizations of the Mediterranean basin. New crops introduced from Asia and the adoption of agriculture profoundly affected early societies across western and northeastern Africa as they transitioned from hunting and gathering in small bands to settled farming communities. Beginning in modern Cameroon and Nigeria, Bantu-speakers spread across central and southern Africa over a two-thousand-year period. Possessing iron tools and weapons, domesticated livestock, and a knowledge of agriculture, these Bantu-speakers assimilated, killed, or drove away the region's previous inhabitants.

Africans in the West African Sahel participated in the trans-Saharan trade, which affected West African society in three important ways: it stimulated gold mining; it increased the demand for West Africa's second-most important commodity, slaves; and it stimulated the development of large urban centers in West Africa.

Similarly, the Swahili peoples along the East African coast organized in city-states traded with Arabia, the Persian Gulf, India, China, and the Malay Archipelago. They depended on Indian Ocean commercial networks, which they used to trade African products for luxury items from Arabia, Southeast Asia, and East Asia. Great Zimbabwe, in southern Africa's interior, traded gold to the coast for the Indian Ocean trade.

The Swahili city-states and the Western Sudan kingdoms were both part of the Islamic world. Arabian merchants brought Islam with them as they settled

CHAPTER LOCATOR | How did Africa's geography shape its history and contribute to its diverse population? | How did agriculture affect life in the western Sudan and central and southern Africa?

292 CHAPTER 10 AFRICAN SOCIETIES AND KINGDOMS

along the East African coast, and Berber traders brought Islam to West Africa. Differing from its neighbors, Ethiopia formed a unique enclave of Christianity in the midst of Islamic societies. The Bantu-speaking peoples of Great Zimbabwe and central and southern Africa generally, were neither Islamic nor Christian.

 **CONNECTIONS** Africa was an integral part of the vast trans-Saharan and Indian Ocean trading networks that stretched from Europe to China. This trade brought wealth to African kingdoms, empires, and city-states that developed alongside the routes. But the trade in ideas more profoundly connected the growing African states to the wider world, most notably through Islam, which had arrived by the seventh century, and Christianity, which developed a foothold in Ethiopia.

Prior to the late fifteenth century Europeans had little knowledge about African societies. All this would change during the European Age of Discovery. Chapter 16 traces the expansion of Portugal from a small, poor European nation to an overseas empire, as it established trading posts and gained control of the African gold trade. Portuguese expansion led to competition, spurring Spain and then England to strike out for gold of their own in the Americas. The acceleration of this conquest would forever shape the history of Africa and the Americas (discussed in Chapters 11 and 15) and intertwine them via the African slave trade that fueled the labor needs of the colonies in the Americas.

LaunchPad

ONLINE DOCUMENT PROJECT

Creating an Ethiopian National Identity

What role did religion play in the formation of Ethiopian identity?

Explore early Ethiopian chronicles, and then complete a quiz and writing assignment based on the evidence and details from this chapter. *See inside the front cover to learn more.*

| What characterized trans-Saharan trade, and how did it affect West African society? | How did the East African city-states compare to the kingdoms of the western Sudan? | ✓ **LearningCurve** Check what you know. |

CHAPTER 10 STUDY GUIDE

 STEP 1 **GET STARTED ONLINE**

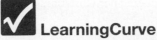 **LearningCurve**

Now that you've read the chapter, make it stick by completing the LearningCurve activity.

STEP 2 **EXPLAIN WHY IT MATTERS**

Put your reading into practice. Identify each term below, and then explain why it matters in world history.

TERM	WHO OR WHAT & WHEN	WHY IT MATTERS
Bantu (p. 272)		
Sudan (p. 273)		
Berbers (p. 275)		
Mogadishu (p. 278)		
stateless societies (p. 279)		
Ghana (p. 280)		
Koumbi Saleh (p. 280)		
Timbuktu (p. 283)		
Aksum (p. 284)		
Swahili (p. 289)		
Kilwa (p. 289)		
Great Zimbabwe (p. 291)		

 **STEP 3** **MOVE BEYOND THE BASICS**

To demonstrate a more advanced understanding of the role of geographic and climatic diversity in African history, fill in the chart below with descriptions of the society, government, and economy of each of Africa's five main climatic zones. In which regions did settled agriculture lead to population growth and urbanization? Which regions had the strongest economic and cultural connections to societies outside of Africa? Which regions were most isolated from the outside world?

	Society	Government	Economy
Fertile northern and southern coastal regions			
Steppe lands			
Deserts			
Savanna			
Tropical rain forests			

STEP 4 **PUT IT ALL TOGETHER**   Now, take a step back and try to explain the big picture. Remember to use specific examples from the chapter in your answers.

GEOGRAPHY AND AGRICULTURE

▶ How did geography and climate shape the spread of agriculture in Africa?

▶ What common characteristics were shared by settled agricultural societies across Africa? What role did Bantu-speaking peoples play in linking diverse African societies?

THE TRANS-SAHARAN TRADE

▶ What role did West Africa play in international commerce between 800 and 1500 C.E.?

▶ How did the growth of the Trans-Saharan trade stimulate political and religious change in West Africa?

KINGDOMS AND EMPIRES

▶ How did Islam shape the political development of West Africa?

▶ Compare and contrast Ethiopia and the East African city-states. How would you explain the differences you note?

LOOKING BACK, LOOKING AHEAD

▶ How has the paucity of indigenous written records shaped our understanding of early African history?

▶ How might the advent of the Atlantic slave trade in the sixteenth century and European imperialism in Africa in the nineteenth century have affected Western assumptions about conditions in Africa prior to 1500?

> **IN YOUR OWN WORDS**

Imagine that you must give an oral report to the class answering the following question: **What role did trade play in the development of African kingdoms and empires?** What would be the most important points and why?

11
THE AMERICAS

2500 B.C.E.–1500 C.E.

> **What similarities and differences were there between the societies of the Americas and other premodern societies around the world?**

Chapter 11 examines the development of American societies prior to contact with other world civilizations. Ancient America was home to diverse and sophisticated societies. At times these societies grew into vast empires. In **Mesoamerica** — the region stretching from present-day Nicaragua to California — the dense urban centers of Maya, Teotihuacan, Toltec, and Mexica city-states and empires featured great monuments, temples, and complex urban planning. Roadways and canals extended trade networks that reached from South America to the Great Lakes region of North America. These achievements were rivaled only in the Andes Mountains of South America. The technological, agricultural, and engineering innovations of ancient Andean civilizations allowed people to make their difficult mountain terrain a home rather than a boundary.

Mesoamerica
▶ The term used to designate the area of present-day Mexico and Central America.

Moche Portrait Vessel A Moche artist captured the commanding expression of a ruler in this ceramic vessel. The Moche were one of many cultures in Peru that developed technologies that were simultaneously useful and beautiful, including brightly colored cloth, hanging bridges made of fiber, and intricately fit stone walls. (Private Collection/Photo © Boltin Picture Library/ The Bridgeman Art Library)

✓**LearningCurve**
After reading the chapter, use LearningCurve to retain what you've read.

> How did ancient peoples of the Americas adapt to, and adapt, their environment?

> What patterns established by early societies shaped civilization in Mesoamerica and the Andes?

> What were the sources of strength and prosperity, and of problems, for the Incas?

> How did the Maya and Teotihuacan develop prosperous and stable societies in the classical era?

> How did the Aztecs build on the achievements of earlier Mesoamerican cultures and develop new traditions to create their large empire?

> What did the European encounter mean for peoples of the major American empires?

> How did ancient peoples of the Americas adapt to, and adapt, their environment?

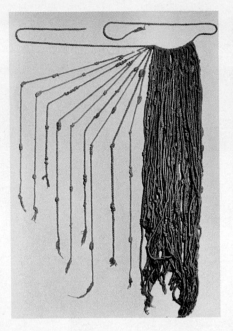

Inca Khipu

Khipus like these (left) were used by communities and by Inca imperial officials to store and communicate data. The dyes, weaves, and knots made by their users recorded data much like contemporary binary computer storage, allowing users (like the seated person) to read information about populations, production, and tribute. (khipu: The Granger Collection, NYC — All rights reserved; illustration: from *Historia y Genealogia Real de los Reyes Incas del Peru, de sus hechos, constumbres, trajes y manera de Gobierno*, known as the *Codice Murua* [vellum], 16th century/Private Collection/The Bridgeman Art Library)

Like people everywhere, civilizations of the Americas interpreted the meaning of the world and their place in the cosmos. They organized societies stratified not just by gender, class, and ethnicity but also by professional roles and wealth, and they adapted to and reshaped their physical and natural world. But they did all this on their own, without outside influences and within a distinct environment.

If the differences between civilizations in the Americas and other world regions are remarkable, the similarities are even more so. By studying the peoples of the Americas before their encounters with other world societies, we gain a clearer view of universal aspects of the human experience.

Trade and Technology

The domestication of crops and animals created an abundance of food and live-stock, which allowed people to take on new social roles and to develop specialized occupations. As cities emerged, they became hubs of a universal human activity:

CHAPTER LOCATOR | **How did ancient peoples of the Americas adapt to, and adapt, their environment?** | What patterns shaped civilization in Mesoamerica and the Andes?

298 CHAPTER 11 THE AMERICAS

ca. 40,000–13,000 B.C.E. Initial human migration to the Americas	**ca. 300–650** C.E. Peak of Teotihuacan's influence
ca. 5000 B.C.E. Intensification of agriculture	**ca. 600–900** C.E. Peak of Maya culture
ca. 2000 B.C.E. Earliest mound building in North America	**ca. 1050–1250** C.E. Construction of mounds at Cahokia
ca. 1500–300 B.C.E. Olmec culture	**ca. 1325** C.E. Construction of Aztec city of Tenochtitlan begins
ca. 1200 B.C.E. Emergence of Chavín culture in the Andes	**ca. 1428–1521** C.E. Aztec Empire dominates Mesoamerica
ca. 100–800 C.E. Moche culture	**ca. 1438–1532** C.E. Inca Empire dominates the Andes

trade. These cities were home to priests who interpreted the nature of our world, as well as a nobility from which kings emerged.

The differences in the development and application of three different kinds of technologies—the wheel, writing and communications systems, and calendars—capture this essential nature of human adaptability.

Before their encounters with other world peoples that began in 1492, societies in Mesoamerica and the Andes did not use wheels. In Mesoamerica there were no large animals like horses or oxen to domesticate as beasts of burden, so there was no way to power wagons or chariots. In the Andes, domesticated llamas and alpacas served as pack animals and were a source of wool and meat. But in the most densely settled, cultivated, and developed areas, the terrain was too difficult for wheeled transportation. Instead Andean peoples developed extensive networks of roads that navigated steep changes in altitude, supported by elaborate suspension bridges made from woven vegetable fibers.

Peoples of the Americas also did not develop an alphabet or character-based writing systems, but this did not mean they did not communicate or record information. Peoples of the Americas spoke thousands of languages. Mesoamericans, beginning with the Olmecs (1500–400 B.C.E.), used pictographic glyphs similar to those of ancient Egyptian writing to record and communicate information. Later civilizations continued to adapt these systems. The Aztecs produced hieroglyphic books written on paper or deerskin.

The Andean innovation for recording information was particularly remarkable. The **khipu** (KEY-pooh) was an assemblage of colored and knotted strings. The differences in color, arrangement, and type of knot, as well as the knots' order and placement, served as a binary system akin to a contemporary computer database. Khipus were used to record demographic, economic, and political information that allowed imperial rulers and local leaders to understand and manage complex data.

Mesoamerican peoples used a sophisticated combination of calendars. These were based on a Calendar Round that combined a 365-day solar calendar with a

khipu

▶ An intricate system of knotted and colored strings used by early Andean cultures to store information such as census and tax records.

What were the sources of strength and prosperity, and of problems, for the Incas?	How did the Maya and Teotihuacan develop prosperous societies in the classical era?	How did the Aztecs build on earlier Mesoamerican cultures and develop new traditions?	What did the European encounter mean for peoples of the major American empires?	☑ LearningCurve Check what you know.

260-day calendar based on the numbers thirteen and twenty, which were sacred to peoples of Mesoamerica. Annual cycles are completed when twenty 13-day bundles converge with thirteen 20-day bundles. Together with the solar calendar, these formed a fifty-two-year cycle whose precision was unsurpassed in the pre-modern world.

Settlement and Environment

The ancient settlers of the Americas migrated from Asia, though their timing and their route are debated. One possibility is that the first settlers migrated across the Bering Strait from what is now Russia to Alaska and gradually migrated southward sometime between 15,000 and 13,000 B.C.E. But archaeological excavations have identified much earlier settlements, perhaps dating to over 40,000 years ago, along the Andes in South America than they have for Mesoamerica or North America. These findings suggest that the original settlers in the Americas arrived instead (or also) as fishermen circulating the Pacific Ocean.

Like early settlers elsewhere in the world, populations of the Americas could be divided into three categories: nomadic peoples, semi-sedentary farming communities, and dense agricultural communities capable of sustaining cities. Urban settlement and empire formation centered around two major regions. The first area was Lake Titicaca, located at the present-day border between Peru and Bolivia. The second area was in the Valley of Mexico on the central plateau of Mesoamerica, where empires emerged from the cities around Lake Texcoco. Access to these large freshwater lakes allowed agriculture to expand through irrigation, which in turn supported large urban populations.

The earliest farming settlements emerged around 5000 B.C.E. These farming communities began the long process of domesticating and modifying plants, including maize (corn) and potatoes. The origins of maize in Mesoamerica are unclear, though it became a centerpiece of the Mesoamerican diet and spread across North and South America. Eaten together with beans, maize provided Mesoamerican peoples with a diet sufficient in protein despite the scarcity of meat. Mesoamericans processed kernels through **nixtamalization**, boiling the maize in a solution of water and mineral lime. The process broke down compounds in the kernels, increasing their nutritional value, while enriching the resulting *masa*, or paste, with dietary minerals including calcium, potassium, and iron.

This masa could be rolled flat on a stone called a *metate* and baked into tortillas. Tortillas played roles similar to bread in wheat-producing cultures: they could be stored, they were light and easy to transport, and they were used as the basic building block of meals. Aztec armies of the fifteenth century could travel long distances because they carried tortillas for sustenance.

Andean peoples cultivated another staple of the Americas, the potato. Potatoes first grew wild, but selective breeding produced many different varieties. For Andean peoples, potatoes became an integral part of a complex system of cultivation at varying altitudes. Communities created a system of "vertical archipelagos" through which they took advantage of the changes of climate along the steep escarpments of the Andes. Different crops could be cultivated at different altitudes, allowing communities to engage in intense and varied farming in what would otherwise have been inhospitable territory.

nixtamalization
▶ Boiling maize in a solution of water and mineral lime to break down compounds in the kernels, increasing their nutritional value.

CHAPTER LOCATOR | How did ancient peoples of the Americas adapt to, and adapt, their environment? | What patterns shaped civilization in Mesoamerica and the Andes?

300 CHAPTER 11 THE AMERICAS

- Highest Elevations: grazing of llamas and alpacas
- Higher Elevations: cultivation of potatoes
- Middle Elevations: terrace cultivation of corn
- Lowlands: cultivation of quinoa, beans, peppers, coca, and cotton
- Coastal Areas: Harvesting of fish and mussels

Communities raised multiple crops and engaged in year-round farming by working at different altitudes located within a day's journey from home. Some of these zones of cultivation were so distant—sometimes over a week's journey—that they were tended by temporary or permanent colonies, called *mitmaq*, of the main settlement.

At higher elevations, members of these communities cultivated potatoes. Arid conditions across much of the altiplano, or high-plains plateau, meant that crops of potatoes could sometimes be planted only every few years. But the climate—dry with daily extremes of heat and cold—could be used to freeze-dry potatoes that could be stored indefinitely. Above the potato-growing zone, shepherds tended animals such as llamas and alpacas.

At middle altitudes, communities used terraces edged by stone walls to extend cultivation along steep mountainsides to grow corn. In the lowlands, they cultivated the high-protein grain quinoa, as well as beans, peppers, and coca. In the lowlands communities also grew cotton, and in coastal areas they harvested fish and mussels. Fishermen built inflatable rafts made of sealskin.

QUICK REVIEW

What were the most striking similarities between the early societies of the Americas and those of Eurasia?

| What were the sources of strength and prosperity, and of problems, for the Incas? | How did the Maya and Teotihuacan develop prosperous societies in the classical era? | How did the Aztecs build on earlier Mesoamerican cultures and develop new traditions? | What did the European encounter mean for peoples of the major American empires? | ✓ LearningCurve Check what you know. |

What patterns established by early societies shaped civilization in Mesoamerica and the Andes?

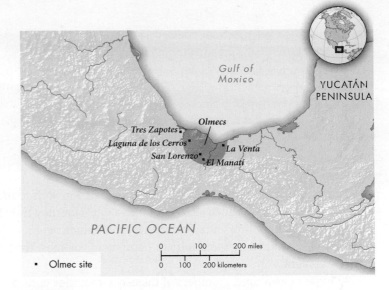

MAP 11.1 ■ The Olmecs, ca. 1500–300 B.C.E.

Olmec civilization flourished in the coastal lowlands of southern Mexico along the Caribbean coast. Olmec patterns of settlement, culture, religion, organization, and trade are known almost solely through excavation of archaeological sites.

Between 1500 and 1200 B.C.E. emerging civilizations in Mesoamerica and the Andes established lasting patterns of production, culture, and social organization that would long influence societies of the Americas. In Mesoamerica, Olmec civilization laid the foundation for future empires. The imprint of Olmec civilization spread across long networks of trade that would one day extend from Central America to the Mississippi Valley and the Great Lakes of North America. In the Andes, Chavín and Moche civilizations formed the early part of a long cycle of centralization and decentralization. This political and economic centralization helped spread technology, culture, and religion.

Olmec Agriculture, Technology, and Religion

Olmecs
▶ The oldest of the early advanced Mesoamerican civilizations.

The **Olmecs** were an early civilization that shaped the religion, trade practices, and technology of later civilizations in Mesoamerica. They flourished in the coastal lowlands of Mexico from 1500 to 300 B.C.E. The Olmecs formed the first cities of Mesoamerica, and these cities served as centers of agriculture, trade, and religion (Map 11.1). Through long-distance trade, the Olmecs spread their culture and technology across Mesoamerica, establishing beliefs and practices that became common to the civilizations that followed.

The Olmecs cultivated maize, squash, beans, and other plants and supplemented their diet with wild game and fish. But they lacked many other resources. In particular, they carried stone for many miles for the construction of temples and for carving massive monuments, many in the shape of heads. Across far-flung networks the Olmecs traded rubber, cacao, pottery, clay figures, and jaguar pelts, as well as the services of artisans such as painters and sculptors, in exchange for

CHAPTER LOCATOR | How did ancient peoples of the Americas adapt to, and adapt, their environment? | **What patterns shaped civilization in Mesoamerica and the Andes?**

obsidian, a volcanic glass that could be carved to a razor-sharp edge and used for making knives, tools, spear tips, and other weapons.

These ties between the Olmecs and other communities spread religious practices, creating a shared framework of beliefs among later civilizations. These practices included the construction of large pyramid temples, as well as sacrificial rituals. In addition to the manner of worship, archaeologists can trace the nature of the deities common in Mesoamerica. Olmec deities, like those of their successors, were combinations of gods and humans, included merged animal and human forms, and had both male and female identities.

The Olmecs also used a Long Count solar calendar—a calendar based on a 365-day year. Archaeologists presume that the existence of the Long Count calendar meant that the Calendar Round combining the 260-day and 365-day years already existed as well. All the later Mesoamerican civilizations used at least one of these calendars, and most used both of them.

Hohokam, Hopewell, and Mississippian Societies

Mesoamerican trading networks extended into southwestern North America, where by 300 B.C.E. the Hohokam people and other groups were using irrigation canals, dams, and terraces to enhance their farming of arid lands (Map 11.2). Like the Olmecs and other Mesoamerican peoples, the Hohokam built ceremonial platforms and played games with rubber balls that were traded over a long distance in return for turquoise and other precious stones. Along with trade goods came religious ideas, including the belief in local divinities who created, preserved, and destroyed. Desert peoples planted crops such as agave, as well as cotton and maize that came from Mexico. Other groups, including the Anasazi (ah-nah-SAH-zee), the Yuma, and later the Pueblo and Hopi also built settlements in this area using large sandstone blocks and masonry to construct thick-walled houses that offered protection from the heat. Eventually drought, deforestation, and soil erosion led to decline in both the Hohokam and Anasazi cultures.

To the east, the Mississippian culture also engaged in monumental mound building beginning around 2000 B.C.E. One of the most important mound-building cultures was the Hopewell (200 B.C.E.–600 C.E.), named for a town in Ohio near the site of the most extensive mounds. Some mounds were burial chambers. Other mounds formed animal or geometric figures. Hopewell earthworks also included canals that enabled trading networks to expand, bringing products from the Caribbean far into the interior. Those trading networks also carried maize, allowing more intensive agriculture to spread throughout the eastern woodlands of North America.

At Cahokia (kuh-HOE-kee-uh), near the confluence of the Mississippi and Missouri Rivers in Illinois, archaeologists have uncovered the largest mound of all, part of a ceremonial center and city that housed perhaps thirty-eight thousand people. Work on this complex of mounds, plazas, and houses began about 1050 C.E. and was completed about 1250 C.E. The largest mound rose in four stages to a height of one hundred feet and was nearly one thousand feet long. On its top stood a large building, used perhaps as a temple.

Cahokia engaged in long-distance trade reaching far across North America and became a highly stratified society. Mississippian mound builders relied on

| What were the sources of strength and prosperity, and of problems, for the Incas? | How did the Maya and Teotihuacan develop prosperous societies in the classical era? | How did the Aztecs build on earlier Mesoamerican cultures and develop new traditions? | What did the European encounter mean for peoples of the major American empires? | ✓ LearningCurve Check what you know. |

303

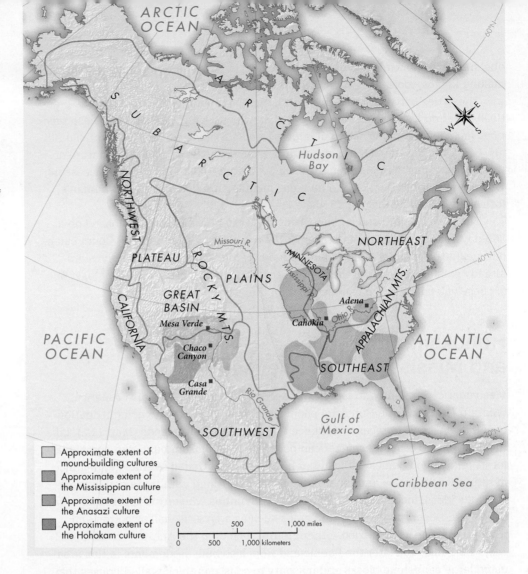

MAP 11.2 ■ Major North American Agricultural Societies, ca. 600–1500 C.E.

Many North American groups used agriculture to increase the available food supply and allow greater population density and the development of urban centers. This map shows three of these cultures: the Mississippian, Anasazi, and Hohokam.

Approximate extent of mound-building cultures

Approximate extent of the Mississippian culture

Approximate extent of the Anasazi culture

Approximate extent of the Hohokam culture

agriculture to support their complex cultures, and by the time Cahokia was built, maize agriculture had spread to the Atlantic coast. Particularly along riverbanks and the coastline, fields of maize, beans, and squash surrounded large, permanent villages containing many houses, all encompassed by walls made of earth and timber.

Kinship and Ancestors in the Andes

As in Mesoamerica, in the Andes social organization and religion shaped ideas of spiritual kinship as well as patterns of production and trade. The *ayllu* (EYE-you), or clan, served as the fundamental social unit of Andean society. Kinship was based on a shared ancestor, or *huaca*, who could be a once-living person whose remains were mummified and preserved, but could also be an animal spirit or a combination of the two. Members of an ayllu considered their huaca as more than a spirit: it was an entity that owned lands the ally's farmers tended, and the huaca served as the center of community obligations such as the pooling of labor.

Ancestor worship provided the foundations of Andean religion and spirituality, served as the basis of authority, and guided food production. All members

CHAPTER LOCATOR | How did ancient peoples of the Americas adapt to, and adapt, their environment? | What patterns shaped civilization in Mesoamerica and the Andes?

CHAPTER 11
304 THE AMERICAS

of the ayllu owed allegiance to *kuracas*, or clan leaders, who typically traced the most direct lineage to the ancestor, or huaca. This lineage made them both temporal and spiritual leaders of their ayllu. An Andean family's identity came from membership in an ayllu's ancestral kinship, and its subsistence came from participation in the broader community's shared farming across vertical climate zones. People often labored collectively and reciprocally.

Andean history unfolded in a cycle of centralization and decentralization. There were three great periods of centralization, which archaeologists call the Early, Middle, and Late Horizon. The Late Horizon, which included the Inca Empire, was the briefest, cut short by the Spanish conquest (see page 323). The first period, the Early Horizon (ca. 1200–200 B.C.E.), centered on the people of Chavín, upland from present-day Lima. The Chavín spread their religion along with technologies for the weaving and dyeing of wool and cotton. Weaving became the most widespread means of recording and representing information in the Andes.

After the end of the Early Horizon, regional states emerged, including **Moche** (MOH-cheh) civilization, which flourished along a 250-mile stretch of Peru's northern coast between 100 and 800 C.E. The Moche people developed complex irrigation systems, with which they raised food crops and cotton. Each Moche valley contained a large ceremonial center with palaces and pyramids surrounded by settlements of up to ten thousand people. Moche artifacts reveal a remarkable skill in metalwork and pottery.

Politically, the Moche were organized into a series of small city-states rather than one unified state, and warfare was common among them. Beginning about 500 the Moche suffered several severe El Niños, changes in ocean current patterns in the Pacific that bring searing drought and flooding. They were not able to respond effectively to the devastation, and their urban population declined.

Pan-Andean cultures re-emerged during the Middle Horizon (500–1000 C.E.), centered to the south in Tiwanaku, near Lake Titicaca, and to the north at Wari, near present-day southern Peru. The city-state of Wari's dominion stretched from the altiplano north of Lake Titicaca to the Pacific coast, drawing on Moche cultural influences. Its reach between mountain and coastal regions led to extensive exchanges of goods and beliefs between ecologically different farming zones. The city-state of Tiwanaku extended its influence in the other direction, south of the lake.

Storms and climate shifts were central to Andean people's worldview because changes in climate, particularly abrupt changes brought by El Niño, could devastate whole civilizations. El Niño disrupted Moche culture and contributed to the decline of Wari and Tiwanaku. As the Middle Horizon ended, the cities of Tiwanaku and Wari endured on a smaller scale, but between 1000 and 1200 C.E. they lost their regional influence. The eras between the Early, Middle, and Late Horizon, known as Intermediate Periods, were times of decentralization in which local cultures and practices re-emerged. It was out of these local developments that new centralizing empires would over time emerge.

Moche
▶ A Native American culture that thrived along Peru's northern coast between 100 and 800 C.E. The culture existed as a series of city-states and was distinguished by an extraordinarily rich and diverse pottery industry.

QUICK REVIEW <

What role did trade play in cultural diffusion in the Americas?

What were the sources of strength and prosperity, and of problems, for the Incas?

How did the Maya and Teotihuacan develop prosperous societies in the classical era?

How did the Aztecs build on earlier Mesoamerican cultures and develop new traditions?

What did the European encounter mean for peoples of the major American empires?

✓ LearningCurve
Check what you know.

> What were the sources of strength and prosperity, and of problems, for the Incas?

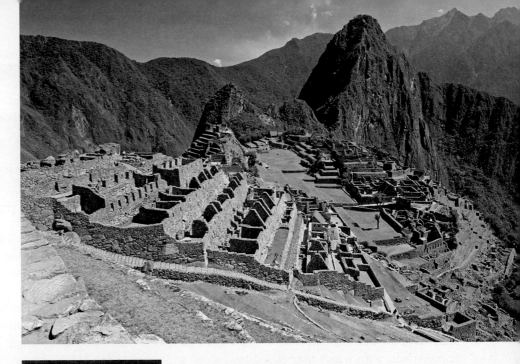

Machu Picchu

The Inca ruins of Machu Picchu rise spectacularly above the steep valley of the Urubamba River. The site was built around 1450 as a royal estate and abandoned after the Spanish conquest. (Tony Camacho/Photo Researchers, Inc.)

Inca

▶ The name of the dynasty of rulers who built a large empire across the Andes that was at its peak around 1500.

I Inca was the name of a governing family of the largest and last Andean empire. The empire, whose people we will call the Incas, was called Tawantinsuyu (TAH-want-een-soo-you), meaning from "from the four parts, one," expressing the idea of a unified people stretching in all directions.

The Inca Model of Empire

In the Late Intermediate Period (1200–1470), the Pan-Andean influences of Wari and Tiwanaku waned. City-states around Lake Titicaca competed and fought with each other. The strongest ones again emerged. To the north, the Chimu claimed the legacy of the Moche and Wari. To the south, the city of Cuzco became the hub of a growing kingdom under the hereditary control of the Inca (Map 11.3). According to their religious, the Inca rulers invented civilization. In reality, they inherited it from the civilizations of the Titicaca basin and the Chimu in the northern coast.

From the 1420s until 1438 Viracocha Inca emerged as the first Inca leader to attempt permanent conquest. Unlike the *sinchis* (SEEN-cheese), or kings, of earlier and rival city-states, Viracocha Inca fashioned himself an emperor, and in adopting the name Viracocha, connected himself to the god of creation. In 1438 rivals invaded Viracocha Inca's territories and he fled. His son, Pachacuti, remained in Cuzco and fended off the invaders. He crowned himself emperor and embarked on a campaign of conquest. Pachacuti Inca (r. 1438–1471) conquered the Chimu near the end of his reign.

CHAPTER LOCATOR | How did ancient peoples of the Americas adapt to, and adapt, their environment? | What patterns shaped civilization in Mesoamerica and the Andes?

306 CHAPTER 11 THE AMERICAS

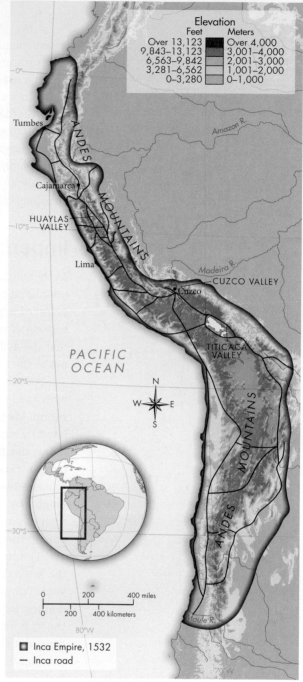

MAP 11.3 ■ The Inca Empire, 1532

Andean peoples turned their stark mountain landscape to their advantage by settling and farming in vertical archipelagos. Settlements were located at temperate altitudes, while farming and herding took place at higher and lower altitudes.

> **MAPPING THE PAST**

ANALYZING THE MAP: In what ways did Andean peoples turn their mountain landscape from an obstacle into a resource? **CONNECTIONS:** What types of geographic features did peoples of the Americas other than the Incas or peoples in other regions of the world adapt to their advantage? How did adaptation to their geography shape other societies?

After conquering the Chimu, Pachacuti instituted practices that quickly expanded the empire across the Andes. He combined Andean ancestor worship with the Chimu system of a split inheritance, a combination that drove swift territorial expansion and transformed Tawantinsuyu into one of the largest empires in the world within less than fifty years. Under the system of ancestor worship, the Incas believed the dead emperor's spirit was still present, and they venerated him through his mummy. Split inheritance meant that the dead emperor retained all the lands he had conquered, commanded the loyalty of all his subjects, and continued to receive tribute. A *panaqa* (pan-AH-kah), a trust formed by his closest relatives, managed both the cult of his mummy and his temporal affairs.

When the ruler died, his corpse was preserved as a mummy in elaborate clothing and housed in a sacred and magnificent chamber. The panaqa of descendants of each dead ruler managed his lands and used his income to care for his mummy, maintain his cult, and support themselves, all at great expense. One of his sons was named the new Inca emperor. He received the title, but not the lands and tribute—nor, for that matter, the direct allegiance of the nobility, bound as it was to the deceased ruler. The new emperor built his own power and wealth by conquering new lands.

Inca Imperial Expansion

The combination of ancestor worship and split inheritance provided the logic and impulse for expanding Inca power. The desire for conquest provided incentives for courageous (or ambitious) nobles: those who succeeded in battle and gained new territories for the state could expect to be richly rewarded. Even common soldiers who distinguished themselves in battle could be rewarded with booty and raised to noble status. Under Pachacuti Inca and his successors, Inca domination was extended by warfare to the frontier of present-day Ecuador and Colombia in the north and to the Maule River in present-day Chile in the south, an area of about 350,000 square miles. Eighty provinces, scores of ethnic groups, and 16 million people came under Inca control.

The Incas pursued the integration of regions they conquered by imposing their language and their gods. Magnificent temples housed images of these gods. Priests led prayers and elaborate rituals, and during occasions such as terrible natural disasters or great military victories they sacrificed humans. The Incas

| What were the sources of strength and prosperity, and of problems, for the Incas? | How did the Maya and Teotihuacan develop prosperous societies in the classical era? | How did the Aztecs build on earlier Mesoamerican cultures and develop new traditions? | What did the European encounter mean for peoples of the major American empires? | ✓ LearningCurve Check what you know. |

Elevation — Feet / Meters: Over 13,123 / Over 4,000; 9,843–13,123 / 3,001–4,000; 6,563–9,842 / 2,001–3,000; 3,281–6,562 / 1,001–2,000; 0–3,280 / 0–1,000

Tumbes · Cajamarca · HUAYLAS VALLEY · Lima · Cuzco · CUZCO VALLEY · TITICACA VALLEY · ANDES MOUNTAINS · PACIFIC OCEAN · Amazon R. · Madeira R. · Maule R.

0   200   400 miles
0   200   400 kilometers

■ Inca Empire, 1532
— Inca road

Quechua

▶ First deemed the official language of the Incas under Pachacuti, it is still spoken by most Peruvians today.

forced conquered peoples to adopt **Quechua** (KEH-chuh-wuh), the official language of the empire, which extinguished many regional languages.

The pressure for growth strained the Inca Empire. Open lands became scarce, so the Incas tried to penetrate the tropical Amazon forest east of the Andes an effort that led to repeated military disasters. Another source of stress came from revolts among subject peoples in conquered territories. Even the system of roads and message-carrying runners couldn't keep up with the administrative needs of the empire. The round trip from the capital at Cuzco to Quito in Ecuador, for example, took from ten to twelve days, so an emperor might have to base urgent decisions on incomplete or out-of-date information. The empire was overextended.

Imperial Needs and Obligations

At its height, the Inca Empire extended over 2,600 miles. The challenges of sustaining an empire with that reach, not to mention one built so fast, required extraordinary resourcefulness. The Inca Empire met these demands by adapting aspects of local culture to meet imperial needs. For instance, the empire demanded that the ayllus, the local communities with shared ancestors, include imperial tribute in the rotation of labor and the distribution of harvested foods.

As each new Inca emperor conquered new lands and built his domain, he mobilized people and resources by drawing on local systems of labor and organization. Much as ayllus had developed satellite communities called mitmaq, populated by settlers from the ayllu in order to take advantage of remote farming areas, the emperor relocated families or even whole villages over long distances to consolidate territorial control or quell unrest. What had been a community practice became a tool of imperial expansion. The emperor also consolidated the empire by regulating marriage, using maternal lines to build kinship among conquered peoples. Inca rulers and nobles married the daughters of elite families among the peoples they conquered.

The reciprocal labor carried out within ayllus expanded into a labor tax called the *mit'a* (MEE-tuh), which rotated among households in an ayllu throughout the year. Tribute paid in labor provided the means for building the infrastructure of empire. Rotations of laborers carried out impressive engineering feats, allowing the vast empire to extend over the most difficult and inhospitable terrain. An excellent system of roads facilitated the transportation of armies and the rapid communication of royal orders by runners. On these roads Inca officials, tax collectors, and accountants traveled throughout the empire, using elaborate khipus to record financial and labor obligations, the output of fields, population levels, land transfers, and other numerical records. Like Persian and Roman roads, these great feats of Inca engineering linked an empire. The government also made an ayllu responsible for maintaining state-owned granaries, which distributed grain in times of shortage and famine and supplied assistance in natural disasters.

> **QUICK REVIEW**

How did the Incas use existing local practices as tools of imperial expansion?

CHAPTER LOCATOR | How did ancient peoples of the Americas adapt to, and adapt, their environment? | What patterns shaped civilization in Mesoamerica and the Andes?

How did the Maya and Teotihuacan develop prosperous and stable societies in the classical era?

In Mesoamerica the classical period (300 C.E. to 900 C.E.) saw major advances in religion, art, architecture, and farming, akin to those of the classical civilizations of the Mediterranean (see Chapters 5 and 6). It saw the rise of many city-states, and although the **Maya** city-states, which peaked between 600 C.E. and 900 C.E., were the longest lasting, others were significant as well. The city of **Teotihuacan** in the Valley of Mexico emerged as a major center of trade (300–650 C.E.). It was followed by the postclassical Toltec Empire (900–1200 C.E.), which adapted the cultural, ritual, and aesthetic practices that influenced later empires like the Aztecs.

Maya Agriculture and Trade

The Maya inhabited the highlands of Guatemala and the Yucatán peninsula in present-day Mexico and Belize. Their physical setting shaped two features of Maya society. First, the abundance of high-quality limestone allowed them to

Maya
▶ A highly developed Mesoamerican culture centered in the Yucatán peninsula of Mexico. The Maya created the most intricate writing system in the Western Hemisphere.

Teotihuacan
▶ The monumental city-state that dominated trade in classical era Mesoamerica.

| What were the sources of strength and prosperity, and of problems, for the Incas? | **How did the Maya and Teotihuacan develop prosperous societies in the classical era?** | How did the Aztecs build on earlier Mesoamerican cultures and develop new traditions? | What did the European encounter mean for peoples of the major American empires? | ✔ LearningCurve Check what you know. |

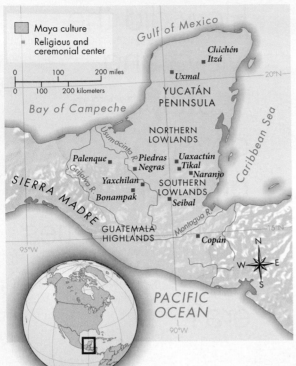

■ The Maya World, 300–900 C.E.

The Maya built dozens of cities linked together in trading networks of roads and rivers. Only the largest of them are shown here.

build monumental architecture. Second, limestone formations created deep natural wells called *cenotes* (say-NOH-tehs), which became critical sources of water in an often-arid environment. The staple crop of the Maya was maize, often raised in small remote plots called *milpas* in combination with other foodstuffs, including beans, squash, chili peppers, some root crops, and fruit trees.

The entire Maya region may have had as many as 14 million inhabitants. Sites like Uxmal, Uaxactún, Copán, Piedras Negras, Tikal, Palenque, and Chichén Itzá (Map 11.4) emerged as independent city-states, each ruled by a hereditary king. These cities produced polychrome pottery and featured altars, engraved pillars, masonry temples, palaces for nobles, pyramids where nobles were buried, and courts for ball games. The largest site, Tikal, may have had forty thousand people and served as a religious and ceremonial center. A hereditary nobility owned land, waged war, traded, exercised political power, and directed religious rituals. Artisans and scribes made up the social level below. Other residents were farmers, laborers, and slaves, the latter including prisoners of war.

At Maya markets, jade, obsidian, beads of red spiny oyster shell, lengths of cloth, and cacao beans served as media of exchange. The extensive trade among Maya communities, plus a common language, promoted unity among the peoples of the region. Merchants traded beyond Maya regions, particularly with the Zapotecs of Monte Albán, in the Valley of Oaxaca, and with the Teotihuacanos of the central valley of Mexico. Since this long-distance trade played an important part in international relations, the merchants conducting it were high nobles or even members of the royal family.

Maya Science and Religion

The Maya developed the most complex writing system in the Americas, a script with nearly a thousand glyphs. They recorded important events and observations in books made of bark paper and deerskin, on pottery, on stone pillars called steles, and on temples and other buildings. Archaeologists and anthropologists have demonstrated that the inscriptions are historical documents that record major events in the lives of Maya kings and nobles.

Surviving Maya books offer a window into religious rituals and practices, as well as Maya astronomy. From observation of the earth's movements around the sun, the Maya used a calendar of eighteen 20-day months and one 5-day month, for a total of 365 days, along with the 260-day calendar based on 20 weeks of 13 days. When these calendars coincided every fifty-two years, the Maya celebrated with feasting, ball-game competitions, and religious observance. These and other observances included blood sacrifice by kings to honor the gods.

The Maya devised a form of mathematics based on the vigesimal (20) rather than the decimal (10) system. More unusual was their use of the number zero, which allows for more complex calculations than are possible in number systems

CHAPTER LOCATOR | How did ancient peoples of the Americas adapt to, and adapt, their environment? | What patterns shaped civilization in Mesoamerica and the Andes?

310 CHAPTER 11 THE AMERICAS

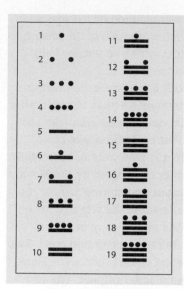

without it. The Maya's proficiency with numbers made them masters of abstract knowledge—notably in astronomy and mathematics.

Between the eighth and tenth centuries the Maya abandoned their cultural and ceremonial centers. Archaeologists attribute their decline to a combination of agricultural failures due to drought, land exhaustion, overpopulation, disease, and constant wars fought for economic and political gain. Royalty also suffered from the decline in Maya civilization. When military, economic, and social conditions deteriorated, their subjects saw the kings as the cause and turned against them.

Decline did not mean disappearance. The Maya ceased building monumental architecture around 900 C.E., which likely marked the end of the era of rule by powerful kings who could mobilize the labor required to build it. The Maya persisted in farming communities, a pattern of settlement that helped preserve their culture and language in the face of external pressures. They resisted invasions from warring Aztec armies by dispersing from their towns and villages and residing in their milpas during invasions. When Aztec armies entered the Yucatán, communities dispersed, leaving Aztec armies with nothing to conquer. This tactic continued to serve the Maya under Spanish colonial rule, with many communities avoiding Spanish domination for generations.

Teotihuacan and the Toltecs

The most powerful city in classical Mesoamerica emerged at Teotihuacan, northwest of the lands of the Maya. By 100 C.E. it had a population of 60,000. At its height, between 300 and 600 C.E., its population reached as high as 250,000. The

| What were the sources of strength and prosperity, and of problems, for the Incas? | **How did the Maya and Teotihuacan develop prosperous societies in the classical era?** | How did the Aztecs build on earlier Mesoamerican cultures and develop new traditions? | What did the European encounter mean for peoples of the major American empires? | ✓ LearningCurve Check what you know. |

311

The Toltecs, ca. 900–1200 C.E.

■ Toltec site
■ Zapotec site

heart of Teotihuacan was a massive ceremonial center anchored by a colossal Pyramid of the Sun, 700 feet wide and 200 feet tall, and a Pyramid of the Moon. Connecting them was the Avenue of the Dead, 150 feet wide and 2 miles long, along which stood the homes of scores of priests and lords.

The monuments of the ceremonial district of Teotihuacan were matched in grandeur by the city's markets, which extended its influence across Mesoamerica. The city's trade empire lay in its control of a resource vital to Mesoamerican society and religion: obsidian, a glasslike volcanic rock that could be worked into objects with both material and spiritual uses. Obsidian knives were used for daily tasks and for important rituals such as the blood sacrifice practiced by the Maya.

Religion followed trade. Teotihuacan was a religious and cultural center whose influence extended over large distances. One factor in the city's success was its ethnic diversity. Teotihuacan grew through the migration of outsiders along trade networks, and these groups built separate ethnic neighborhoods. Two gods that were particularly important to classical period civilizations were Tlaloc (Chac in Maya), the god of rain, and Quetzalcoatl, the plumed serpent. The worship of these deities became an enduring aspect of Mesoamerican religion that the Toltecs and the Aztecs embraced.

Teotihuacan thrived because it controlled trade of the most valuable goods. This helped it grow, and in turn the trade networks it sustained helped other regions in Mesoamerica develop through intensified contact with other groups

The Pyramid of the Sun at Teotihuacan

Built in several stages beginning in about 100 C.E., the Pyramid of the Sun has sides measuring 700 feet long and 200 feet high. Originally it was covered with lime plaster decorated with brightly colored murals. Smaller pyramids surround it in what was the heart of the bustling city of Teotihuacan. (© age fotostock/SuperStock)

CHAPTER LOCATOR | How did ancient peoples of the Americas adapt to, and adapt, their environment? | What patterns shaped civilization in Mesoamerica and the Andes?

CHAPTER 11
312   THE AMERICAS

and the spread of technologies. Over time, improvements in other regions decreased Teotihuacan's comparative advantage, as its trading partners produced increasingly valuable goods, spurring competition. By 600 its influence had begun to decline, and in 650 the residents of the city seem to have burned its ceremonial center in what may have been a revolt against the city's leadership. The city had ceased to be a major trade center by 900 C.E.[1]

The Toltecs (900–1200 C.E.) filled the void created by Teotihuacan's decline. The Toltecs inaugurated a new era, the postclassical, which ended with the Spanish conquest of the Aztec Empire. The postclassical period saw fewer technological or artistic advances. Instead it was a time of intensified warfare in Mesoamerica and a time of rapid and bold imperial expansion through conquest. After the decline of Teotihuacan, the Toltecs entered the Valley of Mexico and settled in Tula. The Toltecs' legend of their origins held that in 968 C.E. their people were led into the valley by a charismatic leader who fused himself to the plumed serpent god and called himself Topiltzin-Quetzalcoatl. In 987, amid infighting, Topiltzin-Quetzalcoatl and his followers were expelled from Tula. They marched south, where they conquered and settled in a Maya region.

The Toltecs built a military empire and gradually absorbed the culture, practices, and religion of their neighbors in the Valley of Mexico. Their empire waned amid war, drought, and famine over the eleventh and twelfth centuries. After the demise of the Toltec Empire, city-states in the Valley of Mexico competed with each other militarily and to cast themselves as the legitimate descendants and heirs of the Toltecs.

QUICK REVIEW

What were the main sources of Maya wealth and power?
What about Teotihuacan?

| What were the sources of strength and prosperity, and of problems, for the Incas? | **How did the Maya and Teotihuacan develop prosperous societies in the classical era?** | How did the Aztecs build on earlier Mesoamerican cultures and develop new traditions? | What did the European encounter mean for peoples of the major American empires? | ✓ LearningCurve Check what you know. |

313

How did the Aztecs build on the achievements of earlier Mesoamerican cultures and develop new traditions to create their large empire?

Huitzilopochtli

This painting of the hummingbird god of war carrying a shield in one hand and a serpent-headed knife in the other was made by Aztec priests in a book written on bark paper about the time of the Spanish conquest. He is shown descending from a step-pyramid, perhaps a reference to the great pyramid in the center of Tenochtitlan, where he was worshipped. (© Foundation for the Advancement of Mesoamerican Studies, Inc., www.famsi.org)

Nahuatl
► The language of both the Toltecs and the Aztecs.

Mexica
► The dominant ethnic group of what is now Mexico, who created an empire based on war and religion that reached its height in the mid-1400s; in the nineteenth century the people became known as Aztecs.

According to their oral tradition, between 1300 and 1345 a group of **Nahuatl**-speaking people, the **Mexica**, migrated southward from what is now northern Mexico, settling on the shores and islands of Lake Texcoco in the central valley of Mexico (Map 11.5). They formed a vast and rapidly expanding empire centered around the twin cities of Tenochtitlan (tay-nawch-TEET-lahn) and Tlatelolco, which by 1500 were probably larger than any city in Europe except Istanbul. This was the Aztec Empire, a network of alliances and tributary states with the Mexica at its core. Examining the means by which they formed and expanded their empire, as well as the vulnerabilities of that empire, can help us build a rich understanding of Mesoamerican society.

The Mexica: From Vassals to Masters

In the early fourteenth century, the Mexica, a migrant, seminomadic group, arrived in the Valley of Mexico. They found an environment that, since the collapse of the Toltec Empire in the twelfth century, had divided into small, fragile

CHAPTER LOCATOR | How did ancient peoples of the Americas adapt to, and adapt, their environment? | What patterns shaped civilization in Mesoamerica and the Andes?

314 CHAPTER 11 THE AMERICAS

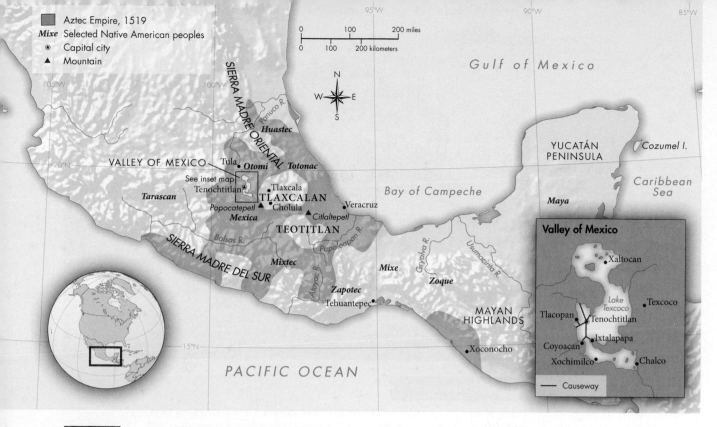

MAP 11.5 ■ The Aztec (Mexica) Empire in 1519

The Mexica migrated into the central valley of what is now Mexico from the north, conquering other groups and establishing an empire, later called the Aztec Empire. The capital of the Aztec Empire was Tenochtitlan, built on islands in Lake Texcoco.

alliances that battled to claim the legacy of the Toltecs. At the moment of their arrival, control over much of the valley lay in the hands of the Tepanec Alliance. The Mexica negotiated the right to settle on a swampy island on Lake Texcoco in exchange for military service to the Tepanecs.

The Mexica adopted the customs of their new region, organizing clan-based communities called *calpolli*, incorporating the deities of their new neighbors, and serving the Tepanecs. They gradually reclaimed land around their island to form two urban centers, Tenochtitlan and Tlatelolco. They adopted a farming technique used in parts of Lake Texcoco called *chinampa* (chee-NAHM-pah) agriculture. Under this system, farmers built up reeds and mud along the margins of Lake Texcoco to gradually extend farming well into the lake.

At its peak, the chinampa farming system formed vast areas of tidy rectangular plots divided by canals that allowed for canoe transportation of people and crops. When the Spanish entered **Tenochtitlan** (which they called Mexico City) in November 1519, they were amazed at this city which seemed to rise straight out of the lake.

Over time, the Mexica improved their standing in the Valley of Mexico by asking a powerful neighboring city-state to name a prince considered to be of noble Toltec descent to rule them, forming a dynasty that would become the most powerful in Mesoamerica. The new ruler, or *tlatoani* (tlah-toh-annie), Acamapichtli (ah-camp-itch-lee), brought the Mexica higher social rank and the ability to form alliances.

Tenochtitlan

▶ A large and prosperous Aztec city that was built starting in 1325. The Spanish admired it when they entered in 1519.

What were the sources of strength and prosperity, and of problems, for the Incas?	How did the Maya and Teotihuacan develop prosperous societies in the classical era?	**How did the Aztecs build on earlier Mesoamerican cultures and develop new traditions?**	What did the European encounter mean for peoples of the major American empires?	✓ LearningCurve Check what you know.

Chinampa Farming

This illustration shows farmers in the Aztec Empire building chinampa farming plots by reclaiming land from Lake Texcoco. Farmers created the plots by packing them with vegetation and mud from the lake, supporting their boundaries by planting willow trees. Chinampas allowed for intensive farming in a region that had limited rainfall, and the canals between them permitted easy transportation. (© Gianni Dagli Orti/Corbis)

By the end of Acamapichtli's reign (1372–1391), the Mexica had fully adapted to their new environment and had adopted the highly stratified social organization that would encourage the ambitions of their own warrior class. Under the rule of Acamapichtli's successors Huitzilihuitl (r. 1391–1417) and Chimalpopoca (r. 1417–1427), the Mexica remained subordinate to the Tepanec Alliance. But in 1427 a dispute over the succession of the Tepanec king created an opportunity for the Mexica.

Taking advantage of the fluid political situation, in 1428 the Mexica formed a coalition with other cities in the Valley of Mexico, besieged the Tepanec capital for nearly three months, and then defeated it. A powerful new coalition had emerged: the Triple Alliance, with the Mexica as its most powerful partner. The Aztec Empire was born.[2]

To consolidate the new political order, Tlatoani Itzcoatl, guided by his nephew Tlacaelel, burned his predecessors' books and drafted a new history. The new history placed the warrior cult and its religious pantheon at the center of Mexica history, making the god of war, Huitzilopochtli, the patron deity of the empire. Huitzilopochtli, "Hummingbird of the South," was a god unique to the Mexica who, according to the new official origin stories of the Mexica people, had ordered them to march south until they found an island where he gave them the sign of an eagle eating a serpent, which appeared to them in Tenochtitlan. (See "Individuals in Society: Tlacaelel," page 318.)

CHAPTER LOCATOR | How did ancient peoples of the Americas adapt to, and adapt, their environment? | What patterns shaped civilization in Mesoamerica and the Andes?

316 CHAPTER 11 THE AMERICAS

Under the new imperial order, government offices combined military, religious, and political functions. Eventually, tlatoanis formalized these functions into distinct noble and common classes. The Valley of Mexico had sustained itself through chinampa agriculture, but as the empire grew, crops provided as tribute from distant conquered peoples increasingly fed the valley's rapidly growing population. The Mexica sustained themselves through military conquest, imposing their rule over a vast part of modern Mexico.

Life in the Aztec Empire

Few sharp social distinctions existed among the Aztecs during their early migrations, but by the early sixteenth century Aztec society had changed. A stratified social structure had emerged, and the warrior aristocracy exercised great authority. Men who had distinguished themselves in war occupied the highest military and social positions in the state. Generals, judges, and governors of provinces were appointed by the emperor from among his servants who had earned reputations as war heroes. These great lords, or *tecuhtli* (teh-COOT-lee), dressed luxuriously and lived in palaces.

Beneath the great nobility of military leaders and imperial officials was the class of warriors. Theoretically, every free man could be a warrior, and parents dedicated their male children to war, burying a male child's umbilical cord with arrows and a shield on the day of his birth. In actuality, the sons of nobles were more likely to become warriors because of their fathers' positions and influence in the state. At the age of six, boys entered a school that trained them for war. They were taught to fight, learned to live on little food and sleep, and to accept pain without complaint. At about age eighteen, a warrior fought his first campaign. If he captured a prisoner for ritual sacrifice, he acquired the title *iyac*, or warrior. If in later campaigns he succeeded in killing or capturing four of the enemy, he became a *tequiua*—one who shared in the booty and was thus a member of the nobility. If a young man failed in several campaigns to capture the required four prisoners, he became a *macehualli* (plural *macehualtin*), a commoner.

The macehualtin were the ordinary citizens—the backbone of Aztec society and the vast majority of the population. Members of this class performed agricultural, military, and domestic services and carried heavy public burdens not required of noble warriors. Government officials assigned them to work on the temples, roads, and bridges. Unlike nobles, priests, orphans, and slaves, macehualtin paid taxes. Macehualtin in the capital, however, possessed certain rights: they held their plots of land for life, and they received a small share of the tribute paid by the provinces to the emperor.

Beneath the macehualtin were the *tlalmaitl*, the landless workers or serfs who provided agricultural labor, paid rents in kind, and were bound to the soil—they could not move off the land. In many ways the tlalmaitl resembled the serfs of western Europe, but unlike serfs they performed military service when called on to do so. Slaves were the lowest social class. Most were prisoners captured in war or kidnapped from enemy tribes. Mexica slaves differed fundamentally from European ones, for they could possess goods; save money; buy land, houses, and even slaves for their own service; and purchase their freedom. If a male slave

| What were the sources of strength and prosperity, and of problems, for the Incas? | How did the Maya and Teotihuacan develop prosperous societies in the classical era? | **How did the Aztecs build on earlier Mesoamerican cultures and develop new traditions?** | What did the European encounter mean for peoples of the major American empires? | ✓ LearningCurve Check what you know. |

317

The hummingbird god Huitzilopochtli was originally a somewhat ordinary god of war and of young men, but in the fifteenth century he was elevated in status among the Mexica. He became increasingly associated with the sun and gradually became the most important Mexica deity. This change appears to have been primarily the work of Tlacaelel, the very long-lived chief adviser to the emperors Itzcóatl (r. 1427–1440), Moctezuma I (r. 1440–1469), and Axayacatl (r. 1469–1481). Tlacaelel first gained influence during wars in the 1420s in which the Mexica defeated the rival Tepanecs, after which he established new systems of dividing military spoils and enemy lands. At the same time, he advised the emperor that new histories were needed in which the destiny of the Mexica people was made clearer. Tlacaelel ordered the destruction of older historical texts, and under his direction the new chronicles connected Mexica fate directly to Huitzilopochtli. Mexica writing was primarily pictographic, drawn and then read by specially trained scribes who used written records as an aid to oral presentation, especially for legal issues, historical chronicles, religious and devotional poetry, and astronomical calculations.

Tlacaelel emphasized human sacrifice as one of the Aztecs' religious duties. (From the *Codex Magliabechiano* [vellum]/Biblioteca Nazionale Centrale, Florence, Italy/ The Bridgeman Art Library)

According to these new texts, the Mexica had been guided to Lake Texcoco by Huitzilopochtli; there they saw an eagle perched on a cactus, which a prophecy foretold would mark the site of their new city. Huitzilopochtli kept the world alive by bringing the sun's warmth, but to do this he required the Mexica, who increasingly saw themselves as the "people of the sun," to provide a steady offering of human blood.

The worship of Huitzilopochtli became linked to cosmic forces as well as daily survival. In Nahua tradition, the universe was understood to exist in a series of five suns, or five cosmic ages. Four ages had already passed, and their suns had been destroyed; the fifth sun, the age in which the Mexica were now living, would also be destroyed unless the Mexica fortified the sun with the energy found in blood. Warfare thus brought new territory under Mexica control and provided sacrificial victims to nourish the sun-god. With these ideas, Tlacaelel created what Miguel León-Portilla, a leading contemporary scholar of Nahua religion and philosophy, has termed a "mystico-militaristic" conception of Aztec destiny.

Human sacrifice was practiced in many cultures of Mesoamerica, including the Olmec and the Maya as well as the Mexica, before the changes introduced by Tlacaelel, but historians believe the number of victims increased dramatically during the last period of Mexica rule. A huge pyramid-shaped temple in the center of Tenochtitlan, dedicated to Huitzilopochtli and the god of rain Tlaloc, was renovated and expanded many times, the last in 1487. To dedicate each expansion, priests sacrificed war captives. Similar ceremonies were held regularly throughout the year on days dedicated to Huitzilopochtli and were attended by many observers, including representatives from neighboring states as well as masses of Mexica. According to many accounts, victims were placed on a stone slab, and their hearts were cut out with an obsidian knife; the officiating priest then held the heart up as an offering to the sun. Sacrifices were also made to other gods at temples elsewhere in Tenochtitlan, and perhaps in other cities controlled by the Mexica.

Estimates of the number of people sacrificed to Huitzilopochtli and other Mexica gods vary enormously and are impossible to verify. Both Mexica and later Spanish accounts clearly exaggerated the numbers, but most historians today assume that between several hundred and several thousand people were killed each year.

Sources: Miguel León-Portilla, *Pre-Columbian Literatures of Mexico* (Norman: University of Oklahoma Press, 1969); Inga Clendinnen, *Aztecs: An Interpretation* (Cambridge: Cambridge University Press, 1991).

QUESTIONS FOR ANALYSIS

1. How did the worship of Huitzilopochtli contribute to Aztec expansion? To hostility toward the Aztecs?
2. Why might Tlacaelel have believed it was important to destroy older texts as he created this new Aztec mythology?

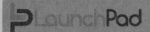

ONLINE DOCUMENT PROJECT
Why did Tlacaelel believe the Aztec Empire needed a new history? Read documents that examine Aztec history and culture, and then complete a quiz and writing assignment based on the evidence and details from this chapter. *See inside the front cover to learn more.*

married a free woman, their offspring were free. Most slaves eventually gained their freedom.

Women of all social classes operated within the domestic sphere. As the little hands of the newborn male were closed around a tiny bow and arrow indicating his warrior destiny, so the infant female's hands were wrapped around miniature weaving instruments and a small broom. Save for the few women vowed to the service of the temple, marriage and the household were a woman's fate, and marriage represented social maturity for both sexes.

The Limits of the Aztec Empire

Mesoamerican empires like that of the Aztecs were not like modern nation-states that consolidate control of the territory within their borders. Instead the Aztec Empire was a syndicate in which the Mexica, their allies, and their subordinates thrived on trade and tribute backed by the threat of force.

When a city succumbed, its captive warriors were marched to Tenochtitlan to be sacrificed. The defeated city was obligated to provide tribute to be distributed within the empire. But conquest stopped short of assimilation. Rulers and nobles remained in place. Subjects were not required to adopt Mexica gods.

The death of a ruler is always a time of uncertainty, and this was especially true in Mesoamerica under the Aztec Empire. For peoples of the Valley of Mexico and beyond, this meant war was sure to arrive. The council of high nobles who served the deceased ruler chose the new tlatoani, who was often the commander of the army. Once the new tlatoani was named, he would embark on a military campaign in order to prove his worthiness.

A success in the tlatoani's inaugural military campaign provided new tribute-paying subjects, produced a long train of sacrificial victims captured in battle, maintained the stability of the empire's alliances, warned off potential foes, and kept conquered areas in subordination. After the successful campaign, the new tlatoani invited the rulers of allied, subject, and enemy city-states alike to his coronation ceremony.

But success was not always possible, as the troubled rule of Tizoc (r. 1481–1486) demonstrated. His wars sometimes resulted in a greater number of casualties among his own forces than of sacrificial victims for his altars. Five years after he was crowned, he was poisoned by his own subjects. His successor, Ahuitzotl (r. 1486–1502), faced the challenge of reinvigorating the empire through renewed displays of strength. To symbolize the restoration of Tenochtitlan's power, he waged wars of conquest that defied precedence in their scale, culminating in two coronation ceremonies, the second of which incorporated sacrificing over eighty thousand captive warriors.

Blood sacrifice was not new to the Aztecs. For centuries Mesoamerican peoples had honored their gods this way. The Aztecs elevated the warrior cult as the central observance. The Mexica believed the earth had been destroyed and re-created four times. The end of creation loomed after their age, the fifth sun. Since this apocalypse might be forestalled through divine intervention, their sacrifice could show that humans were worthy of divine intervention. If ancient deities had given their lives to save the sun, how could mortals refuse to do the same? Their service to the gods culminated on the altar of the temple to Huitzilopochtli, where priests cut into the chests of warriors with their obsidian knives to pull out their beating hearts and raise them in sacrifice to the sun.

Such sacrifice evoked the power of Aztec rulers, but the ceremony observing the end of each fifty-two-year bundle better reflected the Mexica worldview. Had humans sacrificed enough for the gods to intercede and ensure the sun would rise again? In preparation for the end, families broke their earthenware vessels, cleansed their homes, and extinguished all fires. As the new day came, priests made a fire on the chest of a living, powerful captive warrior. Noble warriors lit torches from this new fire, and relayed the noble flame of creation into each hearth in the empire. For the next fifty-two years, all would know the fire in their hearth, like the rising of the sun itself, was the fruit of a sacred warrior sacrifice.

The need for sacrifice, as well as the glorification of the warriors who provided it through battle, was a powerful rationale for the expansion of the Aztec Empire. The role of the Aztecs' sacrifice-based religious system is the subject of scholarly debate: Did the religious system guide imperial expansion? Or did imperial expansion guide the religious system? These views are by no means incompatible: for the Aztecs, the peoples who came under their rule, and the peoples who resisted them, the twin goals of empire building and service to the gods were inseparable.

> **QUICK REVIEW**

What role did warfare play in Mexica society?

CHAPTER LOCATOR | How did ancient peoples of the Americas adapt to, and adapt, their environment? | What patterns shaped civilization in Mesoamerica and the Andes?

320 CHAPTER 11 THE AMERICAS

What did the European encounter mean for peoples of the major American empires?

Construction for the Pino Suárez metro station unearthed the Aztec ceremonial altar of Ehecatl, the Aztec god of wind. (David Hiser/National Geographic/SuperStock)

B By 1500 the Incas and Aztecs strained under the burdens of managing the largest empires the Americas had seen. Both faced the challenges of consolidating their gains, bearing the costs of empire and of the swelling nobility, and waging war in increasingly distant and difficult conditions.

The Fall of the Aztecs

In 1502 Moctezuma II, the last Mexica to rule before the arrival of the Spaniards, was named tlatoani. Moctezuma inherited a strained empire. His predecessors had expanded the empire's reach from the Caribbean coast to the Pacific. At the margins of the empire the Aztecs encountered peoples who were seminomadic or who, like the Maya, abandoned their cities to resist conquest. An empire that had expanded rapidly through conquest found itself with little room to grow.

| What were the sources of strength and prosperity, and of problems, for the Incas? | How did the Maya and Teotihuacan develop prosperous societies in the classical era? | How did the Aztecs build on earlier Mesoamerican cultures and develop new traditions? | **What did the European encounter mean for peoples of the major American empires?** | ✓ LearningCurve Check what you know. |

321

Aztec leaders had sought targets for conquest that were easy to overpower or were strategic for trade, or that possessed resources or produced goods that made for valuable tribute. This created an empire riddled with independent enclaves that had resisted conquest. The most powerful of these was Tlaxcala, at the edge of the Valley of Mexico. In addition, even those areas nominally under Aztec rule retained local leadership and saw themselves as subjected peoples, not as Aztecs.

Finally, the costs of expanding and sustaining the empire had become onerous. Generations of social mobility through distinction in combat had produced a bloated nobility both exempt from and sustained by tribute. Tenochtitlan became dependent on tributary maize in order to feed itself. Materially, the lack of new peoples to conquer meant the empire had little promise of increased prosperity. Spiritually, the dwindling flow of sacrificial victims meant the Mexica might be losing the great cosmic struggle to keep creation from ending.

Faced with these challenges, Moctezuma II reformed the empire. He reduced the privileges (and thus the costs to the empire) of the lesser nobility and narrowed the pathways of social mobility. The austerity he imposed in the imperial capital caused unrest. He also pressed the consolidation of territory by seeking to conquer the autonomous enclaves left by his predecessors. As Moctezuma targeted these enclaves, their ability to resist sapped Mexica resources and strained their morale without producing a corresponding reward for the empire in sacrifice or tribute.

By the time he reached the gates of Tenochtitlan in 1519, the Spanish conquistador Hernán Cortés had forged alliances with foes of the Aztec Empire, particularly Tlaxcala, which had so ably resisted conquest. The Tlaxcalans saw in the foreigners an opportunity that could aid their struggle against the Mexica and formed an alliance with the Spanish. Cortés's band of six hundred Spaniards arrived in Tenochtitlan accompanied by tens of thousands of Tlaxcalan soldiers.

Whatever Moctezuma made of the strangers, he received them as guests, probably because he sought to understand the nature of this encounter and its significance for his empire. Perhaps Moctezuma hesitated, losing the opportunity to act against them. Perhaps he concluded that he had no chance of defeating them, since at that moment most of the men he could count on in battle were tending to their crops and the capital had been so riddled with division and resentment of his reforms that he was powerless to act.

Either way, Cortés and his men managed the encounter skillfully and succeeded in taking Moctezuma prisoner. When the residents of Tenochtitlan rose up to expel the Spaniards, Moctezuma was killed, either at the hands of the Spaniards or by his own subjects, depending on the account. Though the Spaniards were cast out of the city, they left an unwelcome guest, smallpox. The first epidemic of the disease swept through the city in 1520, killing Moctezuma's successor, Cuitlahuac, within a matter of months. Cuauhtemoc, the last tlatoani of the Mexica, was named that same year.

The Aztec Empire and the Mexica people were not defeated by technology, cultural superiority, or a belief that the Europeans were gods. Instead the Mexica suffered a political defeat: they fell because of ruptures in their leadership due to the death of Moctezuma and his successor, as well as the willingness of allies and enemies alike to join with the Spaniards against them when they perceived an opportunity.

CHAPTER LOCATOR | How did ancient peoples of the Americas adapt to, and adapt, their environment? | What patterns shaped civilization in Mesoamerica and the Andes?

322 CHAPTER 11 THE AMERICAS

The Fall of the Incas

In 1525 Huayna Capac Inca, the grandson of Pachacuti Inca, became ill while carrying out a military campaign in present-day Ecuador, at the northern frontier of the empire. His illness was plague, introduced by Europeans waging wars of conquest in Mesoamerica, and it would kill him. But as he waged war, he also received news of the foreigners in the north and anticipated that they would come southward. From his deathbed, he urged his successor to make peace with them.

But peace did not follow Huayna Capac's death. Instead civil war erupted between two of his sons over succession to the throne. Huascar claimed it as the firstborn. His half-brother Atahualpa, Huayna Capac's favorite and an experienced military commander who had accompanied him in his Ecuadorean campaign, claimed it as well. The brothers fought for seven years, turning the empire's armies against each other. In 1532 Atahualpa vanquished and imprisoned his brother and consolidated his rule in Cuzco. That same year a group of Spaniards led by Francisco Pizarro landed on the Peruvian coast, pursuing rumors of a city of gold in the mountains.

Atahualpa agreed through emissaries to meet the Spaniards at the city of Cajamarca in northern Peru. In a demonstration of his imperial authority, he entered Cajamarca carried on a golden litter, accompanied by four military squadrons of eight thousand men each. Atahualpa met the Spanish intending not to fight a battle, but to understand them and hear them out. The meeting between Atahualpa and Pizarro reflected two deeply different worldviews.

In the scuffle that ensued at the meeting, the Spaniards took Atahualpa prisoner, and they eventually executed him. The Spaniards named a new indigenous leader, Manco Capac, whom they hoped to control. But Manco Capac turned against the Spaniards. He, and later his son Tupac Amaru, led resistance against the Spaniards until 1567. Each time the Inca forces besieged a Spanish-controlled city or town, however, their proximity to the Spaniards exposed them to European diseases. They were more successful in smaller-scale attacks, which delayed and limited Spanish colonization, but did not undo it.

QUICK REVIEW <

How did internal political divisions contribute to the fall of both the Aztec and Inca Empires?

What were the sources of strength and prosperity, and of problems, for the Incas?

How did the Maya and Teotihuacan develop prosperous societies in the classical era?

How did the Aztecs build on earlier Mesoamerican cultures and develop new traditions?

What did the European encounter mean for peoples of the major American empires?

✓ LearningCurve
Check what you know.

CHAPTER SUMMARY

The Inca and Aztec Empires that encountered Spanish conquerors were short-lived products of the cycle of centralization and decentralization that had characterized the Andes and Mesoamerica for thousands of years. The empires preceding those of the Incas and Aztecs had been undone when their own people turned against them, when climate changes disrupted them, or when they faced outside competition. What was new in the sixteenth century was that this outside competition came from Europeans.

The civilizations of the Andes and Mesoamerica from which the Incas and Aztecs emerged had remarkable similarities with and differences from other ancient and premodern civilizations in other regions of the world. Indigenous societies of the Americas developed extensive networks of trade. In Mesoamerica and the Andes, the domestication of crops led to the kind of bountiful production that allowed for diversification of labor among farmers, priests, nobles, merchants, and artisans. In these environments, cycles of centralization occurred in which powerful city-states emerged and embarked on campaigns of conquest, bringing vast regions under their political, religious, and cultural influence.

But civilizations of the Americas developed in unique ways as well. This was particularly true in the Andes, where peoples developed specialized patterns of farming in vertical archipelagos in their inhospitable mountain environment. Similarly, though Andean peoples did not develop writing, they instead developed the khipu into a sophisticated system of recording and communicating information.

Ultimately, the history of the peoples of the Americas was defined by their diverse experiences as they coped with varied climates, ecology, and geography. And peoples' experiences of adapting to their environments, and of transforming those environments to meet their needs, shaped the ways they understood their world. These experiences led them to produce precise calendars, highly detailed readings of the stars, and an elaborate architecture of religious beliefs through which they interpreted their relationships to their world and their place in the cosmos.

CONNECTIONS The early sixteenth century marked the end of independent empires of the Americas and the gradual integration of American peoples into global empires seated in Europe. Spaniards were the most motivated and had their greatest success when they encountered dense, organized urban areas. Here they displaced existing overlords as the recipients of tribute in goods and labor. The Spanish were less interested in sparsely settled areas that did not have well-established systems of trade and tribute and were harder to subdue. As a result, European conquest was a surprisingly drawn-out process. Peoples of the Americas resisted conquest until well into the nineteenth century.

The incidental companion of conquest—disease—was also uneven in its effects. Over the course of the sixteenth century, epidemic diseases decimated the population of the Americas, which fell from 50 million to just 5 million. But epidemics of

CHAPTER LOCATOR

How did ancient peoples of the Americas adapt to, and adapt, their environment?

What patterns shaped civilization in Mesoamerica and the Andes?

324 CHAPTER 11
THE AMERICAS

diseases that are spread through human contact, such as measles and smallpox, are primarily urban phenomena: these diseases emerged as ancient cities grew large enough that the diseases could spread quickly among dense populations. As a result, the impact of the diseases brought by Europeans was the most severe and the most destructive in the cities of the Americas.

Since cities faced the brunt of both disease and wars of conquest, the disruptions caused by the encounter were disproportionally felt there. Whole systems of knowledge, sets of artisanal skills, political cultures, and religious thought resided in cities. Thus, as epidemics erupted, many of the most remarkable aspects of American civilizations were lost. Rural peoples and cultures were much more resilient. It was in rural areas that languages, foodways, farming practices, and approaches to healing—indeed whole worldviews—endured and evolved. This process occurred either in isolation from or in dialogue with European cultures, but local practices in rural regions were not obliterated, as they were in major cities. In the end, the European encounter destroyed the urban cultures and systems of knowledge in the Americas.

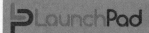

ONLINE DOCUMENT PROJECT
The Making and Remaking of Aztec History

Why did Tlacaelel believe the Aztec Empire needed a new history?

Read documents that examine Aztec history and culture, and then complete a quiz and writing assignment based on the evidence and details from this chapter. *See inside the front cover to learn more.*

| What were the sources of strength and prosperity, and of problems, for the Incas? | How did the Maya and Teotihuacan develop prosperous societies in the classical era? | How did the Aztecs build on earlier Mesoamerican cultures and develop new traditions? | What did the European encounter mean for peoples of the major American empires? | ✔️ **LearningCurve** Check what you know. |

CHAPTER 11 STUDY GUIDE

 STEP 1 | GET STARTED ONLINE

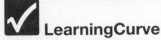 **LearningCurve**

Now that you've read the chapter, make it stick by completing the LearningCurve activity.

STEP 2 | EXPLAIN WHY IT MATTERS

Put your reading into practice. Identify each term below, and then explain why it matters in world history.

TERM	WHO OR WHAT & WHEN	WHY IT MATTERS
Mesoamerica (p. 296)		
khipu (p. 299)		
nixtamalization (p. 300)		
Olmecs (p. 302)		
Moche (p. 305)		
Inca (p. 306)		
Quechua (p. 308)		
Maya (p. 309)		
Teotihuacan (p. 309)		
Nahuatl (p. 314)		
Mexica (p. 314)		
Tenochtitlan (p. 315)		

STEP 3 | MOVE BEYOND THE BASICS

To demonstrate a more advanced understanding of the three major civilizations of the Americas, fill in the chart below with descriptions of the role trade, warfare, and religion played in the society and culture of each civilization. What common characteristics did these civilizations share?

	Trade	Warfare	Religion
Maya			
Aztecs			
Inca			

STEP 4 ▸ PUT IT ALL TOGETHER

Now, take a step back and try to explain the big picture. Remember to use specific examples from the chapter in your answers.

EARLY DEVELOPMENT OF AMERICAN SOCIETIES

▸ How did geography and climate shape migration and settlement patterns in the Americas?

▸ How did the Olmec help lay the foundation for later Mesoamerican societies?

THE CLASSICAL ERA

▸ How did trade link the societies of the Americas during the classical era?

▸ Compare and contrast the classical societies of Mesoamerica and North America. How would you explain the similarities and differences you note?

AZTEC AND INCA EMPIRES

▸ Compare and contrast the imperial expansion of the Aztecs and the Incas. What factors created pressure for continued expansion in each empire?

▸ Compare and contrast imperial government in the Aztec and Inca empires. How did each empire control subject peoples and exploit their labor and resources?

LOOKING BACK, LOOKING AHEAD

▸ What important similarities are there between the histories of the Western and Eastern Hemispheres prior to 1500? How would you account for these similarities?

▸ How might European conquest and colonization of the Americas after 1500 have shaped our view of the civilizations of the Americas as they existed *prior* to 1500?

> IN YOUR OWN WORDS

Imagine that you must give an oral report to the class answering the following question: **What similarities and differences were there between the societies of the Americas and other premodern societies around the world? What would be the most important points and why?**

12
CULTURAL EXCHANGE IN CENTRAL AND SOUTHERN ASIA

300–1400

> **How did Mongol conquests and maritime trade facilitate cultural exchange in central and southern Asia?** Chapter 12 examines the forces that contributed to cultural exchange and transformation in Asia between 300 and 1400. From the fifth century on, groups of nomadic Turks appeared along the fringes of the settled societies of Eurasia. Much more dramatic was the rise of the Mongols in the late twelfth and early thirteenth centuries. Under the leadership of Chinggis Khan, the Mongols subdued one society after another. For a century Mongol hegemony fostered unprecedented East-West trade and contact. Over the course of several centuries, Arab and Turkish armies brought Islam to India. India continued to be the center of a very active seaborne trade, and this trade helped carry Indian ideas and practices to Southeast Asia.

Mongol Woman Women played influential roles among the Mongols. The Mongol woman portrayed in this painting is Chabi, wife of Khubilai Khan. Like other Mongols, she maintained Mongol dress even though she spent much of her time in China. (The Granger Collection, NYC — All rights reserved.)

> What aspects of nomadic life gave the nomads of Central Asia military advantages over nearby settled civilizations?

> How did Chinggis Khan and his successors conquer much of Eurasia, and how did the Mongol conquests change the regions affected?

> How did the Mongol conquests facilitate the spread of ideas, religions, inventions, and diseases?

> What was the result of India's encounters with Turks, Mongols, and Islam?

> How did states develop along the maritime trade routes of Southeast Asia and beyond?

✓ **LearningCurve**

After reading the chapter, use LearningCurve to retain what you've read.

What aspects of nomadic life gave the nomads of Central Asia military advantages over nearby settled civilizations?

Gold Belt Plaques

Like earlier nomads, the Mongols favored art with animal designs, such as these two gold belt plaques, which depict deer under trees or flowers. Belts and horses were often exchanged to seal or commemorate an alliance. (Nasser D. Khalili Collection of Islamic Art, © Nour Foundation. Courtesy of the Khalili Family Trust)

nomads
▶ Groups of people who move from place to place in search of food, water, and pasture for their animals, usually following the seasons.

steppe
▶ Grasslands that are too dry for crops but support pasturing animals; they are common across much of the center of Eurasia.

ONE EXPERIENCE ROME, PERSIA, INDIA, AND CHINA ALL SHARED was conflict with **nomads** who came from the very broad region referred to as Central Asia. This region was dominated by the **steppe**, arid grasslands that stretched from modern Hungary to Mongolia and parts of present northeast China. Initially small in number, the nomadic peoples of this region used their military superiority to conquer first other nomads, then the nearby settled societies. In the process they created settled empires of their own that drew on the cultures they absorbed.

Nomadic Society

Easily crossed by horses but too dry for crop agriculture, the grasslands could support only a thin population of nomadic herders. Following the seasons, they would break camp at least twice a year and move their animals to new pastures, going north in the spring and south in the fall.

In their search for water and good pastures, nomadic groups often came into conflict with other nomadic groups pursuing the same resources, which the two

CHAPTER LOCATOR | **What aspects of nomadic life gave nomads of Central Asia advantages over settled civilizations?** | How did Chinggis Khan conquer Eurasia, and how did Mongol conquests change the region?

330 CHAPTER 12 CULTURAL EXCHANGE IN CENTRAL AND SOUTHERN ASIA

ca. 320–480 Gupta Empire in India	**1030** Turks control north India
ca. 380–450 Life of India's greatest poet, Kalidasa	**ca. 1100–1200** Buddhism declines in India
ca. 450 Huns invade northern India	**ca. 1200–1300** Easter Island society's most prosperous period
ca. 500 Srivijaya gains control of Strait of Malacca	**1206** Temujin proclaimed Chinggis Khan; Mongol language recorded; Delhi sultanate established
ca. 500–1400 India's medieval age; caste system reaches its mature form	**ca. 1240** *The Secret History of the Mongols*
552 Turks rebel against Rouruan and rise to power in Central Asia	**1276** Mongol conquest of Song China
ca. 780 Borobudur temple complex begun in Srivijaya	**ca. 1300** Plague begins to spread throughout Mongol Empire
802–1432 Khmer Empire of Cambodia	**1398** Timur takes control of the Delhi sultanate
ca. 850–1250 Kingdom of the Uighurs	

would then fight over. Groups on the losing end, especially if they were small, faced the threat of extermination or slavery, which prompted them to make alliances with other groups or move far away. Groups on the winning end of inter-tribal conflicts could exact tribute from those they defeated.

To get the products of nearby agricultural societies, especially grain, woven textiles, iron, tea, and wood, nomadic herders would trade their own products, such as horses and furs. When trade was difficult, they would turn to raiding to seize what they needed. Much of the time nomadic herders raided other nomads, but nearby agricultural settlements were common targets as well. The nomads' skill as horsemen and archers made it difficult for farmers and townsmen to defend against them.

Political organization among nomadic herders was generally very simple. Clans—members of an extended family—had chiefs, as did tribes (coalitions of clans). Leadership within a group was based on military prowess and was often settled by fighting. Occasionally a charismatic leader would emerge who was able to extend alliances to form confederations of tribes. Large confederations rarely lasted more than a century or so, however, and when they broke up, tribes again spent much of their time fighting with each other.

The three most wide-ranging and successful confederations were those of the Xiongnu—Huns, as they were known in the West—who emerged in the third century B.C.E. in the area near China; the Turks, who had their origins in the same area in the fourth and fifth centuries C.E.; and the Mongols, who did not become

How did the Mongol conquests facilitate the spread of religions, inventions, and diseases?	What was the result of India's encounters with Turks, Mongols, and Islam?	How did states develop along the maritime trade routes of Southeast Asia and beyond?	✓ LearningCurve Check what you know.

important until the late twelfth century. In all three cases, the entire steppe region was eventually swept up in the movement of peoples and armies.

The Turks

In 552 a group called Turks who specialized in metalworking overthrew their overlords, the Rouruan, whose empire dominated the region from the eastern Silk Road cities of Central Asia through Mongolia. When the first Turkish khagan (ruler) died a few years later, the Turkish empire was divided between his younger brother, who took the western part (modern Central Asia), and his son, who took the eastern part (modern Mongolia). In 576 the Western Turks captured the Byzantine city of Bosporus in the Crimea.

The Eastern Turks frequently raided China and just as often fought among themselves. In the early seventh century the empire of the Eastern Turks ran up against the growing military might of the Tang Dynasty in China and soon broke apart.

In the eighth century a Turkic people called the Uighurs (Wee-gurs) formed a new empire based in Mongolia that survived about a century. It had close ties to Tang China, providing military aid but also extracting large payments in silk. During this period many Uighurs adopted religions then current along the Silk Road, notably Buddhism, Nestorian Christianity, and Manichaeism. In the ninth century this Uighur empire was destroyed by another Turkic people from north of Mongolia called the Kyrghiz. Some Uighurs fled to what is now western China. Setting up their capital city in Kucha, the Uighurs created a remarkably stable and prosperous kingdom that lasted four centuries (ca. 850–1250).

Manichean Priests

Many religions spread through Central Asia before it became predominantly Muslim after 1300. This fragment of a tenth- to twelfth-century illustrated document, found at the Silk Road city of Turfan, is written in the Uighur language and depicts Manichean priests. (Archives Charmet/The Bridgeman Art Library)

Farther west in Central Asia other groups of Turks rose to prominence. Often local Muslim forces would try to capture them, employ them as slave soldiers, and convert them. By the mid- to late tenth century many were serving in the armies of the Abbasid caliphate. Also in the tenth century Central Asian Turks began converting to Islam (which protected them from being abducted as slaves). Then they took to raiding unconverted Turks.

In the mid-eleventh century Turks had gained the upper hand in the caliphate, and the caliphs became little more than figureheads. From there Turkish power was extended into Syria, Palestine, and Asia Minor. In 1071 Seljuk Turks inflicted a devastating defeat on the Byzantine army in eastern Anatolia (see page 245). Other Turkish confederations established themselves in Afghanistan and extended their control into north India (see page 347).

In India, Persia, and Anatolia the formidable military skills of nomadic Turkish warriors made it possible for them to become overlords of settled societies. Just as the Uighurs developed a hybrid urban culture along the eastern end of the Silk Road, the Turks of Central and West Asia created an Islamic culture that drew from both Turkish and Iranian sources. Often Persian was used as the

CHAPTER LOCATOR | **What aspects of nomadic life gave nomads of Central Asia advantages over settled civilizations?** | How did Chinggis Khan conquer Eurasia, and how did Mongol conquests change the region?

administrative language of the states they formed. Nevertheless, despite the presence of Turkish overlords all along the southern fringe of the steppe, no one group of Turks was able to unite them all into a single political unit. That feat had to wait for the next major power on the steppe, the Mongols.

The Mongols

In the twelfth century ambitious Mongols did not aspire to match the Turks or other groups that had migrated west, but rather wanted to be successors to the Khitans and Jurchens, nomadic groups that had stayed in the east and mastered ways to extract resources from China. The Khitans and Jurchens had formed hybrid nomadic-urban states, with northern sections where tribesmen continued to live in the traditional way and southern sections politically controlled by the non-Chinese rulers but settled largely by taxpaying Chinese. The Khitans and Jurchens had scripts created to record their languages and adopted many Chinese governing practices. They built cities in pastoral areas that served as trading centers and places to enjoy their newly acquired wealth. In both the Khitan and Jurchen cases, their elite became culturally dual, adept in Chinese ways as well as in their own traditions.

The Mongols lived north of these hybrid nomadic-settled societies and maintained their traditional ways. They lived in tents called **yurts** rather than in houses. The yurts, about twelve to fifteen feet in diameter, were constructed of light wooden frames covered by layers of wool felt, greased to make them waterproof. The floor of a yurt was covered first with dried grass or straw, then with felt, skins, or rugs. In the center, directly under the smoke hole, was the hearth. A group of families traveling together would set up their yurts in a circle open to the south and draw up their wagons in a circle around the yurts for protection.

The Mongol diet consisted mostly of animal products. The most common meat was mutton, supplemented with wild game. When grain or vegetables could be obtained through trade, they were added to the diet. The Mongols milked sheep, goats, cows, and horses and made cheese and fermented alcoholic drinks from the milk. Wood was scarce, so dried animal dung or grasses fueled the cook fires.

Mongol women had to work very hard and had to be able to care for the animals when the men were away hunting or fighting. They normally drove the carts and set up and dismantled the yurts. They also milked the sheep, goats, and cows and made the butter and cheese. Women, like men, had to be expert riders, and many also learned to shoot. They participated actively in family decisions, especially as wives and mothers. In *The Secret History of the Mongols*, a work written in Mongolian in about 1240, the mother and wife of the Mongol leader Chinggis Khan frequently make impassioned speeches on the importance of family loyalty.

Mongol men kept as busy as the women. They made the carts and wagons and the frames for the yurts. They also made harnesses for the horses and oxen, leather saddles, and the equipment needed for hunting and war, such as bows and arrows. Men also had charge of the horses, and they milked the mares. One specialist among the nomads was the blacksmith, who made stirrups, knives, and other metal tools.

Kinship underlay most social relationships among the Mongols. Normally each family occupied a yurt, and groups of families camping together were usually

yurts
▶ Tents in which the pastoral nomads lived; they could be quickly dismantled and loaded onto animals or carts.

How did the Mongol conquests facilitate the spread of religions, inventions, and diseases?

What was the result of India's encounters with Turks, Mongols, and Islam?

How did states develop along the maritime trade routes of Southeast Asia and beyond?

☑ LearningCurve
Check what you know.

333

related along the male line. More distant patrilineal relatives were recognized as members of the same clan and could call on each other for aid. People from the same clan could not marry each other, so men had to get wives from other clans. When a woman's husband died, she would be inherited by another male in the family. Tribes were groups of clans, often distantly related. Both clans and tribes had chiefs who would make decisions on where to graze and when to retaliate against another tribe that had stolen animals or people. Women were sometimes abducted for brides. When tribes stole men from each other, they normally made them into slaves, and slaves were forced to do much of the heavy work.

Even though population was sparse in the regions where the Mongols lived, conflict over resources was endemic, and each camp had to be on the alert for attacks. Defending against attacks and retaliating against raids was as much a part of the Mongols' daily life as caring for their herds and trading with nearby settlements.

Mongol children learned to ride at a young age. The prime weapon boys had to learn to use was the compound bow, which had a pull of about 160 pounds and a range of more than 200 yards; it was well suited for using on horseback, giving Mongol soldiers an advantage in battle. Other commonly used weapons were small battle-axes and lances fitted with hooks to pull enemies off their saddles.

Hunting was a common form of military training among the Mongols. Each year tribes would organize one big hunt; mounted hunters would form a vast ring perhaps ten or more miles in circumference, then gradually shrink it down, trapping all the animals before killing them.

As with the Turks and other steppe nomads, religious practices centered around the shaman, a religious expert believed to be able to communicate with the gods. The high god of the Mongols was Heaven/Sky, but they recognized many other gods as well. Some groups of Mongols, especially those closer to settled communities, converted to Buddhism, Nestorian Christianity, or Manichaeism.

> QUICK REVIEW

What were the most important similarities and differences between the Mongols and the Turks?

CHAPTER LOCATOR | What aspects of nomadic life gave nomads of Central Asia advantages over settled civilizations? | How did Chinggis Khan conquer Eurasia, and how did Mongol conquests change the region?

CHAPTER 12
334 CULTURAL EXCHANGE IN CENTRAL AND SOUTHERN ASIA

How did Chinggis Khan and his successors conquer much of Eurasia, and how did the Mongol conquests change the regions affected?

IN THE MID-TWELFTH CENTURY the Mongols were just one of many peoples in the eastern grasslands, neither particularly numerous nor especially advanced. Why then did the Mongols suddenly emerge as an overpowering force on the historical stage? One explanation is ecological. A drop in the mean annual temperature created a subsistence crisis. As pastures shrank, the Mongols and other nomads had to look beyond the steppe to get more of their food from the agricultural world. A second reason for their sudden rise was the appearance of a single individual, the brilliant but utterly ruthless Temujin (ca. 1162–1227), later and more commonly called Chinggis Khan (sometimes spelled Genghis or Ghengis).

Chinggis Khan

In Temujin's youth, his father had built a modest tribal following. When Temujin's father was poisoned by a rival, his followers drifted away, leaving Temujin and his mother and brothers in a vulnerable position. Temujin slowly collected followers. In 1182 Temujin was captured and carried in a cage to a rival's camp. After a daring escape, he led his followers to join a stronger chieftain whom his father had

How did the Mongol conquests facilitate the spread of religions, inventions, and diseases?

What was the result of India's encounters with Turks, Mongols, and Islam?

How did states develop along the maritime trade routes of Southeast Asia and beyond?

✓ LearningCurve
Check what you know.

once aided. With the chieftain's help, Temujin began avenging the insults he had received.

Temujin proved to be a natural leader, and as he subdued other nomadic tribes, he built up an army of loyal followers. He mastered the art of winning allies through displays of personal courage in battle and generosity to his followers. To those who opposed him, he could be merciless. He once asserted that nothing gave more pleasure than massacring one's enemies, seizing their horses and cattle, and ravishing their women.

In 1206, at a great gathering of tribal leaders, Temujin was proclaimed **Chinggis Khan**, or Great Ruler. Chinggis decreed that Mongol, until then an unwritten language, be written down in the script used by the Uighur Turks. With this script a record was made of the Mongol laws and customs. Another measure adopted at this assembly was a postal relay system to send messages rapidly by mounted courier, suggesting that Chinggis already had ambitions to rule a vast empire.

With the tribes of Mongolia united, the energies previously devoted to infighting and vendettas were redirected to exacting tribute from the settled populations nearby, starting with the Jurchen (Jin) state that extended into north China. Because of his early experiences with intertribal feuding, Chinggis mistrusted traditional tribal loyalties, and as he fashioned a new army, he gave it a new, nontribal structure. He conscripted soldiers from all the tribes and assigned them to units that were composed of members from different tribes. He selected commanders for each unit whom he could remove at will, although he allowed commanders to pass their posts on to their sons.

After Chinggis subjugated a city, he would send envoys to cities farther out to demand submission and threaten destruction. Those who opened their city gates and submitted without fighting could join the Mongols, but those who resisted faced the prospect of mass slaughter. Not surprisingly many governors of cities and rulers of small states hastened to offer submission.

Chinggis preferred conquest to administration and did not stay in north China to set up an administrative structure. He left that to subordinates and turned his attention westward, to Central Asia and Persia, then dominated by different groups of Turks. In 1218 Chinggis proposed to the Khwarizm shah of Persia that he accept Mongol overlordship and establish trade relations. The shah ordered the envoy and the merchants who had accompanied him killed. The next year Chinggis led an army of one hundred thousand soldiers west to retaliate. Mongol forces destroyed the shah's army and sacked one Persian city after another.

After returning from Central Asia, Chinggis died in 1227 during the siege of a city in northwest China. Before he died, he instructed his sons not to fall out among themselves but instead to divide the spoils.

Chinggis's Successors

Although Mongol leaders traditionally had had to win their positions, after Chinggis died the empire was divided into four states called **khanates**, with one of the lines of his descendants taking charge of each (Map 12.1). Chinggis's third son, Ögödei, assumed the title of khan, and he directed the next round of invasions.

In 1237 representatives of all four lines led 150,000 Mongol, Turkish, and Persian troops into Europe. During the next five years, they gained control of Moscow

---

Chinggis Khan

▶ The title given to the Mongol ruler Temujin in 1206 and later to his successors; it means Great Ruler.

khanates

▶ The states ruled by a khan; the four units into which Chinggis divided the Mongol Empire.

CHAPTER LOCATOR | What aspects of nomadic life gave nomads of Central Asia advantages over settled civilizations? | How did Chinggis Khan conquer Eurasia, and how did Mongol conquests change the region?

CHAPTER 12
336 CULTURAL EXCHANGE IN CENTRAL AND SOUTHERN ASIA

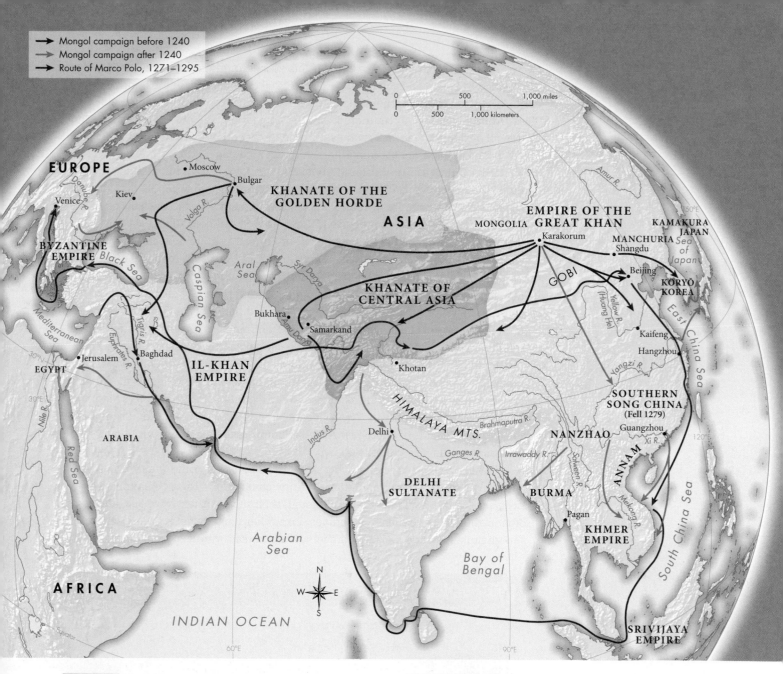

Legend (top left):
- → Mongol campaign before 1240
- → Mongol campaign after 1240
- → Route of Marco Polo, 1271–1295

Map labels:

EUROPE · Moscow · Bulgar · Kiev · Venice · Danube R. · Volga R.

KHANATE OF THE GOLDEN HORDE

ASIA · MONGOLIA · EMPIRE OF THE GREAT KHAN · Karakorum · KAMAKURA JAPAN · MANCHURIA · Shangdu · Amur R. · Sea of Japan

BYZANTINE EMPIRE · Black Sea · Aral Sea · Syr Darya · KHANATE OF CENTRAL ASIA · GOBI · Beijing · KORYŎ KOREA

Mediterranean Sea · Caspian Sea · Bukhara · Samarkand · Amu Darya · Yellow R. (Huang He) · Kaifeng · East China Sea

Tigris R. · Euphrates R. · Baghdad · IL-KHAN EMPIRE · Khotan · Hangzhou

Jerusalem · EGYPT · ARABIA · Nile R. · Red Sea · Indus R. · Delhi · HIMALAYA MTS. · Brahmaputra R. · Ganges R. · Irrawaddy R. · Salween R. · NANZHAO · Guangzhou · Xi R. · SOUTHERN SONG CHINA (Fell 1279) · Yangzi R. · ANNAM · South China Sea

AFRICA · Arabian Sea · DELHI SULTANATE · BURMA · Pagan · Mekong R. · KHMER EMPIRE · Bay of Bengal

INDIAN OCEAN · Equator · SRIVIJAYA EMPIRE

Scale: 0 – 500 – 1,000 miles / 0 – 500 – 1,000 kilometers

MAP 12.1 ■ The Mongol Empire

The creation of the vast Mongol Empire facilitated communication across Eurasia and led to both the spread of deadly plagues and the transfer of technical and scientific knowledge. After the death of Chinggis Khan in 1227, the empire was divided into four khanates ruled by different lines of his successors. In the 1270s the Mongols conquered southern China, but most of their subsequent campaigns did not lead to further territorial gains.

> MAPPING THE PAST

ANALYZING THE MAP: Trace the campaigns of the Mongols. Which ones led to acquisition of territory, and which ones did not?

CONNECTIONS: Would the division of the Mongol Empire into separate khanates have made these areas easier for the Mongols to rule? What drawbacks might it have had from the Mongols' point of view?

---

and Kievan Russia and looted cities in Poland and Hungary. They were poised to attack deeper into Europe when they learned of the death of Ögödei in 1241. To participate in the election of a new khan, the army returned to the Mongols' new capital city, Karakorum.

| How did the Mongol conquests facilitate the spread of religions, inventions, and diseases? | What was the result of India's encounters with Turks, Mongols, and Islam? | How did states develop along the maritime trade routes of Southeast Asia and beyond? | ✓ LearningCurve Check what you know. |

Once Ögödei's son was certified as his successor, the Mongols turned their attention to Persia and the Middle East. In 1256 a Mongol army took northwest Iran, then pushed on to the Abbasid capital of Baghdad. When it fell in 1258, the last Abbasid caliph was murdered, and the population was put to the sword. The Mongol onslaught was successfully resisted, however, by both the Delhi sultanate (see page 347) and the Mamluk rulers in Egypt (see page 246).

Under Chinggis's grandson Khubilai Khan (r. 1260–1294), the Mongols completed their conquest of China. Proceeding deliberately, the Mongols first surrounded the Song empire in central and south China (discussed in Chapter 13) by taking its westernmost province in 1252, as well as Korea to its east in 1258; destroying the Nanzhao kingdom in modern Yunnan in 1254; and then continuing south and taking Annam (northern Vietnam) in 1257. As their invasion moved forward, the Mongols used a variety of forms of battle, employing experts in naval and siege warfare from all over their empire. During their advance toward the Chinese capital of Hangzhou, the Mongols ordered the total slaughter of the people of the major city of Changzhou, and in 1276 the Chinese empress dowager surrendered in hopes of sparing the people of the capital a similar fate.

Having overrun China and Korea, Khubilai turned his eyes toward Japan, launching invasions in 1274 and 1281. On both occasions the Mongols managed to land but were beaten back by Japanese samurai armies. Each time fierce storms destroyed the Mongol fleets. Twelve years later, in 1293, Khubilai tried sending a fleet to the islands of Southeast Asia, including Java, but it met with no more success than the fleets sent to Japan.

Why were the Mongols so successful against so many different types of enemies? Even though their population was tiny compared to the populations of the large agricultural societies they conquered, their tactics, their weapons, and their organization all gave them advantages. Like other nomads before them, they were superb horsemen and excellent archers. Their horses were extremely nimble, able

MONGOL CONQUESTS

1206	Temujin made Chinggis Khan
1215	Fall of Beijing (Jurchens)
1219–1220	Fall of Bukhara and Samarkand in Central Asia
1227	Death of Chinggis
1237–1241	Raids into eastern Europe
1257	Conquest of Annam (northern Vietnam)
1258	Conquest of Abbasid capital of Baghdad; conquest of Korea
1260	Khubilai succeeds to khanship
1274	First attempt at invading Japan
1276	Surrender of Song Dynasty (China)
1281	Second attempt at invading Japan
1293	Mongol fleet unsuccessful in invasion of Java
mid-14th century	Decline of Mongol power

CHAPTER LOCATOR | What aspects of nomadic life gave nomads of Central Asia advantages over settled civilizations? | **How did Chinggis Khan conquer Eurasia, and how did Mongol conquests change the region?**

338 CHAPTER 12 CULTURAL EXCHANGE IN CENTRAL AND SOUTHERN ASIA

to change direction quickly, thus allowing the Mongols to maneuver easily and ride through infantry forces armed with swords, lances, and javelins.

The Mongols were also open to trying new military technologies. To attack walled cities, they learned how to use catapults and other engines of war. At first they employed Chinese catapults, but when they learned that those used by the Turks in Afghanistan were more powerful, they adopted the better model. The Mongols also used exploding arrows and gunpowder projectiles developed by the Chinese.

The Mongols made good use of intelligence and tried to exploit internal divisions in the countries they attacked. Thus in north China they appealed to the Khitans, who had been defeated by the Jurchens a century earlier, to join them in attacking the Jurchens. In Syria they exploited the resentment of Christians against their Muslim rulers.

> **Three Generations of Mongol Conquerors:**

- Chinggis Khan: Led the first round of Mongol conquests
- Ögödei Khan: (Son of Chinggis Khan) Oversaw the westward expansion of the Mongol Empire
- Khubilai Khan: (Grandson of Chinggis Khan) Completed the Mongol conquest of China

The Mongols as Rulers

The success of the Mongols in ruling vast territories was due in large part to their willingness to incorporate other ethnic groups into their armies and governments. Whatever their original country or religion, those who served the Mongols loyally were rewarded.

Since, in Mongol eyes, the purpose of fighting was to gain riches, the Mongols would regularly loot the settlements they conquered, taking whatever they wanted, including the residents. Land would be granted to military commanders, nobles, and army units to be governed and exploited as the recipients wished. Those working the land would be given to them as serfs. The Mongols built a capital city called Karakorum in modern Mongolia, and to bring it up to the level of the cities they conquered, they transported skilled workers from those cities.

The traditional nomad disdain for farmers led some commanders to suggest turning north China into a gigantic pasture after it was conquered. In time, though, the Mongols came to realize that simply appropriating the wealth and human resources of the settled lands was not as good as extracting regular revenue from them. The Mongols gave Chinese methods of taxation a try, but soon political rivals convinced the khan that he would gain even more by letting Central Asian Muslim merchants bid against each other for licenses to collect taxes any way they could, a system called **tax-farming**. Ordinary Chinese found this method of tax collecting much more oppressive than traditional Chinese methods, since there was little to keep the tax collectors from seizing everything they could.

By the second half of the thirteenth century there was no longer a genuine pan-Asian Mongol Empire. Much of Asia was in the hands of Mongol successor states, but these were generally hostile to each other. Khubilai was often at war

tax-farming
▶ Assigning the collection of taxes to whomever bids the most for the privilege.

How did the Mongol conquests facilitate the spread of religions, inventions, and diseases? | What was the result of India's encounters with Turks, Mongols, and Islam? | How did states develop along the maritime trade routes of Southeast Asia and beyond? | ✓ LearningCurve Check what you know.

339

with the khanate of Central Asia, then held by his cousin Khaidu, and he had little contact with the khanate of the Golden Horde in south Russia. The Mongols adapted their methods of government to the existing traditions of each place they ruled, and the regions went their separate ways.

In China the Mongols resisted assimilation and purposely avoided many Chinese practices. The rulers conducted their business in the Mongol language and spent their summers in Mongolia. Khubilai discouraged Mongols from marrying Chinese and took only Mongol women into the palace. Chinese were treated as legally inferior not only to the Mongols but also to all other non-Chinese.

In Central Asia, Persia, and Russia the Mongols tended to merge with the Turkish groups already there and, like them, converted to Islam. Russia in the thirteenth century was not a strongly centralized state, and the Mongols allowed Russian princes and lords to continue to rule their territories as long as they turned over adequate tribute. The city of Moscow became the center of Mongol tribute collection and grew in importance. In the Middle East the Mongol Il-khans (as they were known in Persia) were more active as rulers, again continuing the traditions of the caliphate. In Mongolia itself, however, Mongol traditions were maintained.

In the mid-fourteenth century the Mongol dynasty in China deteriorated into civil war, and in the 1360s the Mongols withdrew back to Mongolia. There was a similar loss of Mongol power in Persia and Central Asia. Only on the south Russian steppe did the Golden Horde maintain its hold for another century.

As Mongol rule in Central Asia declined, a new conqueror emerged, Timur, also known as Tamerlane (Timur the Lame). Not a nomad but a highly civilized Turkish noble, Timur in the 1360s struck out from his base in Samarkand into Persia, north India (see page 347), southern Russia, and beyond. His armies used the terror tactics that the Mongols had perfected, massacring the citizens of cities that resisted. In the decades after his death in 1405, however, Timur's empire went into decline.

> QUICK REVIEW

What were the defining characteristics of Mongol government?

CHAPTER LOCATOR | What aspects of nomadic life gave nomads of Central Asia advantages over settled civilizations? | How did Chinggis Khan conquer Eurasia, and how did Mongol conquests change the region?

Planting Trees

The illustrations in early copies of Marco Polo's book show the elements that Europeans found most interesting. This page illustrates Khubilai's order that trees be planted along the main roads. (Illumination from *Le Livre des Merveilles du Monde* [Travels of Marco Polo], by the Paris studio of the Boucicaut Master, c. 1412/Bibliothèque Nationale, Paris/akg-images)

How did the Mongol conquests facilitate the spread of ideas, religions, inventions, and diseases?

THE MONGOL GOVERNMENTS DID MORE than any earlier political entities to encourage the movement of people and goods across Eurasia. With these vast movements came cultural accommodation as the peoples of Eurasia learned from one another. This cultural exchange involved both physical goods and the sharing of ideas, including the introduction of new religious beliefs and the adoption of new ways to organize and rule the Mongol Empire. It also facilitated the spread of the plague and the unwilling movement of enslaved captives.

The Movement of Peoples

The Mongols had never looked down on merchants the way the elites of many traditional states did, and they welcomed the arrival of merchants from distant lands. Even when different groups of Mongols were fighting among themselves, they usually allowed caravans to pass without harassing them.

The Mongol practice of transporting skilled people from the lands they conquered also brought people into contact with each other in new ways. Besides

| How did the Mongol conquests facilitate the spread of religions, inventions, and diseases? | What was the result of India's encounters with Turks, Mongols, and Islam? | How did states develop along the maritime trade routes of Southeast Asia and beyond? |  LearningCurve Check what you know. |

341

those forced to move, the Mongols recruited administrators from all over. Especially prominent were the Uighur Turks of Chinese Central Asia, whose familiarity with Chinese civilization and fluency in Turkish were extremely valuable in facilitating communication.

One of those who served the Mongols was Rashid al-Din (ca. 1247–1318). A Jew from Persia and the son of an apothecary, Rashid al-Din converted to Islam at the age of thirty and entered the service of the Mongol Il-khan of Persia as a physician. He rose in government service, traveled widely, and eventually became prime minister. Aware of the great differences between cultures, he believed that the Mongols should try to rule in accord with the moral principles of the majority in each land. On that basis he convinced the Mongol khan of Persia to convert to Islam. Rashid al-Din undertook to explain the great variety of cultures by writing a world history more comprehensive than any previously written.

More Europeans made their way as far as Mongolia and China in the Mongol period than ever before. Popes and kings sent envoys to the Mongol court in the hope of enlisting the Mongols on their side in their long-standing conflict with Muslim forces over the Holy Land. European visitors were also interested in finding Christians who had been cut off from the West by the spread of Islam, and in fact there were considerable numbers of Nestorian Christians in Central Asia.

The most famous European visitor to the Mongol lands was the Venetian Marco Polo (ca. 1254–1324). In his *Travels*, Marco Polo described all the places he visited or learned about during his seventeen years away from home. He reported being warmly received by Khubilai, who impressed him enormously. He was also awed by the wealth and splendor of Chinese cities and spread the notion of Asia as a land of riches.

The Spread of Disease, Goods, and Ideas

The rapid transfer of people and goods across Central Asia spread more than ideas and inventions. It also spread diseases, the most deadly of which was the plague known in Europe as the Black Death, which scholars identify today as the bubonic plague. In the early fourteenth century, transmitted by rats and fleas, the plague began to spread from Central Asia into West Asia, the Mediterranean, and western Europe. The confusion of the mid-fourteenth century that led to the loss of Mongol power in China, Iran, and Central Asia undoubtedly owes something to the effect of the spread of the plague and other diseases. (For more on the Black Death, see Chapter 14.)

Traditionally, the historians of each of the countries conquered by the Mongols portrayed them as a scourge. Among contemporary Western historians, it is now more common to celebrate the genius of the Mongol military machine and treat the spread of ideas and inventions as an obvious good. There is no reason to assume, however, that people benefited equally from the improved communications and the new political institutions of the Mongol era. Merchants involved in long-distance trade prospered, but those enslaved and transported hundreds or thousands of miles from home would have seen themselves not as the beneficiaries of opportunities to encounter new cultures but rather as the most pitiable of victims. Moreover, the places that were ruled by Mongol governments for a cen-

CHAPTER LOCATOR | What aspects of nomadic life gave nomads of Central Asia advantages over settled civilizations? | How did Chinggis Khan conquer Eurasia, and how did Mongol conquests change the region?

CHAPTER 12
342 CULTURAL EXCHANGE IN CENTRAL AND SOUTHERN ASIA

tury or more—China, Central Asia, Persia, and Russia—do not seem to have advanced at a more rapid rate during that century than they did in earlier centuries, either economically or culturally.

In terms of the spread of technological and scientific ideas, Europe seems to have been by far the main beneficiary of increased communication, largely because in 1200 it lagged farther behind than the other areas. Chinese inventions such as printing, gunpowder, and the compass spread westward. Persian and Indian expertise in astronomy and mathematics also spread. In terms of the spread of religions, Islam probably gained the most. It came to dominate in Chinese Central Asia, which had previously been Buddhist.

QUICK REVIEW

How did the Mongol conquests contribute to the movement of people across Eurasia?

| How did the Mongol conquests facilitate the spread of religions, inventions, and diseases? | What was the result of India's encounters with Turks, Mongols, and Islam? | How did states develop along the maritime trade routes of Southeast Asia and beyond? | ✅ LearningCurve Check what you know. |

What was the result of India's encounters with Turks, Mongols, and Islam?

Kandariyâ Mahâdeva Hindu Temple

Built around 1050 by a local king in central India, this is one of the best-preserved Hindu temples from the medieval period. The main spire rises 100 feet, and the sides are decorated with more than six hundred stone statues. (Yvan Travert/akg-images)

AFTER THE MAURYAN EMPIRE BROKE APART in 185 B.C.E. (see page 80), India was politically divided into small kingdoms for several centuries. Only the Guptas in the fourth century would emerge to unite much of north India, though their rule was cut short by the invasion of the Huns in about 450. A few centuries later, India was profoundly shaped by Turkish nomads from Central Asia who brought their culture and, most important, Islam to India. Despite these events, the lives of most Indians remained unchanged, with the majority of the people living in villages in a society defined by caste.

The Gupta Empire, ca. 320–480

In the early fourth century a state emerged in the Ganges plain that was able to bring large parts of north India under its control. The rulers of this Indian empire, the Guptas, consciously modeled their rule after that of the Mauryan Empire, and the founder took the name of the founder of that dynasty, Chandragupta. The

CHAPTER LOCATOR | What aspects of nomadic life gave nomads of Central Asia advantages over settled civilizations? | How did Chinggis Khan conquer Eurasia, and how did Mongol conquests change the region?

Guptas united north India and received tribute from states in Nepal and the Indus Valley, thus giving large parts of India a period of peace and political unity.

The Guptas' administrative system was not as centralized as that of the Mauryans. In the central regions they drew their revenue from a tax on agriculture and maintained monopolies on key products such as metals and salt (reminiscent of Chinese practice). They also exacted labor service for the construction and upkeep of roads, wells, and irrigation systems. More distant areas were assigned to governors who were allowed considerable leeway, and governorships often became hereditary. Areas still farther away were encouraged to become vassal states.

The Gupta kings were patrons of the arts. Poets composed epics for the courts of the Gupta kings, and other writers experimented with prose romances and popular tales. India's greatest poet, Kalidasa (ca. 380–450), like Shakespeare, wrote poems as well as plays in verse.

In mathematics, too, the Gupta period could boast of impressive intellectual achievements. The so-called Arabic numerals are actually of Indian origin. Indian mathematicians developed the place-value notation system, with separate columns for ones, tens, and hundreds, as well as a zero sign to indicate the absence of units in a given column. This system greatly facilitated calculation and had spread as far as Europe by the seventh century.

The Gupta rulers were Hindus, but they tolerated all faiths. Buddhist pilgrims from other areas of Asia reported that Buddhist monasteries with hundreds or even thousands of monks and nuns flourished in the cities. The success of Buddhism did not hinder Hinduism with its many gods, which remained popular among ordinary people.

The great crisis of the Gupta Empire was the invasion of the Huns in about 450. Mustering his full might, the Gupta ruler Skandagupta (r. ca. 455–467) threw back the invaders, but they had dealt the dynasty a fatal blow.

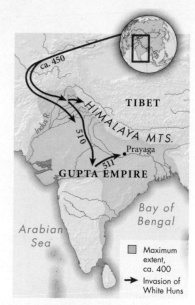

The Gupta Empire, ca. 320–480

India's Medieval Age and the First Encounter with Islam

After the decline of the Gupta Empire, India once again broke into separate kingdoms that were frequently at war with each other. Most of the dynasties of India's medieval age (ca. 500–1400) were short-lived, but a balance of power was maintained between the major regions of India, with none gaining enough of an advantage to conquer the others (Map 12.2).

Political division fostered the development of regional cultures. Literature came to be written in India's regional languages, among them Marathi, Bengali, and Assamese. Commerce continued as before, and the coasts of India remained important in the sea trade of the Indian Ocean.

The first encounters with Islam occurred in this period. In 711 the Umayyad governor of Iraq seized the Sind area in western India (modern Pakistan). The western part of India remained part of the caliphate for centuries, but Islam did not spread much beyond this foothold. During the ninth and tenth centuries Turks from Central Asia moved into the region of today's northeastern Iran and western Afghanistan, then known as Khurasan. Converts to Islam, they first served as military forces for the caliphate in Baghdad, but as its authority weakened

How did the Mongol conquests facilitate the spread of religions, inventions, and diseases?

What was the result of India's encounters with Turks, Mongols, and Islam?

How did states develop along the maritime trade routes of Southeast Asia and beyond?

☑ LearningCurve
Check what you know.

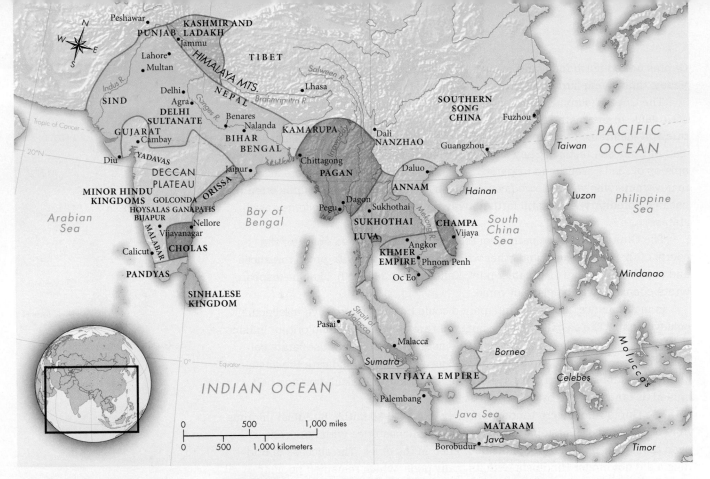

MAP 12.2 ■ **South and Southeast Asia in the Thirteenth Century**
The extensive coastlines of South and Southeast Asia and the predictable monsoon winds aided seafaring in this region. Note the Strait of Malacca, through which most east-west sea trade passed.

(see pages 336–339), they made themselves rulers of an effectively independent Khurasan and frequently sent raiding parties into north India. Beginning in 997 Mahmud of Ghazni (r. 997–1030) led seventeen annual forays into India from his base in modern Afghanistan. Eventually the Arab conquerors of the Sind fell to the Turks. By 1030 the Indus Valley, the Punjab, and the rest of northwest India were in the grip of the Turks.

The new rulers encouraged the spread of Islam, but the caste system (see page 69) made it difficult to convert higher-caste Indians. After an initial period of raids and destruction of temples, the Muslim Turks came to an accommodation with the Hindus, who were classed as a **protected people**, like the Christians and Jews, and allowed to follow their religion. They had to pay a special tax but did not have to perform military service. Local chiefs and rajas were often allowed to remain in control of their domains as long as they paid tribute. Most Indians looked on the Muslim conquerors as a new ruling caste, capable of governing and taxing them but otherwise peripheral to their lives. The myriad castes largely governed themselves, isolating the newcomers.

Nevertheless, over the course of several centuries Islam gained a strong hold on north India, especially in the Indus Valley (modern Pakistan) and in Bengal at the mouth of the Ganges River (modern Bangladesh). Moreover, the sultanate

protected people

▶ The Muslim classification used for Hindus, Christians, and Jews; they were allowed to follow their religions but had to pay a special tax.

CHAPTER LOCATOR | What aspects of nomadic life gave nomads of Central Asia advantages over settled civilizations? | How did Chinggis Khan conquer Eurasia, and how did Mongol conquests change the region?

seems to have had a positive effect on the economy. Much of the wealth confiscated from temples was put to more productive use, and India's first truly large cities emerged. The Turks also were eager to employ skilled workers, giving new opportunities to low-caste manual and artisan labor.

The Muslim rulers were much more hostile to Buddhism than to Hinduism, seeing Buddhism as a competitive proselytizing religion. In 1193 a Turkish raiding party destroyed the great Buddhist university at Nalanda in Bihar. Buddhist monks were killed or forced to flee to Buddhist centers in Southeast Asia, Nepal, and Tibet. Buddhism, which had thrived for so long in peaceful and friendly competition with Hinduism, subsequently went into decline in its native land.

Hinduism, however, remained as strong as ever. South India was largely unaffected by these invasions, and traditional Hindu culture flourished there under native kings ruling small kingdoms. (See "Individuals in Society: Bhaskara the Teacher," page 348.) Devotional cults and mystical movements flourished. This was a great age of religious art and architecture in India. Extraordinary temples covered with elaborate bas-relief were built in many areas.

The Delhi Sultanate

In the twelfth century a new line of Turkish rulers arose in Afghanistan, led by Muhammad of Ghur (d. 1206). Muhammad captured Delhi and extended his control nearly throughout north India. When he fell to an assassin in 1206, one of his generals, the former slave Qutb-ud-din, seized the reins of power and established a government at Delhi, separate from the government in Afghanistan. This sultanate of Delhi lasted for three centuries, even though dynasties changed several times.

A major accomplishment of the Delhi sultanate was holding off the Mongols. Chinggis Khan and his troops entered the Indus Valley in 1221 in pursuit of the shah of Khurasan. The sultan wisely kept out of the way, and when Chinggis Khan left some troops in the area, the sultan made no attempt to challenge them. Two generations later, in 1299, a Mongol khan launched a campaign into India with two hundred thousand men, but the sultan of the time was able to defeat them. Two years later the Mongols returned and camped at Delhi for two months, but they eventually left without taking the sultan's fort. Another Mongol raid in 1306–1307 also was successfully repulsed.

During the fourteenth century, however, the Delhi sultanate was in decline and proved unable to ward off the armies of Timur (see page 339), who took Delhi in 1398. Timur's invasion left a weakened sultanate. The Delhi sultanate endured under different rulers until 1526, when it was conquered by the Mughals, a Muslim dynasty that would rule over most of northern Indian from the sixteenth into the nineteenth century.

Life in Medieval India

Local institutions played a much larger role in the lives of people in medieval India than did the state. Craft guilds oversaw conditions of work and trade, local councils handled law and order at the town or village level, and local castes gave members a sense of belonging and identity.

How did the Mongol conquests facilitate the spread of religions, inventions, and diseases?

What was the result of India's encounters with Turks, Mongols, and Islam?

How did states develop along the maritime trade routes of Southeast Asia and beyond?

☑ LearningCurve
Check what you know.

In India, as in many other societies, astronomy and mathematics were closely linked, and many of the most important mathematicians served their rulers as astronomers. Bhaskara (1114–ca. 1185) was such an astronomer-mathematician. For generations his Brahmin family had been astronomers at the Ujjain astronomical observatory in north-central India, and his father had written a popular book on astrology.

Bhaskara was a highly erudite man. A disciple wrote that he had thoroughly mastered eight books on grammar, six on medicine, six on philosophy, five on mathematics, and the four Vedas. Bhaskara eventually wrote six books on mathematics and mathematical astronomy. They deal with solutions to simple and quadratic equations and show his knowledge of trigonometry, including the sine table and relationships between different trigonometric functions, and even some of the basic elements of calculus. Earlier Indian mathematicians had explored the use of zero and negative numbers. Bhaskara developed these ideas further, in particular improving on the understanding of division by zero.

A court poet who centuries later translated Bhaskara's book titled *The Beautiful* explained its title by saying Bhaskara wrote it for his daughter named Beautiful (Lilavati) as consolation when his divination of the best time for her to marry went awry. Whether Bhaskara did or did not write this book for his daughter, many of the problems he provides in it have a certain charm:

> On an expedition to seize his enemy's elephants, a king marched two yojanas the first day. Say, intelligent calculator, with what increasing rate of daily march did he proceed, since he reached his foe's city, a distance of eighty yojanas, in a week?[*]
>
> Out of a heap of pure lotus flower, a third part, a fifth, and a sixth were offered respectively to the gods Siva, Vishnu, and the Sun; and a quarter was presented to Bhavani. The remaining six lotuses were given to the venerable preceptor. Tell quickly the whole number of lotus.[†]
>
> If eight best variegated silk scarfs, measuring three cubits in breadth and eight in length, cost a hundred nishkas, say quickly, merchant, if thou

The observatory where Bhaskara worked in Ujjain today stands in ruins. (Dinodia Photo Library)

> understand trade, what a like scarf, three and a half cubits long and half a cubit wide will cost.[‡]

In the conclusion to *The Beautiful*, Bhaskara wrote:

> Joy and happiness is indeed ever increasing in this world for those who have *The Beautiful* clasped to their throats, decorated as the members are with neat reduction of fractions, multiplication, and involution, pure and perfect as are the solutions, and tasteful as is the speech which is exemplified.

Bhaskara had a long career. His first book on mathematical astronomy, written in 1150 when he was thirty-six, used mathematics to calculate solar and lunar eclipses or planetary conjunctions. Thirty-three years later he was still writing on the subject, this time providing simpler ways to solve problems encountered before. Bhaskara wrote his books in Sanskrit, already a literary language rather than a vernacular language, but even in his own day some of them were translated into other Indian languages.

---

[*]Quotations from Haran Chandra Banerji, *Colebrooke's Translation of the Lilanvanti*, 2d ed. (Calcutta: The Book Co., 1927), pp. 80–81, 30, 51, 200. The answer is that each day he must travel 22/7 yojanas farther than the day before.

[†]The answer is 120.

[‡]The answer, from the formula $x = (1 \times 7 \times 1 \times 100) / (8 \times 3 \times 8 \times 2 \times 2)$, is given in currencies smaller than the nishka: 14 drammas, 9 panas, 1 kakini, and 6⅔ cowry shells. (20 cowry shells = 1 kakini, 4 kakini = 1 pana, 16 panas = 1 dramma, and 16 drammas = 1 nishka.)

Within a couple of decades of his death, a local ruler endowed an educational institution to study Bhaskara's works, beginning with his work on mathematical astronomy. In the text he had inscribed at the site, the ruler gave the names of Bhaskara's ancestors for six generations, as well as of his son and grandson, who had continued in his profession.

QUESTIONS FOR ANALYSIS

1. What might have been the advantages of making occupations like astronomer hereditary in India?
2. How does Bhaskara link joy and happiness to mathematical concepts?

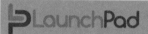

ONLINE DOCUMENT PROJECT

What ideas and beliefs were central to Indian culture? Read a Persian account of medieval India, and then complete a quiz and writing assignment based on the evidence and details from this chapter. *See inside the front cover to learn more.*

Like peasant societies elsewhere, including in China, Japan, and Southeast Asia, agricultural life in India ordinarily meant village life. The average farmer worked a small plot of land outside the village. All the family members pooled their resources under the direction of the head of the family. These joint efforts strengthened family solidarity.

The agricultural year began with spring plowing. The traditional plow, drawn by two oxen wearing yokes and collars, had an iron-tipped share and a handle with which the farmer guided it. Rice, the most important and popular grain, was sown at the beginning of the long rainy season. Beans, lentils, and peas grew during the cold season and were harvested in the spring, when fresh food was scarce. Cereal crops such as wheat, barley, and millet provided carbohydrates and other nutrients. Some families cultivated vegetables, spices, fruit trees, and flowers in their gardens. Sugarcane was another important crop.

Farmers also raised livestock. Most highly valued were cattle, which were raised for plowing and milk, hides, and horns, but Hindus did not slaughter them for meat. Like the Islamic and Jewish prohibition on the consumption of pork, the eating of beef was forbidden among Hindus.

Local craftsmen and tradesmen were frequently organized into guilds, with guild heads and guild rules. The textile industries were particularly well developed. Textiles were produced in large quantities and traded throughout India and beyond. The cutting and polishing of precious stones was another industry associated closely with foreign trade.

In the cities shops were open to the street; families lived on the floors above. The busiest tradesmen dealt in milk and cheese, oil, spices, and perfumes. In addition to these tradesmen and merchants, a host of peddlers shuffled through towns and villages selling everything from needles to freshly cut flowers.

During the first millennium C.E., the caste system reached its mature form. Within the broad division into the four varnas (strata) of Brahmin, Kshatriya, Vaishya, and Shudra (see page 69), the population was subdivided into numerous

Men at Work

This stone frieze from the Buddhist stupa in Sanchi depicts Indian men doing a variety of everyday jobs. Although the stone was carved to convey religious ideas, we can use it as a source for such details of daily life as the sort of clothing men wore while working and how they carried loads. (Dinodia Photo Library)

jati

▶ The thousands of Indian castes.

castes, or jati. Each caste had a proper occupation. In addition, its members married only within the caste and ate only with other members. Members of high-status castes feared pollution from contact with lower-caste individuals and had to undertake rituals of purification to remove the taint.

Eventually Indian society comprised perhaps as many as three thousand castes. Each caste had its own governing body, which enforced the rules of the caste. Those incapable of living up to the rules were expelled, becoming outcastes. These unfortunates lived hard lives, performing tasks that others considered unclean or lowly.

For all members of Indian society regardless of caste, marriage and family were the focus of life. As in China, the family was under the authority of the eldest male, who might take several wives, and ideally sons stayed home with their parents after they married. The family affirmed its solidarity by the religious ritual of honoring its dead ancestors—a ritual that linked the living and the dead, much like ancestor worship in China (see pages 93–94). People commonly lived in extended families: grandparents, uncles and aunts, cousins, and nieces and nephews all lived together in the same house or compound.

Children in poor households worked as soon as they were able. Children in wealthier households faced the age-old irritations of learning reading, writing, and arithmetic. Less attention was paid to daughters than to sons, though in more prosperous families they were often literate. Because girls who had lost their virginity could seldom hope to find good husbands, daughters were customarily married as children, with consummation delayed until they reached puberty.

A wife was expected to have no life apart from her husband. A widow was expected to lead the hard life of the ascetic: sleeping on the ground; eating only one simple meal a day; wearing plain, undyed clothes without jewelry;

CHAPTER LOCATOR | What aspects of nomadic life gave nomads of Central Asia advantages over settled civilizations? | How did Chinggis Khan conquer Eurasia, and how did Mongol conquests change the region?

CHAPTER 12
350 CULTURAL EXCHANGE IN CENTRAL AND SOUTHERN ASIA

and shaving her head. She was viewed as inauspicious to everyone but her children, and she did not attend family festivals. Among high-caste Hindus, a widow would be praised for throwing herself on her husband's funeral pyre. Buddhist sects objected to this practice, called **sati**, but some Hindu religious authorities declared that by self-immolation a widow could expunge both her own and her husband's sins, so that both would enjoy eternal bliss in Heaven.

Within the home the position of a wife depended on her own intelligence and strength of character. Wives were supposed to be humble, cheerful, and diligent, even toward worthless husbands. As in other patriarchal societies, however, occasionally a woman ruled the household. For women who did not want to accept the strictures of married life, the main way out was to join a Buddhist or Jain religious community (see page 188).

sati
▸ A practice whereby a high-caste Hindu woman would throw herself on her husband's funeral pyre.

QUICK REVIEW

How would you characterize Hindu-Muslim relations during India's medieval period?

How did the Mongol conquests facilitate the spread of religions, inventions, and diseases?

What was the result of India's encounters with Turks, Mongols, and Islam?

How did states develop along the maritime trade routes of Southeast Asia and beyond?

✔ LearningCurve
Check what you know.

How did states develop along the maritime trade routes of Southeast Asia and beyond?

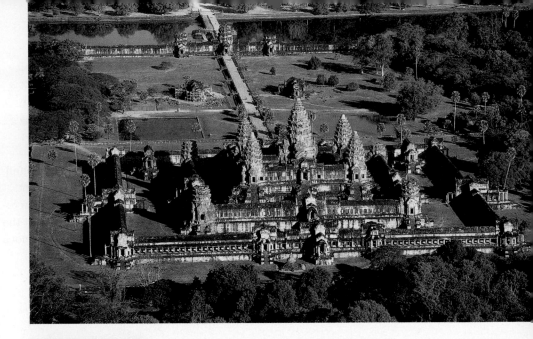

Angkor Wat Temple

The Khmers built several stone temple complexes at Angkor. This aerial view catches something of the scale of the largest of these complexes, Angkor Wat. (© Roy Garner/Alamy)

MUCH AS ROMAN CULTURE SPREAD to northern Europe and Chinese culture spread to Korea, Japan, and Vietnam, in the first millennium C.E. Indian learning, technology, and material culture spread to the mainland and islands of Southeast Asia. The spread of Indian culture was facilitated by the growth of maritime trade, but this interchange did not occur uniformly, and by 1400 there were still isolated societies in this region, most notably in the Pacific islands east of Indonesia.

Southeast Asia is a tropical region that is more like India than China. The topography of mainland Southeast Asia is marked by north-south mountain ranges separated by river valleys. It was easy for people to migrate south along these rivers but harder for them to cross the heavily forested mountains that divided the region into areas that had limited contact with each other. The indigenous population was originally mostly Malay, but migrations over the centuries brought many other peoples, including speakers of Austro-Asiatic (such as Vietnamese and Cambodian), Austronesian (such as Malay and Polynesian), and Sino-Tibetan-Burmese (such as Burmese and possibly Thai) languages, some of whom moved to the islands offshore and farther into the Pacific Ocean.

State Formation and Indian Influences

Southeast Asia was long a crossroads. Traders from China, India, Africa, and Europe either passed through the region when traveling from the Indian to the Pacific Ocean, or came for its resources, notably spices.

The northern part of modern Vietnam was under Chinese political control off and on from the second century B.C.E. to the tenth century C.E. (see page 194), but

CHAPTER LOCATOR | What aspects of nomadic life gave nomads of Central Asia advantages over settled civilizations? | How did Chinggis Khan conquer Eurasia, and how did Mongol conquests change the region?

Indian influence was of much greater significance for the rest of Southeast Asia. The first state to appear in historical records, Funan, had its capital in southern Vietnam. In the first to sixth centuries c.e. Funan extended its control over much of Indochina and the Malay Peninsula. Merchants from northwest India would offload their goods and carry them across the narrowest part of the Malay Peninsula. The ports of Funan offered food and lodging to the merchants as they waited for the winds to shift to continue their voyages. Brahmin priests and Buddhist monks from India settled along with the traders, serving the Indian population and attracting local converts. Rulers often invited Indian priests and monks to serve under them.

After the decline of Funan, maritime trade continued to grow, and petty kingdoms appeared in many places. Indian traders frequently established small settlements, generally located on the coast. Contact with the local populations led to intermarriage and the creation of hybrid cultures. Local rulers often adopted Indian customs and values, embraced Hinduism and Buddhism, and learned **Sanskrit**, India's classical literary language. Sanskrit gave different peoples a common mode of written expression, much as Chinese did in East Asia and Latin did in Europe.

When Indian traders, migrants, and adventurers entered mainland Southeast Asia, they encountered both long-settled peoples and migrants moving southward from the frontiers of China. As in other extensive migrations, the newcomers fought one another as often as they fought the native populations. In 939 the north Vietnamese became independent of China and extended their power southward along the coast of present-day Vietnam. The Thais had long lived in what is today southwest China and north Myanmar. In the eighth century the Thai tribes united in a confederacy and expanded northward against Tang China. Like China, however, the Thai confederacy fell to the Mongols in 1253. Still farther west another tribal people, the Burmese, migrated to the area of modern Myanmar in the eighth century. They also established a state, which they ruled from their capital, Pagan, and came into contact with India and Sri Lanka.

The most important mainland state was the Khmer (kuh-MAIR) Empire of Cambodia (802–1432), which controlled the heart of the region. The Khmers were

Sanskrit
▶ India's classical literary language.

Bayan Relief, Angkor

Among the many relief sculptures at the temples of Angkor are depictions of royal processions, armies at war, trade, cooking, cockfighting, and other scenes of everyday life. In the relief shown here, the boats and fish convey something of the significance of the sea to life in Southeast Asia. (Hervé Champollion/akg-images)

> PICTURING THE PAST

ANALYZING THE IMAGE: Find the boat. What do the people on it seem to be doing? What fish and animals do you see in the picture? Can you find the alligator eating a fish?

CONNECTIONS: Why would a ruler devote so many resources to decorating the walls of a temple? Why include scenes like this one?

| How did the Mongol conquests facilitate the spread of religions, inventions, and diseases? | What was the result of India's encounters with Turks, Mongols, and Islam? | **How did states develop along the maritime trade routes of Southeast Asia and beyond?** | ✔ LearningCurve Check what you know. |

indigenous to the area. Their empire eventually extended south to the sea and the northeast Malay Peninsula. Indian influence was pervasive; the impressive temple complex at Angkor Wat built in the early twelfth century was dedicated to the Hindu god Vishnu. Social organization, however, was modeled not on the Indian caste system but on indigenous traditions of social hierarchy. A large part of the population was of slave status. Generally successful in a long series of wars with the Vietnamese, the Khmers reached the peak of their power in 1219 and then gradually declined.

The Srivijayan Maritime Trade Empire

Srivijaya

▶ A maritime empire that held the Strait of Malacca and the waters around Sumatra, Borneo, and Java.

Far different from these land-based states was the maritime empire of Srivijaya, based on the island of Sumatra in modern Indonesia. From the sixth century on, it held the important Strait of Malacca, through which most of the sea traffic between China and India passed. This state, held together as much by alliances as by direct rule, was in many ways like the Gupta state of the same period in India, securing its prominence and binding its vassals and allies through its splendor and the promise of riches through trade.

Much as the Korean and Japanese rulers adapted Chinese models (see pages 195–196), the Srivijayan rulers drew on Indian traditions to justify their rule and organize their state. The Sanskrit writing system was used for government documents, and Indians were often employed as priests, scribes, and administrators. Indian mythology took hold, as did Indian architecture and sculpture. Kings and their courts, the first to embrace Indian culture, consciously spread it to their subjects.

After several centuries of prosperity, Srivijaya suffered a stunning blow in 1025. The Chola state in south India launched a large naval raid and captured the Srivijayan king and capital. Unable to hold their gains, the Indians retreated, but the Srivijayan Empire never regained its vigor.

Buddhism became progressively more dominant in Southeast Asia after 800. Mahayana Buddhism became important in Srivijaya and Vietnam, but Theravada Buddhism, closer to the original Buddhism of early India, became the dominant form in the rest of mainland Southeast Asia. Buddhist missionaries from India and Sri Lanka played a prominent role in these developments. Local converts continued the process by making pilgrimages to India and Sri Lanka to worship and to observe Indian life for themselves.

The Spread of Indian Culture in Comparative Perspective

The social, cultural, and political systems developed in India, China, and Rome all had enormous impact on neighboring peoples whose cultures were originally not as technologically advanced. Some of the mechanisms for cultural spread were similar in all three cases, but differences were important as well.

In the case of Rome and both Han and Tang China, strong states directly ruled outlying regions, bringing their civilizations with them. India's states did not have comparable bureaucratic reach. Outlying areas tended to be in the hands of local lords who had consented to recognize the overlordship of the stronger state. Moreover, most of the time India was politically divided.

The expansion of Indian culture into Southeast Asia thus came not from conquest and the extension of direct political control but from the extension of

CHAPTER LOCATOR | What aspects of nomadic life gave nomads of Central Asia advantages over settled civilizations? | How did Chinggis Khan conquer Eurasia, and how did Mongol conquests change the region?

354 CHAPTER 12 CULTURAL EXCHANGE IN CENTRAL AND SOUTHERN ASIA

trading networks, with missionaries following along. This made it closer to the way Japan adopted features of Chinese culture, often through the intermediary of Korea. In both cases, the cultural exchange was largely voluntary.

The Settlement of the Pacific Islands

Through most of Eurasia, societies became progressively less isolated over time. But in 1400 there still remained many isolated societies, especially in the islands east of modern Indonesia. As discussed in Chapter 1, *Homo sapiens* began settling the western Pacific islands very early, reaching Australia by 50,000 years ago and New Guinea by 35,000 years ago. The process did not stop there, however. The ancient Austronesians (speakers of Austronesian languages) were skilled mariners who settled numerous islands of the Pacific in subsequent centuries, generally following the coasts. Their descendants, the Polynesians, learned how to sail into the open ocean with only the stars, currents, wind patterns, paths of birds, and perhaps paths of whales and dolphins to help them navigate. They reached Tahiti and the Marquesas Islands in the central Pacific by about 200 C.E.

After reaching the central Pacific, Polynesians continued to fan out, in some cases traveling a thousand or more miles away. They reached the Hawaiian Islands in about 300 C.E., Easter Island in perhaps 1000, and New Zealand not until about 1000–1300. There even were groups who sailed west, eventually settling in Madagascar between 200 and 500.

In the more remote islands, such as Hawai'i, Easter Island, and New Zealand, the societies that developed were limited by the small range of domesticated plants and animals that the settlers brought with them and those that were indigenous to the place. Easter Island is perhaps the most extreme case. Only 15 miles wide at its widest point (only 63 square miles in total area), it is 1,300 miles from the nearest inhabited island (Pitcairn) and 2,240 miles from the coast of South America. At some point there was communication with South America, as sweet potatoes originally from there made their way to Easter Island. The

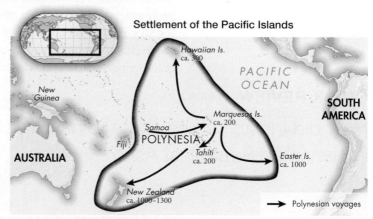

Settlement of the Pacific Islands

community that developed on the island raised chickens and cultivated sweet potatoes, taro, and sugarcane. The population is thought to have reached about fifteen thousand at Easter Island's most prosperous period, which began about 1200 C.E. It was then that its people devoted remarkable efforts to fashioning and erecting the large stone statues that still dot the island.

What led the residents of such a small island to erect more than eight hundred statues, most weighing around ten tons and standing twenty to seventy feet tall? One common theory is that they were central to the islanders' religion and that rival clans competed with each other to erect the most impressive statues. The effort they had to expend to carve them with stone tools, move them to the chosen site, and erect them would have been formidable.

After its heyday, Easter Island suffered severe environmental stress with the decline of its forests. The islanders could not make boats to fish in the ocean, and bird colonies shrank as nesting areas decreased, also reducing the food supply. Scholars still disagree on how much weight to give the many different elements

How did the Mongol conquests facilitate the spread of religions, inventions, and diseases?

What was the result of India's encounters with Turks, Mongols, and Islam?

How did states develop along the maritime trade routes of Southeast Asia and beyond?

✓ LearningCurve
Check what you know.

that contributed to the decline in the prosperity of Easter Island from the age when the statues were erected.

Certainly, early settlers of an island could have a drastic impact on its ecology. When Polynesians first reached New Zealand, they found large birds up to ten feet tall. They hunted them so eagerly that within a century the birds had all but disappeared. Hunting seals and sea lions also led to their rapid depletion. But the islands of New Zealand were much larger than Easter Island, and in time the Maori (the indigenous people of New Zealand) found more sustainable ways to feed themselves, depending more and more on agriculture.

> QUICK REVIEW

How did Indian culture come to have such a strong influence on Southeast Asia?

CHAPTER SUMMARY

The pastoral societies that stretched across Eurasia had the great military advantage of being able to raise horses in large numbers and support themselves from their flocks of sheep, goats, and other animals. Nomadic pastoralists generally were organized on the basis of clans and tribes that selected chiefs for their military talent. Much of the time these tribes fought with each other, but several times in history leaders formed larger confederations capable of coordinated attacks on cities and towns.

From the fifth to the twelfth centuries the most successful nomadic groups on the Eurasian steppes were Turks who gained ascendancy in many of the societies from the Middle East to northern India. In the early thirteenth century, the Mongol leader Chinggis Khan conquered much of Eurasia.

After Chinggis's death, the empire was divided into four khanates ruled by four of Chinggis's descendants. For a century the Mongol Empire fostered unprecedented East-West contact. They encouraged trade and often moved craftsmen and other

CHAPTER LOCATOR | What aspects of nomadic life gave nomads of Central Asia advantages over settled civilizations? | How did Chinggis Khan conquer Eurasia, and how did Mongol conquests change the region?

CHAPTER 12

356 CULTURAL EXCHANGE IN CENTRAL AND SOUTHERN ASIA

specialists from one place to another. The Mongols were tolerant of other religions. As more Europeans made their way east, Chinese inventions such as printing and the compass made their way west. Europe especially benefited from the spread of technical and scientific ideas. Diseases also spread, including the Black Death.

India was invaded by the Mongols but not conquered. After the fall of the Gupta Empire in about 480, India was for the next millennium ruled by small kingdoms, which allowed regional cultures to flourish. For several centuries Muslim Turks formed the Delhi sultanate in north India. Over time Islam gained adherents throughout South Asia. Hinduism continued to flourish, but Buddhism declined.

Throughout the medieval period India continued to be the center of active seaborne trade, and this trade helped carry Indian ideas and practices to Southeast Asia. Local rulers used experts from India to establish strong states, such as the Khmer kingdom and the Srivijayan kingdom. Buddhism became the dominant religion throughout the region, though Hinduism also played an important role. The Pacific islands east of Indonesia remained isolated culturally for centuries.

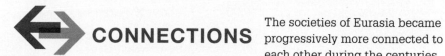 **CONNECTIONS** The societies of Eurasia became progressively more connected to each other during the centuries discussed in this chapter. One element promoting connection was the military superiority of the nomadic warriors of the steppe: first the Turks, then the Mongols, who conquered many of the settled civilizations near them. Invading Turks brought Islam to India. Connection between societies also came from maritime trade across the Indian Ocean and East Asia. Maritime trade was a key element in the spread of Indian culture to both the mainland and insular Southeast Asia. Other elements connecting these societies included Sanskrit as a language of administration and missionaries who brought both Hinduism and Buddhism far beyond their homelands.

East Asia was a key element in both the empires created by nomadic horsemen and the South Asian maritime trading networks. As discussed in Chapter 13, before East Asia had to cope with the rise of the Mongols, it experienced one of its most prosperous periods, during which China, Korea, and Japan became more distinct culturally. China's economy boomed during the Song Dynasty, and the scholar-official class, defined through the civil service examination, came more and more to dominate culture. In Korea and Japan, by contrast, aristocrats and military men gained ascendancy. Although China, Korea, and Japan all drew on both Confucian and Buddhist teachings, they ended up with elites as distinct as the Chinese scholar-official, the Korean aristocrat, and the Japanese samurai.

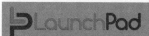

ONLINE DOCUMENT PROJECT

Intellectual and Religious Life in India

What ideas and beliefs were central to Indian culture?

Read a Persian account of medieval India, and then complete a quiz and writing assignment based on the evidence and details from this chapter. *See inside the front cover to learn more.*

| How did the Mongol conquests facilitate the spread of religions, inventions, and diseases? | What was the result of India's encounters with Turks, Mongols, and Islam? | How did states develop along the maritime trade routes of Southeast Asia and beyond? | 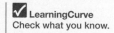 **LearningCurve** Check what you know. |

CHAPTER 12 STUDY GUIDE

 STEP 1

GET STARTED ONLINE

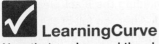 **LearningCurve**
Now that you've read the chapter, make it stick by completing the LearningCurve activity.

 STEP 2

EXPLAIN WHY IT MATTERS

Put your reading into practice. Identify each term below, and then explain why it matters in world history.

TERM	WHO OR WHAT & WHEN	WHY IT MATTERS
nomads (p. 330)		
steppe (p. 330)		
yurts (p. 333)		
Chinggis Khan (p. 336)		
khanates (p. 336)		
tax-farming (p. 339)		
protected people (p. 346)		
jati (p. 350)		
sati (p. 351)		
Sanskrit (p. 353)		
Srivijaya (p. 354)		

 STEP 3

MOVE BEYOND THE BASICS

To demonstrate a more advanced understanding of the connections Central Asian nomads helped forge among the civilizations of Eurasia, fill in the chart below with descriptions of the impact of nomadic invaders on religion, government, and commerce in China and India. What role did nomadic peoples play in stimulating cultural and commercial exchange in China and India?

	Religion	Government	Commerce
Nomadic influences in China			
Nomadic influences in India			

STEP 4 — PUT IT ALL TOGETHER

Now, take a step back and try to explain the big picture. Remember to use specific examples from the chapter in your answers.

CENTRAL ASIAN NOMADS

► What military advantages explain the ability of Central Asian nomads to defeat the large armies of settled peoples?

► In what ways did nomadic and settled peoples cooperate in Eurasia? Under what circumstances did cooperation turn into conflict?

THE MONGOLS

► What light does the rise of Chinggis Khan to power shed on the nature of Mongol politics and society?

► How did Mongol military and political activities accelerate regional exchange? Who gained and who lost as a result of Mongol activities?

INDIA AND SOUTHEAST ASIA

► How did the arrival of Islamic conquerors alter the Indian religious landscape?

► How and why did Indian culture spread in Southeast Asia? How did the relationship between India and Southeast Asia differ from the relationship between China and its neighbors?

LOOKING BACK, LOOKING AHEAD

► How had the settled states of Eurasia responded to the threat posed by nomadic peoples prior to the rise of the Turks and the Mongols? Why did the Turks and the Mongols prove more dangerous than other nomadic confederations?

► How did the Mongols contribute to the process of global integration, a process that accelerated in the centuries after their decline?

> IN YOUR OWN WORDS

Imagine that you must give an oral report to the class answering the following question: **How did Mongol conquests and maritime trade facilitate cultural exchange in central and southern Asia?** What would be the most important points and why?

13

STATES AND CULTURES IN EAST ASIA

800–1400

> **Why did Chinese, Korean, and Japanese society and culture diverge after 800?** Chapter 13 examines developments in East Asia between 800 and 1400. During this period East Asia was the most advanced region of the world. The Chinese economy was strong, and China's methods of production were highly sophisticated. Philosophy and the arts all flourished. China's system of government was also advanced for its time. These strengths were not, however, matched with corresponding military might, and in 1279 China was conquered by the Mongols. During the previous millennium, basic elements of Chinese culture had spread beyond China's borders. Beginning around 800, however, the pendulum shifted toward cultural differentiation as Japan, Korea, and China developed in distinctive ways.

✓ **LearningCurve**
After reading the chapter, use LearningCurve to retain what you've read.

Song Chancellor Known for his stern demeanor, Sima Guang (1019–1086) was an eminent historian and a leading official.

> What made possible the expansion of the Chinese economy, and what were the outcomes of this economic growth?

> How did the civil service examinations and the scholar-official class shape Chinese society and culture, and what impact did the Mongol conquest have on them?

> How did Korean society and culture develop in an age when its northern neighbors were Khitans, Jurchens, and Mongols?

> How did the Heian form of government contribute to the cultural flowering of Japan in the period?

> What were the causes and consequences of military rule in Japan?

> What made possible the expansion of the Chinese economy, and what were the outcomes of this economic growth?

Chinese Paper Money

Chinese paper currency indicated the unit of currency and the date and place of issue. The Mongols continued the use of paper money, as this note from the Mongol period attests. (National Museum of Chinese History, Beijing, China/Ancient Art and Architecture Collection Ltd./The Bridgeman Art Library)

dynastic cycle

▶ The theory that Chinese dynasties go through a predictable cycle from early vigor and growth to subsequent decline as administrators become lax and the well-off find ways to avoid paying taxes, cutting state revenues.

CHINESE HISTORIANS TRADITIONALLY VIEWED dynasties as following a standard cyclical pattern. Founders were vigorous men able to recruit capable followers to serve as officials and generals. Over time, however, emperors born in the palace would get used to luxury and lack the founders' strength and wisdom. Families with wealth or political power would find ways to avoid taxes, forcing the government to impose heavier taxes on the poor. As a result, impoverished peasants would flee, the morale of those in the government and armies would decline, and the dynasty would find itself able neither to maintain internal peace nor to defend its borders.

Viewed in terms of this theory of the **dynastic cycle**, by 800 the Tang Dynasty (see pages 190–191) was in decline. It had ruled China for nearly two centuries, and its high point was in the past. A massive rebellion had wracked it in the mid-eighth century, and powerful enemies were menacing its borders. Many of the centralizing features of the government had been abandoned, with power falling more and more to regional military governors.

CHAPTER LOCATOR | **What made possible the expansion of the Chinese economy, and what were the outcomes?** | How did the civil service examinations and the scholar-official class shape Chinese society?

794–1185 Heian period in Japan	**1120s** First government-issued paper money introduced by Song
804 Two Japanese Buddhist monks, Saichō and Kūkai, travel to China	**1126** Song loss of north China to the Jurchens; Song capital relocated to Hangzhou
935–1392 Koryŏ Dynasty in Korea	**1130–1200** Zhu Xi, Neo-Confucian philosopher
960–1279 Song Dynasty in China; emergence of scholar-official class; invention of movable type	**1185–1333** Kamakura Shogunate in Japan; Zen Buddhism flourishes
995–1027 Fujiwara Michinaga dominant at Heian court	**1234–1368** Mongols' Yuan Dynasty in China
ca. 1000–1010 *The Tale of Genji*	**ca. 1275–1292** Marco Polo travels in China
1119 First reported use of compass	

Historically, Chinese political theorists always assumed that a strong, centralized government was better than a weak one or than political division, but, if anything, the Tang toward the end of its dynastic cycle seems to have been both intellectually and economically more vibrant than the early Tang had been. Less control from the central government seems to have stimulated trade and economic growth.

A government census conducted in 742 shows that China's population was approximately 50 million. Over the next three centuries, with the expansion of wet-field rice cultivation in central and south China, the country's food supply steadily increased, and its population reached 100 million by 1100.

Agricultural prosperity and denser settlement patterns aided commercialization of the economy. Farmers in Song China no longer merely aimed at self-sufficiency. Instead, farmers sold their surpluses and used their profits to buy charcoal, tea, oil, and wine. In many places farmers specialized in commercial crops, such as sugar, oranges, cotton, silk, and tea. The need to transport the products of interregional trade stimulated the inland and coastal shipping industries.

As marketing increased, demand for money grew enormously, leading eventually to the creation of the world's first paper money. To avoid the weight and bulk of coins for large transactions, local merchants in late Tang times started trading receipts from deposit shops where they had left money or goods. The early Song authorities awarded a small set of these shops a monopoly on the issuing of these certificates of deposit, and in the 1120s the government took over the system, producing the world's first government-issued paper money.

With the intensification of trade, merchants became progressively more specialized and organized. They set up partnerships and joint stock companies. In the large cities merchants were organized into guilds according to the type

How did Korean society develop when its northern neighbors were Khitans, Jurchens, and Mongols?	How did the Heian form of government contribute to the cultural flowering of Japan in the period?	What were the causes and consequences of military rule in Japan?	✔ **LearningCurve** Check what you know.

of product sold, and they arranged sales from wholesalers to shop owners and periodically set prices.

Foreign trade also flourished in the Song period. Chinese ships began to displace Indian and Arab merchants in the South Seas, and ship design was improved in several ways. Watertight bulkheads improved buoyancy and protected cargo. Stern-mounted rudders improved steering. Some of the ships were powered by both oars and sails and were large enough to hold several hundred men.

Also important to oceangoing travel was the perfection of the **compass**. The ability of a magnetic needle to point north had been known for some time, but in Song times the needle was reduced in size and attached to a fixed stem (rather than floated in water). In some instances it was put in a small protective case with a glass top, making it suitable for sea travel. The first reports of a compass used in this way date to 1119.

The Song also witnessed many advances in industrial techniques. Heavy industry, especially iron, grew astoundingly. With advances in metallurgy, iron production reached around 125,000 tons per year in 1078, a sixfold increase over the output in 800. Much of the iron was put to military purposes. Mass-production methods were used to make iron armor in small, medium, and large sizes. High-quality steel for swords was made through high-temperature metallurgy. The needs of the army also brought Chinese engineers to experiment with the use of gunpowder. In the twelfth-century wars against the Jurchens (see page 333), those defending a besieged city used gunpowder to propel projectiles at the enemy.

compass

▶ A tool developed in Song times to aid in navigation at sea; it consisted of a magnetic needle that would point north and was placed in a small protective case.

Transplanting Rice

To get the maximum yield per plot and to make it possible to grow two crops in the same field, Chinese farmers grew rice seedlings in a seedbed and then, when a field was free, transplanted the seedlings into the flooded field. Because the Song government wanted to promote up-to-date agricultural technology, in the twelfth century it commissioned a set of twelve illustrations of the steps to be followed. This painting comes from a later version of those illustrations. (*Tilling Rice*, Yuan Dynasty [ink and colour on paper], Qi, Cheng [13th century] [attr. to]/Freer Gallery of Art, Smithsonian Institution, Washington, D.C., U.S.A./The Bridgeman Art Library)

CHAPTER LOCATOR | What made possible the expansion of the Chinese economy, and what were the outcomes? | How did the civil service examinations and the scholar-official class shape Chinese society?

Economic expansion fueled the growth of cities. Dozens of cities had 50,000 or more residents, and quite a few had more than 100,000, very large populations compared to other places in the world at the time. China's two successive capitals, Kaifeng (kigh-fuhng) and Hangzhou (hahng-joh), each had an estimated 1 million residents.

The medieval economic revolution shifted the economic center of China south to the Yangzi River drainage area. This area had many advantages over the north China plain. Rice, which grew in the south, provides more calories per unit of land and therefore allows denser settlement. The milder temperatures often allowed two crops to be grown on the same plot of land, first a summer crop of rice and then a winter crop of wheat or vegetables. The abundance of rivers and streams facilitated shipping, which reduced the cost of transportation and thus made regional specialization economically more feasible.

Ordinary people benefited from the Song economic revolution in many ways. There were more opportunities for the sons of farmers to leave agriculture and find work in cities. Those who stayed in agriculture had a better chance of improving their situations by taking up sideline production of wine, charcoal, paper, or textiles. Energetic farmers who grew cash crops such as sugar, tea, mulberry leaves (for silk), and cotton (recently introduced from India) could grow rich. Greater interregional trade led to the availability of more goods at rural markets.

QUICK REVIEW

How did the Chinese economic revolution
change life in the countryside?

How did Korean society develop when its northern neighbors were Khitans, Jurchens, and Mongols?

How did the Heian form of government contribute to the cultural flowering of Japan in the period?

What were the causes and consequences of military rule in Japan?

✓ LearningCurve
Check what you know.

> How did the civil service examinations and the scholar-official class shape Chinese society and culture, and what impact did the Mongol conquest have on them?

Blue-and-White Jars of the Yuan Period

Chinese ceramics had long been in demand outside China, and an innovation of the Mongol period — decorating white porcelain with underglaze designs in blue — proved especially popular. Persia imported large quantities of Chinese blue-and-white ceramics, and Korean, Japanese, and Vietnamese potters took up versions of the style themselves. (© The Trustees of the British Museum/Art Resource, NY)

IN THE TENTH CENTURY Tang China broke up into separate contending states, some of which had non-Chinese rulers. The two states that proved to be long lasting were the Song, which came to control almost all of China proper south of the Great Wall, and the Liao, whose ruling house was Khitan and which held the territory of modern Beijing and areas north (Map 13.1). Although the Song Dynasty had a much larger population, the Liao was militarily the stronger of the two. In the early twelfth century the Liao state was defeated by the Jurchens, another non-Chinese people, who founded the Jin Dynasty and went on to conquer most of north China, leaving Song to control only the south. After a century the Jin Dynasty was defeated by the Mongols, who extended their Yuan Dynasty to control all of China by 1276.

The Song Dynasty

The founder of the Song Dynasty, Taizu (r. 960–976), was a general whose troops elevated him to emperor (somewhat reminiscent of Roman practice). To make sure

CHAPTER LOCATOR | What made possible the expansion of the Chinese economy, and what were the outcomes? | **How did the civil service examinations and the scholar-official class shape Chinese society?**

that such an act could not happen in the future, Taizu retired or rotated his generals and assigned civil officials to supervise them. In time these civil bureaucrats came to dominate every aspect of Song government and society. The civil service examination system established during the Sui Dynasty (see page 189) was greatly expanded to provide the dynasty with a constant flow of men trained in the Confucian classics.

Curbing the generals' power ended warlordism but did not solve the military problem of defending against the nomadic Khitans' Liao Dynasty to the north. After several attempts to push the Liao back beyond the Great Wall, the Song concluded a peace treaty with them. The Song agreed to make huge annual payments of gold and silk to the Khitans, in a sense paying them not to invade. Even so, the Song rulers had to maintain a standing army of more than a million men. By the middle of the eleventh century military expenses consumed half the government's revenues.

MAP 13.1 ■ East Asia in 1000 and 1200

The Song empire did not extend as far as its predecessor, the Tang, and faced powerful rivals to the north — the Liao Dynasty of the Khitans and the Xia Dynasty of the Tanguts. Koryŏ Korea maintained regular contact with Song China, but Japan, by the late Heian period, was no longer deeply involved with the mainland. By 1200 military families dominated both Korea and Japan, but the borders were little changed. On the mainland the Liao Dynasty had been overthrown by the Jurchens' Jin Dynasty, which also seized the northern third of the Song empire. Because the Song relocated its capital to Hangzhou in the south, this period is called the Southern Song period.

> **MAPPING THE PAST**

ANALYZING THE MAP: What were the countries of East Asia in 1000? What were the major differences in 1200?

CONNECTIONS: What connections do you see between the length of their northern borders and the histories of China, Korea, and Japan?

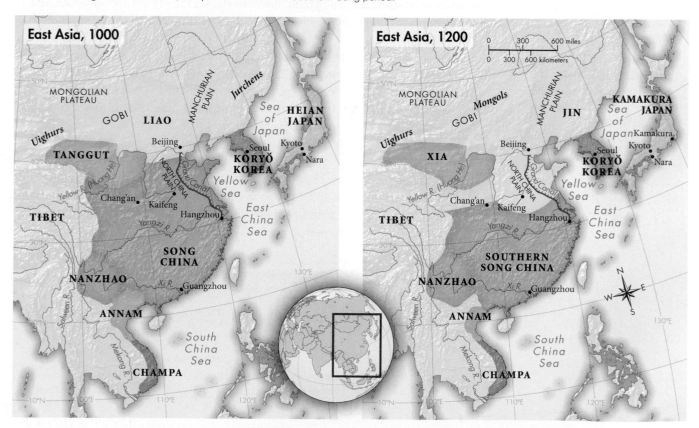

East Asia, 1000

East Asia, 1200

| How did Korean society develop when its northern neighbors were Khitans, Jurchens, and Mongols? | How did the Heian form of government contribute to the cultural flowering of Japan in the period? | What were the causes and consequences of military rule in Japan? | ✓ LearningCurve Check what you know. |

In the early twelfth century the military situation rapidly worsened when the Khitan state was destroyed by another tribal confederation led by the Jurchens, who quickly realized how easy it would be to defeat the Song. When they marched into the Song capital in 1126, they captured the emperor and former emperor and took them and the entire court into captivity. Song forces rallied around one of the emperor's sons who had escaped capture, and this prince re-established a Song court in the south at Hangzhou (see Map 13.1). This Southern Song Dynasty controlled only about two-thirds of the former Song territories, but the social, cultural, and intellectual life there remained vibrant until the Song fell to the Mongols in 1279.

The Scholar-Officials and Neo-Confucianism

The Song period saw the full flowering of one of the most distinctive features of Chinese civilization, the **scholar-official class** certified through highly competitive civil service examinations. This elite was both broader and better educated than the elites of earlier periods in Chinese history. Once the **examination system** was fully developed, aristocratic habits and prejudices largely disappeared.

To prepare for the examinations, men had to memorize the classics. They also had to master specific forms of composition, including poetry, and be ready to discuss policy issues, citing appropriate historical examples. Those who became officials this way had usually tried the exams several times and were on average a little over thirty years of age when they succeeded.

The invention of printing should be given some credit for the trend toward a better-educated elite. Tang craftsmen developed the art of carving words and pictures into wooden blocks, inking the blocks, and pressing paper onto them. Each block held an entire page of text. Such whole-page blocks were used for printing as early as the middle of the ninth century, and in the eleventh century **movable type** (one piece of type for each character) was invented, but it was rarely used because whole-block printing was cheaper. In China, as in Europe a couple of centuries later, the introduction of printing dramatically lowered the price of books, thus aiding the spread of literacy.

Among the upper class the availability of cheaper books enabled scholars to amass their own libraries. Song publishers printed the classics of Chinese literature. Works on philosophy, science, and medicine were also avidly consumed, as were Buddhist texts. Han and Tang poetry and historical works became the models for Song writers. One popular literary innovation was the encyclopedia, which first appeared in the Song period.

scholar-official class
▶ Chinese educated elite that included both scholars and officials. The officials had usually gained office by passing the highly competitive civil service examination. Scholars without office had often studied for the examinations but failed repeatedly.

examination system
▶ A system of selecting officials based on competitive written examinations.

movable type
▶ A system of printing in which one piece of type is used for each unique character.

> ## > The Accomplishments of Notable Scholar Officials:

- Ouyang Xiu: wrote love songs, histories, and the first analytical catalogue of rubbings of ancient stone and bronze inscriptions
- Sima Guang: wrote a narrative history of China, twenty-seven hundred poems, and eight hundred letters; was also an esteemed painter, calligrapher, and theorist of the arts
- Su Song: constructed an eighty-foot-tall mechanical clock that told the time of day, the day of the month, the phase of the moon, and the position of certain stars and planets in the sky

CHAPTER LOCATOR | What made possible the expansion of the Chinese economy, and what were the outcomes? | **How did the civil service examinations and the scholar-official class shape Chinese society?**

On a Mountain Path in Spring

With spare, sketchy strokes, the court painter Ma Yuan (ca. 1190–1225) depicts a scholar on an outing accompanied by his boy servant carrying a lute. The scholar gazes into the mist, his eyes attracted by a bird in flight. The poetic couplet was inscribed by Emperor Ningzong (r. 1194–1124), at whose court Ma Yuan served. It reads: "Brushed by his sleeves, wild flowers dance in the wind. / Fleeing from him, hidden birds cut short their songs." (National Palace Museum, Taipei, Taiwan/photo © AISA/The Everett Collection)

> PICTURING THE PAST

ANALYZING THE IMAGE: Find the key elements in this picture: the scholar, the servant boy, the bird, the willow tree. Are these elements skillfully conveyed? Are there other elements in the painting that you find hard to read?

CONNECTIONS: What do you think is the reason for writing a poetic couplet on this painting? Does it enhance the experience of viewing the painting or detract from it?

The life of the educated man involved more than study for the civil service examinations and service in office. Many took to refined pursuits such as collecting antiques or old books and practicing the arts. In the Song period, the engagement of the elite with the arts led to extraordinary achievement in calligraphy and painting, especially landscape painting. A large share of the social life of upper-class men was centered on these refined pastimes, as they gathered to compose or criticize poetry, to view each other's art treasures, and to patronize young talents. (See "Individuals in Society: Shen Gua," page 370.)

Besides politics, scholars also debated issues in ethics and metaphysics. For several centuries Buddhism had been more vital than Confucianism. Beginning in the late Tang period, Confucian teachers began claiming that the teachings of the Confucian sages contained all the wisdom one needed and that a true Confucian would reject Buddhist teachings. During the eleventh century many Confucian teachers urged students to set their sights not on exam success but on the higher goals of attaining the wisdom of the sages. Metaphysical theories about the workings of the cosmos in terms of *li* (principle) and *qi* (vital energy) were developed in response to the challenge of the sophisticated metaphysics of Buddhism.

Neo-Confucianism, as this movement is generally termed, was more fully developed in the twelfth century by the immensely learned Zhu Xi (joo shee)

Neo-Confucianism
► The revival of Confucian thinking that began in the eleventh century, characterized by the goal of attaining the wisdom of the sages, not exam success.

How did Korean society develop when its northern neighbors were Khitans, Jurchens, and Mongols?

How did the Heian form of government contribute to the cultural flowering of Japan in the period?

What were the causes and consequences of military rule in Japan?

☑ LearningCurve
Check what you know.

INDIVIDUALS IN SOCIETY
Shen Gua

In the eleventh century it was not rare for Chinese men of letters to have broad interests, but few could compare to Shen Gua (1031–1095), a man who tried his hand at everything from mathematics, geography, economics, engineering, medicine, divination, and archaeology to military strategy and diplomacy.

Shen Gua's father was an official and Shen Gua often accompanied him on his assignments, which built up his knowledge of geography. In 1063 he passed the civil service examinations, and in 1066 he received a post in the capital. He eventually held high astronomical, ritual, and financial posts and became involved in waterworks and the construction of defense walls. He was sent as an envoy to the Khitans in 1075 to try to settle a boundary dispute. When a military campaign that he advised failed in 1082, he was demoted and later retired to write.

It is from his book of miscellaneous notes that we know the breadth of his interests. In one note Shen describes how, on assignment to inspect the frontier, he made a relief map of wood and glue-soaked sawdust to show the mountains, roads, rivers, and passes. The emperor was so impressed when he saw it that he ordered all the border prefectures to make relief maps. Elsewhere Shen describes the use of petroleum and explains how to make movable type from clay. Shen Gua often applied a mathematical approach to issues that his contemporaries did not think of in those terms. He once computed the total number of possible situations on a Go board, and another time he calculated the longest possible military campaign given the limits of human carriers, who had to carry their own food as well as food for the soldiers.

Shen Gua is especially known for his scientific explanations. He explained the deflection of the compass from due south. He identified petrified bamboo and from its existence argued that the region where it was found must have been much warmer and more humid in ancient times. He argued against the theory that tides are caused by the rising and setting of the sun, demonstrating that they correlate with the cycles of the moon. He proposed switching from a lunar calendar to a solar one of 365 days, saying that even though his contemporaries would reject his idea, "surely in the future some will adopt my idea." To convince his readers that the sun and the moon

Shen Gua played Go with white and black markers on a grid-like board like this one. (Courtesy of Library of Congress, LC-USZC4-8471/8472)

were spherical, not flat, he suggested that they cover a ball with fine powder on one side and then look at it obliquely. The powder was the part of the moon illuminated by the sun, and as the viewer looked at it obliquely, the white part would be crescent shaped, like a waxing moon. Shen Gua, however, did not realize that the sun and moon had entirely different orbits, and he explained why they did not collide by positing that both were composed of *qi* (vital energy) and had form but not substance.

Shen Gua also wrote on medicine and criticized his contemporaries for paying more attention to old treatises than to clinical experience. Yet he, too, was sometimes stronger on theory than on observation. In one note he argued that longevity pills could be made from cinnabar. He reasoned that if cinnabar could be transformed in one direction, it ought to be susceptible to transformation in the opposite direction as well. Therefore, since melted cinnabar causes death, solid cinnabar should prevent death.

1. How did Shen Gua's travels add to his curiosity about the material world?
2. In what ways could Shen Gua have used his scientific interests in his work as a government official?
3. How does Shen Gua's understanding of the natural world compare to that of the early Greeks? (See pages 128–130.)

LaunchPad

ONLINE DOCUMENT PROJECT

What cultural pursuits interested the scholar-official class? View images from the Song period, and then complete a quiz and writing assignment based on the evidence and details from this chapter. *See inside the front cover to learn more.*

(1130–1200). Besides serving in office, he wrote, compiled, or edited almost a hundred books. Although he was treated as a political threat during his lifetime, within decades of his death his writings came to be considered orthodox, and in subsequent centuries candidates for the examinations had to be familiar with his commentaries on the classics.

Women's Lives in Song Times

Families who could afford it usually tried to keep their wives and daughters within the walls of the house, rather than let them work in the fields or in shops or inns. At home there was plenty for them to do. Not only was there the work of tending children and preparing meals, but spinning, weaving, and sewing were considered women's work as well and took a great deal of time. Families that raised silkworms also needed women to do much of the work of caring for the worms. Within the home women generally had considerable say and took an active interest in issues such as the selection of marriage partners for their children.

Women tended to marry between the ages of sixteen and twenty. Their husbands were, on average, a couple of years older than they were. Marriages were arranged by their parents, who would have either called on a professional matchmaker or turned to a friend or relative for suggestions. Before a wedding took place, written agreements were exchanged, listing the prospective bride's and groom's birth dates, parents, and grandparents; the gifts that would be exchanged; and the dowry the bride would bring.

The young bride's first priority was to try to win over her mother-in-law. One way to do this was to quickly bear a son for the family. Within the patrilineal system, a woman fully secured her position in the family by becoming the mother of one of the men. Every community had older women skilled in midwifery who were called to help when a woman went into labor. If the family was well-to-do, arrangements might be made for a wet nurse to help her take care of the newborn.

Women frequently had four, five, or six children, but likely one or more would die in infancy.

Woman Attendant

The Song emperors were patrons of a still-extant temple in northern China that enshrined a statue of the "holy mother," the mother of the founder of the ancient Zhou Dynasty. The forty-two maids who attend her, one of whom is shown here, seem to have been modeled on the palace ladies who attended Song emperors. (Taiyuan Jinci/Goddess Hall/Uniphoto Press International Japan/Art and Architecture Collection Ltd.)

If a son reached adulthood and married before the woman herself was widowed, she would be considered fortunate, for she would have always had an adult man who could take care of business for her—first her husband, then her grown son.

A woman with a healthy and prosperous husband faced another challenge in middle age: her husband could bring home a **concubine**. Wives outranked concubines and could give them orders in the house, but a concubine had her own ways of getting back through her hold on the husband. The children born to a concubine were considered just as much children of the family as the wife's children, and if the wife had had only daughters and the concubine had a son, the wife would find herself dependent on the concubine's son in her old age.

Neo-Confucianism is sometimes blamed for a decline in the status of women in Song times, largely because one of the best known of the Neo-Confucian teachers, Cheng Yi, once told a follower that it would be better for a widow to die of starvation than to lose her virtue by remarrying. In later centuries this saying was often quoted to justify pressuring widows, even very young ones, to stay with their husbands' families and not remarry. In Song times, however, widows frequently remarried.

It is true that **foot binding** began during the Song Dynasty, but it was not recommended by Neo-Confucian teachers; rather it was associated with the pleasure quarters and with women's efforts to beautify themselves. Mothers bound the feet of girls aged five to eight with long strips of cloth to keep them from growing and to bend the four smaller toes under to make the foot narrow and arched. The hope was that the girl would be judged more beautiful. Foot binding spread gradually during Song times but was probably still largely an elite practice. In later centuries it became extremely common in north and central China, eventually spreading to all classes. Women with bound feet were less mobile than women with natural feet, but only those who could afford servants bound their feet so tightly that walking was difficult.

concubine

▶ A woman contracted to a man as a secondary spouse; although subordinate to the wife, her sons were considered legitimate heirs.

foot binding

▶ The practice of binding the feet of girls with long strips of cloth to keep them from growing large.

CHAPTER LOCATOR | What made possible the expansion of the Chinese economy, and what were the outcomes? | **How did the civil service examinations and the scholar-official class shape Chinese society?**

372 CHAPTER 13 STATES AND CULTURES IN EAST ASIA

China Under Mongol Rule

As discussed in Chapter 12, the Mongols conquered China in stages, gaining much of north China by 1215 and all of it by 1234, but not taking the south till the 1270s. The north suffered the most devastation. The non-Chinese rulers in the north, the Jin Dynasty of the Jurchen thought they had the strongest army known to history. Yet Mongol tactics frustrated them. The Mongols would take a city, plunder it, and then withdraw, letting the Jin take it back and deal with the resulting food shortages and destruction. Under these circumstances, Jurchen power rapidly collapsed.

Not until Khubilai was Great Khan was the Song Dynasty defeated and south China brought under the control of the Mongol's Yuan Dynasty. Non-Chinese rulers had gained control of north China several times in Chinese history, but none of them had been able to secure control of the region south of the Yangzi River, which required a navy. By the 1260s Khubilai had put Chinese shipbuilders to work building a fleet, crucial to his victory over Song (see page 336).

Life in China under the Mongols was much like life in China under earlier alien rulers. Once order was restored, people did their best to get on with their lives. Some were deprived of their land, business, or freedom and suffered real hardship. Yet people still spoke Chinese, followed Chinese customary practices in dividing their family property, made offerings at local temples, and celebrated the new year and other customary festivals. Teachers still taught students the classics, scholars continued to write books, and books continued to be printed.

The Mongols, like other foreign rulers before them, did not see anything particularly desirable in the social mobility of Chinese society. Preferring stability, they assigned people hereditary occupations, occupations that came with obligations to the state. The Mongols also classified the population into four grades, with the Mongols occupying the top grade. Next came various non-Chinese, such as the Uighurs and Persians. Below them were Chinese former subjects of the Jurchen, called the Han. At the bottom were the former subjects of the Song, called southerners.

The reason for codifying ethnic differences this way was to preserve the Mongols' privileges as conquerors. Chinese were not allowed to take Mongol names, and great efforts were made to keep them from passing as Mongols or marrying Mongols. To keep Chinese from rebelling, they were forbidden to own weapons or congregate in public.

As the Mongols captured Chinese territory, they recruited Chinese into their armies and government. Although some refused to serve the Mongols, others argued that the Chinese would fare better if Chinese were the administrators and could shield Chinese society from the most brutal effects of Mongol rule.

Nevertheless, government service, which had long been central to the identity and income of the educated elite in China, was not as widely available under the Mongols. The Mongols reinstituted the civil service examinations in 1315, but filled only about 2 percent of the positions in the bureaucracy through it and reserved half of those places for Mongols.

The scholar-official elite without government employment turned to alternative ways to support themselves. Those who did not have land to live off of found work as physicians, fortune-tellers, children's teachers, Daoist priests, publishers,

| How did Korean society develop when its northern neighbors were Khitans, Jurchens, and Mongols? | How did the Heian form of government contribute to the cultural flowering of Japan in the period? | What were the causes and consequences of military rule in Japan? | ☑ LearningCurve Check what you know. |

373

booksellers, or playwrights. Many took leadership roles at the local level, such as founding academies for Confucian learning or promoting local charitable ventures. Through such activities, scholars without government offices could assert the importance of civil over military values and see themselves as trustees of the Confucian tradition.

Since the Mongols wanted to extract wealth from China, they had every incentive to develop the economy. They encouraged trade both within China and beyond its borders and tried to keep paper money in circulation. They repaired the Grand Canal, which had been ruined during their initial conquest of north China. Chinese industries with strong foreign markets, such as porcelain, thrived. Nevertheless, the economic expansion of late Tang and Song times did not continue under the alien rule of the Jurchens and Mongols.

The Mongols' Yuan Dynasty began a rapid decline in the 1330s as disease, rebellions, and poor leadership led to disorder throughout the country. When a Chinese strongman succeeded in consolidating the south, the Mongol rulers retreated to Mongolia before he could take Beijing. By 1368 the Yuan Dynasty had given way to a new Chinese-led dynasty: the Ming.

> **QUICK REVIEW**

What values and priorities were associated with the scholar-official class?

What made possible the expansion of the Chinese economy, and what were the outcomes?

How did the civil service examinations and the scholar-official class shape Chinese society?

Wooden Blocks for Printing

The Heainsa Buddhist Temple in Korea has preserved the more than eighty thousand woodblocks used to print the huge Buddhist canon in the thirteenth century. The monk shown here is replacing a block. All the blocks are carved on both sides and stabilized by wooden frames that have kept them from warping. (© OUR PLACE THE WORLD HERITAGE COLLECTION, www.ourplaceworldheritage.com)

How did Korean society and culture develop in an age when its northern neighbors were Khitans, Jurchens, and Mongols?

DURING THE SILLA PERIOD, Korea was strongly tied to Tang China and avidly copied China's model (see page 195). This changed along with much else in North Asia between 800 and 1400. In this period Korea lived more in the shadows of the powerful states of the Khitans, Jurchens, and Mongols than of the Chinese.

The Silla Dynasty began to decline after the king was killed in a revolt in 780. For the next 155 years, rebellions and coups d'état followed one after the other, as different groups of nobles placed their candidates on the throne and killed as many of their opponents as they could.

The dynasty that emerged from this confusion was called Koryŏ (KAW-ree-oh) (935–1392). (The English word *Korea* derives from the name of this dynasty.) During this time Korea developed more independently of the China model than it had in Silla times. This was not because the Chinese model was rejected; the Koryŏ capital was laid out on the Chinese model, and the government was closely patterned on the Tang system. But despite Chinese influence, Korean society remained deeply aristocratic.

| How did Korean society develop when its northern neighbors were Khitans, Jurchens, and Mongols? | How did the Heian form of government contribute to the cultural flowering of Japan in the period? | What were the causes and consequences of military rule in Japan? |  LearningCurve Check what you know. |

The founder of the dynasty, Wang Kon (877–943), was a man of relatively obscure background, and he needed the support of the old aristocracy to maintain control. His successors introduced civil service examinations on the Chinese model, as well as examinations for Buddhist clergy, but because the aristocrats were the best educated and the government schools admitted only the sons of aristocrats, this system served primarily to solidify their control.

At the other end of the social scale, the number of people in the serf-slave stratum seems to have increased. This lowborn stratum included not only privately held slaves but also large numbers of government slaves as well as government workers in mines, porcelain factories, and other government industries. Sometimes entire villages or groups of villages were considered lowborn. There were occasional slave revolts, and some freed slaves did rise in status, but prejudice against anyone with slave ancestors was intense. In China and Japan, by contrast, slavery was a much more minor element in the social landscape.

The commercial economy declined in Korea during this period. Except for the capital, there were no cities of commercial importance, and in the countryside the use of money declined. One industry that did flourish was ceramics.

Buddhism remained strong throughout Korea, and monasteries became major centers of art and learning. As in Song China and Kamakura Japan, Chan (Zen) and Tiantai (Tendai) were the leading Buddhist teachings (see page 191). The founder of the Koryŏ Dynasty attributed the dynasty's success to the Buddha's protection, and he and his successors were ardent patrons of the church. The entire Buddhist canon was printed in the eleventh century and again in the thirteenth. As in medieval Europe, aristocrats who entered the church occupied the major abbacies. Monasteries played the same roles as they did in China and Japan, such as engaging in money-lending and charitable works. As in Japan (but not China), some monasteries accumulated military power.

The Koryŏ Dynasty was preserved in name long after the ruling family had lost most of its power. In 1170 the palace guards massacred the civil officials at court and placed a new king on the throne. After incessant infighting among the generals and a series of coups, in 1196 the general Ch'oe Ch'ung-hon took control. The domination of Korea by the Ch'oe family was much like the contemporaneous situation in Japan, where warrior bands were seizing power. Moreover, because the Ch'oes were content to dominate the government while leaving the Koryŏ king on the throne, they had much in common with the Japanese shoguns, who followed a similar strategy.

Korea, from early times, recognized China as being in many ways senior to it, but when strong non-Chinese states emerged to its north in Manchuria, Korea was ready to accommodate them as well. Koryŏ's first neighbor to the north was the Khitan state of Liao, which in 1010 invaded and sacked the capital. To avoid destruction, Koryŏ acceded to vassal status, but Liao invaded again in 1018. This time Koryŏ was able to repel the nomadic Khitans. Afterward a defensive wall was built across the Korean peninsula south of the Yalu River. When the Jurchens and their Jin Dynasty supplanted the Khitans' Liao Dynasty, Koryŏ agreed to send them tribute as well.

As mentioned in Chapter 12, Korea was conquered by the Mongols, and the figurehead Koryŏ kings were moved to Beijing, where they married Mongol princesses, their descendants becoming more Mongol than Korean. This was a time of hardship for the Korean people. In the year 1254 alone, the Mongols enslaved

The Koryŏ Dynasty, 935–1392

CHAPTER LOCATOR

What made possible the expansion of the Chinese economy, and what were the outcomes?

How did the civil service examinations and the scholar-official class shape Chinese society?

CHAPTER 13
376 STATES AND CULTURES IN EAST ASIA

two hundred thousand Koreans and took them away. Ordinary people in Korea suffered grievously when their land was used as a launching pad for the huge Mongol invasions of Japan. In this period Korea also suffered from frequent attacks by Japanese pirates, somewhat like the depredations of the Vikings in Europe a little earlier (see page 390).

When Mongol rule in China fell apart in the mid-fourteenth century, it declined in Korea as well. Chinese rebels opposing the Mongols entered Korea and even briefly captured the capital in 1361. When the Ming Dynasty was established in China in 1368, the Koryŏ court was unsure how to respond. In 1388 a general, Yi Song-gye, was sent to oppose a Ming army at the northwest frontier. When he saw the strength of the Ming, he concluded that making an alliance was more sensible than fighting, and he led his troops back to the capital, where in 1392 he usurped the throne, founding the Chosŏn Dynasty.

QUICK REVIEW <

How did Korean society differ from Chinese society in this period?

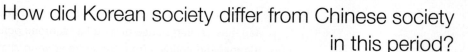

| How did Korean society develop when its northern neighbors were Khitans, Jurchens, and Mongols? | How did the Heian form of government contribute to the cultural flowering of Japan in the period? | What were the causes and consequences of military rule in Japan? | ✓ LearningCurve Check what you know. |

How did the Heian form of government contribute to the cultural flowering of Japan in the period?

The Shogun Minamoto Yoritomo in Court Dress

This wooden sculpture, 27.8 inches tall, was made about a half century after Yoritomo's death for use in a shrine dedicated to his memory. The bold shapes convey Yoritomo's dignity and power. (*Yoritomo [Minamotono-Yoritomo]*, wood with colored painting and quartz eyes, Kamakura Period, 1300/National Museum, Tokyo, Japan/akg-images)

AS DESCRIBED IN CHAPTER 7, during the seventh and eighth centuries the Japanese ruling house pursued a vigorous policy of adopting useful ideas, techniques, and policies from the more advanced civilization of China. The rulers built a capital along Chinese lines in Nara and fostered the growth of Buddhism. Monasteries grew so powerful in Nara, however, that in less than a century the court decided to move away from them and encourage other sects of Buddhism.

The new capital was built about twenty-five miles away at Heian (HAY-ahn; modern Kyoto). Like Nara, Heian was modeled on the Tang capital of Chang'an. For the first century at Heian the government continued to follow Chinese models, but it turned away from them with the decline of the Tang Dynasty in the late ninth century. During the Heian period (794–1185), Japan witnessed a literary and cultural flowering under the rule of the Fujiwara family.

Fujiwara Rule

Only the first two Heian emperors were much involved in governing. By 860 political management had been taken over by a series of regents from the Fujiwara family, who supplied most of the empresses in this period. The emperors contin-

CHAPTER LOCATOR | What made possible the expansion of the Chinese economy, and what were the outcomes? | How did the civil service examinations and the scholar-official class shape Chinese society?

ued to be honored, but the Fujiwaras ruled. Fujiwara dominance represented the privatization of political power and a return to clan politics. Political history thus took a very different course in Japan than in China, where, when a dynasty weakened, military strongmen would compete to depose the emperor and found their own dynasties. In Japan for the next thousand years, political contenders sought to manipulate the emperors rather than supplant them.

The Fujiwaras reached the apogee of their glory under Fujiwara Michinaga (r. 995–1027). Like many aristocrats of the period, he was learned in Buddhism, music, poetry, and Chinese literature and history. He dominated the court for more than thirty years as the father of four empresses, the uncle of two emperors, and the grandfather of three emperors. After ensuring that his sons could continue to rule, he retired to a Buddhist monastery, all the while continuing to maintain control.

By the end of the eleventh century several emperors who did not have Fujiwara mothers had found a device to counter Fujiwara control: they abdicated but continued to exercise power by controlling their young sons on the throne. This system of rule has been called **cloistered government** because the retired emperors took Buddhist orders, while maintaining control of the government from behind the scenes.

cloistered government
▶ A system in which an emperor retired to a Buddhist monastery but continued to exercise power by controlling his young son on the throne.

Aristocratic Culture

A brilliant aristocratic culture developed in the Heian period. In the capital at Heian, nobles, palace ladies, and imperial family members lived a highly refined and leisured life. In their society, niceties of birth, rank, and breeding counted for everything. The elegance of one's calligraphy and the allusions in one's poems were matters of intense concern to both men and women at court. Courtiers did not like to leave the capital, and some like the court lady Sei Shonagon shuddered at the sight of ordinary working people.

In this period a new script was developed for writing Japanese phonetically. Each symbol was based on a simplified Chinese character and represented one of the syllables used in Japanese. Although "serious" essays, histories, and government documents continued to be written in Chinese, less formal works such as poetry and memoirs were written in Japanese. Mastering the new writing system took much less time than mastering writing in Chinese and aided the spread of literacy, especially among women in court society.

In the Heian period, women played important roles at all levels of society. Women educated in the arts and letters could advance at court as attendants to the ruler's empress and other consorts. Women could inherit property from their parents, and they would compete with their brothers for shares of the family property. In political life, marrying a daughter to an emperor or shogun (see page 381) was one of the best ways to gain power, and women often became major players in power struggles.

The literary masterpiece of this period is *The Tale of Genji*, written in Japanese by Lady Murasaki over several years (ca. 1000–1010). This long narrative depicts a cast of characters enmeshed in court life, with close attention to dialogue and personality. Murasaki also wrote a diary that is similarly revealing of aristocratic culture.

The Tale of Genji
▶ A Japanese literary masterpiece about court life written by Lady Murasaki.

Murasaki was one of many female writers in this period. The wife of a high-ranking court official wrote a poetic memoir of her unhappy twenty-year marriage

How did Korean society develop when its northern neighbors were Khitans, Jurchens, and Mongols?

How did the Heian form of government contribute to the cultural flowering of Japan in the period?

What were the causes and consequences of military rule in Japan?

✓ LearningCurve
Check what you know.

379

to him and his rare visits. A woman wrote both an autobiography that related her father's efforts to find favor at court and a love story of a hero who travels to China. Another woman even wrote a history that concludes with a triumphal biography of Fujiwara Michinaga.

Buddhism remained very strong throughout the Heian period. A mission sent to China in 804 included two monks in search of new texts. One of the monks, Saichō, spent time at the monasteries on Mount Tiantai and brought back the Buddhist teachings associated with that mountain (called Tendai in Japanese). Tendai's basic message is that all living beings share the Buddha nature and can be brought to salvation. Once back in Japan, Saichō established a monastery on Mount Hiei outside Kyoto, which grew to be one of the most important monasteries in Japan. By the twelfth century this monastery and its many branch temples had vast lands and a powerful army of monk-soldiers to protect its interests.

Kūkai, the other monk on the 804 mission to China, came back with texts from another school of Buddhism—Shingon, "True Word," a form of **Esoteric Buddhism**. Esoteric Buddhism is based on the idea that teachings containing the secrets of enlightenment had been secretly transmitted from the Buddha. People can gain access to these mysteries through initiation into the mandalas (cosmic diagrams), mudras (gestures), and mantras (verbal formulas). On his return to Japan, Kūkai attracted many followers and was allowed to establish a monastery at Mount Kōya, south of Osaka. The popularity of Esoteric Buddhism was a great stimulus to Buddhist art.

Esoteric Buddhism

▶ A sect of Buddhism that maintains that the secrets of enlightenment have been secretly transmitted from the Buddha and can be accessed through initiation into the mandalas, mudras, and mantras.

> **QUICK REVIEW**

What were the key characteristics of Fujiwara government? How did Fujiwara government represent a departure from Chinese models of political development?

CHAPTER LOCATOR | What made possible the expansion of the Chinese economy, and what were the outcomes? | How did the civil service examinations and the scholar-official class shape Chinese society?

What were the causes and consequences of military rule in Japan?

THE GRADUAL RISE OF A WARRIOR ELITE over the course of the Heian period finally brought an end to the domination of the Fujiwaras and other Heian aristocratic families. In 1156 civil war broke out between the Taira and Minamoto warrior clans based in western and eastern Japan, respectively. Both clans relied on skilled warriors, later called samurai, who were rapidly becoming a new social class. A samurai and his lord had a double bond: in return for the samurai's loyalty and service, the lord granted him land or income. From 1159 to 1181 a Taira named Kiyomori dominated the court, taking the position of prime minister and marrying his daughter to the emperor. His relatives became governors of more than thirty provinces. Still, the Minamoto clan managed to defeat the Taira, and the Minamoto leader, Yoritomo, became **shogun**, or general-in-chief. With him began the Kamakura Shogunate (1185–1333). This period is often referred to as Japan's feudal period because it was dominated by a military class whose members were tied to their superiors by bonds of loyalty and supported by landed estates rather than salaries.

shogun
▶ The Japanese general-in-chief, whose headquarters was the shogunate.

Military Rule

The similarities between military rule in Japan and feudalism in medieval Europe during roughly the same period have fascinated scholars, as have the very significant differences. In Europe feudalism emerged out of the fusion of Germanic and Roman social institutions and flowered under the impact of Muslim and Viking invasions. In Japan military rule evolved from a combination of the native warrior tradition and Confucian ethical principles of duty to superiors.

The emergence of the samurai was made possible by the development of private landholding. The government land allotment system, copied from Tang China, began breaking down in the eighth century (much as it did in China). By the ninth century local lords had begun escaping imperial taxes and control by commending (formally giving) their land to tax-exempt entities such as monasteries, the imperial family, and high-ranking officials. The local lord then received his land back as a tenant and paid his protector a small rent. The monastery or privileged individual received a steady income from the land, and the local lord escaped imperial taxes and control. By the end of the thirteenth century most land seems to have been taken off the tax rolls this way. Unlike peasants in medieval

| How did Korean society develop when its northern neighbors were Khitans, Jurchens, and Mongols? | How did the Heian form of government contribute to the cultural flowering of Japan in the period? | **What were the causes and consequences of military rule in Japan?** | ✓ LearningCurve Check what you know. |

381

Europe, where similar practices of commendation occurred, those working the land in Japan never became serfs. Moreover, Japanese lords rarely lived on the lands they had rights in, unlike English or French lords who lived on their manors.

Samurai resembled European knights in several ways. Both were armed with expensive weapons, and both fought on horseback. Just as the knight was supposed to live according to the chivalric code, so Japanese samurai were expected to live according to **Bushido** (or "way of the warrior"). Physical hardship was accepted as routine, and soft living was despised as weak and unworthy. Disloyalty brought social disgrace, which the samurai could avoid only through *seppuku*, ritual suicide by slashing his belly.

The Kamakura Shogunate derives its name from Kamakura, a city near modern Tokyo that was the seat of the Minamoto clan. The founder, Yoritomo, ruled the country much the way he ran his own estates, appointing his retainers to newly created offices. To cope with the emergence of hard-to-tax estates, he put military land stewards in charge of seeing to the estates' proper operation. To bring order to the lawless countryside, he appointed military governors to oversee the military and enforce the law in the provinces. They supervised the conduct of the land stewards in peacetime and commanded the provincial samurai in war.

Yoritomo's wife, Masako, protected the interests of her own family, the Hōjōs, especially after Yoritomo died. She went so far as to force her first son to abdicate when he showed signs of preferring the family of his wife to the family of his mother. She later helped her brother take power away from her father. Thus the process of reducing power holders to figureheads went one step further in 1219 when the Hōjō family reduced the shogun to a figurehead. The Hōjō family held the reins of power for more than a century until 1333.

The Mongols' two massive seaborne invasions in 1274 and 1281 (see page 336) were a huge shock to the shogunate. Although the Hōjō regents, with the help of a "divine wind" (kamikaze), repelled the Mongols, they were unable to reward their vassals in the traditional way because little booty was found among the wreckage of the Mongol fleets. Discontent grew among the samurai, and by the fourteenth century the entire political system was breaking down. Both the imperial and the shogunate families were fighting among themselves. As land grants were divided, samurai became impoverished.

The factional disputes among Japan's leading families remained explosive until 1331, when the emperor Go-Daigo tried to recapture real power. His attempt sparked an uprising by the great families, local lords, samurai, and even Buddhist monasteries. Go-Daigo destroyed the Kamakura Shogunate in 1333 but soon lost the loyalty of his followers. By 1338 one of his most important military supporters, Ashikaga Takauji, had turned on him and established the Ashikaga Shogunate, which lasted until 1573. Takauji's victory was also a victory for the samurai, who took over civil authority throughout Japan.

Cultural Trends

The cultural distance between the elites and the commoners narrowed a little during the Kamakura period. Buddhism was spread to ordinary Japanese by energetic preachers. Honen (1133–1212) propagated the Pure Land teaching, preaching that paradise could be reached through simple faith in the Buddha

Bushido
▶ Literally, the "way of the warrior"; the code of conduct by which samurai were expected to live.

Kamakura Shogunate, 1185–1333

Mongol invasion, 1274
Mongol invasion, 1281

CHAPTER LOCATOR | What made possible the expansion of the Chinese economy, and what were the outcomes? | How did the civil service examinations and the scholar-official class shape Chinese society?

CHAPTER 13
382   STATES AND CULTURES IN EAST ASIA

and repeating the name of the Buddha Amitabha. His follower Shinran (1173–1263) taught that monks should not shut themselves off in monasteries but should marry and have children. A different path was promoted by Nichiren (1222–1282), a fiery and intolerant preacher who proclaimed that to be saved people had only to invoke sincerely the Lotus Sutra, one of the most important of the Buddhist sutras. These lay versions of Buddhism found a receptive audience among ordinary people in the countryside.

It was also during the Kamakura period that **Zen** came to flourish in Japan. Zen teachings originated in Tang China, where they were known as Chan (see page 191). Rejecting the authority of the sutras, Zen teachers claimed the superiority of mind-to-mind transmission of Buddhist truth. This teaching found eager patrons among the samurai, who were attracted to its discipline and strong master-disciple bonds.

Zen
▶ A school of Buddhism that emphasized meditation and truths that could not be conveyed in words.

Buddhism remained central to the visual arts. Many temples in Japan still house fine sculptures done in this period. In painting, narrative hand scrolls brought to life the miracles that faith could bring and the torments of Hell awaiting unbelievers.

During the Kamakura period, war tales continued the tradition of long narrative prose works. *The Tale of the Heike* tells the story of the fall of the Taira family and the rise of the Minamoto clan. The tale reached a large and mostly illiterate audience because blind minstrels would chant sections to the accompaniment of a lute. The story is suffused with the Buddhist idea of the transience of life and the illusory nature of glory. Yet it also celebrates strength, courage, loyalty, and pride.

After stagnating in the Heian period, agricultural productivity began to improve in the Kamakura period, and the population grew, reaching perhaps 8.2 million by 1333. Much like farmers in contemporary Song China, Japanese farmers adopted new strains of rice, often double-cropped in warmer regions, made increased use of fertilizers, and improved irrigation for paddy rice. Besides farming, ordinary people made their livings as artisans, traders, fishermen, and entertainers. Although trade in human beings was banned, those who fell into debt might sell themselves or their children, and professional slave traders kidnapped women and children. A vague category of outcastes occupied the fringes of society, in a manner reminiscent of India. Buddhist strictures against killing and Shinto ideas of pollution probably account for the exclusion of butchers, leatherworkers, morticians, and lepers, but other groups, such as bamboo whisk makers, were also traditionally excluded for no obvious reason.

QUICK REVIEW ◀

How did competition between aristocratic clans shape
the history of Japan during this period?

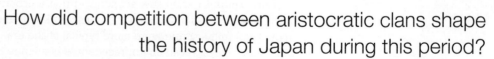

How did Korean society develop when its northern neighbors were Khitans, Jurchens, and Mongols?

How did the Heian form of government contribute to the cultural flowering of Japan in the period?

What were the causes and consequences of military rule in Japan?

✓ LearningCurve
Check what you know.

CHAPTER SUMMARY

The countries of East Asia—China, Japan, and Korea—all underwent major changes in the six centuries from 800 to 1400. In China the loosening of the central government's control of the economy stimulated trade and economic growth. Between 800 and 1100 China's population doubled to 100 million, reflecting in part the spread of wet-field rice cultivation, especially in the south. The economic center of China shifted from the north China plain to the south, the milder region drained by the Yangzi River.

In the Song period, the booming economy and the invention of printing allowed for expansion of the scholar-official class, which came to dominate government and society. Repeatedly, the Song government chose to pay tribute to its militarily powerful neighbors—first the Khitans, then the Jurchens, then the Mongols—to keep the peace. Eventually, however, Song fell to the Mongols.

During the Koryŏ Dynasty, Korea evolved more independently of China than it had previously, in part because it had to placate powerful non-Chinese neighbors. The commercial economy declined, and an increasing portion of the population was unfree, working as slaves for aristocrats or the government. Military strongmen dominated the government, but their armies were no match for the much larger empires to their north. The period of Mongol domination was particularly difficult.

In Heian Japan, a tiny aristocracy dominated government and society. A series of regents, most of them from the Fujiwara family and fathers-in-law of the emperors, controlled political life. The aristocratic court society put great emphasis on taste and refinement. The Heian aristocrats had little interest in life in the provinces, which gradually came under the control of military clans.

After a civil war between the two leading military clans, a military government, called the shogunate, was established. The Kamakura Shogunate was dominated by a military class of samurais. Two invasions by the Mongols caused major crises in military control. Although both times the invaders were repelled, defense costs were high. During this period culture was less centered around the capital, and Buddhism spread to ordinary people.

CONNECTIONS East Asia faced many internal and external challenges between 800 and 1400, and the ways societies responded to them shaped their subsequent histories. In China the first four centuries of this period saw economic growth, urbanization, the spread of printing, and the expansion of the educated class. In Korea and Japan aristocratic dominance and military rule were more typical of the era. All three areas, but especially China and Korea, faced an unprecedented challenge from the Mongols. The challenges of the period did not hinder creativity in the literary and visual arts.

Europe during these six centuries, the subject of the next chapter, also faced invasions from outside; in its case, the pagan Vikings were especially dreaded. Europe had a social structure more like that of Korea and Japan than of China, with less centralization and a more dominant place in society for military men.

CHAPTER LOCATOR | What made possible the expansion of the Chinese economy, and what were the outcomes? | How did the civil service examinations and the scholar-official class shape Chinese society?

384   CHAPTER 13   STATES AND CULTURES IN EAST ASIA

The centralized church in Europe, however, was unlike anything known in East Asian history. These centuries in Europe saw a major expansion of Christendom, both through conversion and migration. Although there were scares that the Mongols would penetrate deeper into Europe, the greatest challenge in Europe was the Black Death and the huge loss of life that it caused.

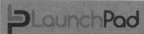

ONLINE DOCUMENT PROJECT
Song Artwork
What cultural pursuits interested the scholar-official class?

View images from the Song period, and then complete a quiz and writing assignment based on the evidence and details from this chapter. *See inside the front cover to learn more.*

How did Korean society develop when its northern neighbors were Khitans, Jurchens, and Mongols?

How did the Heian form of government contribute to the cultural flowering of Japan in the period?

What were the causes and consequences of military rule in Japan?

☑ LearningCurve
Check what you know.

CHAPTER 13 STUDY GUIDE

STEP 1 **GET STARTED ONLINE**

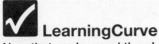 **LearningCurve**

Now that you've read the chapter, make it stick by completing the LearningCurve activity.

STEP 2 **EXPLAIN WHY IT MATTERS**

Put your reading into practice. Identify each term below, and then explain why it matters in world history.

TERM	WHO OR WHAT & WHEN	WHY IT MATTERS
dynastic cycle (p. 362)		
compass (p. 364)		
scholar-official class (p. 368)		
examination system (p. 368)		
movable type (p. 368)		
Neo-Confucianism (p. 369)		
concubine (p. 372)		
foot binding (p. 372)		
cloistered government (p. 379)		
The Tale of Genji (p. 379)		
Esoteric Buddhism (p. 380)		
shogun (p. 381)		
Bushido (p. 382)		
Zen (p. 383)		

STEP 3 **MOVE BEYOND THE BASICS**

To demonstrate a more advanced understanding of the divergence of China, Korea, and Japan in the medieval period, fill in the chart below with descriptions of the major social, political, and cultural developments in the three states during the period covered in this chapter. What role did nomadic peoples play in shaping Chinese, Korean, and Japanese history during this period?

	Society	Politics	Culture
China			
Korea			
Japan			

STEP 4 **PUT IT ALL TOGETHER** Now, take a step back and try to explain the big picture. Remember to use specific examples from the chapter in your answers.

CHINA

▶ In what ways did late Tang and Song China defy the expectations of traditional Chinese historians?

▶ Why, despite its growth and prosperity, did China become increasingly vulnerable to nomadic confederations under the Song?

KOREA

▶ In what ways was Korean society different from Chinese and Japanese society?

▶ How did Korea's leaders react to the presence of powerful nomadic confederations on their borders?

JAPAN

▶ Compare and contrast Japanese elite culture during the Heian period with Chinese elite culture under the Song. How would you explain the differences you note?

▶ How and why did the power of Japanese samurai increase during the medieval period?

LOOKING BACK, LOOKING AHEAD

▶ Compare and contrast the place of China in the East Asian world before and after the period covered in this chapter. How would you explain the differences you note?

▶ From 1500 on, East Asia would face an unprecedented maritime challenge from European states. How might developments in the period covered in this chapter have affected the ability of East Asian states to meet this challenge?

> **IN YOUR OWN WORDS**

Imagine that you must give an oral report to the class answering the following question: **Why did Chinese, Korean, and Japanese society and culture diverge after 800? What would be the most important points and why?**

14
EUROPE IN THE MIDDLE AGES

800–1450

> **What role did clergy, nobles, peasants, and townspeople play in medieval European society?** Chapter 14 examines the development of European civilization in the Middle Ages. Traditionally, the history of Europe has been divided into three periods — ancient, medieval, and modern. At times, the history of other parts of the world has also been fit into this three-period schema as well. Today historians often question the general applicability of such labels, and even the usefulness of the term "Middle Ages" for European history. They assert that the Middle Ages was not simply a period of stagnation between two high points but rather a time of enormous intellectual energy and creative vitality. While agrarian life continued to dominate Europe, political structures that would influence later European history began to form, and Christianity continued to spread.

Hedwig of Silesia Noblewomen in medieval Europe played a wide variety of roles. Hedwig of Silesia conducted diplomatic negotiations, ruled her husband's territory when he was away, founded monasteries, and worked to expand Christianity in eastern Europe. (The John Paul Getty Museum, Los Angeles, Ms Ludwig XI, fol. 12v [detail], Court Atelier of Duke Ludwig I of Liegnitz and Brieg [illuminator], *Vita beatae Hedwigis*, 1353. Tempera colors, colored washes and ink bound between wood boards covered with red-stained pigskin, 34.1 x 24.8 cm.)

> How did medieval rulers restore order and centralize political power?

> How did the Christian Church enhance its power and create new institutions and religious practices?

> What were the causes, course, and consequences of the Crusades?

> How did the lives of common people, nobles, and towns-people differ, and what new commercial developments increased wealth?

> What were the primary educational and cultural developments in medieval Europe?

> Why have the later Middle Ages been seen as a time of calamity and crisis?

✓**LearningCurve**
After reading the chapter, use LearningCurve to retain what you've read.

> How did medieval rulers restore order and centralize political power?

IN 800 CHARLEMAGNE, the most powerful of the Carolingians, was crowned Holy Roman emperor. After his death his empire was divided among his grandsons, and their kingdoms were weakened by nobles vying for power. In addition, beginning around 800 western Europe was invaded by several different groups. Local nobles were the strongest power, and common people turned to them for protection. By the eleventh century, however, rulers in some parts of Europe had reasserted authority and were slowly building centralized states.

Invasions and Migrations

The Vikings were pagan Germanic peoples from Norway, Sweden, and Denmark. They began to make overseas expeditions, which they themselves called *vikings*, and the word came to be used for people who went on such voyages as well. Viking assaults began around 800, and by the mid-tenth century the Vikings had brought large sections of continental Europe and Britain under their sway. In the east they sailed the rivers of Russia as far as the Black Sea. In the west they established permanent settlements in Iceland and short-lived ones in Greenland and Newfoundland in Canada (Map 14.1).

Against Viking ships navigated by experienced and fearless sailors, the Carolingian Empire, with no navy, was helpless. At first the Vikings attacked and sailed off laden with booty. Later, on returning, they settled down and colonized the areas they had conquered, often marrying local women and adopting the local languages and some of the customs.

Along with the Vikings, groups of central European steppe peoples known as Magyars (MAG-yahrz) also raided villages in the late ninth century. Moving westward, small bands of Magyars on horseback reached far into Europe. They subdued northern Italy, compelled Bavaria and Saxony to pay tribute, and penetrated into the Rhineland and Burgundy. They settled in the area that is now Hungary, became Christian, and in the eleventh century allied with the papacy.

From North Africa, the Muslims also began new encroachments in the ninth century. They already ruled most of Spain and now conquered Sicily, driving northward into central Italy and the south coast of France.

From the perspective of those living in what had been Charlemagne's empire, Viking, Magyar, and Muslim attacks contributed to increasing disorder and violence. Italian, French, and English sources often describe this period as one of terror and chaos. People in other parts of Europe might have had a different opinion. In Muslim Spain and Sicily scholars worked in thriving cities, and new crops

CHAPTER LOCATOR | **How did medieval rulers restore order and centralize political power?** | How did the Christian Church enhance its power and create new institutions?

such as cotton and sugar enhanced ordinary people's lives. In eastern Europe states such as Moravia and Hungary became strong kingdoms.

"Feudalism" and Manorialism

The large-scale division of Charlemagne's empire into three parts in the ninth century led to a decentralization of power at the local level. Civil wars weakened the power and prestige of kings, who could do little about regional violence. Likewise, the invasions of the ninth century, especially those of the Vikings, weakened royal authority. The Frankish kings were unable to halt the invaders, and the local aristocracy had to assume responsibility for defense. Thus, in the ninth and tenth centuries, aristocratic families increased their authority in their local territories, and distant and weak kings could not interfere. Common people turned for protection to the strongest power, the local nobles.

    The most powerful nobles were those who gained warriors' allegiance, often symbolized in an oath-swearing ceremony of homage and fealty that grew out of earlier Germanic oaths of loyalty. In this ceremony a warrior (knight) swore his loyalty as a **vassal** to the more powerful individual, who became his lord. In return for the vassal's loyalty, aid, and military assistance, the lord promised him protection and material support. This support might be a place in the lord's household but was more likely land of the vassal's own, called a **fief** (*feudum* in Latin). The fief, which might contain forests, churches, and towns, technically still belonged to the lord, and the vassal had only the use of it. Peasants living on a fief produced the food and other goods necessary to maintain the knight. Most legal scholars and historians have identified these personal ties of loyalty cemented by grants of land as a political and social system they term **feudalism**. In the last

vassal
▶ A knight who has sworn loyalty to a particular lord.

fief
▶ A portion of land, the use of which was given by a lord to a vassal in exchange for the latter's oath of loyalty.

feudalism
▶ A medieval European political system that defines the military obligations and relations between a lord and his vassals and involves the granting of fiefs.

| What were the causes, course, and consequences of the Crusades? | How did the lives of common people, nobles, and townspeople differ? | What were the primary educational and cultural developments in medieval Europe? | Why have the later Middle Ages been seen as a time of calamity and crisis? | ☑ LearningCurve Check what you know. |

MAP 14.1 ■ Invasions and Migrations of the Ninth and Tenth Centuries

This map shows the Viking, Magyar, and Muslim invasions and migrations in the ninth and tenth centuries. Compare it with Map 8.2 (page 219) on the barbarian migrations of late antiquity to answer the following questions.

> MAPPING THE PAST

ANALYZING THE MAP: What similarities do you see in the patterns of migration in these two periods? What significant differences?

CONNECTIONS: How did the Vikings' expertise in shipbuilding and sailing make their migrations different from those of earlier Germanic tribes? How did this set them apart from the Magyar and Muslim invaders of the ninth century?

manorialism

▶ The economic system that governed rural life in medieval Europe, in which the landed estates of a lord were worked by the peasants under the lord's jurisdiction in exchange for his protection.

serf

▶ A peasant who lost his or her freedom and became permanently bound to the landed estate of a lord.

several decades, however, increasing numbers of medieval historians have found the idea of "feudalism" problematic, because the word was a later invention and the system was so varied and changed over time.

The economic power of the warrior class rested on landed estates, which were worked by peasants under a system of **manorialism**. Free farmers surrendered themselves and their land to the lord's jurisdiction in exchange for protection. The land was given back to them to farm, but they were tied to the land by various payments and services. Most significantly, a peasant lost his or her freedom and became a **serf**, part of the lord's permanent labor force. Unlike slaves, serfs were personally free, but they were bound to the land and unable to leave it without the lord's permission.

CHAPTER LOCATOR | How did medieval rulers restore order and centralize political power? | How did the Christian Church enhance its power and create new institutions?

By around 1000 the majority of western Europeans were serfs. In eastern Europe the transition was slower but longer lasting. Western European peasants began to escape from serfdom in the later Middle Ages, at the very point that serfs were more firmly tied to the land in eastern Europe, especially in eastern Germany, Poland, and Russia.

The Restoration of Order

The eleventh century witnessed the beginnings of political stability in western Europe. Foreign invasions gradually declined, and in some parts of Europe lords in control of large territories built up their power even further, becoming kings over growing and slowly centralizing states. In a process similar to that occurring at the same time in the West African kingdom of Ghana (see pages 280–281), rulers expanded their territories and extended their authority by developing larger bureaucracies, armies, judicial systems, and other institutions to maintain control, as well as taxation systems to pay for them. These new institutions and practices laid the foundations for modern national states. Political developments in England, France, and Germany provide good examples of the beginnings of the national state in the central Middle Ages.

The Viking Canute (r. 1016–1035) made England the center of his empire, while promoting a policy of assimilation and reconciliation between Anglo-Saxons and Vikings. At the same time, England was divided into local shires, or counties, each under the jurisdiction of a sheriff appointed by the king. When Canute's heir Edward died childless, there were three claimants to the throne. One of these, Duke William of Normandy, crossed the channel and won the English throne by defeating and killing his Anglo-Saxon rival, Harold II, at the Battle of Hastings in 1066. Later dubbed "the Conqueror," William (r. 1066–1087) limited the power of the nobles and church officials and built a unified monarchy. He retained the Anglo-Saxon institution of sheriff, but named Normans to the posts.

The Norman Conquest, 1066

In 1085 William decided to conduct a systematic survey of the entire country to determine how much wealth there was and who had it. The resulting record, called the *Domesday Book* (DOOMZ-day) from the Anglo-Saxon word *doom*, meaning "judgment," provided William and his descendants with vital information for governing the country.

In 1128 William's granddaughter Matilda married a powerful French noble, Geoffrey of Anjou. Their son, who became Henry II of England, inherited provinces in northwestern France from his father. When Henry married the great heiress Eleanor of Aquitaine in 1152, he claimed lordship over Aquitaine and other provinces in southwestern France as well. The histories of England and France were thus closely intertwined in the Middle Ages.

In the early twelfth century France consisted of a number of nearly independent provinces, each governed by its local ruler. The work of unifying and enlarging France began under Philip II (r. 1180–1223), also known as Philip Augustus. By the end of his reign Philip was effectively master of northern France, and by 1300 most of the provinces of modern France had been added to the royal domain.

In central Europe the German king Otto I (r. 936–973) defeated many other lords to build up his power, based on an alliance with and control of the church. Under Otto I and his successors, a loose confederation stretching from the North Sea to the Mediterranean developed. In this confederation, later called the Holy

What were the causes, course, and consequences of the Crusades?

How did the lives of common people, nobles, and townspeople differ?

What were the primary educational and cultural developments in medieval Europe?

Why have the later Middle Ages been seen as a time of calamity and crisis?

✓ LearningCurve
Check what you know.

Roman Empire, the emperor shared power with princes, dukes, counts, city officials, archbishops, and bishops.

Frederick Barbarossa (r. 1152–1190) of the house of Hohenstaufen tried valiantly to make the Holy Roman Empire a united state. When he tried to enforce his authority over the cities of northern Italy, however, they formed a league against him in alliance with the pope and defeated him. Frederick's absence from the German part of his empire allowed the princes and other rulers of independent provinces to consolidate their power there as well, and Germany did not become a unified state.

Law and Justice

Throughout Europe in the twelfth and thirteenth centuries, the law was a hodgepodge of customs, feudal rights, and provincial practices. Rulers wanted to blend these elements into a uniform system of rules acceptable and applicable to all their peoples, though their success in doing so varied.

The French king Louis IX (r. 1226–1270) was famous for his concern for justice. Each French province, even after being made part of the kingdom of France, retained its unique laws and procedures. But Louis IX created a royal judicial system, establishing the Parlement of Paris, a kind of supreme court that heard appeals from lower courts.

Under Henry II (r. 1154–1189), England developed and extended a common law—a law common to and accepted by the entire country, unique in medieval Europe. Henry's son John (r. 1199–1216), however, met with serious disappointment after taking the throne. A combination of royal debt, increased taxation, and military failures fed popular discontent. A rebellion begun by northern barons grew, and in 1215 the barons forced him to attach his seal to the Magna Carta—the "Great Charter," which became the cornerstone of English justice and law. The Magna Carta was simply meant to assert traditional rights enjoyed by certain groups, but in time it came to signify the broader principle that everyone, including the king and the government, must obey the law.

Statements of legal principles such as the Magna Carta were not how most people experienced the law in medieval Europe. Instead they were involved in actual cases. Judges determined guilt or innocence in a number of ways. In some cases, they ordered a trial by ordeal, in which the accused might be tied hand and foot and dropped in a lake or river. People believed that water was a pure substance and would reject anything foul or unclean. Thus a person who sank was considered innocent, while a person who floated was found guilty. Trials by ordeal were relatively rare, and courts increasingly favored more rational procedures, in which judges heard testimony, sought witnesses, and read written evidence if it was available.

> ## QUICK REVIEW

How did the invasions of the ninth and tenth centuries
shape European society and government?

CHAPTER LOCATOR | How did medieval rulers restore order and centralize political power? | How did the Christian Church enhance its power and create new institutions?

CHAPTER 14
394 EUROPE IN THE MIDDLE AGES

How did the Christian Church enhance its power and create new institutions and religious practices?

KINGS AND EMPERORS were not the only rulers consolidating their power in the eleventh and twelfth centuries; the papacy did as well, although the popes' efforts were sometimes challenged by medieval kings and emperors. Despite such challenges, monasteries continued to be important places for learning and devotion, and new religious orders were founded. Christianity expanded into Europe's northern and eastern regions, and Christian rulers expanded their holdings in Muslim Spain.

Papal Reforms

During the ninth and tenth centuries the church came under the control of kings and feudal lords, who chose church officials in their territories, granting them fiefs that provided an income and expecting loyalty and service in return. Church

| What were the causes, course, and consequences of the Crusades? | How did the lives of common people, nobles, and townspeople differ? | What were the primary educational and cultural developments in medieval Europe? | Why have the later Middle Ages been seen as a time of calamity and crisis? | ✓ LearningCurve Check what you know. |

offices were sometimes sold outright—a practice called *simony*. Although the Roman Church encouraged clerical celibacy, many priests were married or living with women. Wealthy Roman families chose popes from among their members; thus popes paid more attention to their families' political fortunes or their own pleasures than to the church's institutional or spiritual health. Not surprisingly, clergy at all levels who had bought their positions or had been granted them for political reasons provided little spiritual guidance and were rarely models of high moral standards.

Serious efforts to reform the church began in the eleventh century. A series of popes believed that secular or lay control over the church was largely responsible for the lack of moral leadership, so they proclaimed the church independent from secular rulers. The Lateran Council of 1059 decreed that the authority and power to elect the pope rested solely in the college of cardinals, a special group of priests from the major churches in and around Rome.

Pope Gregory VII (pontificate 1073–1085) vigorously championed reform and the expansion of papal power. He ordered all priests to give up their wives and children or face dismissal, invalidated the ordination of church officials who had purchased their offices, and placed nuns under firmer control of male authorities. He believed that the pope was the vicar of God on earth and that papal orders were the orders of God. He emphasized the political authority of the papacy, ordering that any church official selected or appointed by a layperson should be deposed, and any layperson who appointed a church official should be excommunicated—cut off from the sacraments and the Christian community.

European rulers immediately protested this restriction of their power, and the strongest reaction came from Henry IV, the ruler of Germany who later became the Holy Roman emperor. Henry continued to appoint officials, and Gregory responded by excommunicating bishops who supported Henry and threatening to depose him. In January 1077 Henry secured the pope's forgiveness, and Gregory readmitted the emperor into the Christian community. Although Henry bowed before the pope, he actually won a victory, maintaining authority over his subjects and in 1084 being crowned emperor. This victory was temporary, however, for high nobles within the empire took advantage of further conflicts with the pope to enhance their position, siding with the church to gain power.

Monastic Life

Although they were in theory cut off from the world (see page 212), monasteries and convents were deeply affected by issues of money, rank, and power. During the ninth and tenth centuries, many monasteries fell under the control and domination of local feudal lords. Powerful laymen appointed themselves or their relatives as abbots, took the lands and goods of monasteries, and spent monastic revenues.

Medieval monasteries also provided noble boys with education and opportunities for ecclesiastical careers. Although a few men who rose in the ranks of church officials were of humble origins, most were from high-status families. Social class also defined the kinds of religious life open to women. Kings and nobles usually established convents for their female relatives and other elite women, and the position of abbess, or head of a convent, became the most powerful position a woman could hold in medieval society. (See "Individuals in Society: Hildegard of Bingen," page 397.)

CHAPTER LOCATOR | How did medieval rulers restore order and centralize political power?

How did the Christian Church enhance its power and create new institutions?

396 CHAPTER 14
EUROPE IN THE MIDDLE AGES

INDIVIDUALS IN SOCIETY
Hildegard of Bingen

The tenth child of a lesser noble family, Hildegard (1098–1179) was turned over to the care of an abbey in the Rhineland when she was eight years old. There she learned Latin and received a good education. She spent most of her life in various women's religious communities, two of which she founded herself. When she was a child, she began having mystical visions, often of light in the sky, but told few people about them. In middle age, however, her visions became more dramatic: "And it came to pass . . . when I was 42 years and 7 months old, that the heavens were opened and a blinding light of exceptional brilliance flowed through my entire brain. And so it kindled my whole heart and breast like a flame, not burning but warming . . . and suddenly I understood of the meaning of expositions of the books."* She wanted the church to approve of her visions and wrote first to Saint Bernard of Clairvaux, who answered her briefly and dismissively, and then to Pope Eugenius, who encouraged her to write them down. Her first work was *Scivias* (Know the Ways of the Lord), a record of her mystical visions that incorporates extensive theological learning.

Obviously possessed of leadership and administrative talents, Hildegard left her abbey in 1147 to found the convent of Rupertsberg near Bingen. There she produced *Physica* (On the Physical Elements) and *Causa et Curae* (Causes and Cures), scientific works on the curative properties of natural elements; poems; a religious play; and several more works of mysticism. She carried on a huge correspondence with scholars, prelates, and ordinary people. When she was over fifty, she left her community to preach to audiences of clergy and laity, and she was the only woman of her time whose opinions on religious matters were considered authoritative by the church.

Hildegard's visions have been explored by theologians and also by neurologists, who judge that they may have originated in migraine headaches, as she reports many of the same phenomena that migraine sufferers do: auras of light around objects, areas of blindness, feelings of intense doubt and intense euphoria. The interpretations that she develops come from her theological insight and learning, however, not from her illness. That same insight also emerges in her music, which is what she is best known for today. Eighty of her compositions survive — a huge number for a medieval composer — most of them written to

Inspired by heavenly fire, Hildegard begins to dictate her visions to her scribe. The original of this elaborately illustrated copy of *Scivias* disappeared from Hildegard's convent during World War II, but fortunately a facsimile had already been made. (Private Collection/ The Bridgeman Art Library)

be sung by the nuns in her convent, so they have strong lines for female voices. Many of her songs and chants have been recorded recently by various artists and are available on compact disk, as downloads, and on several Web sites.

QUESTIONS FOR ANALYSIS

1. Why do you think Hildegard might have kept her visions secret at first? Why do you think she eventually sought church approval for them?
2. In what ways were Hildegard's accomplishments extraordinary given women's general status in the Middle Ages?

LaunchPad

ONLINE DOCUMENT PROJECT

Why was Hildegard of Bingen considered a worthy instrument for the transmission of God's word? Read excerpts from Hildegard's correspondence, and then complete a quiz and writing assignment based on the evidence and details from this chapter. *See inside the front cover to learn more.*

*From *Scivias*, trans. Mother Columba Hart and Jane Bishop, *The Classics of Western Spirituality* (New York/Mahwah: Paulist Press, 1990).

Routines within individual monasteries varied widely from house to house and from region to region. In every monastery, however, daily life centered on the liturgy or Divine Office, psalms, and other prayers, which monks and nuns said seven times a day and once during the night. Praying was looked on as a vital service. Prayers were said for peace, rain, good harvests, the civil authorities, the monks' and nuns' families, and their benefactors. Monastic patrons in turn lavished gifts on the monasteries, which often became very wealthy, controlling large tracts of land and the peasants who farmed them. The combination of lay control and wealth created problems for monasteries as monks and nuns concentrated on worldly issues and spiritual observance and intellectual activity declined.

In the thirteenth century the growth of cities provided a new challenge for the church. Many urban people thought that the church did not meet their spiritual needs. They turned instead to heresies—that is, to versions of Christianity outside of those approved by the papacy, many of which called on the church to give up its wealth and power. Combating **heresy** became a principal task of new religious orders, most prominently the Dominicans and Franciscans, who preached and ministered to city dwellers; the Dominicans also staffed the papal Inquisition, a special court designed to root out heresy.

Popular Religion

Religious practices varied widely from country to country and even from province to province. But everywhere, religion permeated everyday life.

For Christians, the village church was the center of community life, with the parish priest in charge of a host of activities. People gathered at the church for services on Sundays and holy days, breaking the painful routine of work. The feasts that accompanied celebrations were commonly held in the churchyard. In everyday life people engaged in rituals and used language heavy with religious symbolism. Everyone participated in village processions to honor the saints and ask their protection. The entire calendar was designed with reference to Christmas, Easter, and Pentecost, events in the life of Jesus and his disciples.

The Christian calendar was also filled with saints' days. Saints were individuals who had lived particularly holy lives and were honored locally or more widely for their connection with the divine. People believed that the saints possessed supernatural powers that enabled them to perform miracles, and each saint became the special property of the locality in which his or her relics—remains or possessions—rested. In return for the saint's healing powers and support, peasants would offer prayers, loyalty, and gifts. The Virgin Mary, Christ's mother, became the most important saint.

Most people in medieval Europe were Christian, but there were small Jewish communities scattered through many parts of Europe, as well as Muslims in the Iberian Peninsula, Sicily, other Mediterranean islands, and southeastern Europe. Increasing suspicion and hostility marked relations among believers in different religions throughout the Middle Ages, but there were also important similarities in the ways that each group understood and experienced their faiths. In all three traditions, every major life transition was marked by a ceremony that involved religious officials or spiritual elements. In all three faiths, death was marked by religious rituals, and the living had obligations to the dead, including prayers and special mourning periods.

heresy
▶ An opinion, belief, or action counter to doctrines that church leaders defined as correct; heretics could be punished by the church.

CHAPTER LOCATOR | How did medieval rulers restore order and centralize political power?

How did the Christian Church enhance its power and create new institutions?

398 CHAPTER 14 EUROPE IN THE MIDDLE AGES

The Expansion of Christianity

The eleventh and twelfth centuries saw an expansion of Christianity into Scandinavia, the Baltic lands, eastern Europe, and Spain that had profound cultural consequences. The expansion was accomplished through wars, the establishment of new bishoprics, and the vast migration of Christian colonists into non-Christian territories. More and more Europeans began to think of themselves as belonging to a realm of Christianity that was political as well as religious, a realm they called Christendom.

Christian influences entered Scandinavia and the Baltic lands primarily through the creation of dioceses (church districts headed by bishops). This took place in Denmark and Norway in the tenth and eleventh centuries, and then in Sweden and Finland. In all of these areas, Christian missionaries preached, baptized, and built churches. Royal power advanced institutional Christianity, and traditional Norse religions practiced by the Vikings were outlawed. In eastern Europe the German emperor Otto I (see page 393) planted a string of dioceses along his northern and eastern frontiers, hoping to pacify the newly conquered Slavs in eastern Europe. German nobles built castles and ruthlessly crushed revolts by Slavic peoples.

The church also moved into central Europe, first into Bohemia in the tenth century and from there into Poland and Hungary in the eleventh century. In the twelfth and thirteenth centuries thousands of settlers poured into eastern Europe from the west.

The Iberian Peninsula was another area of Christian expansion. In about 950 Caliph Abd al-Rahman III (912–961) of the Umayyad Dynasty of Córdoba ruled most of the peninsula. Christian Spain consisted of a number of small kingdoms. In the eleventh century divisions and civil wars in the caliphate of Córdoba allowed Christian armies to conquer an increasingly large part of the Iberian Peninsula. By 1248 Christians held all of the peninsula save for the small state of Granada in the south.

Fourteenth-century clerical writers would call the movement to expel the Muslims the **reconquista** (ray-kon-KEES-tah; reconquest)—a sacred and patriotic crusade to wrest the country from "alien" Muslim hands. This religious idea became part of Spanish political culture and of the national psychology. Rulers of the Christian kingdoms of Spain increasingly passed legislation discriminating against Muslims and Jews living under Christian rule, and they attempted to exclude anyone from the nobility who could not prove "purity of blood"—that is, that they had no Muslim or Jewish ancestors.

Spain was not the only place in Europe where "blood" became a way of understanding differences among people and a basis for discriminatory laws. When Germans moved into eastern Europe and English forces took over much of Ireland, they increasingly barred local people from access to legal courts and denied them positions in monasteries or craft guilds. They banned intermarriage between ethnic groups in an attempt to maintain ethnic purity, even though everyone was Christian.

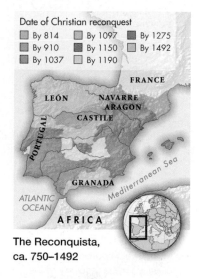

Date of Christian reconquest
- By 814
- By 910
- By 1037
- By 1097
- By 1150
- By 1190
- By 1275
- By 1492

The Reconquista, ca. 750–1492

reconquista
▶ A fourteenth-century term used to describe the long Christian crusade to wrest Spain back from the Muslims; clerics believed it was a sacred and patriotic mission.

QUICK REVIEW ◀

Why did efforts at church reform lead to conflict between secular and religious leaders?

| What were the causes, course, and consequences of the Crusades? | How did the lives of common people, nobles, and townspeople differ? | What were the primary educational and cultural developments in medieval Europe? | Why have the later Middle Ages been seen as a time of calamity and crisis? | LearningCurve Check what you know. |

> What were the causes, course, and consequences of the Crusades?

Córdoba Mosque and Cathedral

The huge arches of the Great Mosque at Córdoba dwarf the cathedral built in its center after the city was conquered by Christian armies in 1236. During the reconquista (see page 399), Christian kings often transformed mosques into churches, often by simply adding Christian elements such as crosses and altars to existing structures. (© dbimages/Alamy)

Crusades
▶ Holy wars sponsored by the papacy for the recovery of the Holy Land from the Muslims.

THE EXPANSION OF CHRISTIANITY in the Middle Ages was not limited to Europe but extended to the eastern Mediterranean in what were later termed the **Crusades**. Occurring in the late eleventh and early twelfth centuries, the Crusades were wars sponsored by the papacy to recover the holy city of Jerusalem from the Muslims.

Background and Motives

In the eleventh century the papacy had strong reasons for wanting to launch an expedition against Muslims in the East. Such an expedition would strengthen his claim to be the leader of Christian society in the West. Moreover, in 1054 a serious theological disagreement had split the Greek Church of Byzantium and the Roman Church of the West. The pope believed that a crusade would lead to strong Roman influence in Greek territories and eventually the reunion of the two churches.

Popes and other church officials gained support for war in defense of Christianity by promising spiritual benefits to those who joined a campaign or died fighting. Preachers communicated these ideas widely and told stories about warrior-saints who slew hundreds of enemies.

Religious zeal led increasing numbers of people to go on pilgrimages to holy places, including Jerusalem. The Arab Muslims who had ruled Jerusalem and the surrounding territory for centuries allowed Christian pilgrims to travel freely, but in the late eleventh century the Seljuk Turks took over Palestine, and pilgrimage became more difficult. The Byzantine emperor at Constantinople appealed to western European Christians for support. The emperor's appeal fit well with

R 14
N THE MIDDLE AGES

papal aims, and in 1095 Pope Urban II called for a great Christian holy war. Urban urged Christian knights who had been fighting one another to direct their energies against those he claimed were the true enemies of God, the Muslims.

The Course of the Crusades

Thousands of people of all classes responded to Urban's call, joining what became known as the First Crusade. The First Crusade was successful, mostly because of the dynamic enthusiasm of the participants, who had little more than religious zeal. They knew little of the geography or climate of the Middle East and could never agree on a leader. Adding to these disadvantages, supply lines were never set up, starvation and disease wracked the army, and the Turks slaughtered hundreds of noncombatants. Nevertheless, the army pressed on, besieging and taking several cities, including Antioch. After a monthlong siege, the Crusaders took Jerusalem in July 1099 (Map 14.2).

With Jerusalem taken, some Crusaders regarded their mission as accomplished and set off for home. Others stayed, setting up institutions to rule local territories and the Muslim population. Four small "Crusader states"—Jerusalem, Edessa, Tripoli, and Antioch—were established, and castles and fortified towns were built in these states to defend against Muslim reconquest.

Between 1096 and 1270 the crusading ideal was expressed in eight papally approved expeditions, though none after the First Crusade accomplished very much. The Muslim states in the Middle East were politically fragmented when the Crusaders first came, and it took them about a century to reorganize. They did so dramatically under Saladin (Salah al-Din), who unified Egypt and Syria. In 1187 the Muslims retook Jerusalem, but the Christians held onto port towns, and Saladin allowed pilgrims safe passage to Jerusalem. From that point on, the Crusader states were more important economically than politically or religiously, giving Italian and French merchants direct access to Eastern products.

After the Muslims retook Jerusalem, the crusading movement faced other setbacks. During the Fourth Crusade (1202–1204), Crusaders stopped in Constantinople, and when they were not welcomed, they sacked the city. The Byzantine Empire splintered into three parts and soon consisted of little more than the city of Constantinople. Moreover, the assault of one Christian people on another, made the split between the churches permanent and discredited the entire crusading movement in the eyes of many Christians.

In the late thirteenth century Turkish armies, after gradually conquering all other Muslim rulers, turned against the Crusader states. In 1291 the Christians' last stronghold, the port of Acre, fell.

Consequences of the Crusades

The Crusades testified to the religious enthusiasm of the High Middle Ages and the influence of the papacy, gave kings and the pope opportunities to expand their bureaucracies, and provided an outlet for nobles' dreams of glory. The Crusades also introduced some Europeans to Eastern luxury goods. They were also a boon to Italian merchants, who profited from outfitting military expeditions as well as from the opening of new trade routes and the establishment of trading communities in the Crusader states.

| What were the causes, course, and consequences of the Crusades? | How did the lives of common people, nobles, and townspeople differ? | What were the primary educational and cultural developments in medieval Europe? | Why have the later Middle Ages been seen as a time of calamity and crisis? | ✓ LearningCurve Check what you know. |

401

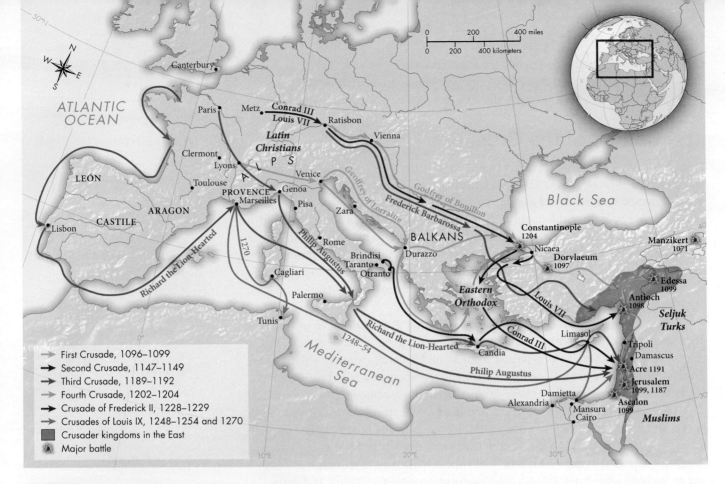

MAP 14.2 ■ The Crusades, 1096–1270

The Crusaders took many different sea and land routes on their way to Jerusalem, often crossing the lands of the Byzantine Empire, which led to conflict with Eastern Christians. The Crusader kingdoms in the East lasted only briefly.

Map legend:
→ First Crusade, 1096–1099
→ Second Crusade, 1147–1149
→ Third Crusade, 1189–1192
→ Fourth Crusade, 1202–1204
→ Crusade of Frederick II, 1228–1229
→ Crusades of Louis IX, 1248–1254 and 1270
▨ Crusader kingdoms in the East
✳ Major battle

Despite these advantages, the Crusades had some seriously negative sociopolitical consequences. For one thing, they proved to be a disaster for Jewish-Christian relations. Inspired by the ideology of holy war, Christian armies on their way to Jerusalem on the First Crusade joined with local mobs to attack Jewish families and communities. Later Crusades brought similar violence, enhanced by accusations that Jews engaged in the ritual murder of Christians to use their blood in religious rites.

Legal restrictions on Jews gradually increased throughout Europe. Jews were forbidden to have Christian servants or employees, to hold public office, to appear in public on Christian holy days, or to enter Christian parts of town without a badge marking them as Jews. They were prohibited from engaging in any trade with Christians except money-lending and were banished from England and France.

The Crusades also left an inheritance of deep bitterness in Christian-Muslim relations. Each side dehumanized the other, viewing those who followed the other religion as unbelievers. The ideal of a sacred mission to conquer or convert Muslim peoples entered Europeans' consciousness and became a continuing goal. When in 1492 Christopher Columbus sailed west, he used the language of the Crusades in his diaries, and he hoped to establish a Christian base in India from which a new crusade against Islam could be launched (see page 464).

> **QUICK REVIEW**

Why did the Crusades undermine relations between Christians and non-Christians?

CHAPTER LOCATOR | How did medieval rulers restore order and centralize political power? | How did the Christian Church enhance its power and create new institutions?

Agricultural Work

In this scene from a German manuscript written about 1190, men and women of different ages are sowing seeds and harvesting grain. All residents of a village, including children, engaged in agricultural tasks. (Rheinisches Landesmuseum, Bonn, Germany/Giraudon/The Bridgeman Art Library)

How did the lives of common people, nobles, and townspeople differ, and what new commercial developments increased wealth?

IN THE LATE NINTH CENTURY medieval intellectuals described Christian society as composed of those who pray (the monks), those who fight (the nobles), and those who work (the peasants). This three-category model does not fully describe medieval society—there were degrees of wealth and status within each group. Also, the model does not take townspeople and the emerging commercial classes into consideration, and it completely excludes those who were not Christian, such as Jews, Muslims, and pagans. Furthermore, those who used the model, generally bishops and other church officials, ignored the fact that each of these groups was made up of both women and men. Despite—or perhaps because of—these limitations, the model of the three categories was a powerful mental construct. Therefore, we can use it to organize our investigation of life in the Middle Ages, broadening it to include groups and issues that medieval authors did not. (See page 396 for a discussion of the life of monks and nuns—"those who pray.")

The Life and Work of Peasants

The men and women who worked the land in medieval Europe made up probably more than 90 percent of the population, as they did in China, India, and other parts of the world where agriculture predominated. The evolution of localized systems of authority into more centralized states had relatively little impact on the daily lives of these peasants except when it involved warfare.

| What were the causes, course, and consequences of the Crusades? | **How did the lives of common people, nobles, and townspeople differ?** | What were the primary educational and cultural developments in medieval Europe? | Why have the later Middle Ages been seen as a time of calamity and crisis? | ✓ LearningCurve Check what you know. |

Medieval theologians lumped everyone who worked the land into the category of "those who work," but in fact there were many levels of peasants, ranging from slaves to free and sometimes very rich farmers. Most peasants were serfs, required to stay in the village and perform labor on the lord's land. Serfs were also often obliged to pay fees on common occurrences, such as marriage or inheritance of property.

Serfdom was a hereditary condition. A person born a serf was likely to die a serf, though many serfs did secure their freedom, and the economic revival that began in the eleventh century (see pages 405–406) allowed some to buy their freedom. Further opportunities for increased personal freedom came when lords organized groups of villagers to migrate to sparsely settled frontier areas or to cut down forests or fill in swamps so that there was more land available for farming. Those who took on this extra work often gained a reduction in traditional manorial obligations and an improvement of their social and legal conditions.

In the Middle Ages most European peasants, free and unfree, lived in family groups in small villages that were part of a manor, the estate of a lord (see page 391). The manor was the basic unit of medieval rural organization and the center of rural life. Within the manors of western and central Europe, villages were made up of small houses for individual families, a church, and perhaps the large house of the lord. Peasant households consisted of one married couple, their children, and perhaps one or two other relatives, such as a grandparent or unmarried aunt. In southern and eastern Europe, extended families were more likely to live in the same household or very near one another. Between one-third and one-half of children died before age five, though many people lived into their sixties.

The arable land of the manor was divided between the lord and the peasantry. A peasant family's land was not usually one particular field but a scattering of strips across many fields, some of which would be planted in grain, some in other crops, and some left unworked to allow the soil to rejuvenate. That way if one field yielded little, strips in a different field might be more bountiful.

The peasants' work was typically divided according to gender. Men and boys were responsible for clearing new land, plowing, and caring for large animals; women and girls were responsible for the care of small animals, spinning, and food preparation. Both sexes harvested and planted. Beginning in the eleventh century water mills and windmills aided in some tasks, especially grinding grain, and an increasing use of horses rather than oxen speeded up plowing.

The mainstay of the diet for peasants everywhere—and for all other classes—was bread. Peasants also ate vegetables; animals were too valuable to be used for food on a regular basis, but weaker animals were often slaughtered in the fall, and their meat was preserved with salt and eaten on great feast days such as Christmas and Easter. Ale was the universal drink of common people.

The Life and Work of Nobles

The nobility, though a small fraction of the total population, influenced all aspects of medieval culture. Nobles generally paid few taxes, and they had power over the people living on their lands. They maintained order, resolved disputes, and protected their dependents from attacks. They appointed officials who oversaw agricultural production. The liberty and privileges of the noble were inheritable, perpetuated by blood and not by wealth alone.

CHAPTER LOCATOR | How did medieval rulers restore order and centralize political power? | How did the Christian Church enhance its power and create new institutions?

CHAPTER 14
404   EUROPE IN THE MIDDLE AGES

The nobles' primary obligation was warfare, just as it was for nobles among the Mexica (see pages 314–317) and samurai in Japan (see page 381). Nobles were also obliged to attend the lord's court on important occasions.

Originally, most knights focused solely on military skills, but around 1200 a different ideal of knighthood emerged, usually termed **chivalry**. Chivalry was a code of conduct in which fighting to defend the Christian faith and protecting one's countrymen was declared to have a sacred purpose. Other qualities gradually became part of chivalry: bravery, generosity, honor, graciousness, mercy, and eventually gallantry toward women, which came to be called "courtly love."

Noblewomen played a large and important role in the functioning of the estate. They were responsible for managing the household's "inner economy"—cooking, brewing, spinning, weaving, and caring for yard animals. When the lord was away for long periods, his wife became the sole manager of the family properties. Often the responsibilities of the estate fell permanently to her if she became a widow.

chivalry
▶ A code of conduct that was supposed to govern the behavior of a knight.

Towns, Cities, and the Growth of Commercial Interests

Most people continued to live in villages in the Middle Ages, but the rise of towns and the growth of a new business and commercial class were central to Europe's recovery after the disorders of the tenth century. Several factors contributed to this growth: a rise in population; increased agricultural output, which provided an adequate food supply for new town dwellers; and enough peace and political stability to allow merchants to transport and sell goods.

Towns in Europe were generally enclosed by walls as were towns in China, India, and the Middle East. Most towns were first established as trading centers, with a marketplace in the middle, and they were likely to have a mint for coining money and a court for settling disputes. Residents bargained with lords to make the town politically independent, which gave them the right to hold legal courts, select leaders, and set taxes.

Townspeople also tried to acquire liberties, above all personal freedom, for themselves. It gradually developed that an individual who lived in a town for a year and a day, and was accepted by the townspeople, was free of servile obligations and status. Thus serfs who fled their manors for towns and were able to find work and avoid recapture became free of personal labor obligations. In this way the growth of towns contributed to a slow decline of serfdom in western Europe.

Merchants constituted the most powerful group in most towns, and they were often organized into merchant guilds, which prohibited nonmembers from trading, pooled members' risks, monopolized city offices, and controlled the economy of the town. Towns became centers of production as well, and artisans in particular trades formed their own **craft guilds**. Members of the craft guilds determined the quality, quantity, and price of the goods produced and the number of apprentices and journeymen affiliated with the guild. Formal membership in guilds was generally limited to men, but women often worked in guild shops without official membership.

craft guilds
▶ Associations of artisans organized to regulate the quality, quantity, and price of the goods produced as well as the number of affiliated apprentices and journeymen.

Artisans generally made and sold products in their own homes, with production taking place on the ground floor. The family lived above the business on the second or third floor. As the business and the family expanded, additional stories were added.

What were the causes, course, and consequences of the Crusades?

How did the lives of common people, nobles, and townspeople differ?

What were the primary educational and cultural developments in medieval Europe?

Why have the later Middle Ages been seen as a time of calamity and crisis?

✓ LearningCurve
Check what you know.

405

Most medieval towns and cities developed with little planning or attention to sanitation. Horses and oxen, the chief means of transportation and power, dropped tons of dung on the streets every year. It was universal practice in the early towns to dump household waste, both animal and human, into the road in front of one's house. Despite such unpleasant aspects of urban life, people wanted to get into medieval towns because they represented opportunities for economic advancement, social mobility, and improvement in legal status.

The Expansion of Trade and the Commercial Revolution

The growth of towns went hand in hand with a revival of trade as artisans and craftsmen manufactured goods for local and foreign consumption. As in the city-states of East Africa (see pages 288–290), most trade centered in towns and was controlled by merchants. They began to pool their money to finance trading expeditions, sharing the profits and also sharing the risks.

Italian cities, especially Venice, led the West in trade in general and completely dominated trade with Asia and North Africa. Merchants from Florence and Milan were also important traders, and they developed new methods of accounting and record keeping that facilitated the movement of goods and money. The towns of Bruges, Ghent, and Ypres in Flanders were leaders in long-distance trade and built up a vast industry in the manufacture of cloth, aided by ready access to wool from England. The availability of raw wool also encouraged the development of cloth manufacture within England itself.

In much of northern Europe, the Hanseatic League (known as the Hansa for short), a mercantile association of towns formed to achieve mutual security and exclusive trading rights, controlled trade. During the thirteenth century perhaps two hundred cities from Holland to Poland joined the league. At cities such as Bruges and London, Hanseatic merchants secured special concessions exempting them from all tolls and allowing them to trade at local fairs. Hanseatic merchants also established foreign trading centers.

These developments added up to what historians of Europe have called the **commercial revolution**, a direct parallel to the economic revolution going on in Song Dynasty China at the same time (see pages 366–368). In giving the transformation this name, historians point not only to an increase in the sheer volume of trade and in the complexity and sophistication of business procedures but also to the new attitude toward business and making money. Some even detect a "capitalist spirit" in which making a profit was regarded as a good thing in itself.

The commercial revolution created a great deal of new wealth, which did not escape the attention of kings and other rulers. Wealth could be taxed, and through taxation kings could create strong and centralized states. Through the activities of merchants, Europeans again saw products from Africa and Asia in city marketplaces, as they had in Roman times. The commercial revolution also provided the opportunity for thousands of serfs in western Europe to improve their social position.

• Principal Hanseatic town
▲ Hanseatic trading partner

The Hanseatic League, 1300–1400

commercial revolution
▶ The transformation of the economic structure of Europe, beginning in the eleventh century, from a rural, manorial society to a more complex mercantile society.

> **QUICK REVIEW**

What are the limitations of the three-category model of medieval society? What aspects of that society does the model fail to capture?

CHAPTER LOCATOR | How did medieval rulers restore order and centralize political power? | How did the Christian Church enhance its power and create new institutions?

What were the primary educational and cultural developments in medieval Europe?

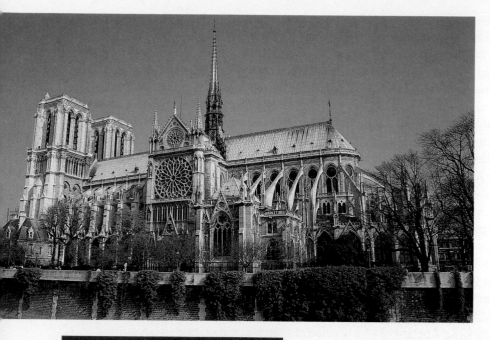

THE TOWNS THAT BECAME centers of trade and production in the High Middle Ages also developed into cultural and intellectual centers. Trade brought in new ideas as well as merchandise, and in many cities a new type of educational institution—the university—emerged. As universities appeared, so did other cultural advancements, such as new forms of architecture and literature.

Universities and Scholasticism

Since the time of the Carolingian Empire, monasteries and cathedral schools had offered the only formal instruction available. In the eleventh century in Bologna and other Italian cities, wealthy businessmen established municipal schools; in the twelfth century municipal schools in Italy and cathedral schools in France developed into much larger universities, a transformation parallel to the opening of madrasas in Muslim cities (see page 000).

The growth of the University of Bologna coincided with a revival of interest in Roman law. The study of Roman law as embodied in Justinian's *Code* (see page 206) had never completely died out in the West, but in the eleventh century

| What were the causes, course, and consequences of the Crusades? | How did the lives of common people, nobles, and townspeople differ? | **What were the primary educational and cultural developments in medieval Europe?** | Why have the later Middle Ages been seen as a time of calamity and crisis? | ✓ LearningCurve Check what you know. |

407

the discovery of a complete manuscript of the code in a library in northern Italy led scholars to study and teach Roman law intently.

At the Italian city of Salerno, interest in medicine had persisted for centuries. Greek and Muslim physicians there had studied the use of herbs as cures and had experimented with surgery. The twelfth century ushered in a new interest in Greek medical texts and in the work of Arab and Greek doctors. Ideas from this medical literature spread throughout Europe from Salerno and became the basis of training for physicians at other medieval universities.

Although medicine and law were important academic disciplines in the Middle Ages, theology was "the queen of sciences." Paris became the place to study theology, and in the first decades of the twelfth century students from all over Europe crowded into the cathedral school of Notre Dame in that city.

University professors were known as "schoolmen" or **Scholastics**. They developed a method of thinking, reasoning, and writing in which questions were raised and authorities cited on both sides of a question. The goal of the Scholastic method was to arrive at definitive answers and to provide a rational explanation for what was believed on faith.

One of the most famous Scholastics was Peter Abelard (1079–1142). Fascinated by logic, Abelard used a method of systematic doubting in his writing and teaching. Abelard was censured by a church council, but he was highly popular with students.

Thirteenth-century Scholastics devoted an enormous amount of time to collecting and organizing knowledge on all topics. These collections were published as summae (SOO-may), or reference books. Thomas Aquinas (1225–1274), a professor at the University of Paris, produced the most famous collection, the *Summa Theologica*, which deals with a vast number of theological questions.

Students lived in privately endowed residential colleges and were considered to be lower-level members of the clergy, so that any student accused of a crime was tried in church, rather than in city, courts. This clerical status, along with widely held ideas about women's lesser intellectual capabilities, meant that university education was restricted to men.

At all universities the standard method of teaching was the lecture. With this method the professor read a passage from the Bible, Justinian's *Code*, or one of Aristotle's treatises. He then explained and interpreted the passage. Examinations were given after three, four, or five years of study, when the student applied for a degree. If the candidate passed, he was awarded the first, or bachelor's, degree. Further study enabled the graduate to try for the master's and doctor's degrees. Degrees were technically licenses to teach. Most students, however, did not become teachers. They staffed the expanding royal and papal administrations.

Cathedrals and a New Architectural Style

In the tenth and eleventh centuries cathedrals were built in a style that resembled ancient Roman architecture, with massive walls, rounded stone arches, and small windows—features later labeled Romanesque. In the twelfth century a new style spread out from central France. It was dubbed **Gothic** by later Renaissance architects. The basic features of Gothic architecture—pointed arches, high ceilings, and exterior supports called flying buttresses that carried much of the weight of

Scholastics

▶ Medieval professors who developed a method of thinking, reasoning, and writing in which questions were raised and authorities cited on both sides of a question.

Gothic

▶ The term for the architectural and artistic style that prevailed in Europe from the mid-twelfth to the sixteenth century.

CHAPTER LOCATOR | How did medieval rulers restore order and centralize political power? | How did the Christian Church enhance its power and create new institutions?

408 CHAPTER 14 EUROPE IN THE MIDDLE AGES

the roof—allowed unprecedented interior light. Stained-glass windows were cut into the stone. Between 1180 and 1270 in France alone, eighty cathedrals, about five hundred abbey churches, and tens of thousands of parish churches were constructed in this new style. They are testimony to the deep religious faith and piety of medieval people and also to the civic pride of urban residents, for towns competed with one another to build the largest and most splendid cathedral.

Vernacular Literature and Drama

Latin was the language used in university education, scholarly writing, and works of literature. By the High Middle Ages, however, no one spoke Latin as his or her first language. The barbarian invasions, the mixture of peoples, and the usual changes in language that occurred over time resulted in a variety of local dialects that blended words and linguistic forms in various ways.

In the High Middle Ages, some authors departed from tradition and began to write in their local dialect, that is, in the everyday language of their region, which linguistic historians call the vernacular. This new **vernacular literature** gradually transformed some local dialects into literary languages, such as French, German, Italian, and English, while other local dialects, such as Breton and Bavarian, remained means of oral communication.

Stories and songs in the vernacular were composed and performed at the courts of nobles and rulers. In southern Europe, especially in Provence in southern France, poets who called themselves troubadours wrote and sang lyric verses celebrating love, desire, beauty, and gallantry. The songs of the troubadours were widely imitated in Italy, England, and Germany, so they spurred the development of vernacular literature there as well. Drama, derived from the church's liturgy, emerged as a distinct art form. Actors performed plays based on biblical themes and on the lives of the saints; these dramas were presented in the towns, first in churches and then at the marketplace. By combining comical farce based on ordinary life with serious religious scenes, plays gave ordinary people an opportunity to identify with religious figures and think about their faith.

Beginning in the fourteenth century a variety of evidence attests to the increasing literacy of laypeople. Wills and inventories reveal that many people, not just nobles, possessed books—mainly devotional texts, but also romances, manuals on manners and etiquette, histories, and sometimes legal and philosophical texts. The spread of literacy represents a response to the needs of an increasingly complex society.

vernacular literature
▶ Literature written in the everyday language of a region rather than Latin; this included French, German, Italian, and English.

QUICK REVIEW <

What trends and values are reflected in the emergence of vernacular literature during this period?

| What were the causes, course, and consequences of the Crusades? | How did the lives of common people, nobles, and townspeople differ? | **What were the primary educational and cultural developments in medieval Europe?** | Why have the later Middle Ages been seen as a time of calamity and crisis? | LearningCurve Check what you know. |

> Why have the later Middle Ages been seen as a time of calamity and crisis?

Procession of Flagellants

In this manuscript illumination from 1349, shirtless flagellants, men and women who whipped and scourged themselves as penance for their and society's sins, walk through the Flemish city of Tournai, which had just been struck by the plague. Many people believed that the Black Death was God's punishment for humanity's wickedness. (The Flagellants at Doornik in 1349, copy of a miniature from the *Chronicle of Aegidius Li Muisis*/Private Collection/The Bridgeman Art Library)

BETWEEN 1300 AND 1450 Europeans experienced a series of shocks: climate change, economic decline, plague, war, social upheaval, and increased crime and violence. Death and preoccupation with death made the fourteenth century one of the most wrenching periods of history in Europe.

The Great Famine and the Black Death

In the first half of the fourteenth century Europe experienced a series of climate changes, especially the beginning of a period of colder and wetter weather that historical geographers label the "little ice age." Its effects were dramatic and disastrous. Population had steadily increased in the twelfth and thirteenth centuries, but with colder weather, poor harvests led to scarcity and starvation. The costs of grain, livestock, and dairy products rose sharply. Almost all of northern Europe suffered a terrible famine between 1315 and 1322, with dire social consequences: peasants were forced to sell or mortgage their lands for money to buy food, and the number of homeless people greatly increased, as did petty crime. An undernourished population was dealt a further blow in 1347 in the form of a virulent new disease, later called the **Black Death** (Map 14.3). The symptoms of

Black Death
▶ The plague that first struck Europe in 1347, killing perhaps one-third of the population.

CHAPTER LOCATOR | How did medieval rulers restore order and centralize political power? | How did the Christian Church enhance its power and create new institutions?

410 CHAPTER 14 EUROPE IN THE MIDDLE AGES

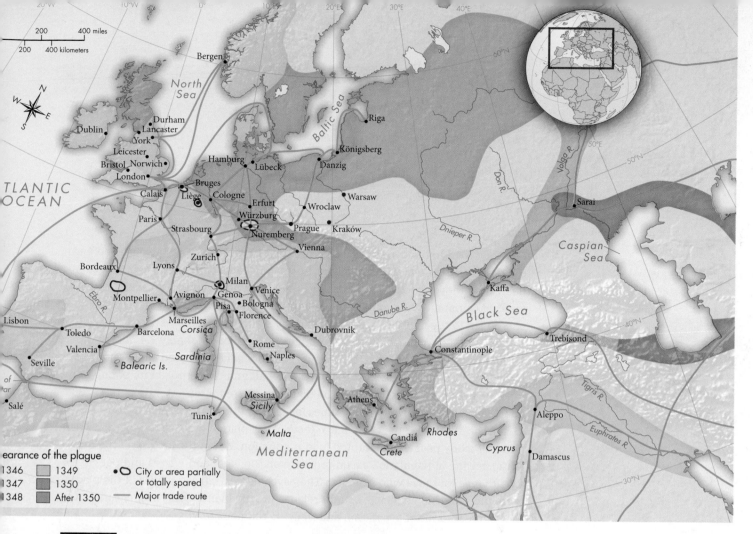

Appearance of the plague

1346		1349	● ◯ City or area partially or totally spared
1347		1350	
1348		After 1350	— Major trade route

MAP 14.3 ■ The Course of the Black Death in Fourteenth-Century Europe

The plague followed trade routes as it spread into and across Europe. A few cities that took strict quarantine measures were spared.

this disease were first described in 1331 in southwestern China, then part of the Mongol Empire (see page 256). From there it spread across Central Asia by way of Mongol armies and merchant caravans, arriving in the ports of the Black Sea by the 1340s. In October 1347 Genoese ships traveling from the Crimea in southern Russia brought the plague to Messina, from which it spread across Sicily and into Italy. From Italy it traveled in all directions.

Most historians and almost all microbiologists identify the disease that spread in the fourteenth century as the bubonic plague, caused by the bacillus *Yersinia pestis*. The disease normally afflicts rats. Fleas living on the infected rats drink their blood and pass the bacteria that cause the plague on to the next rat they bite. Usually the disease is limited to rats and other rodents, but at certain points in history the fleas have jumped from their rodent hosts to humans and other animals.

Most people believed that the Black Death was caused by poisons or by "corrupted air" that carried the disease from place to place. They sought to keep poisons from entering the body by smelling or ingesting strong-smelling herbs,

What were the causes, course, and consequences of the Crusades?	How did the lives of common people, nobles, and townspeople differ?	What were the primary educational and cultural developments in medieval Europe?	**Why have the later Middle Ages been seen as a time of calamity and crisis?**	✓ LearningCurve Check what you know.

411

Initial Stage	Appearance of boil, or *bubo* (growth the size of a nut or an apple in the armpit, the groin, or on the neck)
Secondary Stage	Appearance of black spots or blotches caused by bleeding under the skin
Final Stage	Victim begins to cough violently and spit blood; death follows in two or three days

and they tried to remove the poisons through bloodletting. They also prayed and did penance. Anxiety and fears about the plague caused people to look for scapegoats, and they found them in the Jews, who they believed had poisoned the wells of Christian communities and thereby infected the drinking water. This charge led to the murder of thousands of Jews across Europe.

Of a total English population of perhaps 4.2 million, probably 1.4 million died of the Black Death in its several visits. In Italy densely populated cities endured incredible losses. Florence lost between one-half and two-thirds of its population when the plague visited in 1348. The disease recurred intermittently in the 1360s and 1370s and reappeared many times, as late as the early 1700s in Europe.

In the short term the economic effects of the plague were severe because the death of many peasants disrupted food production. But in the long term the dramatic decline in population eased pressure on the land, and wages and per capita wealth rose for those who survived. The psychological consequences of the plague were profound. Some people sought release in wild living, while others turned to the severest forms of asceticism and frenzied religious fervor.

The Hundred Years' War

While the plague ravaged populations in Asia, North Africa, and Europe, a long international war in western Europe added further death and destruction. England and France had engaged in sporadic military hostilities from the time of the Norman Conquest in 1066 (see page 393), and in the middle of the fourteenth century these became more intense. From 1337 to 1453 the two countries intermittently fought the Hundred Years' War.

The Hundred Years' War had a number of causes. Both England and France claimed the duchy of Aquitaine in southwestern France, and the English king Edward III argued that, as the grandson of an earlier French king, he should have rightfully inherited the French throne. Nobles in provinces on the borders of France who were worried about the growing power of the French king supported Edward, as did wealthy wool merchants and clothmakers in Flanders who depended on English wool.

The war, fought almost entirely in France, consisted mainly of a series of random sieges and raids. During the war's early stages, England was successful, primarily through the use of longbows fired by well-trained foot soldiers against mounted knights and, after 1375, by early cannons. By 1419 the English had advanced to the walls of Paris. But the French cause was not lost. Though England scored the initial victories, France won the war.

CHAPTER LOCATOR | How did medieval rulers restore order and centralize political power? | How did the Christian Church enhance its power and create new institutions?

CHAPTER 14
412 EUROPE IN THE MIDDLE AGES

Siege of the Castle of Mortagne near Bordeaux

This miniature of a battle in the Hundred Years' War shows the French besieging an English-held castle. Medieval warfare usually consisted of small skirmishes and attacks on castles. (from *The Coronation of Richard II to 1387* by Jean de Batard Wavrin/© British Library Board. All Rights Reserved./ The Bridgeman Art Library)

> PICTURING THE PAST

ANALYZING THE IMAGE: What types of weapons are the attackers and defenders using? How have the attackers on the left enhanced their position?

CONNECTIONS: This painting shows a battle that occurred in 1377, but it was painted about a hundred years later and shows the military technology available at the time it was painted, not at the time of the actual siege. Which of the weapons represent newer forms of military technology? What impact would you expect them to have on warfare?

The ultimate French success rests heavily on the actions of Joan, an obscure French peasant girl whose vision and military leadership revived French fortunes and led to victory. Born in 1412 to well-to-do peasants, Joan grew up in a pious household. During adolescence she began to hear voices, which she later said belonged to Saint Michael, Saint Catherine, and Saint Margaret. In 1428 these voices told her that the dauphin of France—Charles VII, who was uncrowned as king because of the English occupation—had to be crowned and the English expelled from France. Joan went to the French court and secured the support of the dauphin to travel, dressed as a knight, with the French army to the besieged city of Orléans.

At Orléans, Joan inspired and led French attacks, and the English retreated. As a result of her successes, Charles made Joan co-commander of the entire army,

What were the causes, course, and consequences of the Crusades?

How did the lives of common people, nobles, and townspeople differ?

What were the primary educational and cultural developments in medieval Europe?

Why have the later Middle Ages been seen as a time of calamity and crisis?

✔ LearningCurve
Check what you know.

413

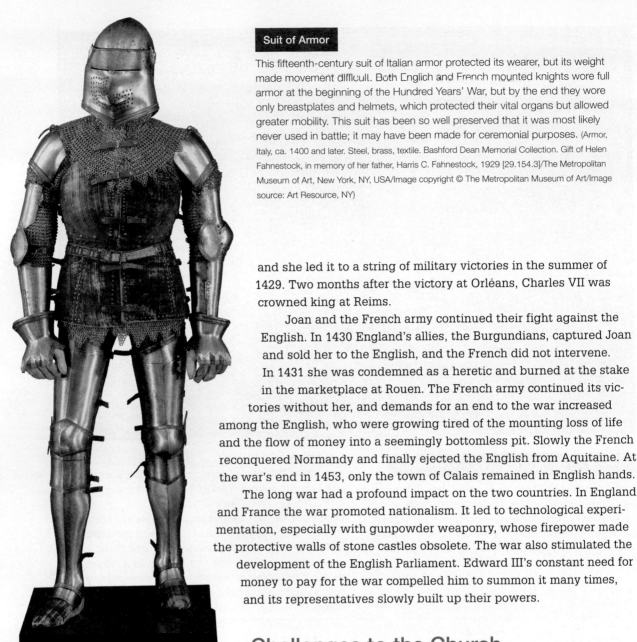

Suit of Armor

This fifteenth-century suit of Italian armor protected its wearer, but its weight made movement difficult. Both English and French mounted knights wore full armor at the beginning of the Hundred Years' War, but by the end they wore only breastplates and helmets, which protected their vital organs but allowed greater mobility. This suit has been so well preserved that it was most likely never used in battle; it may have been made for ceremonial purposes. (Armor, Italy, ca. 1400 and later. Steel, brass, textile. Bashford Dean Memorial Collection. Gift of Helen Fahnestock, in memory of her father, Harris C. Fahnestock, 1929 [29.154.3]/The Metropolitan Museum of Art, New York, NY, USA/Image copyright © The Metropolitan Museum of Art/Image source: Art Resource, NY)

and she led it to a string of military victories in the summer of 1429. Two months after the victory at Orléans, Charles VII was crowned king at Reims.

Joan and the French army continued their fight against the English. In 1430 England's allies, the Burgundians, captured Joan and sold her to the English, and the French did not intervene. In 1431 she was condemned as a heretic and burned at the stake in the marketplace at Rouen. The French army continued its victories without her, and demands for an end to the war increased among the English, who were growing tired of the mounting loss of life and the flow of money into a seemingly bottomless pit. Slowly the French reconquered Normandy and finally ejected the English from Aquitaine. At the war's end in 1453, only the town of Calais remained in English hands.

The long war had a profound impact on the two countries. In England and France the war promoted nationalism. It led to technological experimentation, especially with gunpowder weaponry, whose firepower made the protective walls of stone castles obsolete. The war also stimulated the development of the English Parliament. Edward III's constant need for money to pay for the war compelled him to summon it many times, and its representatives slowly built up their powers.

Challenges to the Church

In times of crisis or disaster people of all faiths have sought the consolation of religion, but in the fourteenth century the official Christian Church offered little solace. While local clergy eased the suffering of many, a dispute over who was the legitimate pope weakened the church as an institution. In 1309 pressure by the French monarchy led the pope to move his permanent residence to Avignon in southern France. This marked the start of seven successive papacies in Avignon. Not surprising, all these popes were French—a matter of controversy among church followers outside France. Also, the popes largely concentrated on bureaucratic and financial matters to the exclusion of spiritual objectives.

In 1376 one of the French popes returned to Rome, and when he died there several years later Roman citizens demanded an Italian pope who would remain

CHAPTER LOCATOR | How did medieval rulers restore order and centralize political power? | How did the Christian Church enhance its power and create new institutions?

in Rome. The cardinals elected Urban VI, but soon regretted their decision. The cardinals slipped away from Rome and declared Urban's election invalid because it had come about under threats from the Roman mob. They elected a French cardinal who took the name Clement VII (pontificate 1378–1394) and set himself up at Avignon in opposition to Urban. There were thus two popes, a situation that was later termed the Great Schism.

The powers of Europe aligned themselves with Urban or Clement along strictly political lines. France recognized the Frenchman, Clement; England, recognized Urban. The rest of Europe lined up behind one or the other. In all European countries the common people were thoroughly confused about which pope was legitimate. In the end the schism weakened the religious faith of many Christians and brought church leadership into serious disrepute.

A first attempt to heal the schism led to the installation of a third pope and a threefold split, but finally a church council meeting at Constance (1414–1418) successfully deposed the three schismatic popes and elected a new leader, who took the name Martin V (pontificate 1417–1431). In the later fifteenth century the papacy concentrated on building up its wealth and political power in Italy rather than on the concerns of the whole church. As a result, many people decided that they would need to rely on their own prayers and pious actions rather than on the institutional church for their salvation.

Allegiance to Rome
Allegiance to Avignon
Official allegiance to Rome but with shifting local allegiances

The Great Schism, 1378–1417

Peasant and Urban Revolts

The difficult conditions of the fourteenth and fifteenth centuries spurred a wave of peasant and urban revolts across Europe. In 1358, when French taxation for the Hundred Years' War fell heavily on the poor, the frustrations of the French peasantry exploded in a massive uprising called the Jacquerie (zhah-kuh-REE). Adding to the anger over taxes was the toll taken by the plague and by the famine that had struck some areas. Artisans, small merchants, and parish priests joined the peasants, and residents of both urban and rural areas committed terrible destruction. For several weeks the nobles were on the defensive, until the upper class united to repress the revolt with merciless ferocity.

Taxes and other grievances also led to the 1381 English Peasants' Revolt, involving tens of thousands of people. The Black Death had dramatically reduced the supply of labor, and peasants had demanded higher wages and fewer manorial obligations. Parliament countered with a law freezing wages and binding workers to their manors. The atmosphere of discontent was further enhanced by popular preachers who proclaimed that great disparities between rich and poor went against Christ's teachings. Moreover, decades of aristocratic violence, much of it perpetrated against the weak peasantry, had bred hostility and bitterness.

In 1380 Parliament imposed a poll tax on all citizens to fund the Hundred Years' War. This tax imposed a greater burden on the poor than on wealthier citizens, and it sparked revolt. The boy-king Richard II (r. 1377–1399) met the leaders of the revolt, agreed to charters ensuring the peasants' freedom, tricked them with false promises, and then proceeded to crush the uprising with terrible ferocity. The nobility tried to use this defeat to restore the labor obligations of serfdom, but they were not successful, and the conversion to money rents continued. In Flanders, France, and England peasant revolts often blended with conflicts

What were the causes, course, and consequences of the Crusades? | How did the lives of common people, nobles, and townspeople differ? | What were the primary educational and cultural developments in medieval Europe? | **Why have the later Middle Ages been seen as a time of calamity and crisis?** | ✓ LearningCurve Check what you know.

415

involving workers in cities. Unrest also occurred in Italian, Spanish, and German cities. In Florence in 1378 the *ciompi*, or poor propertyless wool workers, revolted and briefly shared government of the city with wealthier artisans and merchants. Rebellions and uprisings everywhere revealed deep peasant and worker frustration with the socioeconomic conditions of the time.

> **QUICK REVIEW**

What were the social and economic consequences of the Black Death?

CHAPTER SUMMARY

Invasions by Vikings, Magyars, and Muslims, along with civil wars, created instability in the ninth and tenth centuries. Local nobles became the strongest powers against external threats, establishing a form of decentralized government later known as feudalism. By the twelfth century rulers in some parts of Europe had reasserted authority and were beginning to develop new institutions of government and legal codes that enabled them to assert power over lesser lords and the general population. The papacy also consolidated its power, though these moves were sometimes challenged by kings and emperors. Monasteries continued to be important places for learning and devotion, and new religious orders were founded. A papal call to retake the holy city of Jerusalem led to the Crusades.

The vast majority of medieval Europeans were peasants who lived in small villages and worked their own and their lord's land. Nobles were a tiny fraction of the total population, but they exerted great power over all aspects of life. Medieval towns and cities grew initially as trading centers and then became centers of production.

Towns also developed into cultural and intellectual centers, as trade brought in new ideas as well as merchandise. Universities offered courses of study based on classical models, and townspeople built churches and cathedrals as symbols of their Christian faith and their civic pride. New types of vernacular literature arose in which poems, songs, and stories were written down in local dialects.

In the fourteenth century a worsening climate brought poor harvests, which contributed to an international economic depression and fostered disease. The Black Death caused enormous population losses and social, psychological, and economic consequences. Additional difficulties included the Hundred Years' War, a schism among rival popes that weakened the Western Christian Church, and peasant and worker frustrations that exploded into uprisings.

CHAPTER LOCATOR | How did medieval rulers restore order and centralize political power? | How did the Christian Church enhance its power and create new institutions?

416 CHAPTER 14 EUROPE IN THE MIDDLE AGES

CONNECTIONS Medieval Europe continues to fascinate us today. We go to medieval fairs; visit castle-themed hotels; watch movies about knights and their conquests; play video games in which we become warriors, trolls, or sorcerers; and read stories with themes of great quests set in the Middle Ages. Characters from other parts of the world often heighten the exoticism: a Muslim soldier joins the fight against a common enemy, a Persian princess rescues the hero and his sidekick, a Buddhist monk teaches martial arts techniques. These characters from outside Europe are fictional, but they also represent aspects of reality because medieval Europe was not isolated, and political and social structures similar to those in Europe developed elsewhere.

In reality few of us would probably want to live in the real Middle Ages, when most people worked in the fields all day and even wealthy lords lived in damp and drafty castles. We do not really want to return to a time when one-third to one-half of all children died before age five and alcohol was the only real pain reliever. But the contemporary appeal of the Middle Ages is an interesting phenomenon, particularly because it stands in such sharp contrast to the attitude of educated Europeans who lived in the centuries immediately afterward. They were the ones who dubbed the period "middle." They saw their own era as the one to be celebrated, and the Middle Ages as best forgotten.

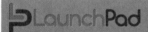

ONLINE DOCUMENT PROJECT

Hildegard of Bingen

Why was Hildegard of Bingen considered a worthy instrument for the transmission of God's word?

Read excerpts from Hildegard's correspondence, and then complete a quiz and writing assignment based on the evidence and details from this chapter. *See inside the front cover to learn more.*

| What were the causes, course, and consequences of the Crusades? | How did the lives of common people, nobles, and townspeople differ? | What were the primary educational and cultural developments in medieval Europe? | Why have the later Middle Ages been seen as a time of calamity and crisis? | ✓ **LearningCurve** Check what you know. |

CHAPTER 14 STUDY GUIDE

STEP 1

GET STARTED ONLINE

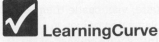 LearningCurve

Now that you've read the chapter, make it stick by completing the LearningCurve activity.

STEP 2

EXPLAIN WHY IT MATTERS

Put your reading into practice. Identify each term below, and then explain why it matters in world history.

TERM	WHO OR WHAT & WHEN	WHY IT MATTERS
vassal (p. 391)		
fief (p. 391)		
feudalism (p. 391)		
manorialism (p. 392)		
serf (p. 392)		
heresy (p. 398)		
reconquista (p. 399)		
Crusades (p. 400)		
chivalry (p. 405)		
craft guilds (p. 405)		
commercial revolution (p. 406)		
Scholastics (p. 408)		
Gothic (p. 408)		
vernacular literature (p. 409)		
Black Death (p. 410)		

STEP 3

MOVE BEYOND THE BASICS

To demonstrate a more advanced understanding of the social structure of medieval Europe, fill in the chart below with descriptions of the characteristics and lifestyle of the medieval peasantry, nobility, and clergy, as well as important developments and trends affecting the group's composition and status. How might you modify this model to create a better picture of the reality of medieval life?

	Characteristics and Lifestyle	Developments and Trends
Peasants		
Nobility		
Clergy		

PUT IT ALL TOGETHER

Now, take a step back and try to explain the big picture. Remember to use specific examples from the chapter in your answers.

POLITICAL CONSOLIDATION AND RELIGIOUS REFORM

▶ What was the relationship between feudalism and manorialism? How did the two systems work together to shape the medieval social and political world?

▶ How and why did the agendas of secular rulers and the papacy clash in the Middle Ages?

SOCIETY, ECONOMY, AND CULTURE

▶ How did serfdom differ from slavery? How and why did Western European peasants gain increased personal liberty over the course of the Middle Ages?

▶ What made the rise of universities possible? How might larger social and economic trends have contributed to their emergence?

THE LATER MIDDLE AGES

▶ What were the social, economic, and cultural consequences of the Hundred Years' War?

▶ What factors combined to undermine European's faith in religious and political authorities? How did peasant and urban revolts reflect this lack of confidence?

LOOKING BACK, LOOKING AHEAD

▶ Argue for or against the following statement. "The Middle Ages are best understood as a period of transition, a low point of decline and disorder between the twin peaks of Classical and Renaissance civilization." What evidence can you present in support of your argument?

▶ What role might the Crusades play in contemporary Muslim-Christian relations? What connections might Muslims or Christians today make between the Crusades and the global policies of Western nations in the twenty and twenty-first centuries?

> IN YOUR OWN WORDS

Imagine that you must give an oral report to the class answering the following question: **What role did clergy, nobles, peasants, and townspeople play in medieval European society? What would be the most important points and why?**

15

EUROPE IN THE RENAISSANCE AND REFORMATION

1350–1600

> In what ways did the Renaissance and Reformation represent breaks from the medieval past? Chapter 15 examines cultural, intellectual, and religious change during Europe's Renaissance and Reformation. While disease, famine, and war marked the fourteenth century in much of Europe, the era also witnessed the beginnings of remarkable changes in many aspects of intellectual and cultural life. First in Italy and then elsewhere, artists and writers thought that they were living in a new golden age, later termed the Renaissance, in which Europeans recaptured the glories of the classical past. Religious reformers carried out even more dramatic changes. In the sixteenth century, long-standing calls for religious reform gained wide acceptance. In a movement termed the Protestant Reformation, Western Christianity broke into many divisions, a situation that continues today.

Portrait of Baldassare Castiglione The author and courtier Baldassare Castiglione directs his calm gaze toward the viewer in this portrait by the renowned Italian Renaissance artist Raphael. Individual portraits like this one expressed the ideals of the Renaissance: elegance, balance, proportion, and self-awareness. (© Samuel Courtauld Trust, The Courtauld Gallery, London, UK/ The Bridgeman Art Library)

✓ LearningCurve
After reading the chapter, use LearningCurve to retain what you've read.

> What were the major cultural developments of the Renaissance?

> What were the key social hierarchies in Renaissance Europe, and how did these hierarchies shape people's lives?

> How did the nation-states of western Europe evolve in this period?

> What were the central ideas of Protestant reformers, and why were they appealing to various groups across Europe?

> How did the Catholic Church respond to the new religious situation?

> What were the causes and consequences of religious violence, including riots, wars, and witch-hunts?

What were the major cultural developments of the Renaissance?

In this detail from a fresco, the Italian painter Lorenzo Lotto captures the mixing of social groups in a Renaissance Italian city. The crowd of men in the left foreground includes wealthy merchants in elaborate hats and colorful coats. Two mercenary soldiers (carrying a sword and a pike) wear short doublets and tight hose stylishly slit to reveal colored undergarments, while boys play with toy weapons at their feet. Clothing like that of the soldiers, which emphasized the masculine form, was frequently criticized for its expense and its "indecency." At the right, women sell vegetables and bread, which would have been a common sight at any city marketplace. (Scala/ Art Resource, NY)

Renaissance
▶ A French word meaning "rebirth," used to describe a cultural movement that began in fourteenth-century Italy and looked back to the classical past.

THE Renaissance WAS CHARACTERIZED by self-conscious awareness among fourteenth- and fifteenth-century Italians, particularly scholars and writers known as humanists, that they were living in a new era. Their ideas influenced education and were spread through the new technology of the printing press. Interest in the classical past and in the individual also shaped Renaissance art in terms of style and subject matter.

Wealth and Power in Renaissance Italy

Economic growth laid the material basis for the Italian Renaissance and its cultural achievements. Ambitious merchants gained political power to match their economic power and then used their money to buy luxuries and hire talent in a **patronage** system. Through this system, cities, groups, and individuals commissioned writers and artists to produce specific works. Thus economics, politics, and culture were interconnected.

The Renaissance began in the northern Italian city of Florence, which possessed enormous wealth as a consequence of its domination of European

patronage
▶ Financial support of writers and artists by cities, groups, and individuals, often to produce specific works or works in specific styles.

CHAPTER LOCATOR | **What were the major cultural developments of the Renaissance?** | What were the key social hierarchies in Renaissance Europe?

422 CHAPTER 15 EUROPE IN THE RENAISSANCE AND REFORMATION

1434–1737 Medici family in power in Florence	**1536** John Calvin publishes *The Institutes of the Christian Religion*
1450s Development of movable metal type in Germany	**1540** Founding of the Society of Jesus (Jesuits)
1469 Marriage of Isabella of Castile and Ferdinand of Aragon	**1545–1563** Council of Trent
1492 Spain conquers Granada; practicing Jews expelled from Spain	**1555** Peace of Augsburg
1508–1512 Michelangelo paints ceiling of the Sistine Chapel	**1558–1603** Reign of Elizabeth I in England
1513 Niccolò Machiavelli writes *The Prince*	**1560–1660** Height of European witch-hunt
1521 Diet of Worms	**1568–1578** Civil war in the Netherlands
1521–1555 Charles V's wars against Valois kings	**1572** Saint Bartholomew's Day massacre
1525 Peasant revolts in Germany	**1598** Edict of Nantes
1527 Henry VIII of England asks Pope Clement VII to annul his marriage to Catherine of Aragon	

banking. Banking profits allowed elite families to control the city's politics and culture. Although Florence was officially a republic, starting in 1434 the great Medici (MEH-duh-chee) banking family held power almost continually for centuries. They supported an academy for scholars and a host of painters, sculptors, poets, and architects. (See "Individuals in Society: Cosimo and Lorenzo de' Medici," page 430.)

In other Italian cities as well, wealthy merchants and bankers built magnificent palaces and became patrons of the arts, hiring not only architects to design and build these palaces but also artists to fill them with paintings and sculptures, and musicians and composers to fill them with music. Attractions like these appealed to the rich, social-climbing residents of Venice, Florence, Genoa, and Rome, who came to see life more as an opportunity for enjoyment than as a painful pilgrimage to Heaven.

This cultural flowering took place amid political turmoil. In the fifteenth century five powers dominated the Italian peninsula: Venice, Milan, Florence, the Papal States, and the kingdom of Naples. These powers competed furiously for territory and tried to extend their authority over smaller city-states. Whenever one Italian state appeared to gain a predominant position within the peninsula, other states combined to establish a balance of power against the threat, thereby preventing long-term political consolidation.

Italian States, 1494

How did the nation-states of western Europe evolve in this period?	What were the central ideas of Protestant reformers, and why were they appealing?	How did the Catholic Church respond to the new religious situation?	What were the causes and consequences of religious violence?	✓ LearningCurve Check what you know.

This division facilitated outside invasions of Italy. These began in 1494 as Italy became the focus of international ambitions and the battleground of foreign armies, and Italian cities suffered severely from continual warfare for decades. Thus the failure of the city-states to form some type of federal system—or at least to establish a common foreign policy—led to centuries of subjugation by outside invaders.

The Rise of Humanism

The Renaissance was a self-conscious intellectual movement. The realization that something new and unique was happening first came to writers in the fourteenth century, especially to the Italian poet and humanist Francesco Petrarch (frahn-CHEH-skoh PEH-trahrk) (1304–1374). Along with many of his contemporaries, Petrarch sought to reconnect with the classical past, and he believed that such efforts were bringing on a new golden age of intellectual achievement.

Petrarch and other poets, writers, and artists showed a deep interest both in the physical remains of the Roman Empire and in classical Latin texts. The study of Latin classics became known as the *studia humanitates*, usually translated as "liberal studies" or the "liberal arts." People who advocated it were known as *humanists*, and their program as **humanism**. Like all programs of study, humanism contained an implicit philosophy: that human nature and achievements were worthy of contemplation. Humanists did not reject religion; instead they sought to synthesize Christian and classical teachings, pointing out the harmony between them.

Humanists and other Renaissance thinkers emphasized individual achievement. They were especially interested in individuals who had risen above their background to become brilliant, powerful, or unique. Such individuals had the admirable quality of *virtù* (vir-TOO), which is not virtue in the sense of moral goodness, but the ability to shape the world around them according to their will. Humanists thought that their recommended course of study in the classics would provide essential skills for all those who would take on this challenge. Just as Confucian officials did in Song China, they also taught that taking an active role in the world and working for the common good should be the aim of all educated individuals.

Humanists put their educational ideas into practice. They opened schools and academies in which pupils began with Latin grammar and rhetoric, went on to study Roman history and political philosophy, and then learned Greek in order to study Greek literature and philosophy. These classics, humanists taught, would provide models of how to write clearly, argue effectively, and speak persuasively. Gradually humanist education became the basis for intermediate and advanced education for well-to-do urban boys and men.

Humanists disagreed about education for women. Many saw the value of exposing women to classical models of moral behavior and reasoning, but they also wondered whether a program of study that emphasized eloquence and action was proper for women, whose sphere was generally understood to be private and domestic. Through tutors or programs of self-study a few women did become educated in the classics.

Humanists looked to the classical past for political as well as literary models. The best-known political theorist of this era was Niccolò Machiavelli (1469–1527),

humanism

▶ A program of study designed by Italians that emphasized the critical study of Latin and Greek literature with the goal of understanding human nature.

CHAPTER LOCATOR | What were the major cultural developments of the Renaissance? | What were the key social hierarchies in Renaissance Europe?

CHAPTER 15
424 EUROPE IN THE RENAISSANCE AND REFORMATION

author of the political treatise *The Prince* (1513). Using the examples of classical and contemporary rulers, *The Prince* argues that the function of a ruler (or a government) is to preserve order and security. To preserve the state, a ruler should use whatever means necessary—brutality, lying, manipulation—but he should not do anything that would make the populace turn against him.

Christian Humanism

In the last quarter of the fifteenth century students from the Low Countries, France, Germany, and England flocked to Italy, absorbed the "new learning" of humanism, and carried it back to their own countries. Northern humanists shared the Italians' ideas about the wisdom of ancient texts and felt even more strongly that the best elements of classical and Christian cultures should be combined. These **Christian humanists**, as they were later called, saw humanist learning as a way to bring about reform of the church and to deepen people's spiritual lives.

The Englishman Thomas More (1478–1535) began life as a lawyer, studied the classics, and entered government service. He became best known for his controversial dialogue *Utopia* (1516). *Utopia* describes a community on an island somewhere beyond Europe where all children receive a good humanist education and adults divide their days between manual labor or business pursuits and intellectual activities. The problems that plagued More's fellow citizens, such as poverty and hunger, are solved by a beneficent government. Furthermore, there is religious tolerance, and order and reason prevail.

Better known by contemporaries than Thomas More was the Dutch humanist Desiderius Erasmus (1466?–1536) of Rotterdam. His fame rested largely on his exceptional knowledge of Greek and the Bible, as well as his many publications. For Erasmus, education was the key to moral and intellectual improvement, and true Christianity was an inner attitude of the spirit, not a set of outward actions.

Christian humanists
▶ Humanists from northern Europe who thought that the best elements of classical and Christian cultures should be combined and saw humanist learning as a way to bring about reform of the church and deepen people's spiritual lives.

Printing and Its Social Impact

The impact of new ideas during this period was magnified by the invention of the printing press with movable metal type. While printing with movable type was invented in China (see page 368), movable *metal* type was actually developed in the thirteenth century in Korea, though it was tightly controlled by the monarchy and did not have the broad impact there that printing did in Europe. Printing with movable metal type developed in Germany in the middle of the fifteenth century. Several metal-smiths, most prominently Johann Gutenberg (ca. 1400–1468), transformed the metal stamps used to mark signs on jewelry into type that could be covered with ink and used to mark symbols onto a page. This type could be rearranged for every page and so used over and over. The printing revolution was also enabled by the ready availability of paper, which was made using techniques that had originated in China and spread from Muslim Spain to the rest of Europe.

The effects of the invention of movable-type printing were not felt overnight. Nevertheless, within a half century of the publication of Gutenberg's Bible of 1456, movable type had brought about radical changes. Historians estimate that somewhere between 8 million and 20 million books were printed in Europe between 1456 and 1500, many more than the total number of books that had been

| How did the nation-states of western Europe evolve in this period? | What were the central ideas of Protestant reformers, and why were they appealing? | How did the Catholic Church respond to the new religious situation? | What were the causes and consequences of religious violence? | ☑ LearningCurve Check what you know. |

produced in the West during the many millennia between the invention of writing and 1456.

Printing transformed both the private and the public lives of Europeans. In the public realm, government and church leaders both used and worried about printing. They printed laws, declarations of war, battle accounts, and propaganda, but they also attempted to censor or ban books and authors whose ideas they thought were wrong.

In the private realm, printing enabled people to read identical books so that they could more easily discuss the ideas that the books contained. Although most of the earliest books and pamphlets dealt with religious subjects, printers produced anything that would sell. Illustrations increased a book's sales, so printers published books full of woodcuts and engravings. Additionally, single-page broadsides and fly sheets allowed public events and "wonders" such as comets and two-headed calves to be experienced vicariously. Since books and other printed materials were read aloud to illiterate listeners, print bridged the gap between the written and oral cultures.

Because many laypeople could not read Latin, printers put out works in vernacular languages, fostering standardization in these languages. Works in these languages were also performed on stage. In London the works of William Shakespeare (1564–1616) were especially popular.

Art and the Artist

No feature of the Renaissance evokes greater admiration than its artistic masterpieces. In Renaissance Italy wealthy merchants, bankers, popes, and princes spent vast sums to commission art as a means of glorifying themselves and their families. Patrons varied in their level of involvement as a work progressed; some simply ordered a specific subject or scene, while others oversaw the work of the artist or architect very closely.

As a result of patronage, certain artists gained great public acclaim and adulation. In the Middle Ages, people believed that only God created, albeit through individuals, and artistic originality was not particularly valued. By contrast, Renaissance artists and humanists came to think that a work of art was the deliberate creation of a unique personality, of an individual who transcended traditions, rules, and theories.

In terms of artistic themes, religious topics remained popular among both patrons and artists. As the fifteenth century advanced and humanist ideas spread more widely, classical themes and motifs figured increasingly in painting and sculpture. Classical styles also influenced architecture, as architects designed buildings that featured arches and domes modeled on the structures of ancient Rome.

The individual portrait emerged as a distinct genre in Renaissance art. Rather than reflecting a spiritual ideal, as medieval painting and sculpture tended to do, Renaissance portraits showed human ideals, often portrayed in a more realistic style. The Florentine sculptor Donatello (1386–1466) revived the classical figure. Leonardo da Vinci (1452–1519) was particularly adept at portraying female grace and beauty. Another Florentine artist, Raphael Sanzio (1483–1520), painted hundreds of portraits, becoming the most sought-after artist in Europe (see page 421).

In the late fifteenth century the center of Renaissance art shifted from Florence to Rome, where wealthy cardinals and popes became active patrons of the

CHAPTER LOCATOR | **What were the major cultural developments of the Renaissance?** | What were the key social hierarchies in Renaissance Europe?

426 CHAPTER 15
EUROPE IN THE RENAISSANCE AND REFORMATION

arts. To meet this demand, Michelangelo Buonarroti (1475–1564) went to Rome from Florence in about 1500 and began the series of statues, paintings, and architectural projects from which he gained an international reputation. Most famously, between 1508 and 1512, he painted religiously themed frescoes on the ceiling and altar wall of the Sistine Chapel.

In both Italy and northern Europe most aspiring artists were educated in the workshops of older artists. By the later sixteenth century formal academies were also established to train artists. Like universities, artistic workshops and academies were male-only settings. Several women did become well known as painters during the Renaissance, but they were trained by their artist fathers and often quit painting when they married.

Women were not alone in being excluded from the institutions of Renaissance culture. Though a few talented artists such as Leonardo and Michelangelo emerged from artisanal backgrounds, most scholars and artists came from families with at least some money. The audience for artists' work was also exclusive, limited mostly to educated and prosperous citizens. In general a small, highly educated minority of literary humanists and artists created the culture of and for a social elite. In this way the Renaissance maintained, and even enhanced, a gulf between the learned minority and the uneducated multitude.

QUICK REVIEW <

Who were the humanists, and what did they believe in?

How did the nation-states of western Europe evolve in this period?	What were the central ideas of Protestant reformers, and why were they appealing?	How did the Catholic Church respond to the new religious situation?	What were the causes and consequences of religious violence?	☑ LearningCurve Check what you know.

> What were the key social hierarchies in Renaissance Europe, and how did these hierarchies shape people's lives?

Laura de Dianti, 1523

The Venetian artist Titian portrays a young Italian woman with a gorgeous blue dress and an elaborate pearl and feather headdress accompanied by a young black page with a gold earring. Slaves from Africa and the Ottoman Empire were common in wealthy Venetian households. (Photographer: Human Bios International AG, CH-8280, Kreuzlingen, www.humanbios.com)

> PICTURING THE PAST

ANALYZING THE IMAGE: How does the artist convey the message that this woman comes from a wealthy family? How does he use the skin color of the slave to highlight the woman's fair skin, which was one of the Renaissance ideals of female beauty?

CONNECTIONS: Household slaves worked at various tasks, but they were also symbols of the exotic. What other elements does Titian include in the painting to represent foreign places and the wealth brought to Venice by overseas trade? What does this painting suggest about Venetian attitudes toward slaves, who were part of that trade?

THE DIVISION BETWEEN THE educated and uneducated was one of many social hierarchies evident in the Renaissance. Other hierarchies built on those of the Middle Ages, but also developed new features that contributed to modern social hierarchies, such as those of race, class, and gender.

CHAPTER LOCATOR | What were the major cultural developments of the Renaissance? | **What were the key social hierarchies in Renaissance Europe?**

Race and Slavery

Renaissance people did not use the word *race* the way we do, but often used *race*, *people*, and *nation* interchangeably for ethnic, national, and religious groups. They did make distinctions based on skin color that were in keeping with later conceptualizations of race, but these distinctions were interwoven with other characteristics when people thought about human differences.

Ever since the time of the Roman Republic, a few black Africans had lived in western Europe. They had come, along with white slaves, as the spoils of war. After the collapse of the Roman Empire and throughout the Middle Ages, Muslim and Christian merchants continued to import black slaves. The black population was especially concentrated in the cities of the Iberian Peninsula. By the mid-sixteenth century blacks, slave and free, constituted roughly 3 percent of the Portuguese population.

In Renaissance Portugal, Spain, and Italy, African slaves supplemented the labor force in virtually all occupations. Slaves also formed the primary workforce on the sugar plantations set up by Europeans on the Atlantic islands in the late fifteenth century (see page 475).

Until their voyages down the African coast in the late fifteenth century, Europeans had little concrete knowledge of Africans and their cultures. They perceived Africa as a remote place, the home of strange people isolated by heresy and Islam from superior European civilization. The expanding slave trade reinforced negative preconceptions about the inferiority of black Africans.

Wealth and the Nobility

By the thirteenth century, and even more so by the fifteenth, the idea of a hierarchy based on wealth was emerging. This was particularly true in cities, where wealthy merchants oversaw vast trading empires, held positions of political power, and lived in splendor rivaling that enjoyed by the richest nobles. (See "Individuals in Society: Cosimo and Lorenzo de' Medici," page 430.)

The development of a hierarchy of wealth did not mean an end to the prominence of nobles, however, and even poorer nobles still had higher status than wealthy commoners. Thus wealthy Italian merchants enthusiastically bought noble titles in the fifteenth century, and wealthy English and Spanish merchants married their daughters and sons into often-impoverished noble families. The nobility maintained its status in most parts of Europe not by maintaining rigid boundaries, but by taking in and integrating the new social elite of wealth.

Gender Roles

Renaissance people would not have understood the word *gender* to refer to categories of people, but they would have easily grasped the concept. Toward the end of the fourteenth century learned men (and a few women) began what was termed the **debate about women**, an argument about women's character and nature that would last for centuries. Misogynist critiques of women from both clerical and secular authors denounced females as devious, domineering, and demanding. In response, several authors compiled long lists of famous and

debate about women
▶ A discussion, which began in the later years of the fourteenth century, that attempted to answer fundamental questions about gender and to define the role of women in society.

| How did the nation-states of western Europe evolve in this period? | What were the central ideas of Protestant reformers, and why were they appealing? | How did the Catholic Church respond to the new religious situation? | What were the causes and consequences of religious violence? | ✔️ LearningCurve Check what you know. |

INDIVIDUALS IN SOCIETY
Cosimo and Lorenzo de' Medici

The Renaissance is often described as a time of growing individualism, a development evidenced in the era's many personal portraits and individual biographies. But a person's family also remained important, even for those at the very top of society. The Medici of Florence were one of Europe's wealthiest families and used their money to influence politics and culture. The Medici got their start in banking in the late fourteenth century, with smart bets on what would happen politically in turbulent Italy and the adoption of the best new business practices. By the early fifteenth century the Medici bank had branches in Rome, Pisa, London, and other important European cities, and it served as the pope's primary banker.

Cosimo (1389–1464) and his grandson Lorenzo (1449–1492) were the most influential Medici. Not content simply with great wealth, Cosimo operated behind the scenes to gain control of the Florentine political system, although he held no office and officially the city remained a republic. Worries about his growing power led the dominant faction of the Florentine city council to exile him, but he took his money and his business with him and was soon asked to return.

Cosimo supported artists and thinkers, sponsoring what became known as the Platonic Academy, an informal group of Florence's cultural elite named in honor of Plato's famous academy in ancient Athens. Here Marsilio Ficino and other humanists translated Plato's works into Latin, making Greek learning available to a much wider European audience. Cosimo collected books and manuscripts from all over Europe, assembling an impressive library within the equally impressive Medici palace that he built in the heart of Florence.

Like his grandfather, Lorenzo was the head of the Medici bank and the de facto ruler of Florence. He, too, survived an attempt to oust him, this one led by the rival Pazzi family. The Pazzi went beyond simply trying to exile the Medici, and instead tried to murder them: Lorenzo was wounded and his brother Giuliano was killed. Medici revenge was swift and many Pazzi were executed, which led the pope — who sided with the Pazzi — to back an invasion of Florence. Lorenzo ended the conflict through personal diplomacy, and the constitution of Florence was modified to favor the Medici.

Lorenzo came to be known during his lifetime — with no irony — as "Lorenzo the Magnificent," primarily for his support for learning and the arts. As they had in Cosimo's day, a group of poets, philosophers, and

Botticelli's *Adoration of the Magi* shows many members of the Medici family and their circle, including the artist himself at the far right. (akg-images/De Agostini Picture Library)

artists spent much of their time at the Medici palace, where Lorenzo patronized writing in Italian as well as humanist scholarship in Latin and Greek. Lorenzo himself wrote love lyrics, sonnets, pastorals, odes, and carnival songs, many of them meditations on nature or on the fleetingness of human life: "Fair is youth and void of sorrow; / But it hourly flies away. / Youths and maids, enjoy today; / Nought ye know about tomorrow." The group included the humanists Ficino and Pico della Mirandola and the artists Michelangelo, Leonardo da Vinci, and Botticelli, all of them influenced by Platonic concepts of beauty and love. Botticelli's *Adoration of the Magi*, painted while he was at the Medici court, shows Cosimo (who was dead by the time the picture was painted) kneeling in front of the Virgin Mary as one of the three kings giving gifts to the infant Jesus, while a black-haired Lorenzo stands with other important Florentines on the right.

As Lorenzo reached his forties, many of the Medici bank branches began to collapse because of bad loans, and his diplomacy was not successful in maintaining a peaceful balance of power. Like many others in Florence, Lorenzo came under the spell of the charismatic preacher Savonarola, who preached that God would punish Italy for its vice and corruption. Lorenzo died before Savonarola's prediction appeared to come true when the French invaded Italy in 1494. The Medici were again ousted, but just as before, they returned, and later became the official and hereditary rulers of Florence and its environs as the Grand Dukes of Tuscany.

QUESTIONS FOR ANALYSIS

1. Renaissance people were fascinated by the quality of virtù, the ability to shape the world around one according to one's will. How did Cosimo and Lorenzo exhibit virtù?
2. The Medici created a model for very wealthy people of how to obtain political and cultural influence. Can you think of more recent examples, including contemporary ones, of those who followed this model?

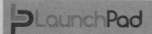

ONLINE DOCUMENT PROJECT

What role did patrons play in shaping Renaissance artistic and intellectual life? Examine paintings and letters by Renaissance artists, and complete a quiz and writing assignment based on the evidence and details from this chapter. *See inside the front cover to learn more.*

praiseworthy women. Some writers, including a few women who had gained a humanist education, were interested not only in defending women but also in exploring the reasons behind women's secondary status. Beginning in the sixteenth century the debate about women also became a debate about female rulers, because in Spain, England, France, and Scotland women served as advisers to child-kings or ruled in their own right.

The dominant notion of the "true" man was that of the married head of household, so men whose class and age would have normally conferred political power but who remained unmarried were sometimes excluded from ruling positions. Actual marriage patterns in Europe left many women unmarried until late in life, but this did not lead to greater equality. Women who worked for wages, as was typical, earned about half to two-thirds of what men did even for the same work. Of all the ways in which Renaissance society was hierarchically arranged—by class, age, level of education, rank, race, occupation—gender was regarded as the most "natural" distinction and therefore the most important one to defend.

QUICK REVIEW

How did Renaissance people use the term *race*? How did ideas of race shape Renaissance society?

> How did the nation-states of western Europe evolve in this period?

Donatello, *Gattamelata*, 1450

The Florentine sculptor Donatello's bronze statue of the powerful military captain nicknamed Gattamelata (Honey-Cat) mounted on his horse was erected in the public square of Padua. The first bronze equestrian statue made since Roman times, the larger-than-life-size work seems to capture in metal the shrewd and determined type of ruler Machiavelli described in *The Prince*. (Scala/Art Resource, NY)

BEGINNING IN THE FIFTEENTH CENTURY monarchs used aggressive methods to build up their governments. As they built and maintained power, they emphasized royal majesty and royal sovereignty and insisted on the respect and loyalty of all subjects.

France

The Black Death and the Hundred Years' War left France drastically depopulated, commercially ruined, and agriculturally weak (see page 412). Nonetheless, Charles VII (r. 1422–1461) revived the monarchy and France. He reorganized the royal council, giving increased influence to middle-class men, and strengthened royal finances through taxes on certain products and on land. Moreover, Charles created the first permanent royal army anywhere in Europe.

CHAPTER LOCATOR | What were the major cultural developments of the Renaissance? | What were the key social hierarchies in Renaissance Europe?

Two further developments strengthened the French monarchy. The marriage of Louis XII (r. 1498–1515) and Anne of Brittany added Brittany to the state. Louis XII's successor, Francis I (r. 1515–1547), and Pope Leo X reached a mutually satisfactory agreement about church and state powers in 1516 that gave French kings the power to control the appointment and thus the policies of church officials in the kingdom.

England

English society suffered severely in the fourteenth and fifteenth centuries. Between 1455 and 1471 adherents of the ducal houses of York and Lancaster waged civil wars over control of the English throne, commonly called the Wars of the Roses. The chronic disorder hurt trade, agriculture, and domestic industry, and the authority of the monarchy sank lower than it had been in centuries.

The Yorkist Edward IV (r. 1461–1483) succeeded in defeating the Lancastrian forces and after 1471 began to reconstruct the monarchy and consolidate royal power. Henry VII (r. 1485–1509) of the Welsh house of Tudor worked to restore royal prestige, to crush the power of the nobility, and to establish order and law at the local level. Under Henry VII the center of royal authority was the royal council. There Henry VII revealed his distrust of the nobility: very few great lords were among the king's closest advisers, who instead were lesser landowners and lawyers. The royal council handled any business the king put before it—executive, legislative, and judicial.

Secretive, cautious, and thrifty, Henry VII rebuilt the monarchy. He encouraged the cloth industry and built up the English merchant marine. He crushed an invasion from Ireland, secured peace with Scotland, and enhanced English prestige through the marriage of his eldest son, Arthur, to Catherine of Aragon, the daughter of Ferdinand and Isabella of Spain. When Henry VII died in 1509, he left a country at peace both domestically and internationally, a substantially augmented treasury, and the dignity and role of the Crown much enhanced.

Spain

While England and France laid the foundations of unified nation-states during the Renaissance, Spain remained a conglomerate of independent kingdoms. Even the wedding in 1469 of Isabella of Castile and Ferdinand of Aragon did not bring about administrative unity. Isabella and Ferdinand were, however, able to exert their authority in ways similar to the rulers of France and England. They curbed aristocratic power by excluding aristocrats and great territorial magnates from the royal council. They also secured from the Spanish pope Alexander VI the right to appoint bishops in Spain and in the Hispanic territories in America, enabling them to establish the equivalent of a national church. In 1492 their armies conquered Granada, the last territory held by Arabs in southern Spain.

Ferdinand and Isabella's rule also marked the start of greater persecution of the Jews. In the Middle Ages, the kings of France and England had expelled the Jews from their kingdoms, and many had sought refuge in Spain. During the long centuries of the reconquista (see page 399), Christian kings in Spain had renewed Jewish rights and privileges; in fact, Jewish industry, intelligence, and money had supported royal power.

How did the nation-states of western Europe evolve in this period?	What were the central ideas of Protestant reformers, and why were they appealing?	How did the Catholic Church respond to the new religious situation?	What were the causes and consequences of religious violence?	☑ LearningCurve Check what you know.

433

In the fourteenth century anti-Semitism in Spain was aggravated by fiery anti-Jewish preaching, by economic dislocation, and by the search for a scapegoat during the Black Death. Anti-Semitic pogroms, violent massacres and riots directed against Jews, swept the towns of Spain, and perhaps 40 percent of the Jewish population was killed or forced to convert. Those who converted were called *conversos* (kuhn-VEHR-sohz) or New Christians. Conversos were often well educated and held prominent positions in government and business.

Such successes bred resentment. Aristocrats resented their financial dependence on conversos, the poor hated the converso tax collectors, and churchmen doubted the sincerity of their conversions. Queen Isabella shared these suspicions, and she and Ferdinand received permission from Pope Sixtus IV to establish an Inquisition to look for conversos who showed any sign of incomplete conversion.

Most conversos identified themselves as sincere Christians; many came from families that had received baptism generations before. In response, officials of the Inquisition developed a new type of anti-Semitism. A person's status as a Jew, they argued, could not be changed by religious conversion, but was in the person's blood and was heritable, so Jews could never be true Christians. Under what were known as "purity of blood" laws, having "pure Christian blood" became a requirement for noble status. Ideas about Jews developed in Spain became important components in European concepts of race.

In 1492, shortly after the conquest of Granada, Isabella and Ferdinand issued an edict expelling all practicing Jews from Spain. Of the community of perhaps 200,000 Jews, 150,000 fled. Absolute religious orthodoxy and "purity of blood" served as the theoretical foundation of the Spanish national state.

The Habsburgs

Because almost all of Europe was ruled by hereditary dynasties, claiming and holding resources involved shrewd marital strategies, for it was far cheaper to gain land by inheritance than by war. The benefits of an advantageous marriage stretched across generations, as can be seen most dramatically with the Habsburgs. The Holy Roman emperor Frederick III, a Habsburg who was the ruler of most of Austria, acquired only a small amount of territory—but a great deal of money—with his marriage to Princess Eleanore of Portugal in 1452. He arranged for his son Maximilian to marry Europe's most prominent heiress, Mary of Burgundy. Through this union with the rich and powerful duchy of Burgundy, the Austrian house of Habsburg, already the strongest ruling family in the empire, became an international power. The marriage of Maximilian and Mary angered the French, and it inaugurated centuries of conflict between the Habsburgs and the kings of France. Within the empire, German principalities that resented Austria's pre-eminence began to see that they shared interests with France.

Maximilian learned the lesson of marital politics well, marrying his son and daughter to the children of Ferdinand and Isabella, the rulers of Spain, much of southern Italy, and eventually the Spanish New World empire. His grandson Charles V (1500–1558) fell heir to a vast and incredibly diverse collection of states and peoples (Map 15.1). Charles was convinced that it was his duty to maintain the political and religious unity of Western Christendom. This conviction would be challenged far more than Charles ever anticipated.

CHAPTER LOCATOR | What were the major cultural developments of the Renaissance?

What were the key social hierarchies in Renaissance Europe?

434 CHAPTER 15
EUROPE IN THE RENAISSANCE AND REFORMATION

Lands inherited by Charles V
Lands gained by Charles V, 1519–1556
States favorable to Charles V
Enemies of Charles V
— Boundary of the Holy Roman Empire

0   150   300 miles
0   150   300 kilometers

N W E S

Spanish holdings, 1550

MAP 15.1 ■ The Global Empire of Charles V, ca. 1556

Charles V exercised theoretical jurisdiction over more European territory than anyone since Charlemagne. He also claimed authority over large parts of North and South America, although actual Spanish control was weak in much of this area.

QUICK REVIEW ‹

How did the monarchs of England, France, and Spain seek to limit the power and autonomy of the nobility?

| How did the nation-states of western Europe evolve in this period? | What were the central ideas of Protestant reformers, and why were they appealing? | How did the Catholic Church respond to the new religious situation? | What were the causes and consequences of religious violence? | ✓ LearningCurve Check what you know. |

What were the central ideas of Protestant reformers, and why were they appealing to various groups across Europe?

Selling Indulgences

A German single-page pamphlet shows a monk offering an indulgence, with the official seals of the pope attached, as people run to put their money in the box in exchange for his promise of heavenly bliss, symbolized by the dove above his head. Indulgences were sold widely in Germany, and they were the first Catholic practice that Luther criticized openly. This pamphlet also attacks the sale of indulgences, calling it devilish and deceitful, a point of view expressed in the woodcut by the peddler's riding on a donkey, an animal that had long been used as a symbol of ignorance. Indulgences were often printed as fill-in-the-blank forms. This one, purchased in 1521, has space for the indulgence seller's name at the top, the buyer's name in the middle, and the date at the bottom. (woodcut: akg-images; indulgence: Visual Connection Archive)

CALLS FOR REFORM IN THE CHURCH came from many quarters in early-sixteenth-century Europe—from educated laypeople and urban residents, from villagers and artisans, and from church officials themselves. This dissatisfaction helps explain why the ideas of Martin Luther found a ready audience. Within a decade of his first publishing his ideas, much of central Europe and Scandinavia had broken with the Catholic Church in a movement that came to be known as the **Protestant Reformation**. In addition, even more radical concepts of the Christian message were being developed and linked to calls for social change.

Protestant Reformation
▶ A religious reform movement that began in the early sixteenth century that split the Western Christian Church.

CHAPTER LOCATOR | What were the major cultural developments of the Renaissance? | What were the key social hierarchies in Renaissance Europe?

436 CHAPTER 15
EUROPE IN THE RENAISSANCE AND REFORMATION

Criticism of the Church

Sixteenth-century Europeans were deeply pious. Many people were also highly critical of the Roman Catholic Church and its clergy. Papal conflicts with rulers and the Great Schism (see page 414) badly damaged the prestige of church leaders. Papal tax collection methods were also attacked, and some criticized the papacy itself as an institution.

In the early sixteenth century, critics of the church concentrated their attacks on clerical immorality, ignorance, and absenteeism. Charges of immorality were aimed at a number of priests who were drunkards, neglected the rule of celibacy, gambled, or indulged in fancy dress. Charges of ignorance applied to barely literate priests who delivered poor-quality sermons.

In regard to absenteeism, many clerics, especially higher ecclesiastics, held several benefices (offices) simultaneously. However, they seldom visited the communities served by the benefices. Instead, they collected revenues from all the benefices assigned to them and hired a poor priest to fulfill their spiritual duties, paying him just a fraction of the income.

There was also local resentment of clerical privileges and immunities. Priests, monks, and nuns were exempt from civic responsibilities, such as defending the city and paying taxes. Yet religious orders frequently held large amounts of urban property. City governments were increasingly determined to integrate the clergy into civic life. This brought city leaders into opposition with bishops and the papacy, which for centuries had stressed the independence of the church from lay control.

Martin Luther

By itself, widespread criticism of the church did not lead to the dramatic changes of the sixteenth century. Those resulted from the personal religious struggle of a German university professor and Augustinian friar, Martin Luther (1483–1546).

Martin Luther was a very conscientious friar, but his scrupulous observance of the religious routine, frequent confessions, and fasting gave him only temporary relief from anxieties about sin and his ability to meet God's demands. Through his study of Saint Paul's letters in the New Testament, he gradually arrived at a new understanding of Christian doctrine. His understanding is often summarized as "faith alone, grace alone, scripture alone." He believed that salvation and justification (righteousness in God's eyes) come through faith, and that faith is a free gift of God, not the result of human effort. God's word is revealed only in biblical scripture, not in the traditions of the church.

At the same time that Luther was engaged in scholarly reflections and professorial lecturing, Pope Leo X authorized a special Saint Peter's indulgence to finance his building plans in Rome. An **indulgence** was a document that substituted for penance. The archbishop who controlled the area in which Wittenberg was located, Albert of Mainz, also promoted the sale of indulgences, in his case to pay off a debt he had incurred to be named bishop of several additional territories. Albert's sales campaign promised that the purchase of indulgences would bring full forgiveness for one's own sins or buy release from purgatory for a loved one.

Luther was severely troubled that many people believed that they had no further need for repentance once they had purchased indulgences. He wrote a letter

indulgence
▶ A papal statement granting remission of a priest-imposed penalty for sin. (No one knew what penalty God would impose after death.)

| How did the nation-states of western Europe evolve in this period? | **What were the central ideas of Protestant reformers, and why were they appealing?** | How did the Catholic Church respond to the new religious situation? | What were the causes and consequences of religious violence? | ✓ LearningCurve Check what you know. |

437

to Archbishop Albert on the subject and enclosed in Latin his "Ninety-five Theses on the Power of Indulgences." His argument was that indulgences undermined the seriousness of the sacrament of penance and competed with the preaching of the Gospel. Luther intended his theses for academic debate, but by December 1517 they had been translated into German and were being read throughout central Europe. Luther was ordered to go to Rome, but he was able to avoid this because the ruler of the territory in which he lived protected him. The pope nonetheless ordered him to recant many of his ideas, and Luther publicly burned the letter containing the papal order. In this highly charged atmosphere, the twenty-one-year-old emperor Charles V summoned Luther to appear before the **Diet of Worms**, an assembly of representatives from the territories of the Holy Roman Empire meeting in the city of Worms in 1521. Luther, however, refused to give in to demands that he take back his ideas.

Protestant Thought and Its Appeal

As he developed his ideas, Luther gathered followers, who came to be called Protestants. At first **Protestant** meant "a follower of Luther," but with the appearance of many other reformers, it became a general term applied to all non-Catholic western European Christians.

Pulpits and printing presses spread the Protestant message all over Germany, and by the middle of the sixteenth century people of all social classes had rejected Catholic teachings and become Protestant. What was the immense appeal of Luther's religious ideas and those of other Protestants?

Educated people and humanists were attracted by Luther's ideas. He advocated a simpler personal religion based on faith, a return to the spirit of the early church, the centrality of the Scriptures in the liturgy and in Christian life, and the abolition of elaborate ceremonies—precisely the reforms the Christian humanists had been calling for. His insistence that everyone should read and reflect on the Scriptures attracted the literate middle classes. Luther's ideas also appealed to

Diet of Worms
▶ An assembly of representatives from the territories of the Holy Roman Empire convened by Charles V in the German city of Worms in 1521. It was here that Martin Luther refused to recant his writings.

Protestant
▶ Originally meaning "a follower of Luther," this term came to be generally applied to all non-Catholic western European Christians.

> Key Differences Between Catholics and Protestants:		
	Catholics	**Protestants**
How is a person saved?	By a combination of faith and good works	By faith alone
Where does religious authority lie?	In the Bible and in the traditional teachings of the church	In the Bible alone
What is the church?	The church is a clerical, hierarchical institution headed by the pope in Rome	The church is a spiritual priesthood of all believers
What is the highest form of Christian life?	The monastic and religious life	Each person should serve God in his or her individual calling

CHAPTER LOCATOR | What were the major cultural developments of the Renaissance? | What were the key social hierarchies in Renaissance Europe?

CHAPTER 15
438 EUROPE IN THE RENAISSANCE AND REFORMATION

townspeople who envied the church's wealth and resented paying for it. After cities became Protestant, the city council taxed the clergy and placed them under the jurisdiction of civil courts.

The printing press also contributed to Luther's fame and success. Many printed works included woodcuts and other illustrations, so that even those who could not read could grasp the main ideas. Hymns were also important means of conveying central points of doctrine, as was Luther's translation of the New Testament into German in 1523.

Luther worked closely with political authorities, viewing them as fully justified in reforming the church in their territories. He instructed all Christians to obey their secular rulers, whom he saw as divinely ordained to maintain order. Individuals may have been convinced of the truth of Protestant teachings on their own, but a territory became Protestant when its ruler, brought in reformers to re-educate the territory's clergy, sponsored public sermons, and confiscated church property. This happened in many of the states of the empire during the 1520s and then moved beyond the empire to Denmark-Norway and Sweden.

The Radical Reformation and the German Peasants' War

In the sixteenth century the practice of religion remained a public matter. The ruler determined the official form of religious practice in his (or occasionally her) jurisdiction. Almost everyone believed that the presence of a faith different from that of the majority represented a political threat to the security of the state.

Some individuals and groups rejected the idea that church and state needed to be united, however, and they sought to create a voluntary community of believers as they understood it to have existed in New Testament times. In terms of theology and spiritual practices, these individuals and groups varied widely, though they are generally termed "radicals" for their insistence on a more extensive break with prevailing ideas. Some adopted the custom of baptizing adult believers—for which they were given the title of "Anabaptists" by their enemies—while others saw all outward sacraments or rituals as misguided. Some groups attempted communal ownership of property. Some reacted harshly to members who deviated from the group's accepted practices, but others argued for complete religious tolerance and individualism.

Religious radicals were met with fanatical hatred and bitter persecution, including banishment and execution. Both Protestant and Catholic authorities felt threatened by the social, political, and economic implications of radicals' religious ideas and by their rejection of a state church. Their community spirit and heroism in the face of martyrdom, however, contributed to the survival of radical ideas.

Another group to challenge state authorities was the peasantry. In the early sixteenth century the economic condition of peasants varied from place to place but was generally worse than it had been in the fifteenth century and was deteriorating. Peasants demanded limitations on the new taxes and labor obligations their noble landlords were imposing. They believed that their demands conformed to the Scriptures and cited Luther as a theologian who could prove that they did.

Wanting to prevent rebellion, Luther initially sided with the peasants. But when rebellion broke out, the peasants who expected Luther's support were soon

| How did the nation-states of western Europe evolve in this period? | **What were the central ideas of Protestant reformers, and why were they appealing?** | How did the Catholic Church respond to the new religious situation? | What were the causes and consequences of religious violence? | ✓ LearningCurve Check what you know. |

disillusioned. Freedom for Luther meant independence from the authority of the Roman Church, not opposition to legally established secular powers. Firmly convinced that rebellion would hasten the end of civilized society, he wrote the tract *Against the Murderous, Thieving Hordes of the Peasants*. The nobility ferociously crushed the revolt, which became known as the German Peasants' War of 1525.

The peasants' war greatly strengthened the authority of lay rulers. Because Luther turned against the peasants who revolted, the Reformation lost much of its popular appeal after 1525, though peasants and urban rebels sometimes found a place for their social and religious ideas in radical groups. Peasants' economic conditions did moderately improve, however.

Marriage and Women's Roles

Luther and other Protestants believed that a priest's or nun's vows of celibacy went against human nature and God's commandments. Luther married a former nun, Katharina von Bora (1499–1532), who quickly had several children. Most other Protestant reformers also married, and their wives had to create a new and respectable role for themselves, pastor's wife. They were living demonstrations of their husband's convictions about the superiority of marriage to celibacy, and they were expected to be models of wifely obedience and Christian charity.

Catholics viewed marriage as a sacramental union that, if validly entered into, could not be dissolved. Protestants saw marriage as a contract in which each partner promised the other support, companionship, and the sharing of mutual goods. They believed that spouses who did not comfort or support one another endangered their own souls and the surrounding community; therefore, most Protestants came to allow divorce. Divorce remained rare, however, because marriage was such an important social and economic institution.

Protestants did not break with medieval scholastic theologians in their view that, within marriage, women were to be subject to men. Men were urged to treat their wives kindly and considerately, but also to enforce their authority, through physical coercion if necessary. A few women took the Protestant idea about the priesthood of all believers to heart and wrote religious pamphlets and hymns, but no sixteenth-century Protestants officially allowed women to hold positions of religious authority.

Because the Reformation generally brought the closing of monasteries and convents, marriage became virtually the only occupation for upper-class Protestant women. Recognizing this, women in some convents fought the Reformation or argued that they could still be pious Protestants within convent walls. Most nuns left, however, and we do not know what happened to them. The Protestant emphasis on marriage made unmarried women (and men) suspect, for they did not belong to the type of household regarded as the cornerstone of a proper, godly society.

The Reformation and German Politics

Criticism of the church was widespread in Europe in the early sixteenth century. Yet such movements could be more easily squelched by the strong central governments of Spain, France, and England. The Holy Roman Empire, in contrast,

CHAPTER LOCATOR | What were the major cultural developments of the Renaissance? | What were the key social hierarchies in Renaissance Europe?

CHAPTER 15
440 EUROPE IN THE RENAISSANCE AND REFORMATION

included hundreds of largely independent states in which the emperor had far less authority than did the monarchs of western Europe. Thus local rulers of the many states in the empire continued to exercise great power.

Luther's ideas appealed to local rulers within the empire for a variety of reasons. Though Germany was not a nation, people did have an understanding of being German because of their language and traditions. Luther frequently used the phrase "we Germans" in his attacks on the papacy, and his appeal to national feeling influenced many rulers. Also, while some German rulers were sincerely attracted to Lutheran ideas, material considerations swayed many others to embrace the new faith. The rejection of Roman Catholicism and the adoption of Protestantism would mean the legal confiscation of valuable church property. Thus many political authorities in the empire used the religious issue to extend their financial and political power and to enhance their independence from the emperor.

The Habsburg Charles V, elected as emperor in 1521, was a vigorous defender of Catholicism, so it is not surprising that the Reformation led to religious wars. Protestant territories in the empire formed military alliances, and the emperor could not oppose them effectively given other military engagements. In southeastern Europe Habsburg troops were already fighting the Ottoman Turks. Habsburg soldiers were also engaged in a series of wars with the Valois (VAL-wah) kings of France. The cornerstone of French foreign policy in the sixteenth and seventeenth centuries was the desire to keep the German states divided. Thus Europe witnessed the paradox of the Catholic king of France supporting Lutheran princes in their challenge to his fellow Catholic, Charles V.

Finally, in 1555, Charles agreed to the Peace of Augsburg, which officially recognized Lutheranism and ended religious war in Germany for many decades. Under this treaty, the political authority in each territory of the Holy Roman

| How did the nation-states of western Europe evolve in this period? | **What were the central ideas of Protestant reformers, and why were they appealing?** | How did the Catholic Church respond to the new religious situation? | What were the causes and consequences of religious violence? | ✓ LearningCurve Check what you know. |

441

Empire was permitted to decide whether the territory would be Catholic or Lutheran. His hope of uniting his empire under a single church dashed, Charles V abdicated in 1556, transferring power over his Spanish and Netherlandish holdings to his son Philip II and his imperial power to his brother Ferdinand.

England's Shift Toward Protestantism

As on the continent, the Reformation in England had economic and political as well as religious causes. The impetus for England's break with Rome was the desire of King Henry VIII (r. 1509–1547) for a new wife. When the personal matter of his need to divorce his first wife became enmeshed with political issues, a complete break with Rome resulted.

In 1527, after eighteen years of marriage, Henry's wife Catherine of Aragon had failed to produce a male child, and Henry had also fallen in love with a court lady-in-waiting, Anne Boleyn. So Henry petitioned Pope Clement VII for an annulment of his marriage to Catherine. When the pope procrastinated in granting the annulment, Henry decided to remove the English Church from papal authority.

Henry used Parliament to legalize the Reformation in England and to make himself the supreme head of the Church of England. Anne had a daughter, Elizabeth, but failed to produce a son, so Henry VIII charged her with adulterous incest and in 1536 had her beheaded. His third wife, Jane Seymour, gave Henry the desired son, Edward, but she died in childbirth. Henry went on to three more wives.

Between 1535 and 1539, Henry decided to dissolve the English monasteries primarily because he wanted their wealth. Hundreds of former church properties were sold to the middle and upper classes, strengthening the upper classes and tying them to the Tudor dynasty, to which Henry belonged. How did everyday people react to Henry's break from the Catholic Church? Recent scholarship points out that people rarely "converted" from Catholicism to Protestantism overnight. Instead they responded to the local consequences of the shift from Catholicism with a combination of resistance, acceptance, and collaboration.

Loyalty to the Catholic Church remained particularly strong in Ireland. Ireland had been claimed by English kings since the twelfth century, but in reality the English had firm control of only the area around Dublin known as the Pale. In 1536, on orders from London, the Irish Parliament, which represented only the English landlords and the people of the Pale, approved the English laws severing the church from Rome. The (English) ruling class adopted the new reformed faith, but most of the Irish people remained Roman Catholic. Irish armed opposition to the Reformation led to harsh repression by the English.

In the short reign of Henry's sickly son Edward VI (r. 1547–1553), strongly Protestant ideas exerted a significant influence on the religious life of the country. The equally brief reign of Mary Tudor (r. 1553–1558), the devoutly Catholic daughter of Catherine of Aragon, witnessed a sharp move back to Catholicism, and many Protestants fled to the continent. Mary's death raised to the throne her half sister Elizabeth (r. 1558–1603) and inaugurated the beginning of religious stability.

Elizabeth had been raised a Protestant, but at the start of her reign sharp differences existed in England. On the one hand, Catholics wanted a Roman Catholic ruler. On the other hand, a vocal number of returning exiles wanted all Catholic elements in the Church of England eliminated. Members of the latter group were

CHAPTER LOCATOR | What were the major cultural developments of the Renaissance? | What were the key social hierarchies in Renaissance Europe?

442 CHAPTER 15 EUROPE IN THE RENAISSANCE AND REFORMATION

called Puritans. Shrewdly, Elizabeth chose a middle course between Catholic and Puritan extremes. The Anglican Church, as the Church of England was called, moved in a moderately Protestant direction.

Calvinism and Its Moral Standards

John Calvin (1509–1564) was born in Noyon in northwestern France. As a young man he studied law, but in 1533 he experienced a religious crisis, as a result of which he converted from Catholicism to Protestantism. Calvin believed that God had specifically selected him to reform the church. Accordingly, he accepted an invitation to assist in the reformation of the city of Geneva. There, beginning in 1541, Calvin worked to establish a Christian society ruled by God through civil magistrates and reformed ministers.

Calvin's ideas are embodied in *The Institutes of the Christian Religion*, first published in 1536 and modified several times afterward. The cornerstone of Calvin's theology was his belief in the absolute sovereignty and omnipotence of God and the total weakness of humanity.

Calvin did not ascribe free will to human beings because that would detract from the sovereignty of God. According to his beliefs, men and women could not actively work to achieve salvation; rather, God decided at the beginning of time who would be saved and who damned. This viewpoint constitutes the theological principle called **predestination**. "This terrible decree," as even Calvin called it, did not lead to pessimism or fatalism. Instead, although Calvinists believed that one's own actions could do nothing to change one's fate, many came to believe that hard work, thrift, and moral conduct could serve as signs that one was among the "elect" chosen for salvation.

Calvin transformed Geneva into a community based on his religious principles. The most powerful organization in the city became the Consistory, a group of laymen and pastors charged with investigating and disciplining deviations from proper doctrine and conduct.

Religious refugees from France, England, Spain, Scotland, and Italy visited Calvin's Geneva, which became the model of a Christian community for many. Subsequently, the Reformed Church of Calvin served as the model for the Presbyterian Church in Scotland, the Huguenot (HYOO-guh-naht) Church in France, and the Puritan Churches in England and New England.

> **predestination**
> ▸ Calvin's teaching that, by God's decree, some persons are guided to salvation and others to damnation; that God has called people not according to their works but according to his purpose and grace.

QUICK REVIEW ◂

What did Lutheranism and Calvinism have in common?
In what ways did they differ?

| How did the nation-states of western Europe evolve in this period? | **What were the central ideas of Protestant reformers, and why were they appealing?** | How did the Catholic Church respond to the new religious situation? | What were the causes and consequences of religious violence? | LearningCurve Check what you know. |

> How did the Catholic Church respond to the new religious situation?

Teresa of Ávila

In this wood carving from 1625, the Spanish artist Gregorio Fernandez shows Saint Teresa book in hand, actively teaching. The influence of her ideas and actions led the pope to give Teresa the title "Doctor of the Church" in 1970, the first woman to be so honored. (Gregorio Fernandez [1576–1636], *Saint Teresa of Ávila*, 1625. Polychromatic Baroque carving on wood, Valladolid, Spain. National Museum of Sculpture/© P. Rotger/Iberfoto/The Image Works)

BETWEEN 1517 AND 1547 Protestantism made remarkable advances. Nevertheless, the Roman Catholic Church made a significant comeback. Many historians see the developments within the Catholic Church after the Protestant Reformation as two interrelated movements, one a drive for internal reform, and the other a Counter-Reformation that actively opposed Protestantism. In both movements, papal reforms and new religious orders were important agents.

Papal Reforms and the Council of Trent

In 1542 Pope Paul III (pontificate 1534–1549) established the Supreme Sacred Congregation of the Roman and Universal Inquisition, often called the Holy Office, with jurisdiction over the Roman Inquisition, a powerful instrument of the Catholic Reformation. The Inquisition had judicial authority over all Catholics and the power to arrest, imprison, and execute.

Pope Paul III also called a general council, which met intermittently from 1545 to 1563 at Trent, an imperial city close to Italy. The decrees of the Council of Trent

CHAPTER LOCATOR | What were the major cultural developments of the Renaissance? | What were the key social hierarchies in Renaissance Europe?

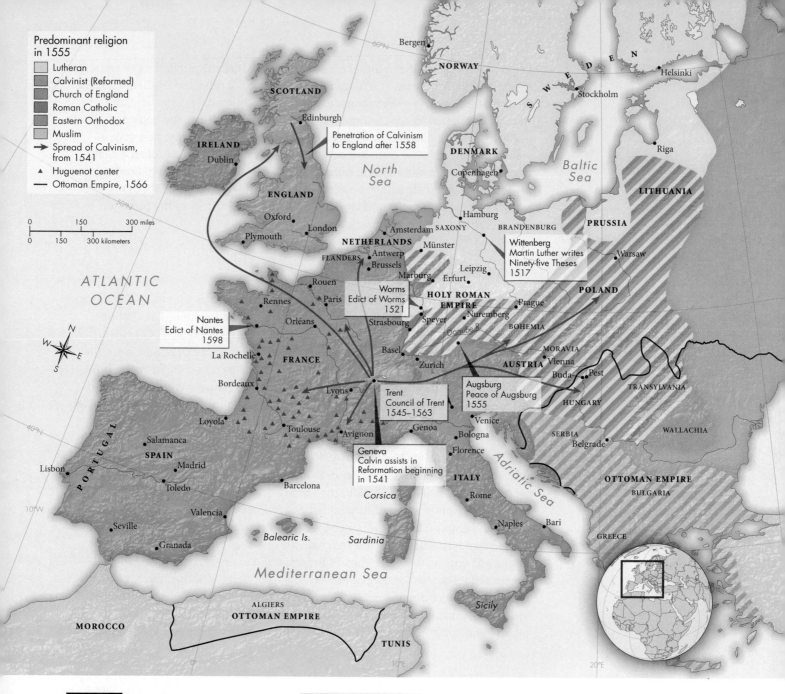

Predominant religion in 1555

- Lutheran
- Calvinist (Reformed)
- Church of England
- Roman Catholic
- Eastern Orthodox
- Muslim
- → Spread of Calvinism, from 1541
- ▲ Huguenot center
- — Ottoman Empire, 1566

Penetration of Calvinism to England after 1558

Wittenberg
Martin Luther writes Ninety-five Theses 1517

Worms
Edict of Worms 1521

Nantes
Edict of Nantes 1598

Trent
Council of Trent 1545–1563

Augsburg
Peace of Augsburg 1555

Geneva
Calvin assists in Reformation beginning in 1541

MAP 15.2 ■ Religious Divisions in Europe, ca. 1555

The Reformation shattered the religious unity of Western Christendom. The situation was even more complicated than a map of this scale can show. Many cities within the Holy Roman Empire, for example, accepted a different faith than did the surrounding countryside; Augsburg, Basel, and Strasbourg were all Protestant, though surrounded by territory ruled by Catholic nobles.

> MAPPING THE PAST

ANALYZING THE MAP: Which countries in Europe were the most religiously diverse? Which were the least diverse?

CONNECTIONS: Where was the first arena of religious conflict in Europe, and why did it develop there and not elsewhere? What nonreligious factors contributed to the religious divisions that developed in sixteenth-century Europe, and to what degree can they explain these divisions?

| How did the nation-states of western Europe evolve in this period? | What were the central ideas of Protestant reformers, and why were they appealing? | **How did the Catholic Church respond to the new religious situation?** | What were the causes and consequences of religious violence? | ✓ LearningCurve Check what you know. |

laid a solid basis for the spiritual renewal of the Catholic Church. It gave equal validity to the Scriptures and to tradition as sources of religious truth and authority. It reaffirmed the seven sacraments and the traditional Catholic teaching on transubstantiation (the transformation of bread and wine into the body and blood of Christ in the Eucharist). It tackled the disciplinary matters that had disillusioned the faithful. The council also required every diocese to establish a seminary for educating and training clergy. Finally, great emphasis was placed on preaching to and instructing the laity, especially the uneducated. For four centuries the doctrinal and disciplinary legislation of Trent served as the basis for Roman Catholic faith, organization, and practice.

New Religious Orders

Just as seminaries provided education, so did new religious orders, which aimed to raise the moral and intellectual level of the clergy and people. The Ursuline (UHR-suh-luhn) order of nuns, founded in 1535 by Angela Merici (1474–1540), attained enormous prestige for its education of women. The Ursulines were the first women's religious order concentrating exclusively on teaching young girls, with the goal of re-Christianizing society by training future wives and mothers. After receiving papal approval in 1565, the Ursulines rapidly spread to France and the New World.

Jesuits

▶ Members of the Society of Jesus, founded by Ignatius Loyola and approved by the papacy in 1540, whose goal was the spread of the Roman Catholic faith through humanistic schools and missionary activity.

Another important new order was the Society of Jesus, or **Jesuits**. Founded by Ignatius Loyola (1491–1556) in 1540, this order played a powerful international role in strengthening Catholicism in Europe and spreading the faith around the world. Under Loyola's leadership, the Society of Jesus developed into a highly centralized, tightly knit organization whose professed members vowed to go anywhere the pope said they were needed. They established schools that adopted the modern humanist curricula and methods and that educated the sons of the nobility as well as the poor. The Jesuits attracted many recruits and achieved phenomenal success for the papacy and the reformed Catholic Church, carrying Christianity around the world. Within Europe the Jesuits brought almost all of southern Germany and much of eastern Europe back to Catholicism. Also, as confessors and spiritual directors to kings, Jesuits exerted great political influence.

> **QUICK REVIEW**

What reforms were enacted by the Council of Trent?

CHAPTER LOCATOR | What were the major cultural developments of the Renaissance? | What were the key social hierarchies in Renaissance Europe?

446   CHAPTER 15   EUROPE IN THE RENAISSANCE AND REFORMATION

What were the causes and consequences of religious violence, including riots, wars, and witch-hunts?

Massacre of the Huguenots, 1573

The Italian artist Giorgio Vasari depicts the Saint Bartholomew's Day massacre in Paris, one of many bloody events in the religious wars that accompanied the Reformation. Here Admiral Coligny, a leader of the French Protestants (called Huguenots), is hurled from a window while his followers are slaughtered. This fresco was commissioned by Pope Gregory XIII to decorate a hall in the Vatican Palace in Rome. Both sides used visual images to win followers and celebrate their victories. (Giorgio Vasari [1511–1574], Sala Regia, Apostolic Palace, Vatican City/De Agostini Picture Library/The Bridgeman Art Library)

IN 1559 FRANCE AND SPAIN signed the Treaty of Cateau-Cambrésis, which ended the long conflict known as the Habsburg-Valois wars. However, over the next century religious differences led to riots, civil wars, and international conflicts. Especially in France and the Netherlands, Protestants and Catholics opposed one another through preaching, teaching, and violence. This era also saw the most virulent witch persecutions in European history, as both Protestants and Catholics tried to make their cities and states more godly.

How did the nation-states of western Europe evolve in this period?

What were the central ideas of Protestant reformers, and why were they appealing?

How did the Catholic Church respond to the new religious situation?

What were the causes and consequences of religious violence?

✓ LearningCurve
Check what you know.

French Religious Wars

The costs of the Habsburg-Valois wars, waged intermittently through the first half of the sixteenth century, forced the French to increase taxes and borrow heavily. King Francis I's treaty with the pope (see page 432) gave the French crown a rich supplement of money and offices and also a vested financial interest in Catholicism. Significant numbers of French people, however, were attracted to Calvinism. Calvinism drew converts from among reform-minded members of the Catholic clergy, the industrious middle classes, and artisan groups. Additionally, some French nobles became Calvinist. By the middle of the sixteenth century perhaps one-tenth of the French population had become **Huguenots**, the name given to French Calvinists.

Huguenots

▶ French Calvinists.

Both Calvinists and Catholics believed that the others' books, services, and ministers polluted the community. Preachers communicated these ideas in sermons, triggering religious violence. Armed clashes between Catholic royalist nobles and Calvinist antimonarchical nobles occurred in many parts of France.

Calvinist teachings called the power of sacred images into question, and mobs in many cities destroyed statues, stained-glass windows, and paintings. Catholic mobs responded by defending the sacred images, and crowds on both sides killed their opponents, often in gruesome ways.

A particularly savage Catholic attack on Calvinists took place in Paris on August 24, 1572 , Saint Bartholomew's Day. The occasion was the marriage of the king's sister Margaret of Valois to the Protestant Henry of Navarre, which was intended to help reconcile Catholics and Huguenots. Instead Huguenot wedding guests in Paris were massacred, and other Protestants were slaughtered by mobs. Violence spread to the provinces, where thousands were killed. The Saint Bartholomew's Day massacre led to a civil war that dragged on for fifteen years.

politiques

▶ Catholic and Protestant moderates who sought to end the religious violence in France by restoring a strong monarchy and granting official recognition to the Huguenots.

What ultimately saved France was a small group of moderates of both faiths called **politiques** (POH-lee-teeks) who believed that only the restoration of a strong monarchy could reverse the trend toward collapse. The politiques also favored officially recognizing the Huguenots. The death of the French queen Catherine de' Medici, followed by the assassination of her son King Henry III, paved the way for the accession of Henry of Navarre, a politique who became Henry IV (r. 1589–1610).

Henry's willingness to sacrifice religious principles to political necessity saved France. He converted to Catholicism but also, in 1598, issued the Edict of Nantes (nahnt), which granted liberty of conscience (freedom of thought) and liberty of public worship to Huguenots in 150 fortified towns. By helping restore internal peace in France, the reign of Henry IV and the Edict of Nantes paved the way for French kings to claim absolute power in the seventeenth century.

Civil Wars in the Netherlands

In the Netherlands a movement for church reform developed into a struggle for Dutch independence. The Catholic emperor Charles V had inherited the seventeen provinces that compose present-day Belgium and the Netherlands (see page 434). In the Netherlands, as many other places, Lutheran ideas took root.

CHAPTER LOCATOR | What were the major cultural developments of the Renaissance? | What were the key social hierarchies in Renaissance Europe?

448 CHAPTER 15
EUROPE IN THE RENAISSANCE AND REFORMATION

Charles V had grown up in the Netherlands, however, and he was able to limit the impact of the new ideas. Charles V abdicated in 1556 and transferred power over the Netherlands to his son Philip II, who had grown up in Spain. Although Philip, like his father, opposed Protestantism, Protestant ideas spread in the Netherlands.

By the 1560s Protestants in the Netherlands were primarily Calvinists. When Spanish authorities attempted to suppress Calvinist worship and raised taxes, it sparked riots and a wave of iconoclasm. In response, Philip II sent twenty thousand Spanish troops, and from 1568 to 1578 civil war raged in the Netherlands between Catholics and Protestants and between the seventeen provinces and Spain. Eventually the ten southern provinces came under the control of the Spanish Habsburg forces. The seven northern provinces, led by Holland, formed the Union of Utrecht (the United Provinces), and in 1581 they declared their independence from Spain. The north was Protestant, and the south remained Catholic. Philip did not accept the independence of the north, and war continued. England was even drawn into the conflict, supplying money and troops to the United Provinces. Hostilities ended in 1609 when Spain agreed to a truce that recognized the independence of the United Provinces.

The Great European Witch-Hunt

Insecurity created by the religious wars contributed to persecution for witchcraft, which actually began before the Reformation in the 1480s but became especially common about 1560. Both Protestants and Catholics tried and executed those accused of being witches.

The heightened sense of God's power and divine wrath in the Reformation era was an important factor in the **witch-hunts**, but other factors were also significant. In the later Middle Ages, scholars and officials added a demonological component to existing ideas about witches. For them, the essence of witchcraft was making a pact with the Devil that required the witch to do the Devil's bidding. Witches were no longer simply people who used magical power to do harm and get what they wanted, but rather people used by the Devil to do what he wanted.

Trials involving this new notion of witchcraft as diabolical heresy began in Switzerland and southern Germany in the late fifteenth century; became less numerous in the early decades of the Reformation, when Protestants and Catholics were busy fighting each other; and then picked up again about 1560, spreading to much of western Europe and to European colonies in the Americas. Scholars estimate that during the sixteenth and seventeenth centuries somewhere between 100,000 and 200,000 people were officially tried for witchcraft, and between 40,000 and 60,000 were executed.

Though the gender balance of the accused varied widely in different parts of Europe, between 75 and 85 percent of those tried and executed were women, whom some demonologists viewed as weaker and so more likely to give in to the Devil. Tensions within families, households, and neighborhoods also played a role in witchcraft accusations, as grievances and jealousies led to accusations. Suspects were questioned and tortured by legal authorities, and they often implicated others.

witch-hunts
▶ Campaign against witchcraft in early modern Europe and European colonies in which hundreds of thousands of people, mostly women, were tried, and many of them executed.

| How did the nation-states of western Europe evolve in this period? | What were the central ideas of Protestant reformers, and why were they appealing? | How did the Catholic Church respond to the new religious situation? | **What were the causes and consequences of religious violence?** | ✓ LearningCurve Check what you know. |

449

Even in the sixteenth century a few individuals questioned whether witches could ever do harm, make a pact with the Devil, or engage in the wild activities attributed to them. Furthermore, doubts about trial procedures and the use of torture to extract confessions gradually spread among the same type of religious and legal authorities who had so vigorously persecuted witches. By about 1660 prosecutions for witchcraft had become less common.

> **QUICK REVIEW**

What sparked the French wars of religion? How were they brought to an end?

CHAPTER SUMMARY

The Renaissance was characterized by self-conscious awareness among educated Europeans, particularly scholars and writers known as humanists, that they were living in a new era. Central to humanists were interest in the Latin classics, belief in individual potential, education for a career of public service, and, in northern Europe, the reform of church and society. Their ideas spread as a result of the development of the printing press with movable metal type, which revolutionized communication. Interest in the classical past and in the individual shaped Renaissance art in terms of style and subject matter, and patrons provided the money needed for an outpouring of painting, sculpture and architecture. Social hierarchies in the Renaissance developed new features that contributed to the modern social hierarchies of race, class, and gender. In politics, feudal monarchies gradually evolved into nation-states, as rulers used war, diplomacy, new forms of taxation, centralized institutions, and strategic marital alliances to build up their power.

Many individuals and groups had long called for reforms in the Catholic Church, providing a ready audience in the early sixteenth century for the ideas of Martin Luther. Luther and other reformers, called Protestants, developed a new understanding of Christian doctrine that emphasized faith and grace; Protestant ideas spread rapidly through preaching, hymns, and the printing press; and soon western Europe was split religiously. Local situations influenced religious patterns. In England the king's need for a church-approved divorce triggered the break with Rome, while in France and eastern Europe the ideas of John Calvin gained wide acceptance. By the middle of the sixteenth century the Roman Catholic Church had begun a process of internal reform along with opposing Protestants intellectually, politically, militarily, and institutionally. This reinvigorated Catholic Church would carry Christian ideas around the world, while in Europe religious differences led to riots, witch persecutions, civil wars, and international conflicts.

CHAPTER LOCATOR | What were the major cultural developments of the Renaissance? | What were the key social hierarchies in Renaissance Europe?

450 CHAPTER 15
EUROPE IN THE RENAISSANCE AND REFORMATION

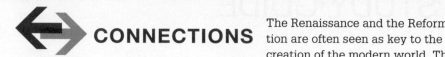

CONNECTIONS The Renaissance and the Reformation are often seen as key to the creation of the modern world. The radical changes of these times contained many elements of continuity, however. Artists, humanists, and religious reformers looked back to the classical era and early Christianity for inspiration. Political leaders played important roles in cultural and religious developments, just as they had for centuries in Europe and other parts of the world.

The events of the Renaissance and Reformation were thus linked with earlier developments, and they were also closely connected with another important element in the modern world: European exploration and colonization (discussed in Chapter 16). Renaissance monarchs paid for maritime expeditions, expecting a large share of any profits gained and increasingly viewing overseas territory as essential to their own reputations and to a strong state. Moreover, for many, European expansion had a religious dimension and was explicitly linked to the spread of Christianity around the world. The desire for fame, wealth, and power that was central to the Renaissance, and the religious zeal central to the Reformation, were thus key to the European voyages and to colonial ventures as well.

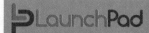

ONLINE DOCUMENT PROJECT

Cosimo and Lorenzo de' Medici

What role did patrons play in shaping Renaissance artistic and intellectual life?

Examine paintings and letters by Renaissance artists, and complete a quiz and writing assignment based on the evidence and details from this chapter. *See inside the front cover to learn more.*

| How did the nation-states of western Europe evolve in this period? | What were the central ideas of Protestant reformers, and why were they appealing? | How did the Catholic Church respond to the new religious situation? | What were the causes and consequences of religious violence? | ☑ **LearningCurve** Check what you know. |

451

CHAPTER 15 STUDY GUIDE

STEP **1**

GET STARTED ONLINE

LearningCurve

Now that you've read the chapter, make it stick by completing the LearningCurve activity.

STEP **2**

EXPLAIN WHY IT MATTERS

Put your reading into practice. Identify each term below, and then explain why it matters in world history.

TERM	WHO OR WHAT & WHEN	WHY IT MATTERS
Renaissance (p. 422)		
patronage (p. 422)		
humanism (p. 424)		
Christian humanists (p. 425)		
debate about women (p. 429)		
Protestant Reformation (p. 436)		
indulgence (p. 437)		
Diet of Worms (p. 438)		
Protestant (p. 438)		
predestination (p. 443)		
Jesuits (p. 446)		
Huguenots (p. 448)		
politiques (p. 448)		
witch-hunts (p. 449)		

STEP **3**

MOVE BEYOND THE BASICS

To demonstrate a more advanced understanding of the key differences between Catholic and Protestant beliefs and practices by filling in the chart below with descriptions of Catholic and Protestant views of salvation, the nature and role of the clergy, and the nature and role of the church. How did Protestant beliefs challenge Catholic institutions?

	View of Salvation	Nature and Role of Clergy	Nature and Role of the Church
Protestantism			
Catholicism			

STEP 4 — PUT IT ALL TOGETHER

Now, take a step back and try to explain the big picture. Remember to use specific examples from the chapter in your answers.

THE RENAISSANCE

▶ How did Renaissance ideas about individuals and their potential differ from those that prevailed in the Middle Ages?

▶ How did political and economic considerations shape the emergence, development, and spread of the Renaissance?

THE PROTESTANT REFORMATION

▶ How did Protestantism differ from earlier calls for theological and institutional reform of the Catholic Church? What explains Protestantism's remarkable success?

▶ What groups found Protestantism most appealing? Why?

THE CATHOLIC REFORMATION AND RELIGIOUS VIOLENCE

▶ Should the Catholic Reformation be considered a success? Why or why not?

▶ What connections can you make between the various forms of religious violence (riots, wars, witchcraft trials) that plagued sixteenth- and seventeenth-century Europe? What common factors and conditions contributed to each of these types of religious violence?

LOOKING BACK, LOOKING AHEAD

▶ How did medieval developments prepare the way for the Renaissance and the Reformation? What were the most important areas of continuity between medieval and early modern Europe?

▶ Many scholars and thinkers have seen the Renaissance and Reformation as marking the beginning of the "modern" Western world. Do you agree with this assessment? Why or why not?

> IN YOUR OWN WORDS

Imagine that you must give an oral report to the class answering the following question: **In what ways did the Renaissance and Reformation represent breaks from the medieval past? What would be the most important points and why?**

16
THE ACCELERATION OF GLOBAL CONTACT
1450–1600

> **What new global connections were forged in the fifteenth and sixteenth centuries?** Chapter 16 examines the causes, course, and effects of European expansion in the fifteenth and sixteenth centuries. Before 1500 Europeans were relatively marginal players in a centuries-old trading system that linked Africa, Asia, and Europe. By 1550 the European search for better access to Asian trade goods had led to a new overseas empire in the Indian Ocean and the accidental discovery of the Western Hemisphere. With this discovery South and North America were drawn into an international network of trade centers and political empires, which Europeans came to dominate. The era of globalization had begun, creating new political systems and forms of economic exchange as well as cultural assimilation, conversion, and resistance.

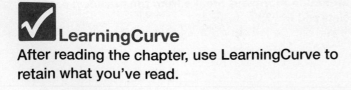

LearningCurve
After reading the chapter, use LearningCurve to retain what you've read.

Nezahualpilli At the time of the arrival of Europeans, Nezahualpilli was ruler of the city-state of Texcoco, the second most important city in the Aztec Empire after Tenochtitlan. (Nezahualpilli, portrait from *Codex Ixtlilxochitl*, 1582, pigment on European paper/Bibliothèque Nationale, Paris, France/De Agostini Picture Library/akg-images)

> What was the Afroeurasian trade world like prior to the era of European exploration?

> Why and how did Europeans undertake ambitious voyages of expansion?

> What was the impact of Iberian conquest and settlement on the peoples and ecologies of the Americas?

> How was the era of global contact shaped by new commodities, commercial empires, and forced migrations?

> How did new encounters shape cultural attitudes and beliefs in Europe and the New World?

> What was the Afroeurasian trade world like prior to the era of European exploration?

The Port of Calicut in India

The port of Calicut, located on the west coast of India, was a center of the Indian Ocean spice trade during the Middle Ages. Vasco da Gama arrived in Calicut in 1498 and obtained permission to trade there, leading to hostilities between the Portuguese and the Arab traders who had previously dominated the port. (Private Collection/The Stapleton Collection/The Bridgeman Art Library)

THE AFROEURASIAN TRADE WORLD linked the products and people of Europe, Asia, and Africa in the fifteenth century. The West was not the dominant player in this trading system. Nevertheless, wealthy Europeans were eager consumers of luxury goods from the East, which they received through Italian middlemen.

The Trade World of the Indian Ocean

The Indian Ocean was the center of the Afroeurasian trade world, serving as a crossroads for commercial and cultural exchanges between China, India, the Middle East, Africa, and Europe (Map 16.1). From the seventh through the four-teenth centuries, the volume of this trade steadily increased, declining only dur-ing the years of the Black Death.

Merchants congregated in a series of multicultural, cosmopolitan port cities strung around the Indian Ocean. Most of these cities had some form of autono-mous self-government, and mutual self-interest had largely limited violence and attempts to monopolize trade. The most developed area of this commercial web was made up of the ports surrounding the South China Sea. In the fifteenth cen-tury the port of Malacca became a great commercial entrepôt (AHN-truh-poh), a trading post to which goods were shipped for storage while awaiting redistribu-tion to other places.

CHAPTER LOCATOR | **What was the Afroeurasian trade world like prior to the era of European exploration?** | Why and how did Europeans undertake ambitious voyages of expansion?

456 CHAPTER 16
THE ACCELERATION OF GLOBAL CONTACT

1271–1295	**1519–1522**
Marco Polo travels to China	Magellan's expedition circumnavigates the world
1443	**1521**
Portuguese establish first African trading post at Arguin	Cortés conquers Aztec Empire
1492	**1533**
Columbus lands on San Salvador	Pizarro conquers Inca Empire
1494	**1571**
Treaty of Tordesillas ratified	Spanish establish port of Manila in the Philippines
1518	**1602**
Atlantic slave trade begins	Dutch East India Company founded

The Mongol emperors opened the doors of China to the West, encouraging Europeans like the Venetian trader and explorer Marco Polo to do business there. Marco Polo's tales of his travels from 1271 to 1295 fueled Western fantasies about the Orient.

After the Mongols fell to the Ming Dynasty in 1368, China entered a period of agricultural and commercial expansion, population growth, and urbanization (see pages 612–619). Historians agree that China had the most advanced economy in the world until at least the beginning of the eighteenth century.

China also took the lead in exploration, sending Admiral Zheng He's fleet as far west as Egypt. Each of his seven expeditions from 1405 to 1433 involved hundreds of ships and tens of thousands of men (see page 633). The purpose of the voyages was primarily diplomatic, to enhance China's prestige and seek tribute-paying alliances. The high expense of the voyages in a period of renewed Mongol encroachment led to the abandonment of the maritime expeditions after the deaths of Zheng He and the emperor.

China's decision to forego large-scale exploration was a decisive turning point in world history, one that left an opening for European states to expand their role in Asian trade. Nonetheless, Zheng He's voyages left a legacy of increased Chinese trading in the South China Sea and Indian Ocean.

Another center of Indian Ocean trade was India, the crucial link between the Persian Gulf and the Southeast Asian and East Asian trade networks. The subcontinent had ancient links with its neighbors to the northwest. Trade among ports bordering the Indian Ocean was revived in the Middle Ages by Arab merchants who circumnavigated India on their way to trade in the South China Sea.

The inhabitants of India's Coromandel coast traditionally looked to Southeast Asia, where they had ancient trading and cultural ties. Hinduism and Buddhism arrived in Southeast Asia from India during the Middle Ages, and a brisk trade between Southeast Asian and Coromandel port cities persisted from that time until the arrival of the Portuguese in the sixteenth century. India itself was an important contributor of goods to the world trading system. Most of the world's pepper was grown in India, and Indian cotton and silk textiles were also highly prized.

What was the impact of Iberian conquest and settlement on the peoples of the Americas?	How was the era of global contact shaped by new commodities and forced migrations?	How did new encounters shape cultural attitudes and beliefs in Europe and the New World?	✔ LearningCurve Check what you know.

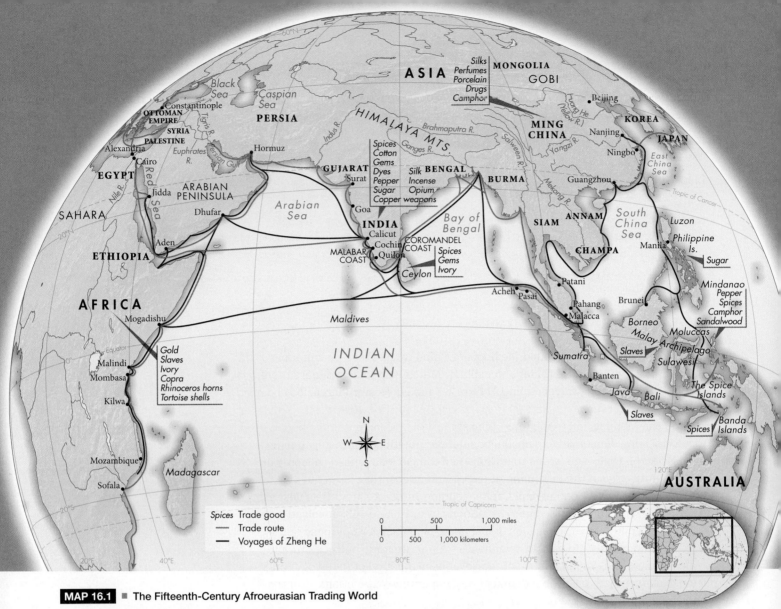

MAP 16.1 ■ The Fifteenth-Century Afroeurasian Trading World

After a period of decline following the Black Death and the Mongol invasions, trade revived in the fifteenth century. Muslim merchants dominated trade, linking ports in East Africa and the Red Sea with those in India and the Malay Archipelago. The Chinese admiral Zheng He followed the most important Indian Ocean trade routes on his voyages (1405–1433), hoping to impose Ming dominance of trade and tribute.

Peoples and Cultures of the Indian Ocean

Indian Ocean trade connected peoples from the Malay Peninsula (the southern extremity of the Asian continent), India, China, and East Africa, among whom there was an enormous variety of languages, cultures, and religions. In spite of this diversity, certain sociocultural similarities linked these peoples, especially in Southeast Asia.

In comparison to India, China, or even Europe after the Black Death, Southeast Asia was sparsely populated. People were concentrated in port cities and in areas of intense rice cultivation. Another difference between Southeast Asia and

CHAPTER LOCATOR | **What was the Afroeurasian trade world like prior to the era of European exploration?** | Why and how did Europeans undertake ambitious voyages of expansion?

CHAPTER 16
458 THE ACCELERATION OF GLOBAL CONTACT

India, China, and Europe was the higher status of women—their primary role in planting and harvesting rice gave them authority and economic power. At marriage, which typically occurred around age twenty, the groom paid the bride (or sometimes her family) a sum of money called **bride wealth**, which remained under her control. This practice was in sharp contrast to the Chinese, Indian, and European dowry, which came under the husband's control. Property was administered jointly, in contrast to the Chinese principle and Indian practice that wives had no say in the disposal of family property. All children, regardless of gender, inherited equally.

Respect for women carried over to the commercial sphere. Women participated in business as partners and independent entrepreneurs. When Portuguese and Dutch men settled in the region and married local women, their wives continued to play important roles in trade and commerce.

In contrast to most parts of the world other than Africa, Southeast Asian peoples had an accepting attitude toward premarital sexual activity and placed no premium on virginity at marriage. Divorce carried no social stigma and was easily attainable if a pair proved incompatible. Either the woman or the man could initiate a divorce.

bride wealth

► In early modern Southeast Asia, a sum of money the groom paid the bride or her family at the time of marriage. This practice contrasted with the dowry in China, India, and Europe, which the husband controlled.

> **> Common Features of Southeast Asian Societies:**

- Austronesian languages
- Diet based on rice, fish, palms, and palm wine
- Rice, harvested by women, as the staple of the diet
- Fishing as the chief male occupation

Trade with Africa and the Middle East

On the east coast of Africa, Swahili-speaking city-states engaged in the Indian Ocean trade, exchanging ivory, rhinoceros horn, tortoise shells, copra (dried coconut), and slaves for textiles, spices, cowrie shells, porcelain, and other goods. The most important cities were Mogadishu, Mombasa, and Kilwa, which had converted to Islam by the eleventh century.

West Africa also played an important role in world trade. In the fifteenth century most of the gold that reached Europe came from the Sudan region in West Africa. Transported across the Sahara by Arab and African traders on camels, the gold was sold in the ports of North Africa. Other trading routes led to the Egyptian cities of Alexandria and Cairo.

Inland nations that sat astride the north-south caravan routes grew wealthy from this trade. In the mid-thirteenth century the kingdom of Mali emerged as an important player on the overland trade route. In later centuries, however, the diversion of gold away from the trans-Sahara routes would weaken the inland states of Africa politically and economically.

Gold was one important object of trade; slaves were another. Long before the arrival of Europeans, Arab and

Mansa Musa

This detail from the Catalan Atlas of 1375, a world map created for the Catalan king, depicts a king of Mali, Mansa Musa, who was legendary for his wealth in gold. European desires for direct access to the trade in sub-Saharan gold helped inspire Portuguese exploration of the west coast of Africa in the fifteenth century. (Detail from the *Catalan Atlas*, 1375 [vellum], by Abraham Cresques (1325–1387)/Bibliothèque Nationale, Paris, France/The Bridgeman Art Library)

What was the impact of Iberian conquest and settlement on the peoples of the Americas?

How was the era of global contact shaped by new commodities and forced migrations?

How did new encounters shape cultural attitudes and beliefs in Europe and the New World?

☑ LearningCurve
Check what you know.

African merchants took West African slaves to the Mediterranean to be sold in European, Egyptian, and Middle Eastern markets and also brought eastern Europeans to West Africa as slaves. In addition, Indian and Arab merchants traded slaves in the coastal regions of East Africa.

The Middle East served as an intermediary for trade between Europe, Africa, and Asia and was also an important supplier of goods for foreign exchange. Two great rival empires, the Persian Safavids and the Turkish Ottomans, dominated the region, competing for control over western trade routes to the East. By the mid-sixteenth century the Ottomans had established control over eastern Mediterranean sea routes to trading centers in Syria, Palestine, Egypt, and the rest of North Africa.

Genoese and Venetian Middlemen

Europe constituted a minor outpost in the world trading system, for European craftsmen produced few products to rival those of Asia. However, Europeans desired luxury goods from the East, and in the late Middle Ages such trade was controlled by the Italian city-states of Venice and Genoa. Venice had opened the gateway to Asian trade in 1304, when it established formal relations with the sultan of Mamluk Egypt and started operations in Cairo. Because Eastern demand for European goods was low, Venetians funded their purchases through shipping and trade in firearms and slaves.

Venice's ancient trading rival was Genoa. By 1270, Genoa dominated the northern route to Asia through the Black Sea. From then until the fourteenth century, the Genoese expanded their trade routes as far as Persia and the Far East.

In the fifteenth century, with Venice claiming victory in the spice trade, the Genoese shifted focus from trade to finance and from the Black Sea to the western Mediterranean. When Spanish and Portuguese voyages began to explore the western Atlantic (see page 461), Genoese merchants, navigators, and financiers provided their skills and capital to the Iberian monarchs.

A major element of Italian trade was slavery. Merchants purchased slaves in the Balkans of southeastern Europe. After the loss of the Black Sea trade routes—and thus the source of slaves—to the Ottomans, the Genoese sought new supplies of slaves in the West, eventually seizing or buying and selling the Guanches (indigenous peoples from the Canary Islands), Muslim prisoners and Jewish refugees from Spain, and, by the early 1500s, both black and Berber Africans. With the growth of Spanish colonies in the New World, Genoese and Venetian merchants became important players in the Atlantic slave trade.

> **QUICK REVIEW**

What role did the peoples of Southeast Asia play in the Afroeurasian trade world? What role did Europeans play?

CHAPTER LOCATOR | What was the Afroeurasian trade world like prior to the era of European exploration? | Why and how did Europeans undertake ambitious voyages of expansion?

CHAPTER 16
460 THE ACCELERATION OF GLOBAL CONTACT

Why and how did Europeans undertake ambitious voyages of expansion?

Pepper Harvest

To break the monotony of their bland diet, Europeans had a passion for pepper, which — along with cinnamon, cloves, nutmeg, and ginger — was the main object of the Asian trade. We can appreciate the fifteenth-century expression "as dear as pepper": one kilo of pepper cost 2 grams of silver at the place of production in the East Indies and from 1 to 10 grams of silver in Alexandria, Egypt; 14 to 18 grams in Venice; and 20 to 30 grams at the markets of northern Europe. Here natives fill vats, and the dealer tastes a peppercorn for pungency. (Bibliothèque Nationale, Paris, France/Archives Charmet/The Bridgeman Art Library)

AS EUROPE RECOVERED after the Black Death, new European players entered the scene with novel technology, eager to spread Christianity and to undo Italian and Ottoman domination of trade with the East. A century after the plague, Iberian explorers began the overseas voyages that helped create the modern world, with immense consequences for their own continent and the rest of the planet.

Causes of European Expansion

European expansion had multiple causes. The first was economic. By the middle of the fifteenth century Europe was experiencing a revival of population and economic activity after the lows of the Black Death. This revival created renewed demand for luxuries, especially spices, from the East. The fall of Constantinople and the subsequent Ottoman control of trade routes created obstacles to fulfilling these demands. European merchants and rulers eager for the profits of trade thus needed to find new sources of precious metal to exchange with the Ottomans or trade routes that bypassed the Ottomans.

| What was the impact of Iberian conquest and settlement on the peoples of the Americas? | How was the era of global contact shaped by new commodities and forced migrations? | How did new encounters shape cultural attitudes and beliefs in Europe and the New World? |  LearningCurve Check what you know. |

461

Religious fervor and the crusading spirit were another important catalyst for expansion. Just seven months separated Isabella and Ferdinand's conquest of the emirate of Granada, the last remaining Muslim state on the Iberian Peninsula, and Columbus's departure across the Atlantic. Overseas exploration thus transferred the militaristic religious fervor of the reconquista (reconquest) to new non-Christian territories. As they conquered indigenous empires, Iberians brought the attitudes and administrative practices developed during the reconquista to the Americas.

A third motivation was the dynamic spirit of the Renaissance. Like other men of the Renaissance era, explorers sought to win glory for their exploits and demonstrated a genuine interest in learning more about unknown waters. The detailed journals kept by European voyagers attest to their fascination with the new peoples and places they visited.

The people who stayed at home had a powerful impact on the voyages of discovery. Merchants provided the capital for many early voyages and had a strong say in their course. To gain authorization and financial support for their expeditions, they sought official sponsorship from the Crown. Competition among European monarchs for the prestige and profit of overseas exploration thus constituted another crucial factor in encouraging the steady stream of expeditions that began in the late fifteenth century.

The small number of Europeans who could read provided a rapt audience for tales of fantastic places and unknown peoples. Cosmography, natural history, and geography aroused enormous interest among educated people in the fifteenth and sixteenth centuries. One of the most popular books of the time was the fourteenth-century text *The Travels of Sir John Mandeville*, which purported to be a firsthand account of the author's travels in the Middle East, India, and China.

Technology and the Rise of Exploration

Technological developments in shipbuilding, navigation, and weaponry enabled European expansion. Since ancient times, most seagoing vessels had been narrow, open boats called galleys, propelled by slaves or convicts manning the oars. The need for sturdier craft, as well as population losses caused by the Black Death, forced the development of a new style of ship that would not require much manpower. Over the course of the fifteenth century the Portuguese developed the **caravel**, a small, light, three-mast sailing ship with triangular lateen sails. The caravel was much more maneuverable than the galley. When fitted with cannon, it could dominate larger vessels.

This period also saw great strides in cartography and navigational aids. Around 1410 Arab scholars reintroduced Europeans to **Ptolemy's** *Geography*. Written in the second century, the work synthesized the geographical knowledge of the classical world. It represented a major improvement over medieval cartography, but it also contained significant errors. Unaware of the Americas, Ptolemy showed the world as much smaller than it is, so that Asia appeared not very far to the west of Europe.

The magnetic compass made it possible for sailors to determine their direction and position at sea. The astrolabe, an instrument invented by the ancient Greeks and perfected by Muslim navigators, was used to determine the altitude

caravel

▶ A small, maneuverable, three-mast sailing ship developed by the Portuguese in the fifteenth century that gave the Portuguese a distinct advantage in exploration and trade.

Ptolemy's *Geography*

▶ A second-century-C.E. work that synthesized the classical knowledge of geography and introduced the concepts of longitude and latitude. Reintroduced to Europeans in 1410 by Arab scholars, its ideas allowed cartographers to create more accurate maps.

CHAPTER LOCATOR | What was the Afroeurasian trade world like prior to the era of European exploration? | **Why and how did Europeans undertake ambitious voyages of expansion?**

CHAPTER 16
462 THE ACCELERATION OF GLOBAL CONTACT

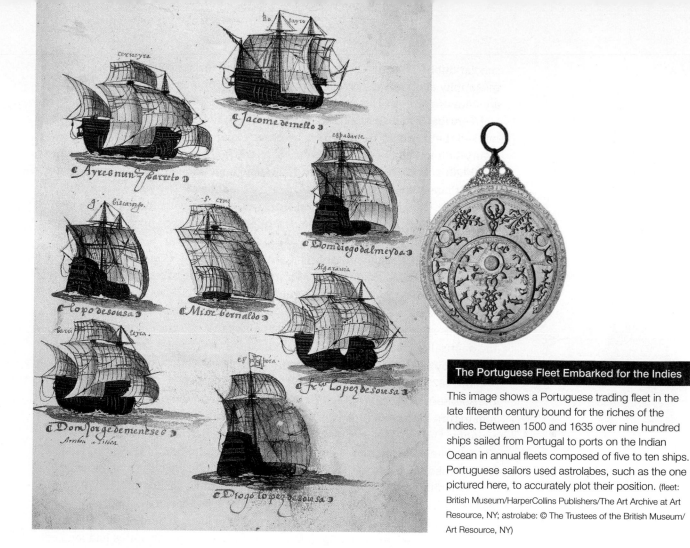

The Portuguese Fleet Embarked for the Indies

This image shows a Portuguese trading fleet in the late fifteenth century bound for the riches of the Indies. Between 1500 and 1635 over nine hundred ships sailed from Portugal to ports on the Indian Ocean in annual fleets composed of five to ten ships. Portuguese sailors used astrolabes, such as the one pictured here, to accurately plot their position. (fleet: British Museum/HarperCollins Publishers/The Art Archive at Art Resource, NY; astrolabe: © The Trustees of the British Museum/Art Resource, NY)

of the sun and other celestial bodies. It permitted mariners to plot their latitude, that is, their precise position north or south of the equator.

Like the astrolabe, much of the new technology that Europeans used on their voyages was borrowed from the East. Gunpowder, the compass, and the stern-post rudder were Chinese inventions. Advances in cartography also drew on the rich tradition of Judeo-Arabic mathematical and astronomical learning in Iberia. In exploring new territories, European sailors thus called on techniques and knowledge developed over centuries in China, the Muslim world, and trading centers along the Indian Ocean.

The Portuguese in Africa and Asia

For centuries Portugal was a small and poor nation on the margins of European life. Yet Portugal had a long history of seafaring and navigation. Blocked from access to western Europe by Spain, the Portuguese turned to the Atlantic. Nature favored the Portuguese: winds blowing along their coast offered passage to Africa, its Atlantic islands, and, ultimately, Brazil.

In the early phases of Portuguese exploration, Prince Henry (1394–1460), a dynamic younger son of the king, played a leading role. A nineteenth-century

| What was the impact of Iberian conquest and settlement on the peoples of the Americas? | How was the era of global contact shaped by new commodities and forced migrations? | How did new encounters shape cultural attitudes and beliefs in Europe and the New World? | ✓ **LearningCurve** Check what you know. |

scholar dubbed Henry "the Navigator" because of his support for the study of geography and navigation and for the annual expeditions he sponsored down the western coast of Africa.

Portugal's conquest of Ceuta, an Arab city in northern Morocco, in 1415 marked the beginning of European overseas expansion. In the 1420s, under Henry's direction, the Portuguese began to settle the Atlantic islands of Madeira (ca. 1420) and the Azores (1427). In 1443 they founded their first African commercial settlement at Arguin in North Africa. By the time of Henry's death in 1460, his support for exploration had resulted in thriving sugar plantations on the Atlantic islands, the first arrival of enslaved Africans in Portugal (see page 475), and new access to African gold.

The Portuguese next established fortified trading posts, called factories, on the gold-rich Guinea coast and penetrated into the African continent all the way to Timbuktu (Map 16.2). By 1500 Portugal controlled the flow of African gold to Europe. In contrast to the Spanish conquest of the Americas (see page 468), the Portuguese did not establish large settlements in West Africa or seek to control the political or cultural lives of those with whom they traded. Instead they sought to profit by inserting themselves into pre-existing trading systems.

In 1487 Bartholomew Diaz (ca. 1451–1500) rounded the Cape of Good Hope at the southern tip of Africa (Map 16.2), but storms and a threatened mutiny forced him to turn back. A decade later Vasco da Gama (ca. 1469–1524) succeeded in rounding the Cape while commanding a fleet in search of a sea route to India. With the help of an Indian guide, da Gama reached the port of Calicut in India. He returned to Lisbon with spices and samples of Indian cloth, having proved the possibility of lucrative trade with the East via the Cape route. Thereafter, a Portuguese convoy set out for passage around the Cape every March.

Lisbon became the entrance port for Asian goods into Europe, but this was not accomplished without a fight. Muslim-controlled port city-states had long controlled the rich trade of the Indian Ocean, and they did not surrender it willingly. From 1500 to 1515 the Portuguese used a combination of bombardment and diplomatic treaties to establish trading factories at Goa, Malacca, Calicut, and Hormuz, thereby laying the foundation for a Portuguese trading empire in the sixteenth and seventeenth centuries. The acquisition of port cities and their trade routes brought riches to Portugal, but, as in Africa, the Portuguese had limited impact on the lives and religious faith of peoples beyond Portuguese coastal holdings.

Inspired by the Portuguese, Spain had also begun the quest for empire. Theirs was to be a second, entirely different mode of colonization leading to large-scale settlement and the forced assimilation of huge indigenous populations.

Spain's Voyages to the Americas

Christopher Columbus, a native of Genoa, was an experienced seaman and navigator. He had worked as a mapmaker in Lisbon and had spent time on Madeira. He was familiar with such fifteenth-century Portuguese navigational aids as *portolans*—written descriptions of the courses along which ships sailed—and the use of the compass as a nautical instrument.

Columbus was also a deeply religious man. He had witnessed the Spanish conquest of Granada and shared fully in the religious fervor surrounding that event. Like the Spanish rulers and most Europeans of his age, Columbus under-

CHAPTER LOCATOR | What was the Afroeurasian trade world like prior to the era of European exploration? | **Why and how did Europeans undertake ambitious voyages of expansion?**

CHAPTER 16
464 THE ACCELERATION OF GLOBAL CONTACT

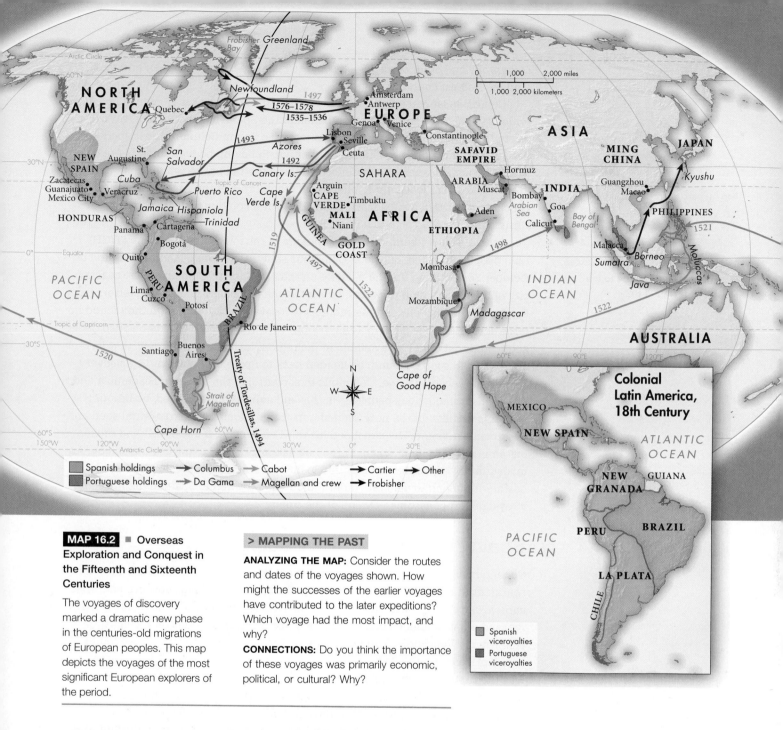

MAP 16.2 ■ Overseas Exploration and Conquest in the Fifteenth and Sixteenth Centuries

The voyages of discovery marked a dramatic new phase in the centuries-old migrations of European peoples. This map depicts the voyages of the most significant European explorers of the period.

> MAPPING THE PAST

ANALYZING THE MAP: Consider the routes and dates of the voyages shown. How might the successes of the earlier voyages have contributed to the later expeditions? Which voyage had the most impact, and why?

CONNECTIONS: Do you think the importance of these voyages was primarily economic, political, or cultural? Why?

stood Christianity as a missionary religion that should be carried to all places of the earth.

Rejected for funding by the Portuguese in 1483 and by Ferdinand and Isabella in 1486, Columbus finally won the support of the Spanish monarchy in 1492. Buoyed by the success of the reconquista and eager to earn profits from trade, the Spanish crown agreed to make him viceroy over any territory he might discover and to give him one-tenth of the material rewards of the journey.

Columbus and his small fleet left Spain on August 3, 1492. Columbus dreamed of reaching the court of the Mongol emperor, the Great Khan, not realizing that the Ming Dynasty had overthrown the Mongols in 1368. Based on Ptolemy's

What was the impact of Iberian conquest and settlement on the peoples of the Americas? | How was the era of global contact shaped by new commodities and forced migrations? | How did new encounters shape cultural attitudes and beliefs in Europe and the New World? | ✓ LearningCurve Check what you know.

Columbus's First Voyage to the New World, 1492–1493

Geography and other texts, he expected to pass the islands of Japan and then land on the east coast of China.

Columbus landed on an island in the Bahamas on October 12, which he christened San Salvador and claimed on behalf of the Spanish crown. In a letter he wrote to Ferdinand and Isabella on his return to Spain, Columbus described the natives as handsome, peaceful, and primitive. Believing he was somewhere off the east coast of Japan, in what he considered the Indies, he called them "Indians," a name that was later applied to all inhabitants of the Americas. Columbus concluded that they would make good slaves and could quickly be converted to Christianity.

Scholars have identified the inhabitants of the islands as the Taino (TIGH-noh) people. From San Salvador, Columbus sailed southwest, landing on Cuba on October 28. Deciding that he must be on the mainland of China near the coastal city of Quinsay (now Hangzhou), he sent a small embassy inland with letters from Ferdinand and Isabella and instructions to locate the city. Although they found no large settlement, the sight of Taino people wearing gold ornaments on Hispaniola suggested that gold was available in the region. In January, confident that its source would soon be found, he headed back to Spain to report on his discovery.

On his second voyage, Columbus took control of the island of Hispaniola and enslaved its indigenous peoples. On this and subsequent voyages, he brought with him settlers for the new Spanish territories, along with agricultural seed and livestock. Arriving in Hispaniola on his third voyage, he found revolt had broken out against his brother, whom Columbus had left behind to govern the colony. An investigatory expedition sent by the Spanish crown arrested Columbus and his brother for failing to maintain order. Columbus returned to Spain in disgrace and a royal governor assumed control of the colony.

Spain "Discovers" the Pacific

Columbus never realized the scope of his achievement: that he had found a vast continent unknown to Europeans, except for a fleeting Viking presence centuries earlier. The Florentine navigator Amerigo Vespucci (veh-SPOO-chee) (1454–1512) realized what Columbus had not. Writing about his discoveries on the coast of modern-day Venezuela, Vespucci stated: "Those new regions which we found and explored with the fleet . . . we may rightly call a New World." This letter was the first document to describe America as a continent separate from Asia. In recognition of Amerigo's bold claim, the continent was named for him.

To settle competing claims to the Atlantic discoveries, Spain and Portugal turned to Pope Alexander VI. The resulting **Treaty of Tordesillas** (tawr-duh-SEE-yuhs) in 1494 gave Spain everything to the west of an imaginary line drawn down the Atlantic and Portugal everything to the east.

The search for profits determined the direction of Spanish exploration and expansion in South America. Because its profits from Hispaniola and other Caribbean islands were insignificant compared to Portugal's enormous riches from the Asian spice trade, Spain renewed the search for a western passage to Asia. In 1519 Charles V of Spain commissioned Ferdinand Magellan (1480–1521) to find a direct sea route to Asia. Magellan sailed southwest across the Atlantic to Brazil, and after a long search along the coast he located the strait off the southern tip of South America that now bears his name (see Map 16.2). After passing through

Treaty of Tordesillas

▶ The 1494 agreement giving Spain everything west of an imaginary line drawn down the Atlantic and giving Portugal everything to the east.

CHAPTER LOCATOR | What was the Afroeurasian trade world like prior to the era of European exploration? | **Why and how did Europeans undertake ambitious voyages of expansion?**

466 CHAPTER 16 THE ACCELERATION OF GLOBAL CONTACT

the strait, his fleet sailed north up the west coast of South America and then headed west into the Pacific.

Terrible storms, disease, starvation, and violence haunted the expedition. Magellan himself was killed in a skirmish in the Malay Archipelago, and only one of the five ships that began the expedition made it back to Spain. This ship returned home in 1522 with only eighteen men aboard, having traveled from the east by way of the Indian Ocean, the Cape of Good Hope, and the Atlantic. The voyage—the first to circumnavigate the globe—had taken close to three years.

Despite the losses, this voyage revolutionized Europeans' understanding of the world by demonstrating the vastness of the Pacific. Magellan's expedition also forced Spain's rulers to rethink their plans for overseas commerce and territorial expansion. The westward passage to the Indies was too long and dangerous for commercial purposes. Thus Spain soon abandoned the attempt to oust Portugal from the Eastern spice trade and concentrated on exploiting its New World territories.

Early Exploration by Northern European Powers

Spain's northern European rivals also set sail across the Atlantic during the early days of exploration, searching for a northwest passage to the Indies. In 1497 John Cabot (ca. 1450–1499), a Genoese merchant living in London, landed on Newfoundland. The next year he returned and explored the New England coast. These forays proved futile, and at that time the English established no permanent colonies in the territories they explored.

News of the riches of Mexico and Peru later inspired the English to renew their efforts. Between 1576 and 1578 Martin Frobisher (ca. 1535–1594) made three voyages in and around the Canadian bay that now bears his name. Frobisher brought a quantity of ore back to England with him in hopes that it contained precious metals, but it proved to be worthless.

Early French exploration of the Atlantic was equally frustrating. Between 1534 and 1541 Frenchman Jacques Cartier (1491–1557) made several voyages and explored the St. Lawrence region of Canada, searching for a passage to the wealth of Asia. When this hope proved vain, the French turned to a new source of profit within Canada itself: trade in beavers and other furs. As had the Portuguese in Asia, French traders bartered with local peoples whom they largely treated as autonomous and equal partners. French fishermen also competed with the Spanish and English for the schools of cod they found in the Atlantic waters around Newfoundland.

QUICK REVIEW

How did the Portuguese lay the foundation for European overseas expansion?

What was the impact of Iberian conquest and settlement on the peoples of the Americas?	How was the era of global contact shaped by new commodities and forced migrations?	How did new encounters shape cultural attitudes and beliefs in Europe and the New World?	✓ LearningCurve Check what you know.

What was the impact of Iberian conquest and settlement on the peoples and ecologies of the Americas?

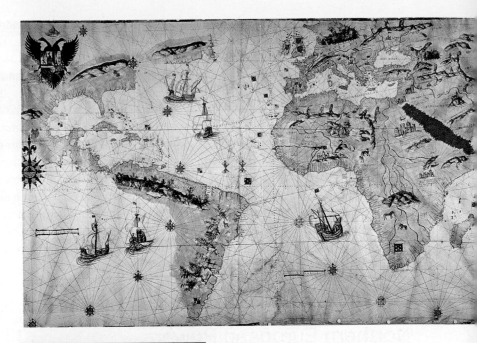

Juan Vespucci's World Map, 1526

As chief pilot to the Spanish crown, Juan Vespucci oversaw constant revisions to royal maps necessitated by ongoing voyages of discovery and exploration. This map shows the progress of Spanish knowledge of the New World some thirty years after Columbus. (The Granger Collection, NYC — All rights reserved.)

BEFORE COLUMBUS'S ARRIVAL, the Americas were inhabited by thousands of groups of indigenous peoples with distinct languages and cultures. These groups ranged from hunter-gatherer tribes organized into tribal confederations to settled agriculturalists to large-scale empires connecting bustling cities and towns. The best estimate is that the peoples of the Americas numbered between 35 and 50 million in 1492. Their lives were radically altered by the arrival of Europeans.

Spanish Conquest of the Aztec and Inca Empires

conquistador
▶ Spanish for "conqueror"; a Spanish soldier-explorer, such as Hernán Cortés or Francisco Pizarro, who sought to conquer the New World for the Spanish crown.

In the first two decades after Columbus's arrival in the New World, the Spanish colonized Hispaniola, Cuba, Puerto Rico, and other Caribbean islands. Based on rumors of a wealthy mainland civilization, the Spanish governor in Cuba sponsored expeditions to the Yucatán coast of the Gulf of Mexico, including one in 1519 under the command of the **conquistador** (kahn-KEES-tuh-dawr) Hernán Cortés (1485–1547). Alarmed by Cortés's ambition, the governor decided to withdraw his support, but Cortés quickly set sail before being removed from command. Cortés and his party landed on the Mexican coast on April 21, 1519. His

CHAPTER LOCATOR | What was the Afroeurasian trade world like prior to the era of European exploration? | Why and how did Europeans undertake ambitious voyages of expansion?

CHAPTER 16
468 THE ACCELERATION OF GLOBAL CONTACT

camp soon received visits by delegations of Aztec leaders bearing gifts and news of their great emperor.

The Mexica Empire, also known as the **Aztec Empire**, comprised the Mexica people and the peoples they had conquered. At the time of the Spanish arrival, the empire was ruled by Moctezuma II (r. 1502–1520), from his capital at Tenochtitlan (tay-nawch-teet-LAHN), now Mexico City. The Aztecs were a sophisticated civilization with an advanced understanding of mathematics, astronomy, and engineering. As in European nations at the time, a hereditary nobility dominated the army, the priesthood, and the state bureaucracy and reaped the gains from the agricultural labor of the common people.

Within weeks of his arrival, Cortés acquired translators who provided vital information on the empire and its weaknesses. (See "Individuals in Society: Doña Marina / Malintzin," page 470.) Through his interpreters, Cortés learned of strong local resentment against the Aztec Empire. Realizing that he could exploit dissensions within the empire to his own advantage, Cortés forged an alliance with Tlaxcala (tlah-SKAH-lah), a subject kingdom of the Aztecs. In October a combined Spanish-Tlaxcalan force occupied the Aztec city of Cholula, second largest in the empire, and massacred thousands of inhabitants. Strengthened by this victory, Cortés formed alliances with other native kingdoms. In November 1519, with a few hundred Spanish men and some six thousand indigenous warriors, he marched on Tenochtitlan.

Moctezuma's response to the arrival of the Spanish was weak and hesitant. Unlike other native leaders, he refrained from attacking the Spaniards but instead welcomed Cortés and his men into Tenochtitlan. Moctezuma was apparently deeply impressed by Spanish victories and believed the Spanish were invincible. When Cortés took Moctezuma hostage, the emperor's influence crumbled. During the ensuing attacks and counterattacks, Moctezuma was killed. The Spaniards and their allies escaped from the city suffering heavy losses. Cortés quickly began gathering forces and making new alliances against the Aztecs. In May 1521 he led a second assault on Tenochtitlan, leading an army of approximately one thousand Spanish and seventy-five thousand native warriors.[1]

The Spanish victory in late summer 1521 was hard-won and was greatly aided by the effects of smallpox, which had devastated the besieged population of the city. After establishing a new capital in the ruins of Tenochtitlan, Cortés and other conquistadors began the systematic conquest of Mexico.

More remarkable than the defeat of the Aztec Empire was the fall of the remote **Inca Empire** in Peru. Living in a settlement perched more than 9,800 feet above sea level, the Incas were isolated from the Mesoamerican civilization of the Aztecs. The Incas' strength lay largely in their bureaucratic efficiency. They divided their empire into four major regions, each region into provinces, and each province into districts. Officials at each level used the extensive network of roads to transmit information and orders. The Incas used a complex system of colored and knotted cords, called khipus, for administrative bookkeeping.

By the time of the Spanish invasion, however, the Inca Empire had been weakened by a civil war over succession and an epidemic of disease, possibly smallpox, spread through trade with groups in contact with Europeans. The Spanish conquistador Francisco Pizarro (ca. 1475–1541) landed on the northern coast of Peru on May 13, 1532, the very day the Inca leader Atahualpa (ah-tuh-WAHL-puh) won control of the empire. As Pizarro advanced across the Andes toward Cuzco, the capital of the Inca Empire, Atahualpa was also heading there for his coronation.

Aztec Empire
▶ Also known as the Mexica Empire, a large and complex Native American civilization in modern Mexico and Central America that possessed advanced mathematical, astronomical, and engineering technology.

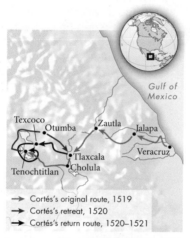

Invasion of Tenochtitlán, 1519–1521

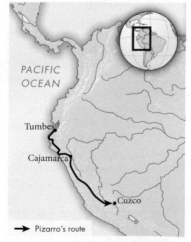

The Conquest of Peru, 1532–1533

Inca Empire
▶ The vast and sophisticated Peruvian empire centered at the capital city of Cuzco that was at its peak in the fifteenth century.

| What was the impact of Iberian conquest and settlement on the peoples of the Americas? | How was the era of global contact shaped by new commodities and forced migrations? | How did new encounters shape cultural attitudes and beliefs in Europe and the New World? | 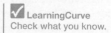 LearningCurve Check what you know. |

INDIVIDUALS IN SOCIETY
Doña Marina / Malintzin

In April 1519 Hernán Cortés and his followers received a number of gifts from the Tabasco people after he defeated them, including a group of twenty female captives. Among them was a young woman the Spanish baptized as Marina, which became Malin in the Nahuatl (NAH-wha-tuhl) language spoken in the Aztec Empire. Her high status and importance were recognized with the honorific title of *doña* in Spanish and the suffix *-tzin* in Nahuatl. Bernal Díaz del Castillo, who accompanied Cortés and wrote the most important contemporary history of the Aztec Empire and its conquest, claimed that Doña Marina (or Malintzin) was the daughter of a leader of a Nahuatl-speaking tribe. According to his account, the family sold Marina to Maya slave traders as a child to protect the inheritance rights of her stepbrother.

Marina possessed unique skills that immediately caught the attention of Cortés. Fluent both in Nahuatl and Yucatec Maya (spoken by a Spanish priest accompanying Cortés), she offered a way for him to communicate with the peoples he encountered. She quickly learned Spanish as well and came to play a vital role as an interpreter and diplomatic guide. Indigenous pictures and writings created after the conquest depict Malintzin as a constant presence beside Cortés as he negotiated with and fought and killed Amerindians. The earliest known images show her interpreting for Cortés as he meets with the Tlaxcalan lord Xicotencatl, forging the alliance that would prove vital to Spanish victory against the Aztecs. Malintzin also appears prominently in the images of the *Florentine Codex*, an illustrated history of the Aztec Empire and its conquest created near the end of the sixteenth century by indigenous artists working under the direction of Friar Bernardino de Sahagún. All the images depict her as a well-dressed woman standing at the center of interactions between the Spanish and Amerindians.

Malintzin bore Cortés a son, Don Martín Cortés, in 1522 and accompanied him on expeditions to Honduras between 1524 and 1526. It is impossible to know the true nature of their personal relationship. Cortés was married to a Spanish woman in Cuba at the time, and Malintzin was a slave, in no position to refuse any demands he made of her. Cortés recognized their child and provided financial support for his upbringing. Malintzin later married one of Cortés's Spanish followers, Juan Jaramillo, with whom she had a daughter. It is unknown when and how she died.

Bernal Díaz gave Malintzin high praise. In his history, written decades after the fact, he described her as beautiful and intelligent, revered by native tribesmen, and devotedly loyal to the Spanish. He stated repeatedly that it would have been impossible for them to succeed without her help. Cortés mentioned Malintzin only twice in his letters to Spanish king Charles V. He acknowledged her usefulness as his interpreter but described her only as "an Indian woman of this land," giving no hint of their personal relationship. No writings from Malintzin herself exist.

Doña Marina translating for Hernán Cortés. (The Granger Collection, NYC — All rights reserved)

Malintzin is commonly known in Mexico and Latin America as La Malinche, a Spanish rendering of her Nahuatl name. She remains a compelling and controversial figure. Popular opinion has often condemned La Malinche as a traitor to her people, whose betrayal enabled the Spanish conquest and centuries of subjugation of indigenous peoples. Other voices have defended her as an enslaved woman who had no choice but to serve her masters. As the mother of a *mestizo* (mixed-race) child, she has also been seen as a founder of the mixed-race population that dominates modern Mexico. She will always be a reminder of the complex interactions between indigenous peoples and Spanish conquistadors that led to the conquest and the new culture born from it.

QUESTIONS FOR ANALYSIS

1. Why was the role of interpreter so important in Cortés's conquest of the Aztec Empire? Why did Malintzin become such a central figure in interactions between Cortés and the Amerindians?
2. What options were open to Malintzin in following her path? If she intentionally chose to aid the Spanish, what motivations might she have had?

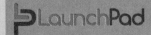

ONLINE DOCUMENT PROJECT

How did Spanish and Amerindian artists depict Malintzin? Examine Spanish and Amerindian representations of Malintzin's role in the conquest, and then complete a quiz and writing assignment based on the evidence and details from this chapter. *See inside the front cover to learn more.*

Like Moctezuma in Mexico, Atahualpa sent envoys to greet the Spanish. Motivated by curiosity about the Spanish, he intended to meet with them to learn more about them and their intentions. Instead the Spaniards ambushed and captured him, extorted an enormous ransom in gold, and then executed him in 1533. The Spanish then marched on to Cuzco, profiting, as with the Aztecs, from internal conflicts and forming alliances with local peoples. When Cuzco fell in 1533, the Spanish plundered immense riches in gold and silver.

A combination of factors made it possible for tiny Spanish forces to bring down the mighty empires of the Americas: the boldness and audacity of conquistadors like Cortés and Pizarro; the military superiority endowed by Spanish firepower and horses; the fervent belief in a righteous Christian God imparted by the reconquista; division within the Aztec and Inca Empires that produced native allies for the Spanish; and, of course, the devastating impact of contagious diseases among the indigenous population. Ironically, the well-organized, urban-based Aztec and Inca Empires were more vulnerable to wholesale takeover than more decentralized and fragmented groups like the Maya, whose independence was not wholly crushed until the end of the seventeenth century.

Inca Women Milking Cows

This illustration of Inca women milking cows is from a collection of illustrations by a Spanish bishop that offers a valuable view of life in Peru in the 1780s. (From *Codex Trujillo*, Bishop Baltasar Jaime Martínez Compañón, Palacio Real, Madrid, Spain/Photo: Albers Foundation/ Art Resource, NY)

Portuguese Brazil

Unlike Mesoamerica or the Andes, the territory of Brazil contained no urban empires but instead had roughly 2.5 million nomadic and settled people divided into small tribes and many different language groups. In 1500 the Portuguese crown named Pedro Álvares Cabral commander of a fleet headed for the spice trade of the Indies. En route, the fleet sailed far to the west, accidentally landing on the coast of Brazil, which Cabral claimed for Portugal under the terms of the Treaty of Tordesillas.

In the 1520s Portuguese settlers brought sugarcane production to Brazil. They initially used enslaved indigenous laborers on sugar plantations, but the rapid decline in the indigenous population soon led to the use of forcibly transported Africans. In Brazil the Portuguese thus created a new form of colonization in the Americas: large plantations worked by enslaved people. This model of slave-worked sugar plantations would spread throughout the Caribbean in the seventeenth century.

Colonial Administration

By the end of the sixteenth century the Spanish and Portuguese had successfully overcome most indigenous groups and expanded their territory throughout modern-day Mexico, the southwestern United States, and Central and South America. In Mesoamerica and the Andes, the Spanish had taken over the cities and tribute systems of the Aztecs and the Incas, basing their control on the prior existence of well-established polities with organized tribute systems.

What was the impact of Iberian conquest and settlement on the peoples of the Americas?	How was the era of global contact shaped by new commodities and forced migrations?	How did new encounters shape cultural attitudes and beliefs in Europe and the New World?	 LearningCurve Check what you know.

While early conquest and settlement were conducted largely by private initiatives, the Spanish and Portuguese governments soon assumed more direct control. In 1503 the Spanish granted the port of Seville a monopoly over all traffic to the New World and established the House of Trade, or *Casa de Contratación*, to oversee economic matters. In 1523 Spain created the Royal and Supreme Council of the Indies, with authority over all colonial affairs subject to approval by the king. Spanish territories themselves were divided initially into two **viceroyalties**, or administrative divisions: New Spain, created in 1535; and Peru, created in 1542. In the eighteenth century, two new viceroyalties, New Granada and La Plata, were created (see Map 16.2).

Within each territory, the viceroy, or imperial governor, exercised broad military and civil authority. The viceroy presided over the *audiencia* (ow-dee-EHN-see-ah), a board of judges that served as his advisory council and the highest judicial body. As in Spain, settlement in the Americas was centered on cities and towns. In each city, the municipal council, or *cabildo*, exercised local authority.

In Portugal, the India House in Lisbon functioned much like the Spanish House of Trade, and royal representatives oversaw its possessions in West Africa and Asia, as did governors in Spanish America. To secure the vast expanse of Brazil, however, the Portuguese implemented a distinctive system of rule, called **captaincies**, in the 1530s. These were hereditary grants of land given to nobles and loyal officials who bore the costs of settling and administering their territories. Over time, the Crown secured greater power over the captaincies, appointing royal governors to act as administrators.

Throughout the Americas, the Catholic Church played an integral role in Iberian rule. The papacy allowed Portuguese and Spanish officials greater control over the church than was the case at home, allowing them to appoint clerics and collect tithes. This control helped colonial powers use the church as an instrument to indoctrinate indigenous people (see page 479).

Indigenous Population Loss and Economic Exploitation

From the time of Christopher Columbus in Hispaniola, the conquerors of the New World made use of the **encomienda system** to profit from the peoples and territories they encountered. This system was a legacy of the methods used to reward military leaders in the time of the reconquista. First in the Caribbean and then on the mainland, conquistadors granted their followers the right to employ groups of Native Americans as laborers and to demand tribute payments from them in exchange for providing food, shelter, and instruction in the Christian faith.

A 1512 Spanish law authorizing the use of the encomienda called for indigenous people to be treated fairly, but in practice the system lead to terrible abuses. Spanish missionaries publicized these abuses, leading to debates in Spain about the nature and proper treatment of indigenous people (see page 479). King Charles V responded to such complaints in 1542 with the New Laws, which set limits on the authority of encomienda holders.

The New Laws provoked a revolt among elites in Peru and were little enforced throughout Spanish territories. Nonetheless, the Crown gradually gained control over encomiendas in central areas of the empire and required indigenous people

CHAPTER LOCATOR | What was the Afroeurasian trade world like prior to the era of European exploration? | Why and how did Europeans undertake ambitious voyages of expansion?

472   CHAPTER 16
THE ACCELERATION OF GLOBAL CONTACT

to pay tributes in cash, rather than in labor. To respond to a shortage of indigenous workers, royal officials established a new government-run system of forced labor, called *repartimiento* in New Spain and *mita* in Peru. Administrators assigned a certain percentage of the inhabitants of native communities to labor for a set period each year in public works, mining, agriculture, and other tasks.

Spanish systems for exploiting the labor of indigenous peoples were both a cause of and a response to the disastrous decline in the numbers of such peoples that began soon after the arrival of Europeans. Some indigenous people died as a direct result of the violence of conquest and the disruption of agriculture and trade caused by warfare. The most important cause of death, however, was infectious disease. Having little or no resistance to diseases brought from the Old World, the inhabitants of the New World fell victim to smallpox, typhus, influenza, and other illnesses.

The pattern of devastating disease and population loss established in the Spanish colonies was repeated everywhere Europeans settled. Overall, population declined by as much as 90 percent or more but with important regional variations. In general, densely populated urban centers were worse hit than rural areas and tropical, low-lying regions suffered more than cooler, higher-altitude ones.

Colonial administrators responded to native population decline by forcibly combining dwindling indigenous communities into new settlements and imposing the rigors of the encomienda and the repartimiento. By the end of the sixteenth century the search for fresh sources of labor had given birth to the new tragedy of the Atlantic slave trade (see page 598).

Patterns of Settlement

The century after the discovery of silver in 1545 marked the high point of Iberian immigration to the Americas. Although the first migrants were men, soon whole families began to cross the Atlantic, and the European population began to increase through natural reproduction. By 1600 American-born Europeans, called *Creoles*, outnumbered immigrants.

Iberian settlement was predominantly urban in nature. Spaniards settled into the cities and towns of the former Aztec and Inca Empires as the native population dwindled through death and flight. They also established new cities in which settlers were quick to establish urban institutions familiar to them from home: city squares, churches, schools, and universities.

Despite the growing number of Europeans and the rapid decline of the native population, Europeans remained a small minority of the total inhabitants of the Americas. Iberians formed sexual relationships with native women leading to a substantial population of mixed Iberian and Indian descent known as *mestizos* (meh-STEE-zohz). The large-scale arrival of enslaved Africans, starting in Brazil in the mid-sixteenth century, added new ethnic and racial dimensions to the population (see pages 598–603).

QUICK REVIEW

What factors help explain the conquest of the mighty Inca and Aztec Empires by the Spanish?

| **What was the impact of Iberian conquest and settlement on the peoples of the Americas?** | How was the era of global contact shaped by new commodities and forced migrations? | How did new encounters shape cultural attitudes and beliefs in Europe and the New World? | ✔ LearningCurve Check what you know. |

How was the era of global contact shaped by new commodities, commercial empires, and forced migrations?

A New World Sugar Refinery in Brazil

Sugar was the most important and most profitable plantation crop in the New World. This image shows the processing and refinement of sugar on a Brazilian plantation. Sugarcane was grown, harvested, and processed by African slaves who labored under brutal and ruthless conditions to generate enormous profits for plantation owners. (Bibliothèque Nationale, Paris, France/Giraudon/The Bridgeman Art Library)

THE CENTURIES-OLD AFROEURASIAN trade world was forever changed by the European voyages of discovery and their aftermath. For the first time, a truly global economy emerged in the sixteenth and seventeenth centuries, and it forged new links among far-flung peoples, cultures, and societies.

The Columbian Exchange

The travel of people and goods between the Old and New Worlds led to an exchange of animals, plants, and diseases, a complex process known as the **Columbian exchange**. As we have seen, the introduction of new diseases to the Americas had devastating consequences. But other results of the exchange brought benefits not only to the Europeans but also to native peoples.

Everywhere they settled, the Spanish and Portuguese brought and raised wheat. Grapes and olives brought over from Spain did well in parts of Peru and Chile. Perhaps the most significant introduction to the diet of Native Americans

Columbian exchange
▶ The exchange of animals, plants, and diseases between the Old and the New Worlds.

CHAPTER LOCATOR | What was the Afroeurasian trade world like prior to the era of European exploration? | Why and how did Europeans undertake ambitious voyages of expansion?

474 CHAPTER 16
THE ACCELERATION OF GLOBAL CONTACT

came via the meat and milk of the livestock that the early conquistadors brought with them, including cattle, sheep, and goats. The horse enabled both the Spanish conquerors and native populations to travel faster and farther and to transport heavy loads more easily.

In turn, Europeans returned home with many food crops that became central elements of their diet. Crops originating in the Americas included tomatoes, squash, pumpkins, peppers, and many varieties of beans, as well as tobacco. One of the most important of such crops was maize (corn). By the late seventeenth century, maize had become a staple in Spain, Portugal, southern France, and Italy, and in the eighteenth century it became one of the chief foods of southeastern Europe and southern China. Even more valuable was the nutritious white potato, which slowly spread from west to east, contributing everywhere to a rise in population.

While the exchange of foods was a great benefit to cultures across the world, the introduction of European pathogens to the New World had a disastrous impact on the native population. The wave of catastrophic epidemic disease that swept the Western Hemisphere after 1492 can be seen as an extension of the swath of devastation wreaked by the Black Death in the 1300s, first on Asia and then on Europe. The world after Columbus was thus unified by disease as well as by trade and colonization.

Sugar and Early Transatlantic Slavery

Two crucial and interrelated elements of the Columbian exchange were the transatlantic trade in sugar and slaves. Throughout the Middle Ages, slavery was deeply entrenched in the Mediterranean, but it was not based on race. How, then, did black African slavery enter the European picture and take root in South and then North America? In 1453 the Ottoman capture of Constantinople halted the flow of European slaves from the eastern Mediterranean. Additionally, the successes of the Christian reconquest of the Iberian Peninsula drastically diminished the supply of Muslim captives. Cut off from its traditional sources of slaves, Mediterranean Europe turned to sub-Saharan Africa, which had a long history of slave trading.

As Portuguese explorers began their voyages along the western coast of Africa, one of the first commodities they sought was slaves. While the first slaves were simply seized by small raiding parties, Portuguese merchants soon found that it was easier and more profitable to trade with African leaders, who were accustomed to dealing in enslaved people captured through warfare with neighboring powers. From 1490 to 1530 Portuguese traders brought between three hundred and two thousand enslaved Africans to Lisbon each year.

In this stage of European expansion, the history of slavery became intertwined with the history of sugar. Population increases and greater prosperity in the fifteenth century led to increasing demand for sugar. The establishment of sugar plantations on the Canary and Madeira Islands in the fifteenth century testifies to this demand.

Sugar was a particularly difficult crop to produce for profit, requiring constant, back-breaking labor. The invention of roller mills to crush the cane more efficiently meant that yields could be significantly augmented, but only if a sufficient labor force was found to supply the mills. Europeans solved the labor problem by forcing first native islanders and then transported Africans to perform the backbreaking work.

| What was the impact of Iberian conquest and settlement on the peoples of the Americas? | **How was the era of global contact shaped by new commodities and forced migrations?** | How did new encounters shape cultural attitudes and beliefs in Europe and the New World? | ✓ LearningCurve Check what you know. |

475

The Transatlantic Slave Trade

The transatlantic slave trade that would ultimately result in the forced transport of over 12 million individuals began in 1518, when Spanish king Charles V authorized traders to bring enslaved Africans to New World colonies. The Portuguese brought the first slaves to Brazil around 1550. After its founding in 1621, the Dutch West India Company transported thousands of Africans to Brazil and the Caribbean, mostly to work on sugar plantations. In the late seventeenth century, with the chartering of the Royal African Company, the English began to bring slaves to Barbados and other English colonies in the Caribbean and mainland North America.

Before 1700, when slavers decided it was better business to improve conditions, some 20 percent of slaves died on the voyage from Africa to the Americas.[2] The most common cause of death was dysentery induced by poor-quality food and water, lack of sanitation, and intense crowding. On sugar plantations, death rates among enslaved people from illness and exhaustion were extremely high. Driven by rising demands for plantation crops, the tragic transatlantic slave trade reached its height in the eighteenth century.

The Birth of the Global Economy

With Europeans' discovery of the Americas and their exploration of the Pacific, the entire world was linked for the first time in history by seaborne trade. The opening of that trade brought into being three successive commercial empires: the Portuguese, the Spanish, and the Dutch.

In the sixteenth century the Portuguese controlled the sea route to India (Map 16.3). From their bases at Goa on the Arabian Sea and at Malacca on the Malay Peninsula, ships carried goods to the Portuguese settlement at Macao. From Macao Portuguese ships loaded with Chinese silks and porcelains sailed to Japan and the Philippines, where Chinese goods were exchanged for Spanish silver from New Spain. Throughout Asia the Portuguese traded in slaves. They also exported horses from Mesopotamia and copper from Arabia to India; from India they exported hawks and peacocks for the Chinese and Japanese markets. Back to Portugal they brought Asian spices that had been purchased with textiles produced in India and with gold and ivory from East Africa. They also shipped back sugar from their colony in Brazil, produced by African slaves whom they had transported across the Atlantic.

Becoming an imperial power a few decades later than the Portuguese, the Spanish were determined to claim their place in world trade. This was greatly facilitated by the discovery of immense riches in silver in the Americas. Silver poured into Europe through the Spanish port of Seville, contributing to steep inflation across Europe. Demand for silver also created a need for slaves to work in the mines.

The Spanish Empire in the New World was basically land based, but across the Pacific the Spaniards built a seaborne empire centered at Manila in the Philippines. The city of Manila served as the transpacific bridge between Spanish America and China. In Manila Spanish traders used silver from American mines to purchase Chinese silk for European markets.

In the seventeenth century the Dutch challenged the Spanish and Portuguese Empires. The Dutch East India Company was founded in 1602 with the stated

CHAPTER LOCATOR | What was the Afroeurasian trade world like prior to the era of European exploration? | Why and how did Europeans undertake ambitious voyages of expansion?

476 CHAPTER 16 THE ACCELERATION OF GLOBAL CONTACT

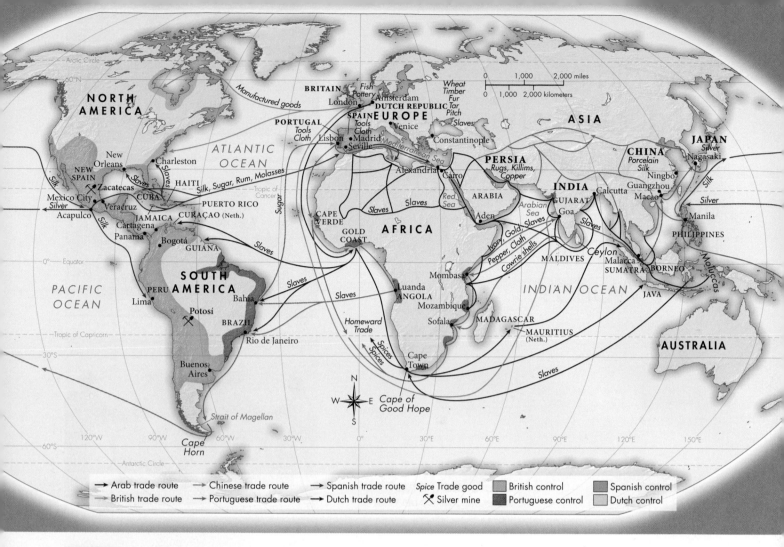

MAP 16.3 ■ Seaborne Trading Empires in the Sixteenth and Seventeenth Centuries

By the mid-seventeenth century trade linked all parts of the world except for Australia. Notice that trade in slaves was not confined to the Atlantic but involved almost all parts of the world.

intention of capturing the spice trade from the Portuguese. Drawing on their commercial wealth and long experience in European trade, by the end of the century the Dutch emerged as the most powerful worldwide seaborne trading power (see Chapter 19).

QUICK REVIEW ◄

How did European demand for sugar stimulate the expansion of the transatlantic slave trade?

| What was the impact of Iberian conquest and settlement on the peoples of the Americas? | **How was the era of global contact shaped by new commodities and forced migrations?** | How did new encounters shape cultural attitudes and beliefs in Europe and the New World? | ✓ LearningCurve Check what you know. |

> How did new encounters shape cultural attitudes and beliefs in Europe and the New World?

Español con India, Mestizo.

Mestizo con Española, Castizo.

5

6

Mulato con Española, Morisco.

Morisco con Española, Chino.

9

10

Lobo con China, Cibaro.

Gibaro con Mulata, Albarazado.

13

14

Sambaigo con Loba, Calpamulato.

Calpamulato con Cambuja, Tente en el Aire.

Mixed Races

The unprecedented mixing of peoples in the Spanish New World colonies inspired great fascination. An elaborate termin-ology emerged to describe the many possible combinations of indigenous, African, and European blood, which were known collectively as *castas*. This painting belongs to a popular genre of the eighteenth century depicting couples composed of individuals of different eth-nic origin and the children produced of their unions. (Schalkwijk/Art Resource, NY)

> PICTURING THE PAST

ANALYZING THE IMAGE: What do these images suggest about the racial composition of the population of Spanish America and the inter-action of people with different racial and ethnic backgrounds? Who do you think the audience might have been, and why would viewers be fascinated by such images?

CONNECTIONS: What elements of this chapter might suggest that these are romanticized or idealized depic-tions of relations among different racial and ethnic groups?

THE AGE OF OVERSEAS EXPANSION heightened Europeans' contacts with the rest of the world. These contacts gave birth to new ideas about the inherent supe-riority or inferiority of different races. Religion became another means of cultural contact, as European missionaries aimed to spread Christianity in both the New World and East Asia. The East-West contacts also led to exchanges of influential cultural and scientific ideas.

CHAPTER LOCATOR

| What was the Afroeurasian trade world like prior to the era of European exploration? | Why and how did Europeans undertake ambitious voyages of expansion? |

Religious Conversion

Converting indigenous people to Christianity was one of the most important justifications for European expansion. The first missionaries to the New World accompanied Columbus on his second voyage, and more than 2,500 Franciscans, Dominicans, Jesuits and other friars crossed the Atlantic in the following century. Later French explorers were also accompanied by missionaries.

Catholic friars were among the first Europeans to seek an understanding of native cultures and languages as part of their effort to render Christianity comprehensible to indigenous people. They were also the most vociferous opponents of abuses committed by Spanish settlers.

Religion had been a central element of pre-Columbian societies, and many, if not all, indigenous people were receptive to the new religion that accompanied the victorious Iberians. In addition to spreading Christianity, missionaries taught indigenous peoples European methods of agriculture and instilled obedience to colonial masters. Despite the success of initial conversion efforts, authorities could not prevent the melding together of Catholic teachings with elements of pagan beliefs and practices.

European Debates About Indigenous Peoples

Iberian exploitation of the native population of the Americas began from the moment of Columbus's arrival in 1492. Denunciations of this abuse by Catholic missionaries, however, quickly followed, inspiring vociferous debates in both Europe and the colonies about the nature of indigenous peoples and how they should be treated. Bartolomé de Las Casas (1474–1566), a Dominican friar and former encomienda holder, was one of the earliest and most outspoken critics of the brutal treatment inflicted on indigenous peoples.

Mounting criticism in Spain led King Charles V to assemble a group of churchmen and lawyers to debate the issue in 1550 in the city of Valladolid. One side of the **Valladolid debate**, led by Juan Ginés de Sepúlveda, argued that conquest and forcible conversion were both necessary and justified to save indigenous people from the horrors of human sacrifice, cannibalism, and idolatry. To counter these arguments, Las Casas and his supporters depicted indigenous people as rational and innocent children, who deserved protection and tutelage from more advanced civilizations.

Elsewhere in Europe, audiences also debated these questions. Eagerly reading denunciations of Spanish abuses by critics like Las Casas, they derived the **Black Legend** of Spanish colonialism, the notion that the Spanish were uniquely brutal and cruel in their conquest and settlement of the Americas. This legend helped other European powers overlook their own record of colonial violence and exploitation.

New Ideas About Race

At the beginning of the transatlantic slave trade, most Europeans grouped Africans into the despised categories of pagan heathens or Muslim infidels. As Europeans turned to Africa for new sources of slaves, they drew on beliefs about Africans' primitiveness and barbarity to defend slavery.

Valladolid debate

▶ A debate organized by Spanish king Charles V in 1550 in the city of Valladolid that pitted defenders of Spanish conquest and forcible conversion against critics of these practices.

Black Legend

▶ The notion that the Spanish were uniquely brutal and cruel in their conquest and settlement of the Americas, an idea propagated by rival European powers.

| What was the impact of Iberian conquest and settlement on the peoples of the Americas? | How was the era of global contact shaped by new commodities and forced migrations? | **How did new encounters shape cultural attitudes and beliefs in Europe and the New World?** | ✓ LearningCurve Check what you know. |

479

Over time, the institution of slavery fostered a new level of racial inequality. Africans gradually became seen as utterly distinct from and wholly inferior to Europeans. In a transition from rather vague assumptions about Africans' non-Christian religious beliefs and general lack of civilization, Europeans developed increasingly rigid ideas of racial superiority and inferiority to safeguard the growing profits gained from plantation slavery. Black skin became equated with slavery itself as Europeans at home and in the colonies convinced themselves that blacks were destined by God to serve them as slaves in perpetuity. Support for this belief went back to the Greek philosopher Aristotle's argument that some people are naturally destined for slavery and to biblical associations between darkness and sin.

After 1700 the emergence of new methods of observing and describing nature led to the use of science to define race. Although previously the term referred to a nation or an ethnic group, henceforth "race" would be used to describe supposedly biologically distinct groups of people whose physical differences produced differences in culture, character, and intelligence. Biblical justifications for inequality thereby gave way to allegedly scientific ones (see page 736).

> **QUICK REVIEW**

How did European ideas about race change over the course of the early modern period?

CHAPTER SUMMARY

Prior to Columbus's voyages, well-developed trade routes linked the peoples and products of Africa, Asia, and Europe. Overall, Europe played a minor role in the Afroeurasian trade world. As the economy and population recovered from the Black Death, Europeans began to seek more direct and profitable access to the Afroeurasian trade world. Technological developments such as the invention of the caravel and the magnetic compass enabled explorers to undertake ever more ambitious voyages.

In the aftermath of their conquest of the Aztec and Inca Empires, the Spanish established new forms of governance to dominate native peoples and exploit their labor. The arrival of Europeans brought enormous population losses to native communities, primarily through the spread of infectious diseases. Disease was one element of the Columbian exchange, a complex transfer of germs, plants, and animals between the Old and New Worlds. These exchanges contributed to the creation of the first truly global economy. Tragically, a major component of global trade was the transatlantic slave trade, in which Europeans transported Africans to labor in the sugar plantations and silver mines of the New World. European nations vied for supremacy in global trade, with early Portuguese success in India and Asia being challenged first by the Spanish and then by the Dutch.

CHAPTER LOCATOR | What was the Afroeurasian trade world like prior to the era of European exploration? | Why and how did Europeans undertake ambitious voyages of expansion?

480 CHAPTER 16
THE ACCELERATION OF GLOBAL CONTACT

Increased contact with the outside world led Europeans to develop new ideas about cultural and racial differences. Debates occurred in Spain and its colonies over the nature of the indigenous peoples of the Americas and how they should be treated. Europeans had long held negative attitudes about Africans; as the slave trade grew, they began to express more rigid notions of racial inequality and to claim that Africans were inherently suited for slavery. Religion became another means of cultural contact, as European missionaries aimed to spread Christianity in the New World.

CONNECTIONS Just three years separated Martin Luther's attack on the Catholic Church in 1517 and Ferdinand Magellan's discovery of the Pacific Ocean in 1520. Within a few short years western Europeans' religious unity and notions of terrestrial geography were shattered. In the ensuing decades Europeans struggled to come to terms with religious differences among Protestants and Catholics at home and with the multitudes of new peoples and places they encountered abroad.

Even as the voyages of discovery contributed to the fragmentation of European culture, they also played a role in state centralization and consolidation in the longer term. Henceforth, competition to gain overseas colonies became an integral part of European politics. While Spain's enormous profits from conquest ultimately led to a weakening of its power, over time the Netherlands, England, and France used profits from colonial trade to help build modernized, centralized states.

Two crucial consequences emerged from this era of expansion. The first was the creation of enduring contacts among five of the seven continents of the globe—Europe, Asia, Africa, North America, and South America. From the sixteenth century onward, the peoples of the world were increasingly entwined in divergent forms of economic, social, and cultural exchange. The second was the growth of European power. Europeans controlled the Americas and gradually assumed control over existing trade networks in Asia and Africa. Although China remained the world's most powerful economy until at least 1800, the era of European dominance was born.

⯈LaunchPad

ONLINE DOCUMENT PROJECT
Interpreting Conquest

How did Spanish and Amerindian artists depict Malintzin?

Examine Spanish and Amerindian representations of Malintzin's role in the conquest, and then complete a quiz and writing assignment based on the evidence and details from this chapter. *See inside the front cover to learn more.*

| What was the impact of Iberian conquest and settlement on the peoples of the Americas? | How was the era of global contact shaped by new commodities and forced migrations? | How did new encounters shape cultural attitudes and beliefs in Europe and the New World? | ✔ **LearningCurve** Check what you know. |

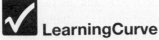
CHAPTER 16 STUDY GUIDE

GET STARTED ONLINE

STEP 1

 LearningCurve

Now that you've read the chapter, make it stick by completing the LearningCurve activity.

EXPLAIN WHY IT MATTERS

STEP 2

Put your reading into practice. Identify each term below, and then explain why it matters in world history.

TERM	WHO OR WHAT & WHEN	WHY IT MATTERS
bride wealth (p. 459)		
caravel (p. 462)		
Ptolemy's *Geography* (p. 462)		
Treaty of Tordesillas (p. 466)		
conquistador (p. 468)		
Aztec Empire (p. 469)		
Inca Empire (p. 469)		
viceroyalties (p. 472)		
captaincies (p. 472)		
encomienda system (p. 472)		
Columbian exchange (p. 474)		
Valladolid debate (p. 479)		
Black Legend (p. 479)		

MOVE BEYOND THE BASICS

STEP 3

To demonstrate a more advanced understanding of the nature and impact of Spanish exploration and conquest in the Americas, fill in the chart below with descriptions of the motives behind Spanish expansion across the Atlantic. Next, identify key Spanish conquests and discoveries and the institutions of Spanish rule in the Americas. Finally, describe the impact of Spanish conquest in the New World and Europe. How do the motives you listed help explain the course of Spanish expansion in the New World?

Motives	Conquests and Discoveries	Institutions of Spanish Rule	Impact in the New World and Europe

STEP 4 — PUT IT ALL TOGETHER

Now, take a step back and try to explain the big picture. Remember to use specific examples from the chapter in your answers.

THE AFROEURASIAN TRADE WORLD BEFORE COLUMBUS

▶ Which states were at the center of global trade prior to 1492? Why?

▶ Why were Europeans at a trading disadvantage prior to 1492? How did geography limit European participation in world trade? What role did Europe's economy and material culture play in this context?

DISCOVERY AND CONQUEST

▶ In your opinion, what was the most important motive behind European expansion? What evidence can you provide to support your position?

▶ What was the Columbian exchange? How did it transform both Europe and the Americas?

CHANGING VALUES AND BELIEFS

▶ How did European expansion give rise to new ideas about race?

▶ How did expansion complicate European's understanding of themselves and their place in the world?

LOOKING BACK, LOOKING AHEAD

▶ If Europe was at the periphery of the global trading system prior to 1492, where was it situated by the middle of the sixteenth century? What had changed? What had not?

▶ What connections can you make between our own experience of globalization in the twenty-first century and the experience of globalization in the sixteenth century? In what ways are the experiences similar? In what ways do they differ?

> IN YOUR OWN WORDS

Imagine that you must give an oral report to the class answering the following question: **What new global connections were forged in the fifteenth and sixteenth centuries?** What would be the most important points and why?

ENDNOTES

Chapter 4
1. Patricia Buckley Ebrey, ed., *Chinese Civilization: A Sourcebook*, 2d ed., revised and expanded (New York: Free Press, 1993), p. 33. All quotations from this work reprinted and edited with the permission of The Free Press, a Division of Simon & Schuster, Inc. Copyright © 1993 by Patricia Buckley Ebrey. Copyright © 1981 by The Free Press. All rights reserved.

Chapter 9
1. Quoted in B. F. Stowasser, "The Status of Women in Early Islam," in *Muslim Women*, ed. F. Hussain (New York: St. Martin's Press, 1984), p. 25.
2. F. E. Peters, *A Reader on Classical Islam* (Princeton, N.J.: Princeton University Press, 1994), p. 250.
3. R. Hillenbrand, "Cordoba," in *Dictionary of the Middle Ages*, vol. 3, ed. J. R. Strayer (New York: Scribner's, 1983), pp. 597–601.

Chapter 10
1. T. Spear, "Bantu Migrations," in *Problems in African History: The Precolonial Centuries*, ed. R. O. Collins et al. (New York: Markus Weiner Publishing, 1994), p. 98.
2. J. S. Trimingham, *Islam in West Africa* (Oxford: Oxford University Press, 1959), pp. 6–9.
3. R. A. Austen, "The Trans-Saharan Slave Trade: A Tentative Census," in *The Uncommon Market: Essays in the Economic History of the Atlantic Slave Trade*, ed. H. A. Gemery and J. S. Hogendorn (New York: Academic Press, 1979), pp. 1–71, esp. p. 66.
4. Pekka Masonen and Humphrey J. Fisher, "Not Quite Venus from the Waves: The Almoravid Conquest of Ghana in the Modern Historiography of Western Africa," *History in Africa* 23 (1996): 197–232.
5. See H. G. Marcus, *A History of Ethiopia*, updated ed. (Berkeley: University of California Press, 2002), pp. 17–20.
6. Ibn Battuta, *The Travels of Ibn Battuta, A.D. 1325–1354*, vol. 1, ed. H. A. R. Gibb (London: University Press, 1972), pp. 379–380.
7. Austen, "The Trans-Saharan Slave Trade," p. 65; J. H. Harris, *The African Presence in Asia* (Evanston, Ill.: Northwestern University Press, 1971), pp. 3–6, 27–30; P. Wheatley, "Analecta Sino-Africana Recensa," in Neville Chittick and Robert Rotberg, *East Africa and the Orient* (New York: Africana Publishing, 1975), p. 109.

Chapter 11
1. Ross Hassig, *War and Society in Ancient Mesoamerica* (Berkeley: University of California Press, 1992), p. 81, 85.
2. Ross Hassig, *Aztec Warfare* (Norman: University of Oklahoma Press, 1988), p. 143.

Chapter 16
1. Thomas Benjamin, *The Atlantic World: Europeans, Africans, Indians and Their Shared History, 1400–1900* (Cambridge: Cambridge University Press, 2009), p. 141.
2. Herbert S. Klein, "Profits and the Causes of Mortality," in *The Atlantic Slave Trade*, ed. David Northrup (Lexington, Mass.: D. C. Heath, 1994), p. 116.

INDEX

Go-Daigo, 382

Goddesses. *See also* Polytheism
  Athena, 125, 126(i), 128(t)
  Hera, 128(t)
  Isis, 46, 137, 152(i), 156
  Peace, 157(i)
  Tyche, 137
  Venus, 155(i)

Gods. *See also* Myths; Pharaohs;
    Polytheism; Religions; Sacrifices;
    Spirits
  Agni, 69
  Ahuramazda, 58
  Apollo, 83, 128, 128(t)
  Ares, 128(t)
  bronze mirror, Han Dynasty, 180(i)
  Di, 94, 110
  division of labor, 27
  Ehecatl, 321(i)
  Greek religion, 128, 128(t)
  Heaven/Sky, 334
  Horus, 49
  Huitzilopochtli (hummingbird god),
    314(i), 316, 318, 319, 320
  Krishna, 75, 77
  Marduk, 42, 196
  Mars, 148
  Mesopotamians, 39
  Olympian, 128, 128(t)
  Osiris, 46, 58, 137
  Quetzalcoatl, 312, 313
  Rome foundation myths and, 148
  Shinto (Way of the Gods), **196**–197, 383
  social hierarchy, 27
  sun-gods
    Amon, 45, 48
    Amon-Ra, 45
    Aten, 48, 49
    pyramids and, 45
    Ra, 45, 48
    Shamash, 42, 42(i)
  Taiyi (astral god), 110
  Tlaloc, 312, 318
  Topiltzin-Quetzalcoatl, 312, 313
  Vishnu, 71(i), 348, 354
  Zeus, 128, 128(t)

Gold belt plaques, 330(i)

Golden age. *See also* Renaissance
  golden age of Chinese philosophy (500–
    200 B.C.E.), 91(t), 104, 111, 113
  Latin literature (reign of Augustus), 158

Good works, 438(t)

Goose and boy (statue, Hellenistic period),
  115(i)

Gospels, 165, 215, 438. *See also* New
    Testament

Gothic style, **408**–409

Goths, 222
  Ostrogoths, 218, 219(m), 222
  Visigoths, 205(m), 218(i), 219(m), 226,
    235(t), 238

Government. *See* Laws; *specific entries*

Gracchus, Gaius, 154

Gracchus, Tiberius, 154, 158(m)

Grace
  Augustine's view, 216
  "faith alone, grace alone, scripture
    alone," 437

Granada
  Patio of the Lions at Alhambra, 244(i)
  Spain conquers (1492), 423(t), 433, 462

Grand Canal, **190**, 190(m), 374

Great Famine in Europe (1315–1322), 391(t),
  410

Great Friday Mosque, Jenne, 282(i)

"Great house," 45. *See also* Pharaohs

Great Mosque at Córdoba, 400(i)

Great Mosque at Kilwa, 290(i)

Great Mosque in Isfahan, 248(i)

Great Rift Valley, 7(m), 272, 284

Great Royal Wives, 49

Great Schism, 391(t), 415(m), 437

Great Silk Road. *See* Silk Road

Great Wall, Qin Empire, **177**–178, 177(t),
  179(m), 180, 198

Great Zimbabwe, 269(t), 276(m), 279(i),
  291–292, 293

Greek civilization (3500–30 B.C.E.), 114–143
  Alexander the Great
    conquests, 133(m)
    control of Gandhara kingdom, 78(i)
    death, 114, 131, 132
    debates, with Indian philosophers, 79
    enters Indus Valley (326 B.C.E.), 62,
      65(t), 79
    Hellenization, **133**–134
    military campaigns (336–324 B.C.E.),
      117(t)
    Persian Empire conquest, 57, 79, 80(m),
      131
    Philip II of Macedonia (father), 131,
      132, 140
  Antigonid dynasty, 117(t), 132
  Archaic Period, 117(t), 120–123
  Athens
    archons, 123
    arts (fifth century B.C.E.), 125–126,
      126(i)
    Delian League, 125, 125(m)
    evolution of, 123
    family life, 126–127
    marriage, 127
    Peloponnesian War, 117(t), 124, 125,
      132, 143
    Pericles, 117(t), 125, 126(i)
    philosophy, 128–130
    political institutions developed (700–
      500 B.C.E.), 117(t)
    sexual relations, 126–127
  big picture, 143(i)
  chronology, 117(t)
  Classical Greece (ca. 500–338 B.C.E.)
    Carolingian Renaissance and, 227
    in chronology, 117(t)
    map (ca. 450 B.C.E.), 118(m)
    religion, 128
    warfare (499–404 B.C.E.), 124–125,
      143
  CONNECTIONS, 141
  Dark Age (ca. 1100–800 B.C.E.), 117(t),
    119, 140
  explosive flamethrower, 204(i), 207
  Helladic period (ca. 3000–1200 B.C.E.),
    116–118
    in chronology, 117(t)
    periodization, 114

Hellenic Greece (ca. 1200–323 B.C.E.)
  in chronology, 117(t)
  civil wars (323– ca. 300 B.C.E.), 117(t),
    125, 132
  colonization (ca. 750–550 B.C.E.), 121,
    122(m), 146
  origins, 114, 143
  Persian Wars (499–479 B.C.E.), 117(t),
    125(m), 126(i)
  religious procession, 124(i)

Hellenistic period, **131**–141
  Delos (island), 131(i)
  Gandhara art, 78(i)
  mystery religions, 128, 136, 137, 141
  philosophy, 137, 139
  polis to monarchy (404–200 B.C.E.),
    132
  religion, 136–137
  sciences, 139–140
  terra-cotta figurine, Myrina (200 B.C.E.),
    136(i)
  trade, 134–135

horticulture (4000 B.C.E.), 21

Minoans (ca. 2000–1200 B.C.E.)
  Crete (ca. 1500 B.C.E.), 118(m)
  described, 116–118, 117(t)
  fall, 118
  Linear A, 116
  Mycenaeans and, 116–118

Mycenaeans (ca. 2000–1200 B.C.E.)
  described, 116–118, 117(t)
  Linear B writing, 117
  map (ca.1300 B.C.E.), 118(m)
  Minoans and, 116–118

overview, 114

periodization, 114

polis (plural *poleis*)
  Acropolis of Athens, 125, 126(i)
  democracy, **121**
  described, **120**–123
  development of (ca. 800–500 B.C.E.),
    117(t), 120
  hoplites, 120(i), **121**, 124, 132
  oligarchy, **121**
  organization, 120–121
  overseas expansion, 121, 122(m)

Seleucid dynasty, 117(t), 153

Sparta
  growth of, 122–123
  helot revolt, 122
  Peloponnesian War, 117(t), 124, 125,
    132, 143
  political institutions developed (750–
    500 B.C.E.), 117(t)

summary, 140–141

Greek fire, explosive liquid, 204(i), 207

Gregory I (pope), 222

Gregory VII (pope), 396

Gregory XIII (pope), 447(i)

Griffon vulture
  bone flute (33,000 B.C.E.), 16(i)
  on Scythian saddlecloth (fifth century
    B.C.E.), 57(i)

Gupta Empire (ca. 350–480), 331(t), 344–
  345, 345(m)

Gutenberg, Johann, 425

Gutenberg's Bible, 425

Gutenberg's printing press, 425–426

reform of Qin Empire, 176–177, 198
tomb, with ceramic soldiers (Qin
Empire), 176(i)
Zhou aristocracy, 178
Great Wall, **177**–178, 177(t), 179(m), 180,
198
Legalism, 109, 178, 201
Li Si, 176–177, 178
map (221 B.C.E.), 103(m)
Mengchang and, 100
Records of the Grand Historian, 177(t),
180, 181
unification (221–206 B.C.E.), 176–178,
177(t)
Warring States Period, 102, 103,
103(m)
Quechua, 308
Queen Mother, 274
Quetzalcoatl (god), 312, 313
Qur'an, **235**, 235(t). *See also* Islam

Ra (sun-god), 45, 48
Race concept
European expansion, 479–480
Renaissance, 429
scientific definition, 480
Racism, anti-Semitism
Inquisition and, 434
Spain (fourteenth century), 434
Radical Reformation, 439–440
al-Rahman III, Abd, 399
Ramadan, 236
Ramayana, 69, 77, 85, 119
Ramesses II, 48
Rape
of Lucretia, 148
wergeld and, 220
Raphael, 421(i), 426
al-Rashid, Harun, 241–242, 254–255
Rats, Black Death and, 342, 411
Reality, ultimate. *See also* Enlightenment
(spirituality); Truth
Brahman, **70**, 75
Dao, **108**
Rebirth. *See* Afterlife; Enlightenment;
Reincarnation; Renaissance
Reconquista (750–1492)
Americas, 462, 465, 471, 472
Christian crusade in Spain, 235(t), 391(t),
399, 399(m), 400(i)
Records of the Grand Historian (Sima
Qian), 177(t), **180**, 181
Reformation. *See* Catholic Reformation;
Protestant Reformation
Reincarnation. *See also* Afterlife
Cleopatra and Isis, 156
Jainism, 72
karma, **70**, 72, 84, 104, 188
mystery religions, 84
Christianity *versus*, 166
cult of Isis, 137
defined, **128**
Hellenistic period, 128, 136, 137, 141
Roman Empire, 141, 165, 166
Pure Land school, 191, 382–383
samsara, 70
Vedas, 84
Relics, 76(i), 81(i), 210(i), 224, 398. *See also*
Saints

Reliefs. *See also* Sculpture
Angkor temples, 353(i)
Ara Pacis, 157(i)
Bayan relief, Angkor, 353(i)
female spirit from Indian stupa, 63(i)
iconoclastic controversy, 216
India's medieval age, 347
Religions. *See also* Buddhism; Christianity;
Goddesses; Gods; Hinduism;
Islam; Jainism; Judaism; Myths;
Polytheism; Sacrifices; Spirits
animism
Africa, 274, 278, 283, 289
defined, **15**
Mansa Musa's reign, 283
Paleolithic era, 15–16
Classical Greece, 128
Hellenistic era, 136–137
Manichaeism, 332, 332(i), 334
Maya culture, 310–311
mystery religions
Christianity *versus*, 166
cult of Isis, 137
defined, **128**
Hellenistic period, 128, 136, 137, 141
Roman Empire, 141, 165, 166
Olmecs, 302–303
Shinto (Way of the Gods), **196**–197. 383
syncretistic, 165
Zhou Dynasty, 99, 101
Zoroastrianism
described, **58**
dhimmis, 248
Islam and, 260, 262
Mahayana Buddhism and, 58, 74
state religion, Sassanid Persians, 206
Religious orders
Dominicans, 398, 479
Franciscans, 398, 479
Jesuits, 423(t), **446**
Remus and Romulus, foundation myth, 148,
158
ren (ultimate Confucian virtue), **105**
Renaissance
arts, 426–427
big picture, 453(i)
Carolingian Renaissance, 227
chronology, 423(t)
CONNECTIONS, 451
cultural developments, 422–427
debate about women, **429**, 431
defined, **422**
gender roles, 429, 431
humanism, **424**–425
Italian Renaissance, 421(i), 422–424,
423(m)
Medici family, 423, 423(t), 430–431
overview, 420–421
printing, 425–426
race concept, 429
slavery, 429
social hierarchies, 428–431
summary, 450
wealth and power, 422–424, 423(m),
429
Renovatio romani imperi, 227
Republic. *See* Roman Republic
Resurrection, of Jesus, 165
Retreats, glaciers, 2, 5(t), 6, 10, 13, 18

Revolutions
Agricultural Revolution, **17**–21, 31
commercial revolution, **406**, 406(m)
Song Dynasty's economic revolution,
365
"Rhapsody on the Two Capitals" (Ban Gu),
181
Rice, transplanting, Song Dynasty, 364
Richard II, 415
Right actions, Eightfold Path, 74
Rig Veda, 65(t), **68**
Rock painting
cattle grazing in Tassili n'Ajjer, 271(i)
shaman (50,000 B.C.E.), 3(i)
Roma et Augustus cult, 157
Roman Catholic Church. *See* Catholic
Church
Roman Empire (ca. 1000 B.C.E.–400 C.E.),
144–173. *See also* Byzantine Empire;
Roman Republic; Roman Senate;
Rome
Antigonid dynasty overthrown (168
B.C.E.), 117(t)
Antonine emperors, 147(t), 161
big picture, 173(i)
Christianity
acceptance, 166–167, 170
evolution, 166–167
Paul of Tarsus, 166
rise in, factors, 164–165
spread, 166
chronology, 145(t), 147(t)
CONNECTIONS, 171
Constantine (emperor)
Edict of Milan, 147(t), 170
New Rome, 169
Nicene Creed, 205(t), 211
Persian Empire's cultural influence,
169
political reforms, Roman Empire,
147(t), 168
reconstruction of empire, 147(t)
sarcophagus of Helena, 210(i)
daily life, 161
Diocletian, 147(t), 168, 169, 210
division (293 C.E.), 169, 169(m)
Egypt conquered (30 B.C.E.), 117(t)
expansion, 162–163
Flavians, 147(t), 161
gladiatorial combat
Coliseum in Rome, 160(i)
Etruscans, 148
mosaic (fourth century C.E.), 168(i)
Roman Empire, 160(i), 161, 168(i)
Han Dynasty and, 163, 184
Julio-Claudians, 147(t), 161
overview, 144–145
pax Romana, 147(t), **160**–163
Pompeii
Mount Vesuvius eruption, 145(i), 161
two triremes race, temple of Isis,
152(i)
Woman from Pompeii (fresco), 145(i)
prosperity in provinces, 162
summary, 170–171
Theodosius, 147(t), 170, 205(t), 211
Theodosius II, 205
third-century crisis, 147(t), 168–170
Romanesque, 408

About the Authors

John P. McKay (Ph.D., University of California, Berkeley) is professor emeritus at the University of Illinois. He has written or edited numerous works, including the Herbert Baxter Adams Prize-winning book *Pioneers for Profit: Foreign Entrepreneurship and Russian Industrialization, 1885–1913.*

Patricia Buckley Ebrey (Ph.D., Columbia University), professor of history at the University of Washington in Seattle, specializes in China. She has published numerous journal articles and *The Cambridge Illustrated History of China*, as well as several monographs. In 2010 she won the Shimada Prize for outstanding work of East Asian Art History for *Accumulating Culture: The Collections of Emperor Huizong.*

Roger B. Beck (Ph.D., Indiana University) is Distinguished Professor of African and twentieth-century world history at Eastern Illinois University. His publications include *The History of South Africa*, a translation of P. J. van der Merwe's *The Migrant Farmer in the History of the Cape Colony, 1657–1842*, and more than a hundred articles, book chapters, and reviews. He is a former treasurer and Executive Council member of the World History Association.

Clare Haru Crowston (Ph.D., Cornell University) teaches at the University of Illinois, where she is currently associate professor of history. She is the author of *Fabricating Women: The Seamstresses of Old Regime France, 1675–1791*, which won the Berkshire and Hagley Prizes. She edited two special issues of the *Journal of Women's History*, has published numerous journal articles and reviews, and is a past president of the Society for French Historical Studies.

Merry E. Wiesner-Hanks (Ph.D., University of Wisconsin-Madison) taught first at Augustana College in Illinois, and since 1985 at the University of Wisconsin-Milwaukee, where she is currently UWM Distinguished Professor in the department of history. She is the coeditor of the *Sixteenth Century Journal* and the author or editor of more than twenty books, most recently *The Marvelous Hairy Girls: The Gonzales Sisters and Their Worlds* and *Gender in History*. She is the former Chief Reader for Advanced Placement World History.

Jerry Dávila (Ph.D., Brown University) is Jorge Paulo Lemann Professor of Brazilian History at the University of Illinois. He is the author of *Dictatorship in South America; Hotel Trópico: Brazil and the Challenge of African Decolonization*, winner of the Latin Studies Association Brazil Section Book prize; and *Diploma of Whiteness: Race and Social Policy in Brazil, 1917–1945*. He has served as president of the Conference on Latin American History.